International
Handbook
on
Abortion

International Handbook on Abortion

EDITED BY

Paul Sachdev

GREENWOOD PRESS
NEW YORK • WESTPORT, CONNECTICUT • LONDON

Library of Congress Cataloging-in-Publication Data

International handbook on abortion.

Bibliography: p.
Includes index.
1. Abortion—Cross-cultural studies—Handbooks,
manuals, etc.   2. Abortion—Government policy—
Handbooks, manuals, etc.   3. Abortion—Law and
legislation—Handbooks, manuals, etc.   I. Sachdev,
Paul.
HQ767.I668   1988   363.4'6   87–11994
ISBN 0–313–23463–9 (lib. bdg. : alk. paper)

British Library Cataloguing in Publication Data is available.

Library of Congress Catalog Card Number: 87–11994
ISBN: 0–313–23463–9

First published in 1988

Greenwood Press, Inc.
88 Post Road West, Westport, Connecticut 06881

Printed in the United States of America

The paper used in this book complies with the
Permanent Paper Standard issued by the National
Information Standards Organization (Z39.48–1984).

10 9 8 7 6 5 4 3 2 1

To Christopher Tietze (1908–84), whose passion for social justice and untiring devotion to the cause of reproductive freedom spared a multitude from compulsory parenthood.

CONTENTS

PREFACE

Because of the role abortion plays in influencing contraceptive and fertility behavior, governments make deliberate attempts to regulate abortion practices and availability through the enactment of abortion laws ranging from the very permissive to the very restrictive. A host of considerations prompts legislative decisions along this continuum: demographic patterns; population size; religious, socioeconomic, attitudinal, age, and sex distribution of people in reproductive years; and sexual and contraceptive profiles. In the last two decades many countries have made significant alterations in conditions governing the availability of abortion that have had far-reaching consequences for millions of women around the globe in their freedom to make reproductive choices. These legislative activities provided an impetus for a comprehensive examination of a complex interplay of myriad factors in different sociopolitical systems and how they impact on the practice of abortion.

The *International Handbook on Abortion* represents a unique work of its kind, for it assembles in a single volume data (some of which were hard to find) from all continents on the general pattern of the legal status, indications for abortion, service delivery, abortion incidence, fertility trends, and the profile of contracepting and aborting women.

The Handbook provides thirty-three chapters covering Africa, Asia, Eastern and Western Europe, Latin America and the Caribbean, the Middle East, the Nordic countries, North and South America, and Oceania. Each chapter, written specifically for this volume by leading authorities in the field, surveys in depth the following topical areas:

—The historical development of abortion policy

—The role of the medical profession, news media, religious and women's organizations, and other pressure groups in the legislative enactments

—The attitudes over time of the medical community and of the public to abortion policies

—Demographic data concerning women who seek abortions such as incidence, age, parity, marital status, gestation period, pre- and postcontraceptive use, and repeat abortions

—Abortion among special groups such as teenagers and ethnic minorities

—The impact of abortion on fertility behavior, and family planning policy and programs

—Illegal abortion: incidence, complications, morbidity

—Abortion research

If the book assists educators, researchers, administrators, public health officials, and human service providers in enhancing their understanding of this culturally and geographically universal social practice and in guiding future research, it has achieved its mission.

The Handbook avoids arguments concerning the moral and religious aspects of abortion. Since it presents data on laws and policies on abortion, and their impact on fertility behavior, it can appeal to academics and lay readers on both sides of the controversy.

I owe a special debt of gratitude to the contributors for their thoughtful chapters and for their ungrudging willingness to implement my editorial comments. I feel a unique sense of camaraderie with each of them.

Needless to say, it was an arduous task to identify, locate, and solicit chapters from the most prominent experts in each country. The most valuable and generous assistance in the matter was rendered by the late Dr. Christopher Tietze whose colossal stature in the international community and personal contact with some of the contributors brought forth the most enthusiastic response. He sustained his zeal for the project until his death in 1984. As a tribute to Chris's prodigious contribution to human fertility and its control, I feel privileged to dedicate this Handbook to his memory.

To my colleagues Dr. J. Victor Thompson and Professor Jeffrey Bulcock I feel grateful for their many critical and helpful comments on my chapters. Dr. Stanley K. Henshaw was generous in giving his assistance, generally. I am most thankful to him.

Finally, to my wife, Sudarshan, I am eternally grateful for her massive support and encouragement at critical moments. Her instructive comments and immeasurable patience were vital to the completion of this work.

International
Handbook
on
Abortion

1

ABORTION TRENDS: AN INTERNATIONAL REVIEW

Paul Sachdev

An estimated 40 million abortions are legally performed each year in the world, or one pregnancy is terminated for every two births (*Globe and Mail*, 18 December 1986). More than three-quarters of the world's population resides in countries that have laws permitting induced abortion under certain circumstances. In the past few years some countries have either extended grounds for abortion or have relaxed the enforcement of illegal abortion statutes, while others have moved from permissive to moderate legal status of abortion. These legislative changes have spawned variations in abortion trends, the demography of abortion seekers, and their impact on fertility behavior. This chapter provides an overview of these significant developments in different regions of the world. Table 1.1 (below) presents information on the legal status of abortion, the abortion rates, and the characteristics of abortion seekers for selected countries and years.

LEGAL STATUS OF ABORTION

In most jurisdictions laws permit induced abortion, but conditions regulating the practice range from limited prohibition to an elective abortion at the request of the pregnant woman (see table 1.1). Under limited prohibition, grounds are generally not specific, but abortion is permitted by case-law on defense of necessity, that is, to save the pregnant woman's life. Most countries of Islamic faith (e.g., Indonesia, Bangladesh), half of the countries in Africa (e.g., Nigeria, the Republic of South Africa), about two-thirds of the countries of Latin America, and three countries in Western Europe (i.e., Belgium, Ireland, and Malta) fall under these prohibitive statutes. These countries make up about one-quarter of the world's population (Tietze & Henshaw, 1986). However, governments in several countries (e.g., Indonesia, South Africa, Latin America and the Caribbean, Korea) where strict penal prohibition is in force show leniency in enforcing the law; consequently, physicians evidencing good faith are seldom prosecuted for inducing the termination of pregnancy for broad medical grounds. Likewise, in order to avoid confrontation with religious fundamentalists, some Muslim countries (e.g., Bangladesh) have opted to circumvent the Criminal Code by introducing abortion services in the guise of menstrual regulation (MR) as a component of family planning programs.

Thirty-nine percent of the world's population live in countries that have statutes broad enough to permit termination of pregnancy on request, usually during the first trimester. However, the gestational limit prescribed for termination for social reasons does not apply to abortions performed on medical grounds even up to and beyond the twentieth week. This category is represented by an assortment of countries from different regions, including Cuba, Denmark, Finland, the German Democratic Republic (GDR), Greece, the Netherlands, Norway, Singapore, Sweden, the United States, and Yugoslavia.

In some countries such as Denmark, the GDR, Norway, Italy, and Cuba, a pregnant minor must obtain a prior consent of her parent or guardian. A few countries (e.g., New Zealand, Sweden, the Federal Republic of Germany [FRG], and Italy) require preabortion counseling, while others (e.g., GDR, Italy, the Netherlands, and Israel) require a waiting period of up to one week following application and before the procedure. In the FRG and Czechoslovakia a pregnant woman is counseled on government assistance if she wishes to continue her pregnancy.

Nearly one-quarter of the world's population is governed by laws that authorize abortion on sociomedical grounds, that is, where social factors such as inadequate income, poor housing, and unmarried status are considered risks to the mother's health if her pregnancy is allowed to continue. Countries such as the FRG, India, Japan, most of the countries of Eastern Europe, and the United Kingdom fall in this category. Some of these countries interpret sociomedical grounds broadly enough so that abortions, mostly at an early stage, are available almost on request. In India, for example, the failure of contraception constitutes justification for termination of the pregnancy on the grounds that it is likely to adversely affect the mental health of the pregnant woman. However, the gestational limits on pregnancy termination vary widely from a period less than twelve weeks in Cuba, Czechoslovakia, Finland, and FRG, to twenty-four weeks in Japan, Singapore, and Israel. (Israel does not prescribe any gestational limit, but in practice abortions are permitted up to twenty-two weeks.)

Access to legal abortion is relatively easy in most Asian countries since there are very few regulations and administrative requirements. In a few countries such as China and Korea, governments have introduced a variety of incentives such as paid leave and subsidies for nourishment to encourage women to use abortions as a means of fertility regulation. In China, where the official policy stressed until recently the one-child family, abortion is viewed as one of the four planned birth operations, the other three being vasectomy, tubal ligation, and the insertion of an intrauterine device (IUD). In Korea abortion is widely practiced despite restrictive laws, and the government encourages abortion use by providing subsidies to private clinics if abortion is performed concurrently with sterilization or if the pregnancy resulted from IUD failure.

Early abortions, usually up to the tenth week, are permitted on juridical (such as rape or incest), eugenic, or fetal indications (genetic defects or other impairment of the fetus) in some countries of Latin America such as Colombia, Chile, Brazil, Peru, El Salvador, and Jamaica.

The concept of health as a ground for providing abortion is either narrowly defined to mean that the pregnancy poses a threat to a women's physical health as in several Latin American countries, Africa, Belgium, Ireland, Bangladesh, Indonesia, and Sri Lanka, or interpreted broadly to mean that the pregnancy might endanger or is likely to endanger her physical or mental health. In some countries, such as Canada, the concept is left vague and unspecified, and its interpretation, whether narrow or broad, is left to the discretion and judgment of abortion committees.

HISTORICAL DEVELOPMENT OF ABORTION POLICY

In most countries legislative reforms took place in the last ten years and were stimulated by a convergence of social, political, and demographic factors. In the Western countries, Australia, and New Zealand, these factors included a phenomenal number of illegal abortions and their resulting serious health risks, an alarming proportion of unwanted pregnancies among unmarried women, advocacy of human rights groups for control over their own fertility, and concern for the quality of life. Countries such as Canada, Australia, and New Zealand which share the United Kingdom's religious values and social and political structure were also influenced by the legislative changes in British abortion laws. In October 1967 the British Parliament passed a bill authorizing abortion on broad grounds which, in fact, is the most progressive of the modern liberal statutes in Western Europe. The role of the medical profession in the abortion reform movement is noteworthy. Initially, medical associations in most of these countries were opposed to changes in the restrictive statutes because of their fear of losing control over abortion services if regulations were relaxed to allow paramedics to perform abortions. Later, they reversed their position approving more liberal laws. Changes in abortion laws were generally preceded by fierce debates among parliamentarians, and professional and lay people on both sides of the controversy. Because of the difficulty in resolving the polemic issue, the laws were passed by a very close vote.

The issue of the legalization of abortion was not as polemic in most countries of Asia (e.g., India, Japan, Korea, and China) and Cuba as it was in the Western countries where the Roman Catholic church has been the most vigorous and articulate opponent to reform. In Bangladesh and Korea the governments successfully mollified the resistance of religious fundamentalist groups by avoiding the enactment on liberal grounds. But in practice, the restrictive measures are deliberately ignored, and abortion is performed as a routine practice in both countries. In Indonesia where abortion is prohibited, Muslim fundamentalists neither prosecute nor oppose physicians for performing an abortion as long as they carry out their professional duty.

These countries' efforts to change abortion laws were stimulated by their desire to curtail population growth which they were unable to halt through family planning measures. Abortion was regarded as the most effective and efficient solution to runaway fertility rates and to depressed economic and health standards. Curiously, most governments in Africa, including the white government of South Africa, are reluctant to relax their repressive abortion laws because of vigorous opposition from religious groups and tribal elders, although they are faced with a nagging problem of rampant population growth, unwanted teenage pregnancies, and limited contraceptive services and usage.

The socialist countries of Eastern Europe were motivated to liberalize their abortion laws because of an alarming increase in illegal abortions and the consequent problems of maternal mortality and morbidity. But their efforts were spurred by the example of the Soviet Union which pioneered in the liberalization of repressive abortion laws in 1920 by permitting abortions at the request of the woman involved. The GDR, however, followed a different pattern that was characterized by an initial three-year period of relaxation of repressive laws to combat illegal abortions which increased in the wake of World War II. This phase was followed by restrictive measures in 1950; somewhat broader interpretation in 1965; and, finally, legalization of abortion on request in 1972. Since there were no organized and vocal religious groups in these countries, except in Poland, religious opposition was virtually absent. In Poland the factors that prompted changes in abortion laws more closely resembled those in the West than those in the socialist bloc countries. For example, professional bodies and the public debated the issue, and the media sensitized the public to the need for reform and created awareness for the rights of women to control their own fertility.

While the rising fertility rate was the chief impetus for policy change in Asia and Cuba, sharp declines in birth rates in Eastern European countries caused their governments to adopt more restrictive grounds for abortion. In Czechoslovakia, for example, the 1973 decree restricted access to induced abortion by requiring that all applications for abortion, except those on medical grounds, be approved by a commission. In Hungary, begining in 1974 abortion on request has been available to single, married, or previously married women who meet certain conditions.

DEMOGRAPHY OF ABORTION

Eastern and Central Europe

In terms of the incidence of abortions performed worldwide, the available statistics reveal that China and the Soviet Union combined contribute the largest number of legal abortions, estimated at 25 million, to the overall total (Tietze & Henshaw, 1985, p. 29). Currently, about two out of every three pregnancies end in abortion in the Soviet Union (*Abortion Research Notes*, 1987, p. 1). Based on the data available for the most recent year, China and most socialist countries of Europe posted abortion rates ranging from 34.5 abortions per 1,000 women aged fifteen to forty-four for Czechoslovakia to 62.9 for China to 75.7 for Yugoslavia and to 181 for the Soviet Union. These rates were much higher than those reported by other countries (see table 1.1).

The pattern in abortion trends in Eastern Europe (e.g., Czechoslovakia, GDR, Hungary, Poland, and Yugoslavia) is marked by fluctuations with abortion rates making a steep rise following the liberalization of their abortion laws during the 1950s (1965 for GDR), thus replacing illegal abortions and unwanted births with easily accessible legal abortions. Of these countries, Hungary registered the biggest jump, peaking at 90.6 abortions per 1,000 women in 1969, when it outstripped its birth rate by more than 8 points. Yugoslavia, Czechoslovakia, and Poland, in that order, posted lower abortion rates than Hungary. After a brief period of modest increase, abortion rates started to decline in response to the use of the contraceptive pill and IUDs which were widely disseminated during these years under government pronatalist programs. These measures stabilized abortion rates for a couple of years after which they began to increase gradually. The trend is continuing in contrast to that in most Western countries where the rates have started to show a downward trend. In European countries abortion apparently continues to be used as the primary method of fertility control as the governments have now diminished emphasis on contraceptive efforts. (The official figures on abortion incidence in Poland are highly deficient because of underreporting by private clinics where the majority of abortions are performed.)

In general, these countries experienced a sharp decline in their birth rates during the first years following abortion legislation. The drop in the birth rates was almost ten times the decline that occurred in Western Europe. Evidently, this reflects the effect of abortion, at least in the beginning, since most couples in these countries relied on traditional methods of birth control, especially coitus interruptus. In Czechoslovakia, the pill and IUDs were not available until the 1960s, and most women used abortion for family spacing and limitation. In Poland the government's first concerted efforts to promote modern contraception did not get underway until 1957. Contraceptive services still lag behind needs. Hungary adopted population policy measures only in 1973 to promote use of oral contraception and IUDs and to increase their availability. In Yugoslavia the official recognition of family planning policy did not come until 1969. Despite the increasing availability of the pill and IUD, coitus interruptus still remains the most widely used contraceptive method throughout Eastern Europe. Although modern methods of contraception are now replacing abortions as the primary means of fertility regulation, the availability of inexpensive and easy abortion and a pill scare have slowed this development.

The Americas

Of the North American countries, Canada's abortion rate (9.2 per 1,000 women fifteen to forty-four years) and abortion ratio (16.2 abortions per 100 live births) were almost one-third those of the United States which posted 28.0 and 41.1, respectively, in 1985. The lower Canadian rates may be attributed to restrictive Canadian abortion laws and inadequate services. There is also a higher contraceptive use, especially of the pill by unmarried women, than in the United States. The fact that many abortions performed in free-standing clinics in Ontario and Quebec as well as those conducted on Canadian women in the United States are not included may also partly explain the lower rates in Canada.

Cuba is the only country in Latin America that performs a large number of abortions (139,588 in 1984) under its permissive abortion system established in the mid–1960s. The abortion rate reached its peak at 69.5 in 1974 when, along with the birth rate, it started to drop. The decline continued until 1981. The birth rate fell by more than 44 percent and the fertility rate by 31.2 percent during this period. The marked drop in the fertility rate suggests an abortion effect. Between 1981 and 1982 the abortion rate and general fertility took a precipitous upturn (over 13 percent), which is believed to be the result of the increased proportion of sexually active teenagers in the population and high marriage rates (David, 1983) Cuba's abortion rate at 59 abortions per 1,000 women aged fourteen to fifty-five continues to remain one of the highest in the world after that of the USSR, Romania, Yugoslavia, Bulgaria, and China.

Although abortion is prohibited by law in most Latin American countries, women who need an abortion and are able to pay for it have no difficulty finding a competent physician. Professionals performing abortions carry newspaper advertisements in many cities. However, poor women usually end up with an unskilled backstreet abortionist. The incidence of illegal abortions is impossible to ascertain with any degree of accuracy. One conservative estimate places the number between 1 to 8 million a year; the actual figure may be twice that. The number of illegal abortions is steadily escalating as an increased proportion of young single people are becoming sexually active at an earlier age, often without taking contraceptive precaution. Government-sponsored family planning education and services are highly inadequate in most countries such as Brazil, Argentina, Ecuador, Paraguay, and Peru. In some regions of a country they are virtually nonexistent. At the current rate of growth (about 3 percent annually), the population in the entire region is expected to swell from the present level of 380 million to 600 million by the year 2000.

Nordic Countries

The legal abortion trends in the Nordic countries (Denmark, Finland, Norway, and Sweden) are strikingly similar. In 1983 their abortion rates ranged between 12.1 for Finland and 18.6 abortions per 1,000 women for Denmark. The abortion rates showed marked increases following the liberalization of laws in these countries until they reached a peak of around 20–27 in the mid–1970s. Thereafter the rates have been steadily dropping except for Sweden which reported minor fluctuations between 1979 and 1980. The decline in the abortion rates was the highest for Finland with 46 percent, followed by 31.4 percent for Denmark, 21.5 percent for Norway, and 11.4 percent for Sweden. The same period witnessed a corresponding drop in the number of conceptions among married women, suggesting the effect of increased use of contraception. However, the number of abortions outstripped the number of unplanned pregnancies among teenagers.

The United Kingdom and Western European Countries

England's abortion rate and ratio are substantially lower than those in the United States or in some countries of Northern and Eastern Europe. But they are higher than in Canada, Bangladesh, India, Finland, the FRG, and the Netherlands. After peaking at 11.7 in 1973 the abortion rate in the United Kingdom began to drop between 1974 and 1976 in response to aggressive national family planning programs. The abortion rate started to accelerate again after a three-year period of stabilization as more women reverted to traditional, less effective methods of contraception because of the pill scare. The abortion figures for England reflect the inclusion of women from other countries who go to England to obtain abortions under its liberal system.

The Netherlands' abortion rate, averaging around 6 abortions per 1,000 women, is lower than that of all the Western nations. Its number and rates follow the ebb and flow pattern seen in other Western European countries. In 1984 its rate reverted to the 1979 level when it was 5.6 abortions per 1,000 women. A sizable number of Belgian women (4,900 in 1984) travel to the Netherlands to seek pregnancy termination because abortion is illegal in their own country.

In the FRG, about one-half of all abortions are currently performed in private clinics, a trend that is increasing because private clinics offer greater anonymity, a short stay, and administrative informality. Some women travel to neighboring countries such as the Netherlands, England, and Austria where they can obtain less encumbered abortions. Vexing regulations and staid bureaucratic procedures make the FRG one of the three Western countries where abortions are most difficult to obtain.

In Italy, the official statistics misrepresent the exact number of legal abortions because of a flawed reporting system and wide regional differences. Nevertheless, its abortion rate of 19.0 per 1,000 women and its abortion ratio of 38.0 per 100 live births in 1984 were higher than those in some countries in Europe such as Denmark, France, Finland, England and Wales, and the FRG, all of which have longer histories of permissive abortion system. Italy's birth rate has dropped markedly in recent years, and this trend continues, signifying that abortion is the most frequently used method of limiting family size. The use of the most effective methods of contraception control—the pill and IUD—is extremely low except among better educated couples. Furthermore, compared to most other

European countries, in Italy few teenagers resort to abortion, perhaps owing to the legal barrier which the requirement of parental consent imposes on them.

Israel with its abortion rate of 26 per 1,000 Jewish women is in the middle compared to Eastern, Western, and North European countries, but is closer to that of Denmark and the United States (white women). The fertility rate among Jewish women declined sharply until 1979, a change attributed chiefly to abortion use. Although restricted until 1977, abortions were easily available. Since 1979 greater emphasis has been placed on modern contraceptive methods; the trend in declining fertility rate also slowed down until it reversed in 1982. The level of contraceptive usage among Jewish women is the same as that of most Western countries, but the discrepancy in their fertility rates is due largely to the family size norm which favors larger families than is the case in most other Western nations.

Asia and Africa

Among all Asian countries, China had the highest abortion rate at 62.9 per 1,000 women in 1983, which mirrors its permissive abortion laws, strict birth quota requirement, and low contraceptive usage. Although Japan has the most permissive abortion system in the world, its abortion rate of 21.5 per 1,000 women is lower than that of China and Singapore (28.1). This is in large part due to widespread and effective contraception. Its abortion rate has been steadily falling since its peak year in 1955 in response to the Japanese government's continual emphasis on comprehensive family planning education and the dissemination of contraceptive devices. Concerned about the phenomenal drop in the birth rate, the government of Singapore is now discouraging abortions by offering sizeable tax incentives to couples giving birth to a third child.

India and Bangladesh reported substantially lower rates in 1981—2.7 and 1.6, respectively. In both countries the incidence of abortion can be much higher as the implementation of laws authorizing abortion has been extremely slow, especially in rural areas. In Bangladesh, the social stigma associated with menstrual regulation (MR) inhibits reporting, especially by private physicians. MRs up to ten or twelve weeks are widely practiced throughout government hospitals, and health and family planning complexes, and their number has sharply increased —by 1,400 percent between 1976 and 1984.

In the first five years since the abortion laws in India were liberalized in 1972, the number of medical terminations of pregnancies (MTPs) climbed over 1,000 times. Over 500,000 MTPs were performed in 1983–84, representing an increase of 45 percent during the preceding five years. But this frequency does not represent the true demand as a sizable proportion of the Indian population is unaware of the availability of legalized abortion. As in Bangladesh there is a heavy emphasis on contraceptive counseling and on concurrent contraceptive measures, including sterilization and insertion of IUDs. About one-quarter of women seeking abortion accept sterilization, and another 28 percent accept IUDs. Currently, the government of India is contemplating introducing a variety of disincentive and incentive schemes to stimulate rapid decline in fertility through a combined use of abortion and contraception.

Although abortions are illegal in South Korea except for medical and philanthropic reasons, they have been routinely performed by gynecologists since 1962. About one-half of South Korean wives had experienced an induced abortion by 1982. Compared to other developing countries in the region, South Korea's annual population growth rate dropped sharply from 2.9 percent in 1962 to 1.56 percent in 1980. The deceleration in the growth rate was achieved chiefly by easily available, inexpensive, safe, induced abortions; widespread use of modern contraceptives—the pill, IUD, condom, sterilization; and postponement of marriage.

In Singapore, after a steep rise in the initial years following the legalization of abortion laws, the rates have stabilized at around 28 abortions per 1,000 women in the last six years. Roughly 44.8 percent of births are presently averted annually under its most liberal abortion law, which is largely responsible for Singapore achieving its targeted demographic goals sooner than expected.

Abortions in South Africa are available under broad eugenic and juridical indications, but very few abortions, only 689, were performed in 1985. Four-fifths of the abortions were performed on white women, suggesting that nonwhite women do not have the same access to lawful abortions. The repressive abortion laws and uneven access to abortion services drive thousands of women, estimated at 200,000 annually, to backstreet abortions. A number of privileged women travel to Britain to procure an abortion. In Nigeria and in most African states, clandestine abortions are also increasingly performed because of a strict ban on legal abortion. About 50 percent of medical complications reported in hospital emergencies are attributed to backstreet abortions. The incidence of clandestine abortions can also be traced to an acute lack of contraceptive knowledge and services in most African countries.

Oceania

In the countries of Oceania, New Zealand recorded a lower abortion rate at 9.7 abortions per 1,000 women than Australia with a rate of 15.2 in 1984. New Zealand's abortion rate is quite low compared to that of most other countries with low birth rates, suggesting that induced abortion is not used as a major means of fertility regulation. Its abortion rate has been quite steady. Only minor fluctuations have occurred since the enactment of its abortion law in 1977, except during 1978–79 when a significant number of New Zealand women, especially single women aged twenty to twenty-four, traveled to Australia to obtain abortions.

Estimates of the incidence of abortions in Australia vary considerably, and complete statistics are available only for South Australia. In the mid–1970s, the period following the legalization of abortion, the number and abortion rate rose sharply, mostly among younger women under twenty. Since 1978 the abortion rate has tended to drop, from around 14 per 1,000 women aged fifteen to forty-four to 13.2 in 1984. The incidence also showed a slight drop in all age groups except among women twenty to twenty-nine years old. In terms of marital status, the proportion of total abortions in single or formerly married women increased from 47 percent to 74 percent in 1984 (*Abortion Research Notes*, 1987, p. 3). Australian women rely heavily on contraception to control their fertility, with over 80 percent reporting having ever used a contraceptive method. Surprisingly, the most common methods are coitus interruptus, natural methods, and spermicides (30 percent), which are highly unreliable; the pill and condom are used by only 12 percent of women.

GENERALIZATIONS

1. One of the most significant abortion trends in many countries was an initial radical upswing in the number and rate of induced abortions following the enactment of liberal abortion laws. This was largely due to replacement of illegal abortions by legal abortions. The proportion of increase in the number of abortions generally corresponded with the degree of permissiveness of the law and the availability of abortion services; the more permissive the laws and the more widespread abortion services, the higher the increase. Thereafter, the numbers and rates began to taper off or show a moderate decline. The downward shift often reflected the widespread use of modern contraceptive methods mostly by married women or those couples living in a stable relationship. In the late 1970s abortion rates generally began to take an upturn following the pill scare, which induced many women to revert to traditional or less effective methods of birth control.

Changes in demographic factors such as age, sex, age at marriage, and reproductive norms also contribute to abortion trends. For example, the addition of a significant number of sexually active adolescent females to the women in their reproductive years can be a crucial factor in raising demand for abortion.

2. During the initial period following liberalization of abortion laws, more married than single women sought abortions in order to space births. Once they completed their desired family size, they resorted to a more permanent method of family limitation (e.g., sterilization). Since an increasing number of young women are becoming sexually active at an earlier age and often without contraceptive precaution, they tend to rely heavily on abortion as a means of preventing unintended motherhood. Thus, while the proportion of married women seeking abortion is steadily decreasing, single women continue to constitute a large proportion of the abortion seekers. Recently, the proportion of women under twenty and over twenty-nine years of age undergoing abortions has declined because of greater contraceptive vigilance in these age groups. The above phenomena are more common in most Western countries, North America, and Oceania.

3. The experiences of Eastern European countries, Singapore, China, and Cuba demonstrate that contraceptives (including surgical methods) alone do not

achieve the target fertility reduction without a concurrent heavy reliance on induced abortion—legal or illegal. Initially, abortion is used as a primary method of fertility regulation, but over time it is used only to compensate for contraceptive failure. A mass educational campaign can foster attitudinal changes in reproductive norms and behavior, while incentive and disincentive programs appreciably increase the possibility that the target population will utilize abortion and contraceptive services. India, for example, has been making vigorous efforts in the past decade to reduce its birth rate through widespread use of abortion and contraception. But to date the results have not been encouraging. In the hope of making its population utilize these services effectively, the Indian government is contemplating the launching of elaborate programs of incentives and disincentives.

4. Notwithstanding the significant role of abortion in fertility decline, no government that had enacted permissive abortion laws advocated a continual use of abortion as a primary method of birth control. Abortion, it was hoped, would eventually be replaced by efficient contraception. To reduce women's reliance on abortion, all countries directed their efforts toward comprehensive family planning programs either in concert with abortion services or following the target reduction in fertility rates. In the GDR a woman is given contraceptive counseling and is required to report to a family planning center soon after her abortion. In the FRG the government recently announced strict counseling provisions.

In 1973 Hungary adopted a comprehensive population policy aimed at prevention rather than interruption of undesired pregnancies. These measures have resulted in effective contraceptive practices that have reduced considerably the reliance of Hungarian women on abortion. For example, one-quarter of married women had at least one abortion before the age of forty in 1985, as contrasted with one-third of them in the 1970s (*Abortion Research Notes*, 1987, p. 2). In Poland immediately after the 1956 Abortion Act was adopted, health service centers launched a program designed to instruct women in how to prevent unwanted pregnancy, and every new mother was required to receive family planning instructions. Polish women still rely heavily on rhythm, which is unprecedented in Europe. The government has recently established a program of providing counseling on contraception and sexuality and devices. Israel has placed a great emphasis on modern contraceptive methods since the sharp decline in Jewish fertility in 1979. Cuba has recently adopted a policy designed to promote equal access to abortion and contraception. In Bangladesh the emphasis is on post-MR acceptance of contraceptive methods. In Czechoslovakia a woman is given instructions on contraception and sterilization at the time of abortion.

5. As a further safeguard against improper practice, laws in all countries stipulate regulatory procedures that guide abortion practices. Most countries (e.g., the FRG, Canada, Italy, GDR, Hungary, New Zealand, and Czechoslovakia) require that the procedure be carried out in a hospital or in an approved institution. Some have statutory bodies to approve applications and oversee the process. A few countries (e.g., Israel, Yugoslavia, and India) impose additional

requirements if abortion is performed in the second trimester. However, a necessary corollary of these unencumbered regulations is the painful fact that women seeking abortion have little or no freedom to make independent decisions and are actually or potentially subjected to obstacles ranging from the torpor of bureaucratic red tape to the strong resistance of the service providers.

6. Legislative reforms in most countries are generally not matched by an adequate service delivery, thus creating inequality of access to legal abortion, especially for poor or socially disadvantaged women as in Australia, Canada, the FRG, India, Italy, New Zealand, and the United States. Consequently, many women who want an abortion are forced to travel a considerable distance to other regions or to another country. Others are compelled to resort to illegal abortions available through paramedics or untrained personnel (e.g., countries of Latin America and the Caribbean).

7. Abortion continues to be a divisive and highly polemic political issue in many countries (e.g., Canada, the United States, and Western Europe) that have liberalized laws because religious fundamentalists, Christian, Muslim, and Jew, resist abortion for any reasons. Consequently, their governments are under increasing pressure to adopt more restrictive grounds for abortion or to institute a total ban on the availability of the procedure. Despite fierce controversy, women in all societies continue to practice abortion, legally or illegally, as a solution to their problem pregnancies.

CHARACTERISTICS OF PATIENTS

Of the abortion seekers, the largest proportion of terminations occurs among women aged twenty to thirty-four. In the early years following the introduction of liberal abortion legislation, the number of women under twenty years of age seeking abortions increased, reaching as high as 30 percent in some countries such as Canada, New Zealand, and the United States. But more recently their incidence has either declined or leveled off except in Asian countries. In terms of a single unit year, women aged eighteen to nineteen in countries such as Canada, England and Wales, Finland, New Zealand, Norway, and the United States post a higher abortion rate than those in either the preceding or following age groups. Among Western countries except the Netherlands and New Zealand, Canada records lower teenage abortion rates (per 1,000 women under twenty), ranging from 1.4 to 28.1 percent. In Asian countries such as Japan, India, Singapore, Bangladesh, and South Korea, teenagers undergoing abortion constitute a very small proportion of abortion seekers compared to the countries of the West. Their number is now on the rise because of increasing numbers of sexually active teenagers in the Asian population.

Currently married women account for the highest proportion of abortion seekers in Bangladesh (almost all), India (93 percent), Singapore (85 percent), Czechoslovakia (78 percent), Italy (71 percent), and Hungary (70 percent). Other countries have recorded a proportion of 50 percent or less. The United States

(20 percent), Canada (22 percent), and New Zealand (26 percent) registered the lowest figures. The proportion of married women seeking abortion has been declining in many countries over the past few years except Czechoslovakia, Hungary, and Norway.

Abortion among Special Groups

There are also significant variations in the abortion rates among ethnic groups in a given country. In the United States, for example, the abortion rate per 1,000 nonwhite women (mostly blacks) is more than twice (2.4 percent) as high as that for white women. In New Zealand, Maori, and the Pacific Islands, the aborting women are older, of higher parity, have a higher fertility rate, and are more likely to use induced abortion as a means of family limitation than Caucasian women of European descent. In Canada, French Canadian women have the lowest birth rate (13.2 per 1,000 population in 1985) and the smallest family size—1.5 children. In Quebec, the teenage pregnancy rate (21.5 births plus abortions per 1,000 women fifteen to nineteen) are consistently among the lowest of all other provinces. French Canadians rely more heavily on contraception and use abortion as a complement to family planning, particularly in the case of failed contraception. Quebec, with a population of 26.4 percent of the total in 1981, contributed 13.9 percent of the therapeutic abortions performed on Canadian women in that year.

Unlike the minority in Canada, Surinamese women in the Netherlands, who make up one-quarter of all residents seeking abortion, post a much higher abortion rate than that of native Dutch women. Likewise, in Sweden, immigrant women from countries in the Eastern Mediterranean record an abortion rate that is almost twice that of Swedish women. This is largely due to their nonacceptance of birth control methods.

Gestation Period

With increased public awareness and acceptance of abortion, and improved health education on the relative safety of early abortion, more women tend to present themselves for an early termination of their pregnancies. Thus, in all countries, first-trimester terminations up to thirteen weeks of gestation constitute a large majority—up to 90 percent—of the abortions performed. The proportion of pregnancy terminations occurring in the second trimester, up to twenty weeks, is 12 to 18 percent in England and Wales, India, and Australia. Cumbersome procedures, inadequate services, the requirement of a second medical opinion, and the need for referrals are among the factors causing delay in seeking an early abortion in these countries. The proportion of late terminations is directly linked with the level of difficulty created by bureaucratic procedures, committee requirements, and unwieldy application processes. Nowhere is the effect of the simplification of procedures on the reduction of delay in seeking an abortion so evident as in Sweden. In 1979 Sweden relaxed its requirements considerably and eased its procedures, enabling women to apply for an abortion directly to a gynecology clinic at a hospital. This resulted in a spectacular drop in the mean duration of pregnancy at termination from 14.1 weeks in 1968 to 9.9 weeks in 1980. Put differently, the percentage of first-trimester abortions, which was 43 percent in 1968, climbed to 80 percent in 1973 and to 95.5 percent in 1984. In Hungary, the government relaxed some abortion indications and procedures in July 1986, enabling a woman to obtain authorization from the committee chair rather than the full committee. Abortion on request is now available to women aged over thirty-five instead of forty as was prescribed previously (*Abortion Research Notes*, 1987, p. 4).

The proportion of second-trimester abortions is almost the same in Canada and the United States—11 percent. The proportion is even lower in Sweden and Japan where elective abortions are now permitted up to eighteen and twenty-four weeks, respectively.

Late abortions are more common among young single women and among the economically and socially disadvantaged. These women are either ignorant of the facilities or cannot afford to travel away from their home, or they are unaware of or unwilling to recognize their pregnancy. The requirement of parental consent can sometimes contribute to the delay.

REPEAT ABORTIONS

The percentage of women who reported having had at least one previous induced abortion has steadily increased in most countries since abortion laws were relaxed. Hungary is an exception. These numbers are more likely underreported since they are based on verbal reporting by patients who might be reluctant to disclose this information.

Based on the information available, it seems that increases in multiple abortions have occurred particularly in countries that experienced increases in the abortion rate. In addition, there has been a general increase in the proportion of women in the population who have experienced an abortion, which makes them more susceptible to a repeat abortion.

The percentage of women having at least one prior abortion is highest in Eastern European countries, ranging from 45 percent (among married women) in Czechoslovakia to 50 percent in Yugoslavia and to 75 percent among Russian women. Among Western countries, the United States registers the highest percentage of women with recent abortions, almost 37 percent. Other countries report significantly lower percentages of repeat abortions, with a high of 20 percent for Canada and a low of 14 percent for England and Wales. Among the Nordic countries, Sweden has the highest percentage of women with prior abortions, almost the same as that in the United States, but 10 percentage points higher than that in Norway, Finland, and Denmark.

Among the countries of Asia, Singapore and South Korea tie for the highest level, with almost 35 percent of the aborting women having had an earlier abortion. India ranks the lowest in percentage, ranging from 5 to 15 percent.

New Zealand and Australia post the same proportion—12 to 13 percent—of women having experienced a repeat abortion. Repeat abortions are more common among older women than among younger women.

The proportion of women seeking repeat abortions, especially abortions of third or higher orders, is expected to increase in most countries as more women begin to engage in sex at an earlier age, often without an effective or frequent contraceptive protection. Increased coital frequency generally involving multiple partners, coupled with the pill scare, has forced many women in Western countries to rely on less effective methods of contraception; as a result, these women are further exposed to the risk of unwanted pregnancies. In many Asian and Eastern European countries, inadequate contraceptive services compound the risk of unwanted impregnation. As legal abortion becomes more accessible and acceptable, more women are likely to use this method as a supplement to, if not as a substitute for, contraception. It has also been observed that women who are motivated to control their fertility are likely to make more frequent use of both contraceptives and abortion as complementary methods. Furthermore, the fertility norm favoring smaller family size and changing childbearing patterns have increased the probability that abortion will be used for family spacing and limitation.

REFERENCES

Abortion Research Notes. Bethesda, Md.: Transnational Family Research Institute, July 1987, *16* (1–2).

David, H. P. Cuba: Low fertility, relatively high abortion . . . *Intercom*, July-August 1983, 5–6.

Tietze, C., & Henshaw, S. K. *Induced abortion: A world review, 1986* (6th ed.). New York: Alan Guttmacher Institute, 1986.

Table 1.1
Grounds for Abortion, Abortion Rates, Marital Status, and Number of Cases by Previous Abortions and Gestation Period: Selected Areas and Years

Area and Year	Grounds for Abortion	Abortion Rate per 1000 women 15-44	Marital Status		Previous Abortions 1+	Gestation Period under 13 weeks
			Single	Currently Married		
			Percent		percent	percent
North America						
Canada	2					
1974		9.6	58.2	31.3	7.9	78.8
1980		11.4	65.2	23.7	15.6	86.0
1984		10.2	66.6	22.0	20.1	88.0
1985		9.2	66.8	21.8	20.4	88.9
Cuba	6					
1974		69.5	-	-	-	-
1980		47.1	-	-	-	-
1984		58.7	-	-	-	-
United States	6					
1974		19.3	72.4*	27.6	15.2	88.0
1980		29.3	79.4*	20.6	32.9	91.0
1983		28.5	81.3	18.7	38.8	90.5
1985		28.0	-	-	-	-
South America						
Brazil	1, 4	-	-	-	-	-
Chile	1	-	-	-	-	-
Ecuador	1, 4	-	-	-	-	-
Peru	2	-	-	-	-	-

1 = Medical (life); 2 = Medical (health); 3 = Eugenic (fetal); 4 = Juridical (rape, incest); 5 = Socioeconomic; 6 = On request
* Previously married and never-married women are combined.

Table 1.1 (Continued)

Area and Year	Grounds for Abortion	Abortion Rate per 1000 Women 15-44	Marital Status Single	Currently Married	Previous Abortions 1+	Gestation Period Under 13 weeks
			Percent		Percent	Percent
Europe						
Belgium	1					
1979		-	37.0	57.0	-	-
1981		-	53.7	39.3	-	-
1982			52.9	40.4	-	-
Czechoslovakia	2, 3, 4, 5					
1974		26.4	16.9	76.6	-	99.5
1980		31.1	12.2	80.6	-	99.5
1984		34.5	13.2	78.4	-	99.5
Denmark	6					
1974		24.2	34.0	57.9	-	97.4
1980		21.8	49.5 (1981)	42.3	-	98.2
1984		18.4	52.7 (1983)	39.5	-	(1983) 97.5
Finland	2, 3, 4, 5					
1974		28.8	-	-	(1973) 14.6	87.8
1980		13.8	56.2	35.3	21.5	95.4
1983		12.0	59.1	32.1	22.6	95.8
German Federal Republic	2, 3, 4, 5					
1977		4.1	29.7	61.6	-	-
1980		6.6	39.3	54.1	-	-
1984		6.4	43.7	50.2	-	-

Table 1.1 (Continued)

Area and Year	Grounds for Abortion	Abortion Rate per 1000 Women 15-44	Marital Status		Previous Abortions 1+	Gestation Period Under 13 weeks
			Single	Currently Married		
				Percent	Percent	Percent
German Dem.Republic	6					
1974		28.8	-	-	-	-
1980		24.4	-	-	-	-
1984		26.2	-	-	-	-
Greece	2, 3	-	-	-	-	-
Hungary	2, 3, 4, 5					
1969		90.6	13.2	82.9	-	-
1974		44.3	23.0	70.2	56.7	99.0
1980		36.3	20.4	71.1	49.9	99.0
1984		37.1	(1983) 20.4	70.0	49.2	98.8
Italy	6					
1979		15.9	24.1	75.9	-	98.3
1980		18.7	28.0	72.0	-	99.9
1984		19.0	(1983) 26.6	73.4	(1983) 24.9	
Netherlands	6					
1974		6.2	-	-	-	-
1980		6.7	50.6	41.5	-	-
1984		5.9	56.2	36.2	19.1	99.2
Norway	6					
1974		20.0	-(1975)53.1		('78)18.5	-
1980		16.1	52.2	40.5	21.8	96.9
1984		15.9	49.3	43.5	23.1(1983)	97.1
Poland	2, 4, 5					
1974		18.2	-	-	-	-
1980		16.6	-	-	-	-
1984		16.5	-	-	-	-

Table 1.1 (Continued)

Area and Year	Grounds for Abortion	Abortion Rate per 1000 Women 15-44	Marital Status Single	Currently Married	Previous Abortions 1+	Gestation Period Under 13 weeks
			Percent		Percent	Percent
Sweden	6					
1974		19.2	53.7	35.8	8.8(1975)	86.7
1980		20.7	-	-	27.5	94.9
1984		17.7	-	-	33.5	95.5
United Kingdom	2, 3, 5					
1974		11.6	48.8	41.3	5.8	82.8
1980		12.8	53.8	34.7	10.2	82.1
1984		12.8	60.4	28.8	14.2(1983)	86.1
Yugoslavia	6					
1975		59.5	-	-	-	-
1980		71.4	-	-	-	-
1984		75.7	-	-	-	-
Asia						
Bangladesh	1					
1975-76		0.3	-	-	-	-
1980-81		1.6	-	-	-	-
1984-85		3.4	-	-	-	-
China,Peoples Republic	6					
1974		26.0	-	-	-	-
1980		44.1	-	-	-	-
1983		62.9	-	-	-	-
India	2, 3, 4, 5					
1974-75		0.8	5.9	92.8	6.5(75-76)	76.0
1980-81		2.7	-	-	-	86.0
1982-83		-	-	-	-	85.0

19

Table 1.1 (Continued)

Area and Year	Grounds for Abortion	Abortion Rate per 1000 Women 15-44	Marital Status		Previous Abortions 1+	Gestation Period under 13 weeks
			Single	Currently Married		
			Percent		Percent	Percent
Indonesia	1	-	-	-	-	-
Israel	2, 3, 4					
1979		23.2	-	-	-	-
1980		21.1	-	-	-	-
1984		25.7	-	68.0	-	-
Japan	2, 3, 4, 5					
1974		25.5	-	-	-	-
1980		22.5	-	-	-	-
1983		21.5	-	-	-	-
Korea,Republic	2, 3, 4					
1973		105.4	-	30.0	-	-
1978		124.2	-	49.0	-	-
1982		-	-	49.6	53.0[+]	-
Singapore	6					
1974		13.6	10.5	88.4	-	-
1980		28.4	24.7	74.1	23.3	93.5
1983		28.1	26.0	72.8	35.3	95.8
Sri Lanka	1	-	-	-	-	-
Africa						
Nigeria	1	-	-	-	-	-
South Africa	2, 3, 4					
1981		0.1	44.4	48.3	-	-
1982		0.1 (1983-85)	40.0	52.0	-	-

20

Table 1.1 (Continued)

Area and Year	Grounds for Abortion	Abortion Rate per 1000 Women 15-44	Marital Status		Previous Abortions 1+	Gestation Period under 13 weeks
			Single	Currently Married		
			Percent		Percent	Percent
Oceania						
Australia	2, 3, 5					
1980		13.9	(1979) 58.0	29.0	-	-
1982		13.4	61.0	27.0	13.6	-
New Zealand	2, 3, 4					
1976		7.1	56.7	30.1	5.7	-
1980		8.6	59.5	25.3	7.4	91.9
1984		9.7	-	-	12.2(1983)	-

+ Based on larger cities only

21

2

AUSTRALIA

Stefania Siedlecky

The history of abortion in Australia parallels that of other Western countries from which its population and culture are largely derived. The generation to 1911 went through a demographic revolution (Hicks, 1978, p. 157). In 1903 a Royal Commission on the Decline of the Birthrate was appointed in the State of New South Wales (NSW) to investigate the causes of the fertility decline. It was reported that abortifacients and contraceptives were freely advertised and sold. One doctor reported a Melbourne hospital study which revealed that 50 percent of the women had had a previous abortion (Hicks, 1978, pp. 35–36). Doctors and clergy joined the debate on both sides. Concern was directed to the "selfish and immoral" use of contraception and abortion.

Little accurate information is available on the previous incidence of illegal abortion, but morbidity and mortality were high. Abortionists' fees were exorbitant, and many women resorted to unskilled or self-abortion. In 1939 the Report of the Director-General of Health in NSW warned of the "serious menace to life and health caused by the enormous number of abortions and abortal sepsis" (Report of the Director-General, 1940, p. 51), which accounted for 22 percent of maternal deaths and 2.53 percent of all female deaths in women aged fifteen to forty-four.

The debate continued with varying degrees of virulence and emerged more seriously in the 1960s, stimulated by the new women's movements and the debate in Britain which resulted in the introduction of legal abortion in 1967. Humanist societies called public meetings and established Abortion Law Reform Associations and women's groups in the states. One of these, Children by Choice, in Queensland became not only a pressure lobby, but also an abortion referral service.

In 1969 in South Australia (SA), the Criminal Law Consolidation Act was amended, laying down conditions for abortion to be lawfully performed. Common law judgments in Victoria and NSW led to the definition of "lawful" in relation to abortion, and a more liberal interpretation of the law became possible. Following an attempt to introduce similar laws into the Australian Capital Territory (ACT), a Royal Commission on Human Relationships (RCHR) was established in 1974 to inquire into all "aspects of male and female relationships as far as these matters are relevant to the powers and function of the Australian Parliament and Government" (RCHR, 1976, p. 6). The Commission found that there was no clear majority favoring prohibition of abortion; that current laws had no clear policy; and that "more liberal laws could help to overcome some of the worst abuses which occur under restrictive laws" (1977, p. 136).

Since 1974, in the new liberalized climate, free-standing abortion clinics have been opened in NSW, Victoria, and Queensland. In the early years these organizations were subject to various police investigations. "Pro-choice" groups such as the National Abortion Action Campaign have been established, as well as a doctors' group, the Abortion Providers Federation of Australia. Opposed to abortion reform are various "pro-life" groups such as Festival of Light and the Doctors Who Respect Human Life. The pro-life groups form a cohesive opposition with links in other countries. Their tactics have included parliamentary action, confrontation of local government and parliamentary candidates, letter and media campaigns, intimidation of clinic staff and clients, and actual damage to clinic properties. However, the results of the 1983 elections would seem to indicate that the antiabortion lobby had little or no effect on the election outcome.

LEGAL STATUS OF ABORTION

Australian state laws on abortion are based on the English law of 1861 and the McNaghten judgment of 1938 (*R* v. *Bourne*) which in effect states that abortion is not unlawful if the doctor believes it is necessary to save the life of the mother or to prevent her becoming a "mental and physical wreck" (Finlay & Sihombing, 1978). The laws fall into three categories:

1. In two states, Victoria and NSW, abortion comes under common law. Common law rulings in Victoria (Menhennit J. in *R* v. *Davidson*, 1969) and NSW (Levine J. in *R* v. *Wald*, 1972) have found that abortion is not unlawful if the doctor honestly believes on reasonable grounds that abortion is necessary to preserve the life or physical or mental health of the mother. In NSW "health" also includes the effects of social or economic stresses. ACT follows NSW law.

2. In Tasmania, Queensland, and Western Australia, abortion comes under the Criminal Code. There have been no such rulings, but there is a statutory exemption from the English 1861 act, where the operation is performed on an unborn child for the preservation of the mother's life, if the performance of the operation is reasonable, having regard to the patient's state at the time and to all the circumstances of the case.

3. In South Australia (1969) and the Northern Territory (NT) (1974), additional clauses have been added which make abortion lawful where there is risk to the life or physical or mental health of the mother or risk of serious handicap to the child. The opinion of two doctors is required except in emergency cases to save the life of the mother.

In SA the operation must be carried out in a prescribed hospital; there is a limit of twenty-eight weeks gestation, and the woman must have a residential qualification of two months, not necessarily current.

In the NT the abortion must be carried out by a gynecologist or obstetrician up to fourteen weeks gestation, or by any doctor, up to twenty-three weeks, to prevent grave injury to the woman's physical or mental health. The place of operation is not specified.

Both South Australia and the Northern Territory have a conscience clause that does not affect any duty to participate in treatment to save the pregnant woman's life or to prevent grave injury to her mental or physical health. In the NT, the consent of the woman, or a guardian in the case of a minor, is required. In the other states there is no consent clause, and laws regarding consent for any medical procedure apply. No state requires the consent of the spouse or putative father.

Only SA requires notification of all abortions. Consequently, this is the only state where comprehensive statistics are available. NSW has the most "liberal" position of all states regarding abortion. The NSW attorney-general confirmed the position on abortion in 1974 (RCHR, 1977, Vol. 3, p. 138). In 1976 charges against a doctor at a women's health center were dropped on the decision of the NSW attorney-general, and there have been no further prosecutions.

Australian governments generally have pronatalist policies. No Australian government has a stated policy on abortion reform, and there has been a reluctance to make further changes in the law since 1974, leaving any later decisions to the courts. In 1977 following an inquiry into abortion, the federal government introduced an ordinance preventing the establishment of free-standing clinics in the ACT. Attempts to repeal or amend this ordinance have failed; attempts to introduce new legislation in the federal parliament to restrict medical benefit payments for abortion, or to limit funding for family planning clinics that refer for abortion have also failed. Amendments to the Human Rights Commission Bill of 1979 and the Sex Discrimination Bill of 1982 sought to restrict abortion by incorporating the rights of the fetus from the time of contraception. These amendments were defeated, as was a bill introduced in the Queensland Parliament in 1980 to severely restrict abortion in the state.

Meanwhile, in 1982 a court decision overruled a decision by the NSW minister for health not to approve an abortion for a fifteen-year-old girl in an institution (*K* v. *Minister for Youth and Community Services*), and in 1983 a court decision refused an injunction application by a Queensland man to prevent his girlfriend from having an abortion (*Attorney-General of Queensland and Kerr* v. *T.*).

ILLEGAL ABORTION

Before 1969, most abortions were illegal. Although little information is available, estimates as high as 100,000 per year were reported to the Royal Commission. Deaths from illegal abortion have probably been underreported. In 1936 abortion accounted for 33 percent of all maternal deaths (see table 2.1).

Deaths from abortion declined from 14.7 per 100,000 females aged fifteen to forty-four in 1936 to 0.1 per 100,000 in 1975 and nil in 1981. The decline has been due to better techniques, to introduction of blood transfusion and antibiotics, to the changing attitudes of doctors since the mid–1960s, and to the more liberal interpretation of "legal" abortion.

ATTITUDES TOWARD ABORTION

The abortion debate cuts across all political parties, and all religious and social groups, and polarizes the community. Protagonists of abortion reform argue that restrictive laws encourage abuses; that the law is uncertain, discriminatory, and a denial of women's rights and does not apply uniformly in all states. Their opponents argue that human life is sacred from the moment of conception and that abortion is immoral and can only be justified in the rare case of extreme risk to the mother's life. The large mass of people do not participate in campaigns but have expressed support for legal availability of abortion in opinion polls. Although the Catholic church is most closely identified with opposition to abortion law reform, not all Catholics adopt this attitude and a large number of Catholics accept abortion even under liberal conditions (table 2.2). Among non-Catholics there is a wide range of opinion, and a number of churchmen have played a prominent role in the movements favoring liberalization of abortion laws.

Attitudes of the media have varied, with some presenting a balanced view and others giving greater publicity to the antiabortion lobby. Over the past twenty years a number of surveys and media polls have been carried out on attitudes toward abortion, including a major survey in 1980 at the time of the attempt to introduce restrictive regulation into the Queensland Parliament (*Australian Women's Weekly*, 1980). Even allowing for distortion, the trend toward more liberal attitudes is obvious (table 2.2).

Two household surveys in Melbourne in 1971 (Caldwell, 1972, p. 44) and 1977 (Department of Demography, 1979) showed a similar trend among married women; among the unmarried, in 1979, 9 percent of both males and females opposed abortion, 57 percent approved, and 32 percent approved under certain conditions.

Doctors' attitudes have changed along with those of the community, and, since 1967, many have gained experience in legal abortion in the United Kingdom. A survey of general practitioners in Tasmania in 1976 showed that 7 percent would not refer for abortion and 92 percent would refer where there was a substantial risk to the mother's life, including 40 percent who would refer on request (Davey, 1976, p. 37). Catholic doctors were least likely to refer on request. In 1968 the National Health and Medical Research Council (NH&MRC)

made recommendations on abortion which were later embodied in the SA legislation (NH&MRC, 1969).

The Australian Medical Association (AMA), reflecting the diverse views of its membership, has no set policy on abortion. In 1972 the resolution of the World Medical Council was incorporated into the AMA Code of Ethics (AMA, 1972, p. 94). In 1974, at the request of the AMA, abortion was added to the list of services eligible for health insurance benefits. One Catholic Health Insurance fund was exempted from paying these benefits.

In 1973 the NSW Branch of the AMA published ethical guidelines that were adopted by the NSW Medical Defence Union (AMA, 1974, p. 11). Briefly, these include the need for a second medical opinion except in urgent cases, written consent of the woman and her husband if married, and, in the case of an unmarried minor, the guardian. Under age sixteen the parents/guardian should be consulted even if the girl forbids it, except where the doctor considers there is a grave threat to the girl's life. These guidelines are more cautious than the legal interpretation allows in NSW.

In 1979 the AMA opposed the motion in Parliament to limit the scope of medical benefits paid for abortion and reaffirmed the principle that termination of pregnancy, when legally performed, was a medical service. The AMA took a similar position when the Queensland Pregnancy Termination Control Bill was introduced in 1980 (NH&MRC, 1969, p. 11). Improvement in technology and acceptance of abortion as a medical procedure have resulted in more doctors openly performing abortions in properly equipped hospitals and clinics. This development has virtually eliminated illegal abortion and has brought the cost into line with other medical services.

There has been a gradual change in the indications for abortion from medical/ fetal to psychosocial (84 percent in 1971 and 98 percent in 1982) (Annual Reports, SA, 1972–82). This has caused concern among antiabortionists who see it as a move toward abortion on demand.

There is still considerable disadvantage to women in some states and some country areas where restrictive attitudes persist. Even in the "liberal" states, Catholic hospitals severely restrict or prohibit abortion, and large public hospitals impose limits on the numbers performed. Many women travel to major cities or even interstate to obtain abortions in free-standing clinics.

DEMOGRAPHY OF ABORTION

Incidence

Estimates of the incidence of abortion in Australia vary considerably and are likely to be exaggerated, either to press the case for law reform or to emphasize the need for stricter controls. The Royal Commission estimated that 60,000 abortions were carried out each year (Vol. 3, p. 195). Current estimates may be made from two sources, as shown in table 2.3.

Figure 2.1
Age-Specific Abortion Rates, South Australia, 1972–82

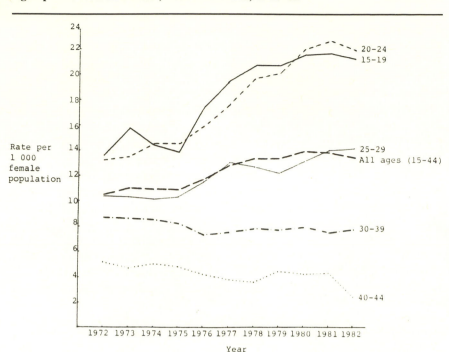

Source: Australian Department of Health, Canberra.

1. Health insurance estimates which include only cases where medical benefits have been paid. Fluctuations reflect changes in health insurance and the level of reporting, as well as incidence.

2. Estimates based on notifications in South Australia (Annual Reports, SA) which include all clients, insured and uninsured. Data for 1976 only suggest a net loss from SA interstate of about 7.5 percent. No subsequent figures are available.

In 1984 medical benefits were paid for 54,600 abortions, compared with an estimate based on SA figures of around 46,500 for 1982–83. Expressed differently, the number of abortions in 1984 represented an abortion rate of 15.2 abortions per 1,000 women aged fifteen to forty-four and an abortion ratio of approximately 22.7 per known pregnancies. In 1985 the number of abortions rose to 56,400. Assuming 20 percent underestimation, the number of abortions appears to be fewer than many estimates indicate. The trends in incidence in various age groups in SA are shown in figure 2.1, and the Australia-wide trend appears similar. In the mid–1970s there was a rapid rise in abortions, most marked among the age group fifteen to twenty-four, which followed the extension of the Medical Benefits Schedule to include abortion in 1974 and the introduction of Medibank (universal health insurance) in 1975. The rise may reflect an increasing transfer from clandestine to open legal abortion as well as an increase in rates. Since 1978 the incidence has stabilized and may be declining, particularly in older women.

Gestation

When a second medical opinion is required, there may be delays in performing the abortion. In SA, 86 percent of abortions were carried out before twelve weeks in 1971 and 90 percent in 1977; the proportion above fifteen weeks remained at 5 percent (Godfrey, 1980, p. 32). In 1982, 92 percent of abortions were carried out by vacuum aspiration compared with 78 percent in 1974. Hysterectomy declined from 5 percent of cases in 1971 to 0.25 percent in 1982 (Annual Reports, SA).

Age, Parity, and Marital Status

Information for this analysis is taken from SA data and reports from three free-standing clinics which show considerable consistency: Preterm, Sydney (Snyder & Wall, 1976); Population Services International, Sydney (Johnston & Roberts, 1978); and Fertility Control Centre, Melbourne (Wainer, n.d.).

SA data show that in 1982 30 percent of abortions occurred in teenagers (table 2.4), most of whom were unmarried. By comparison, in 1982 only 7.2 percent of all births were to teenagers. Table 2.4 also shows the relative increase in abortions among unmarried women between 1970 and 1982 from 47 percent to 75 percent. The percentage of never-married and formally married who sought abortion in 1984 remained unchanged (*Abortion Research Notes*, 1987, p. 3). The relative decline of abortion among older age groups and married women reflects their better contraceptive practice and the increasing use of sterilization among those over age thirty. The Royal Commission (1977, p. 201) found that abortions fell into two main groups:

—Young never-married women with no children, mainly aged fifteen to twenty-four
—Married women with two or more children

About half of all abortion clients have had no children. Migrant and Catholic women were represented in all groups, but were less likely to be in the unmarried teenage group and more likely to seek abortion after two or more children. There was some overlap in these groups since many migrant women are Catholics. Overall, Catholics were represented in similar or slightly higher proportions than the general population, and Protestants slightly less. Those of no stated religion were overrepresented.

Contraceptive Use

There is a high level of contraceptive use in Australia, but unwanted pregnancy may result from irregular use or use of less reliable methods. Over 80 percent of clients had ever used contraception, ranging from 50 percent among fourteen to sixteen year olds to 90 percent among women aged over twenty-one years. These figures were an improvement on earlier studies. Never-married women and Catholic women currently practicing their religion were less likely to have ever used a contraceptive method. Oral contraception was the most common method ever used by all religious groups, followed by the condom, coitus interruptus, and spermicides. There were differences related to cultural practice and levels of education. There was a higher level of use of coitus interruptus among less educated women, many of whom were migrants. Protestant and Catholic women had similar levels of use of the natural methods.

At the time of conception, over half of the married women were using contraception, but over 70 percent of never marrieds and previously married women were not using any method. The most common method reported was coitus interruptus (30 percent), followed by natural methods, spermicides, oral pills, and condoms (each about 12 percent). Half of the women aged over twenty-one years and 75 percent of those under that age were not using any method. Following abortion, 97 percent of women intended to use a contraceptive method, 72 percent choosing oral contraceptives, 12 percent an IUD, 8 percent sterilization, and 5 percent other methods. Catholic women were less likely to choose an oral contraceptive and more likely to choose an IUD.

In South Australia in 1982, 8 percent of women had a concurrent sterilization, including 3 percent of those under age thirty years, 30 percent between ages thirty and thirty-nine, and 49 percent aged forty years and over.

REPEAT ABORTIONS

Caldwell (1972, p. 78) found that in 1971 5 percent of married Melbourne women acknowledged that they had had or tried to procure an abortion. The AWW survey in 1980 showed that 16 percent of women aged thirty-five to forty-four years and 7 percent aged fifteen to nineteen years had had a previous abortion. This may be a distorted sample. Snyder and Wall (1976) found that 16 percent of Preterm clients had had one or more induced abortions (p. 11). In 1979, 10 percent of clients were "repeat abortions" (Mougne, Edwards, & Nolan, 1980, p. 33).

In South Australia in 1982, 13.6 percent of women undergoing abortion reported one or more previous abortions compared with 13.2 percent in 1977 and 10.4 percent in 1971 (Godfrey, 1980, p. 56). A higher rate of previous abortion was reported among Catholic women than among Protestants, as well as among migrants compared to Australian-born women (Johnston & Roberts, 1978, p. 31).

It would appear that abortion clients represent an "at risk" group with higher rates of previous abortion than the general community. Mougne et al. (1980) concluded that the present rate of repeat abortions was not a cause for concern (p. 33).

ABORTION AND FERTILITY REGULATION

Australia has an aging population. Demographic trends since 1900 have been characterized by declining mortality and, except for major fluctuations following the two world wars, a declining birth rate. Net reproduction rates fell below replacement during the economic depression of the 1930s and again in the late 1970s (DIEA, 1983). Australian women have a long record of fertility control going back to the end of the nineteenth century, and Australia has relied heavily on immigration for its population growth. Australia's demographic transition occurred before the advent of modern contraceptive technology. Withdrawal was the most frequently used method during the 1930s (Caldwell, 1982, p. 239). Caldwell considers that "the beginning of the Australian fertility decline took the form of a contraceptive revolution, not an abortion one" (p. 251). This should not underestimate the impact of abortion which, as shown above, was a matter of social and public health concern.

Between 1971 and 1981, 11 percent of the decline in births was achieved by an increase in legal abortions and 89 percent by better contraceptive use reducing the number of pregnancies. Even among teenagers, increase in abortions accounted for 38 percent of the decline in births, and contraception for 62 percent (table 2.5).

Family planning organizations date back to 1926. The first birth control clinic was opened in 1933, but only in 1970, coincident with the introduction of the SA abortion legislation, did a state government (SA) adopt a policy on family planning as a means of reducing the need for abortion. The federal government first supported family planning in 1973, including support for natural family planning, and in 1974 introduced its Family Planning Program. Other state governments followed. All medical family planning services attract health insurance benefits. Following the introduction of Medicare in February 1984, family planning clinic services are now, in effect, provided free of charge. Since 1973 oral contraceptives have been available as a pharmaceutical benefit, and other contraceptives have been free of sales tax.

In 1973 the age of majority was lowered to eighteen years which has made it easier and more acceptable for teenagers to obtain family planning advice and abortion. There is currently an investigation into the rights of minors to seek confidential medical advice and to give consent for medical procedures including abortion (Law Reform Commission, 1981).

It is difficult to measure the impact of government policy initiatives among other social trends occurring at the same time. Certainly, government support has legitimized family planning and has encouraged the acceptance and use of family planning services.

ABORTION RESEARCH

Apart from surveys of the free-standing clinics, little research has been published in Australia since 1970. In 1973 Miller examined South Australian abortions in the first two years following the new legislation (Miller, 1973, pp. 825–830). In this period there was only one abortion death which was not due to therapeutic abortion. In the previous six years, abortion had been the major cause of maternal death. Miller found one or more significant complications in 49 percent of cases and emphasized the need for stringent restriction after twelve weeks (p. 825). The SA reports show that in 1982 early complications were reported in only 3 percent of cases, and 2 percent were admitted over the next six weeks with retained products.

Weston found little psychiatric disturbance attributable to abortion (1973). Long-term followup studies are difficult to mount in terms of cost and mobility of clients.

A study of clients attending Children by Choice, Brisbane, in 1974 and 1980 (Bourne & Kerr, 1982) showed a history of previous abortion in 6 percent of women in 1974 and 18 percent in 1980. In 1980, over 70 percent were under age twenty-five; 97 percent of those under age twenty were not married.

Ratten and Beischer (1979) found that therapeutic abortion was followed by a higher incidence of second-trimester abortion or premature labor in the next pregnancy than a previous spontaneous abortion. A later study (Furness, 1983) did not find an increased incidence of either cervical incompetence or premature labor in subsequent pregnancies among women who had had a previous therapeutic abortion.

CONCLUSION

A trend toward more liberalized community attitudes to abortion in Australia has been reflected in some changes in abortion laws and in their wider interpretation. There has been a shift from illegal, unskilled, and self-induced abortion to "legal," skilled abortion openly performed in well-equipped hospitals and clinics. The result has been the virtual disappearance of illegal abortion and the high rates of morbidity and mortality that accompanied it. Cases of postabortal sepsis and hemorrhage occur very rarely. Abortion has not replaced contraception as a means of fertility control. The rate of abortion appears to have reached a plateau and may be declining; therefore, the dire predictions of the antiabortion lobby have not been realized.

SUMMARY

In Australia abortion laws fall within the jurisdiction of the various states. Since 1969 law changes and judgments in several states have laid down conditions under which abortion may be lawfully performed. The changes have occurred as a result of community support for more liberal abortion laws. Statistics show that one-third of abortions are performed on teenagers and about half on unmarried women, and that Catholic women differ little from other women in their use of abortion.

Liberalization of the abortion law has not fulfilled the grave predictions of its opposition. Instead, following an initial rise, legal abortion rates have stabilized and may be declining, even among teenagers. Mortality from abortion, previously the largest single cause of maternal death, is now almost nil. Morbidity has also declined with safer techniques and better equipped facilities. Nevertheless, there is still a strong, vigorous opposition to abortion which carries on a constant campaign at all levels.

No Australian government, either state or federal, has a policy on reform of abortion law, and there is a reluctance to make further changes to the existing laws. Attempts to introduce legislation to liberalize or restrict abortion have been unsuccessful, and it appears that future changes will come from legal judgments.

REFERENCES

Abortion Research Notes. Bethesda, Md.: Transnational Family Research Institute, July 1987, *16* (1–2).

Annual Reports of the Committee appointed to Examine and Report on Abortions notified in South Australia, 1971–1981. Adelaide: Government Printer, South Australia, 1972–82.

Australian Medical Association. Annual report 1971. Supplement. *Medical Journal of Australia*, 1972, 2(9).

———, NSW Branch. Therapeutic abortion. *Monthly Bulletin*, August 1974.

Bourne, A., & Kerr, J. The characteristics of two samples of women seeking abortion in Queensland. *Australian Journal of Social Issues*, 1982, *17*, 3, 207–219.

Caldwell, J. Australian attitudes towards abortion: Survey evidence. In N. Haines (Ed.), *Abortion—repeal or reform*. Canberra: Australian National Unviersity, 1972.

———. Fertility control. In *Population of Australia*. Country Monograph Series No. 9, Vol. 1. New York: United Nations, 1982. (U.N. Doc. No. ST/ESCAP/210.)

Davey, M. The role of Tasmanian general practitioners in the provision of contraception, abortion and sexual counselling services. Unpublished thesis, University of Tasmania, 1976.

Department of Demography, Melbourne Survey, 1977. Canberra: Australian National University, 1979, Parts 1–3. (Unpublished.)

Department of Immigration and Ethnic Affairs. *Review of Australia's demographic trends*. Canberra: Australian Government Publishing Service, 1983.

Finlay, H., & Sihombing, J. *Family planning and the law* (2d ed.). Pt. II: Abortion. Sydney: Butterworths, 1978.

Furness, E. T. Therapeutic abortion, premature labour and cervical incompetence (letter). *Medical Journal of Australia*, 1983, *2*, 604.

Godfrey, B. *Termination of pregnancy in South Australia, 1970–1977*. Adelaide: South Australian Health Commission, 1980.

Hicks, N. *"This sin and scandal," Australia's population debate 1891–1911*. Canberra: Australian National University Press, 1978.

Johnston, J., & Roberts, D. *Catholic women and abortion*. Sydney: Catholic Family Life Program, 1978.

Law Reform Commission of Western Australia. Uniform law for the provision of medical services for minors. Terms of Reference 1981.

Miller, J. M. Medical abortion in South Australia: A critical assessment of early complications. *Medical Journal of Australia*, 1973, *1*, 825–830.

Mougne, C., Edwards, I., & Nolan, D. The increase of repeat abortions—A study at Preterm. *New Doctor*, August-October 1980, *17*, 32–35.

National Health and Medical Research Council, *Report of the 67th session*. Canberra: Commonwealth Government Printing Office, 1969.

Ratten, G., & Beischer, N. The effects of termination of pregnancy on maturity of subsequent pregnancy. *Medical Journal of Australia*, 1979, *1*, 479–480.

Report of the Director-General of Public Health, NSW, for 1939. Sydney: Government Printer, 1940.

Royal Commission on Human Relationships. *Interim report*. Canberra: Australian Government Publishing Service, 1976, *3*, 199.

————. *Final report*, Vol. 3. Canberra: Australian Government Publishing Service, 1977.

Snyder, E., & Wall, S. *Abortion in Sydney: A perspective on change*. Sydney: Preterm Foundation, 1976.

"The voice of the Australian woman" says: "Abortion should be freely available." *Australian Women's Weekly*, May 7, 1980, 12–13; 15–17.

Wainer, J. Abortion: The experience of a freestanding clinic in Melbourne. East Melbourne: Fertility Control Clinic. Submission to the Royal Commission on Human Relationships, No. 73, 1977.

Weston, F. Psychiatric sequelae to legal abortion in South Australia. *Medical Journal of Australia*, 1973, *1*, 350–354.

Table 2.1
Maternal and Abortion Deaths, Australia, 1931–81

Year	Rates/100,000 Live Births				
	Maternal		Abortion		Abortion as %
	Deaths	Rate	Deaths	Rate	Maternal Deaths
1931	650	548.5	185	156.1	28.5
1936	696	599.6	233	200.7	33.4
1941	490	364.2	125	92.9	25.5
1951	203	105.0	36	18.6	17.7
1961	108	45.0	24	10.0	22.2
1971	51	18.5	11	4.0	21.6
1981	25	10.6	0	0	-

Source: Australian Bureau of Statistics: Demography Bulletins, 1931–61; Causes of Death, 1966–81.

Table 2.2
Changes in Attitudes: Should Abortion Be Available?

	% responses	No	Yes,	Yes
			Subject to conditions	
1968 National Gallup Poll[1]		11	72	13
1980 AWW[2] - Catholic		16	41	43
Protestant		3	34	63
All		6	32	62

[1] Reported in Wainer, note 8.
[2] *Australian Women's Weekly*, note 2.

Table 2.3
Estimated Abortion Rates per 1000 Women Aged Fifteen to Forty-four

Year	Health Insurance[1]	S.A. Data[2]
1980	13.2	13.9
1981	13.2	13.8
1982	12.2	13.4

[1] Supplied by Australian Department of Health.
[2] Annual Reports, SA.

Table 2.4
Characteristics of Abortion Clients, South Australia

	% distribution		
Age	1970	1979	1982
Under 20 years	15	32	30
20-29 years	41	43	50
30+	44	25	20
Marital Status			
Never married	38	58	61
Married, de facto	53	29	27
Widowed etc.	9	13	14

Figures rounded.
Source: Annual Reports, SA, 1970–82.

Table 2.5
Estimated Total Pregnancy Rate, Australia, 1971 and 1981[1]

	Age group under 20 years		20-24 years		All ages 15-44	
	1971	1981	1971	1981	1971	1981
Births	54.6	27.1	176.1	104.5	101.1	67.5
Abortions[2]	11.3	21.7	13.8	22.7	10.1	13.9
Total pregnancies	65.9	48.8	189.9	127.2	111.2	81.4

[1] Rates per 1,000 female population in age group.
[2] Based on SA rate. Assumes Australia-wide rate is similar.
Source: Australian Department of Health.

3

BANGLADESH

Halida Akhter

HISTORICAL DEVELOPMENT OF ABORTION POLICY

The population of Bangladesh is now around 100 million, with an estimated growth rate of 2.6 percent annually. Its population density is one of the highest in the world at over 600 persons per square kilometer. The age structure of the population gives a high dependency ratio (93 percent) with 45 percent of the population below fifteen years. The total fertility rate remains high, estimated at 5.8 in 1985. Extended breastfeeding practice leads to relatively long birth intervals of approximately three years. Early marriage is still the norm. More than 50 percent of women get married by the age of sixteen (1981). The health status of the population is unacceptably low: the country has an estimated infant mortality of 125 per 1,000 live births and maternal mortality of 5.7 per 1,000 live births (1975). At least a quarter of this high maternal mortality is due to complications of indigenously induced abortions.

Under the Penal Code of 1860, induced abortion is permitted in Bangladesh only to save the life of the mother. In 1972 the law was waived for women raped during the War of Liberation. Abortions were performed in a few district hospitals under the guidance of expert teams from Bangladesh, India, the United Kingdom, and the United States. In 1976 legalization of first-trimester abortion on broad medical and social grounds was proposed, but legislative action was not taken.

In 1974 the government encouraged the introduction of menstrual regulation (MR) services in a few isolated family planning clinics. In 1978 the Pathfinder Fund initiated an MR training and services program in seven government medical colleges and two government district hospitals. Training was given to government doctors and paramedics (Family Welfare Visitors, FWVs) and a few private doctors. In 1979 the government included MR in the national family planning program and encouraged doctors and paramedics to provide MR services in all government hospitals, health and family planning complexes (Government Circular, 1979). Citing a Law Institute paper, the government noted that MR is not regulated by the Penal Code, since pregnancy is difficult or impossible to prove. Rather, MR is said to be an "interim method of establishing nonpregnancy" for a woman at risk of being pregnant, whether or not she actually is pregnant (Bangladesh Institute of Law and International Affairs, 1979).

By 1984 about 2,100 doctors (government and private) and 2,200 government FWVs had been trained in MR (table 3.1). Reported MR procedures rose from 4,000 in 1975–76 to 50–60,000 per year in 1983–84 (table 3.2), but the actual number may be much higher. The social stigma attached to MR and abortion may inhibit reporting, and the reporting system is in any case poor. It may also be assumed that a large number of MRs are performed in private practice and are not reported. Trained providers are dispersed throughout the country, primarily in government health complexes and centers at various administrative levels. Unfortunately, adequate records have not been kept, and the exact number and location of trained providers are not known. A study involving 376 physicians in 173 rural health complexes, 44 hospitals, and 26 nonhospital centers, including family planning centers, found that about half of them provide pregnancy termination services, MR services, and referral for pregnancy termination services (table 3.3) (Rosenberg et al., 1981).

The government provides considerable support in the form of clinic space, salaries, and equipment for MR training and services (Government Memo, 1979, 1980). Until 1983 external funds were available from the United States Agency for International Development (USAID), the Pathfinder Fund, and the Population Crisis Committee. Because of the U.S. government's stance on abortion, in 1983–84 almost all nongovernment programs stopped providing MR services in order to protect their USAID funds. At present only three programs, two quasigovernment and one nongovernment, train government health personnel (doctors and FWVs) in the MR procedure. The government in its Third Five-Year Plan (1985–90) proposes to extend MR facilities (trained staff and equipment) to rural health complexes throughout the country.

ATTITUDES TOWARD ABORTION

Few studies have been done on attitudes toward abortion in Bangladesh (table 3.4). In the 1975 Bangladesh Fertility Survey, extreme approval or disapproval of abortion was minimal. Among 6,513 married women interviewed, 88 percent approved abortion in cases of rape, 88 percent in cases of premarital pregnancy, and 53 percent in cases of danger to the mother's life. Younger women were more favorably disposed toward abortion than older women (Bangladesh Fertility Survey, 1978).

These findings were similar to those revealed in a study of the attitudes of rural health facilities toward abortion (Rosenberg et al., 1981). Nearly all of the 376 physicians approved the use of abortion to preserve the health of the women.

Over three-quarters approved if the pregnancy resulted from rape; more than 60 percent if the pregnancy was extramarital; and about 60 percent for women who become pregnant during lactational amenorrhea or for pregnant grandmothers. In 1975 a total of 388 married male professionals in urban areas were asked whether they approved of abortion as a means of family planning in Bangladesh (Choudhury, 1975). More than half of these Bangladesh elites (university faculty members, government officials, research scholars, and owners of private firms) favored abortion as a means of family planning. In a pretesting of a Bangladesh Fertility Survey (BFS) questionnaire, 280 ever married women were interviewed, and findings were similar to those from the BFS (Ahmed, 1979). The highest majority of women approved abortion for pregnancy due to rape and premarital pregnancy. Abortion to save the mother's life was approved by 53 percent, but only 17 percent of the women agreed it was acceptable for economic reasons. In 1980 a cross section of 1,130 currently married women in metropolitan Dhaka favored abortion under selected situations (Choudhury, 1980). As many as 50 percent of these women endorsed abortion in at least three situations: (1) if the life of the mother was endangered, (2) if the baby was expected to be born defective, and (3) if a woman was raped.

The mass media, especially daily and weekly newspapers, published several articles on abortion in the late 1970s which highlighted the sufferings of complicated cases at large hospitals, described the consequences of abortions by untrained providers, and listed clinics and health facilities that provided abortion or MR services (Bichitra, 1977; Hassan, 1976; Choudhury, 1975). These articles published interviews with service providers, eminent physicians, women's leaders, political leaders, government officials, and policymakers to expose people to the issue. Since the late 1970s no additional studies have been done.

LEGAL STATUS OF ABORTION

As early as 1976 the Bangladesh National Population Policy attempted to legalize first-trimester abortions on broad medical and social grounds (Choudhury & Susan, 1975). As of 1985 this policy had not been implemented, and restrictive legislation remains in effect.[1] Nevertheless, a memorandum from the Population Control and Family Planning Division (PCFPD) states categorically that "menstrual regulation" (MR) is one of the methods used in the national Family Planning Program. The memorandum quotes a report from the Institute of Law (1979) to the effect that MR does not come under the provision of Penal Code Section 312 in regard to abortion because pregnancy cannot be established. The Bangladesh Institute of Law report (1979) also mentioned the following:

Moreover, many Family Planning Clinics are carrying out the post-conceptive method of "Menstrual Regulation" as a means of birth control which does not come under section 312 of the Penal Code. Under statutory scheme, pregnancy is an essential element of the crime of abortion, but the use of menstrual regulation makes it virtually impossible for the prosecutor to meet the required proof. In our country menstrual regulation (M.R.) is being carried out till the tenth week following a missed menstrual period, and after that patients are referred as abortion cases. M.R. is now recognised as an interim method of establishing non-pregnancy for the woman who is at risk of being pregnant. Whether or not she is, in fact, pregnant is no longer an issue. (p. 31)

The Bangladesh government's Population Control and Family Planning Division (PCFPD) circular states that MR is included in the official policy and that a necessary logistic support for MR services and training will be provided by the Division.[2] Another Bangladesh PCFPD memorandum (1980) permits that MR can be performed by an MR-trained registered medical practitioner and by any FWV who has specific training in MR.[3] It also specifies that an FWV should perform MR only up to eight weeks from the last menstrual period, that is, four weeks from the missed menstrual period under supervision of a physician.[4] Any case with a longer duration must be referred to a trained doctor. In many government-supported clinics the procedure is performed by paramedics (Bhatia & Ruzicka, 1980). The Second Five-Year Plan released in 1980 envisaged that MR facilities would be provided through the family planning clinics, welfare centers, all health centers, and hospitals (Akhter & Rider, 1984b).

DEMOGRAPHY OF MENSTRUAL REGULATION

Since 1974 many family planning clinics have been providing MR services as a backup for contraceptive failure. With an increasing number of trained providers and improvement of the MR reporting system, the reported MR procedures have risen to 50,000–60,000 per year. Published data on the characteristics of those who accept MR are very limited. Very few published articles and only locally published working reports document the characteristics of MR acceptors at clinics providing such services (table 3.5).

Several studies have shown that the women undergoing MR are predominantly younger. Their husbands' and their own educational background suggest that they have a relatively high socioeconomic status. Their mean age is 25.6 years, and they average seven years of schooling, which is much higher than the national average (Akhter & Rider, 1983). At the time they requested MR they had, on the average, three prior pregnancies. Similarly, the MR clients of a Bangladesh village-based family planning program in Matlab were also considerably younger than other women in the population who used contraceptives (Bhatia & Ruzicka, 1980). Almost all clients were reported to be currently married. Since nearly everyone in Bangladesh marries at a very early reproductive age and premarital sex is socially unacceptable, pregnancy termination for unmarried women is unlikely to be reported.

POST–MR CONTRACEPTION

Because MR service is viewed as a backup for contraceptive failure, most clinics emphasize contraceptive counseling and post-MR acceptance of a contraceptive method. In several clinic populations after MR, overall contraceptive use improves, and couples switch to more effective methods. Akhter and Rider (1984a) compared three years of birth control practices of 1,172 women who underwent MR and 499 others who accepted contraceptives only from an urban clinic in Bangladesh. Although about 60 percent of the women in the sample were followed up, the three-year overall continuation rate was higher in the MR group (64 percent) that in the non-MR group (62 percent). When subsample groups were compared, the observed difference was far greater in the same direction. In addition, among the women who did not desire any more children, the continuation rate in the MR group was significantly higher than that of the non-MR group (80 percent versus 68 percent). In several other urban and rural studies, it was found that most of the MR acceptors adopted some form of contraception shortly after they had MR. Although several studies on MR showed that fewer than half of the women who had MR ever used contraceptives previously, a large majority accepted a more effective contraceptive method after they had MR (Akhter & Rider, 1984a; Ahmed & Kabir, 1984).

Only one study documented the subsequent resort to MR during a three-year period following use of MR procedures (Akhter & Rider, 1984b). Three-year contraceptive use data available for 558 women who obtained MR and 228 women who obtained only contraceptives were compared. Of the 558 women who had MR, 21 had at least another abortion in a three-year period after they had MR. The cumulative induced abortion rate was 4.3 percent among the MR acceptors compared to 3.5 per 100 pregnancies in the comparison group. During the observed three-year period, women in the MR group did not obtain abortion significantly more often than women in the comparison group. These findings indicate effective contraceptive practice following MR at least for this urban population. It seems to support similar findings (Bhatia & Ruzicka, 1980) and thus also supports Bernard's (1977) contention that the abortion or MR experience appears to serve as a key in learning to regulate fertility. Overall findings suggest a complementary relationship between MR and contraceptive services. The easy availability of a multimethod service after MR seems important in promoting effective contraception (Akhter & Rider, 1984b).

INDUCED/ILLEGAL ABORTION

Because abortion is illegal in Bangladesh, very little documentation is available on the incidence of induced abortion. Whatever scant information is available comes from mortality and morbidity records of hospital admissions and a single survey of health workers in rural areas. A survey of rural health workers (Measham, Obaidullah, & Rosenberg, 1981) and hospital admission records indicates that induced abortion is common in Bangladesh (Begum, Khan, & Jahan, 1978). These abortions are responsible for a substantial number of maternal deaths. The health worker interview study estimated that 780,000 abortions were performed in Bangladesh in 1978. This figure is an extrapolation from 7,800 deaths due to complications of induced abortion based on a fatality rate of 1 percent (Measham, Obaidullah, & Rosenberg, 1981).

In an interview of seven selected indigenous abortion practitioners in rural Bangladesh, the practitioners presented a wide-range of statistics on the number of abortions they perform (Islam, 1981). Their performance ranged from a minimum of three to four cases in eight to nine years of the practitioner's career to a maximum of 1,000 induced abortions. Some perform several cases per month. One of them had performed 10 to 15 cases during the previous three years, and others 50–60 to 200–300 cases.

COMPLICATIONS OF INDUCED ABORTION

Although menstrual regulation has become increasingly available in recent years, in rural areas the service cannot deal with the large number of unwanted pregnancies. Clandestine abortion is still widely practiced in Bangladesh, especially in rural areas. Approximately half of the admissions to gynecology departments of major urban hospitals are due to complications of abortion (Begum, Khan, & Jahan, 1978). These complications are frequently related to abortions performed by untrained personnel using nonmedically approved procedures. A large proportion of women with induced abortion were admitted with sepsis, temperature, and pelvic infection, which may be a consequence of unsanitary procedures uses in inducing abortion.

Nearly half of the complicated abortions were induced by inserting objects such as a stick or a root into the uterus or by vigorous physical activities. The most common practice was to insert a tree root into the uterus and leave it in place until an abortion or complications ensued. Insertion of foreign bodies was about five times as common as the use of oral preparations, the next most common method (Jabeen, 1978).

Very little is known about the characteristics of women who obtain abortions from indigenous practitioners. Some information is available from referral hospitals which admitted women with serious abortion complications. In pooled data from three medical college hospitals and one clinic, the Bangladesh Fertility Research Program documented the characteristics and complications of abortion patients. On admission, most of these facilities reported patients as married with an average age of 25.5 and a mean parity of 3.5. They reported a mean number of 2.7 living children (Waliullah et al., 1981).

The complications of illegal abortion affect not only individual women or the family but also medical institutions and society as a whole. Treating these complications consumes substantial quantities of such scarce resources as hospital beds, blood for transfusion, costly medicines, and the time of trained medical personnel which could be better utilized treating other medical conditions. A study of 491 induced abortion cases admitted in the Dhaka Medical College Hospital during 1977–80 showed that the mean duration of a hospital stay for all the women was six days (Khan et al., 1984). In two other such studies at Chittagong Medical College (Begum, Khan, & Jahan, 1978) and Salimullah Medical College, the mean hospital stay was two to three days for both induced and spontaneous abortion cases.

Approximately 26 percent of maternal deaths are caused by abortion practices (Chen et al., 1975). Due to the extremely weak maternal and child health service delivery system, statistics are almost nonexistent. Although these large referral hospitals provide data on complications and causes of deaths, rates could not be calculated owing to lack of denominator data. The rural health worker survey study estimated that in 1978 at least 7,800 women died as a result of complications of induced abortion (Rochat et al., 1981).

In any country the legal status of abortion usually influences the specific abortion techniques used and thus the subsequent risk to women. In Bangladesh, unwanted pregnancies appear to pose a particular problem for women with large families and to a lesser extent for unmarried women. Population-based complication rates for illegal abortion cannot be determined because of the lack of data. However, some indications of the extent of complications and the extent of mortality that have been obtained by short survey and by observing hospital admissions for septic incomplete abortions may lead one to conclude that abortion is common to Bangladesh. Most complications may be attributed to abortions performed by untrained practitioners using unsafe, nonmedically approved procedures.

By comparing the characteristics of women who received MR and those who were admitted for serious abortion complications, one can observe that MR clients have higher education, are younger, and are largely urban dwellers compared to the induced abortion complication group. Apparently, MR is not reaching high parity, less educated, and poor women.

SUMMARY

Bangladesh has an unacceptable maternal mortality rate of 5.7 per 1,000 live births. At least a quarter of this high maternal mortality is due to complications of abortions induced by indigenous practitioners. In 1978 several researchers estimated that at least 800,000 induced abortions occurred every year in Bangladesh. The country's restrictive abortion law does not permit abortion except to save the mother's life. During the 1970s attempts were made to legalize abortion, but no legislative action was taken. In 1979 the government included menstrual regulation (MR) in the National Family Planning Program. By 1984 the government trained more than 4,000 doctors and paramedics in MR and began to provide logistics support for the service nationwide. Although grossly underreported, the nationally reported number of MR procedures in ten-year period rose from 4,000 to 60,000 per year in 1984. The women who undergo MR are found to be considerably younger, have had about three prior pregnancies, and come from a higher socioeconomic class than the contraceptive users. Most MR recipients seem to become more effective contraceptive users after they have had MR. However, the characteristics of women receiving MR are different from those who become victims of complications of abortion. Even as late as 1978, a health worker survey estimated that at least 8,000 women were dying every year from induced abortion, which presumably is a very small proportion of the actual number. The common practice is to induce abortion by inserting objects in the uterus or by performing vigorous physical exercise which leads to serious complications. These complications not only are a burden to the woman's family but also drain scarce medical resources. Many advocate making legally approved abortion services by trained personnel widely available in order to save many women's lives.

NOTES

1. The abortion law of Bangladesh was patterned after British colonial law, and the influence of Islam may be the basis for its maintenance. Some scholars, however, interpret the Holy Quran as permitting abortion up to 120 days (sixteen weeks) (Al-Qaliqili, 1977) and believe that the current law is unduly restrictive. Other predominantly Muslim countries have widely varying laws ranging from one that permits abortion on request up to twelve weeks of gestation (Tunisia) to another that forbids abortion under any circumstances (Indonesia).

2. Government of People's Republic of Bangladesh Population Control and Family Planning Division Circular No. FP/Misc–26/79/278 (600), issued on 31 May 1979, announced that by 1982 all the headquarters of the country should be equipped with facilities to provide all types of family planning services such as MR, sterilization, the IUD, and other contraceptive methods. Government of People's Republic of Bangladesh Population Control and Family Planning Division Memo No. 5–14/MCH-FP/Trg/79 dated 8 December 1979, Subject: MR Program.

3. Government of People's Republic of Bangladesh Population Control and Family Planning Division Memo No. 5–14/MCH/FR/trg./80, Subject: Guidelines for Menstrual Regulation (MR). This memo provided guidelines to regulate the services and ensure technical standards, including who can perform MR, criteria for MR training, national program support and supervision system.

4. Government of People's Republic of Bangladesh Population Control and Family Planning Division Memo No. 5–14/MCH-FR/Trg/79, National Institute of Population Research and Training. Subject: Arrangement for MR training for doctors and FWVs.

REFERENCES

Ahmad, R. Attitude toward induced abortion in Bangladesh. *Quarterly Journal of the Bangladesh Institute of Development Studies*, 1979, 7 (4).

Ahmed, T., & Kabir, M. A retrospective study on complications in M.R.—An investigation of socio-cultural causes. Contraceptive Practice in Bangladesh: Safety issues, Report of Multi-Institutional Contraceptive Safety Research Program, Dhaka, December 1984.

Akhter, H. H., and Rider, R. V. Menstrual regulation versus contraception in Bangladesh: Characteristics of the acceptors. *Studies in Family Planning*, December 1983, *14* (12, Pt. 1), 318–323.

————. Continuation of contraception following menstrual regulation—A Bangladesh experience. *Journal of Biosocial Science*, 1984a, *16*, 137–151.

————. Menstrual Regulation and contraception in Bangladesh: Competing or complementary? *International Journal of Obstetrics and Gynecology*, 1984b, *22*, 137–143.

Al-Qaliqili, Sheikh Abdullah, the Grand Mufti of Jordan. Fatwa: Family Planning in Islam. Islam and Family Planning. Dhaka: Directorate of Population Control and Family Planning, Government of the People's Republic of Bangladesh, 1977.

Bangladesh Fertility Survey. First report, Ministry of Health and Population Control, Population Control and Family Planning Division. Government of the People's Republic of Bangladesh, Dhaka, 1978.

Bangladesh Institute of Law and International Affairs. Dhaka Report on Legal Aspects of Population Planning in Bangladesh, Chapter 11—Abortion. 1979, p. 31.

Bangladesh Planning Commission, 1980. The second five-year-plan, Dhaka, Ministry of Planning, Para XVII/87.

Bangladesh Population Control and Family Planning Division (PCFPD). Memo no. 5–14/MCH-FP/80, 1980.

Begum, S. F., Khan, A. R., & Jahan, S. A study of 1003 induced and spontaneous abortion patients treated at Dhaka Medical College. Bangladesh Technical Report No. 8, Bangladesh Fertility Research Program, August-October, 1978.

Bernard, R. P. Contraception and abortion. In M. Potts, P. Diggory, & J. Peel (Eds.), *Abortion*, 490–491. New York: Cambridge University Press, 1977.

Bhatia, S., & Ruzicka, L. T. Menstrual regulation clients in a village-based family planning programme. *Journal of Biosocial Science* 1980, 12–31.

Bhuiyan, N., Begum, R., & Begum, S. Characteristics of abortion cases admitted in Chittagong Medical College Hospital in 1978. Technical Report No. 33, 1978.

Bichitra, Dhaka, August 1977.

Chen, L. C., Gesche, M. C., & Ahmed, S. Maternal mortality in rural Bangladesh. *Studies in Family Planning*, 1975, *5*, 331–334.

Choudhury, R. H. Attitude of some elites towards introduction of abortion as a method of family planning in Bangladesh. *Quarterly Journal of the Bangladesh Institute of Development Studies*, October 1975, *3* (4).

————. Attitudes towards legalization of abortion among a cross-section of women in metropolitan Dacca. *Journal of Biosocial Science*, 1980, *12*, 417–428.

Choudhury, Zaffrullah, & Susan. Abortion in Bangladesh. *The Bangladesh Times*, Dhaka, 3 and 5 May 1975.

Government of the People's Republic of Bangladesh, Population Control and Family Planning Division, *Bangladesh National Population Policy*. Dhaka: Government of Bangladesh, 1976.

Hassan, S. Should abortion be legalized? Desperate women seek quack's help. *The Bangladesh Times*, 13–14 December 1976.

Islam, S. *Indigenous abortion practitioners in rural Bangladesh*. Women for Women: A Research Study Group, Dhaka, 1981.

Jabeen, S. Maternal mortality in Sir Salimullah Medical College (Mitford Hospital) from October, 1976-September, 1978. *Magazine '77*, Sir Salimullah Medical College, 1978, 31–34.

Jabeen, S., Nazmul, S., & Ahmed, G. A study of the abortion related cases admitted in Sir Salimullah Medical College Hospital. Dhaka, Technical Report No. 35, 1979.

Khan, A. R., Begum, S. F., Covington, D. L., Janowitz, B., James, S., & Potts, M. Risks and cost of illegally induced abortion in Bangladesh. *Journal of Biosocial Science*, January 1984, *16* (1), 89.

Measham, A. R., Obaidullah, M., & Rosenberg, M. J. Complications from induced abortion in Bangladesh related to types of practitioners and methods, and impact on morbidity. *Lancet* 24 January 1981, 199–202.

Rochat, R. W., Jabeen, S., & Rosenberg, M. J. Maternal and abortion related deaths in Bangladesh, 1978–79. *International Journal of Obstetrics and Gynecology*, 1981, *19*, 155–164.

Rosenberg, M. J., Rochat, R. W., Jabeen, S., Measham, A. R., Obaidullah, M., & Khan, A. R. Attitudes of rural Bangladesh physicians toward abortion. *Studies in Family Planning*, August-September 1981, *12* (8–9).

Waliullah, S., & Al-Sabir, Ahmed. A study on menstrual regulation programme in two clinics. *Contraceptive practice in Bangladesh: Safety issues*, Report of Multi-Institutional Contraceptive Safety Research Program, Dhaka, December 1984.

Waliullah, S., Begum, S. F., Suraiya, J., Barua, A., Rahman, S., & Ahmad, N. Abortion patients of three medical college hospitals and a clinic in Bangladesh. Paper presented at the Sixth Contributors' Conference of Bangladesh Fertility Research Program, Dhaka, December 1981.

Table 3.1
Distribution of Trained Physicians and Paramedics (FWV*) by MR Training Centers, Bangladesh

Name and Location of MR training centres	Year MR training started	Total trained up to 1984	
		Doctor	FWV
Mohammadpur Fertility Services and Training Centre, Dhaka	1975	89	698
Dhaka Medical College Hospital	1979	628	–
Sir Salimullah Medical College Hospital	1979	499	46
Chittagong Medical College Hospital	1979	164	195
Rangpur Medical College Hospital	1980	126	193
Sher-e-Bangla Medical College Hospital, Barisal	1981	150	163
Sylhet Medical College Hospital	1981	152	146
Mymensingh Medical College Hospital	1981	155	236
Pabna Sadar Hospital	1981	87	188
Khulna Sadar Hospital	1981	94	196
Bangladesh Women's Health Coalition Clinics	1982	+	131
Total		2,144	2,196

* Family Welfare Visitors, a paramedic group.
+ Do not train doctors.

Source: Data compiled by Bangladesh Association for Prevention of Septic Abortion (BAPSA) and published in its quarterly MR newsletter, May 1985.

Table 3.2
National Statistics for MR Services Reported During 1975–85

Year	Number of MRs performed
1975–76	4,408
1976–77	6,687
1977–78	6,135
1978–79	4,412
1979–80	10,479
1980–81	28,041
1981–82	42,427
1982–83	58,579
1983–84	56,728
1984–85	68,600

Source: Directorate of Population Control bulletin. The statistics on the performance of MR services are collected as a part of family planning and MCH service by the Management Information System (MIS) unit of the Directorate of Population Control.

Table 3.3
Reproductive Services Provided by Physician Respondents in Past Year: Abortion Attitude Survey, Bangladesh, 1978–79 ($n = 376$)

Type of Services	Percent providing service[a]
One or more services below	92.0
Delivery	82.1
Referral for pregnancy termination	45.2
Pregnancy termination (abortion at 12 or more weeks of gestation)	45.2
Menstrual regulation (abortion up to 12 weeks of gestation)	31.6
IUD insertion	10.9

[a]Totals do not add to 100 because of multiple responses.
Source: Rosenberg et al., 1981, pp. 318–321.

Table 3.4
Summary Table of Studies Conducted in Bangladesh on Attitude Toward Abortion

Key Authors	Population Interviewed	Most common reasons for approving abortion
1. Bangladesh Fertility Survey, 1975	Survey of 6513 married women of reproductive age	1) rape (88.3%) 2) premarital pregnancy (87.6%)
2. Choudhury, 1975	388 married male professionals in urban areas	56% responded in favour of introducing abortion as a method of family planning.
3. Ahmad Ranna, 1979	280 ever married, urban and rural women (pretesting of BFS questionnaire)	1) rape (89%) 2) premarital conception (88%)
4. Rosenberg, 1981	376 Physicians in 1973 rural health complexes, 44 hospitals and 26 non hospital centers including family planning centers	1) pregnancy dangerous to a woman's health (95%) 2) pregnancy before marriage (79%)
5. Choudhury, 1980	1130 currently married fecund women of metropolitan Dhaka-working & non working	1) endangers life of the wife (70%) 2) woman is raped (43%) 3) child crippled (48%)

Table 3.5
Summary Table on Demographic Characteristics of Women Who Have Undergone MR

Key author year of publications	Number of women and types of clinics	Mean age in years	Mean parity/ gravidity	Number of years of schooling	
				Wife /	Husband
1. Akhter, 1983	2821 (one urban)	25.6	3.5	7.2	11.2
2. Waliullah, 1984	442 (two urban)	26.4	3.2	7.2	10.6
3. Tofayel, 1984	611 (20 rural, 10 urban)	27.5	2.8	7.4	11.0

4

BELGIUM

Marleen Temmerman, Jean-Jacques Amy, and Michel Thiery

HISTORICAL DEVELOPMENT OF ABORTION POLICY

Belgium is one of the very few European countries that still enforces a strict abortion law. The present law is based on the Napoleonic Penal Law (1810) which prohibits abortion under any circumstances. An additional law aimed at increasing the birth rate in the country was enacted in 1923. This law prohibited any help or information concerning matters of abortion and contraception. Abolition of this law was sought in 1966 but in vain.

In the early 1970s the public debate on abortion flared up. To be sure, abortions had formerly been performed: wealthy women would be attended by their private gynecologist, or they could go to a foreign country (in sequence: Switzerland, the United Kingdom, and the Netherlands), whereas the lower social class had to resort to local illegal abortionists, risking the serious complications inherent to the instillation of saponaceous solutions or the insertion of sharp objects into the uterus. The medical records of one of the university hospitals in Brussels reveals a decrease in the admissions following incomplete abortion from 128 in 1969 to 20 in 1979 (Vekemans & Dohmen, 1982).

In 1971 a first bill authorizing the liberalization of abortion was presented to Parliament by the socialist W. Calewaert. During the same year, Dr. W. Peers, a gynecologist in Namur, openly started to perform abortions on social and economic grounds. Two years later Dr. Peers was arrested. A massive protest movement emerged both within and outside the country. Petitions for liberalized abortion were signed by more than 300,000 people. Thousands of letters and telegrams reached Dr. Peers in jail, and after thirty-three days of imprisonment he was released.

In 1973 the provision that forbade dispensing information on contraceptives was abolished, and in 1974 a leaflet on contraception and planned parenthood was edited and circulated by the Ministry of Health. In 1975 the government set up a Royal Commission for the Study of Ethical Problems whose conclusions were submitted in 1976. The majority of the commission—thirteen out of twenty-five members—recommended the depenalization of abortion. However, the minority of twelve members submitted a separate report defending the application of the existing law except in case of therapeutic (medically indicated) abortion.

Meanwhile, the abortion movement grew, and in 1976 the main subject on the "Women's Day" was abortion; depenalization of abortion, and the performance of abortion at the woman's request and at social security rates were two of the main themes.

In the mid–1970s the "Pro-Vita" movement (member of the European Federation "Europa Pro Vita") appeared on the scene in Belgium, assuming the defense of the rights of the embryo and the fetus. Their spokespersons belonged to the conservative and Roman Catholic (RC) fraction of society, and they requested strict application of the law.

Although several proposals to suspend or mitigate the law were made in Parliament, no changes resulted. In 1981 the public prosecutor of the Brussels area decided to prosecute again. Since then, a number of women, doctors, and social workers have been given suspended sentences of one to eighteen months' imprisonment. Some of them were later acquitted by the Court of Appeals. Other lawsuits are still pending. In 1982 suspension of the law was asked in Parliament but rejected by a slim majority. On the other hand, a national demonstration on the theme of liberalizing abortion attracted only about 3,000 people.

Over the last twelve years at least fifteen clinics have openly performed abortion in Brussels and the French-speaking part (Wallonia) of the country. In the Flemish-speaking part of Belgium (Flanders), four outpatient clinics and one hospital have adopted a similar attitude. Thus, in Belgium access to abortion differs for Flemish-speaking and French-speaking women. Flanders, the most northern part of the country, is Catholic and conservative. For about fifteen years abortion problems confronting the Flemings have to a great extent been solved in the Netherlands, whereas Brussels and Wallonia, being more progressive in this matter, have attempted to face the issue by themselves.

LEGAL STATUS OF ABORTION

The Law as It Stands

According to Belgian Penal Law, abortion is liable to severe punishment, regardless of why it is performed. The applicable provisions are to be found in the Penal Code, Book II, Title VII: "of crimes and offences against the order of the family and against public decency," of which chapter I is entitled "Abortion." This chapter includes articles 348 to 353, which ban abortion, without any exception being made. Both the (voluntary) performer and the (consenting) woman are subject to two to five years of imprisonment in addition to a fine. Lesser punishments are applied if the abortion was accidentally provoked through battery, if the abortion fails, or if attenuating circumstances can be invoked. On the contrary, heavier charges are imposed on the performer if the woman did not consent (maximum ten years), if the woman dies (maximum fifteen years), or if the abortionist belongs to the medical or paramedical profession (five years added to all punishments; maximum twenty years). As noted earlier, this strict abortion law goes back to the Napoleonic Penal Code of 1810, at which time Belgium was part of France. It was adopted with minor changes in the Belgian Penal Code in 1867.

An additional provision is to be found in Chapter VII (public offense of good morals) of the same title; Article 383, introduced in 1923, pertains to abortion, pornography, and anticonception. It forbids all publicity and help regarding abortion. As already mentioned, the restrictions concerning anticonception were abolished in 1973. Since 1867 and 1923, the provisions on abortion have not been changed, although their application tends to differ from the letter of the law.

Application of the Law

Public Prosecution

The public prosecutor plays a crucial role in the application of the law: it is within his or her discretionary powers not to seek prosecution in certain cases. For instance, traditionally an abortion performed to save the woman's life is not prosecuted. On the other hand, clandestine abortion is almost always prosecuted.

Medical abortion falls in neither of these categories. As explained above, it came into focus in the beginning of the 1970s. In 1974, in view of the violent public reaction to Dr. Peers's arrest and of the proposed reform of the law, the minister of justice used his influence on the public prosecutors, and this resulted in a general suspension of prosecution. (Due to separation of powers, it is not within the power of the minister to order the public prosecutor, who is part of the judiciary, to withhold from prosecuting.) During this period, complaints were received and investigations made, but no case of medical abortion was brought to a criminal court.

In 1978, however, the public prosecutor of the Brussels area reinitiated proceedings, claiming that plans for law reform in Parliament should not uphold the action of justice for too long. In the rest of the country, a lenient attitude was still being observed. Once again the minister of justice used his influence, and the proceedings were suspended at the court level. But in 1981 Parliament still had not assumed its responsibilities in this matter, and so the trials started in Brussels.

Court Proceedings

In September 1981 doctors, patients, and others involved in abortion (e.g., parents who had consented to their daughter's abortion) stood trial before the Brussels criminal court. Several convictions were obtained. Professor Pierre-

Olivier Hubinont, head of the Department of Obstetrics and Gynecology of the University Hospital Saint-Pierre in Brussels, was given a suspended sentence of eighteen months imprisonment. In June 1983 the Court of Appeals reversed all of these sentences. The court ruled that the accused could not be held responsible for violating a law that had been in disuse for so long that it could have been thought to be no longer applicable. But in September of that same year, the criminal court of Brussels gave a gynecologist who had performed an abortion on a fourteen-year-old girl a suspended sentence of one month imprisonment. This judgment was appealed, but the appeal was rejected in March 1983. Since then several investigations on abortion cases have been conducted in the Brussels area and in other parts of the country as well. A gynecologist was arrested in 1984, being accused of having performed an abortion on a fourteen-year-old girl. He spent nine days in jail, and he was scheduled to appear in court in 1987.

Law in the Making

Since the early 1970s the Belgian Parliament has periodically discussed abortion bills, but as a result of strong political divisions on this matter, the law has remained unchanged. Two types of law proposals can be distinguished: (1) bills that seek to change or suppress the law permanently; (2) bills that, in view of the present prosecutions and convictions, would suspend the application of the law temporarily.

Proposals for Permanent Change

In 1966 the above-mentioned abolition of Article 383 (prohibiting help and publicity concerning abortion) was put to a vote but did not gather a majority. Five years later socialist Senator Willy Calewaert proposed a law that would have legalized abortion on medical, psychological, and socioeconomic grounds, subject to approval by two or three doctors, one of whom had to be a gynecologist. As was true of all other bills, it failed in Parliament.

Since then, some twenty bills have been proposed, primarily from the socialist or liberal faction in Parliament. As a result of political instability (each time the government falls, Parliament is disbanded and all bills have to be reintroduced), most of these projects were never debated in public.

Only once did the government show concern for the issue of abortion. In 1974 an Ethical Commimssion was created. The majority and minority reports submitted by the commission were never really used or discussed in Parliament, due to another change in the government.

Proponents of liberalization of the Belgian abortion law (Herman-Michielsens et al., 1981) and those in favor of a more far-reaching depenalization (Detiège et al., 1981) have finally agreed to the concurrent introduction of one law proposal. At the time of this writing, this proposal is being discussed in the ad hoc Commission of the Senate (Lallemand et al., 1986); it still awaits discussion in the House of Representatives (Detiège & Moureaux, 1986). This bill seeks to legalize the performance of abortion on women up to fifteen weeks of pregnancy, without imposing further restrictions. A delay of six days would be required between the moment the decision was made and termination of pregnancy, which would have to be performed by a physician either in a specialized consultation center or in a hospital. After fifteen weeks of pregnancy, abortion would be allowed only if continuation of the pregnancy would pose a serious danger for the physical or psychological health of the woman, or if a serious fetal anomaly was diagnosed.

The Detiège Bill (1981) goes much further: it proposes to legalize abortion on demand, without imposing restrictions, examination panels, or delays. Clandestine (nonmedical) abortion would remain punishable.

Proposals for Temporary Suspension

Since 1974 twelve bills have been proposed to stop prosecutions by suspending the application of the penal law. The first of these bills, which sought to suspend prosecutions, were found to be unconstitutional, inasmuch as Parliament was not entitled to suspend the execution of existing law (which Parliament itself had not found necessary to amend). Later bills therefore tended to suspend the penal law itself, which would be unconstitutional. None of the bills succeeded in Parliament, though some came very close; in 1982, with several cases pending before the criminal court, the opponents to legalized abortion carried the vote with only three votes difference. Some liberal members of the government who had previously claimed to be in favor of liberalization voted with their Catholic coalition partners against the proposal. Moreover, a few socialist Members of Parliament had refrained from voting, arriving in Parliament late that very day.

ATTITUDES TOWARD ABORTION

Since 1972 Belgian public opinion with regard to abortion has shifted toward less severe laws, or even toward complete liberalization (Dequeecker, 1978; ISCOP, 1978; Van de Weghe et al., 1976).

The Roman Catholic church takes a very restrictive view, and several bishops have issued warnings against spreading information on contraception and abortion.

In inquiry conducted among politicians in 1978 showed that no political party was homogeneous regarding abortion; the majority of the Members of Parliament stated that they were personally in favor of depenalization (CRISP, 1982). The difference between personal opinion and votes in Parliament (where depenalization was rejected) may be explained by the imperatives of party coherence and the will to avoid a government crisis. The public opinion tolerance poll about abortion (1978), published in 1982, shows the division in public opinion between the different regions. Inhabitants of Brussels are the highest in tolerance, while Flanders seems to be the most conservative part of the country, as illustrated in table 4.1. Yet according to a more recent opinion poll (1984), 87 percent of women members of the (Flemish) Christian Democratic party were in favor of liberalizing the law.

Robert Legros (1985), former president of the high court, stated in unambiguous terms that abortion had been de facto depenalized in Belgium, as women residing in Belgium could have their pregnancy terminated in a neighboring country without risking prosecution.

DEMOGRAPHY OF ABORTION

Levels and Trends

Since it is illegal to terminate pregnancy in Belgium, it is impossible to give precise information on the demography of medical abortion.

Extrapolating from data on the clinical effectiveness of contraceptives used in Belgium, Cliquet and Schoenmaekers estimated the annual number of abortions to be between 19,000 and 34,000 a year (CGGS, 1979; Schnabel 1976) about 30,000 annual abortions. These estimates were based on the number of Belgian women who traveled to the Netherlands for abortion. Verheye, Thiery, and Cliquet (1982) collated information from outpatient clinics in the Netherlands, the United Kingdom, and the French-speaking part of Belgium, which led them to estimate an abortion rate of between 13,400 and 15,900 a year. If these figures are correct, there would be about one induced abortion for each nine to ten births in Belgium.

Existing statistics about abortions performed in Belgium are based on data collated by the Action Group of Outpatient Clinics Performing Abortion (GACEHPA). This organization advises women on contraception and helps those confronted with psychosexual problems; it is active in preventing clandestine abortion and in the fight to obtain total liberalization. GACEHPA clinics (which now number sixteen) keep standardized medical records, which are the basis of overall statistics. Their most recent study deals with 3,789 applications for abortion in Belgium during the year 1979, 3,266 of which were actually carried out; two-thirds took place in outpatient clinics and one-third in hospitals (Vekemans & Dohmen, 1982).

In Belgium, abortions are performed by gynecologists or general practitioners with special training in the technique of suction curettage under paracervical block. For second-trimester abortion the hospital gynecologist may use such techniques as intra-amniotic instillation of hypertonic saline solution, prostaglandins or—very rarely—hysterotomy.

The study conducted by Verheye, Thiery, and Cliquet pertains to 3,409 Belgian women who aborted in the Netherlands in the first six months of 1979. These data were collated by STIMEZO (the Dutch Assoociation for Medical Abortion) which gathers information concerning abortion performed in a network of Dutch abortion clinics, through a system of continuing registration. These data thus represent only part of the total number of abortions performed in the Netherlands.

Abortions performed in several hospital departments and by private practitioners should be added to this figure (Vekemans & Dohmen, 1982). Moreover, an estimated 400 Belgian women still travel to the United Kingdom, a figure that is considerably less than that of a few years ago when 2,000 or 3,000 women residing in Belgium went to the United Kingdom for abortion (Kols et al., 1982). This decrease took place because women up to twenty or twenty-two weeks gestation may now be aborted in some Belgian or Dutch hospitals.

Ketting's results published in 1983 provide information on all abortions performed in the Netherlands during 1982 (Ketting & Leliveld, 1983). The decrease in the number of Belgian women who are being aborted in the Netherlands is striking: it diminished from 12,000 in 1975 to 6,300 in 1982. About 75 percent of these women are Flemish, and about 10 percent are immigrants from Turkey or Northern Africa. The decrease in the number of abortions performed in the Netherlands on women residing in Belgium is due partly to an overall decrease in the number of abortions done on these women and partly to a relative increase in the number of these procedures being done in Belgium.

Age

Table 4.2 shows the age distribution of the patients. The median group in the GACEHPA study was twenty to twenty-four years of age (Vekemans & Dohmen, 1982); in the STIMEZO report of the same year (Verheye et al., 1982; Ketting & Leliveld, 1983) it was thirty to thirty-four. Yet a trend toward younger age groups has been observed in recent years, which can be explained by the fact that adolescents are sexually active at a younger age. By comparing the GACEHPA data (Vekemans & Dohmen, 1982) with national statistics (Ministère de la Santé Publique et de la Famille, 1980) in 1979, it appeared that women were overrepresented in the age group twenty to thirty-four.

Marital Status

The marital status of women in the GACEHPA study (Vekemans & Dohmen, 1982), those treated over several years by STIMEZO (Verheye et al., 1982; Ketting & Leliveld, 1983), and national statistics (Ministère de la Santé Publique et de la Famille, 1980) are shown in table 4.3. Single, divorced, and widowed women are more numerous in the group applying for abortion than is the case nationwide.

Parity

Forty to 50 percent of the group under consideration did not yet have children. Only 8 to 9 percent had three and only 4 to 7 percent of the applicants had four or more children. About one-third of women applying for abortion are taking care of two or more children already (Vekemans & Dohmen, 1982; Ketting & Leliveld, 1983).

Religion

According to the GACEHPA data, about 22 percent of women requesting termination of pregnancy claim to have no religion. Among the others, 68 percent are Roman Catholic, but three-fourths of them do not regularly attend church. Eight percent are Muslims and 2 percent Protestants. Roman Catholic leaders are acting against abortion, yet they do not seem to be influential enough to keep their flock from having an abortion performed (Vekemans & Dohmen, 1982).

Gestational Age

One of the most important risk factors of abortion is advanced gestational age. According to the GACEHPA data, the duration of pregnancy is most frequently between six and ten weeks (70.5 percent) (Vekemans & Dohmen, 1982). STIMEZO reports a high number of second-trimester abortions (26 percent) performed on young unmarried girls between the ages of fifteen and nineteen, due to the denial of the problem, doubts, fear to reveal the unwanted pregnancy, and lack of information on the location of abortion clinics (Verheye, Thiery, & Cliquet, 1982).

Socioeconomic Status

The average monthly per capita income of the patients in GACEHPA study is less than $400 US for about three-quarters of the women. Fifty-five percent of the patients attended school up to the age of fifteen; 33 percent finished secondary school; and 12 percent went to college (Vekemans & Dohmen, 1982).

Reasons for Abortion

The GACEHPA asked the patients what their main reasons were for wanting to have their pregnancy interrupted. A summary of these reasons is given in table 4.4; each reason mentioned is expressed as a percentage of all the reasons given. (Each patient could indicate one or more of forty-four motivations given in the inquiry.)

Social and economic reasons were cited by 40 percent. Problems in the relationship with the partner were also frequently invoked. Only 5 percent of the women did not want children at all, and 91 percent claimed to want children at a later date. Most of the women requesting abortion said they would have continued their pregnancy if they had been living under better social and economic circumstances, or if they had had a better relationship. Rape, incest, risk of fetal malformations, and risk for the health of the mother were rarely invoked. Thus, liberalizing abortion solely for these reasons would have very little impact on the legal status of most currently performed abortions (Vekemans & Dohmen, 1982).

Data which Van Kets and Thiery (1975) collated in 1975 are not in complete agreement with the above findings, but the authors acknowledged that they pertained to a small and highly selected group of women who had applied for abortion at the University Hospital in Ghent in 1972–74. As many as 82 of the 172 requests filed had a medical motivation.

ABORTION AND CONTRACEPTION

According to GACEHPA statistics, almost half of the patients were not using any contraceptive at the moment of conception (table 4.5). Nevertheless, 63 percent had used an effective contraception before: in most cases, the woman herself decided to abandon its use, but in about 10 percent it was the result of medical advice. Frequently, stopping the pill was not followed by the adoption of other contraceptive measures. Only 7 percent of women with an unwanted pregnancy had never used any method of birth control before (Vekemans & Dohmen, 1982).

Ketting and Leliveld (1983) found that the Belgian abortion patient uses less effective or ineffective contraceptive methods, even though Belgium has the highest consumption of pills in the world. (Thirty-one percent of all Belgian women between fifteen and forty-four years of age take the pill, as opposed to 29.5 percent of all Dutch women, see Kols et al., 1982.) Consumption of oral contraceptives is the highest among married women betwteen the ages of twenty and twenty-four, and decreases among women thirty to thirty-four years of age and thereafter, probably reflecting the fear of age-related morbidity which the media relentlessly publicizes.

In 96 percent of all abortions, an effective birth control method was begun or prescribed on the day the abortion was performed, the main methods being hormonal contraception (64 percent) and the IUD (32 percent). In 1.2 percent, a method was advised but not prescribed; 2.1 percent of the women refused contraception; and in 0.7 percent no discussion of contraception took place. Tubal ligation is preferred by married, divorced, or widowed women over thirty years of age (Ketting & Leliveld, 1983). Thus, abortion very often leads the woman to reassess her behavior and is a strong motivation to resort to a more effective contraceptive technique. However, thorough followup is necessary for proper guidance.

ABORTION AND ADOLESCENTS

More than 50 percent of Brussels' sexually active youths under eighteen years of age use contraceptives (Vekemans & Dohmen, 1982). Girls of seventeen to eighteen years old usually take the pill, whereas younger girls do not use con-traception at all.

According to the GACEHPA results, 259 girls aged thirteen to eighteen years applied for abortion in 1979 (mean age = seventeen years). Among those girls, about 17 percent were less than ten weeks pregnant, but in a nonnegligible fraction gestational age was more than fourteen weeks. About 4.6 percent were not certain who the father was. They usually came to the clinic accompanied by a member of their family or a friend. Twenty-five percent of those girls were employed, but only 10 percent earned more than $400 US a month. Two-thirds of the girls were students, and about 60 percent did not have any personal income. Thirty-nine percent had a stable relationship, whereas 33 percent were having casual affairs. Eighty-eight percent of the fathers were bachelors; of the 51 percent employed, 54 percent earned more than $400 US. These young people used contraceptives but frequently the less effective types. The majority of these girls were primigravidae, who were not opposed to having children, but who wanted to have them later. About 4 percent of these young girls were seeking a second abortion, a figure that emphasizes the problem of contraceptive guidance.

REPEAT ABORTION

Little information is available on repeat abortion. According to the STIMEZO inquiry (1982), 213 of 1,667 women (12.8 percent) were having a second or third abortion. Compared to patients without a previous pregnancy, more of these women (about 2 percent) used contraception, but the discontinuation rate of the pill was high. The fact that even women with repeat abortions, conscious of the need for birth control, fail to continue using contraception is disquieting and has important implications for those responsible for giving contraceptive advice.

ABORTION RESEARCH

Apart from the GACEHPA inquiry in 1979, little research has been done on abortion in Belgium (Vekemans & Dohmen, 1982).

Avants and Piot (1983) assessed the prevalence of genital infections and the frequency of infectious complications in a group of 170 women requesting abortion in a medical center in Flanders. *Chlamydia trachomatis* was isolated in 12 percent of these women and in *Neisseria gonorrhoeae* 0.6 percent. Following the abortion performed by vacuum aspiration under paracervical block at less than twelve weeks' amenorrhea, 5.5 percent developed salpingo-oöphoritis and 3 percent endometritis. There was a strong correlation between an infection with *C. trachomatis* before abortion and the appearance of infectious complications after the suction curettage. No such relation was found with any other microorganism. Depending on the prevalence of *C. trachomatis* in a given population, screening followed by selective treatment or prophylactic use of antimicrobial medication is thought to be indicated.

ILLEGAL ABORTION

As would be expected, few data are available on clandestine abortion in Belgium. According to Cliquet et al. (1976), fewer than 0.5 percent of the clandestine abortions are brought to court. Because the outpatient clinics and hospitals disregard the legal status of abortion and provide good medical care, the admission rate of women suffering from complications of clandestine abortion has dropped dramatically.

SUMMARY

In spite of the repressive legislation in Belgium, 15,000 to 20,000 Belgian women seek an abortion in or outside the country annually. The most frequently invoked reasons for having the abortion are socioeconomic and social problems. The majority of these women already have children or want to have children in the future. Although most women have a good knowledge of contraception, the discontinuation rate is high.

The results of pilot studies suggest that registration of standardized data is necessary.

The present law forbids abortion and makes no exception. While prosecutions are in progress, a bill aiming at legalizing the law is awaiting discussion in Parliament. Public opinion regarding abortion is divided, but the majority wants a more liberal law.

ACKNOWLEDGMENTS

The authors are indebted to MP Leona Detiège, Dr. Marcel Vekemans, and Hendrik Dierick for advice, and to Ms. Bea Pion for expert secretarial assistance.

REFERENCES

Avonts, D., & Piot, P. Genital infections in women undergoing therapeutic abortion. *European Journal of Obstetrics, Gynecology and Reproductive Biology*, 1985, *20*, 53.

CGGS. Scientific follow-up of pregnancy termination. Annual report, 1978, p. 54.

Cliquet, R., Thiery, M., & Deven, F. Induced abortion: An interdisciplinary study with respect to policy alternatives in Belgium. *Population and family in the Low Countries I*. Leyden: Martinus Nijhoff, 1976.

Courrier hebdomadaire du CRISP, European Election Study. European Parties Middle Level Elites. 1982, p. 962.

Dequeecker, I. Abortus: De vrouw beslist [Abortion: the woman's decision]. *Vrouw en Socialisme*, 1, Uitgavefonds Leon Lesoil, 1978.

Detiège, L., & Moureaux, Ph. *Bill concerning the interruption of pregnancy*. Introduced in the House of Representatives on 19 June 1986.

Detiège, L., Risopoulos, B. J., Neyts-Uyttebroeck, A. M., Brouhon, H., Klein, E., Deleuze, O., & Nagels, J. *Bill concerning the interruption of pregnancy and the suspension of articles 350, 351, 352, 353 and 383, paragraph 5 and following of the Penal Code*. Introduced in the House of Representatives on 15 December 1981.

Herman-Michielsens, L., Mayence-Goossens, J., Henrion, R., Pede, J., Vanderpoorten, H., & Waltniel, L. *Project of Law to alter articles 350, 351, 352 and 353 of the*

Penal Code and to regulate some cases of interruption of pregnancy. Introduced in the Belgian Senate on 20 March 1981.

Une enquête de l'ISCOP. L'avortement et l'opinion publique Belge [Public opinion toward abortion in Belgium]. *Pourquoi-Pas*, 13 April 1978.

Ketting, E., & Leliveld, J. Abortus en anticonceptie anno 1982 [Abortion and contraception in 1982] *STIMEZO Onderzoek*, 1983.

Kols, A., Rinehart, W., Piotrow, P. T., Doucette, L., & Quillin, W. F. Oral contraceptives in the 1980s. *Population Reports*, May-June 1982, Series A, No. 6.

Lallemand, R., Herman-Michielsens, L., Wyninckx, J., Henrion, R., Vaes, J. F., Aelvoet, M., Lepaffe, J., Pataer, P., & Rifflet-Knauer, M. *Bill concerning the interruption of pregnancy, the modification of articles 348, 350 and 351, and the suspension of articles 352 and 353 of the Penal Code*. Introduced in the Belgian Senate on 6 March 1986.

Legros. R. Le Problème de l'avortement et la logique juridique. *Journal des Procès*, 18 October 1985, *70*, 14.

Ministère de la Santé Publique et de la Famille. Annuaire Statistique de la Santé Publique, Exercice 1980 [Ministry of Public Health and Family, Statistics of Public Health, Year 1980], Belgium.

De publieke opinie tolerant inzake abortus [The public opinion tolerance about abortion]. *Knack*, April 1978.

Schnabel, P. Poliklinische abortus: een vergelijking tussen Nederlandse en Belgische abortusclienten [Out-patient abortion: A comparison between Dutch and Belgain abortion patients]. *Bevolking en Gezin*, 1976, *2*, 183.

STIMEZO Zeeuws Vlaanderen: Jaarverslag 1982 (Annual Report 1982, STIMEZO-Zeeuws Vlaanderen), 1982.

Van de Weghe, M., Van Egmond, H., de Poorter, A. M., Carlier, A., & Thiery, M. Een opinieonderzoek betreffende abortus arte provocatus [A poll about abortion]. *Tijdschrift voor Geneeskunde*, 1976, *32*, 8.

Van Kets, H., & Thiery, M. Motivatie van aanvraag tot abortus arte provocatus. [Motivation for requests of interruption of pregnancy]. *Tijdschrift voor Geneeskunde*, 1975, *24*, 1217.

Vekemans, M., & Dohmen, B. Induced abortion in Belgium: Clinical experience and psychological observations. *Studies in Family Planning*, 1982, *13*, 355.

————. Interruption de grossesse chez des adolescentes âgées de 13 à 18 ans. Analyse clinique et sociologique de 295 cas [Abortion in adolescents between 13 and 18 years. Clinical and sociological analysis of 295 cases]. *Gynécologie, Obstétrique et Biologie de la Reproduction*, 1984, *13*, 21.

Verheye, C., Thiery, M., & Cliquet, R. Zwangerschaps-afbreking bij Belgische vrouwen in Nederland [Abortion on Belgian women in the Netherlands]. *Tijdschrift voor Geneeskunde*, 1982, *38*, 1.

Table 4.1

Percentage of People from the Different Parts of Belgium Who Would Approve of Abortion Being Performed on the Following Grounds[a]

	1	2	3	4	5	6
FLANDERS	90	73	24	42	22	23
BRUSSELS	91	87	59	81	48	53
WALLONIA	90	80	34	60	22	25

[a] One or more reasons for having an abortion.
1. Woman's life being endangered.
2. Risk of a malformed child.
3. Financial constraints posing hazards to a good education.
4. Rape.
5. Husband of the woman is not the procreator.
6. Unmarried woman.

Table 4.2
Age Distribution of Belgian Women Requesting an Abortion (GACEHPA, 1979; STIMEZO, 1979–82) as Compared to National Statistics, 1980

Age Group (Years)	National Statistics	Abortion Requests Gacehpa 1979 (%)	Abortion Requests Stimezo (%)		
			1979	1981	1982
14	3.3	0.3			
15 – 19	16.8	15.6	12.9	14.7	15.5
20 – 24	16.6	29.7	25.6	25.1	23.6
25 – 29	15.8	23.8	28.7	19.4	20.7
30 – 34	15.1	17.4	21.8	19.2	19.3
35 – 39	11.8	8.4	11.0	14.4	14.7
40 – 44	12.7	4.0		7.2	6.3
45 – 48	8.0	0.8			

Source: Vekemans & Dohmen, 1982; Ketting & Leliveld, 1983.

Table 4.3
Marital Status of Belgian Women Requesting Abortion (GACEHPA, 1979; STIMEZO, 1979–82) as Compared to National Statistics, 1980

Marital Status	National Statistics (%)	Abortion Requests Gacehpa 1979 (%)	Abortion Requests Stimezo (%)		
			1979	1981	1982
Single	31	45	37	53.7	52.9
Married	67	47*	57	39.3	40.4
Divorced or widowed	2	6	5	7	6.6
Unknown	–	2	–	–	–

* 42 percent are living with their husband, whereas 5 percent are separated.

Table 4.4
Reasons for Requesting an Abortion (GACEHPA, 1979)

Reason	Percentage
Economic Reasons (e.g. inadequate income)	24.0%
Social problems (e.g. single woman, student)	16.1%
One or both partners too young, too old, or unstable relationship	15.2%
"Inconvenient" pregnancy (e.g. family completed)	13.0%
Subjective considerations (e.g. fear, refusal of pregnancy, refusal to have a child, without further explanation)	11.5%
Health problems (e.g. physical or emotional wellbeing of the woman or of the partner, mental instability, suicidal risk)	6.8%
Legal problems (e.g. rape, incest, adulterous pregnancy)	2.2%
Family problems (e.g. parents oppose a wedding)	3.0%
Contraceptive failure of normally effective or normally ineffective method.	3.2%
Other reasons – not specified.	5.0%

Source: Vekemans & Dohman, 1982.

Table 4.5

Contraceptive Use during the Cycle in Which Conception Occurred (GACEHPA, Belgium, 1979; STIMEZO, Belgian Women in the Netherlands, 1979–82)

Method Used	GACEHPA 1979 (%)	STIMEZO 1979 (%)	STIMEZO 1982 (%)
No contraceptives used	48.6	33.3	25.3
Withdrawal and/or periodic abstinence	26.4[a]	31.0	34.7
Pill	15.5[b]	22.0	21.6[d]
Condom (with or without spermicide)	3.8	7.1	7.2[e]
I.U.C.D.	3.5[c]	3.3	3.5
Spermicide only	1.2		
Diaphragm	0.5		
Medroxyprogesterone acetate (150 mg every 3 months)	0.3	3.6	1.7
Sterilization (male or female)	0.2		

[a] 50 percent of the users admitted incorrect use.
[b] 78.2 percent of the users admitted incorrect use.
[c] 12.5 percent of these I.U.C.D's were found intracervically.
[d] These 21.6 percent are further subdivided as follows:
    5.7 percent who forgot their pill
    9.8 percent who stopped without taking any other form of contraception
    2.8 percent who stopped and changed to withdrawal or periodic abstinence
    0.4 percent who stopped and changed to condoms or diaphragm
    2.9 percent were real pill failures.
[e] 2.8 percent were due to failed condom contraception.
Source: Vekemans & Dohman, 1982; Ketting & Leliveld, 1983.

5

CANADA

Paul Sachdev

HISTORICAL DEVELOPMENT OF ABORTION POLICY

Prior to August 1969, abortion was lawful under Section 251 of the Criminal Code of Canada, when, "in good faith, considered necessary to preserve a woman's life."[1] Thus, the law recognized abortion on the ground of strict necessity and was largely vague on specific indications. The Canadian movement to widen and clarify the grounds for abortion was rooted in the convergence of unique forces and circumstances. The specific impetus for changes in the Criminal Code came from factors such as the dreadful plight of a sizable number of desperate women seeking back alley abortions, the thalidomide tragedies of the early 1960s, epidemic unwanted pregnancies both among married and unmarried women, the doctrine of separation of law and private morality, and emphasis on the right of women to control their own fertility. Furthermore, Canadians have been traditionally influenced by British and U.S. legal events and theories. In October 1967 the British Parliament passed a bill permitting abortions under broad circumstances, and about the same time, several states in the United States liberalized their abortion laws. These developments bolstered the Canadian public and professional interest in reforming the country's abortion laws.

The mass media played a key role in catalyzing changes in political and social attitudes toward greater acceptance of legalized abortion. In the early 1960s the much heralded women's magazine, *Chatelaine*, launched a scathing attack against the legal prohibition of abortion and continued the campaign for a decade through its editorials. But the most vociferous supporter of legal abortion in Canada was the English-language newspaper, the *Globe and Mail*, which through its series of articles and editorials denounced the existing abortion laws as unsound, outmoded, and unenforceable as the vast number of abortions were being performed illegally without effective interdiction. The paper also supported the women's ideology and argued that abortion was a matter of private morality, a woman's right, and therefore it was improper to allow any religious beliefs or ethical standards to influence the issue.

At the same time, the liberalization of abortion was being fiercely debated in the United States and was strongly supported by magazines like *Redbook* and *Time*. These magazines, which were also read by Canadian public, added to the fervor for reformation of Canada's abortion laws.

Two major Protestant bodies—the United and the Anglican churches of Canada—approved abortion first as an emergency measure and later for broader circumstances. It was a remarkable coincidence that the abortion issue was being debated at a time of sexual permissiveness. The Canadian Parliament passed two equally controversial and sensitive laws in 1969 that broadened the grounds for divorce and legalized the sale of contraceptives. The debate on these issues made the public more pluralistic in its outlook on standards of behavior. Significantly, the major Protestant churches did not find these developments offensive to Christian doctrine, whereas the Roman Catholic church remained resolutely opposed to these laws for their own adherents.

In addition to the Roman Catholic church, another influential group that opposed the legalization of abortion was the Canadian Medical Association (CMA). The medical profession's opposition to abortion may be traced to the medical code of ethics embodied in the 2,500-year-old Hippocratic Oath which interdicted all doctors from causing abortion through any means including instruments or drugs.

The CMA did an about-face in 1965 when it approved abortion to preserve the woman's life or physical or mental health. Interestingly, the CMA's position on abortion progressively swung toward liberalism and in 1971 went beyond the scope of the current abortion laws when it advocated socioeconomic reasons as grounds for obtaining abortion. In 1973 the CMA issued a call favoring abortion on demand and deleted from the Hippocratic Oath all references proscribing abortifacients.

Strong support for abortion law reform came from yet another powerful professional body, the Canadian Bar Association (CBA), which endorsed the utilitarian philosophy implying rational distinction between the more useful and less useful lives and stressed the separation of religion, morality, and civil laws.

The antagonists objected to liberalizing abortion law for three main reasons: First, abortion is an act of violence against innocent, defenseless life, and it is, therefore, contrary to the state's fundamental principle and duty to preserve life and protect those without power. Second, matters of life and death which the Criminal Code embodies are not the moral standards of a particular group or sect, but are the cornerstones of the Canadian democratic system and humanistic values. They asserted that the state, by legalizing abortion, would act against the common good. They rejected the utilitarian argument by stressing that the humanness of the unborn life and that of the already born was not different;

therefore, for the state to allow the more powerful to kill the less viable was tantamount to approving the principle of might makes right and the end justifies the means.

In response to the public debate, the government of Canada set up a Parliamentary Standing Committee in October 1967 to review the existing abortion law. The committee received submissions and briefs from a variety of professional and religious groups and reviewed public opinion. Three findings are of special importance here. First, a number of doctors characterized a woman's desire to seek preterm termination as irresponsible and senseless. Second, even some women who had undergone abortions wanted the indications for abortion to be broad, but not broad enough to permit abortion on demand. Third, none of the briefs by professional or public bodies recommended abortion for socioeconomic reaons (Pelrine, 1971, p. 33).

After an acrimonious and emotionally charged debate, the bill was passed by the Commons on 14 May 1969 by a vote of 149 to 55 and received royal assent on 28 August 1969. The bill as passed was considered the best compromise, and by no means did it represent a consensus. The act permits a therapeutic abortion if the continuation of the pregnancy "would or would be likely to endanger the woman's life or health." The act requires that abortions must be carried out in an approved or accredited hospital that has a therapeutic abortion committee consisting of no fewer than three qualified medical practitioners. The practitioner performing the abortion cannot be a member of the committee that approves the woman's application by a majority vote.

There are serious flaws in the amended abortion law. First, it represents no major change in the existing abortion practice, nor does it expand the legal grounds. It merely ensures that, unlike before, the legality of abortion will be established prior to termination by a formal mechanism, that is, a therapeutic abortion committee, and it will be carried out in an accredited or approved hospital. Second, the term "health" which was added to the existing law is vague and thus is subject to interpretation. Some hospital committees invoke a broader definition of health to include mental and emotional states, while others allow abortions on a pregnancy deemed a threat to the woman's life only. In this sense, the law creates inequity in making abortion services available to women seeking termination of their pregnancies.

Third, since hospitals are not required to set up therapeutic committees, the law renders the abortion services uneven across the country. In addition, under pressure from community or antiabortion groups, hospitals in some provinces have either curtailed abortion services or have entirely withdrawn them. As of 1 January 1985, there were 250 hospitals with therapeutic abortion committees, down from a maximum of 274 in 1975. Of these hospitals about one-sixth (14.6 percent) performed no abortions during 1985. Thirty-nine hospitals, or 15.4 percent, performed almost three out of every four abortions performed in Canada during that year, thus creating a service overload. Abortions are not provided in Canada's nearly 300 Roman Catholic hospitals (Pelrine, 1971, p. 37), and in

Prince Edward Island a woman cannot obtain a legal abortion (*Globe and Mail*, 5 June 1986). The only hospital in Newfoundland that offers abortion services has for some time been unable to find a gynecologist to perform therapeutic abortions (*Evening Telegram*, 16 August 1986). In Ontario, unlike other provinces, some doctors charge women a heavy fee (up to $400) for making referrals to hospital abortion committees.

Fourth, many women face delay in getting their applications approved because of the bureaucratic red tape involved in the committee system. Long delays can necessitate a second-trimester abortion, thus compounding the risks to the woman. Fifth, in requiring the hospital committees to decide for the woman whether she should continue her pregnancy, the law infringes on the individual sovereignty and personal freedom to make free choices. Finally, the law does not specify the gestational limit for the purpose of inducing termination which puts the onus on individual committees to set their limits. Thus, some committees permit only first-trimester abortions, while others allow terminations right up to the commencement of the process of birth.

Almost two decades after the law was proclaimed, the debate over federal abortion law continues to rage between those who think the existing Criminal Code provisions are too liberal and those who think they are too restrictive, unprincipled, and unfair. A spirited challenge to the federal abortion laws came in 1973 from Dr. Henry Morgentaler, a passionate crusader for abortion on demand who admitted publicly to performing 5,000 abortions in his Montreal clinic in defiance of the law. (Abortion is legal if done in an accredited hospital with the approval of the hospital therapeutic abortion committee.) Dr. Morgentaler was tried three times on a charge of performing abortions illegally and acquitted each time by a French-Canadian Catholic jury. Recognizing that the current law was unenforceable, the new Quebec minister of justice in the government of Parti-Quebcoi decided not to prosecute any qualified physician performing abortions under proper medical conditions and urged the federal government to amend it to bring it in line with the needs of modern society. Quebec is thus the only province where abortions are legally available in provincially approved free-standing clinics, thus effectively exempting over one-quarter of the country's population from the provisions of the Criminal Code.

Buoyed by his court victories, Dr. Morgentaler has taken his crusade to other provinces to test the law. He established abortion clinics in Ontario and was tried on a charge of illegal abortion and acquitted again by a jury in 1984. He continues to face new criminal charges and vociferous antiabortion lobbies.

More recently, the abortion debate has been further fueled by the Canadian Charter of Rights enacted in 1982 which protects the rights of all persons. Some Canadian courts have recently extended the same rights to the unborn child under the charter in tort, property, and equity cases, thus opening the possibility that abortion might wind up in the Supreme Court of Canada. On the other hand, antiabortionists, emboldened by the lower courts' decisions as well as the rising new moral militancy in the United States supported by the Reagan Administration, have spirited their crusade against legal abortion. To avoid another divisive national debate, the Conservative government has set up a commission known as the Task Force on the Status of the Fetus. The commission is presently reviewing the various aspects of the abortion law, including a policy on the fetus, and will suggest changes that could meet wider agreement between opposing groups (*Globe and Mail*, 24 June 1986).

ATTITUDES TOWARD ABORTION

To determine how Canadian adults view elective abortions, three Gallup Polls were undertaken in 1975, 1978, and 1983. The items included in all three polls were identical so that they yielded an attitudinal pattern that could be compared over an eight-year period. The surveys show that despite the intensification of pro-choice and pro-life movements fueled by Dr. Henry Morgentaler's foray into the abortion debate and the greater visibility of their polar positions in the media, the attitudes of Canadians toward abortion have remained largely unchanged over time.

As shown in table 5.1, all three surveys noted that, while a vast majority of Canadians (eight out of ten) consistently approve of legalized abortion in general, three-fifths support it on selective grounds. Only about one-sixth of all Canadians reject abortion under any circumstances, and nearly one in four are in favor of it for any reason. Thus, the average Canadian does not subscribe to two extreme positions represented by the pro-life and pro-choice groups.

An analysis of responses of Canadians who endorsed abortion only under certain circumstances reveals that hard reasons such as the risk of a child's deformity or danger to the woman's own health elicited substantially greater support—over 60 to 86 percent, respectively—compared with less than one-fifth for soft or discretionary grounds such as economic plight or the first-trimester pregnancy. Thus, the polls clearly indicate strong support for extending the hard grounds in the existing law to include birth defects for permitting abortion.

Sociodemographic variations in Canadian attitudes in the Gallup Poll of 1983 show that education and religion appear to be the strongest predictor of attitude toward abortion. As education increases, opposition to legal abortion on all four grounds (i.e., mother's health, birth defect, financial straits, first-trimester pregnancy) decreases. Persons associated with Protestant churches or who claim affiliation with no religion are more approving of abortion under these four conditions than those professing the Catholic faith. Although Catholics do not endorse abortion for wider circumstances, a large majority of them, 66 percent, do find it acceptable when the mother's life or health is in danger as is permitted under the current law (Boyd, 1985).

As with religion, there are sex differences in attitudes toward abortion. Differences between genders are small insofar as abortion is rendered legal for reasons of mother's health or life. However, female respondents are less supportive of abortions performed during the first trimester or for economic reasons than men are. Age and marital status also seem to determine variations in the level of acceptance of abortion under specific circumstances. For example, younger Canadians, thirty-nine years or under, are more favorable to abortion on selective grounds than are their older counterparts. Singles emerge with the highest level of support for abortion under specific conditions, while persons widowed or divorced indicate the lowest level. In short, while the degree of support for abortion under specific circumstances varies among Canadians by education, age, marital status, and religion with higher endorsement coming from the more educated, younger, single, and non-Catholic, their differences tend to be accentuated when soft reasons of financial plight or the first-trimester pregnancy are invoked.

On 15 June 1985 *The Globe and Mail*, the national daily newspaper, conducted its own survey, the Globe-Crop Poll, of 2,044 adult Canadians and their attitudes toward abortion. Its results closely match those of the 1983 Gallup Poll except in one respect. The Crop Poll asked its respondents to agree or disagree with the statement, "Every woman who wants an abortion should be able to have one." A majority, 53 percent, agreed with the statement implying an unequivocal approval of abortion for any reason. This compares with 23 percent of the respondents in the Gallup Poll of 1983 who endorsed abortion under any circumstances. This discrepancy is due to the phrasing of the question in the Crop Poll which effectively elicited its respondents' views on the "right" of every woman to obtain an abortion rather than the legality of abortion as probed in the Gallup Poll. It is one thing to support freedom of choice as a general principle, but it is another thing whether one should be permitted to exercise choice without constraints.

When the responses to questions that were similar in both surveys are compared, however, their findings are strikingly in agreement. Almost the same proportion of respondents in both surveys (78 percent in the Crop Poll and 76 percent in the Gallup Poll) believed that it should be possible for a pregnant woman to obtain a legal abortion if approved by a therapeutic abortion committee in an accredited or approved hospital. In addition, both surveys consistently reported that a vast majority of Canadians—87 percent in the Crop Poll and 74 percent in the 1983 Gallup Poll—approved abortion where the mother's health was in danger. The relationships between education, gender, city size, and levels of support for legal abortion have been found to be similar in both surveys.

Another survey of national opinion on abortion was undertaken in 1977 by the Committee on the Operation of the Abortion Law which was set up to review the working of the law (Justice Department, 1977). Its findings more or less confirmed those of the 1978 Gallup Poll. It reported that about one out of every four respondents rejected abortion under any circumstances. Females were more reserved in their endorsement of abortion on request than men were—16 percent versus 23 percent. Slightly more females (71 percent) than males (67 percent) favored abortion in case of danger to the mother's life (p. 257)

DEMOGRAPHY OF ABORTION

Data Source

Following the legalization of abortion, statistics on therapeutic abortions have been compiled nationally by Statistics Canada which coordinates the work in cooperation with the participating hospitals. The figures do not include induced abortions performed in nonhospital settings (e.g., clinics and doctor's offices) in the province of Quebec, Ontario, or any other province in Canada. The statistics available between 1970 and 1973 relate to the counts and rates only, but from 1974 onward information also includes the selected demographic and medical characteristics on the aborting women.

Levels, Trends, and Incidence

The number of abortions among Canadian women increased fourfold from 11,152 in 1970 to 65,043 in 1979. As shown in table 5.2, the biggest jump— 177.3 percent—in a single year was recorded in 1971, the year after legalization of abortion, followed by moderate increases ranging between 4 and 11 percent in the number of therapeutic abortions each year until 1979. The period 1980– 85 witnessed minor fluctuations in the number of abortions, with no more than a 2 percent change over the previous year. The exception, however, was 1983 when the number plunged sharply to 61,750 abortions, or 6.7 percent less than in 1982. It rose again to 62,247 in 1984, but in 1985 the number returned to the 1983 low.

Expressed in terms of abortion rates (per 1,000 women aged fifteen to forty-four and abortion ratios (per 100 live births), there was a steady and sharp rise in both between 1970 and 1978 as shown in table 5.2. The spectacular jump in abortion rates, nearly 300 percent, from 2.5 to 9.6, was posted during the initial four years following the enactment of the amended law. Between 1974 and 1979 the increases were moderate, one-fifth, from 9.6 to 11.6 in 1979, the peak year in abortion rates. Thereafter the abortion rate started to dip slightly but hovered around 11 until 1983 when it took a sharp drop to 10.2 abortions per 1,000 women fifteen to forty-four years. Another drop followed in 1985 when the abortion rate reached 9.2 abortions per 1,000 women. The initial steep rise may in part be due to the replacement of illegal abortions by legal abortions. The number of legal abortions dropped as the demand for illegal abortions subsided and the use of contraception increased.

Note also in table 5.2 that abortion ratios rose faster than abortion rates, which accounted for an almost fourfold increase between 1970 and 1982, compared with a five-fold rise for abortion ratios during the same period—from 3 to 17.8 abortions for every 100 live births. There were 16.5 abortions for every 100 live births in 1984, a slight drop from 1982. However, if 3,484 abortions done on

Canadian women in the United States and the estimated 2,500 abortions performed in free-standing clinics in Montreal (Nolte, 1983) are added, the total
number of therapeutic abortions will amount to 68,231 in 1984, with an abortion
rate of 11.2 per 1,000 women fifteen to forty-four years, or 18.1 abortions for
every 100 live births.

Variations within Canada

The data presented in table 5.3 on abortion rates and abortion ratios by provinces and territories show great variations across the country from a low of 0.4
abortions in Prince Edward Island (PEI) to a high of 19.7 abortions for every
1,000 women fifteen to forty-four in North West Territories (NWT) in 1985.
Similarly, abortion ratios (per 100 live births) also demonstrate wide variations
in 1985 from a low of 0.5 abortions in PEI to a high of 26.1 in British Columbia.

The differences among provinces in rates have held sway over the period
1970–85 partly because of the disparity that exists in the availability of abortion
services. Three provinces—British Columbia, Ontario, and Yukon (or NWT)—
have consistently made a major contribution to the national abortion rates and
abortion ratios with their higher than national averages during the same period.
Two provinces—Newfoundland and Quebec, and Yukon Territory—made the
biggest gains during the period 1970–82 with sixteen-, fourteen-, and tenfold,
respectively.

Age, Parity, and Marital Status

Data on the selected demographic profile of women seeking abortion are
presented in table 5.4. As shown, there has been little change in the characteristics
of the women seeking abortion during the period 1974–85 for which the information is available. A typical abortee is very young, unmarried without previous
deliveries, and seeks termination in the first trimester. Of 60,518 therapeutic
abortions in 1985, two-thirds (66.8 percent) were performed on single women.
This represents an increase of 14.8 percent since 1974 matched by a decrease
of 30.3 percent abortions on married women from 31.3 percent in 1974 to 21.8
percent to total therapeutic abortions in 1985. There has been a steady decline
in the percentage of abortions performed for teenage women under twenty years—
from one-third in 1974 to less than one-quarter in 1985. The percentage of
therapeutic abortions to the total also declined during the same period for women
over thirty-nine years from 3.3 to 2.1 percent. This decrease was offset by an
increase in the proportion of abortions for women twenty to twenty-nine and
thirty to thirty-nine years of age. In 1985 women twenty to twenty-nine years
contributed 55 percent to the total number, up from 47.8 percent in 1974. The
proportion of therapeutic abortions among women thirty to thirty-nine rose by
14.3 percent in 1985 from 17.5 percent in 1974 (table 5.4).

Increasingly, more women are seeking earlier abortions. While fewer than
eight out of every ten (78.8 percent) pregnancies terminated in 1974 were under
thirteen weeks of gestation, there were almost 9 (89 percent) terminations with

the same gestation period in 1985. Likewise, the abortion cases with a gestation period of thirteen weeks and over decreased from 21.2 percent of total abortions in 1974 to 11.0 percent in 1985. Married women and older women twenty years and above are more likely than single and younger women under twenty to seek first-trimester abortions. But this difference has been narrowing over time. For example, the percentage of pregnancy terminations with gestation periods of under thirteen weeks to total abortion cases increased for single women by 15.7 percent from 75.8 percent in 1974 to 87.7 percent in 1985, while the increase for married women was about 10 percent during the same period as shown in table 5.5.

Similarly, during 1974–1985, the number of abortions performed on women under thirteen weeks gestation in relation to the total increased by 16.6 percent for women under twenty years compared with an increase of 10.3 percent for older women at least twenty years of age.

As more single and younger women are undergoing therapeutic abortions, this proportion of women with no previous deliveries at pregnancy termination is also increasing. There were 57.2 percent abortions in 1974 to women with zero previous deliveries, and this proportion increased steadily to 62.4 percent in 1980 before it dropped to 62 percent in 1981. It continued to slip until the proportion reached 59.1 percent in 1985.

If the distribution is considered in terms of marital status and age, therapeutic abortions with no previous deliveries continue to be more common among single and younger women under twenty, although their proportion has been slipping since 1974 (see table 5.4). Single women with no previous delivery accounted for 87 percent to total abortions in 1974, and this proportion dropped to 83.9 percent in 1980, 82.3 percent in 1982, and 78.1 percent in 1985. Likewise, of the women under twenty undergoing therapeutic abortion in 1974, over 90 percent (91.6 percent) of them had no previous deliveries at pregnancy termination, and this proportion dropped to 88.7 percent in 1985.

REPEAT ABORTIONS

During the period between 1974 and 1985 there has been an upward trend among women having at least one previous abortion. As shown in table 5.6, the percentage of women who reported having at least one previous induced abortion increased by 160 percent—from 7.8 percent in 1974 to 20.3 percent in 1985.

Older women twenty to twenty-nine and thirty to thirty-nine continue to be the major contributors to the high percentage of women with previous induced abortions. Their percentages rose to almost one-quarter each in 1985 from 1974 when they accounted for about one-tenth in relation to abortions performed on these women. In contrast, of the abortions performed on teenagers under twenty, 8.8 percent were repeat terminations in 1985, up from 4.2 percent in 1974.

In general, it is suspected that the number of women with repeat abortions is underreported because of possible reluctance to unveil this information. For instance, in the National Patient Survey of 1976, 18 percent of patients admitted having prior induced abortions (Justice Department, 1977, p. 354). The incidence of repeat abortions is expected to rise continually because of women's earlier sexual debut and their high frequency of sexual activity with multiple partners, their irregular or less effective use of contraceptives, the higher fecundity level, and the greater availability and acceptance of legal abortion services. Furthermore, more women are seeking abortion as a direct consequence of the general annual increase in the proportion of women in the reproductive years, thus creating an enlarged pool of women at risk of having a repeat abortion. In addition, those who have experienced an abortion are more likely to have another if they encounter an unwanted pregnancy (Tietze, 1983, p. 61).

The Canadian trend is not dissimilar to trends reported in other countries where abortions are legal. Tietze (1983) reviewed the international status on repeat abortions and concluded that the demand for repeat abortion, especially of third and higher orders, has increased at much higher rates than the first abortion. He hypothesized that the diffeence between the first abortion rates and repeat abortion rates will widen as the degree of heterogeneity of the female population (i.e., age, marital status, and parity) and their need for and accessibility of abortion services increases.

It is misleading to interpret the increased incidence of abortion and especially repeat abortions as a reflection of these women's indifference to birth control methods and their acceptance of abortion as the primary method of regulating fertility. In fact, the research evidence indicates the contrary. According to the National Patient Survey, referred to above, a little less than half of the women (47.3 percent) who had a repeat abortion reported using contraception at the time of conception (Justice Department, 1977, p. 352). Tietze (1983), having surveyed the contraceptive prevalence among abortees, contended that it is the women on contraceptives who are more likely to have an abortion rather than those who are nonusers of birth control.

Are the women with repeat abortions different from those with first abortions? Berger et al. (1981) did a comparative analysis of the women who sought initial or repeat abortions at the Montreal General Hospital between July 1972 and June 1978 and found that the repeaters were older, better educated, more likely to be currently or once married, more accepting of legal abortion, and had more frequent intercourse than women experiencing their first abortions. But neither group differed in terms of religious background or degree of religious commitment, psychological adjustment, relationship with the sexual partner, and attitude toward sexuality. Nor did they differ in the proportion of those using less effective contraceptive methods or in their reasons for not using contraception during the month of conception. The authors concluded that women having an initial or repeat abortion are more similar than dissimilar (p. 168).

ABORTION AND ADOLESCENTS

Teenage pregnancies and abortions are of particular interest to public health officials because of the extra psychological and physical health risks they present to the patient (see, for example, Furstenberg et al., 1981; Stuart & Wells, 1982). Although the proportion of abortions to teenagers under age twenty has steadily declined by more than one-quarter (27.3 percent) between 1974 and 1985, from 31.5 percent to 22.9 percent of total abortions, teenagers are still the major contributors to the overall yearly number, compared to all age categories except women twenty to twenty-four years (see table 5.4). In terms of abortion rates there were 16.2 therapeutic abortions for every 1,000 females under twenty years in 1982, compared with 9.9 abortions for every 1,000 women twenty years and above (see table 5.7 below). Although the abortion rate for teenagers dropped to 14.5 in 1985, it was still 5.5 percentage points higher than that for women twenty years and over.

Teenagers even show much higher rates than do women twenty years and older when the number of abortions per 100 live births in the respective groups are compared. The data are presented in table 5.8.

As indicated in the table, in 1985 there were 62.5 abortions for every 100 live births to teenagers compared with 13.6 abortions for 100 live births to women twenty years and above. The rates in the respective groups have remained quite stable since 1979.

As mentioned above, more teenagers than women twenty years and above are seeking early abortions (see table 5.5). Moreover, between 1974 and 1985 teenagers showed a much smaller increase in the percentage of those with at least one previous induced abortion in relation to women twenty years and older having at least one previous abortion. As shown in table 5.6, while teenagers with at least one previous induced abortion increased by 4.6 percentage points during the period, women aged twenty to twenty-nine and thirty to thirty-nine increased by 13.2 and 17.3 percentage points, respectively.

In comparison with most Western countries where abortions are legal, the Canadian teenage abortion rates (per 1,000 women under twenty) are lower, ranging from 1.4 to 28.1 percentage points except for the Netherlands and New Zealand.

ABORTION IN FRANCOPHONE QUEBEC

Francophones are the largest—26.4 percent—minority culture in the Canadian mosaic. Eight out of every ten French Canadians lives in the province of Quebec and distinguish themselves from anglophones in cultural and ethnic heritage, ancestry, and politics.

In addition, the fertility of much of the francophone population differs markedly from that of other provinces. Quebec is the only province that recorded a steady decline in birth rate (per 1,000 population)—from 15.4 in 1980 to 13.3

in 1985 which was the lowest in the country (*Vital Statistics*, 1980–85). If we focus on the number of births per woman (i.e., total fertility rate), French Canadian women not only had the smallest family size—1.5 children—in 1983, but the decline in their childbearing was dramatic since 1957 when it was 4.0 births per woman (Romaniuc, 1984, p. 14).

As shown in table 5.9, teenage pregnancy rates (births plus abortions per 1,000 women aged fifteen to nineteen) in Quebec also remained the lowest among all provinces—22.4 in 1971 and 21.5 in 1984. In comparison, Ontario, British Columbia, Alberta, and Manitoba, the other four large provinces that make up more than 60 percent of the population of Canada, experienced a much higher pregnancy rate of 41.4, 47.3, 53.3, and 54.0, respectively, in 1984.

In view of Quebec's low fertility rate, it is particularly significant to examine the sexual activity of this province. Quebec's falling birth rate may suggest either (1) less sexual activity or (2) high sexual activity coupled with high contraceptive prevalance.

No national study has been done that provides comparative information by province. A few studies based on high school and college samples, however, show sketchy trends in sexual and contraceptive practices in a few regions. These studies suggest that in the late 1970s the level of sexual activity among Quebec's teenagers was slightly higher than that in other provinces (Hobart, 1980). Similar trends were confirmed by two studies conducted in the early 1980s involving students at a community college in suburban Montreal, Quebec, and at high schools in Calgary, Alberta. In the Montreal study, Frappier (1981) found that 55 percent of the males and 53 percent of the female respondents had had coital experience compared with 33 percent of the respondents (both sexes) in the Calgary study (Meikle et al., 1985). More recently, a national survey on attitudes toward explicit sex in the media found Quebecers more relaxed than Ontarians about sex on television (*Globe and Mail*, 9 June 1986, p. 1).

Given the high sexual profile of young Quebecers, which obviously makes them vulnerable to unwanted pregnancies, it can be assumed that they rely heavily on the use of abortion and contraceptive services as a means of controlling their fertility. In the following section, we will examine the prevalence of abortion rates and contraceptive usage in Quebec.

Of the four largest provinces, Quebec with its population of 26.4 percent of the total in 1981 contributed 13.9 percent of the therapeutic abortions performed that year in Canada, while Ontario (pop. 35.4 percent), British Columbia (pop. 11.3 percent), and Alberta (pop. 9.2 percent) contributed disproportionately more than their population. Their respective share in 1981 was 47.0, 19.6, and 10.3 percent of the total. In terms of abortion rates and abortion ratios, Quebec ranked eighth among provinces, with 5.8 abortions for every 1,000 women fifteen to forty-four or 11.0 abortions for every 100 live births in 1985. (See table 5.3.) Likewise, Quebec's teenage abortion rate of 7.1 (per 1,000 women under twenty) was less than one-half the national rate which stood at 14.5 in 1985 and was the lowest after New Brunswick with 3.1 abortions.[3] (See table 5.7.)

Since its proportion of abortion and the rate of abortion in the general population as well as among teenagers are one of the lowest in the country, it is not surprising that Quebec records one of the lowest abortion rates for teenage pregnancies. For example, in 1984 Quebec teenagers terminated 33.5 percent of their pregnancies compared to 48 percent, 47.3 percent, and 34 percent, respectively, for the other three large provinces, British Columbia, Ontario, and Alberta.

With high prevalence of sexual activity and low abortion rates, it seems that Quebec adolescents rely more heavily on contraceptive means to prevent unwanted pregnancies. Like the studies on sexual activity, the data on contraceptive practices are scarce. The only study available on contraceptive prevalence among teenagers was done by Dupras and Levy (1981) in individual high schools in Quebec. In eight different studies between 1970 and 1976, the authors found that the proportion of students reporting use of a contraceptive method at initial intercourse ranged from around one-third to two-thirds. In comparison, slightly more than one-third of the high school students in Ontario who were engaging in first intercourse used some kind of contraceptive device.

A survey was conducted in Quebec in 1971 to study the contraceptive practices of married women up to age forty-five who were followed up again in 1976. In the five-year period, the Quebec women had shown much less reliance on such traditional methods as periodic abstinence, withdrawal, and chemical contraception and had increasingly accepted the highly effective IUD and condom methods. Ten percent fewer women, however, were using the pill in 1976 than they were in 1971, but the acceptance of sterilization for contraception had risen dramatically from 2.4 percent in 1971 to an estimated 37.8 percent of the couples who had opted for this method in 1976 (Henripin et al., 1981; Laprierre-Adamyck & Marcil-Gratton, 1981). In contrast, the Canadian women in the national study conducted by the Committee on the Operation of Abortion Law were more accepting of chemical barriers and the pill and less reliant on more effective methods such as the condom, IUD, and sterilization (Justice Department, 1977).

Based on the above discussion, it appears that the low marital and nonmarital fertility among Quebec women is largely attributable to their disciplined and effective use of contraceptive methods as the first line of defense and that abortion is invoked as a backup measure.

While abortion and modern contraceptive technology play a significant role in Quebec's low fertility and pregnancy rates, nevertheless, certain changes in the Quebecer's procreative norms concerning the timing of childbearing, child spacing, and family size preference seem to have catalyzed their motivation and ability to achieve their childbearing targets. Women in Quebec, for instance, reveal a marked tendency toward higher age of childbearing and wider intervals between births. The average interval from marriage to the first child, which was twenty-three months for women married between 1951 and 1960, lengthened to twenty-eight months for women married between 1966 and 1970. Likewise, the average spacing between the first and second births extended from thirty-two to forty-three months for the same two marriage periods (Romaniuc, 1984, p. 27). Associated with this change in spacing is a sharp decline in higher parity fertility. The proportion of women who expect to have only two children has risen dramatically, almost twofold, from 17 percent for those married between 1920 and 1945 to 45 percent for those married between 1966 and 1971 (Romaniuc, 1984, p. 33). In the absence of national statistics on the timing of fertility and child spacing, the Quebec data, however, cannot be compared with trends in other provinces.

ABORTION AND FERTILITY REGULATION

Population Dynamics

Canada's crude birth rate which stood at 28.0 births per 1,000 population in 1956, the peak year of the postwar baby boom, has since been steadily declining. By 1978 it had plunged to 15.3 and has mostly stabilized at that level except a slight drop to 15.0 in 1983 and 1984 and to 14.9 in 1985, the last year for which statistics are available. Not only has Canada experienced a decline in overall fertility, but its descending reproductive level is also manifest in each age group of women fifteen to thirty-four, except among the older cohort thirty to thirty-nine years old, as shown in table 5.10.

In terms of total fertility rate, the number of births per woman fall from about 4 in the late 1950s to less than 1.7 in 1984, which is below the replacement level of 2.1 births (*Vital Statistics*, 1984). Demographers characterize the current phase of the fertility pattern of Canadian women as a baby bust.

The decline in Canada's birth rate has largely resulted from a low level of fertility among married women. While the marital fertility rate (per 1,000 women fifteen to forty-nine) dipped dramatically by 44.8 percent from 162.6 in 1956 to 89.7 births in 1982, the nonmarital fertility rate (per 1,000 unmarried women fifteen to forty-four) increased by one-half during the same period from 16 to 24 births for every 1,000 unmarried women (Romaniuc, 1984, Table 2.6; *Vital Statistics*, 1961, 1982). If we add the number of out-of-wedlock pregnancies that end in therapeutic abortions, the nonmarital fertility rate will rise to almost twice as much. For instance, between 1974 and 1985, 527,285 unwed pregnancies were terminated via abortions and there were as many births, 537,018, to unmarried women during the same period.

A sizable proportion of out-of-wedlock pregnancies (live births plus abortions) occur to single teenage girls under twenty. The combined numbers of births and therapeutic abortions to unmarried teenagers stood at 27,018 in 1974 and at 36,667 in 1980, an increase of more than one-third (35.7 percent). Thereafter the numbers slipped slightly to 35,557 in 1982 and to 29,570 in 1985 (*Vital Statistics*, Therapeutic Abortions, 1974 to 1985).

There are many reasons for the growing number of pregnancies among unmarried women. A substantial number of young women from the baby boom generation has entered the reproductive years. The proportion of fifteen- to nineteen-year-old women went up from 21 percent in 1951 to 28 percent in 1976. Likewise, the proportion of never-married women twenty to twenty four grew from 40 percent in 1961 to 51 percent in 1981 (Romaniuc, 1984, pp. 37–38). At the same time, greater sexual activity, particularly among single women beginning at an earlier age, coupled with the trend toward later marriage, exposes these women to an increased risk of an out-of-wedlock pregnancy. Another growing phenomenon—cohabitation—amoung young adults increases the frequency of sexual intercourse and thus the risk of impregnation. Based on the last census in 1981, couples who admitted to living in common law unions represented 8.7 percent of families, or more than twice as many as in 1971 (*Globe and Mail*, 4 July 1986). Greater acceptance of motherhood without the benefit of marriage may also have weakened their prevention resolve. In the national population survey of 1976, referred to above, 28.2 percent of the sexually active women over fifteen years old and 33.3 percent of those aged fifteen and under did not use any contraceptive means. Of the married women, 23 percent were nonusers of contraceptives (Justice Department, 1977, p. 347). The surveys commissioned by Planned Parenthood Federation of Canada in 1984 found a higher percentage of nonusers among its respondents, which is 35 percent for unmarried women and 47 percent for men aged twenty-five to thirty-four years (*Tellus*, 30 September 1984, p. 27; *Tellus*, Spring 1985, p. 6). The contraceptive pill which was ever used by two-thirds of single women in the 1976 survey was reportedly used only by 17.3 percent of teenagers in the Canada Health Survey conducted on a random sample of Canadians in 1979 (Health and Welfare, Canada, 1981). Single women are abandoning the pill because of publicized health hazards and are increasingly relying on less effective contraceptive methods of withdrawal and chemical barriers which make them highly vulnerable to unintended pregnancies and thus to seeking therapeutic abortions as a backup measure. On the other hand, married and never married women are switching to more effective methods of fertility control—sterilization and IUD (Justice Department, 1977, pp. 344–350; Romaniuc, 1986, p. 42). This partially explains the occurrence of a higher proportion of abortions—two-thirds—among single women.

Besides more effective contraception, low fertility among married women is attributed to yet another significant demographic correlate—the changes in these women's perspective on procreative behavior. Because of higher educational goals and career orientation, women now tend to marry later in life and delay childbearing until their late twenties or even early thirties. They are also electing to have fewer children and at longer intervals. Nearly four out of every ten married women prior to 1876 had at least six children. Today, hardly 3 percent of married women prefer this family size (Romaniuc, 1984, p. 31). In the 1960s, the average age at which women had their first child was 23.5 years, which rose to almost twenty-five years in 1980 (Romaniuc, 1984, p. 27). The proportion of first-time mothers in the thirty to thirty-four, thirty-five to thirty-nine, and forty to forty-four age groups was 14 percent, 9 percent, and 7 percent, respectively, in 1970, which rose in 1982 to 26, 19, and 16 percent in the respective age groups (Romaniuc, 1984, p. 30). Another demographic trend is the significant increase in the number of well-educated, career-oriented women who are choosing to forego motherhood permanently. An estimated 5 to 10 percent of all Canadian married women are remaining childless by choice (Veevers, 1980). Some demographers project that as many as 16 percent of young Canadian women may forego maternity (Strohmenger & Lavoie, 1982).

Certain sociological changes, such as decline in marriage and remarriage rates and soaring divorce incidence, may have an influence on reproductive behavior that may not be as distinct and perceptible as the role of late parenting, lower nuptuality, child spacing, and voluntary childlessness, but nonetheless they do exert a depressing effect, though subtly, on marital fertility.

Family Planning Services

Until 18 August 1969, the dissemination of information about birth control or the sale of devices was prohibited under federal law, although the ban was not strictly enforced and contraceptives had been available at pharmacies and were prescribed by doctors. With the amendment to the Criminal Code of Canada, the federal government was actively involved in the public information, training, and research in family planning. In 1972 the Family Planning Division was set up in the Department of National Health and Welfare to implement these activities in cooperation with provincial and municipal governments and voluntary agencies. Since health care and welfare services are provincial matters, ultimate responsibility for providing family planning services rested with the provincial governments. Because of budgetary constraints and low priority for family planning, the division was phased out in 1979, leaving the responsibility for continuing the services in the hands of the provinces. These services are provided largely by family planning divisions in each province, Planned Parenthood Association and other voluntary agencies, university health services, as well as private practitioners. However, because of the federal government's low commitment, the number of family planning centers is extremely limited, especially in the Prairies and Maritime provinces, and are unevenly located across Canada. Many are operating under considerable fiscal constraints. Cost, however, is no barrier to receiving contraceptive counseling, and sometimes even devices through a physician, since health services are guaranteed to every Canadian citizen or landed immigrant under the universal health care system.

In general, there is public acceptance of family services for married couples, but their support undergoes a rapid attrition for single persons who, it is feared, may interpret these services as society's approval of their sexual activity which the opponents regard as immoral.

There is a controversy surrounding not only the target groups who should receive family planning services, but also the type of methods that should be disseminated. Recognizing the Roman Catholic church's traditional strong opposition to all kinds of barrier methods, the federal government has been promoting natural birth control known as the Ovulation or Billings method through research funds to Serena (Service de Regulation des Naissances), a Quebec-based national agency (*Globe and Mail*, 24 June 1986). This method is gaining increased acceptance from women who are tired of the inconvenience, pain, bleeding, and unknown side-effects of current contraceptives.

One controversy that continues to rage centers on the issue of providing birth control information and devices to sexually active minors without parental consent. Retarded adolescents present a special dilemma to health professionals. A national survey of family practitioners and obstetrician/gynecologists conducted in 1980 found that 43 percent of those surveyed were reluctant or unwilling to provide birth control services to single minors without parental consent (*Tellus*, Spring 1985, p. 25).

Another controversial and divisive issue is the desirability of sex education programs in the schools. Initiatives in teaching sex education are hampered by lack of consensus on the definition, objectives, and contents in the school curriculum. According to a national survey of Canadian schools conducted by the Planned Parenthood Federation of Canada and a Gallup Poll in 1984, only 50 percent of schools offered this program, less than one-quarter had separate courses in the subject, one in five adults were given the ''facts of life'' during their growing up years, and less than 50 percent were aware of more than five methods of birth control. On the other hand, 83 percent of Canadian adults supported the teaching of sex education in schools, and 94 percent believed that parents should discuss sex and sexual behavior with their children (*Tellus*, September 1984, p. 25). Interestingly, the rate of endorsement for a high school-based sex education program remained consistently high in the Canadian Gallup Polls conducted in 1943 (76 percent), 1949 (72 percent), 1964 (75 percent), 1969 (73 percent), 1974 (73.1 percent) (Meikle et al., 1985). Unlike these Gallup Polls, a survey done in Calgary in 1979–80 involved only parents with school-going children and examined their attitudes toward providing birth control information to teenagers in school. The results, based on 1,062 replies, indicated that eight out of ten respondents favored such educational programs, but only one-half (53.5 percent) of them supported the idea of making birth control devices accessible to teenagers (Meikle et al., 1985, p. 103).

SUMMARY

A unique convergence of social and political forces led to the amendment in the Criminal Code of Canada in 1969 which did not bring about the much hoped for changes in the existing abortion practice except that abortions can now be legally performed only if the pregnancy would likely endanger the woman's life or health. The abortion services are uneven across the country because the law does not require hospitals to set up therapeutic abortion committees that must approve a woman's application. The availability of services also depends on whether the hospital committee interprets the terms "health" and gestational limits liberally or conservatively. Only one-sixth of the country's non-Catholic hospitals perform three-fourths of all abortions.

In the last ten years a large majority (66 percent) of Canadians have consistently endorsed abortion under certain circumstances, but generally will not approve it on request or for socioeconomic reasons.

The demand for abortion increased fourfold in the first seven years following its legalization, but since 1976 the percentage increase has been quite moderate. The abortion rates have fluctuated over time around 11 per 1,000 women, fifteen to forty-four years, or 16 abortions for every 100 live births. But these rates vary widely from province to province.

Abortions continue to be very common among single women, especially those under twenty who contributed about one-qurter to the total abortions in 1984. In 1982, 16.2 abortions were performed for every 1,000 females under twenty, compared with 9.9 abortions for women twenty years and above, or 62.2 abortions for every 100 live births to teenagers, compared with 14.5 abortions for every 100 live births to women twenty and older. Increasingly, more women are seeking earlier abortions, but it is more common among married women and older women at least twenty years of age. Older women also more often seek repeat abortions, although the percentage of all women with at least one previous induced abortion increased by 150 percent between 1974 and 1984.

Canada's declining birth rate has largely resulted from the low level of fertility among married women who use highly effective contraception, sterilization, and the IUD, and have changed their perspective on procreative behavior. However, the fertility rate has been increasing among unmarried women, as has their abortion rate which is largely due to a substantial increase in the proportion entering the reproductive years, high sexual activity, and their use of less effective methods of contraception. There is no evidence that these women use abortion as a primary method of pregnancy control.

Abortion continues to be a highly controversial and divisive issue, and the pro-life forces have intensified their campaign to make the availability of abortion in Canada more restrictive.

NOTES

1. For an excellent and detailed review of the historical background of the abortion policy in Canada, see Alphonse de Valk, "Abortion Politics: Canadian Style," in Paul Sachdev (Ed.), *Abortion: Readings and research* (Toronto: Butterworths, 1981).

2. As this book was going to press, the Supreme Court of Canada, in a landmark decision on January 28, 1988, struck down the federal abortion law, effectively allowing abortion on demand. The Court ruled that the law threatened the health of women by permitting arbitrary delays and unfair disparities in access to abortion across the country.

3. Prince Edward Island's abortion rate of 0.7 in 1984 is misleading because its only hospital that performs abortion has not approved a single application since October 1982, thus forcing women to seek abortion elsewhere in the country or in the United States. In

1985 an estimated 650 PEI women sought abortion outside the province (*Globe and Mail*, 5 June 1986).

REFERENCES

Berger, C., Gold, Gillett, P., Andres, D., & Kinch, R. Repeaters: Different or unlucky? In Paul Sachdev (Ed.), *Abortion: Readings and research.* Toronto: Butterworths, 1981.

Boyd, Monica. How the people feel: Canadian attitudes on abortion. Paper presented at the 1985 Annual Meeting of the Canadian Population Society, Montreal, 1985.

Dickens, Bernard M. Legal aspects of abortion. In Paul Sachdev (Ed.), *Abortion: Readings and research.* Toronto: Butterworths, 1981.

Dupras, A., & Levy, J. J. *La sexualite et la contraception chez les cegepiens.* In J. J. Levy & A. Dupras (Eds.), *La sexualite au Quebec: Perspectives contemporaines.* Longueil, Quebec: Editions IRIS, 1981.

Frappier, J. In Edward S. Herold (Ed.), *Sexual behavior of Canadian young people.* Markham, Ontario: Fitzhenry & Whiteside, 1984.

Furstenberg, F., Jr., Lincoln, F. R., & Menken, J. (Eds.). *Teenage sexuality, pregnancy and childbearing.* Philadelphia: University of Pennsylvania Press, 1981.

Health and Welfare, Canada, & Statistics Canada. *The health of Canadians: Report of the Canada Survey.* Catalogue 82–538E, Ottawa, 1981.

Henripin, J., Huot, P. M., Lapierre-Adamcyk, E., & Marcil-Gratton, N. *Les enfants qu'on n'a plus au Quebec.* Montreal: University of Montreal Press, 1981.

Henripin, J., & Lapierre-Adamcyk, E. *La fin de la revanche des berceaux: Qu'en pensent les quebecoises?* Montreal: University of Montreal Press, 1974.

Herold, Edward S. *Sexual behavior of Canadian young people.* Markham, Ontario: Fitzhenry & Whiteside, 1984.

Hobart, Charles W. The courtship process: Premarital sexual attitudes and behavior. In G. N. Ramu (Ed.), *Courtship, marriage and the family in Canada.* New York: Gage Publishing, 1980.

Justice Department, Canada. *Report of the committee on the operation of the abortion law.* Catalogue J2–3Q/1977, Supply and Services Canada, Ottawa, 1977.

Lapierrre-Adamcyk, E., & Marcil-Gratton, N. La Sterilizasion au Quebec, 1971–1979. Rapport de recherche. Montreal: University of Montreal Press, 1981.

Meikle, S., Peitchinis, J. A., & Pearce, K. *Teenage sexuality.* San Diego, Calif.: College-Hill Press, 1985.

Nolte, Judith. Canadian abortion statistics aren't complete. *News*, Journal of Planned Parenthood Federation of Canada, 1983, *1* (1).

Pelrine, Eleanor Wright. *Abortion in Canada.* Toronto: New Press, 1971.

Romaniuc, A. *Fertility in Canada: From baby-boom to baby-bust.* Catalogue 91–524E, Supply and Services Canada, Ottawa, 1984.

Sachdev, Paul. Problems of fertility control among Canadian women. In Paul Sachdev (Ed.), *Abortion: Readings and research.* Toronto: Butterworths, 1981.

———. Counselling single abortion patients: A research overview and practice implications. In Paul Sachdev (Ed.), *Perspectives on abortion.* Metuchen, N.J.: Scarecrow Press, 1985.

Statistics Canada. *Therapeutic abortions.* Catalogue 82–211 Annual.

———. *Vital statistics, births and deaths*, Catalogue 82–204 Annual.

Strohmenger, C., & Lavoie, Y. L'infeconite au Canada: Niveau et tendances. Paper presented at 50eme Congres de l'association Canadienne-francaise pour l'avancement des sciences, 1982.

Stuart, Irving R., & Wells, Carl F. (Eds.) *Pregnancy in adolescence.* New York: Van Nostrand Reinhold Co., 1982.

Tellus, Journal of Planned Parenthood Federation of Canada, September 1984; Spring 1985; Autumn 1985.

Tietze, Christopher. *Induced abortion: A world review, 1983.* New York: Population Council, 1983.

Valk, Alphonse de. Abortion politics: Canadian style. In Paul Sachdev (Ed.), *Abortion: Readings and research.* Toronto: Butterworths, 1981.

Veevers, Jean E. *Childless by choice.* Toronto: Butterworths, 1980.

Table 5.1

Attitudes Toward Abortion under All, Some, or No Circumstances, Canada, 1975–83

	Poll #378 July 1975 Question 10A	Poll #410 March 1978 Question 3A	Poll #475:1 July 1983 Question 13A
	Do you think abortions should be legal under any circumstances, legal only under certain circumstances or illegal in all circumstances?		
N. Total	1039	1037	1062
Percent, Total	100	100	100
Legal under any circumstances	23	16	23
Legal only under certain circumstances	60	69*	59
Illegal in all circumstances	16	14	17
Don't know, no response	1	1	1

*Higher percentage of support compared with 1975 and 1978 polls was due to the question ordering effect.

Source: Boyd, 1985, table 1. Reprinted with permission.

Table 5.2
Selected Demographic Characteristics of Canadians, Abortion Rates, Abortion Ratios, 1970–85

Year	Total pop (in mil).	Total female pop in mil.	Total women 15–44 in mil.	Crude birth rate per 1,000 pop.	Total abortion for Can. resident	Percent increase over last year	Abortion rate (per 1,000 women 15–44	Percent change over previous year	Abortion ratio (per 100 live births	Percent change over previous year	Total fertility rate per 1,000 women[1]
1970	21.3	10.6	4.6	17.5	11,152	-	2.5	-	3.0	-	2,331
1971	21.6	10.8	4.7	16.8	30,923	177.3	6.6	185.0	8.5	186.7	2,167
1972	21.8	10.9	4.8	15.9	38,853	25.6	8.2	24.2	11.2	30.2	2,024
1973	22.1	11.0	4.9	15.5	43,201	11.2	8.9	8.5	12.6	12.5	1,931
1974	22.4	11.2	5.9	15.6	48,136	11.4	9.6	7.9	13.7	8.7	1,875
1975	22.8	11.4	5.2	15.8	49,311	2.4	9.6	0	13.7	0	1,852
1976	23.0	11.5	5.3	15.7	54,478	10.5	10.3	7.3	15.1	10.2	1,825
1977	23.2	11.7	5.4	15.5	57,564	5.7	10.6	2.9	15.9	5.3	1,806
1978	23.5	11.8	5.5	15.3	62,290	8.2	11.3	6.6	17.4	9.4	1,757
1979	23.7	11.9	5.6	15.5	65,043	4.4	11.6	2.7	17.8	2.3	1,764
1980	23.9	12.1	5.7	15.5	65,751	1.1	11.5	-0.9	17.7	-0.6	1,746
1981	24.7	12.3	5.9	15.3	65,053	-1.1	11.1	-3.5	17.5	-1.1	1,704
1982	24.7	12.4	6.0	15.1	66,254	1.8	11.1	0	17.8	1.7	1,694
1983	24.9	12.6	6.0	15.0	61,750	-6.7	10.2	-8.1	16.5	-7.3	1,680
1984	25.1	12.2	6.1	15.0	62,247	0.8	10.2	0	16.5	0	1,686
1985	25.4	12.8	6.2	14.8	60,928	-2.1	9.2	-2.9	16.2	-1.8	1,669

[1] Excluding Newfoundland.
Source: Statistics Canada, *Vital Statistics*, Births and Deaths, catalogue 84–204, annual; Statistics Canada, *Therapeutic Abortions*, catalogue 82–211, annual.

Table 5.3
Legal Abortion Rates, Abortion Ratios by Provinces in Canada: 1970–85 (Therapeutic Abortions for Canadian Residents Performed in Canada Only)

Legal Abortion Rates
(Per 1,000 Females Aged 15–44 Years)

	1970	1971	1972	1973	1974	1975	1976	1977	1978	1979	1980	1981	1982	1983	1984	1985
Nfld.	0.2	0.7	1.2	1.7	1.6	1.5	3.5	3.9	4.2	4.9	4.0	3.5	3.4	3.4	2.7	2.9
PEI	0.8	1.8	2.0	1.8	2.1	3.0	2.2	1.7	2.2	1.7	0.8	1.0	0.9	0.5	0.4	0.4
N.S.	1.7	4.0	5.1	5.5	6.1	5.7	6.9	7.0	7.7	7.8	8.4	8.5	8.4	8.2	8.2	8.0
N.B.	0.6	1.1	1.4	2.5	3.1	2.5	2.6	2.8	2.9	2.8	2.8	2.7	1.5	1.6	1.6	1.8
Que.	0.4	1.4	2.0	2.2	3.1	3.8	4.8	5.0	5.1	5.6	5.7	5.6	6.0	5.8	5.9	5.8
Ont.	3.4	9.7	11.8	12.9	13.7	13.3	14.2	14.3	14.8	15.2	15.1	14.7	14.9	13.4	13.1	12.5
Man.	1.2	4.1	5.8	6.0	5.6	5.9	6.3	6.9	8.1	7.0	6.8	6.9	7.3	7.0	9.1	9.2
Sask.	1.2	4.2	5.9	6.8	6.5	6.8	5.9	6.3	7.4	8.0	7.5	7.7	7.5	6.4	5.4	5.1
Alb.	3.4	8.9	10.8	10.9	11.4	10.8	11.9	12.5	13.9	13.9	13.8	12.0	11.2	10.8	11.2	11.0
B.C.	6.6	15.5	17.2	18.3	19.0	18.4	19.3	19.7	21.3	21.1	20.2	19.3	18.8	17.2	16.7	16.4
Yukon	1.6	2.0	11.2	17.3	14.6	15.7	15.8	16.8	19.5	21.9	19.2	18.8	19.8	14.7	14.8	
N.W.T	..	..	5.7	6.4	9.4	11.9	11.1	12.9	13.7	12.2	15.8	18.6	17.1	18.4	19.7	
CANADA	2.4	6.7	8.2	8.9	9.6	9.6	10.3	10.6	11.3	11.6	11.5	11.1	11.1	10.2	10.2	9.9

Table 5.3 (Continued)

Abortion Ratios
(Per 100 Live Births)

	1970	1971	1972	1973	1974	1975	1976	1977	1978	1979	1980	1981	1982	1983	1984	1985
Nfld.	0.2	0.6	1.0	1.6	1.6	1.6	3.8	4.4	5.1	6.3	5.2	4.6	5.0	5.4	4.5	4.9
PEI	0.9	1.9	2.2	2.2	2.6	4.0	2.9	2.2	3.0	2.4	1.2	1.4	1.4	0.7	0.6	0.5
N.S.	1.8	4.5	6.2	7.0	8.2	7.7	9.7	10.5	11.6	12.2	13.4	14.0	13.7	13.5	13.8	13.6
N.B.	0.6	1.2	1.6	3.0	3.8	3.2	3.4	3.7	4.2	4.1	4.4	4.2	2.3	2.6	2.7	3.1
Que.	0.6	2.1	3.4	3.7	5.0	6.0	7.5	7.9	8.3	8.7	9.2	9.5	10.7	10.7	11.1	11.0
Ont.	4.1	12.4	16.2	18.3	20.0	19.8	21.8	22.6	24.2	25.2	25.1	24.9	25.1	22.4	21.5	20.7
Man.	1.3	4.6	6.8	7.4	8.2	7.6	8.3	9.4	11.4	10.0	9.9	10.0	10.7	10.2	13.4	13.4
Sask.	1.3	4.7	6.7	8.2	7.8	8.4	7.1	7.5	9.0	9.7	9.2	9.5	9.2	7.8	6.7	6.5
Alb.	3.6	10.2	13.3	13.8	14.7	13.7	15.0	16.4	18.5	18.6	17.9	15.8	14.7	14.2	15.1	14.9
B.C.	7.9	20.2	23.7	26.7	28.3	27.8	29.9	30.7	33.5	33.1	31.6	30.4	29.4	27.0	26.1	26.1
Yukon	1.3	1.6	10.6	18.1	12.7	18.9	17.6	24.5	21.0	22.6	26.3	22.9	23.6	20.9	16.8	20.5
N.W.T.	..	..	3.6	4.2	7.2	8.1	7.6	8.6	11.1	11.0	9.7	13.7	16.0	13.7	15.7	17.7
CANADA	3.0	8.5	11.2	12.6	13.7	13.7	15.1	15.9	17.4	17.8	17.7	17.5	17.8	16.5	16.5	16.2

Source: Statistics Canada, *Therapeutic Abortions*, 1983–85, catalogue 82–211, annual.

Table 5.4

Percentage Distribution of Abortions by Selected Sociodemographic Characteristics, Canada, 1974–85

Characteristics	1974	1975	1976	1977	1978	1979	1980	1981	1982	1983	1984	1985
Total abortions	41,227	49,033	54,097	57,131	61,806	64,569	65,243	64,554	65,812	61,326	61,822	60,518
Age												
Under 15 years	1.2	1.2	1.2	1.2	1.0	1.0	0.9	0.8	0.8	0.8	0.7	0.8
15–19 "	30.3	30.1	29.5	29.6	29.5	29.4	28.8	27.5	26.0	24.1	22.9	22.1
20–24 "	29.3	29.1	29.6	30.3	30.9	31.5	31.8	32.3	32.8	33.3	33.5	33.5
25–29 "	18.5	19.4	19.8	19.4	19.3	19.3	19.6	19.9	20.4	20.8	21.3	21.5
30–34 "	10.7	10.7	10.9	11.2	11.3	11.3	11.6	12.0	12.2	12.6	12.7	13.0
35–39 "	6.8	6.4	6.1	5.8	5.7	5.4	5.3	5.5	5.9	6.4	6.9	7.0
40–44 "	3.0	2.8	2.6	2.2	2.1	1.8	1.8	1.8	1.8	1.8	1.8	1.9
over 44 "	0.3	0.2	0.3	0.4	0.3	0.2	0.2	0.2	0.2	0.2	0.2	0.2
Marital Status												
Single	58.2	58.4	58.4	60.2	61.3	64.0	65.2	65.8	65.3	66.1	66.6	66.8
Married	31.3	31.4	30.7	29.0	27.3	24.7	23.7	23.0	23.0	22.4	22.0	21.8
Other and unknown	10.6	10.2	10.9	10.8	11.4	11.3	11.0	11.3	11.7	11.5	11.4	11.3
Gestation Weeks												
Under 9 weeks	20.8	22.4	24.1	23.8	24.7	24.5	24.7	25.5	25.9	27.7	29.5	31.8
9–12 "	58.0	58.9	59.0	60.4	59.9	61.3	61.4	61.1	61.0	60.2	58.5	57.1
13–16 "	14.0	13.3	11.8	11.0	11.1	10.3	10.4	9.9	9.7	8.8	8.6	7.7
17–20 "	6.0	5.2	5.0	4.5	4.1	3.7	3.4	3.2	3.2	3.1	3.1	3.0
Over 20 "	1.2	0.2	0.2	0.3	0.2	0.2	0.2	0.2	0.2	0.2	0.3	0.3
No. of Previous Deliveries												
0	57.2	57.3	57.6	59.0	59.7	61.7	62.4	62.0	61.7	60.9	59.7	59.1
1	14.3	14.3	15.0	15.6	15.7	15.5	15.7	15.9	16.4	17.1	17.6	17.8
2	14.2	14.5	14.7	14.0	13.9	13.3	13.1	13.6	13.4	13.8	14.1	14.3
3 or more	13.0	11.8	10.6	9.3	8.3	7.3	6.9	6.4	6.2	6.2	6.3	6.3
unknown	1.4	2.0	2.0	1.9	2.3	2.2	1.9	2.1	2.3	2.0	2.3	2.5

Table 5.4 (Continued)

Previous Induced Abortions

0	91.0	88.9	87.4	86.1	84.4	83.7	82.6	81.4	79.9	78.7	77.9	76.9
1	7.0	7.6	8.8	9.8	11.0	11.9	12.8	13.6	14.5	15.4	15.7	16.2
2 or more	1.0	1.0	1.2	1.4	1.9	2.1	2.5	2.7	3.0	3.5	3.8	4.1
Unknown	2.0	2.5	2.7	2.6	2.7	2.3	2.1	2.3	2.5	2.3	2.6	2.7

Previous Deliveries - Percent to Total Cases
For Selected Years

Marital Status	1974			1977			1980		
	0	1+	Unkn	0	1+	Unkn	0	1+	Unkn
Single	87.0	12.0	1.0	84.9	13.0	2.1	83.9	13.9	2.2
Married	16.0	83.0	1.0	17.9	80.3	1.8	19.4	79.3	1.3
Other and unknown	22.0	76.0	1.0	25.6	72.6	1.8	27.4	70.9	1.6

Marital Status	1981			1982			1984		
	0	1+	Unkn	0	1+	Unkn	0	1+	Unkn
Single	82.9	14.8	2.3	82.3	15.3	2.4	79.3	NA	NA
Married	18.5	80.0	1.5	19.5	78.6	1.9	17.8	80.3	3.9
Other and Unknown	28.5	69.5	2.0	29.5	68.4	2.1	NA	NA	NA

NA = Information not available.

91

Table 5.4 (Continued)

Previous Deliveries - Percent to Total Cases for Selected Years

Age	1974			1977			1980		
	0	1+	Unkn	0	1+	Unkn	0	1+	Unkn
Under 20	91.6	7.1	1.3	90.6	7.8	1.8	90.6	7.3	2.1
20 - 29	54.2	44.4	1.4	56.4	41.4	2.2	61.1	37.0	1.9
30 - 39	12.8	85.7	1.5	17.4	80.7	1.9	23.0	75.4	1.5
40+	6.8	91.8	1.4	8.9	89.6	1.5	11.3	87.0	1.6

Age	1981			1982			1984			1985		
	0	1+	Unkn	0	1+	Unkn	0	1+	Unkn	0	1+	Unkn
Under 20	90.1	7.6	2.3	89.3	8.1	2.6	88.7	8.4	2.9	88.7	8.5	2.8
20 - 29	61.2	36.9	2.0	61.8	36.1	2.1	60.8	37.0	2.2	59.9	37.6	2.5
30 - 39	24.4	73.6	2.0	25.3	72.5	2.1	26.5	71.6	1.9	27.5	70.4	2.1
40+	14.1	83.6	2.3	13.1	84.9	2.0	14.0	84.4	1.6	14.5	83.5	1.9

Source: Statistics Canada, *Therapeutic Abortions*, catalogue 82–211, annual.

Table 5.5
Therapeutic Abortions by Gestation Period and Marital Status, 1974–85

Per cent cases with gestation period as
Pourcentage des cas ou la période de gestation était de

	Under 13 weeks / Moins de 13 semaines												13 weeks and over / 13 semaines et plus											
	1974	1975	1976	1977	1978	1979	1980	1981	1982	1983	1984	1985	1974	1975	1976	1977	1978	1979	1980	1981	1982	1983	1984	1985
Cases – Total –	78.8	81.3	83.1	84.2	84.6	85.9	86.0	86.6	86.9	87.9	88.0	89.0	21.1	18.7	16.9	15.8	15.4	14.1	14.0	13.4	13.1	12.1	12.0	11.0
Marital status- Etat matrimonial:																								
Single – Celibataire	75.8	78.5	80.1	81.5	82.1	83.8	84.3	85.0	85.4	86.6	86.8	87.7	24.2	21.5	19.9	18.5	17.9	16.2	15.7	15.0	14.6	13.4	13.2	12.3
Married– Mariee	84.3	86.4	88.6	89.7	90.0	90.8	90.4	90.7	90.9	91.2	91.1	92.3	15.7	13.6	11.4	10.3	10.0	9.2	9.6	9.3	9.1	8.8	8.9	7.7
Other and unknown – Autres et inconnu	79.0	81.7	83.8	84.6	85.4	86.9	86.6	87.3	87.5	89.2	88.8	90.2	21.0	18.3	16.2	15.4	14.6	13.1	13.4	12.7	12.5	10.8	11.2	9.8
Age- Age:																								
Under 20 years– Moins de 20 ens	71.1	74.0	75.2	77.3	77.7	79.4	80.4	81.0	80.7	82.2	82.0	82.9	28.9	26.0	24.8	22.7	22.4	20.6	19.6	19.0	19.3	17.8	18.0	17.1
20 years and over – and et plus	82.3	84.6	86.6	87.3	87.6	88.7	88.4	88.8	89.2	89.8	89.8	90.8	17.7	15.4	13.4	12.7	12.4	11.3	11.6	11.2	10.8	10.2	10.2	9.2
20-29 years – ans	81.4	83.5	85.6	86.2	86.6	87.8	87.2	87.6	88.2	88.7	88.7	89.7	18.6	16.5	14.4	13.8	13.4	12.2	12.8	12.4	11.8	11.3	11.3	10.3
30-39 evars ans	85.0	97.3	89.5	90.2	90.8	91.4	92.1	92.2	92.1	92.8	92.9	93.5	15.0	12.7	10.5	9.8	9.2	8.6	7.9	7.8	7.9	7.2	7.1	6.5
40 years and over – ans et plus	82.3	86.6	85.9	87.9	88.0	88.6	88.1	89.8	90.1	90.6	90.8	91.9	17.7	13.4	14.1	12.1	12.0	11.4	11.9	10.2	9.9	9.4	9.2	8.1

Source: Statistics Canada, *Therapeutic Abortions*, catalogue 82–211, annual.

93

Table 5.6
Percentage Distribution of Previous Induced Abortion Cases by Age, 1974–85

	1974			1975			1976			1977			1978			1979		
	0	1+	unkn	0	1+	unkn	0	1+	unkn	0	1+	unkn	0	1+	unkn	0	1+	unkn
Total 100	90.7	7.8	1.5	88.9	8.6	2.5	87.4	10.0	2.7	86.1	11.3	2.6	84.4	12.9	2.7	83.7	14.0	2.3
Under 20	94.6	4.2	1.2	93.7	4.5	3.8	92.9	4.9	2.1	92.4	5.7	1.9	92.0	6.0	2.7	91.0	6.7	2.3
20 - 29	88.4	10.0	1.6	86.4	10.8	2.8	84.2	12.9	2.9	83.0	14.1	2.9	NA	NA	NA	80.3	17.3	2.4
30 - 39	89.8	8.4	1.6	86.7	10.5	2.8	86.6	10.5	2.9	83.2	13.6	3.2	NA	NA	NA	80.4	17.6	2.0

	1980			1981			1982			1983			1984			1985		
	0	1+	unkn	0	1+	unkn	0	1+	unkn	0	1+	unkn	0	1+	unkn	0	1+	unkn
Total 100	82.6	15.2	2.1	81.4	16.3	2.3	79.9	17.5	2.5	78.7	18.9	2.3	77.9	19.5	2.6	76.9	20.3	2.7
Under 20	90.5	7.3	2.2	90.3	9.4	2.3	89.6	7.8	2.6	NA	NA	NA	88.9	8.2	2.9	88.3	8.8	2.9
20 - 29	79.4	18.4	2.2	78.3	19.5	2.2	77.0	20.5	2.4	NA	NA	NA	75.1	22.4	2.5	74.1	23.2	2.7
30 - 39	78.4	19.5	2.0	76.0	21.6	2.5	74.1	23.3	2.7	NA	NA	NA	72.1	25.4	2.5	71.7	25.7	2.6

NA = Information not available.
Source: Statistics Canada, *Therapeutic Abortions*, catalogue 82–211, annual.

Table 5.7

Teenage Therapeutic Abortion Rates[a] (per 1,000 Females Aged Fifteen to Nineteen Years), Canada and Provinces, and Abortion Rates (per 1,000 Females Aged Twenty and Above), Canada, 1974–85

Province	1974	1975	1976	1977	1978	1979	1980	1981	1982	1983	1984	1985
Canada												
Under 20	13.6	13.7	14.6	15.3	16.3	17.0	16.9	16.2	16.2	14.7	14.7	14.5
20 & above	8.4	8.4	9.1	9.4	9.9	10.1	10.1	9.9	9.9	9.3	9.3	9.0
Newfoundland	1.5	1.7	5.0	6.6	6.2	8.0	6.2	5.3	5.2	5.2	4.4	5.1
Prince Edward Island	3.3	6.1	3.9	2.7	2.9	3.2	2.0	1.4	1.5	0.3	0.7	0.4
Nova Scotia	9.8	9.4	11.5	11.7	12.7	13.3	14.0	13.5	14.2	12.9	13.2	12.9
New Brunswick	4.9	4.8	4.4	4.2	4.8	4.9	5.4	4.9	2.5	3.0	2.5	3.1
Quebec	3.0	3.6	4.5	4.7	5.0	5.8	6.2	6.4	6.9	6.6	7.2	7.1
Ontario	19.7	19.6	20.5	20.9	21.6	22.6	22.8	21.9	22.6	20.2	19.6	18.6
Manitoba	10.6	9.4	9.9	10.8	12.8	10.8	10.6	11.1	11.8	10.9	14.7	16.1
Saskatchewan	11.8	12.8	10.8	11.5	14.3	14.1	13.7	13.5	12.6	11.0	10.4	7.9
Alberta	18.6	18.4	20.1	21.3	24.1	24.2	23.6	20.9	18.4	17.4	18.1	18.1
British Columbia	28.9	28.5	28.8	31.5	32.2	32.3	30.2	29.5	27.8	23.8	22.7	23.5
Yukon	23.3	26.0	23.0	30.9	23.6	29.2	30.0	30.0	31.0	37.8	20.0	29.0
Northwest Territories	16.1	15.8	14.3	13.6	15.4	18.0	15.4	23.2	30.4	23.5	24.6	31.2

[a] Rates based on all therapeutic abortions on females aged under twenty years and female population aged fifteen to nineteen years.

Source: Statistics Canada, *Therapeutic Abortions*, catalogue 82–211, annual; Statistics Canada, *Vital Statistics*, Births and Deaths, catalogue 84–204, annual.

Table 5.8
Therapeutic Abortion Ratios (100 Live Births to Females under Twenty Years and to Females Aged Twenty Years and Above), 1974–85

CANADA Age	1974	1975	1976	1977	1978	1979	1980	1981	1982	1983	1984	1985
Under 20	38.8	39.4	43.9	48.3	55.2	61.8	62.3	62.7	62.2	60.1	61.5	62.5
20 years & above	11.0	11.0	12.1	12.6	13.8	14.0	13.8	14.1	14.5	13.7	13.8	13.6

Source: Statistics Canada, *Therapeutic Abortions*, catalogue 82–211, annual; Statistics Canada, *Vital Statistics*, Births and Deaths, 84–204, annual.

Table 5.9
Teenage Pregnancy Rates (Births Plus Abortions per 1,000 Women Aged Fifteen to Nineteen), Canada and Provinces, 1971, 1981, 1984

Year	Canada	Provinces							
		P.E.I.	New Brunswick	Quebec	Ontario	Manitoba	Saskatchewan	Alberta	British Columbia
1971*	51.1	50.2	57.5	22.4	63.4	62.4	57.4	70.2	78.7
1981*	44.2	35.0	40.1	25.5	45.6	51.3	62.7	65.1	59.4
1984**	36.3	38.8	33.8	21.5	41.4	54.0	59.4	53.3	47.3

* Stanley K. Henshaw, ''Canada,'' Unpublished paper, 1985, table 3, p. 36.
** Statistics Canada, *Vital Statistics*, Deaths and Births, catalogue 84–204, post-census annual estimates, catalogue 91–210; Statistics Canada, *Therapeutic Abortions*, catalogue 82–211, annual.

Table 5.10
Age-Specific Fertility Rate (per 1,000 Women) by Age Group for Selected Years, Canada, 1966–85

Year	15–19	20–24	25–29	Age Group 30–34	35–39	40–44
1966	48.2	169.1	163.5	103.3	57.5	19.1
1971	40.1	134.4	142.0	77.3	33.6	9.4
1976	33.3	110.3	129.9	65.6	21.1	4.3
1979	27.9	101.8	130.8	69.1	19.5	3.4
1980	27.6	100.1	129.4	69.3	19.4	3.1
1981	26.4	96.7	126.9	68.0	19.4	3.2
1982	26.5	95.4	124.7	68.0	20.2	3.1
1983	24.9	92.4	124.6	70.5	20.5	3.0
1984	24.4	88.8	126.0	73.3	21.5	3.0
1985	23.7	85.3	125.3	74.6	21.8	3.0

Source: Statistics Canada, *Vital Statistics*, Births and Deaths, catalogue 84–204, annual.

6

CHINA

Chi-hsien Tuan

HISTORICAL DEVELOPMENT OF ABORTION POLICY

Apart from miscarriage due to physiological causes, induced abortion must have been in existence in China for a long time. Although incontrovertible evidence for this statement is not easily available, common sense endorses its plausibility. The major justification may be stated succinctly as "Life necessitates it." Conditions that require abortion to end an unwanted pregnancy existed in the past as they are prevalent today; hence, ways must have been sought to meet the demand in ancient China.

Ancient medical books are the best sources that may attest to the existence of induced abortion. The earliest record of abortion is the *Shen Nong Bencao Jing* (Shen Nong's Classics of Herbal Medicine), mentioned by the well-known Tang Chinese physician Sun Simao (682–581 B.C.). In his book *Qian Jin Yao Fang* (Thousands of Important Gold Prescriptions), Dr. Sun's quotation of the Shen Nong text evidently indicates that the Chinese were practicing abortion at least over 2,000 years ago (Himes, 1963).

Prescriptions for contraception and abortion can be found in the twenty-four-volume book *Fu Ren Da Quan Liang Fang* [Encyclopedia of Effective Prescriptions for Women], written by Chen Zimin of the Southern Song Dynasty (700 to 800 years ago). The book contains 260 topics together with their discussion, and prescriptions. The fact that the book includes the heading Duan Chan Fang Lun [studies on prescriptions of contraception] is significant. In Book 13:7, Dr. Chen revealingly states: "married women have difficulties at the time of childbirth. Some bear offspring unceasingly but desire to stop this, therefore, prescriptions are written so that they may be prepared for use." He further illustrates his point by quoting three prescriptions from *Qian Jin Yao Fang*, one of which is entitled Qian Jin Qu Tai (Thousands of Gold Prescriptions for Abortion). This constitutes definite evidence that the Chinese medical profession had been trying to meet the people's demand for abortion as early as 1,300 years ago. The prescription uses barley leaves as the main ingredient and assures that "The fetus will become like rice gruel and the mother will be without any suffering" (Himes, 1963).

Another important physician who practiced herbal medicine was Tang Shenwei of the Northern Song Dynasty (about 1108 A.D.) who in his comprehensive book *Chong Xiu Zheng He Zheng Nei Ben Cao* observed that "Mercury will . . . cause abortion" (Himes, 1963, pp. 109–112). Many Chinese medicines have an abortive effect and many Chinese drugs contain warnings that pregnant women should not take them.

Whether the old prescriptions are effective and safe may be questionable, but all the same they irrefutably establish the notion that abortion was in demand in ancient China and that ways had been sought to meet this demand.

This does not in any way suggest that the demand for abortion was *prevalent* in old China. Until recently, the Chinese attitude has been predominantly pronatalistic. Common to all the major schools of thought as well as religious inclination in China, including Confucianism, Buddhism, and Taoism, is reverence for the preservation of life. This is well attested by a very popular saying handed down among the Chinese from generation to generation: "The virtue of the heaven lies in its fondness for life." So *ren* or benevolence has been established as the virtue of ethics to guide one's conduct and to perfect one's spiritual life, which means that one should have kindness, love, affection, and devotion, as well as forgiveness and pity. The ethics of *ren* runs counter to the act of abortion. As Confucianism treasures *li* above all things, that is, the appropriateness of relationships and conduct among peoples, abortion finds no place in the formalities of the divine order of *li*. But practical life is harsh, and people must adapt themselves to harshness. Although the Chinese highly respected the divine order of *li* or propriety, prompted by necessity they admitted an act contrary to the heavenly spirit. The digression of the cold act of abortion from the divine principle of benevolence and *li* created a market. Thus, even to this day, practitioners nicknamed "Huang lu hi-shen" (yellow-green physicians, i.e., charlatans or quacks) prosper in Hong Kong and Taiwan for the very reason that abortion on grounds other than humanitarianism is illegal, yet in great demand.

The traditional attitude toward abortion was not a social issue decided by law, but rather a private family affair guided by an individual's ethical code. The matter was left almost totally to the discretion of women whose knowledge of their own menstruation and incidental abortion were primarily secrets. They could choose not to impart the information to others. However, as abortion requires the skill of a second party as well as cost, infanticide which requires neither skill nor cost emerged as an alternative to supersede abortion and became a frequent practice in times of stress.

The shift from abortion to infanticide resulted primarily from poverty as well as from lack of medical know-how. Its irregular usage as a solution to unwanted pregnancies also indicates that in traditional custom and thought there was no insurmountable hindrance that would block the way for the Chinese masses to accept modern abortion for the purpose of population control. After all, in comparison with infanticide, abortion is a much more palatable act. Abortion has never become a national issue for the Chinese on the mainland. The government endorsed it in the 1950s, with only minimal ethical objection to its employment as a birth control measure and practically nonexistent religious opposition. Of course, with the powerful government's restrictive measures against the traditional ethics and religion they could hardly play a negative role in hindering abortion. This does not mean, however, that contemporary China has never countenanced different opinions on the matter of population policy and abortion.

The ethical approach to fertility was eventually formalized in the form of law after the termination of the dynastic rule. In 1935 the Nationalist government prohibited abortion (Chow, 1970), but the law was rarely enforced, either because of the Nationalist government's inability (before 1949) or because of deliberate negligence of governmental duty (after 1949 in Taiwan). In Taiwan where the Nationalists still hold power, induced abortion, though illegal, is easily available on the black market. In fact, the official antiabortion stance has been so weakened that Taiwan is actually at the verge of legalizing it.

Since 1949, abortion as an integral part of China's population policy has undergone dramatic changes on the mainland. The Marxists were originally pronatalist, and so the government they formed in China naturally adhered to their vital doctrines, which accorded well with the Chinese traditional ideology. But this policy could not be maintained very long. By 1954 the government was alarmed by the unexpected statistics revealed by China's first Census of 1953, which gave an enormous total population figure of 582 million. In August 1953 the State Council in Beijing instructed the Ministry of Health to make preparations for the spread of contraception and approved the Regulations on Contraception and Abortion, revised by the Ministry of Health (Shi, 1980). Abortion was officially accepted as the means to end an unwanted pregnancy. The adoption of abortion as a contraceptive means to control population growth was not extraordinary inasmuch as it was the only alternative for checking growth in China. But it indeed marked a remarkable shift on an issue that was of historical significance in both the socialist ideology and the traditional culture.

The necessity of abortion in accomplishing population control and the government's awareness of population combined to make its acceptance inevitable. In the 1950s development in China was still at the traditional level of the peasant economy and modernization was but a distant dream. Yet population doubled in about thirty years, and any birth control program without abortion as a backup measure could not cope with the urgency of population pressure. Preparing a contraceptive program on a massive scale required a great deal of work, yet cutting the growth rate was an urgent need that could not be put off indefinitely. Abortion was seen as a reliable measure that could yield immediate results while the reproductive couples were adapting to the notion of contraception. The official decision to accept abortion was a sober response to existing conditions and marked an important development from the point of both Chinese tradition and the country's ideological doctrine.

To appreciate the impact of population policy in general on abortion, first we must understand the process and function of the planned birth model which China has developed during the last thirty years. The Chinese Constitution stipulated a law on planned births which required that both the government and individual citizens practice planned births. Pregnancy is legalized in China, and one cannot have a pregnancy without a birth quota. From the very start, the Chinese communist government assumed a decisive role in the matter of population control, which was in the care of the Health Ministry before 1974. Since then, controlling population growth rate has been part of the plan of the national economy. China spent about six years organizing an extensive national network of planned birth work linking the central government in Beijing with the grass-roots organs of the neighborhood committee in the urban areas and production brigade in the rural areas. This office is devoted exclusively to birth planning and has a full-time staff.

The government's role as initiator and executor of population control programs, together with its decision-making authority on family size, gives rise to a problem: unless there is a dependable means, the plan to control population cannot be fulfilled. Since 1974 when planned births started to be included in the planning of the national economy, a birth permit or quota began to be allocated to couples of reproductive age. Although the Chinese education-persuasion model of communication functions effectively, it cannot successfully deal with all the cases that can occur, especially in a country that has over 250 million women of reproductive age. Many women who become pregnant without a birth quota hide their pregnancies and are not noticed until later in the pregnancy. In cases of contraceptive failure, abortion is the only solution.

The function of abortion has undergone some unique changes in China. Before 1974 abortion functioned as in other countries: as purely a backup measure to deal with unwanted pregnancies. Although it certainly reduced population growth, it was not relied on as a means to achieve an exact goal set for a planned decline in growth. Least of all, it had never been used to enforce the birth quota requirement. After 1974, the birth quota for each couple was set at no more than two births, and so abortion assumed a more important role in accomplishing the target quota. Since 1979 when the single-child family policy was implemented, abortion began to assume a function that it has never experienced anywhere else. Thus we see that before about 1974, abortion was allowed for pregnancies within thirteen weeks. Mid- or longer term abortion was hardly allowed. The legalization of pregnancy necessitates reconsideration of the old convention, and what is termed *Dai Yue Fen Yin Chan* (later month abortion) has to be considered. Thus, when the mother's safety is assured, the abortion of pregnancies over three months has begun to be practiced. This demonstrates the rising importance of abortion in cases where birth control plans become vital and exact. Although the Chinese authorities maintain that the increasing prevalence and efficiency of contraception have reduced the number of abortions, the unprecedented tightening of a birth quota for each couple undoubtedly places greater reliance on abortion. Because of its exceptional role, abortion has become a problem of serious concern. The government decided abortion was a sensitive issue and so allowed no information on it for external disclosure. Many problems which other countries have hardly experienced with regard to abortion have emerged in China.

One major problem derives primarily from the contradiction between the individual's and the government's concept of the most desirable family size. Some people want two rather than the prescribed one child. Sex prejudice also plays a nasty role. A couple can have only one child, and in the majority of cases in China a son is preferred. In extreme cases, some fanatic parents have tried to exploit the loophole of the local planned birth regulations in each area which allows a couple to have another birth quota if the only child dies. Some have been known to kill their daughter in hope of getting another chance to try for a son. More worrying cases may arise from induced abortion. Abortion used to be made for higher orders of pregnancies, but in one recent case a woman with a first pregnancy applied for abortion because medical pretests showed it was a female fetus. In areas where such cases were found the sex ratio at birth was above 120. While the accuracy of such an incidence may be questionable, this technique of detecting the sex of a pregnancy at a very early stage is worrisome. If it is available to the population, it will enhance the tradition of son preference and thus may disrupt the natural balance of sex ratio at birth. It would also challenge the government's ability to execute the policy of abortion according to parity because some people may use the sex of a pregnancy to determine whether to have an abortion. Before a solution to the problem can be worked out, it is necessary to examine every aspect of abortion and its relation to the planned birth policy.

In the 1950s abortions could be performed only in the hospital by qualified doctors. This was consistent not only with tradition, but also with medical conditions. In the 1960s the vacuum aspiration machine was so perfected that it no longer required highly skilled doctors to operate and was viable enough economically for the government to be able to spread it to the countryside. But as abortion for second-trimester pregnancies gains more attention, more highly skilled doctors may be needed in both rural and commune hospitals.

Abortion in China is not only free, but is also rewarded. The planned birth regulations of Guangdong, for example, stipulate that fourteen paid days for recuperation are granted to a woman after abortion, seventeen paid days if an IUD is inserted simultaneously with abortion, and thirty-five paid days if sterilization is done at the same time. Women who terminate a pregnancy after the first trimester and simultaneously agree to sterilization are awarded fifty-one paid days. Women who have abortions are awarded subsidies for nourishment by their respective organizations where they work (GPROPB, 1980). With regard to planned birth, especially abortion, different opinions have been expressed internally against the ill effects of population policy. Such opinions used to be heard in the medical world, where abortion was opposed on the grounds of safety. But today the medical profession is completely absorbed in the work of planned birth and is devoted to technical consultations and safe therapeutic operations. As the planned births policy gains momentum, the Federation of Women has become a major pressure group for women.

DEMOGRAPHY OF ABORTION

Incidence

Data on the extent of induced abortion can be traced to 1971, when China was preparing to extend a planned birth program to rural areas where 80 percent of its population reside. Table 6.1 shows that in 1971 there were 21 abortions per 1,000 women aged fifteen to forty-four. During the seven year period 1972–78, the number stabilized at around 26. In 1979 the figure rose rapidly, and by 1982 it jumped to 55. In 1983 the figure continued rising, reaching about 63 abortions per 1,000 women in this age group. This was over 1.4 times higher than the level prevalent before 1978. Abortion figures for 1983 are estimates based on reports from nineteen provinces and municipalities, and may be different from the actual numbers of the whole country. In comparison with figures before 1982, and specifically judging from the energy the government exerted to cut births in 1983, there is no doubt, however, that the 1983 increase of abortions must be substantial. It must also be pointed out that the Chinese data on abortion are reasonably reliable, for abortion data are records of operations done by the health department. Abortion records are the basis on which the health department is reimbursed by the planned births office. Therefore, both parties are careful about the accuracy of the records. This may be the basic assurance for the quality of data. This is not to say that deliberate mistakes are not made. Because money is involved, the health department may be inclined to exaggerate the figures. In contrast, in other countries abortion is often considerably underreported. But exaggerations in China are not believed to be serious enough to impair the credibility of the data.

Changes in abortion trends in China are associated with the development of the country's population policy. In 1971, for example, on the eve of the decision to extend the planned birth program to cover the vast countryside, the abortion rate was 2 percent. This figure reflects the fact that planned births had already penetrated into the countryside, because abortion rates in 1972–78 were generally not much higher. The average level of 2.7 percent in this period corresponded to the level which prevailed when the family size was targeted at two. The decision to extend the planned birth program to cover the countryside did not affect the abortion rate as much as the single-child family policy did in 1979, demonstrating a growing reliance on fulfilling the planned target of birth reduction on abortion. These changes in abortion rates are consistent with China's policy changes.

Because China is a country where children are generally born in wedlock, the abortion rate for married women aged fifteen to forty-four may be more meaningful here. As shown in table 6.1, column 3, in 1971 each currently married woman had 0.036 abortions, a figure that stabilized at around 0.045 in 1972 through 1978, as in the case of reproductive women as shown in column 2. In 1982 it rose to 0.094 and in 1983 to 0.108.

But in 1982, 69.5 percent of married women between the ages of fifteen and forty-nine were practicing planned births. Abortions due to the failure of contraceptive methods accounted for about half of the total operations in the 1979–82 period. The other half were performed on women who were not current users of contraception (Qiu et al., 1983). Based on this information, the abortion rate for current contraceptive users was estimated at 0.06 for 1980, 0.07 for 1982, and 0.08 for 1983. The corresponding figures for nonusers were 0.12, 0.15, and 0.18, respectively. The abortion rate for noncontraceptive users was about 1.0 to 1.2 times higher than that of the contraceptive users. But of all the nonusers (accounting for 30.5 percent of married women who were still of reproductive age), 20 percent were infertile, 5 percent were either divorced or widowed, 34 percent were women who were in planned pregnancy, and the rest (40 percent) were women who should have but did not use contraceptives and were responsible for the other half of the abortions. In other words, each noncontraceptive user had 0.96 abortions in 1980, 1.25 in 1982, and 1.43 in 1983 (Qiu et al., 1983). This is about seven times higher than that of the contraceptive users. Therefore, to reduce abortion, the main task lies in persuading these nonusers, accounting for 12.2 percent of all married reproductive women, to adopt contraception.

For current contraceptive users, abortion by cause of failure is given in table 6.2. About 42 percent of abortions performed on current contraceptive users for the years 1979–82 were due to the IUD falling out, and 23 percent were due to women who got pregnant with the IUD. Altogether, of the 65 percent of abortions of contraceptive users, 34 percent of total abortions were caused by IUD failure, giving an effective contraceptive rate of 92.4 percent for 1983. As the IUD is the method of choice for half the current contraceptive users, its effective rate is of vital importance in reducing abortion. Efforts are constantly being made to improve the efficacy of the IUD. A report in September 1983 shows that the effective rate rose to 94.2 percent (Jian Kang Bao, 1983) in 1983 against 90.1 percent in 1978.

Although the Chinese are reluctant to release any data on abortion, their abortion level is apparently no higher than that in some other countries. In terms of ratio of abortions per 100 live births (table 6.1, column 4) China started from 15 percent in 1971 and rose to 84 percent in 1983. The highest figures were for the USSR with 275 percent in 1965, Hungary with 139 percent (1964), Romania with 408 percent (1965), and Bulgaria with 98 percent (1979). A medium estimate gives 120 percent for Japan in 1975. China's level is about twice as high as

Singapore's (45 percent in 1981) (Tietze, 1983), where most of the people are Chinese.

In terms of absolute numbers, China recorded 3.9 million abortions in 1971 which rose to about 15 million in 1983, an increase of almost 285 percent in thirteen years. The annual increase rate was very uneven, however, and fluctuated drastically—a phenomenon that resulted primarily from the bureaucratic requirement of incessant boosting and strict supervision from the central government. However, the arithmetic mean increase rate for the number of abortions per year from 1972 to 1983 was 14 percent, whereas after the change of population factor in the denominator is eliminated, the increase rate was 11 percent (calculated from table 6.1, column 2).

The effect of abortion on births is immediate as is shown in table 6.3, column 4. The abortion rate per 1,000 population as a percentage of the birth rate started from 15 percent in 1971 and increased gradually to 24 percent in 1975. In 1977–78 the figure was about 30 percent and in 1980 54 percent. The figure dropped a little in 1981 and then rose again in 1982 until by 1983 it was 68 percent. The effect of abortion on the natural increase rate is even more impressive. If each pregnancy is assumed to result in one live birth, the natural increase rate per year would be 2.3 percent instead of 1.5 percent from 1971 to 1983. The would-be rate is over 50 percent higher than the reported rate.

Demographic Profile

The following discusses abortion by mother's age and parity. Data in table 6.4 show that the number of abortions per 100 pregnancies for Beijing urban women is associated with the order of pregnancy. The degree of association depends on the women's exposure to the planned birth program as well as their ages. Women over age sixty-one began to be exposed to birth control when they were already over forty. Still the higher percentages of abortion are found in the higher order of conception, and in the younger age groups, showing that the effects of the planned birth program have reached them. As one moves from older age cohorts to younger ones, the percentages rise rapidly with higher orders of pregnancy. Among women fifty-one years of age, the highest percentage is no more than 60 percent. For women forty-one years old, the percentages of abortion for a pregnancy order of six and higher are 100 percent, and the figure rises sharply from the third pregnancy (from almost 60 percent to 86 percent) to the fifth. The reproductive experiences of this group of women correspond to those which held when two children per woman were considered adequate. Women aged thirty-five had also spent some of their reproductive life in the same period. But the effect of single-child family policy began to have a strong effect on their reproductive behavior. The percentage of abortions for the third pregnancy was as high as 97 percent. But for the youngest age group, the single-child family rule had a decided effect on fertility. The abortion rate for the second pregnancy was 100 percent.

The number of abortions per 100 pregnancies for each group of women (see

table 6.4) reflects a relation between the abortion rate and the age of women.
In the last row in this table, the mean number of pregnancies for the different
age groups which ever aborted during their whole reproductive life is given. It
is shown that the highest figure was 0.77 abortions for each woman aged forty-
one years.

The figures in column 8 of table 6.4 are for Chinese women aged twenty to
forty-nine (1979) who migrated to Hong Kong during the ten years prior to 1979.
They were mostly from the rural areas of Guangdong Province. Interpretation
of this information is difficult, as such data are rare in China. The age-specific
number of ever-aborted pregnancies per married woman must be added. They
are as follows: none for women twenty to twenty-four, 0.21 for women twenty-
five to twenty-nine, 0.37 for women thirty to thirty-four, 0.49 for women thirty-
five to thirty-nine, 0.91 for women forty to forty-four, and 0.50 for forty-five
to forty-nine-year-old women. The mean number of ever-aborted pregnancy for
women of reproductive age is 0.37 per woman. For the urban case in Beijing,
the mean number of ever-aborted pregnancies per ever-pregnant woman was
0.64, while it was 0.50 per married woman. If women below twenty-four (twenty-
five for Beijing) are excluded, the number of abortions ever experienced per
married woman would be 0.64, while the figure for the Chinese woman who
went to Hong Kong would be 0.41, the first figure being about 60 percent higher
than the second. This difference may be due not only to geography, but also to
urban and rural divisions (as most of the women found in Hong Kong were
mainly from the rural areas) as well as to time differences. The difference is
consistent with the report that about 38.1 percent of urban contraceptive users
adopt less effective means such as pills and condoms, while only 9.7 percent
do so in rural areas (Qiu et al., 1983).

Finally, since abortion has been officially upgraded in the interest of population
control, abortion of midterm pregnancies, that is, pregnancies between three and
six months gestation, has been performed under conditions assuring the safety
of the aborting women. Although no overall figure can be given, data fragments
can be quoted. Among Beijing's 93,879 cases of abortion in 1978, 8,577 cases
were midterm abortions, accounting for 9.1 percent of total abortions (Qian et
al., 1980). An article about PengXian, Sichuan, reports that the Health Center
of Qingjian Commune has a record of 277 cases of abortion in 1978, 47 percent
of which were termed *yinchan* (i.e., midterm abortion), while in 1980, there
were 159 cases of abortion of which 14 percent were midterm abortion (Xin &
Zhiliang, 1982).

SUMMARY

Since the mid–1950s the Chinese attitude toward abortion has shifted from
an antiabortion ethical tradition to a very liberal position. Abortion has become
an integral component of the country's overall population policy and has become
an adopted measure for birth control. The importance of abortion increased with

the rapid development of the population control policy. Its function evolved from a purely backup measure to end an unwanted pregnancy to a necessary instrument for implementing the single-child family policy. The abortion rate rises sharply the higher order the pregnancy. However, the overall abortion level is not extraordinary in comparison with the levels of Eastern European countries and Japan. The chief reason is the government's stress on preventive contraception, with a consequent high user rate of effective contraceptive means.

Abortion is free and rewarded. It is under the management of a unique and tight government planned birth program that functions very effectively throughout China.

REFERENCES

Beijing Xichenqu Funu Butong Shiqi Shengyo Zhuangkuang De Huiguxing Diaocha. *Population and Economics*, China, 1983, No. 1.

Chow, L. P. Abortion in Taiwan. In Robert E. Hall (Ed.), *Abortion in a changing world*, Vol. 1. New York: Columbia University Press, 1970.

Guangdong Provincial Regulations on Planned Birth. *Nanfang Ribao*. China, 13 February 1980.

Himes, Norman E. *Medical history of contraception*. New York: Gamut Press, 1963, pp. 109–112.

Jian Kang Bao. China, 9 September 1980, and 29 September 1983.

Qian Linjuan, Xu Bing, & Huang Shuyuan. Current conditions and tasks of population development in Beijing City. *Renkou Yanjiu (Population Research)*, China, 1980, No. 1, p. 44.

Qiu Shuhua, Wu Shutao, & Wang Meizhen. *Contraceptive status of reproductive women*. Monograph by the *Journal of Population and Economics*, Beijing Economics College, China, 1983, pp. 130–136.

Shi Chengli. Survey of the planned birth work since 1949—Exploring the history of planned birth activities of our country. *Xibei Renkou (Northwest Population)*, China, 1980, No. 2, pp. 33–48.

Shi Chengli & Wang Jian. Exploring the process of changes of planned birth policy of our country. *Xibei Renkou (Northwest Population)*, China, 1983, No. 3, pp. 49–51.

Xin Dan, & Peng Zhiliang. Experience of PengXian, Sichuan in practicing the responsibility system of contraceptive techniques. *Renkou Yanjui (Population Research)*, China, 1982, No. 6, p. 32.

Zhang Guoshen. The current situation of marital status of women in reproductive period. Monograph by the *Journal of Population and Economics*, Beijing Economics College, China, 1983, pp. 109–110.

Table 6.1
Rates and Ratios of Abortion, China Mainland, 1971–83

Year (1)	No. of Abortions Per 1,000 Women in Ages 15-44 (2)	No. of Abortions Per 1,000 Still Married Women in Ages 15-44 (3)	No. of Abortions Per 1,000 Live Births (4)	No. of Abortions Per 1,000 Population (5)	Increase Rate (%) Change of Abortions in a Year as % of the No. of Abortions in the Preceding Year (6)	Change of Rate in Colum 2 of a Year as % of the Preceding Year (7)
1971	20.9	35.7	152.3	4.6	–	–
1972	25.3	43.3	187.6	5.6	23.1	21.1
1973	26.7	45.7	207.5	5.8	6.2	5.5
1974	26.0	44.5	223.0	5.5	-2.5	-2.6
1975	26.5	45.3	241.7	5.5	2.0	1.9
1976	24.6	42.0	255.9	5.1	-6.7	-7.2
1977	26.4	45.1	292.7	5.5	10.3	7.3
1978	26.3	44.9	308.9	5.6	3.1	-.4
1979	37.3	63.8	454.9	8.1	45.7	41.8
1980	44.1	75.4	540.3	9.7	21.3	18.2
1981	39.3	67.2	418.5	8.8	-8.7	-10.9
1982	55.0	94.0	584.2	12.3	42.8	44.0
1983	62.9	107.6	840.0	14.3	17.4	14.4

Source: Abortion figures for 1971–82 are from *Wei Seng Nienyian, 1983* (Beijing People's Health Press, 1983). The figure for 1983 was estimated from information given by *Jian Kang Bao*, 29 September 1983. Numbers of women 14–44 are estimated from the age distribution in 1978. Still-married women are worked out from information given by Quan Guo Qian Fen Zhi Yi Ren Kou Sheng Yo Lu Chou Yang Diao Cha Fen Xi (Beijing: Renkou Yu Jinji Zhuankan, 1983), pp. 109–110. Population and birth figures are from *China Statistics Year Book* (Beijing: Statistics Press, 1983).

Table 6.2

Abortions by Causes of Failures as a Percentage of Total Abortions of Contraceptive Users, China, 1979–82

Causes	1979	1980	1981	1982
Fallout of IUD	42.4	44.2	40.1	41.0
Pregnancy with IUD	24.2	22.6	22.9	23.4
Failure in Pills	15.9	17.3	22.1	21.2
Failure in Male Sterilization	7.1	7.5	5.0	3.7
Failure in Female Sterilization	2.4	1.9	1.0	1.3
Failure due to Condom Defects	3.5	3.0	4.5	4.0
Other Failures	4.5	3.5	4.5	5.5
Total	100.0	100.0	100.1	100.1
Abortions of Contraceptive Users as % in Total Abortions	50.31	53.06	54.36	51.03

Source: Calculated from data given by Qiu Shuhua et al., 1983.

Table 6.3
Effect of Abortion on the Birth Rate

Year	No. of Live Births Per 1,000 Population	No. of Live Births and Abortions Per 1,000 Population	Column (3) as % of Column (2)	Natural Increase Rate Per 1,000	Would-Be Natural Increase Rate Without Abortion Per 1,000	Column (6) as % in Column (5)
(1)	(2)	(3)	(4)	(5)	(6)	(7)
1971	30.7	35.3	115	23.3	27.9	120
1972	29.8	35.4	119	22.2	27.8	125
1973	27.9	33.7	121	20.9	26.7	128
1974	24.8	30.3	122	17.5	23.0	131
1975	23.0	28.5	124	15.7	21.2	135
1976	19.9	25.0	126	12.7	19.8	156
1977	18.9	24.4	129	12.1	17.6	145
1978	18.3	23.8	130	12.0	17.6	147
1979	17.8	25.9	146	11.6	18.8	162
1980	18.0	27.7	154	11.8	21.5	182
1981	20.9	29.7	142	14.6	23.4	160
1982	21.1	33.4	158	14.5	26.8	185
1983	18.6	32.9	177	11.5	25.8	224

Source: Birth rates, except for 1980, are from *China Statistics Yearbook*, 1983. In 1980 there were 14.22 million registered births. There were also 2.71 million births that went unregistered because they were born without a birth quota. The birth rate of 1980 was calculated on a total of 17.63 million births. Figures for 1983 are based on information given by *Ta Kung Pao* (Overseas edition), 2 May 1984.

Table 6.4

Number of Abortions per 100 Pregnancies by Order of Pregnancy and Age of Women

Order of Pregnancy (1)	West City District, Beijing						Women from China in Hong Kong Ages 20-49, 1979 (8)
	Age in 1981						
	25 (2)	35 (3)	41 (4)	51 (5)	61 (6)	67 (7)	
1	10.0	.4	0.0	0.0	.8	1.2	4.9
2	100.0	31.4	9.5	1.8	.8	1.3	2.4
3		96.7	59.2	8.3	.9	1.5	35.7
4		96.8	83.8	25.9	7.6	6.6	51.2
5		100.0	85.7	35.0	14.7	7.0	63.6
6		100.0	100.0	40.5	22.0	3.1	81.8
7				60.0	19.2	-	100.0
8				57.1	25.0	11.1	-
Total	18.2	31.4	26.7	13.3	7.8	5.6	27.0
No. of Ever Pregnant Women	60	256	266	229	128	82	281
Mean No. of Pregnancies Ever Aborted Per Ever Pregnant Woman	.20	.69	.77	.55	.39	.29	.37

Source: Figures for columns 2 through 7 are derived from data on pregnancy and birth given in Beijing Xi Chengqu Funu Butong Shizi Shengyo Zhuan Kuang De Huiguxing Diaocha, *Population and Economics*, 1983, No. 1. Figures in column 8 are from a survey conducted by the East-West Population Institute.

7

CUBA

Paula E. Hollerbach

HISTORICAL DEVELOPMENT OF ABORTION POLICY

Throughout the twentieth century, and especially since the mid–1960s, the availability of abortion has been a significant factor in Cuba's declining fertility. Since 1965 Cuba has experienced a sharp decrease in fertility, representing the final stage of its demographic transition since the onset of fertility declined in the 1920s. Policies liberalizing access to abortion have been enacted since the mid–1960s, but since the mid–1970s efforts have been undertaken to reduce the incidence of abortion by substituting the use of effective contraceptive methods. The actual effect of induced abortion on fertility is comparatively less than that of other factors inhibiting fertility, such as marriage patterns and contraceptive prevalence. However, as of the late 1970s, Cuba had one of the highest abortion ratios in the world, approximately 429 abortions per 1,000 pregnancies in 1983, indicating that the decline of fertility has been accomplished by a heavy reliance on induced abortion as a backup method in situations of contraceptive nonuse or failure.

This chapter focuses on the demographic consequences of abortion and abortion legislation in Cuba. In the first section, recent trends in Cuban fertility are reviewed, and in the second section, the legal status of abortion and government policies on fertility regulation are examined. The third section considers the demography of legal abortion: the effect of liberalized abortion legislation on fertility and maternal mortality, the medical sequelae of abortion, and the characteristics of women requesting abortion. In the fourth section, the fertility-inhibiting effects of nuptiality, contraceptive prevalence and effectiveness, the incidence of induced abortion, and the duration of postpartum infecundability are identified.

FERTILITY TRENDS

Cuba was among the first Latin American nations to experience a transition to low fertility. Beginning in the 1920s and ending in 1958, fertility consistently declined in Cuba, relatively rapidly through the late 1940s and more gradually through the 1950s. The crude birth rate (the number of births per 1,000 population) declined from 38 in 1920–24 to 32 in 1940–45 and to 28 by the early 1950s (Hollerbach & Diaz-Briquets, 1983).

In the postrevolutionary period, three distinct trends have emerged with regard to fertility. During the postrevolutionary baby boom period, which lasted from 1959 to 1964, the crude birth rate increased from 28 per 1,000 population to 35. The general fertility rate (births per 1,000 women fifteen to forty-four) increased from 127 births per 1,000 women of reproductive age in 1959 to 165 births in 1964, triggered by increased childbearing among younger women. The baby boom was followed by a slow decline in fertility from 1965 to 1973, except in 1971 which registered a slight rise. By 1973 the crude birth rate (25) and general fertility rate (122) had finally approached prerevolutionary levels, and by 1981, the crude birth rate had reached an extremely low level of 14 births per 1,000 population, rising slightly to 16.6 births in 1984. The general fertility rate declined from 122 in 1973 to 60.6 births per 1,000 women aged fifteen to forty-four in 1981 and then rose to 69.9 in 1984. By 1981 the lifetime fertility rate of 1,818 births per 1,000 women of reproductive age was well below the replacement level (2,000 births per 1,000 women).

LEGAL STATUS OF ABORTION AND GOVERNMENT POLICIES ON FERTILITY REGULATION

Prior to 1870 legislation pertaining to the provision of abortion existed in various statutes with contradictory interpretations. To remedy the situation, specific legislation was enacted, dating back to the Spanish Penal Code of 1870, which was later incorporated into the Cuban Penal Code of 1879 and the Social Defense Code of April 1936. According to the 1936 code, abortion was prohibited except on grounds of grave danger to the woman's life or health; on juridical grounds (pregnancy following rape or abduction without marriage); or on eugenic grounds (anticipated physical or mental impairment).

Early statistics on the incidence of abortion are lacking. However, the conditions constituting high risk to a woman's health were not defined by the law, but merely required the concurrence of two physicians. Thus, abortion was available in large urban areas, especially in Havana, where physicians charged moderate fees according to the social class of their clients. Abortions were also available through unskilled practitioners for even lower fees.

The early practice of abortion in Cuba was in part due to the relatively weak influence of institutional religion during the prerevolutionary period as well as the well-developed structure of the medical health system. A variety of social surveys reviewed by Dominguez (1978) show that the majority of the urban population and a substantial proportion of the rural population identified themselves as Catholics. However, the majority did not attend services regularly or formalize their marriages in church. Thus, Catholicism was weaker in Cuba than in other Latin American countries during the mid–1950s. Despite this secularism, religious beliefs associated with Afro-Cuban sects have had a characteristically strong influence, especially in the rural areas and within the lower class. However, there is little evidence that any of these religions has strongly influenced fertility preferences or fertility limitation. Prior to the revolution, Cuba's medical health system was highly developed through mutualist insurance plans and a fairly extensive system of public hospitals and dispensaries, which accounts in part for the low infant mortality and high life expectancy attained by the population, as well as the availability of abortion services especially in urban areas.

During the immediate postrevolutionary period, however, the antiabortion law was more strictly enforced. The nation's postrevolutionary baby boom was partially offset by emigration, which reached an early peak between 1960 and 1962, interrupted in late 1962 by the missile crisis. The emigration of private physicians during this period (officially reported as 2,000 to 3,000 of the previously existing 6,300 physicians), increased the difficulty and cost of obtaining an abortion, resulting in greater reliance on unskilled practitioners and a rise in maternal mortality. During this period, a shortage of contraceptive supplies also developed following the economic blockade of the island. As a result of these developments, the incidence of illegal abortion increased, and between 1962 and 1965 clandestine abortion accounted for nearly one-third of all maternal deaths (other causes included traumatic births and infections).[1] Thus, in late 1964 the Social Defense Code was amended to make the conditions for abortion more flexible through the adoption of the World Health Organization's definition of health: "a state of complete physical, mental and social well-being and not merely the absence of disease or infirmity" (WHO, 1970). These criteria, which became the medical norms for termination of pregnancy established by the Ministry of Public Health, have resulted in greater access to abortion since 1965 through the national public health system.

The recent decline in Cuban fertility experienced by women in all age groups has been facilitated by government policies designed to provide equal access to abortion and contraception and to reduce infant mortality. The Cuban government has established targets for the reduction in infant, child, and maternal mortality, and has concentrated medical personnel and services in the less developed regions in order to achieve these goals. After a period during which infant mortality showed littled general trend (40 per 1,000 in 1965, 39 per 1,000 in 1970), the 1970s saw a period of sharp decline with a provisional rate of 15.0 by 1984, the lowest infant mortality rate in Latin America.[2] From 1966 to 1980 maternal mortality declined 42 percent, from 91 deaths per 100,000 live births in 1966 to 53 deaths in 1980 and a provisional rate of 40 deaths in 1981.

The Cuban government has not set specific targets for fertility reduction. However, the government has established a variety of objectives related to fertility regulation. Briefly summarized, these include: the reduction of the frequency of abortion and repeat abortion; prevention of high-risk pregnancies; improved quality of maternal/child health/family planning services through the use of more effective contraceptives and increased coverage to reduce differentials in regional availability; and prevention of the transmission of genetically determined illness (UNFPA, 1982b).

Under the new Penal Code of 1 November 1979, which covers all laws and not just those relating to abortion and health, punishment has been established for *illegal* abortions (loss of physician's license and imprisonment). Illegal abortions are defined as those performed without the permission of the woman, for profit, outside hospitals, or against the regulations established by the Ministry of Public Health. This new Penal Code reflects a change in law, but not in practice, since the age and gestation guidelines pertaining to the provision of abortion remain unchanged. Additional norms regarding appropriate abortion techniques and length of hospital stay will also be established in the near future.

At present, most abortions are performed in provincial maternity hospitals and general medical-surgical hospitals by vacuum aspiration or surgical curettage. Abortions up to twelve weeks of gestation are performed solely at the woman's request for single women eighteen years of age and older and married women, and consent of the partner is not required. Single women under the age of eighteen require parental permission for an abortion, according to the norms of the Ministry of Public Health. However, in reality, such approval is not always necessary. Abortions after twelve weeks are also performed, requiring validation by the director of the institution and approval of the obstetrician-gynecologist, which is usually forthcoming.

DEMOGRAPHY OF ABORTION

Cuban data on abortion pertain primarily to aggregate national statistics on total abortions, legal abortions, and other abortions, tabulated on an annual basis, as well as abortion-related mortality. Although abortion data will be tabulated by age group in the near future, at present no such tabulations are available.

Table 7.1 presents national data on the incidence of abortion during 1968–84, a period of increased access to legal abortion and sharply declining fertility. The table includes numbers of live births, legal abortions, other abortions, annual rates of live births and abortions per 1,000 women fifteen to forty-four years of age, and the corresponding general fertility rates per 1,000 women fifteen to forty-four years of age for the period 1968–84.[3] Total abortions have been divided into legal and "other" (a category that includes spontaneous abortions, some therapeutic curettages related to uterine and gynecological diseases, and incomplete illegal abortions requiring medical treatment). This categorization pertains to the data for 1968–80. The data on other abortions available for 1981–84 are provisional estimates (see note to table 7.1).

As noted in table 7.1, between 1968 and 1971 the general fertility rate (the number of births per 1,000 women of reproductive age) fluctuated between 143 and 148. Since then it has fallen consistently to 60.6 in 1981, rising to 69.9 in 1984. Increasing access to legal abortion sharply reduced the incidence of illegal abortions during this period: in 1968 other abortions represented substantially more than one-half of the total abortions reported; by 1980 other abortions had been reduced through the greater availability of legal abortion to only about one-fifth of all abortions, indicating that the "other" category now includes primarily spontaneous abortions.

Effect of Liberalization of Abortion Legislation on Fertility

The number of legal abortions increased from 28,485 in 1968 to a high of 131,536 in 1974, and subsequently declined to 103,974 in 1980. By 1984 the number of legal abortions had again increased to 139,588, and the number of births had also increased to 166,281—about 22 percent above the 1981 figure.[4] As illustrated in table 7.2, increased availability of legal abortion has also reduced the incidence of total abortion mortality, which increased from 13.7 deaths per 100,000 live births in 1960 to a high of 25 in 1969 (62 total abortion deaths) and subsequently declined steadily to 3.4 deaths per 100,000 live births in 1978 (5 deaths). In 1980 this figure increased to 15.3 deaths per 100,000 live births. The rise is in part attributable to a sudden increase in deaths associated with legal abortion: among the 72 maternal deaths from all causes recorded in 1980, 21 were associated with all types of abortion and 8 with legal abortion; the legal abortion mortality rate increased to 7.7 in 1980. Anesthetic or septic shock, sepsis, and heart failure were the main causes of the 1980 abortion-related deaths. Recent international data suggest an average of 1 death per 100,000 abortion procedures within a hospital setting. Thus, the recent Cuban figure is about eight times higher than might be expected (UNFPA, 1982b). In 1981 the total abortion mortality rate had again declined to 9.5 deaths per 100,000 live births (13 deaths). Moreover, the lifetime mortality rates are still extremely low, indicating that the effect of induced abortion on overall mortality is comparatively minor from a demographic perspective. Cuba's nonabortion mortality rate of 31 deaths per 100,000 live births is still considerably below the earlier figures recorded for 1968–69 (58–60 deaths), in part because of the integrated maternal-child health program.

With the reduction in the incidence of illegal procedures, the incidence of legal abortion rose. As noted in table 7.1, the legal abortion rate per 1,000 women aged fifteen to forty-four rose from 17 in 1968 to 70 in 1974. Expressed as the average number of legal abortions per woman during her lifetime at prevailing incidence levels, the rate increased from 0.5 abortions per woman in 1968 (a lifetime abortion rate of 501 abortions per 1,000 women fifteen to forty-four) to 2.1 abortions in 1974.

After that point, largely because of the greater availability and use of effective contraceptive methods, the legal abortion rate declined to an estimated 47 in 1980, or 1.4 abortions per woman, and a lifetime abortion rate of 1,416 per 1,000 women fifteen to forty-four. Regardless of legislation, a lifetime rate of 1,000 per 1,000 women has been suggested as a probable minimum for a country with moderately effective contraception and a rate of 200 per 1,000 for a country with highly effective contraception (Tietze & Bongaarts, 1975). The provisional legal abortion rate rose somewhat to 54 in 1983 and 59 in 1984 (1.8 abortions per woman).

Throughout this period, however, the abortion ratio showed substantial and consistent annual increases. From 103 in 1968, the ratio rose to 432 per 1,000 pregnancies in 1980, and then declined slightly to 429 in 1983, indicating that fertility decline has been accomplished by a heavy reliance on induced abortion as a backup method in situations of contraceptive nonuse or failure (Hollerbach, 1980). Recent abortion estimates show that only four countries had higher abortion ratios than Cuba's during the late 1970s: Bulgaria (495 in 1979), Japan (547 in 1975), Romania (498 in 1979), and the USSR (700 in 1970) (Tietze, 1983). The abortion ratio for Havana is higher than the overall rate for Cuba, and the reported incidence is generally higher in urban than in rural areas of the country. By 1978–80 abortions in Ciudad de la Habana represented 29 to 30 percent of all abortions (Direccion Provincial de Estadisticas, Ciudad de la Habana, n.d.).

Medical Sequelae

Although data on abortion are available on the national level and abortion data exist within each institution, no national data on the epidemiology of and complications associated with abortion have been compiled. Similarly, information on the incidence of repeat abortion and complications and characteristics of abortion recipients is limited to small-scale studies in selected polyclinics and hospital settings, and representative studies at the national level are unavailable.

A study conducted in the America Arias teaching hospital of gynecology and obstetrics in Havana indicated that among 2,205 women obtaining abortion by dilatation and curettage, only 1.8 percent experienced complications when the procedure was performed by specialists, and 1.1 percent when the procedure was performed by residents (who performed low-risk abortions). The most common complication was pelvic inflammation; the second most prevalent was retained tissue, more common in abortions to nulliparous and primiparous women (Rodriguez Castro, 1978). A second study of 8,678 abortions performed in the Eusebio Hernandez Hospital of Marianao, Havana, showed that 2.6 percent of abortions involved retained tissue; in 31 cases uterine perforations occurred, and in one case, a maternal death followed hysterectomy (Rodriguez Castro, 1978).

National data on the incidence of second-trimester abortion in Cuba are also unavailable. However, a recent study conducted in the Ramon Gonzalez Coro Gynecology and Obstetrics Hospital in Havana from 1974 to 1977 reported that second-trimester abortions constituted only 1.5 percent to 2 percent of all induced abortions during that time. Among these women, 75 percent of the abortion patients who were younger than twenty sought abortions for social reasons. Among the women thirty or more years of age, this proportion was only 38 percent; 45 percent sought abortion for medical indications (Valdes Vivo et al., 1978).

Characteristics of Women Requesting Abortion

A study conducted in a municipality of Havana, averaging between 6,000 and 7,000 abortions annually, provides additional information on abortion trends by age, showing that abortion is used primarily by women aged twenty and older. Over time, however, there has been a slight increase in the proportion of younger women having abortions—from 18 percent in 1976 to 21 percent in 1977 and 24 percent in 1978 (from 1,078 to 1,223 abortions over the three years), probably owing to an increase in the proportion of single women age fifteen to nineteen and a recent decline in their age-specific fertility (Rodriguez Castro, 1978).

RELATIVE IMPACT OF CONTRACEPTION, NUPTIALITY, AND ABORTION ON FERTILITY

Contraceptive Prevalence

Some indication of recent trends in contraceptive use can be gained from results of a survey conducted in 1980 in Arroyo Naranjo, a semirural area at the edge of the city of Havana, with a sample of 732 women in union aged fifteen to forty-four (Vila & Alvarez, 1980). This survey shows a higher figure than surveys conducted in the early 1970s of contraceptive use among urban women in union: 68 percent were current users, and 60 percent were using the three most effective methods—IUD (37 percent), sterilization (16 percent), or the pill (7 percent). In the early 1970s four area contraceptive prevalence surveys showed that only an estimated 33 to 49 percent of urban women in union were using effective methods. Thus, by 1980 the increased availability of government-supplied methods (primarily the pill, the IUD, and sterilization) appears to have resulted in reduced reliance on less effective methods, higher contraceptive prevalence, and greater access to contraceptive services.

Nuptiality

Marital fertility is also affected by a variety of factors relating to nuptiality: the average age at first union and marital status, or the proportion of women in union. Between 1970 and 1979 a trend toward the postponement of unions was evident in Cuba. The mean age at first union for males increased 0.5 years from 23.4 to 23.9, and for females 0.7 years from 19.5 to 20.2. Although the number of men and women entering reproductive age increased with the aging of the baby boom cohort, the proportion of the population aged fifteen to forty-nine currently in union declined somewhat to 65 percent of women and 56 percent of men in 1979, in comparison to 68 percent and 56 percent, respectively, in 1970.

Decomposition of the Proximate Determinants of Fertility

The level of fertility in a society is determined primarily by four factors, termed the proximate determinants of fertility. Utilizing a model developed by Bongaarts (1982), the fertility effects of the most important proximate determinants are measured through four indexes: the index of marriage (C^m), the index of contraception (C^c), the index of abortion (C^a), and the index of postpartum infecundability (C^i). These indexes assume values between 0, if fertility inhibition is complete, and 1, if the variable has no fertility-inhibiting effect. A summary of the decomposition of the proximate determinants follows. A more complete explanation of the general model is provided elsewhere (Bongaarts, 1982; Bongaarts & Potter, 1983); detailed application of the model to Cuban data is discussed in Hollerbach and Diaz-Briquets (1983).

The lower the value of any index, the larger its relative fertility-modifying effect. As illustrated in table 7.3, which provides measures of the intermediate fertility variables, the indexes, and the total, marital, and natural marital fertililty rates for Cuba, the effect of contraception is the most significant (0.519), followed by the effect of marriage patterns (0.693). The fertility-inhibiting effects of these two factors is significantly greater than the effect of either abortion (0.789) or postpartum infecundability (0.897).

Utilizing the data available in table 7.3, the model estimate of the total fertility rate is estimated as $C^m \times C^c \times C^a \times C^i \times TF$, equivalent to 3.89. This derived estimate is only slightly higher than the total fertility rate of 3.77 originally calculated for all women aged fifteen to forty-nine and within an acceptable range of variation.

The data provided in table 7.3 on other societies with TFRs of 3.0 to 4.5 are subject to large sampling errors because of the small number of populations included in the averages. Comparisons of these societies and Cuba show that Cuba's prevalence of contraceptive use is higher, while the use-effectiveness of contraception is similar, given the high proportion of women using traditional methods at the time. However, not surprisingly, Cuba has a much higher total induced abortion rate and a shorter duration of postpartum infecundability. With respect to the indexes, contraception and especially induced abortion are more significant determinants of the total fertility rate in Cuba than they are in other Phase III societies with similar fertility levels; marriage and postpartum infecundability are less significant.

SUMMARY

Cuba's fertility decline since 1965, accelerating since 1973, has been greatly facilitated by government policies to increase access to legal abortion since the mid–1960s and promote the availability of modern contraceptives since the mid–1970s.

Increasing access to legal abortion has sharply reduced the incidence of illegal abortions and the number of deaths and death rates associated with abortion. The legal abortion rate per 1,000 women aged fifteen to forty-four rose from 17 in 1968 to 70 in 1974; the total abortion rate increased from 0.5 abortions per woman in 1968 to 2.1 abortions in 1974, owing to the availability of abortion services and a relaxation of use or method failure associated with traditional contraceptive methods.

Despite widespread access to legal abortion, decomposition of the proximate determinants of fertility for the 1970–73 period indicates that the fertility-inhibiting effect of contraception is the most significant, followed by the effect of marriage patterns. These two factors are significantly more important than the effect of abortion and postpartum infecundability, which is the least significant.

By 1980 the increased availability of government-supplied contraceptives (primarily pills, intrauterine devices, and sterilization) and concerted efforts to educate Cuban women on fertility regulation had resulted in reduced reliance on less effective methods, higher contraceptive prevalence, and greater access to contraceptive services, especially in the less developed provinces, and a decline in the incidence of abortion and the legal abortion rate which reached 47 in 1980, or 1.4 abortions per woman. The provisional legal abortion rate rose somewhat to 59 in 1984, or 1.8 abortions per woman. However, during the same period the abortion ratio continued to rise, from 103 in 1968 to 432 per 1,000 pregnancies in 1980, declining to 429 in 1983, indicating that fertility decline has been accomplished by a heavy reliance on induced abortion as a backup method in situations of contraceptive nonuse or failure.

NOTES

The author wishes to thank John Bongaarts, Sergio Diaz-Briquets, Kenneth H. Hill, and Christopher Tietze for their comments and suggestions on this chapter. Portions of this chapter also appear in the volume *Fertility Determinants in Cuba* by P. E. Hollerbach and S. Diaz-Briquets. Report No. 26 of the Committee on Population and Demography (Washington, D.C.: National Academy Press, 1983). The author wishes to thank the director of the National Academy Press for permission to reprint selected portions of the text in this chapter. The author also wishes to thank Robert J. Lapham, Study Director of the Panel on Fertility Determinants, and the Committee on Population and Demography, for permission to reproduce the tables appearing in this volume.

1. National data on the incidence of abortion prior to 1968 have not been tabulated. Although the conditions allowing abortion were liberalized in late 1964, educational efforts were initially directed to high-parity women. Access to abortion during these years was dependent on the disposition of the director of the institution; access to physicians

was reduced because of emigration, and clandestine abortion continued. Therefore, the data provided in table 7.1 for 1968–69 probably underestimate the actual incidence of abortion.

2. Indirect estimates of child mortality based on the 1979 National Demographic Survey suggest an infant mortality level of around 35 for 1976–77, with no apparent decline in infant mortality during the latter 1970s. However, given the statistical consistency in the previous mortality estimates, the evidence that birth and death registration was virtually complete in the late 1960s and early 1970s, and lack of evidence that the official registration system has sharply deteriorated, the official sequence of infant mortality statistics is accepted, with the qualification that it is not independently supported and requires final confirmation from surveys in the early 1980s (Hollerbach & Diaz-Briquets, 1983).

3. The lifetime rates for abortion and fertility were estimated by multiplying the annual rates by 30, the average number of years lived between the ages of fifteen and forty-five since age-specific abortion rates are unavailable. The demographic terms for these lifetime rates are "total fertility rate" and "total abortion rate," and are sometimes computed per woman rather than per 1,000 women.

4. The factors underlying the recent increase in both births and abortions during 1981 and 1984 are unknown, although plausible explanations may be provided. First, the proportion of women aged fifteen to nineteen and twenty to twenty-four has increased because the children born during the baby boom period in the early 1960s have arrived at reproductive age. The age-specific fertility rates among women in the prime reproductive years (age fifteen to nineteen and twenty to twenty-four) dropped sharply between 1976 and 1981. However, recent age-specific fertility data for 1982–1984 show that an increase in fertility has occurred within these two age groups. The effect of the Mariel sealift in 1980 and the emigration of 125,000 Cubans to the United States during that time would have had some dampening effect on fertility through shifts in the age and sex composition of the population. However, the migration also had a countervailing pronatalist effect among younger couples who had previously postponed marriage or childbearing due to the urban housing shortage, resulting in higher marriage rate from 1980 to 1984. Previous waves of emigration during the early 1960s and early 1970s had also been accompanied by the redistribution of existing housing and higher marriage rates. A final explanation may be a temporary shortage in oral contraceptives, due to a temporary closing of the production factory in 1981. Thus, supply problems in the availability of fertility regulation may also partially explain the recent rise in fertility and the higher incidence of abortion.

REFERENCES

Bongaarts, J. The fertility-inhibiting effects of the intermediate fertility variables. *Studies in Family Planning*, 1982, *13*(6/7), 179–180.

Bongaarts, J., & R. G. Potter, *Fertility, biology, and behavior: An analysis of the proximate determinants*. New York: Academic Press, 1983.

Comite Estatal de Estadisticas, Instituto de Investigaciones Estadisticas. *Anuario demografico 1984*. La Habana: Comite Estatal de Estadisticas, 1984.

David, H. P. Cuba: Low fertility, relatively high abortion. *Intercom*, 1983, *11*(7/8), 5–6.

Direccion Provincial de Estadisticas, Ciudad de la Habana (n.d.). Unpublished manuscript cited in Gonzalez Perez, n.d.

Dominguez, J. I. *Cuba: Order and revolution.* Cambridge, Mass.: Belknap Press of Harvard University Press, 1978.

Gonzalez de la Cruz, V. Conocimiento y uso de metodos anti-conceptivos. Resultados obtenidos mediante encuestas sobre fecundidad. *Revista Cubana de Administracion de Salud,* 1980, *6*(1), 31–38.

Gonzalez Perez, G. Aspectos sociodemograficos del aborto: Estudios recientes en Ciudad de la Habana. Unpublished manuscript, n.d.

Hollerbach, P. E. Recent trends in fertility, abortion, and contraception in Cuba. *International Family Planning Perspectives,* 1980, *6*(3), 97–106.

Hollerbach, P. E., & Diaz-Briquets, S. *Fertility determinants in Cuba.* Report No. 26 of the Committee on Population and Demography. Washington, D.C.: National Academy Press, 1983.

Junta Central de Planificacion, Comite Estatal de Estadisticas (JUCEPLAN, C.E.E.). *Anuario estadistico de Cuba, 1980.* La Habana: Comite Estatal de Estadisticas, 1981.

Ministerio de Salud Publica de Cuba. *Informe anual 1978.* La Habana: Ministerio de Salud Publica de Cuba, 1979.

———. *Informe anual 1979.* La Habana: Ministerio de Salud Publica de Cuba, 1980.

———. *Informe anual 1980.* La Habana: Ministerio de Salud Publica de Cuba, 1981.

———. *Informe anual 1981.* La Habana: Ministerio de Salud Publica de Cuba, 1982.

Nortman, D. L., & Hofstatter, E. *Population and family planning programs: A compendium of data through 1978* (10th ed.). New York: Population Council, 1980.

Population Reference Bureau. Cuban abortions still high. *Population Today,* 1986, *14*(5), 4.

Rodriguez Castro, R. Complicaciones del aborto a corto plazo. In B. Arce & P. Pujol-Amat (Eds.), *Reproduccion humana y regulacion de la fertilidad.* Barcelona: Espaxs, 1978.

Tietze, C. *Induced abortion, 1983* (5th ed.). New York: Population Council, 1983.

Tietze, C., & Bongaarts, J. Fertility rates and abortion rates: Simulations of family limitations. *Studies in Family Planning,* 1975, *6*(5), 114–120.

United Nations, Department of International Economic and Social Affairs. *World population prospects: Estimates and projections as assessed in 1982.* Population Studies No. 86. New York: United Nations, 1985.

United Nations, Population Division. *Population by sex and age for regions and countries 1950–2000 as assessed in 1973: Medium variants.* New York: United Nations, 1976.

United Nations Fund for Population Activities (UNFPA). *Evaluation of UNFPA Programme in Cuba: Projects CUB/73/P01 and CUB/79/P01/P02/P03/P04 (1975–81).* New York: United Nations Fund for Population Activities, 1982a.

———. *Evaluation of UNFPA Programme in Cuba (1975–81). Appendix II.B. Evaluation of the contraception, abortion and related research/evaluation components of the Cuban MCH Programme and of UNFPA contributions to that Programme.* New York: United Nations Fund for Population Activities, 1982b.

Valdes Vivo, P., Forte Manilla, J., Saavedra Vega, J., Terrero Encarnacion, A., & Sanchez Texido, C. Metodos extra-amnioticos para la terminacion del embarazo.

In B. Arce & P. Pujol-Amat (Eds.), *Reproduccion humana y regulacion de la fertilidad*. Barcelona: Espaxs, 1978.

Vila, E., & Alvarez, M. *Encuesta de fecundidad. Arroyo Naranjo 1980. Resultados anticipados de variables seleccionadas*. La Habana: Ministerio de Salud Publica de Cuba, 1980.

World Health Organization (WHO). *Spontaneous and induced abortion: Report of a WHO scientific group*. WHO Technical Report Series, No. 461. Geneva: World Health Organization, 1970.

Table 7.1

Number of Women Aged Fifteen to Forty-four, Number of Live Births and Abortions, Abortion Rates and Ratios, and General Fertility Rate, Cuba, 1968–84

Year	Women 15–44 (in 1,000s)	Live Births	Legal Abortions	Other Abortions	Total Abortions[a]	Legal Abortion Rate[b]	Total Abortion Rate[b]	Legal Abortion Ratio[c]	General Fertility Rate
1968	1,708	251,857	28,485	43,424	71,909	16.7	42.1	103	147.5
1969	1,731	246,005	46,080	47,420	93,500	26.6	54.0	160	142.1
1970	1,754	237,019	70,521	42,485	113,006	40.2	64.4	222	135.1
1971	1,788	256,014	84,823	36,224	121,047	47.4	67.7	252	143.2
1972	1,822	247,997	100,045	34,056	134,101	54.9	73.6	297	136.1
1973	1,858	226,005	112,107	32,069	144,176	60.3	77.6	343	121.6
1974	1,893	203,066	131,536	33,718	165,254	69.5	87.3	399	107.3
1975	1,920	192,941	126,107	33,510	159,617	65.7	83.1	399	100.5
1976	1,974	187,555	121,415	31,039	152,454	61.5	77.2	405	95.0
1977	2,029	168,960	114,829	30,647	145,476	56.6	71.7	420	83.3
1978	2,086	148,249	110,431	27,420	137,851	52.9	66.1	431	71.1
1979	2,144	143,551	106,549	25,546	132,095	49.7	61.6	432	67.0
1980	2,205	136,900	103,974	24,896	128,870	47.2	58.4	432	62.1
1981[d]	2,247	136,211	108,559	24,108[d]	132,667[d]	48.3	59.0	423	60.6
1982[d]	2,290	159,759	126,745	25,813[d]	152,558[d]	55.3	66.6	438	69.8
1983[d]	2,334	165,284	124,791	25,853[d]	150,644[d]	53.5	64.5	429	70.8
1984[d]	2,378	166,281	139,588	26,994[d]	166,582[d]	58.7	70.1	—	69.9

[a]Total abortions equal legal abortions plus other abortions.

[b]Procedures per 1,000 women 15–44.

[c]Legal abortions per 1,000 pregnancies (abortions plus those live births taking place during a twelve-month period commencing six months later than the period in which abortions were measured).

[d]Data for 1981 to 1984 are provisional. Moreover, the previously published data on other abortions for 1981–84 include diagnostic curettages, that is, procedures performed for the diagnosis of pathology, which have been excluded in the tabulations of other abortions. Therefore, the current estimates of total abortions for 1981 to 1984 have been derived by excluding the relative proportion of diagnostic curettages (42%) among total abortions.

—Data unavailable.

Source: Age data, 1968–74, United Nations (1976); age data 1975–84, United Nations (1985); abortion data, David (1983), Population Reference Bureau (1986), Rodríguez Castro (1978); all other data, C.E.E. (1984), JUCEPLAN, C.E.E. (1981), Ministerio de Salud Pública de Cuba (1979, 1981), UNFPA (1982b). Author's calculations.

Table 7.2
Measures of Abortion-Related and Nonabortion-Related Maternal Mortality, Cuba, 1968–82

Year	Maternal Mortality Rate[a]	Total Abortion Mortality Rate[a]	Non-Abortion Mortality Rate[a]	Legal Abortion Mortality Rate[b]	Total Abortion Deaths	Legal Abortion Deaths	Total Abortion Deaths per 100,000 Women 15–44	Legal Abortion Deaths per 100,000 Women 15–44	Lifetime Rate per 1,000 Women[d] Legal Abortions	Live Births
1968	83.0	24.6	58.4	—	62	1	3.6	0.06	501	4425
1969	85.0	25.2	59.8	—	62	—	3.6	—	798	4263
1970	70.5	21.5	49.0	—	51	—	2.9	—	1206	4053
1971	67.6	11.3	56.3	—	29	1	1.6	0.06	1422	4296
1972	52.0	10.9	41.1	—	27	0	1.5	0.00	1647	4083
1973	55.3	12.4	42.9	1.2	28	3	1.5	0.16	1809	3648
1974	58.1	14.8	43.3	—	30	1	1.6	0.05	2085	3219
1975	68.4	11.9	56.5	—	23	2	1.2	0.10	1971	3015
1976	47.5	10.7	36.8	—	20	0	1.0	0.00	1845	2850
1977	49.1	8.9	40.2	1.1	15	3	0.7	0.15	1698	2499
1978	45.2	3.4	41.8	—	5	0	0.2	0.00	1587	2133
1979	51.5	9.8	41.7	—	14	—	0.6	—	1491	2010
1980	52.6	15.3	37.3	7.7	21	8	1.0	0.36	1416	1863
1981[c]	40.4	9.5	30.9	—	13	—	0.6	—	1449	1818
1982[c]	—	—	—	—	—	—	—	—	1659	2094

[a]Per 100,000 live births. The total abortion mortality rate takes into account all maternal deaths associated with abortions (legal and all other abortions; the nonabortion mortality rate excludes these factors).

[b]Per 100,000 legal abortions.

[c]Provisional data.

[d]Lifetime rate estimated by multiplying annual rate by 30.

—Data unavailable.

Source: Age data 1968–74, United Nations (1976); age data 1975–82, United Nations (1985); abortion data, David (1983), Rodriguez Castro (1978); all other data, C.E.E. (1984), JUCEPLAN, C.E.E. (1981), Ministerio de Salud Publica de Cuba (1979, 1980, 1981, 1982), UNFPA (1982a). Statistics on mortality on file at the World Health Organization data bank in June 1980, supplied by Dr. H. Hansluwka.

Table 7.3

Measures of the Intermediate Fertility Variables, the Indexes, and the Total, Marital, and Natural Marital Fertility Rates, Cuba, 1972, and Countries in Phase III of a Synthetic Transition (TFR 3.0–4.5)

Measures	Cuba	Phase III Societies[a]
Prevalence of contraceptive use	0.53	0.40
Use-effectiveness of contraception	0.84	0.86
Total induced abortion rate	1.65	0.38
Postpartum infecundability (in months)	3.79	8.50
Index of marriage	0.693	0.551
Index of contraception	0.519	0.630
Index of induced abortion	0.789	0.961
Index of postpartum infecundability	0.897	0.763
Total fertility rate	3.77	3.88
Total marital fertility rate	5.45	7.05
Model estimate of total fertility rate	3.89	—
Total natural marital fertility rate[b]	13.72	11.67

[a]The data were obtained by averaging data from four countries; see Bongaarts (1982, table 4).

[b]Estimated as 15.3 times the index of postpartum infecundability.

8

CZECHOSLOVAKIA

Jiři Šráček

HISTORICAL DEVELOPMENT OF ABORTION POLICY

Czechoslovakia was established as a sovereign state on 28 October 1918 upon the division of the Austro-Hungarian monarchy after World War I. The Austro-Hungarian monarchy was a Roman Catholic state where abortion was illegal and heavily punished in accordance with Act 117/1852 of the Empire Code. Nevertheless, illegal abortion was frequently performed. Demographers (Srb & Trojanová, 1978) estimate that at the turn of the century more than 100,000 abortions were performed annually in the area of present-day Czechoslovakia.

After 1918 the new state of Czechoslovakia took over the act prohibiting abortion from the Austro-Hungarian Empire Code, the only amendment being to Section 144 of the 77/1920 Official Code which allowed abortion to save the life of a woman. Modern-minded physicians, the progressive woman's movement, and leftists and left-wing artists joined in an effort to allow induced abortion on medical and social grounds, but the more powerful conservative political parties and the established Roman Catholic church prevented any liberalization. Hence, illegal abortions continued despite prosecution, the number climbing to over 200,000 during the Great Depression.

After World War II under the new social order, the Abortion Act was liberalized. The new Criminal Law 86/1950 permitted abortions not only when the woman's life was endangered, but also for serious health and genetic failures. No social grounds were included as yet, and so illegal abortions continued to be carried out at approximately 100,000 per year (Vojta, 1961).

The principal change in the law came in 1957 when the liberal Abortion Act 68/1957 was passed and became effective on 1 January 1958. Passage of the act was preceded by two years of comprehensive public discussions.

The main input to the bill came from the Soviet Union. The act was passed primarily to enhance family development care which was being undermined by life-threatening illegal abortions performed by unskilled persons outside the health establishment. In addition to medical and genetic grounds, other grounds meriting special attention were introduced.

The act thus obviated the need for the woman to self-abort or visit an illegal practitioner. At the same time, the compulsory registration of all abortions (the act distinguishes between spontaneous, legal, and illegal abortions) permits statistical evaluation and followup. As a result, practically all abortions are now performed in hospitals by skilled gynecologists, thereby decreasing the morbidity and mortality figures for women.

Because of its easy availability, the abortion rate has been increasing rapidly. Moreover, abortions are performed free of charge, and there is no need to have a permanent address to apply for the abortion. In 1962 Order 126/1962 was issued which allowed a woman to make her application only to the district commissioner in the district in which she was residing.

After a brief decline in 1963 and 1964, the abortion rate rose again reaching a peak in 1969, followed by another decline in 1973. In 1976 abortions again increased until 1984. This pattern of fluctuation can be traced to the government's new pronatalist measures.

In 1968 Czechoslovakia officially became the federation of two republics: the Czech Socialist Republic and the Slovak Socialist Republic. This change was reflected in the abortion legislation, with each republic issuing its orders and methodological instructions in connection with the Abortion Act.

In 1971 the Government Population Commission was established comprising twenty-nine members and presided over by a deputy premier of the federal government (Population Policy in Czechoslovakia, 1974). The commission analyzes population development in Czechoslovakia and provides draft measures for the government so that quantitative and qualitative population developments may be observed. At its annual meetings the commission deals with activities related to abortion.

LEGAL STATUS OF ABORTION

As noted above, the liberal Abortion Act (Zákon 68, 1957) became effective on 1 January 1958 for both the Czech Socialist Republic and the Slovak Socialist Republic. The act provides that the abortion can be performed only if the woman concerned gives her consent and if her application for abortion has been approved by the Abortion Commission at the district or regional national committee. The abortion can be performed only in a health establishment.

An abortion can be authorized for medical reasons as well as for specific special circumstances. Any abortion performed without previous authorization is prohibited. The Ministry of Health, in conjunction with the Ministry of Justice, issues orders and methodological instructions relating to the grounds concerned and to the Abortion Commission's performance and activities.

In 1983 the following orders and methodological instructions became effective:

in the Czech Socialist Republic Order 71/1973 (Vyhláška 71, 1973), Order 80/ 1980 (Vyhláška 80, 1980), and Methodological Instruction 6/1980 (Metodické opatřeni 6, 1980). Methodological Instruction 14/1982 (Metodické opatřeni 14, 1982) deals with the termination of early pregnancies and has been effective since 1 September 1982. The Slovak Socialist Republic has implemented Order 72/1973 (Vyhláška 72, 1973), Order 141/1982 (Vyhláška 141, 1982), and Methodological Instruction 9/1983 (Metodické opatrenia 9, 1983). The methodological instruction dealing with termination of early pregnancy is at present being prepared in the Slovak Socialist Republic.

The amendments to these orders contain a list of medical grounds for terminating a pregnancy. Abortions that are performed on medical grounds are free of charge. The orders specify the special grounds for performing an abortion, especially the following:

1. Woman's age over forty years

2. At least three living children

3. Pregnancy because of a rape or other crime

4. Difficult situation arising from pregnancy for an unmarried woman

5. Loss of the husband or his serious health condition

6. Housing and financial difficulties

7. Breakdown of the family unit

The existence of the last three conditions enable even the married woman without children or with only one child to obtain an abortion.

No abortion is permitted if total gestation is more than twelve weeks (counting from the first day after the last menstruation); if an acute or chronic disease exists which will increase the risk of the abortion procedure; or if the pregnant woman has obtained an induced abortion within the previous twelve months.

Certain exceptions are possible. The pregnancy may be interrupted in spite of contraindications if by continuing the pregnancy the woman's life would be threatened. The twelve-week restriction may be extended to sixteen weeks if the woman has contracted rubella or if the rubella cannot be excluded. In addition, for women who have at least three children the term between the two abortions may be shortened from twelve to six months. Finally, in the event of genetic problems, the pregnancy may be terminated up to the twenty-sixth week of pregnancy.

Abortions granted on the grounds of special attention cost Kčs 200 to 800. The commission determines the amount of the charge according to individual economic situations. Accordingly, the commission may decide on no charge if the woman is indigent.

The pregnant woman seeking abortion must first consult her gynecologist. Following the examination, the gynecologist instructs the woman as to the risks of abortion and the possible complications and sequelae, especially pointing out the danger to fertility, if any. He or she records the application form for the abortion, and the woman states the grounds of her application and signs it. After informing the woman about the necessary documents, the gynecologist sends her to the commission appropriate to her permanent address. A worker or a student may make application to the District Commission in her place of employment or school address.

The commission is an administrative arm of the National Committee and has three members: the chairman, who is the National Committee deputy; the chief gynecologist of the Department of Obstetrics and Gynecology; and a psychologist, sociologist, or jurist.

The commission discusses the reasons for the abortion with the woman and offers her counsel, if needed. In the majority of cases the abortion is approved; only 3.4 to 5.7 percent of all applications are turned down. If the application is refused, the woman may reapply to the higher Regional Commission. Approximately 70 percent of women whose application is refused reapply, and in 50 percent of these cases the Regional Commission revises the District Commission's decision.

The commission presents the woman with information on contraception and sterilization and determines the charge at the same time. The commission also determines the day on which the woman is to be admitted to the hospital. The abortion is performed by a skilled gynecologist under sterile conditions and with general anesthesia. Approximately one-third of all abortions are performed by vacuum aspiration and two-thirds by dilatation and curettage (Havránek, 1976, 1982). The woman is hospitalized for two to four days. Before being discharged, she is again instructed about contraception and sterilization, and she signs this instruction. If the woman is employed, she is disabled for three to seven days.

In recent years early pregnancy termination (menstrual regulation) has been initiated on an ambulatory basis without anesthesia and hospitalization. The commission's authorization is needed for this procedure; this usually leads to delays, thus increasing the risk. Consequently, an amendment to the Abortion Act dealing with menstrual regulation has been requested (Šráček & Uzel, 1975; Havránek, 1979, 1982).

ATTITUDES TOWARD ABORTION

Since the Abortion Act became operative in 1958, public attitudes toward abortion have changed. The people have come to regard it as simply another birth control method. The high abortion rate indicates that to some extent abortion is utilized in the place of contraception. The Roman Catholic church's attempts to reverse this trend have met with no success.

The majority of gynecologists (Kviz, 1978; Fukalová, 1979), except some chiefs of university departments, favor liberalizing abortion; specifically, they advocate eliminating the commission's authorization as well as the six- to twelve-month limitation for the next abortion. The commission could act as an advisory organ, helping the woman find the most suitable solution for her particular situation.

Terminating a pregnancy over twelve weeks gestation would then be possible on medical grounds only, the decision belonging to a commission consisting of physicians. Another proposal is to enact an amendment dealing with family planning (Šráček, Uzel, & Fukalová, 1975; Stěpán, 1981) that would cover the principal requirements relating to reproduction problems, including induced abortion.

DEMOGRAPHY OF ABORTION

The abortion rate and abortion ratio for Czechoslovakia are shown in table 8.1. The comparatively high abortion rate reflects, in part, the unavailability of the pill and the IUD at the time the liberalized Abortion Act was put into effect. Hence, until the 1960s when modern contraceptive methods became available, most women utilized abortion for child spacing and family limitation.

Since 1970 statistics have been collected on the use of oral contraceptives and the IUD. (See table 8.2.) Today, 6.3 percent and 15.0 percent of women of fertile age use oral contraceptives and the IUD, respectively.

Some restrictive measures concerning the Abortion Act—orders issued in 1973—were instituted to encourage the use of contraception over abortion for fertility control. Passage of the orders in 1973 was followed by the rise in the number of oral contraceptive and IUD users. At the same time condom sales have increased, reaching 15 million in 1982. On the other hand, the failure of oral contraceptive and IUD users constitutes medical grounds for abortion, which is then approved and performed without charge. The idea is to perform an abortion only when contraception fails.

An analysis of the grounds discussed during negotiations by the Abortion Commission shows that 26.7 percent of abortions were performed on medical grounds, including IUD failure, 19.9 percent because of the large number of children, 15.1 percent because the woman was unmarried, 14.4 percent because of financial reasons, 8.1 percent because of housing difficulties, 2.4 percent because of breakdown of the family unit, 0.3 percent because of the loss of the husband or his serious health condition, 0.01 percent because of rape or other crime, and 10.8 percent because of other grounds in 1982 (*Zdravotnická statistika ČSSR, Potraty, 1982*).

In 1982 the percentage distribution of legal abortions by age of the woman at the termination was as follows: nineteen years or less 6.3 percent, twenty to twenty-four years 19.2 percent, twenty-five to twenty-nine years 28.9 percent, thirty to thirty-four years 25.6 percent, thirty-five to thirty-nine years 15.0 percent, forty years or more 4.7 percent.

The majority (73.7 percent) of all abortions were obtained by women aged twenty to thirty-four, and the highest proportion (28.9 percent) by women aged twenty-five to twenty-nine, an age span in which today's two-children family norm is usually reached. The proportion of women under age twenty is low and represents 6.3 percent, and under age fifteen only 0.03 percent. Women aged forty-five or older obtained 0.28 percent (*Zdravotnická statistika ČSSR, Potraty, 1982*).

The percentage distribution of legal abortions by parity—by surviving children in Czechoslovakia—was as follows in 1982 (*Zdravotnická statistika ČSSR, Potraty, 1982*): women without a surviving child 11.0 percent, with one surviving child 16.0 percent, with two 48.4 percent, with three 18.9 percent, with four 3.9 percent, and with five and more 1.6 percent.

Women applying for abortion without surviving children represent a minority. Only under exceptional circumstances can a married woman without children or with a single child obtain an abortion. The highest proportion of abortions (48.4 percent) is represented by women with two surviving children, which is today's ideal family size.

The percentage distribution of legal abortions by marital status at termination in 1982 was as follows (*Zdravotnická statistika ČSSR, Potraty, 1982*): never married (single) women 12.3 percent, currently married women including women in informed unions 79.9 percent, widows 0.9 percent, and divorced women 6.7 percent.

The proportion of never married (single) women obtaining abortion remains low because premarital pregnancies are often resolved by marriage. The proportion of married women remains high. The majority of currently married women obtaining abortion, 56.0 percent, have two surviving children, which corresponds to the established two-child family norm in Czechoslovakia.

With regard to the social structure, 33.0 percent of all legal abortions in 1982 were obtained by workwomen, 33.7 percent by employees, 2.3 percent by co-operative farmwomen, and 25.4 percent by housekeeping women (*Zdravotnická statistika ČSSR, Potraty, 1982*).

The percentage distribution of legal abortions in 1982 by weeks of gestation was as follows (*Zdravotnická statistika ČSSR, Potraty, 1982*): eight weeks or less 56.4 percent, nine to twelve weeks 42.4 percent, thirteen to sixteen weeks 0.3 percent, seventeen weeks or more 0.1 percent. Second-trimester abortions are very rare in Czechoslovakia because the Abortion Act permits abortion after twelve weeks of gestation only for medical and genetic indications. The mortality following legal abortion is very low and reflects the virtual limitation of legal abortions in Czechoslovakia to the first trimester.

ABORTION AND FERTILITY REGULATION

In 1982, Czechoslovakia's population totaled 15,369,091 (midyear estimate); 3,254,188 women were in the fifteen to forty-four age group. The Communist party of Czechoslovakia and the government of Czechoslovakia regard population developments as a vital factor in the country's general development. The country's population policy is pronatalist, and pronatalist measures have been adopted to provide favorable quantitative and qualitative population development (Population Policy in Czechoslovakia, 1974).

Because abortion has been so heavily used for fertility regulation (2,451,867 abortions were performed from 1958 to 1982), efforts have been made to replace abortion by contraception, reserving abortion exclusively for contraceptive failure.

ABORTION AND ADOLESCENTS

Great care is taken with abortions performed on adolescents and primigravidae in which the risk of complications and sequelae is higher than among older women. The percentage of abortions at all ages obtained by women under twenty years of age in 1982 was 6.3 percent, under age fifteen only 0.03 percent, age fifteen to seventeen 2.0 percent, and eighteen to nineteen 4.3 percent. The percentage of abortions obtained by primigravidae was 9.7 (*Zdravotnická statistika ČSSR, Potraty, 1982*).

Systematic parenthood and health education programs aimed particularly at the young generation are carried out to improve contraceptive knowledge as well as to increase awareness of abortion risk.

REPEAT ABORTIONS

Statistics on repeat abortions in Czechoslovakia are available for only married women. In 1982 (*Zdravotnická statistika ČSSR, Potraty, 1982*), of all married women undergoing legal abortion 54.7 percent obtained their first abortion and 45.3 percent a repeated one. This represents a high proportion of repeaters, including 30.8 percent with one prior abortion, 10.1 percent with two, and 4.2 percent with three or more. To lower the proportion of repeaters, the Abortion Commission and the gynecologist performing the procedure are required to instruct the woman on contraception.

ABORTION RESEARCH

Since the liberalized Abortion Act became effective, many studies have been carried out on morbidity connected with abortion and its impact on subsequent fertility (Černoch, 1960, 1964; Kulich, Šauer, & Šimek, 1961; Kolářová, Kohoutek, & Novosad, 1964; Dráč, 1970; Fuchs et al., 1970; Heczko, Gazárek, & Jirátko, 1970; Belák, 1972).

Studies on better and safer techniques of abortion, especially on vacuum aspiration, have been carried out (Bruchác, Vierik, & Sirotný, 1964; Chalupa, 1964; Vojta, 1967; Havránek, 1979; Hamann, 1981; Uzel & Šráček, 1981). The outcome of refused abortion for the child has also been examined (Matějček, Dytrych, & Schüller, 1975). Results of the abortion research are used to improve abortion techniques and to prevent the morbidity connected with abortion.

SUMMARY

In Czechoslovakia the liberalized Abortion Act became effective on 1 January 1958. Abortion is an integral part of primary health care within the care of mother and child. Until 31 December 1984, 2,451,867 abortions were performed on medical grounds and on grounds meriting special attention. In 1985 the abortion ratio was 53 abortions per 100 live births—up from 50 in 1984.

The majority of women and men accept abortion as a method of fertility regulation; it is widely used as a method of child spacing as well as for family limitation. The aim of the socialist government is to replace abortion by contraception as a primary method of fertility regulation, reserving abortion for contraceptive failure only.

REFERENCES

Balák, K. Poznámky ke škodlivosti interrupci u primigravid. *Československá Gynekologie*, 1972, *37*, 585.

Brucháč, D., Vierik, J., & Sirotny, E. Nový sposob umelého prerušenia tehotnosti pomocou vakuového exhaustora. *Československá Gynekologie*, 1964, *29*, 83–86.

Černoch, A. Problematika umělého přerušeni těhotenství. *Československá Gynekologie*, 1960, *25*, 646–649.

———. Symposion o problémech interrupce a antikoncepce. *Československá Gynekologie*, 1964, *29*, 593–597.

Chalupa, M. Gebrauch des Vakuum zur künstlichen Schwangerschaftsunterbrechung. *Zentralblatt für Gynakologie*, 1964, *86*, 1803–1808.

Dráč, P., & Nekvasilová, Z. Předčasné ukončeni těhotenství po předcházejícím umělém přerušení. *Československá Gynekologie*, 1970, *35*, 332–333.

Fuchs, V., Dráč, P., Brutar, V., & Houdek, J. Insuficience hrdla děložního ve vztahu k předchozí interrupci. *Československá Gynekologie*, 1970, *35*, 365–366.

Fukalová, D. Znovu k problematice činnosti interrupčních komisí. *Československá Gynekologie*, 1979, *44*, 752–754.

Hamann, B. Zkušenosti s aspirační kyretou pro ukončení časnáeho těhotenství-miniinterrupce. *Československá Gynekologie*, 1981, *46*, 480.

Havránek, F. Přehled o technice umělého přerušení těhotenství. *Československá Gynekologie*, 1976, *41*, 616–620.

———. Umělé přerušení raných stadií těhotenství (regulace menstruace, mini-interrupce). *Československá Gynekologie*, 1979, *44*, 374–378.

———. *Interruptio graviditatis*. Praha: Avicenum Zdravotnické Nakladatelství, 1982.

Heczko, P., Gazárek, F., & Jirátko, K. Vliv interrupce první gravidity na gestaci. *Československá Gynekologie*, 1970, *35*, 333–334.

Kolářová, O., Kohoutek, M., & Novosad, D. Následky po umělém přerušení těhotenství. *Československá Gynekologie*, 1964, *29*, 608–613.

Kulich, V., Šauer, J., & Šimek, J.Interrupce jako příčina izoimunizace v systému ABO. *Československá Gynekologie*, 1961, *26*, 506–510.

Kviz, D. Zamyšlení nad dvaceti lety platnosti zákona č. 68/57 Sb. *Československá Gynekologie*, 1978, *43*, 452–453.

Matějček, Z., Dytrych, Z., & Schüller, V. Pražská studie o dětech narozených z nechtěného těhotenství. *Psychológia a patopsychológia dieťaťa*, 1975, 229–246, 291–306.

Metodické opatřeni 6. Věstník Ministerstva zdravotnictví České socialistické republiky, 1980, *28*, 29–36.

Metodické opatřeni 14. Věstník Ministerstva zdravotnictví České socialistické republiky, 1982, *30*, 129–130.

Metodické opatrenie 9. Vestník Ministerstva zdravotníctva Slovenskej socialistickej republiky, 1983, *30*.

Population Policy in Czechoslovakia. Prague: Orbis, 1974.

Šráček, J., & Uzel, R. Je možno v našich podmínkách léčit sekundární amenorrhoeu metodou regulace menstruace? *Československá Gynekologie*, 1975, *40*, 510–511.

Šráček, J., Uzel, R., & Fukalová, D. Některé právní otázky spojené s plánovaným rodičovstvím. *Československá Gynekologie*, 1975, *40*, 715–716.

Srp, V., & Trojanová, H. *Potratovost v ČSSR v letech*, 1958–1977. Praha: FSÚ, 1978.

Štěpán, J. Právní aspekty výzkumu a praxe na úseku regulace porodnosti. *Československá Gynekologie*, 1981, *46*, 493–494.

Tietze, C., & Henshaw, S. K. *Induced abortion: A world review, 1986* (6th ed.). New York: Alan Guttmacher Institute, 1986.

Uzel, R., & Šráček, J. Naše zkušenosti s jednorázovou aspirací obsahu dutiny děložní. *Československá Gynekologie*, 1981, *46*, 489–490.

Vojta, M. Die Abortsituation in der Tschechoslowakischen Sozialistischen Republik. In K.-H. Mehlan (Ed.), *Internationale Abortsituation Abortbekämpfung Antikonzeption.* Leipzig: VEB Georg Thieme, 1961.

————. A critical view of vacuum aspiration: a new method for the termination of pregnancy. *Obstetrics and Gynecology*, 1967, *30*, 28–34.

Vyhláška č. 71. Sbírka zákonů 1973. Praha: 1973.

Vyhláška č. 72. Sbírka zákonů 1973. Praha: 1973.

Vyhláška č. 80. Sbírka zákonů 1980. Praha: 1980.

Vyhláška č. 141. Sbírka zákonů 1982. Praha: 1982.

Zákon č. 68 o umělém přerušení těhotenství. Sbírka zákonů 1957. Praha: 1957.

Zdravotnická statistika ČSSR. Potraty, 1982 and all earlier volumes since 1965. Praha: Ústav zdravotnických informcí a statistiky, 1983.

Table 8.1
Number of Legal Abortions, Abortion Rates, Abortion Ratios, Czechoslovakia, 1954-84

Year	Number of Abortions	Abortion Rate per 1,000		Abortion Rate per 100	
		Total Population	Women 15-44	Live Births	Known Pregnancies
1954	2,798	0.22	1.0	1.1	1.1
1955	2,123	0.16	0.8	0.8	0.8
1956	3,117	0.23	1.1	1.2	1.2
1957	7,300	0.5	2.7	2.9	2.8
1958	61,418	4.6	22.8	28.0	21.9
1959	79,131	5.8	29.3	36.5	26.7
1960	88,288	6.5	32.5	40.5	28.8
1961	94,306	6.8	34.1	43.2	30.1
1962	89,800	6.5	31.5	40.3	28.7
1963	70,546	5.1	24.1	29.0	22.5
1964	70,698	5.0	23.6	29.8	22.9
1965	79,591	5.6	26.3	35.4	26.1
1966	90,263	6.3	29.6	41.2	29.2
1967	96,421	6.7	31.4	45.2	31.1
1968	99,886	7.0	32.4	45.6	31.3
1969	102,797	7.1	33.1	45.7	31.4
1970	99,766	6.9	32.3	42.7	29.9
1971	97,271	6.8	31.4	39.8	28.5
1972	91,292	6.3	29.2	34.7	25.8
1973	81,233	5.6	25.9	28.0	21.9
1974	83,055	5.7	26.4	28.6	22.3
1975	81,671	5.5	25.9	29.8	22.9
1976	84,589	5.7	26.8	29.4	22.7
1977	88,989	5.9	27.9	31.8	24.1
1978	92,545	6.1	29.1	33.6	25.1
1979	94,486	6.2	29.5	36.0	26.4
1980	100,170	6.5	31.1	42.1	29.6
1981	103,517	6.7	32.1	43.5	30.3
1982	107,638	7.0	33.1	46.1	31.5
1983	108,700	7.1	33.1	48.1	32.5
1984	113,800	7.4	34.5	51.0	33.8

Sources: Vojta, 1961; Statistická knižnice, 1982; Tietze & Henshaw, 1986; *Zdravotnická statisticka ČSSR. Potraty, 1982*, and earlier volumes since 1965.

Table 8.2
Number of Oral Contraceptive Users and IUD Users in Czechoslovakia, 1970–82

Year	OC Users	IUD Users
1970	36,495	82,600
1971	43,582	92,441
1972	55,770	91,791
1973	112,289	239,311
1974	129,082	271,638
1975	175,144	306,244
1976	188,162	322,981
1977	201,924	347,471
1978	213,882	368,181
1979	228,123	377,085
1980	231,585	413,312
1981	213,223	456,919
1982	204,289	488,499

Source: Ostav zdravotnických informaci a statistiky v Praze. Unpublished data, Praha: 1983.

9

DENMARK

Lars Heisterberg

HISTORICAL DEVELOPMENT OF ABORTION POLICY

Until 1939 induced abortion in Denmark was punishable according to the Penal Code unless it was performed to avert a serious threat to the woman's health or life. During the preceding decades, the sexual reform movement in Denmark had been started as part of a larger international movement. Its program centered on birth control and sexual information, but later it also involved possibilities for legal abortion. Since the goals of the movement were equal social rights for women and the emancipation of women, several feminist groups were involved in it. The foremost group, the Danish Feminist Society (Dansk Kvindesamfund), however, could not accept abortion as a means of promoting equal rights for women, an attitude that was more harmful to the society than the reform for legal abortion.

During the 1930s the discrepancy between abortion practice and the law became evident even to the politicians, and a parliamentary commission was appointed. Four indications for legal abortion were discussed: (1) medical; (2) eugenic; (3) ethical; and (4) social. The first three provoked no objections, but the fourth, which would permit legal abortion when the pregnancy involved a risk for permanent reduction of the woman's social position, elicited public protest. As a result, social indication was dropped, and in its place the medical indication was expanded to include conditions other than actual disease. Thus it was rephrased the sociomedical indication. The interpretation of the indications was to a large extent handed over to the National Council for the Unmarried Mother and Her Child (Mødrehjælpen) which was started on private initiative in approximately 1910 but was connected to the new abortion law of 1939 as a consulting institution.

The law was revised in 1956, and a proper sociomedical indication was established. A new fourth indication was added for cases where the mother was evaluated as being unable to take care of the child. Councils consisting of a social worker and two physicians, one of which was to be a psychiatrist in association with the local branches of the National Council, were established with the object of evaluating applications from women seeking abortions.

Public pressure for free abortion led to the third abortion law in 1970 which generally liberalized the indications and introduced a purely social indication. The gestational age limit was lowered from the former sixteen weeks to twelve. With a 96 percent permission rate for the women applying for abortion, the new law only survived three years, and in 1973 permission for abortion up to and including the twelfth gestational week was given freely.

LEGAL STATUS OF ABORTION

Under the present abortion law all female residents in Denmark are eligible for an induced abortion. After the twelfth gestational week, the woman's application must be evaluated by the aforementioned council. Permission for abortion after the twelfth week can be granted if (1) the pregnancy is the result of a criminal act; (2) the pregnancy involves a risk for deterioration of the woman's health; (3) the child will suffer seriously because of disease; (4) the woman, afflicted by mental, psychic, or somatic disease, cannot attend to the child; (5) the woman cannot take care of the child because of her youth or immaturity; or (6) the pregnancy will involve such a serious strain on the woman that for her sake and that of her family the pregnancy should be terminated. Abortion is performed without the need for permission if the pregnancy is a threat to the life of the woman. Adolescents under the age of eighteen need the consent of a parent or guardian, but the council can decide if under special circumstances such a consent can be waived. The council's decision can be appealed through a central board. The physician to whom the woman states her request for abortion must inform her of supportive possibilities in the event she wishes to continue her pregnancy, as well as the abortion procedure and risks associated with it. The abortion can only be performed by a physician at a public hospital, and expenses connected with the abortion are covered through public taxes.

ATTITUDES TOWARD ABORTION

Birth control was not a public topic in Denmark until about 1920. Literature on how to avoid more pregnancies had been circulating among the population since the turn of the century, but a law passed in 1906 with the intention of counteracting the immoral tendencies in society forbade public advertising for the sale of articles concerned with hindering the consequences of intercourse. One had to talk cautiously about the subject of birth control.

Because the Malthusian League in Great Britain and its affiliated organizations in Europe based their work for population control on Malthus's conservative theories concerning overpopulation, rather than on practical birth control, the working class and the political left wing created its own organizations and agitators. Sexual information became a means to obtain social and economic equality for the working class in general and women in particular. The author and syndicalist Chr. Christensen, the female author Thit Jensen, and the physician J. H. Leunbach traveled throughout the country and spread the ideas of Wilhelm Reich, Havelock Ellis, Norman Haire, and others at public meetings, and in newspapers and pamphlets. They sought to establish so-called sexual clinics where women received instruction in contraceptive methods and ways to obtain abortion. The fear that only the well-to-do would practice birth control with a consequent deterioration of the genes of humanity gave the debate a eugenic content. This was one of the subjects which the medical profession debated in periodicals during the second decade of this century.

Another subject which brought the profession into public debate was whether or not the women ought to receive instruction in contraceptive methods from persons other than doctors. Physicians, who were opposed to general instruction in birth control, claimed that the use of contraceptive methods would result in illegitimate and promiscuous sexual connections and general immorality. Moreover, an acceptance of contraception as a means of birth control could lead to public pressure for liberal abortion. The politicians were concerned with the declining birth rate, from 75,000 to 65,000 births per year during the period 1925–35, and appointed a committee that was to contrive measures to oppose this tendency.

Dr. Leunbach envisioned his main task as one of disseminating knowledge about fertility regulation in the indigent part of the population for eugenic as well as socioeconomic purposes. Because of two lawsuits in which he was charged as party to criminal abortion, he became a national figure in Denmark in the 1930s. He was acquitted in 1935, but the following year he was sentenced to three months in prison and loss of civil rights for five years. The court cases and their exposure of the conditions for women seeking to have an abortion, criminal if necessary, probably influenced public opinion to view contraception and abortion as acceptable methods of population control. At any rate, by far the largest majority of the Danish medical profession according to a questionnaire study in 1933 was willing to instruct their female clientele, including unmarried women, in contraceptive methods.

In 1936 the parliamentary commission that preceded the first abortion law of 1939 was appointed. The 1930s thus marked a shift in the opinion of the general population as well as the medical profession and the politicians. Since then the development has largely been to adjust the abortion laws to public attitudes and the actual use of existing indications. More liberal laws have been passed in accordance with the belief of the majority of the population that abortion is an acceptable means of fertility regulation. The present law has been in existence since 1973; an editorial in the periodical for members of the Danish Medical Association, *Ugeskrift for Læger*, states: ''The law of 1973 has come to stay. It hardly needs to be changed.''

DEMOGRAPHY OF ABORTION

Levels, Trends, and Incidence

The number of applications steadily increased from the first abortion law in 1939 until 1950, stabilizing at about 8,000 per year, after which a new increase to 10,000 in 1972 and 12,000 in 1973 was seen. In contrast, the percentage of permissions increased throughout the entire period, reaching 82 percent in 1973. The number of legal abortions after the abortion law of 1973 rose initially from almost 25,000 in 1974 to nearly 27,000 in 1976 when the total number started to decline to about 23,000 in 1979 and to 20,742 in 1984. The number further decreased to 19,919 in 1985, the lowest figure since liberalization of abortion laws in 1973.

Abortion rates followed a similar pattern as illustrated in table 9.1. The highest rate for the entire 1974–85 period was observed among women aged eighteen to twenty-four years. The largest reductions in abortion rates have fallen in the age groups fifteen to seventeen and thirty to thirty-nine years.

Age, Parity, and Marital Status

The percentage distribution of abortions by parity and age is depicted in table 9.2, and the number of legal abortions by marital status and age in table 9.3. The headings "not stated" and "unmarried" contain a large number of women living in a common law marriage. In a survey from Copenhagen in 1978 (Rasmussen, 1983), age, parity, and marital status have been separated into eight different groups of women and abortion rates per 1,000 women in the survey area for each group calculated (table 9.4). It appears that women below the age of twenty and single women have the highest abortion rates.

Socioeconomic Status and Education

In two studies from the city of Aarhus (Wohlert & Møller-Larsen, 1978) and Copenhagen (Rasmussen, 1983), the socioeconomic conditions have been compared between pregnant women seeking abortion and pregnant women planning delivery. In the Aarhus study, a significantly higher proportion of unskilled workers and students was observed in the group of women seeking abortion, and this group had more threatened social conditions than women planning delivery. The Copenhagen study compared abortion rates, that is, how many pregnant women in each of the aforementioned eight groups chose to have an abortion. The women with a husband or partner, below thirty-five years of age, and with fewer than two children seldom chose abortion and thus were considered to have a relatively free choice between abortion and delivery. Consequently, the survey could investigate which factors other than age, parity, and marital status were of significance for the choice of abortion. For women with no children, the abortion rate was higher for women with twelve years of schooling than for women with nine years. Women in educational positions had a generally higher abortion rate. Unemployed women had a higher abortion rate only when they already had one child. Women with one child and whose husband or partner was an unskilled worker had higher abortion rates. A part-time job did not influence the abortion rate. A low income was associated with a high abortion rate, as was the size of the residence in relation to number of inhabitants. Conception within three years from delivery of the first child involved a high abortion rate, and women in relationships of short duration also had high abortion rates.

Gestational Age

The percentage distribution of gestational age in relation to woman's age can be seen in table 9.5. For all age groups 75 to 80 percent of the abortions are performed before the eleventh gestational week. As previously mentioned, the groups seeking abortion after the twelfth week must apply for permission to have an abortion. In 1981 there were 740 applications for abortion after the twelfth week of pregnancy. Eighty-three (11 percent) were refused. The actual number performed was 604, so about 50 women probably chose not to have the abortion. The youngest and oldest age groups tended to exceed the twelfth week limit more often than other age groups.

Contraceptive Use

Several studies have investigated the use of contraception among Danish women undergoing legal abortion (Wohlert & Møller-Larsen, 1979; Sidenius, et al., 1983; Diederich et al., 1976; Lundvall, 1976). Only one of these (Sidenius et al., 1983) looked into the actual use of contraception half a year after the abortion. Among the 2,553 women included in all four studies, only 16 percent used safe contraceptive methods (IUD, oral, or sterilization) before abortion. Among 230 women interviewed six months after the abortion, this percentage had increased to 73. A note of caution is needed here since the number of women interviewed was small compared to the total number of applicants and represented only one of the studies (table 9.6).

ABORTION AND FERTILITY REGULATION

The Danish population was 5.123 million in 1980 and 5.122 in 1981, of which 2.596 million were women and of these 1,238,200 were between fifteen and forty-nine years of age (137,355 were between forty-five and forty-nine years). From surveys undertaken by the Institute for Social Medicine in 1977–78 (Sundhedsstyrelsen, 1982), it is known that oral contraceptives were used by 30 to 35 percent, the IUD by 15 to 20 percent, and the more traditional methods, the diaphragm, condom, and the withdrawal method, by 45 percent. Approximately 6,700 women corresponding to 0.5 percent of fertile women have been sterilized each year since 1973 when sterilization became available to all men and women twenty-five years of age or older. Nearly 7,000 men have been sterilized each year in the same period. In the same survey about 70 percent of the women claimed they used contraception consistently. As illustrated in table 9.7, the total number of conceptions has been declining during the period 1976–81. The number of deliveries for a calendar year is compared to the number of abortions registered from 1 July the previous year to 30 June in the calendar year so that the conception period is approximately the same. Both the number of deliveries and the number of abortions have been falling, but as the number of deliveries has decreased relatively more than the number of legal abortions (19 percent versus 16 percent) a larger proportion of the conceptions has ended in legal abortion. The number of spontaneous abortions treated in hospitals has been fairly constant. It has been claimed (Rasmussen, 1983) that the reduction in deliveries is a consequence of a reduction in planned pregnancies, while a corresponding drop in the number of unplanned pregnancies has not taken place. Consequently, the number of children is not entirely regulated by use of abortion. That the decline in conceptions is not simply a matter of distribution of safe contraceptive methods can be inferred from estimates of the use of oral contraceptives and IUDs compared to the number of conceptions. Until 1973 the number of pregnancies increased despite the use of the pill and IUD. Since 1975 the decline in conceptions has continued in spite of stabilized consumption of the pill and use of the IUD. The large percentage of traditional contraceptive methods still in use is a difficult factor to assess. Variations of distribution of women among age groups, changes in the age at sexual debut, and variations in coital frequency are other factors that present problems in evaluation.

In the last decade Danish women have tended to have fewer children. The women are older at their first delivery, and more women choose not to have any children at all. This change is reflected in the increase in the percentage of women having no children at the time of their first abortion (table 9.8). Another indication can be extracted from the figures shown in table 9.9 where the percentage of pregnancies ending in an abortion has been increasing for the age groups twenty to twenty-four years and decreasing for the age groups thirty to thirty-four and thirty-five to thirty-nine years.

ABORTION AND SPECIAL GROUPS

Teenage abortions have always attracted special interest for several reasons. For most teenagers it is their first pregnancy, and the majority will want to have a child later in life. Therefore, complications are considered very serious in this group. Contraceptive failure is considered of significance for these young girls who have a long life of fertility ahead of them. Consequently, it is satisfying to note that the abortion rate decreased significantly for the age group fifteen to seventeen years during the 1974–82 period, although the rate for the age group eighteen to nineteen years did not drop more than the total rate (table 9.1). However, almost one-fifth of all abortions in Denmark in 1980 and 1981 were performed on teenagers, with 10 percent occurring to those between eighteen and nineteen years old. At the same time, an increasing percentage of pregnancies was being terminated by abortion, from 53 percent in 1976 to 61 percent in 1982 (table 9.9).

REPEAT ABORTIONS

It has been said that women seeking abortion constitute a certain group that is signified by lack of use of contraception. One method of testing this hypothesis is to investigate the frequency of repeat abortions. A study conducted in 1979 (Wohlert & Møller-Larsen, 1979) revealed that 80 percent of women seeking abortion versus 94 percent of pregnant controls planning delivery had no previous abortion, 14 percent versus 6 had one, and 5 percent versus 1 had two or more legal abortions. This difference was statistically significant. During the four-year period 1975–78, almost 94,000 women in Denmark had legal abortions. Of these, 91 percent had one abortion, 8 percent had two, and less than 1 percent had more than two induced abortions (Sundhedsstyrelsen, 1982). There seems to have been no change in the percentage during the four-year period, whereas the percentage with a second abortion doubled when the period was extended from twelve to twenty-four months. The highest percentage of women with repeat abortion was among those with the highest abortion and delivery rate, namely, in the age group twenty to twenty-nine years. Approximately 0.5 percent had two repeat abortions within twenty-four months after the first.

ABORTION RESEARCH

Research on abortion in Denmark since 1975 has concentrated on acute complications and sequelae and associated risk factors, midtrimester abortion techniques, contraceptive use in abortion-seeking women, and socioeconomic factors leading to the choice of abortion. An increased frequency of postabortal infection was found to be associated with the presence of *Chlamydia trachomatis* in the cervix at the time of abortion (Westergaard, Philipsen, & Scheibel, 1982) or a history of pelvic inflammatory disease (Sonne-Holm et al., 1981). In the latter double-blind study, prophylactic penicillin/ampicillin reduced the frequency of infection, whereas prophylactic doxycycline was shown to decrease the postabortal frequency of infection in women with *Chlamydia* (Møller et al., 1981). Possible risk factors with regard to postabortal complications have been assessed (Heisterberg, et al., 1982). Long-term sequelae following legal abortion dealing with pregnancy complications, risk of spontaneous abortion, and fertility were investigated in a thesis (Obel, 1979). Positive findings included increased frequency of bleeding before twenty-eight weeks of gestation, increased frequency of retained placental tissue, and increased frequency of infants below 2,501 grams after dilatation of the cervix to more than 12 mm and after repeat curettage. Abortions complicated by infections were associated with a longer period before desired pregnancy occurred. Several authors (Bostofte & Legarth, 1981; Lange

& Gammelgaard, 1982; Gregersen & Pedersen, 1974) have reported their experiences with different midtrimester abortion methods, including intra- and extra-amniotic prostaglandin $F_2\alpha$ or compared intracervical prostaglandin E_2 gel and intra-amniotic prostaglandin $F_2\alpha$ in a randomized trial that demonstrated the equal efficacy of the two methods but fewer side-effects with the intracervical prostaglandin gel (Sørensen & Wolf, 1983). Contraceptive use among women seeking abortion was investigated by Wohlert and Møller-Larsen (1979), Sidenius et al. (1983), and Diederich et al. (1976). The main findings were that these women had used more different types of contraception, that the conceptions occurred during shifts from one form of contraception to another, and that very few women used no contraception at all. Two studies compared the socioeconomic conditions of women seeking abortion to women planning delivery (Rasmussen, 1983; Wohlert & Møller-Larsen, 1979). It was demonstrated that women undergoing abortion did not constitute a risk group with regard to birth control, but happened to be in a situation where a pregnancy was unwanted and thus chose to terminate it.

Abortion research in Denmark has also included comparison of the effect of local and general anesthesia on blood loss, and findings were that local anesthesia gave minimum blood loss (Møller, Hansen, & Mommsen, 1978). The advantages of inserting an IUD at abortion were not outweighed by increased risk of complications (Skouby, 1976). The postabortion rate of admission to psychiatric hospital was observed to be 18 per 10,000 women obtaining abortion and the postdelivery rate to be 12 per 10,000 women carrying to term (David, Rasmussen, & Holst, 1981).

In 1983–84 abortion research in Denmark concerned itself, among other things, with identifying risk groups for postabortal infection which might benefit from prophylaxis, as well as different forms of prophylaxis.

ABORTION MORTALITY

Denmark's mortality rate during the 1967–76 period was reported to be 2.7 per 100,000 abortions; there were four deaths in connection with 149,300 abortions (WHO, 1978). For the twelve-year period 1970–81, 248,314 legal abortions were performed and three deaths were reported. According to the death certificates, one woman died from cor pulmonale one and a half years after a legal abortion which was complicated by a pulmonary embolus; one woman was found dead after an apparent attempt of self-induced abortion with water. Autopsy revealed an air embolus of 100 ml in the right cardiac ventricle and a pregnancy in the eighth month; finally, one woman died from hemorrhage and sepsis in connection with placental abruption and subsequent abortion. Thus, one and possibly two deaths can be attributed to induced abortion, giving a legal abortion mortality rate of 0.4 or 0.8 per 100,000 abortions. These figures are perhaps minimal. Delayed deaths as a consequence of a complication caused by a legal termination may not be registered on the official Danish death certificate as a death connected with a legal abortion. The possibility that such cases have existed cannot be clarified without coordination of the official abortion register and death register.

SUMMARY

The first Danish abortion law was passed in 1939 and revised in 1956, 1970, and 1973, at which point abortion up to and including the twelfth gestational week was allowed freely. Permission for abortion after the twelfth week could be granted on several indications.

The 1920s and 1930s marked the beginning of a public debate on contraception and abortion in Denmark and mainly originated from a quest for equal social rights for women. Thus, a social indication for abortion was involved early in the discussion.

The number of abortions in 1982 was around 21,000 and has generally decreased since 1976. Single women below twenty years of age had the highest abortion rate, but several socioeconomic factors were involved in their choosing abortion. Approximately 16 percent of women seeking abortion used safe contraception, but six months after an abortion 70 percent did.

The number of conceptions had been falling during the 1976–81 period, but the use of contraceptive methods was not found to be the only explanation for this decrease. Other nonassessable factors were involved. Danish women chose to have fewer children; the women were older when they chose to give birth; and the abortion rate among teenagers decreased the most compared to other age groups. An investigation of repeat abortions revealed that very few women used abortion as a substitute for contraception. This was confirmed in a socioeconomic survey among abortion-seeking women and controls planning delivery.

Abortion research in Denmark from 1975 has focused on risk factors associated with infectious complications, the effect of long-term sequelae on subsequent pregnancies and fertility, second-trimester abortion techniques, contraceptive use among the abortion clientele, and socioeconomic factors leading to abortion.

The abortion mortality rate for the 1970–81 period was 0.4 to 0.8 per 100,000 abortions.

REFERENCES

Bostofte, E., & Legarth, J. Termination of midtrimester pregnancies induced by hypertonic saline and prostaglandin $F_2\alpha$. *Acta Obstetricia et Gynecologica Scandinavica*, 1981, *60*, 575–578.

David, H. P., Rasmussen, N. K., & Holst, E. Postpartum and postabortion psychotic reactions. *Family Planning Perspectives*, 1981, *13*, 88–92.

Diederich, P., Møller, B. R., Hansen, J. T., & Oram, V. Legal termination of pregnancy. *Ugeskrift for Læger*, 1976, *138*, 355–359.

Gregersen, E., & Pedersen, P. H. The incidence of abortion after the 12th week of pregnancy employing prostaglandin $F_2\alpha$ administered extra-amnially. *Ugeskrift for Læger*, 1974, *136*, 1292–1295.

Heisterberg, L., Sonne-Holm, S., Andersen, J. T., Hebjørn, S., Dyring-Andersen, K., & Hejl, B. L. Risk factors in first-trimester abortion. *Acta Obstetricia et Gynecologica Scandinavica*, 1982, *61*, 357–360.

Knudsen, L. B. Development in the number of legal terminations of pregnancy. *Ugeskrift for Læger*, 1983, *145*, 3753–3758.

Lange, A. P., & Gammelgaard, J. Induction of second trimester abortion with intra-amniotic prostaglandin $F_2\alpha$ *Ugeskrift for Læger*, 1982, *144*, 946–949.

Lundvall, F. Legal termination of pregnancy in 1,000 women. *Ugeskrift for Læger*, 1976, *138*, 363–369.

Møller, B. R., Ahrons, S., Laurin, J., & Mårdh, P-A. Pelvic infection after elective abortion associated with Chlamydia trachomatis. *Obstetrics and Gynecology*, 1981, *59*, 210–213.

Møller, B. R., Hansen, J. T., & Mommsen, S. Effect of general and local anesthesia on blood loss during and after therapeutic abortion. *Acta Obstetricia et Gynecologica Scandinavica*, 1978, *57*, 133–135.

Obel, E. B. Long-term sequelae following legally induced abortion. Ph.D. diss., University of Copenhagen, 1979. Lægeforeningens Forlag, 1979.

Rasmussen, N. K. Abort—et valg? Copenhagen: FADL's Forlag, 1983. (English summary.)

Sidenius, K., Rasmussen, N. K., Boesen, E. M., & Pedersen, H. The contraceptive habits of women applying for termination of pregnancy. *Ugeskrift for Læger*, 1983, *145*, 3721–3724.

Skouby, S. O. Insertion of intra-uterine devices at termination of pregnancy. *Ugeskrift for Læger*, 1976, *138*, 339–341.

Sonne-Holm, S., Heisterberg, L., Hebjørn, S., Dyring-Andersen, K., Andersen, J. T., & Hejl, B. L. Prophylactic antibiotics in first-trimester abortions: a clinical, controlled trial. *American Journal of Obstetrics and Gynecology*, 1981, *139*, 693–696.

Sørensen, S. S., & Wolf, P. Randomized trial of intracervical prostaglandin E_2 gel and intraamniotic prostaglandin $F_2\alpha$ for induction of second-trimester abortion. Manuscript submitted for publication, 1983.

Sundhedsstyrelsen. Statistik om prævention og aborter 1981. Copenhagen, 1982. (English legends and summary.)

Tietze, C., & Henshaw, S. K. *Induced abortion: A world review, 1986* (6th ed.). New York: Alan Guttmacher Institute, 1986.

Westergaard, L., Philipsen, T., & Scheibel, J. Significance of cervical Chlamydia trachomatis infection in postabortal pelvic inflammatory disease. *Obstetrics and Gynecology*, 1982, *60*, 322–325.

Wohlert, M., & Møller-Larsen, F. The significance of social factors in the choice of legal termination of pregnancy. *Ugeskrift for Læger*, 1978, *140*, 1835–1840.

———. The contraceptive habits of women applying for termination of pregnancy. *Ugeskrift for Læger*, 1979, *141*, 1863–1866.

World Health Organization. Induced abortion. Technical Report Series 623. Geneva, 1978.

Table 9.1
Age-Related Number of Legal Abortions per 1,000 Women, 1974–85

	15-17	18-19	20-24	25-29	30-34	35-39	30-44	>45	15-44	15-49
1974	19		28	29	30	23	11	1	–	21
1975	24		32	32	32	25	12	1	–	24
1976	22	33	32	30	28	22	11	1	–	23
1977	21	33	30	28	27	22	10	1	–	22
1978	19	32	29	25	23	19	9	1	–	20
1979	18	31	29	25	22	19	9	1	–	19
1980	17	31	29	25	22	18	9	1	22	19
1981	15	30	30	25	21	17	9	1	21	18
1982	13	27	29	24	20	15	8	1	19	17
1983	18		29	23	19	15	–	–	19	–
1984	–	–	–	–	–	–	–	–	16	–
1985	–	–	–	–	–	–	–	–	15	–

Source: Sundhedsstyrelsen, 1982; Tietze & Henshaw, 1986.

Table 9.2
Percentage Distribution of Legal Abortions by Age and Parity, 1981

Parity	15-19	20-24	25-29	30-34	35-39	40-44	>45	Total
0	94	62	28	11	7	5	4	40
1	6	26	27	21	13	11	8	19
2	0	10	36	46	45	36	25	26
3	0	1	8	17	25	31	38	10
≥4	0	0	1	5	10	18	24	4
Total	100	99	100	100	100	101	99	99

Source: Sundhedsstyrelsen, 1982.

Table 9.3
Number of Legal Abortions by Marital Status and Age, 1981

Marital Status	15-19	20-24	25-29	30-34	35-39	40-44	>45	Total
Unmarried	3,127	3,165	1,403	590	229	52	2	8,568
Married	79	763	1,589	2,078	1,892	835	98	7,334
Previously Married	6	140	348	415	358	141	13	1,421
Not stated	829	1,339	1,137	1,046	714	298	33	5,456
Total	4,041	5,467	4,477	4,129	3,193	1,326	146	22,779

Source: Sundhedsstyrelsen, 1982.

Table 9.4
Abortion Rates for Women Grouped with Regard to Marital Status, Age, and Parity, Copenhagen, 1978

Marital Status	Age	Parity	Abortion/rate/1,000 women in area
Married or permanent partnership	20	0	38
		1	-
	20-34	0	14
		1	32
		≥2	30
	≥35	≤1	8
		≥2	11
Single			39
Total			25

Source: Rasmussen, 1983.

Table 9.5
Percentage Distribution of Legal Abortion by Age and Gestational Age, 1981

Gestational Week	15–19	20–24	25–29	30–34	35–39	40–44	45	Total
≤6	1	2	2	2	2	2	3	2
7–8	28	32	35	35	37	36	34	33
9–10	45	45	45	44	44	44	40	44
11–12	21	19	17	16	15	15	20	18
>12	5	2	2	2	2	3	4	3

Source: Sundhedsstyrelsen, 1982.

Table 9.6
Pre- and Postabortal Contraception in Four Danish Studies, 1976–83

Method	Preabortal 1)	2)	3)	(%) 4)	Total %	Postabortal(%) 1)
No contraception	1	12	62	44	35	5
Withdrawal/safe period	1	1	1	1	1	1
Condom	51	30	21	21	31	12
Diaphragm	7	5	4	11	8	5
Chemical agents	11	–	9	6	6	2
IUD	7	8	1	3	4	27
Oral	21	32	2	4	12	34
Sterilization	1	–	–	0	0	12
Unknown	0	12	0	0	3	0
Number patients	414	531	698	1,000	2,553	230

Source: Sidenius et al., 1983; Wohlert & Møller-Larsen, 1979; Diederich et al., 1976; Lundvall, 1976.

Table 9.7
Number of Conceptions, 1976–81

	1976	1977	1978	1979	1980	1981
Deliveries	65,050	61,650	61,750	59,500	56,950	52,840
Legal abortions	27,100	28,400	24,500	23,250	23,550	22,800
Spontaneous hospital abortions	7,700	8,575	9,125	8,975	8,440	8,000
Total conceptions	99,850	96,625	95,375	91,725	88,940	83,640
Legal abortions in percent of legal abortions and deliveries	29	30	28	28	29	30

Source: Knudsen, 1983.

Table 9.8
Percentage Distribution of Legal Abortion in Age Groups Twenty to Twenty-four Years and Twenty-five to Twenty-nine Years with Zero Parity, 1974–82

	20-24 years	25-29 years	15-49 years
1974	42	13	27
1978	56	21	36
1981	62	28	40
1982	64	30	41

Source: Sundhedsstyrelsen, 1982; Knudsen, 1983.

Table 9.9
Percentages of Pregnancies Ending in Legal Abortions by Age Groups, 1976–82

	15-19	20-24	25-29	30-34	35-39	≥40	Total
1976	53	21	20	33	56	77	29
1977	54	21	20	33	57	80	30
1978	55	21	17	30	53	80	28
1979	57	21	17	29	52	78	28
1980	58	23	18	30	52	79	30
1981	60	24	18	30	51	79	30
1982	61	25	18	28	50	81	30

Source: Knudsen, 1983.

10

FINLAND

Pirkko Niemelä

HISTORICAL DEVELOPMENT OF ABORTION POLICY

Before 1950 Finland had no particular law concerning abortion. An abortion was considered a crime unless an emergency situation could be proved. The World Health Organization (WHO) has classified the abortion laws of different countries in the following way (WHO, 1971):

1. Abortion is not allowed under any circumstances
2. Abortion is allowed only on medical grounds
3. Medical-social and ethical grounds are taken into consideration in addition to the medical grounds
4. Abortion is allowed on social grounds
5. Abortion is performed when a pregnant women asks for it

Within the WHO classification, Finland could then be classified in category 2.

The 1950 Law

On 1 June 1950 Finland got its first abortion law, which can be classified in WHO category 3. According to this law, abortion was granted on medical grounds (i.e., when the pregnancy or childbirth would cause a serious risk to the woman's physical or psychological health because of illness, defect, or weakness); on ethical grounds (i.e., when the intercourse leading to pregnancy happened against the woman's will, or when the woman was under sixteen years of age at the time of conception); and on eugenic grounds (i.e., the mother or the father had a severe hereditary physical or mental defect or illness). For an abortion on medical or ethical grounds, an abortion decision was needed from two physicians—the physician performing the abortion and the physician appointed by the National Board of Health for abortion decisions. For an abortion on eugenic grounds, as well as when the pregnancy was over four months, permission for abortion was needed from the National Board of Health.

Rising Dissatisfaction

In the 1960s there was a rising dissatisfaction with the 1950 law, particularly within the women's liberation movement and the political left wing, for example, "Group Nine," a group dedicated to sexual equality. In addition, many physicians were actively expressing their dissatisfaction through Finnish medical journals. The first group to officially suggest the liberalization of the abortion law was the Finnish Women's Democratic Union.

Finnish Opinion before the New Law

In 1969 a Finnish medical journal commissioned George Gallup to perform a study on opinions concerning abortion. One thousand individuals representing the Finnish population in terms of age, gender, social class, and abode were interviewed individually. One hundred and seven trained interviewers gathered the data in forty cities or towns and in fifty-two places in the countryside. The findings were as follows: 2 percent thought abortion should be forbidden under any circumstances, 27 percent wanted abortion permitted only in cases of very serious risk to the mother's life, 10 percent wanted abortion granted for less serious health reasons, 26 percent believed abortion should also be allowed for economic and social reasons, 29 percent thought the woman should make the decision, and 6 percent expressed no opinion.

Urban residents were more permissive than rural people, and men were more liberal in their views than women. Persons with higher education and/or higher income also were more permissive, as were the young versus the old. Five percent of older respondents were irrevocably opposed to abortion.

Similar results were obtained in a study performed in 1970 by the major Finnish nonparty newspaper. In the countryside 45 percent and in the cities 60 percent were in favor of easier abortion. Among those with the most education, 71 percent would have permitted abortion more easily than the 1950 law did; among factory workers 58 percent; and among farmers 34 percent. This study also took into consideration preference for political party. Two-thirds of those who supported the Social Democrats or Communists favored easier abortion, as did 59 percent of Conservative party and 36 percent of Agrarian party supporters.

The Public Debate

Opinions expressed in newspaper editorials at the height of the debate on the abortion law have been studied by Helga Suutarinen (1972) who analyzed the editorials of all fifty-eight Finnish newspapers that appear at least five times a week. The papers generally espoused a more permissive abortion law, and discussed the case for and against completely free abortion. They often dealt with the specific grounds for abortion, for example, social indicators and age limits. Sixty percent of the editorials concerning abortion also favored birth control.

The left party newspapers leaned most heavily toward a more permissive abortion law. The Agrarian party newspapers were not as negative toward the new law as were the party supporters; half of their editorials favored a more permissive law, and about half were neutral on the issue. They generally supported the social grounds but were against completely free abortion. The spirit of the Conservative newspaper editorials was close to that of the Agrarian papers, and the editorials of nonparty papers were similar to those of the left party papers.

The Making of the New Law

In 1967 the Finnish cabinet appointed a committee to work on a new abortion law. The committee's report, ready in 1968, did not favor completely free abortion, nor did it believe that social grounds did not by themselves warrant an abortion. The committee recommended that an abortion be allowed when the woman was under sixteen or over forty at the moment of conception. It suggested accepting the social-medical grounds and liberalized eugenic grounds. It further recommended a law regulating fertility in order to make counseling and birth control available to everyone at a low cost. It also suggested that fertility regulation and sexual education be included in the school curriculum and that medical staff give counseling about birth control after abortion.

The government further liberalized the committee's suggestions. For example, it recommended that abortion would also be granted solely on social grounds, if the women's living conditions would make childbirth and child care an "unbearable" strain. The government also suggested that the lower age limit should be seventeen instead of sixteen.

The Finance Committee gave the law its final content and form. It modified the social grounds, allowing an abortion when childbirth and child care would constitute a "considerable" strain for a woman. The Finance Committee further suggested that abortion be permitted for women forty years of age or with four or more children. It also enabled abortion to be performed by any physician in public practice.

The Parliament accepted the law as formulated by the Finance committee by a vote of 113 to 56. All the left-wing parties, that is, the Social Democrats and the Communists, voted unanimously for the new law. The Agrarian Center party mostly voted against it, as did the Conservative party. Most members of the small liberal parties, the Liberal party and the Swedish party, voted for the law.

LEGAL STATUS OF ABORTION

Grounds for Abortion

The new abortion law, which came into force on 1 June 1970, can be classified in WHO category 4 (WHO, 1971). According to the law, an abortion is granted to a woman asking for it

1. when pregnancy or childbirth would risk her life or health because of illness, physical defect, or weakness (medical grounds).

2. when childbirth and child care would be a considerable strain on her and her family economically and socially (social grounds). Such strain can be caused by conditions such as the following:

—The woman's civil status, family relationships, and the living conditions of the earlier children in the family, and the effects of child care and rearing on them

—The economic situation of the woman and her family

—The probable effects of childbirth and care on her work and studies

—The effects of childbirth and care on her significant relationships, including the marital one

—The effects of childbirth and care on her future plans

—The woman's opinion of the child's father's willingness and ability to participate in child care and rearing

—Limitations to care for and rear the child caused by her age or immaturity, or her or her family member's ill-health or handicap

—Limitations to care for and rear the child caused by her or her family member's continuous use of alcohol, criminality, or asocial way of life.

3. when she is made pregnant against her will (ethical grounds).

4. when she was not yet seventeen years of age or was over forty or already had four children at the moment of conception.

5. when there is reason to expect the child to be mentally defective or to have a difficult illness or physical defect (eugenic grounds).

6. when illness, disturbed psychological functioning, or a comparable factor of one or both parents seriously limits their capacity to take care of the child.

For the actual frequency of the use of abortion grounds, see table 10.1 which gives the statistics from the National Board of Health. (These statistics are used throughout this chapter when not otherwise indicated.)

Practice

In order to obtain an abortion on grounds 1, 2, 3, and 6 above, the approval of two physicians is needed, whereas for 4 only the approval of one physician is needed. An abortion based on eugenic grounds requires the permission of the National Board of Health up to the twentieth week of gestation. When eugenic grounds are used, the sterilization of the woman also has to be considered if there is reason to assume that the child might be mentally defective because of the woman's low intellectual ability.

With any legalized physician in public practice being allowed to grant an abortion, the number of physicians allowed to grant an abortion increased from 530 to 4,100.

According to the law, each abortion must be reported to the National Board of Health on a specific form. (All the data in this chapter were obtained through these reports.)

Change in the Law

The 1970 law was modified on 1 July 1979, after which an abortion was allowed after the twelfth week of pregnancy only in the case of the woman's illness or physical defect as well as on up to the twentieth week on eugenics grounds. (Before the amendment, the time limit was the sixteenth week of gestation.) However, when the woman is younger than seventeen years or if there is another compelling reason, the National Board of Health can grant the abortion later, though not after the twentieth week of pregnancy. The abortion law permits any legalized physician to induce an abortion in any period of gestation if the mother's life or health is at risk.

ATTITUDES TOWARD ABORTION

After the Abortion Act was ratified in 1970, the storm of opinions surrounding abortion calmed down. Today most political parties do not have any program concerning abortion.

The Christian Party

Only the Christian party has an active interest in the abortion issue. This small party, registered in 1970, has three members among the 200 members of the Finnish Parliament. The Christian party opposes abortion and advocates its use solely on medical grounds.

The State Church

Most Finns belong to the State Church (Lutheran), but very few are active members. In 1978 the church's Family Committee suggested a more restrictive law so that abortion would not be granted on purely social grounds. This suggestion was not taken into account in the 1979 law change.

Women's Groups

Today many women's groups are fairly passive about abortion inasmuch as it is considered to be practically free. However, some women believe they should have the sole right of decision about their own bodies, including pregnancy and abortion, without interference from medical authorities. Union, one of the oldest and most influential of the women's groups in Finland, states in its program: "All women should have the right themselves to decide about sterilization and abortion."

Physicians

Some physicians and nurses oppose abortions and so do not want to perform them. They would like a law that would give each person on the medical staff a free choice to decide whether or not to perform abortions. In 1971 the Association for Young Physicians conducted a study of the opinions of its 2,110 members and found that more than two-thirds (67.6 percent) advocated giving the physician the right to refuse to perform an abortion on grounds other than risk of the mother's life. In 1974 the Physicians' Christian Association asked its members to sign the following statement: "Because of my deep personal conviction I refuse to give permission or perform an abortion without serious medical reasons." Of the 230 members 70 signed.

Health Nurses and the General Public: A Comparison

A study of the opinions of health nurses working in the antenatal centers, delivery rooms (i.e., midwives), postnatal wards, and child-care centers was done by Niemelä et al. (1981). Three hundred and eighty-two health nurses attending a yearly midwives convention in 1980 gave their opinions for the five statements presented in table 10.2.

In order to compare the health nurses' and nonprofessionals' opinions, the same statements were given in 1982 to mothers and fathers visiting the antenatal and child-care centers in Turku for routine checkups. A total of 263 mothers and 157 fathers, among them 140 couples, gave their ratings. The differences between mothers, fathers, and health nurses were tested by the t-test, and the effects of age, education, and so on, by analyses of variance. Only differences significant at least on $p<0.05$ level are mentioned below.

Forty-seven percent of mothers and 38 percent of fathers agreed with the first statement, "Abortion is granted today too easily in Finland," whereas 31 percent of mothers and 36 percent of fathers did not agree. Many had no opinion on the issue. According to this sample, the 1970 law quite well represents fathers' opinions, while somewhat more mothers think the law is too lenient. The difference between mothers and fathers is not statistically significant.

Significantly more ($p<0.001$) health nurses than fathers or mothers stated that abortion was granted too easily. Over 70 percent agreed with the statement and fewer than 20 percent did not agree.

With regard to the second statement, "The woman has to be allowed to decide herself about an abortion, without a doctor's consent," only a fourth of the mothers and fathers agreed. Over 60 percent disagreed.

The health nurses answered a somewhat different statement: "The woman has to be allowed to decide herself about the abortion, without the husband's consent or the doctor's consent." Some nurses said that the husband's and doctor's consent are very different things. Therefore, "the husband's consent" was later dropped out of the statement. This difference in statements apparently explains why the health nurses were in greater agreement ($p<0.001$) with this statement than were the parents. According to the nurses, a woman does not need her partner's consent for an abortion.

More mothers and fathers than health nurses ($p<0.001$) agreed with the third statement, "For the women it is better to choose an abortion than an unwanted child."

Over 70 percent of the mothers and fathers and over 80 percent of the health nurses disagreed with the fourth statement, "A woman who chooses an abortion is not fit to be a mother." There was no statistical difference between the parents and the nurses.

The fifth statement, "A woman who chooses an abortion or gives her child away will always suffer from guilt," was agreed with by 41 percent of mothers, 37 percent of fathers, and 43 percent of health nurses. There were no statistically significant differences between parents and nurses. Many said they did not know: 32 percent of mothers, 35 percent of fathers, and 23 percent of nurses.

Attitudes toward abortion do not form a single dimension. The correlations between the statements are fairly low, varying between $r = -0.43 - +0.42$ for the mothers; between $r = -0.52 - +0.42$ for the fathers; and $r = -0.16 - +0.33$ for the health nurses. For example, those who think that abortion is granted too easily today in Finland do not blame a woman who chooses an abortion.

Age, education, type of work, and marital status, however, were consistently related to the opinions expressed by the statements. Age was related to the first, second, and fourth opinions. It was the youngest fathers and mothers (under twenty-five years of age) as well as the youngest health nurses (under thirty-five years of age) who were most against abortion. Education was related to the first, fourth, and the fifth opinions. The fathers with least education were most opposed to abortion, and the mothers with an academic education were most in favor of abortion. Marital status was related to the second, third, and fourth statements. Those married were most against abortion. The health nurses' work was related to the second and third statements. The nurses working in the delivery room or postnatal ward were more in favor of abortion, while the nurses working in the antenatal centers or child-care centers were more against abortion. Apparently, the midwives and nurses working with mothers when they are most insecure as mothers are more in favor of abortion than the nurses whose work is not immediately connected with the moment a woman becomes a mother.

The mothers and fathers of the sample were either expecting a baby or had at least one child under seven years of age. This sample might therefore be expected to be stricter about abortion than the Finnish people in general, as the persons in the sample had chosen to be parents. The data indicate that the Finnish abortion law fairly reflects the present opinions of the general public.

DEMOGRAPHY OF ABORTION

Incidence of Legal Abortions

Table 10.3 shows the incidence of legal abortions in Finland before and after the 1970 act. After the 1970 act, the number of induced abortions increased from 7.8 in 1969 to 21.4 abortions per 1,000 women fifteen to forty-four in 1972. This statistic aroused much concern until the abortion numbers began to decrease again in the mid–1970s. Table 10.3 shows that the highest percentage of legal abortions (22.4) came in 1973, that is, three years after the act. The preliminary statistics for 1982 and 1983 show that the decreasing trend continues.

Age

Table 10.4 shows that during recent years the rate of induced abortions has decreased in every age group.

Marital Status

Statistics on the marital status of women with induced abortion in 1983 are as follows: 32.1 percent were married, 8.2 percent were legally divorced, and 0.6 percent widowed. A little less than one-half (49.1 percent) were unmarried, but this number also included women who were cohabiting with their male partners.

Gestation

Table 10.5 shows the effects of the 1979 law change, suggesting that most abortions are performed before the twelfth week of pregnancy. In 1983, 95.8 percent of all abortions were performed in the first trimester. A study by Kokkonen and Rönnberg (1973) showed the social factors were not related to the time of abortion.

Education and Socioeconomic Status

The statistics of the National Board of Health do not reveal the education or the socioeconomic status of women asking for a legal abortion. Therefore, two studies comparing women choosing an abortion and women choosing to have the baby are consulted here. Ritva Pesonen (1974) compared 191 women who were in a Helsinki hospital for an abortion in 1973 (''the abortion group'') with 193 women who came to a Helsinki antenatal center (''the control group''). Elina Rautanen et al. (1980) similarly compared 99 women with an induced abortion with 100 women who had had a child. This study was performed in 1974, also in Helsinki, and the women were similarly contacted in a hospital and in an antenatal center. In both studies the women were over eighteen years of age.

According to Pesonen (1974), the women with an abortion had lower education than the women in the control group. Of the first group, 62 percent and of the second, 38 percent had only primary school education. Ten percent of the abortion group and 33 percent of the control group had at least a high school education. The women as well as their partners in the abortion group had lower income than those in the control group. The abortion group had lower quality housing than the control group. Finally, 15 percent of the women with an abortion and 30 percent of the control group were owner-occupiers.

The results of Rautanen et al. (1980) support the above findings. According to their study, too, the women who had an abortion had lower education. Among the abortion group, 11 percent had university education and 20 percent vocational training. In the control group the corresponding figures were 29 percent and 25 percent.

Contraceptive Use

The birth control methods used by the women undergoing an abortion are presented in table 10.6. According to Pesonen (1974), no woman in either the abortion or control group was negative toward use of contraceptives. Women in both groups were well informed about contraceptives. The women who had an abortion reported that at the moment of conception they did not have birth control devices at hand or that application of birth control methods would have interfered with sexual pleasure. The women in the abortion group had used somewhat less reliable methods than the women in the control group, but after the abortion they intended to use more reliable methods: about three-fifths of the abortion group and 45 percent of the control group were planning to use either the pill or an IUD. The results of Rautanen et al. (1980) are very similar. There was little difference between the groups as to the uses of contraception: 64 percent of both groups used the pill, and 5 percent of the abortion group and 6 percent of the control group had used an IUD. The difference between the studies of the Helsinki population and the overall country statistics given in table 10.6 are probably due to the differences in the birth control practices of different parts of the country.

ABORTION AND FERTILITY REGULATION

Table 10.3 shows that the abortions peaked in 1973, after which the number of abortions has been decreasing steadily. This trend reflects the Finnish family planning policy. The 1970 Abortion Act included a law specifying what information the performing physician was to give after an abortion as well as a law about sterilization. Two years later, in 1972, the National Board of Health directed that family planning instruction be given to all women asking for birth control in health centers, which are within easy access of everyone in Finland.

The nurses working in health centers are now trained to interview every woman who comes in for birth control advice in order to find the best method for her. After the interview the physician inserts an IUD, gives the pill, or recommends some other method. The IUD and diaphragm are given free. The first IUD checkup is given three months later and yearly thereafter. Only the copper IUD is used. The pills are first given free for three months, and thereafter, with the checkup, for six months after which the physician gives a prescription. The followup is done mainly by nurses. The initial interview and the checkups are mainly for singling out the women for whom the use of the pill would be risky.

The effects of the Finnish family planning program can be regarded as good.

Forty-eight percent of fertile women are estimated to use safe methods, either the pill or an IUD; 32 percent are estimated to use an IUD, 16 percent the pill, 32 percent the condom, 5 percent spermicides and condom, and an estimated 15 percent none of these methods. Because of the personal family planning advice and the directives against pills with high estrogens (in 1973 the products containing over 50 micrograms were forbidden in Finland), the negative effects caused by the pill have decreased. The use of the IUD has doubled since 1974.

Family planning information and consultation are given not only in the health centers but also, for example, in schools and colleges and are recommended to be given in the army.

ABORTION AND ADOLESCENTS

Table 10.4 above shows that the adolescent abortion rate is not very high. Actually, the number of both pregnancies and abortions among adolescents is decreasing (see table 10.7 and Kosunen & Rimpelä, 1983.)

Several studies conducted in the wake of a large increase in abortions soon after the liberal abortion law of 1970 was passed have shown that adolescent abortions are not due to lack of knowledge about reproductive physiology or contraceptives (Widholm et al., 1974; Räsänen, 1979; Ruusuvaara, 1983). Rather, lack of contraceptive use is due to lack of motivation.

Several studies of adolescent abortions have described the family background and the sexual relations of the young abortees. The most recent study, by Leena Ruusuvaara (1983), compared 201 abortees under eighteen years of age with 185 school girls of the same age who had not had an abortion (the control group). Nearly half of the girls in the abortion group and a third of the control group came from broken homes. The girls who had abortions more often said that their fathers were strict and/or indifferent. They also reported more conflicts in the family than did the controls.

A strict and/or indifferent father may be one reason why a girl starts a sexual relationship earlier: she is seeking love and appreciation. Ruusuvaara (1983) found that the girls in the abortion group had started a sexual relationship earlier and that they had sexual intercourse more regularly than did the controls. Their sexual partners were also older. In both groups the girls said they were in love with their sexual partners.

In Ruusuvaara's study (1983), 15 percent of abortees and 16 percent of control girls had never used contraception. Nineteen percent of the abortion group had used unsafe methods, that is, coitus interruptus and "safe periods." The method most commonly used was the condom. In both groups there was some lack of motivation about contraceptive use. The occurrence of pregnancies in the abortion group was probably due to the higher frequency of intercourse in the abortion group rather than to the difference in the use of birth control.

During the last few years, there has been a significant change toward better use of contraceptives. An earlier study by Widholm et al. (1974) on the abortions of adolescent girls who were living in the same region as Leena Ruusuvaara's (1983) interviewees showed that at that time 74 percent of the girls had not used contraceptives. The decrease of nonuse from 74 percent as estimated by Widholm et al. (1974) to 15 percent as estimated by Ruusuvaara (1983) is remarkable. A recent change to the use of more reliable contraceptives has been documented in an ongoing and so far unpublished study by Matti Rimpelä, within which a nationally representative sample of adolescents has been interviewed about their health habits. According to this study, 6.7 percent of the sixteen-year-old girls used the pill in 1981 and 7.5 percent in 1983. The corresponding figures for the eighteen-year-old girls were 22 percent in 1981 and 25.7 percent in 1983.

It is now acknowledged in Finland that giving information about contraceptives only is not a sufficient measure. This information should be linked with education about human relationships, sexual partnerships, and family, and it should be given in a personal way. According to Ruusuvaara's study (1983), the girls in both groups felt that the school nurse had given the best information.

REPEAT ABORTIONS

Although the absolute number of abortions has decreased since 1973, there has been a relative increase in the number of women having previous abortions— from 14.6 percent to 22.6 percent in 1983.

A study by Niemelä et al. (1981) investigated the factors underlying repeat abortions. Thirty women expecting a second abortion were compred with twenty-nine women who had successfully prevented conception after a first abortion. It was found that both groups improved their contraceptive practices after the first abortion, but the women now having their second abortion soon went back to their earlier neglect of contraceptives. Thus, the inefficient use of contraceptives after the first abortion was not due to lack of information about contraceptives or to their unavailability. Comparison between the two groups showed that the difference in the use of contraception was not due to differences in educational level but to the developmental level of personality structures. The women having their second abortion rated lower in control of impulsivity, emotional balance, realism, self-esteem, and stability of life as well as capacity for more integrated personal relationships. These personality factors were found to be related to differences in growth conditions in childhood, for example, the family atmosphere.

ABORTION RESEARCH

Methods of inducing abortion have been studied and developed by an international research group including Thomas Kerenyi and Arpad Csapo from the United States and Martti Pulkkinen and Asko Kivikoski from Finland. In the 1960s this group was developing the abortion method whereby hypertonic saline is injected intra-amniotically, resulting in abortion in thirty hours in 97 percent of patients. Because this method can be used late in pregnancy, it has made the minor section unnecessary and has thus saved many women from a surgical operation (Pulkkinen, 1969; Pulkkinen & Kivikoski, 1969).

The use of prostaglandins was also developed by this group. Prostaglandin (PGE-PGF) was injected, for example, intra-amniotically (Csapo et al., 1976). A further development was the "menstrual induction" method, that is, a woman is given prostaglandin immediately after the diagnosis of pregnancy (Csapo et al., 1980). Many different forms of prostaglandins were tried out; PGE_2, called sulproston, was finally chosen (Pulkkinen, 1979).

Different forms of prostaglandin and ways of administering it have been tried out in several Finnish studies. For example, P. Kajanoja et al. (1975) studied the side-effects and complications of prostaglandin given intravenously or extra-amniotically. Induction of prostaglandin vaginally has been studied by Mandelin and Kajanoja (1978).

A comparison of different abortion methods by Mandelin (1983) shows that the standard methods, VA and MR, are equally safe and have nearly the same complication rate. Psychic disturbances after abortion were found to occur less frequently in earlier terminations. The restoration of ovulation was rapid after all types of first-trimester terminations, and abortion was not found to have any substantial harmful effect on subsequent pregnancy.

ILLEGAL ABORTIONS

The number of illegal abortions can be estimated only by means of the number of patients who come to gynecological wards for reasons other than an induced legal abortion or spontaneous abortion. Table 10.8 presents the number of these patients and shows that the number of suspected illegal abortions has decreased significantly since the Abortion Act of 1970.

SUMMARY

In 1970 Finland got a liberal abortion law, according to which abortion may also be permitted solely on social grounds. This law seems to correspond fairly well to Finnish public opinion about abortion. Only the Christian party wants a stricter law, and some women's groups, for example, the Union, are striving for a completely free abortion law.

After the liberalization of abortion, the incidence of abortion increased and was highest in 1973. After that, the number of abortions began to decrease, due to fertility regulation programs that give individual advice and to some extent free birth control pills and devices throughout the country's health centers. As a result of fertility regulation programs in health centers and schools, adolescent abortions are also decreasing.

Several Finnish studies show that the lack of use of contraceptives in Finland is not due to ignorance about, or unavailability of, birth control devices, but that the reasons lie deeper in psychosocial and psychological factors.

ACKNOWLEDGMENTS

I wish to thank Ms. Pirkko Waenerberg for collecting information, Ms. Anja Rasimus at the Finnish National Board of Health for checking the statistics and information, and Ms. Arja Mäkelä for typing the manuscript.

REFERENCES

Csapo, A. I., Hertzeg, J., Pulkkinen, M., Kaihola, H.-L., Zoltan, I., Zillac, M., & Mocsary, P. Termination of pregnancy with double prostaglandin impact. *American Journal of Obstetrics and Gynecology*, 1976, *124*, 1–13.

Csapo, A. I., Pescin, E. K., Sauvage, J. P., Pulkkinen, M. O., Lampe, L., Godenyi, S., Laajoki, V., & Kivikoski, A. Menstrual induction in preference to abortion. *The Lancet*, 1980, *1*, 90–91.

International Digest of Health Legislation, 1970, *21* (3).

Kajanoja, P., Jungner, G., Seppälä, M., Karjalainen, O., & Widholm, O. Prostaglandin induction of midtrimester abortions: Three years' experience of 626 cases. *Acta Obstetricia et Gynecologica Scandinavica (Stockholm)*, Suppl., 1975, *37*, 51–56.

Kokkonen, J., & Rönnberg, L. Raskaudenkeskeytyspotilaiden raskauden kestoon vaikuttavia tekijöitä [Factors influencing the gestation of abortion patients]. *Suomen Lääkärilehti*, 1973, *28*, 3123–3127.

Kosunen, E., & Rimpelä, M. Teini-ikäisten raskaudet ja raskauden keskeytykset Suomessa vuosina 1965–81 [Teenage pregnancies and abortions in Finland 1965–81]. *Suomen Lääkärilehti*, 1983, *38*, 2748–2753.

Mandelin, M. *Induced abortion*. Helsinki, 1980.

Mandelin, M., & Kajanoja, P. Induction of second trimester abortion: Comparison between vaginal 15-methyl-$PGF_2\alpha$ A methyl ester and intra-amniotic $PGF_2\alpha$. *Prostaglandins*, 1978, *16*, 995–1001.

Niemelä, P. *A study of midwives as a source of the stereotypic mother image*. Manila: World Federation for Mental Health Congress, Workshop on Sex Roles, 1981.

Niemelä, P., Lehtinen, P., Rauramo, L., Hermansson, R., Karjalainen, R., Mäki, H., & Storå, C. Å. The first abortion—and the last? A study of the personality factors underlying repeated failure of contraception. *International Journal of Gynaecology and Obstetrics*, 1981, *19*, 193–200.

Official statistics of Finland XI: 78. Health Services. Yearbook of National Board of Health, 1985.

Pesonen, R. Synnyttävien ja abortin saaneiden naisten välisistä eroista [Differences between women giving birth and aborting]. *Helsingin Lääkärilehti*, 1974, *22*, No. 3, 28–33.

Pulkkinen, M. O. The significance of progesteron: its regulatory effect on the myometrium. In G.E.W. Wolstenholm & J. Knight (Eds.), *Ciba Foundation Study Group no. 34*. London: J. A. Churchill, 1969.

———. The clinical development of sulproston for pregnancy termination. International Sulprostone Symposium, Vienna Nov. 1978. In K. Fiebel, A. Schneider, & H.

Würfel (Eds.), *Medico-Scientific series of Schering AG Berlin and Bergkam*, 1979, 77–84.

Pulkkinen, M. O., & Kivikoski, A. A quantitative study of the accelerated evolution of uterine activity, induced by intra-amniotic hypertonic saline. *International Journal of Gynaecology and Obstetrics*, 1969, *7*, 279–293.

Räsänen, E. Abortin saaneet alle 17-vuotiaat [Abortees under 17 years]. *Suomen Lääkärilehti*, 1979, *34*, 1601–1606.

Rautanen, E., Widholm, O., Ruusuvaara, L., & Kantero, R.-L. Mikä saa naisen valitsemaan abortin? [What makes a woman choose an abortion?] *Duodecim*, 1980, *96*, 1328–1336.

Ruusuvaara, L. *Teenage abortions: Family background, sexual experience and contraceptive use*. Helsinki, 1983.

Suutarinen, H. Vuoden 1970 aborttilaki sanomalehtien pääkirjoituksissa [The 1970 abortion law in newspaper editorials]. Unpublished M.A. thesis in Social Politics, University of Helsinki, 1972.

Tietze, C., & Henshaw, S. K. *Induced abortion: A world review, 1986* (6th ed.). New York: Alan Guttmacher Institute, 1986.

WHO: Abortion laws. Report of a WHO Scientific Group. Geneva, 1971.

Widholm, O., Kantero, R.-L., & Rautanen, E. Medical and social aspects of adolescent pregnancies. *Acta Obstetricia et Gynecologica Scandinavica (Stockholm)*, 1974, *53*, 347–353.

Table 10.1

Percentage Distribution of Grounds for Induced Abortion

Grounds	1981	1982
1. Medical	3.4	3.3
2. Social	78.5	79.7
3. Ethical	0.0	0.1
4. Age less than 17	7.0	7.1
Age 40 years or more	7.5	6.9
4 children	2.4	2.0
5. Eugenic	0.9	0.7
6. Restricted ability to take care of children	0.3	0.2
	100.0	100.0
	(14120)	(13861)

Source: Yearbook of National Board of Health, 1985.

Table 10.2

Percentage of Respondents Agreeing with Statements Concerning Abortion

	Agree	Agree somewhat	Cannot say	Disagree somewhat	Disagree
1. Abortion is granted today too easily in Finland					
Mothers (n=263)	25.1	22.1	22.1	15.2	15.6
Fathers (n=157)	21.3	16.8	25.8	14.2	21.9
Nurses (n=382)	51.8	22.5	6.5	10.5	8.6
2. The woman has to be allowed to decide herself about an abortion without a doctor's permission					
Mothers (n=263)	14.2	11.5	11.1	23.8	39.5
Fathers (n=157)	16.8	11.6	5.8	23.2	42.6
Nurses (n=382)	38.7	15.0	3.9	13.9	28.4
3. For the women it is better to choose an abortion than an unwanted child					
Mothers (n=263)	31.6	17.5	20.9	15.2	14.8
Fathers (n=157)	25.0	26.3	25.0	9.6	14.1
Nurses (n=382)	21.6	14.5	19.2	18.9	25.8
4. A woman who chooses an abortion is not fit to be a mother					
Mothers (n=263)	9.1	3.4	10.6	20.2	56.7
Fathers (n=157)	5.8	5.8	12.3	16.8	59.4
Nurses (n=382)	3.4	5.3	8.7	22.5	60.1
5. A woman who chooses an abortion or gives her child away will always suffer from guilt					
Mothers (n=263)	18.3	22.8	31.9	14.1	12.9
Fathers (n=157)	17.9	19.9	34.6	12.2	15.4
Nurses (n=382)	20.1	23.2	23.2	18.5	14.9

Source: Niemelä, 1981.

Table 10.3
Number of Legal Abortions, Abortion Rates, and Abortion Ratios, 1969–84

Year	Number of Abortions	Abortion Rates per 1,000 women 15–44	Abortion Ratios per 100 live births
1969	8,200	7.79	12.4
1970	14,800	14.61	24.1
1971	20,600	20.22	33.7
1972	22,100	21.36	38.4
1973	23,400	22.37	38.8
1974	22,800	21.68	36.2
1975	21,500	20.30	31.6
1976	19,800	18.63	30.0
1977	17,800	16.66	27.7
1978	16,900	15.76	26.5
1979	15,800	14.67	25.1
1980	15,000	13.84	24.0
1981	14,100	12.94	21.8
1982	13,900	12.56	20.8
1983	13,400	12.04	20.2
1984	13,645	-	21.0

Source: *Yearbook of National Board of Health*, 1985; Tietze & Henshaw, 1986.

Table 10.4
Legal Abortions per 1,000 Women by Corresponding Age

Age	1977	1979	1981	1982	1983
14	0.9	0.9	0.8	1.0	0.2*
15	5.1	5.1	4.7	4.5 ⎫	
16	13.6	12.8	11.8	12.5 ⎬	
17	24.1	24.7	20.3	21.8 ⎭	10.0
18	26.8	26.3	25.0	24.3 ⎫	
19	28.0	28.1	26.8	25.7 ⎭	13.0
20–24	22.0	20.4	18.4	18.7	18.4
25–29	16.1	13.8	11.5	11.1	11.0
30–34	14.6	11.8	10.3	9.9	9.3
35–39	13.4	10.4	9.7	9.0	9.1
40–44	10.3	8.9	7.6	7.0 ⎫	
45–49	1.8	1.7	1.7	1.3 ⎭	7.5

*14 or less.
Source: *Yearbook of National Board of Health*, 1985.

Table 10.5
Percentage Distribution of Abortions Performed by Weeks of Gestation

Weeks	1978		1980		1982	
-6	3.7		15.5		14.6	
7	10.1		21.0		20.6	
8	19.5		22.6		22.7	
9	19.9	82.5	17.3	94.9	18.3	95.2
10	17.7		12.2		12.9	
11	11.6		6.3		6.1	
12	7.7		0.5		0.2	
13	3.0		0.5		0.6	
14	2.7		1.1		0.9	
15	2.0	17.2	0.9	5.0	0.7	
16	0.8		0.6		0.7	
17-	1.0		1.4		1.4	
Unknown	0.3		0.0		0.3	
Total	100.0		100.0		100.0	
	(16928)		(15037)		(13861)	

Source: Yearbook of National Board of Health, 1985.

Table 10.6
Percentage Distribution of Women Using Contraceptives before the Conception Leading to Abortion

Contraceptive	1980	1981	1982
Pill	4.6	4.9	5.2
IUD	10.9	10.6	9.9
Condom	41.8	40.1	41.5
None	32.3	33.5	33.0
Other	4.9	6.2	4.0
Unknown	5.4	4.7	6.4
Total	100.0	100.0	100.0
	(15037)	(14120)	(13861)

Source: Yearbook of National Board of Health, 1985.

Table 10.7

Frequency (1/1,000/Year) of Pregnancies (Whether Terminating in Childbirth or Abortion) and of Abortions Related to Age

Age	Pregnancies (1/1000)			Abortions (1/1000)		
	1975–76	1980–81	Change	1975–76	1980–81	Change
15	6.6	5.3	−20%	5.2	4.5	−14%
16	21.3	17.5	−18%	14.8	13.2	−11%
17	46.7	33.4	−29%	25.5	21.5	−16%
18	70.8	52.9	−25%	29.5	25.5	−14%
19	91.7	72.3	−21%	28.8	27.6	− 4%

Source: Kosunen & Rimpelä, 1983.

Table 10.8

Number of Abortion Patients Other Than Legally Induced Abortion Treated in Inpatient Departments of Hospitals

Dgn.	ICD, 8	1969	1972	1980	1981	1982
No 642	Other than legally induced abortion (criminal and induced abortion NOS)	366	65	16	20	15
No 644	Abortion not specified as induced or spontaneous	1487	568	51	51	47

Source: *Yearbook of National Board of Health*, 1985.

11

GERMAN DEMOCRATIC REPUBLIC

K. H. Mehlan

HISTORICAL DEVELOPMENT OF ABORTION POLICY

In Germany after World War I, fertility regulation was practiced mainly by illegal abortions. Thousands of women died from clandestine abortions. In Parliament the Communist party fought without any success against Section 218 (anti-Abortion Law), which remains in force today in the German Federal Republic. In some towns birth control clinics were opened, one of the first and best recommended of which was the clinic founded by H. Lehfeldt, F. Hirsch, and F. Teilhaber in Berlin. Clinics were also established in Hamburg and Dresden.

When Hitler came to power in 1933, the use of contraception was prohibited by police decree and the production of contraceptives was terminated. Abortionists were condemned to death. In addition, many generations of physicians educated at German medical schools were instructed that contraception would be dangerous to the health of the woman. This notion persists even today. For example, the leading textbook of gynecology in Germany by Stoeckel, 13th edition, 1965, p. 735, reads as follows (in translation): ''Contraception is an epidemic and the doctor has to fight against it with all his power.'' Another context discusses the health-damaging effects of contraception. This false education of doctors over a period of more than twenty-five years was a severe obstacle to the regulation of fertility. First, therefore, it was necessary to change the attitudes of physicians in this field.

In 1935 the German Association of Gynecology prohibited the Gräfenberg ring. Ernst Gräfenberg immigrated to the United States in 1936 from Berlin. Hundreds of women had used his ring as protection against pregnancy. Gesenius reported in 1960 that after 1945 he had removed many Gräfenberg rings from women in menopause who never had complications with the ring. In 1932

Gräfenberg and the histologist R. Meyer reported on the additional contraceptive effect of silver and gold with the ring (Lehfeldt, 1981).

LEGAL STATUS OF ABORTION

Concern for the life and health of women led to a temporary relaxation of strictly medical grounds for abortion. To reduce the number of illegal abortions in the aftermath of World War II, in 1947 restrictions in the abortion law were temporarily relaxed in most districts of the German Democratic Republic (GDR) to include social indications as well as eugenic reasons. The number of legal abortions increased to 26,360 in 1950 (see table 11.1).

The temporary liberal rules of 1947 were rescinded at the end of 1950 by the law entitled "Protection of mother and child and the right of women" (Gesetz-blätter der DDR, 1 Oct. 1950, p. 1037). Section 11 of this law states:

In order to protect the health of women and to make for an increase in the number of births, the artificial interruption of pregnancy shall only be made where the *life or health* of the pregnant woman *would be seriously endangered* if she carried the child to full term or where one of the parents suffers from a serious hereditary disease. The interruption of pregnancy for any other reason is forbidden and will be punished by imprisonment.

A pregnant woman could address her request for abortion to a district commission, which had to reply within fourteen days. The commission consisted of the medical district officer (chairman), a gynecologist, a physician, a public health officer, a social worker, and a representative of the local women's organization. If a request was denied, the woman could appeal to a regional commission.

After 1950 the status of abortion in the GDR became more strict than that of any other European socialist country. The incidence of induced abortion was reduced from one abortion per one live birth in 1947 to one abortion per three live births in 1954 (Mehlan, 1955). The number of legal abortions remained stable until 1964—700 to 800 per year, or 0.5 abortions per 100 live births. This decrease led to a corresponding increase in the number of illegal abortions and an increase of life births on the other hand. The birth rate in 1963 was 17.6.

The different interpretations of the law by the 250 local commissions were unsatisfactory. Thus, in March 1965 permissive instructions were added to the law of 1950 (Instruction Section 11, 1965). In some districts only 20 percent of all requests were granted and in others up to 80 percent (Mehlan & Falkenthal, 1965). The new facilities for early termination of pregnancies allowed abortion under the following circumstances:

1. If the pregnant woman's life or physical or psychological health is at grave risk if the pregnancy continues to term or as a consequence of the strain of bearing and rearing the child

2. If the pregnant woman is forty years of age

3. If the pregnant woman is under sixteen

4. If the pregnant woman has already had four children at intervals of less than fifteen months, and is pregnant again within six months of her last confinement

5. If the pregnant woman, whether living alone or with her husband, already has to care for five or more children

6. If the pregnancy is the result of a criminal act

7. If diagnosis indicates a high probability that the child will be mentally defective or suffer from serious abnormalities

Pregnancy had to be terminated by gynecologists in hospitals; there was no charge. Every aborted woman was required to report soon afterwards to a family planning center for contraceptive counseling; home visits were made to encourage compliance (Lellbach, 1968).

As a result of the more liberal interpretation of the law, the legal abortion rate increased to about 9.0 per 100 births in 1971. With more extensive propaganda for contraception since 1965, there appeared to be a short increase in the abortion rate until 1971 (see table 11.1). Abortions increased faster than births in the age groups up to twenty-one years, among the unmarried, among women with one child or none, and in large towns (Mehlan & Schüler, 1978).

The abortion law was further liberalized until abortion on request finally became available.

The current Law on the Interruption of Pregnancy was implemented in the GDR on 9 March 1972 (Gesetzblätter der DDR, 15 March 1972). Its provisions are as follows:

§ 1. A woman has the right to decide on termination on her own responsibility. An abortion may only be carried out by a doctor in a recognized clinic within twelve weeks' duration of pregnancy. The doctor is obliged to explain the risks of the operation to the woman and to advise her on contraception for the future.

§ 2. A pregnancy of more than twelve weeks' duration may only be terminated if there are grave risks to the life of the woman or if other serious medical reasons exist. The decision will be made by a commission of medical specialists.

§ 3. Termination is normally prohibited if there has been a previous abortion within six months. In such cases approval may only be granted by a specialist commission of doctors.

§ 4. An abortion, including preparation and any postoperative treatment, counts as sickness for the purposes of employment and social insurance regulations.

§ 5. The appropriate social insurance is responsible for the treatment and care required in connection with the interruption of the pregnancy. All contraceptives and advice are free of charge.

In the regulations of the law of 15 March 1972 and the instructions of the Ministry of Health, 1972, No. 4 is mentioned:

The woman addressing a request for interruption is to be given opportunity to present her request orally to her family doctor, gynecologist, hospital physician, or counseling center for pregnant women. The oral request of the woman is juridically speaking of the same value as a written application.

If a woman is below eighteen years of age an approval by her legal guardian is required.

The operation must be performed within one week after the application of the pregnant woman by an experienced gynecologist in a state hospital. The woman must stay in hospital up to three days.

The head of the gynecological department is responsible that the pregnancy is no longer than twelve weeks, that there are no contraindications, that the conditions for operation are good, and the operation is not against the desire of the woman. She is informed before the operation about possible complications and after it about the use of contraceptives.

If the medical inspection offers a medical contraindication or the pregnancy is more than twelve weeks, or the interval of the last interruption is less than six months, the case must be referred for decision to a regional commission for pregnancy interruption.

Permanent members of this commission are a physician, a gynecologist, a doctor of social medicine, and the Medical Regional Officer as chairman.

The abortion legislation was accompanied by sociopolitical measures to give social benefits and professional support to mothers with children, such as family allowances, higher lump sum payment, and one year paid leave after delivery.

In the GDR promoting the desire for children and the right to limit the number of children are two sides of the same coin.

ATTITUDES TOWARD ABORTION AND CONTRACEPTION

In the GDR there is a close relationship between abortion, family planning, and family policy.

Immediately after World War II, not only Section 218, but also directions against the use of contraceptives was abolished. Information, praxis, and availability of contraception were zero. In addition, medical personnel were uninformed and unskilled. At that time the only method of regulating fertility was the induced abortion.

In 1956 Professor K. H. Mehlan founded the Institute for Hygiene of the University of Rostock Medical School, which worked closely with the Ministry of Health and professional and public organizations in fostering family planning. The main research questions during his twenty-five years of directorship were as follows:

—How to influence poeple's attitudes toward family planning?

—What kind of services would best meet local conditions and customs?

—How to make available contraceptive methods that would satisfy the variety of personal preferences of different individuals and couples?

—How would successful family practice improve the health and welfare of the family?

In 1960 the Rostock institute organized the first European International Conference on Abortion and Family Planning. This meeting with specialists from twenty countries was a milestone in further legalization of abortion laws and in expanded use of contraceptives worldwide.

In May 1963 Professor Mehlan and his colleagues founded the Association for ''Ehe und Familie'' (Efa), (Marriage and Family), which is a member of the International Planned Parenthood Federation. (Henceforth in this chapter it will be referred to a the GDR Family Planning Association (FPA).) Its aims are as follows:

—To improve the health of women and mothers which may be endangered by illegal abortions, insufficient birth spacing, too many children, and other conditions

—To secure reproduction of the population by promoting the wish for children. State interests will correspond to a healthy and harmonious family

—To educate for marriage and family responsibilities; support sex education for youth to reduce the number of early marriages, illegitimate births, and divorces; and to promote the stability of marriage and the family

—To promote the harmony, health, and welfare of the family, including the use of contraceptives, and treatment of sexual disturbances

In December 1965 the Family Law was passed, requiring that the Ministry of Public Health establish the medical branch of marriage and family counseling, called Marriage and Sexual Advisory Centers. To facilitate international communication, these centers will be referred to as Family Planning Centers (FPC), although their work is more extensive, for example, by cooperation with communities, youth groups, women's organizations, and public health services.

DEMOGRAPHY OF ABORTION

Levels, Trends, and Incidence

Immediately after World War II, when Hitler's harsh restrictions on abortion were finally repealed and replaced by liberal laws, the abortion rate increased to a moderately high level, primarily because of postwar conditions. Table 11.1 shows the increase in legally performed abortions to 1950. At the same time, the number of abortions treated in hospitals (called ''other hospital abortions'') increased from 54,000 in 1946 to 89,000 in 1949, decreasing to 63,000 in 1954 (Mehlan, 1955a). Most of these abortions were induced at home and completed in hospitals.

From 1946 to 1950 the total number of abortions nearly equaled the number of live births. By the restrictive decree in 1950, legal abortion was allowed only on medical grounds. Legal abortion declined from a moderately high level in 1950 to very low levels in the early 1960s. Abortion praxis was very restrictive, but based on an investigation conducted by Mehlan (1961) clandestine abortions were still high. Between 1963 and 1972, abortion figures for the whole GDR were not registered, except those for the district of Rostock. Here the number of legal abortions increased from 87 in 1963 (abortion rate = 0.5) to 1,162 in 1971 (abortion rate = 6.4) (see table 11.1).

After the more liberal abortion law was passed in 1965, the abortion rate doubled in the district of Rostock. Later investigations confirmed that these abortion rates and ratios were similar for the whole GDR (Mehlan et al., 1979).

After the liberalization of the abortion statutes on 9 March 1972, there was a fivefold increase of legal abortion in the GDR over 1971 (figure 11.1). This "legalization effect" could be observed in nearly all countries with legal abortion. Other hospital abortions decreased in 1972 by 40 percent. The sudden increases of legal abortions immediately after legalization reflects, on the one hand, the replacement of illegal abortion by legal abortion and, on the other hand, the possibility of applying for an abortion. The change from illegal to legal abortions is evident in the obvious decrease of maternal mortality after abortion in 1973 when it was 1 death per 100,000 legal abortions compared to 31 in 1971 and in a decreasing number of suicides of pregnant women as well.

Nearly all countries with legal abortion reached their peak only within ten to twenty years. In the GDR, however, a steady decrease of legal abortions started only one year after legalization, as shown in figure 11.2.

In spite of the restrictive abortion law, the birth rate has decreased since 1964. This is true for many European countries with and without legalization. Births in the GDR increased again from 1974, as a result of sociopolitical measures. Legalization of abortion in the GDR hitherto had no influence on the birth rate.

A comparison of the abortion rates of some socialist countries shows the GDR among the countries with relatively low ratios. The data are presented in table 11.2. Table 11.3 demonstrates that six years after legalization, the number of abortions decreased by 33 percent. This decrease is caused primarily by the behavior of women aged twenty to twenty-nine. Abortions in this age group decreased with births and an increasing use of contraceptives. The group is characterized by positive attitudes to responsible parenthood (Mehlan & Schüler, 1978).

Since 1979 the number of legal abortions has increased slowly from 76,000 to 92,000, followed by a slight increase of the abortion rate and ratio. This moderate increase had no influence on births (1974 = 179,000; 1983 = 242,000 live births).

Table 11.4 shows the incidence of legal abortions in the district of Rostock for the years 1973–84. The abortion rates and especially the ratios are a little higher than the average of the whole GDR. The birth rate in all years was always 2 to 3 percent higher than the birth rate of the GDR. In addition, the number of women using safe contraceptive methods is increasing. The main reason could be the age structure of women in fertile age in this district. The percentage distribution of legal *abortions by the woman's age* in the last twenty-five years in the GDR shows (table 11.5) that until 1970 more than 60 percent of all

Figure 11.1
Abortion Rate and Ratio and Fertility Rate, District of Rostock, 1965–84

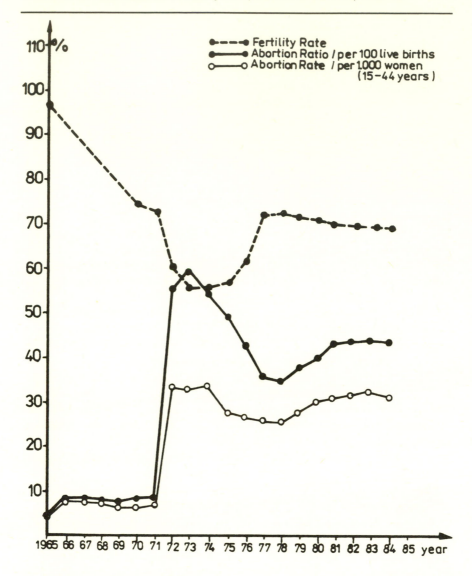

Source: Mehlan, 1979, p. 85.

abortions were obtained by women aged thirty and above before legalization took place. After 1972 there was a shift to younger age groups. More than one-third of all legal abortions were performed on women below twenty-five years of age. In spite of overcoming social and cultural differences between rural and

Figure 11.2
Abortion Rate (Legal Abortions per 1,000 Population in Socialist Countries, 1956–84)

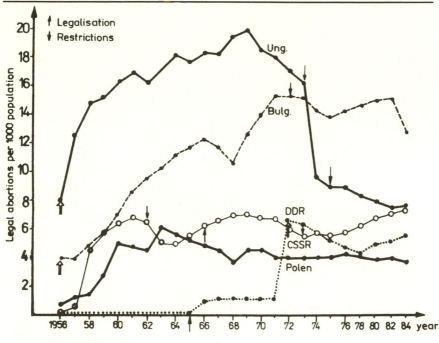

Source: Mehlan, 1979, p. 85.

urban districts, the abortion rates still differ. More abortions take place in urban than in rural communities. This illustrates a very slow change of reproductive behavior. Urban families tend to consist of two children or only one, while families in rural areas tend to comprise two or three children (Mehlan et al., 1979).

Age, Parity, and Marital Status

Analyzing the outcome of pregnancy according to age groups demonstrates the known increases of abortions with increasing age of women (table 11.6). Women with two or more children accounted for 70 percent of all abortions in 1975. In 1973, 39 percent of all pregnancies in the GDR were terminated by abortions; in 1982 the ratio decreased to 27 percent (see table 11.1).

The percentage distribution of the number of pregnancies terminated by legal abortion reveals major differences during the last twenty-five years. The most numerous abortees are women with two children in their third pregnancy. Since legalization in 1972, the number of women interrupting their first pregnancy has been increasing, as shown in table 11.7.

Data on marital status are available only until 1956. No reports on age, parity, or marital status appeared after 1976. According to the *Statistical Yearbook* of the GDR (1984) we know that the proportion of women never married has increased since 1972. The proportion of wanted or desired children out-of-wedlock increased from 12 percent in 1972 to 32 percent in 1982 in the GDR and up to 61 percent in 1983 in Berlin.

Contraceptive Use

With regard to contraceptive use, there is a high correlation between abortion and contraceptive experience. This can be noted in the GDR because both contraception and abortion are freely available. Table 11.8 demonstrates the use of oral contraceptives in the district of Rostock for the years 1977–83.

In the GDR the following brands of oral contraceptives are manufactured by VEB Jenapharm: Ovosiston, Sequenz-Ovosiston, Non Ovlon, Gravistat, Deposiston, and Minisiston. Next to the oral contraceptives in popularity is the IUD (Cupper T, Nova T, or Dana Cupper). Its use has increased in the last ten years. Mehlan (1979) estimated that in 1981, 7 to 8 percent of women of reproductive age were using IUDs. Condoms or other barrier methods are not as commonly used.

The authorization of abortions on request in March 1972 was followed by a steady increase in the use of effective contraceptives, accompanied by a decrease in the use of legal abortions and an increase in live births. The increase in births was the result of the government's high social and political benefits for mothers with children.

As in some other countries such as the United States, Great Britain, and the Federal Republic of Germany, there is no dramatic fluctuation (i.e., a sharp decrease followed by a sharp increase) in the use of the pill in the GDR. The legalization of abortion has positively influenced attitudes and behavior with regard to contraceptives because medical personnel and other institutions are now very interested in combating legal abortion with active education, motivation, and praxis in contraception.

Table 11.9 shows that beginning in 1975 pregnancy, birth, and abortion rates increased, as did the use of oral contraceptives and the IUD. This paradox reflects the multiple factors that determine the level of known pregnancies. The increase in the pregnancy rate reflects the higher number of wanted children.

The legal abortion rate among adolescents in the GDR has been stable since 1972 and 1982 except in the district of Rostock where it increased from 20 in 1972 to 24 abortions per 1,000 teenage females in 1980. In the age group below eighteen, abortion rates are increasing, whereas women aged eighteen to nineteen have fewer abortions and more births and use contraceptives more frequently (Mehlan & Schüler, 1979).

ABORTION AND FERTILITY REGULATION

To show the population dynamics of the GDR, it will be useful to review the basic demographic data of the GDR. The total population in 1950 was 18.4

million compared with 16.7 million in 1983. There has been a significant change in age structure since 1960. The proportion of persons of working age increased from 61.3 percent in 1960 to 64.6 percent in 1982, and the number of old age pensioners rose from 17.6 percent in 1960 to 20.5 percent in 1982. The mean life expectancy increased from 66.5 years to 69.0 years between 1960 and 1981 for men, and from 71.3 years to 75.7 years for women. The crude marriage rate was 9.7 per 1,000 in 1960 and 7.3 per 1,000 in 1982. The average age of marriage for bachelors was 23.9 in 1960 and 23.5 in 1980; the corresponding figures for spinsters were 22.5 and 21.4. The mean difference in age at marriage was about 1.35 in 1965 but increased to 2.7 in 1981. The crude divorce rate was 1.4 per 1,000 in 1960 and 3.0 per 1,000 in 1983. The birth rate has undergone different changes. In 1946 it was 10.4, the first being in 1959 with a birth rate of 16.9. This was followed by a steady increase to 17.6 in 1963, followed by a constant decrease of 10.6 in 1974. During the last years following abortion legislation combined with sociopolitical measures, the birth rate increased to 14.0 in 1983. The population growth rate is below zero.

The number of "wanted" children born out-of-wedlock is increasing and was 32 percent in 1983. There is a trend to unmarried partnership.

The government has made great efforts to increase facilities for young children to support working mothers. In 1983 there were 68 places in crèches per 100 children up to three years of age, 93 places in kindergartens for 100 children aged four to six years, and 82 places in school nurseries per 100 children aged seven to eleven years. These nurseries are largely supported by the state: parents are required only to pay on average 1.0 percent of the family income.

The GDR's policy on family planning was well delineated in a speech which the minister for health, Professor Dr. L. Mecklinger, gave at the Rostock Conference in October 1967. In summary, he made the following points:

—Family planning is a task of the total society and is integrated into public health services, especially to protect mother and child.

—Every woman has the right to determine when she prefers to give birth; she also has the right to obtain an abortion as well as access to contraceptives.

—Each family has the right to determine the number of children it desires.

—There is no pressure for births.

—The woman has the opportunity to reproduce but not the duty.

—Each individual has the right to receive information about preventing pregnancy.

—All physicians have the duty to counsel married couples and unmarried individuals and to prescribe contraceptives.

In May 1966 the GDR Ministry of Public Health, in collaboration with the Family Planning Association (FPA) promulgated an order establishing Family Planning Centers (FPCs) in all districts of the country. In 1967 the Ministry affirmed the guiding principles for FPCs as elaborated by the FPA, especially by Dolberg and Geissler (1966). They are now the legal basis for the activities of physicians and for anyone engaged in family planning. The result has been an integration of family planning into the GDR public health services.

In 1969 there were approximately 200 FPCs. In accordance with their comprehensive goals, these centers are staffed by full- or part-time physicians, psychologists, and social workers with consultants available from other specialties, including gynecology and psychiatry. Not all centers are fully staffed, and some are opened for only limited time periods during the week. The GDR Ministry of Health provides a budget for the payment of staff and maintenance. All methods of contraception, including the pill and coils, are available. No charges are made for services rendered. The number of FPCs is expected to reach 300 by 1990 (1 per 12,000 women of fertile age).

According to Mehlan (1968), the following tasks are assigned to the FPCs:

—Education toward family life and promotion of positive attitudes toward children

—Family planning counseling and advice on contraception, birth spacing, regulation of date of pregnancy, and number of children

—Counseling and therapy in the case of sexual disturbances

—Prevention of illegal and legal abortion by supplying contraceptive advice and by taking women into dispensary care

—Advice in cases of infertility and genetic counseling

—Treatment of medically caused disturbances in marriage

Contraceptive methods were seldom mentioned in German medical publications, newspapers, radio, or television until 1967 because methods were not available and medical personnel were neither informed nor skilled. One of the first tasks of the FPA was to change the attitudes of the medical personnel and the public toward contraception by dispensing information on contraceptive means, methods, and use through different communications.

In cooperation with the Ministry of Health, the FPA organized annual postgraduate training courses for doctors in Rostock. All methods of fertility regulation were intensively discussed. About 16,000 doctors and staff of the FPA clinics hitherto used this training possibility. The participants were motivated and initiated for progressive action in family planning. The FPA also organized training courses for the GDR Academy of Continuing Medical Education to qualify physicians in the specialty of family planning.

Sex education is being integrated into primary and secondary school curricula; information on contraception is included.

Until 1963 public discussions of sex were considered taboo; now the subject is popular. Members of the FPA and the FPC staff use all public media for propagating family planning and for offering discussion groups, lectures, and individual consultations.

REFERENCES

Dolberg, G., and Geissler, A. Sum Aufbau der ärztlich-psychologischen Ehe- und Sexualberatung als Bestandteil der Ehe und Familienplanung. *Dtsch. Ges. Wesen*, 1966 (21), 1768–1775.

Familiengesetzbuch der DDR [Code of family law of the German Democratic Rep.]. Berlin: Staatsverlag, 1965.

Gesenius, H. Internationale Abortsituation. In K. H. Mehlan (Ed.). VEB Georg Thieme Verlag. Leipzig, 1961.

Gesetzblätter der Deutschen Demokratischen Republik (DDR). 27.9. Law on the Protection of Mothers and Children. 1950, 1037–1041.

––––––. Teil I 15. Legalisieurung des Abortes in der DDR (abortion law), 1972, 149–151.

––––––. Teil II 12. Instruktionen zum Gesetz vom 5. März 1972, 149–151.

Häublein, H. G. Institut für Sozialhygiene "Maxim Gorki." Berlin. Personal information, 1982.

Lehfeldt, H. New Experiences with IUD's. Paper presented at the University of Rostock, August 1981 (unpublished).

Lellbach, H. Wiederholte Anträge auf Interruptio. In K. H. Mehlan, (Ed.), Artz und Familienplanung, 1968.

Mecklinger, L. Mitverantwortung und Aufgaben des Arztes bei der Familienplanung. Paper presented. 3. Rostocker Fortbildungstage, Ehe- und Sexualberatung. K. H. Mehlan, Arzt und Familienplanung, 1968.

Mehlan, K. H. Die Problematik der Schwangerschaftsunterbrechung auf Grund der sozialen Indikation DDR 1948/54. Ph.D., Humboldt Universität, Berlin, 1955a. (Copies available at all university libraries in the GDR.)

––––––. Abortstatistik und Geburtenhäufigkeit in der DDR. *Dtsch. Ges Wesen*, 1955b, no. 10, 1648–1659.

––––––. Die Schwangerschaftsunterbrechungen in der DDR in den Jahren 1946–50. Ärzteblatt Schleswig Holstein, 1956, no. 9, 22–28.

––––––. Das Bild der Schwangerschaftsunterbrechung in der DDR. *Dtsch. Ges. Wesen*, 1958 (13), 595–601.

––––––. Internationale Abortsituation. VEB Georg Thieme Verlag, Leipzig, DDR, 1961.

––––––. Probleme der Ehe- und Sexualberatung. VEB Volk und Gesundheit, Berlin, 1966.

––––––, ed. Arzt und Familienplanung. VEB Volk and Gesundheit, Berlin, 1968.

––––––. Auswirkungen der Legalisierung des Abortes im Bezirk Rostock (DDR). *Dtsch. Ges. Wesen*, 1974 (29), 2216–2219.

––––––. Fertilitätsregulierung eine Aufgabe der WHO. *Wissenschaftliche Zeitschrift der Wilhelm-Pieck-Universität Rostock*, 1979 (28), 739–753.

––––––. Fertilitätsprobleme im Bezirk Rostock 1972–1983. Paper presented at the meeting of FPA in Berlin, February 1984 (unpublished).

––––––. Legal abortions in socialist countries of Europe. Paper presented at the Christopher Tietze International Symposium, Berlin-West, 21/22 September 1985.

Mehlan, K. H. & Falkenthal, S. Der lagale Abort in der DDR 1953–1962. *Dtsch. Ges. Wesen*, 1965 (20), 1163–1167.

Mehlan, K. H. & Schüler, Ch. Die Abortsituation in der DDR 1972–1977 im Bezirk Rostock, speziell der Teenager. Sozialhygiene Report, 1978 (1), 9–20.

Mehlan, K. H., et al. Abortentwicklung und reproduktives Geschehen im Bezirk Rostock 1972–1977. *Dtsch. Ges. Wesen*, 1979 (52), 665–670.
Statistische Jahrbücher der DDR 1955. Annual until 1984.
Tietze, C. *Induced abortion: A world review 1983* (5th ed.). New York: Population Council, 1983.

Table 11.1
Number of Legal Abortions, Abortion Rates, and Abortion Ratios, German Democratic Republic, by Years and Characteristics

Years	Number of abortions[1]	Abortion Rate per 1,000 Total population	Abortion Rate per 1,000 Women 15-44	Abortion Ratio per 100 Live births[2]	Abortion Ratio per 100 Known pregnancies[3]	Clandestine abortions[4]
1948[5]	17,500	1.57	5.3	5.6	7.3	64,000
1949	26,300	1.55	6.2	8.4	7.8	76,000
1950	26,400	1.9	6.4	8.6	7.9	84,000
1951	5,000	0.27	1.2	1.6	1.6	68,000
1952	3,600	0.20	0.9	1.2	1.2	62,000
1953	2,400	0.13	0.6	0.8	0.8	64,000
1954	1,700	0.1	0.4	0.6	0.6	60,000
1955	1,200	0.07	0.3	0.4	0.4	
1956[6]	1,000	0.06	0.3	0.4	0.4	
1957	900	0.05	0.3	0.3	0.3	
1958	900	0.05	0.3	0.3	0.3	
1959	800	0.04	0.2	0.3	0.3	
1960	800	0.04	0.2	0.3	0.3	
1961	800	0.04	0.2	0.3	0.3	
1962[7]	700	0.04	0.2	0.3	0.3	
1963[7a]	87	0.01	0.5	0.5	0.5	
1964	128	0.02	0.7	0.7	0.7	
1965	625	0.1	3.6	3.7	3.6	
1966	1,207	1.42	7.1	7.5	7.2	
1967	1,239	1.45	7.2	8.3	7.7	
1968	1,180	1.39	6.8	8.1	7.6	
1969	1,078	1.26	6.1	7.8	7.4	
1970	1,114	1.31	6.2	8.5	7.8	
1971	1,162	1.25	6.4	8.9	8.8	
1972[8]	114,000	6.7	33.1	57.0	37.4	
1973	110,800	6.5	32.2	61.9	38.8	
1974	99,700	5.9	28.8	53.3	35.6	
1975	87,800	5.2	25.2	48.0	31.9	
1976	81,900	4.9	23.3	41.8	29.5	
1977	78,900	4.7	22.5	35.4	26.1	
1978[9]	76,202	4.5	21.5	32.8	24.7	
1979	86,522	5.2	23.8	36.7	26.8	
1980[10]	88,600	5.3	24.4	36.1	26.5	
1981	90,300	5.4	24.8	38.0	27.5	
1982	90,400	5.4	24.9	37.6	27.3	
1983	92,500	5.5	25.5	39.3	27.5	
1984	96,200	5.8	26.2	41.1	28.0	

[1]All numbers rounded. [2]Statistisches Jahrbuch der DDR. [3]Live births plus. [4]1948–54: Mehlan, 1955. [5]1948–55: Mehlan, 1955. [6]1946–55: Mehlan, 1956. [7]1953–62: Mehlan & Falkenthal, 1965. [7a]Number of legal abortions only for district of Rostock for 1963–77. [8]Mehlan, 1974. [9]1972–78: Mehlan & Schüler, 1978. [10]Häublein, 1982.

Table 11.2
Legal Abortions per 1,000 Live Births (Abortion Ratio), Selected Socialist Countries, 1956–84 (Four-year Interval)

Year	Bulgaria	CSSR	GDR	Hungary	Poland
1956	14	12	3	464	16
1960	400	405	3	1129	337
1964	719	298	7	1393	312
1968	647	456	83	1310	289
1972	986	347	590	1161	230
1976	880	305	418	505	215
1980	974	413	361	620	199
1984	950	510	411	691	190

Source: Mehlan, 1985.

Table 11.3
Legal Abortions, GDR, Selected Years

Year	Total (in thous)	Decrease	Rate (per 1000 women 15-44)	Ratio (per 100 live births)
1972	114.0	=100	33	57
1973	110.8		32	62
1974	99.7		29	56
1975	87.8		25	48
1976	81.9		23	42
1977	78.0	= 68	22	35
1978	76.2	= 66	22	33
1980	80.6		24	36
1982	90.4		25	38
1984	96.2	= 84	26	41

Source: Mehlan, 1985.

Table 11.4
Number of Legal Abortions, Abortion Rates, and Abortion Ratios, District of Rostock (GDR), 1972–84

Years	Number of Abortions[1]	Total Population	Abortion Rate per 1,000 Women 15–44	Live Births	Abortion Ratio per 100 Known Pregnancies[2]
1972	6111	7.0	33.0	55.2	35.2
1973	6168	7.1	32.9	59.7	37.3
1974	5746	6.6	33.2	54.9	35.4
1975	5428	6.2	27.0	49.8	33.2
1976	5175	5.8	26.4	43.3	27.0
1977	5115	5.8	25.7	36.1	26.5
1978	5159	5.8	25.5	35.7	26.3
1979	5543	6.2	27.3	38.2	27.6
1980	6061	6.8	29.8	40.4	28.8
1981	2636	7.0	30.6	43.6	30.4
1982	6346	7.0	31.3	44.1	30.6
1983	6390	7.1	31.6	44.3	30.5
1984	6470	7.2	32.2	44.8	30.6

[1]District Medical Office for Statistics, Rostock.
[2]Statistische Jahrbücher der DDR, 1973–83.

Table 11.5

Percentage Distribution of Legal Abortions by Age of Women at Termination, GDR, Selected Years

Years	-19	20-24	25-29	30-34	35-40	40 or more
1948[1)	3.1	16.4	28.3	18.8	22.8	10.6
1956[2)	2.8	12.4	23.7	27.1	22.3	11.7
1972[4)	12.3	23.1	18.5	24.8	15.7	5.6
1976[3)	13.5	20.5	19.2	19.4	19.9	7.6

Source: Mehlan, 1958 (1, 2, 4); Mehlan, 1979 (3).

Table 11.6

Legal Abortion Ratio by Age of Women at Conception, GDR

Years	-19	20-24	25-29	30-34	35-40	40 or more
1973	20.0	24.1	47.0	61.8	76.8	87.5
1974	20.2	21.0	42.2	61.5	77.5	88.2
1975	18.8	17.5	35.9	59.8	76.5	88.3

Source: Tietze, 1983.

Table 11.7

Percentage Distribution of Legal Abortions by Parity, Number of Terminated Pregnancies, GDR, Selected Years

Years	1	2	3	Pregnancies 4	5	6 or more
1948/50	13.2	20.3	25.4	17.6	10.5	13.2
1956	11.2	13.8	19.4	20.4	13.6	21.6
1972	19.0	23.0	29.0	29.0		
1976	18.0	26.0	33.0	23.0		

Source: Mehlan, 1955; Tietze, 1983.

Table 11.8
Users of Oral Contraceptives per Year and Women Aged Fifteen to Forty-five, District of Rostock, 1977–83

Year	1977	1978	1979	1980	1981	1982	1983
Total number of women 15–45	198,545	201,632	202,632	203,273	203,269	202,786	202,550
Number of women using orals	58,120	60,643	78,425	80,316	79,909	80,828	82,005
Percent of users	29.3	30.2	38.7	39.5	39.3	40.0	40.5

Source: Mehlan, 1984.

Table 11.9

Development of Different Fertility Regulation Factors in the GDR and the District of Rostock for the Years 1975–83 (1975 = 100; Increase Until 1983 in Percent)

	GDR	Rostock
Number of pregnancies	25%	28%
Number of live births	35%	32%
Number of legal abortions	5%	17%
Number of pill users	45%	60%

Source: Mehlan, 1984.

12

FEDERAL REPUBLIC OF GERMANY

Gerhard Kraiker

HISTORICAL DEVELOPMENT OF ABORTION POLICY

The laws laid down in the first Penal Code passed by Germany in 1871 retained their validity for decades. According to these laws as set down in Paragraph 218, any individual found guilty of participating in an act of abortion was liable to a sentence of one to five years of penal servitude. Thus, the penalty for abortion was the same as that for infanticide. But under Kaiser Wilhelm and primarily during the period of the Weimar Republic (1919–33), the workers' movement made many attempts to abolish, or at least to moderate, the abortion laws (*Arbeiterbewegung*, 1973; Joachimsen, 1971). These attempts failed, however, because of resistance from the middle-class conservative parties.

This resistance stemmed not only from the moral interests which imposed on women a natural obligation to bear children, but also from fears that making abortion legal would cause a decline in the population growth rate (Heinsohn et al, 1979). The sole change in the law came in 1926 when the Supreme Court legalized abortion on medical grounds.

During the last phase of the fascist regime, abortion was considered a capital offense. Anyone "who progressively impaired the vitality of the German people" (*Verordnung zum Schutz von Ehe*, 1943) was threatened with the death penalty. Abortion was permitted only when the pregnancy was considered undesirable from the point of view of racist ideology. The laws laid down in the 1920s remained uncontested until the beginning of the Socialist-Liberal Coalition (1969), composed of the German Socialist Democratic party (SPD) and the Free Democratic party (FDP).

Radical and Moderate Reform Objectives

In the second half of the 1960s, a fundamental opposition arose in the Federal Republic, as in other Western industrial countries, which was vehemently opposed to authoritarian structures in the society and state, the family, and the educational system, and which called for the recognition of democratic principles in all walks of life. This opposition was composed mainly of the young, but after the preliminary impact, many of their demands found sympathy with the older population. This opposition led in large measure to the beginning of a new political era with the Socialist-Liberal Coalition in 1969.

The new government's program sought to liberate the penal law from its numerous archaisms from the time of Kaiser Wilhelm. This objective was furthered by a series of concrete proposals for reform published by a group of liberal professors of law in 1970, as well as through the national alliance of liberal or socialist-minded women's groups to form the organization "Aktion 218." The agreement of these law professors was not unanimous, however. The majority recommended the so-called trimester regulation, that is, the freedom to decide for or against an abortion within the first three months of pregnancy, which the SPD had previously supported during the Weimar Republic. A minority of the professors of law rejected the idea of the trimester regulation in favor of abortion if "pregnancy means an insupportable burden for the mother" or if it occurs to a woman under sixteen years and in cases where material provision for other children could be endangered by the birth of another child (*Alternativ-Entwurf eines Strafgesetzbuches*, 1970). The aim of the women's group was to abolish Paragraph 218 altogether. The group argued that woman has a sovereign right to decide whether or not she wishes to bear a child (see Kraiker, 1983, pp. 100–114). It was principally women with academic qualifications and students who agitated against the abortion law. Of course, it was only a matter of time before women's groups from the trade unions and the Socialist Democratic party joined them. Other organized women's associations, excluding Catholic women's organizations, also voted for reform but of a less far-reaching nature. They argued in favor of the trimester regulation. The already existing and proposed means of financial support for single mothers did not serve to lessen the burden of raising a child to any noticeable extent. The activists pointed out the serious negative consequences which unwanted children could bring women: the abandonment of work and with it economic independence, continuation of social inequality in professional life, social isolation caused by confinement to the household, fewer opportunities to break free from broken marriages, discrimination toward unmarried mothers. At a hearing before the German Parliament (Bundestag), the spokesman for "Aktion 218" stressed reports of violence against unwanted children by parents or caretakers and reported that 56 percent of unmarried mothers were compelled to return to work eight weeks after the birth of the child and to make provision for the care of the infant at least during their working hours (*Protokolle des Bundestagssonderausschusses für die Strafrechtsreform*, 1972, p. 2354).

Liberal publications like *Stern* and *Der Spiegel* supported the women's campaign by publishing the names of hundreds of famous women who themselves admitted to having had an abortion, as well as reports from physicians who had assisted at abortions. The result of all this publicity was that in the summer of 1971 in an opinion poll carried out by the Allensbach Demographic Institute a slight majority of the population (56 percent) proved to be in favor of the complete legalization of abortion whereas only 29 percent voted against (Noelle-Neumann, 1974, pp. 245–246). In March 1971 only 46 percent had been in favor of legalization, compared with the year 1949 when it had been a mere 16 percent (Noelle-Neumann, 1956, p. 18).

Meanwhile, all the political parties were in agreement that reform was necessary. The high rates of illegal, medically dangerous abortions, estimated between 200,000 and 1 million, the increasing numbers of abortions of German women abroad in neighboring countries with more liberal legalization, plus the fact that the existing laws could hardly be enforced by the police authorities, all led to this consensus.

The motives, however, were varied; some were more concerned with re-establishing the authority of the law, others with readapting the laws to suit the changing values of society, which included an acknowledgment of the positive interest value of sexuality as opposed to the propagation function and the right of the woman to determine her own life.

Accordingly, the concrete proposals for reform differed greatly. No party was prepared to accept complete abolition of the abortion laws such as the women's movement demanded. Nor was any party prepared to support the reasoning of the autonomous women's groups which asserted that protective intervention on the part of the state after the third month of pregnancy was superfluous, because it is in any case in the interest of the woman's health and a matter of the physician's responsibility to terminate the pregnancy at the earliest date possible. They argued further that an abortion of a child capable of living outside the mother's womb could not be considered a case of infanticide (Kraiker, 1983, p. 104).

The reform proposals from the Free Democratic party went furthest. The Free Democrats were prepared to grant women legal immunity to reach a decision within the first three months of pregnancy. The Socialist Democratic party was torn between opposite poles within their women's groups: those who wished to implement the trimester regulation, and the Catholics in the party who were led by the minister for justice and were only prepared to accept medical grounds as justification for the termination of pregnancy, but not social hardship (the social indication) (Kraiker, 1983, pp. 61–67). The Christian Democratic Union (CDU) and the Christian Social Union (CSU) adopted the position of the Catholic church but asserted it less rigidly, that the individual has been given a preordained scale of values which the state is morally bound to protect, if necessary, against the empirical moral consciousness of the population. Their fear was that progressive liberalization, which would go even as far as involving a transfer of costs to the health-insurance companies, could lead to the misuse of abortion as a means of contraception. The major doubt cast in this line of reasoning on the woman's ability to take the abortion decision even in permissible cases underlined the fears of the Christian parties; medical counselors should ultimately make the decision and not the women themselves (Kraiker, 1983, pp. 55–59).

Opponents of Reform

The principal opponent of reform was the Catholic church. The church tried to make its influence felt on the public through pastoral letters written by its bishops, through sermons, and through its own newspapers with circulation in the millions. Whereas at the time of the Weimar Republic Catholics represented a minority compared with the Protestants, today they are a numerical majority because of the partition of Germany and because of a higher birth rate in the Federal Republic. However, the strong political unity of Catholicism in the 1950s has been considerably diminished by the growing tendency toward secularization in politics. Nevertheless, the Catholic church remains an important political factor in the Federal Republic, making its considerable influence felt over Christian parties on matters of basic ideology (Kraiker, 1972). The Protestant church has much more difficulty exerting political influence because it is composed of many theologically and administratively autonomous creeds, and its way of thinking is widely recognized to be less doctrinaire. In the first decades of the federal republic, the Protestant church often joined with the Catholic church in promoting its own interests, and once again its official representatives followed the Catholics in their rejection of reform of the abortion laws.

The Catholic bishops demanded legal protection of the unborn child from the moment of its conception. The unborn child was not to be regarded as part of the mother's body which she could dispose of as she pleased (*Stellungnahme der Deutschen Bischofskonferenz zur Strafrechtsreform*, 1970). A report published one year later by the Commission of German Bishops admitted, however, that morality and the law were not always compatible and declared that it was humane as well as legally justifiable, in the case of risk to life or permanent damage to the health of the mother, that the termination of pregnancy should not be punishable by law. Even under these circumstances, however, the termination of pregnancy could not be regarded as ethically justified (*Stellungnahme* vom 23.06, 1971). With this report the official Catholic church gave a clear indication of how far it was prepared to go in giving its approval to the legislators. The Catholic-Protestant Statement of December 1970 did not allow any further freedom of decision in this matter. The statement, however, regarded the legal protection of life from the moment of conception as a moral obligation of universal validity to which the legislator is constitutionally bound (*Evangelisch-katholische Stellungnahme* vom 10.12, 1970). The bishops accused women who had publicly admitted to having abortions performed for reasons of personal and material convenience, and they further reproached them with being proud of their crime against human life (*Wort der Deutschen Bischofskonferenz* vom 23.09, 1971).

Although the Catholic and Protestant churches seemed to form a unified block of resistance to reform because of the common declarations of their bishops, in the course of time very different positions became visible within the Protestant church. Here the majority was even prepared to allow the decision in serious cases of conflict to be a matter of conscience on the part of women and physicians; furthermore, this decision should prevail over the state's obligation to protect unborn life. Cases of conflict were primarily considered to be those involving psychological or physical risk to the life of the mother, or pregnancy after a case of rape. Abortion on eugenic grounds was not usually regarded as a matter for conflict, and the social indications for abortion were only supported by a minority of church representatives (Kraiker, 1983, pp. 53–55).

During the pre-parliamentary discussion, the next strongest group of opponents to liberalization of abortion, after the two main church bodies, was the organization of physicians. Whereas the Association of General Practitioners declared its general opposition to reform, gynecologists considered an extended regulation of abortion grounds to be feasible. A serious problem from the physicians' point of view was obviously the discrepancy between their oath to save life and the demand to terminate growing life. The Report of the International Association of Physicians (1970) had already drawn attention to the supreme moral obligation for medical practitioners as summarized in the Geneva oath, "I swear to hold human life from the moment of its conception in the highest regard" (*Stellung-nahme* vom 22.08, 1970). The interpretation of this principle of conduct within the reform discussion related in the conclusion that physicians should only perform an abortion in medically justified borderline cases and oppose abortions carried out on purely social or psychological grounds.

Most of all, the physicians feared a regulation that would give women too much responsibility for their decision to terminate a pregnancy and the doctors only the responsibility for performing the abortion. The physician's usual position of authority in the doctor-patient relationship would have to be maintained at all costs, as the representative of the doctors emphasized at a hearing before the German Parliament (*Protokolle des Bundestagssonderausschusses für die Straf-rechtsreform*, 1972, p. 2266). The physicians demanded expert assessment of the cases either by two specialists or by a suitably specialized counseling institution in order to legitimize their decision to terminate a pregnancy. This demand was directed, on the one hand, against those doctors who abuse the physicians' professional norms, whether for commercial reasons or because of a feeling of identification with women in distress. On the other hand, the demand arose from the doctors' need for a legal safeguard, just as the clause exists in nearly all medico-legislative proposals that a doctor who negligently or mistakenly performs an abortion is punishable by law (Kraiker, 1983, pp. 59–61).

Stages in the Process of Political Reform

In February 1972 the Socialist-Liberal government (SPD/FDP) introduced the draft of a bill into Parliament (Bundestag) which provided for termination of pregnancy on medical grounds, eugenic grounds (in the case of congenital diseases), criminal grounds (in case of rape), and on grounds of social distress.

Medical grounds were to be considered valid in cases not only of physical but also psychological risk to the mother's life.

The social indication was to remain restricted to cases of serious external distress that could not be averted by other means. The physician in attendance was legally bound to seek the advice of a second doctor authorized by the professional organization and to keep a written record of the results of this consultation (*Gesetzentwurf der Bundesregierung* vom 15.05, 1972). The draft produced a compromise within the largest government party, the SPD. In the course of this legislative period, Parliament came to no further decisions concerning abortion, and the government left it to the parliamentary parties to submit a new draft in the following legislative period when the Socialist-Liberal parties were once again in the majority. Meanwhile, the pressure of public opinion for more far-reaching reforms had become so great that the coalition parties introduced a bill in March 1973, the essence of which was to revive the trimester regulation. According to this draft, women were obliged to seek preabortion counseling at an institution authorized by the state. The costs of this counseling and of legal abortions were to be borne by the health insurance companies (*Gesetzentwurf der SPD/FDP-Fraktionen* vom 21.03, 1973). In June 1973 the bill passed through Parliament with a narrow majority, and, although the Council of Federal States (Bundesrat) in which the Christian parties were in the majority voted against it, the bill became law in June 1974. But this situation was short-lived as the opposition took the case before the Supreme Constitutional Court (Bundesverfassungsgericht) because of its alleged incompatibility with the Constitution. The Supreme Court, composed mainly of conservative judges, passed a decree by which the law was temporarily rescinded.

At the beginning of the 1970s, three supreme courts in Western countries were required to pronounce judgment on the legality of abortion. In France and Austria the respective supreme courts sanctioned the conformity of the trimester regulation with their Constitutions. The U.S. Supreme Court forbade a legal application of the indication regulation for the first four months—in other words it passed the same judgment as the other courts. In view of these judgments in countries with a similar social structure as West Germany, it could have been expected that the German Constitutional Court would not obstruct the successful reform of the abortion laws that had been taking place worldwide since the 1960s. But the majority decision proclaimed on 25 February 1975 proved that this expectation had been only too optimistic. Admittedly, the Supreme Court did not oppose every aspect of reform and went beyond the concept of the appellant Christian parties by binding the legislator to the framework of the above-mentioned government draft of 1972. However, it rejected the trimester regulation as incompatible with the basic rights laid down in the Constitution. The Supreme Constitutional Court (Bundesverfassungsgericht) justified this difference with the judgments of the other supreme courts in the above-mentioned countries with the argument that because of the historical experience encountered under National Socialism a more value-oriented order had been established in the Constitution of the Federal Republic, based on the idea "that man possesses his own independent values in the order of creation" (Mehrheits-Urteil, 1975, p. 67). Thus, the Supreme Court applied a religious-metaphysical significance to the basic rights of the Constitution, which in a predominant pluralistic secular society was bound to create an extremely problematic situation.

The majority of the judges regarded growing life as an autonomous legal good that must be safeguarded by the Constitution in accordance with the norms of basic law, namely, that "Everyone has the right to life, liberty and security of person" (Article 2), and "the dignity of the human being is inviolable. It is the duty of any government to respect and protect it" (Article 1). With reference to legal history, the court acknowledged a difference in the state's legal obligation to protect existing life as opposed to unborn life, but considered this difference to be of less consequence. The judges' conception of the state's protective duty was based on the norms of basic law which not only called for subjective defense on the part of the state but also embodied an objective order of values. The judges considered that this protective commitment also applied to pregnant mothers. The judges, while agreeing that the woman's right to the free and full development of her personality was equally in need of protection, argued that this right was restricted by the embryo's right to life. Since in the opinion of the judges the embryo is not a part of the mother but already an independent being, even though it is not capable of life outside the womb, the woman's right to self-determination cannot be an acceptable justification for abortion. Abortion is not a private affair but always has a social dimension which necessitates regulations on the part of the state, even during the first three months of pregnancy.

The legislators were therefore bound by the injunctions of the Supreme Court, and the bill introduced into Parliament by the government in 1976 was drafted accordingly. Once again it included all indication cases and laid down in cases of abortion on criminal and social grounds that the termination has to take place within the first twelve weeks of pregnancy. For all other indications, a period of twenty-two weeks has been set. The woman is legally bound to consult a physician other than the one who performs the abortion or else an authorized institution. The law requires that counselors inform the mother of all available state and private support when the child is born. The abortion may only be performed in hospitals or specially authorized institutions. No physician or member of a hospital staff can be forced to take part in such an operation, except when the life of the mother is at risk. This law is still valid today (*Strafrecht-sanderungsgesetz* vom 18.05, 1976).

CURRENT STATUS OF THE REFORMED ABORTION LAW

According to the law and the regulations laid down by the Federal States for its implementation, the following conditions are imposed on a woman seeking legal abortion in West Germany:

1. She must find a physician who takes a decision upon the indication according to the grounds involved. This can be her family doctor, a gynecologist, or another physician. In a small number of cases, the physician may be consulted in the institution which is also responsible for preabortion counseling as, for example, Pro Familia's family planning organization in Bremen.

2. The mother requires written proof that she has received social counseling; this must take place at least three days before the termination of pregnancy. Approximately 1,000 advisory organizations and a further 1,000 physicians are qualified as counselors.

3. The mother must find a hospital, clinic, or obstetrician to carry out the termination. The physician may not be the doctor who decided on the indication or the one who acted as preabortion counselor. The physician who performs the abortion must give the mother detailed information about the medical risks involved and must obtain her express written consent.

The provisions for the official authorization of abortion, for preabortion counseling, and the financial support of counseling organizations differ greatly from state to state within the Federal Republic. In the predominantly Catholic states, Bavaria and Baden-Wuttemberg, abortions may only be performed in state hospitals because there is supposedly no demand for abortions in private clinics or practices. Similarly, in other Christian Democratic Union (CDU) governed states abortions are rarely permitted outside hospitals. This considerably aggravates the situation for women seeking abortion in these states, especially since a survey showed that, of the 241 hospitals surveyed, 170 refused to perform an abortion on the grounds of social distress and further expressed strong reservations about pregnancy terminantion for other indication (*Bericht der Kommission*, 1980, p. 92).

Given the pronounced hierarchical structure of West German hospitals, senior physicians or administrative bodies (church, religious orders) often generalize the legitimate right of doctors and hospital staff to refuse to perform or assist at an abortion in certain cases by applying it to all pregnancy terminations and to all medical personnel. As a result, women from Catholic states must often seek an abortion either in SPD-controlled states where the number of private practices available for abortions is considerably greater or in neighboring countries (Pro Familia, Bremen, 1978). Currently, half of the abortions are performed in hospitals, and the other half in private practices or clinics. Several factors are responsible for the present trend toward the latter option, namely, the above-mentioned negative attitude of many state hospitals, prolonged periods of convalescence in hospitals, the higher level of anonymity in private practices, and last, but not least, the improved level of fees for pregnancy terminations which since 1981 has made gynecologists more willing to provide abortion services. The fact that in some Federal States abortions performed in private practices must be carried out within the first eight weeks of pregnancy (although the law allows a period of twenty-two weeks for the eugenic indication and twelve weeks for the criminal and social indications) has proved no obstacle to women seeking abortion. This difference in the availability of abortion exists not only between Catholic and non-Catholic regions, but also between rural and urban areas. In urban areas abortion is more available even in the Catholic south (Ketting & van Praag, 1985, p. 77).

Variations in the availability of abortions between the states also exist with regard to obligatory preabortion counseling. In Catholic states the authorization and financial support of counseling organizations are not determined by the demand for abortion because this would mean that nondenominational institutions such as Pro Familia would predominate; the conformity of the counseling with Catholic ideology is decisive in this case. In the greater number of Catholic states, the counseling organizations are called on to unreservedly preserve unborn life by pointing out to women ways and means of alleviating situations of distress and by positively influencing them to preserve life. The Protestant and non-denominational counseling organizations are also concerned with offering assistance. Their goal, however, is to help women make their own decisions and to respect those decisions.

It is self-evident that counseling should be available for pregnant women who are contemplating abortion, and it should emphasize the possibility of finding a solution to their real or anticipated problems in giving birth to a child. Considerable debate still surrounds the compulsion to receive counseling, to which the Federal Constitutional Court (Bundesverfassungsgericht) and others gave their approval. On the one hand, the majority of women report that they personally found counseling far less unpleasant than they had expected; on the other hand, only 2.3 percent felt that counseling had presented new perspectives. About 85 percent had already decided on abortion before counseling, usually after discussion with individuals close to them (*Bericht der Kommission*, 1980, p. 142). The system of counseling and determination of indications as laid down by the judiciary and accordingly regulated in practice brought not only regional disadvantages with it but also class tensions. Given the relatively difficult access to information, the necessity of coping with complicated formalities, and finally having to defend one's own decision vis-à-vis physicians who in the last resort must make the final decision themselves—these three factors mean that upper- and middle-class women have a far greater chance of obtaining abortions than women from the lower classes or from other countries.

In order to simplify the complicated procedures that precede abortion, which women have often felt to be a deliberate provocation, the family planning organization Pro Familia has set up an experimental center in Bremen, the smallest SPD-governed Federal State. With this model all the procedural steps for abortion could be undertaken in a single institution (Amendt, 1978; Ketting & van Praag, 1985, p. 74). This center also offers advice on sex education, contraception, and guidance on partner relationships. The fierce polemic which the founding of this center caused and the financial constraints which were imposed on it prove that the opponents of abortion regard the complex preabortion procedure as a welcome hurdle which women must overcome. Nevertheless, centers of this kind have in the meantime also been founded in Hamburg and Nordrhein-Westfalen (Müller & von Paczensky, 1982).

Government Measures to Prevent Abortions

In the course of the reform dispute, nearly all parties have emphasized that it is scandalous that social hardship should be the cause for the high number of abortions in a comparatively prosperous society such as the Federal Republic. Although the Conservatives still maintain that the sacrifice which parents must make is unavoidable, they too considered an improvement in government support for families and unmarried mothers to be essential. Government aid, which to this day has been forthcoming, was one of the arguments within the Christian parties against a revocation of reform after the change of government.

The years following the new abortion legislation were marked by an economic crisis which, compared with the early 1970s, caused a decline in the employment situation and the income power of a large number of the population of West Germany and as a result led to a reduction of state aid for pregnant women instead of the unanimously favored increase.

In 1982 the Socialist-Liberal government cut back the family allowance considerably, and in 1983 the Conservative-Liberal coalition further reduced the financial aid available to working mothers during maternity leave. Meanwhile, the Conservative-Liberal government has introduced some compensatory measures, such as an increase in family allowance for the first-born child and an increase in tax-relief for children. Reasons for these new measures were the extremely low birth rate in West Germany, on the one hand, and the relatively high number of abortions among women in the eighteen to thirty age group (see table 12.4 below) on the other. The institution "Mutter und Kind—Schutz des ungeborenen Lebens" (Mother and Child—Protection of Unborn Life), founded by the government in 1984, has capital resources of 50 million Marks at its disposal and offers pregnant women in need of financial aid a child-care allowance of 600 Marks per month for a period of ten months after the birth. It also offers leave of absence for the same period of time for either the mother or father of the child. Related to this leave of absence is earnings compensation as well as a guarantee that employment will be resumed. The woman's movement criticizes the new child-care allowance, which is a substitute for maternity benefits and therefore only new for working mothers, as a means of pushing women out of professional life back into the traditional housewife role. They say that what is offered as financial aid is in reality nothing more than a premium for childbearing based on population policy (Pfarr, 1985).

Apart from the lack of effectiveness of these government measures and the aim at which they are directed, they only affect one aspect of the complex motives that women have when they seek an abortion, however important this one aspect may be in individual cases. In the latest survey approximately half of the women asked said that they were seeking an abortion on financial grounds. The survey was carried out in 1980. In the meantime financial motives have probably come to play an even greater role. Nevertheless, many other factors may lie behind this motive, as well as behind the personal reasons which two-thirds of women also claim as a motive for seeking abortion. Short-term financial assistance cannot compensate for any of these factors. The major difference between the women's and the advisers' perception of financial and personal reasons (see table 12.1) points to the almost impenetrable complexity of the motives.

The Conservatives argue that pregnant women who receive short-term government aid should therefore no longer require an abortion on grounds of social hardship and only grave social distress should be regarded as a legitimate motive for abortion.

The Continuing Conflict in the Post-Reform Period

The Supreme Court's reform raised abortion out of the dangerous obscurity of illegality, reduced the rate of complications during abortions from 14 percent to 1.8 percent, and lessened the need for women seeking abortion to go abroad, as shown in table 12.2.

The reform fell short of the expectations of almost all women's groups at the beginning of the 1970s. With this law and its implementation the German Federal Republic, along with Belgium and Switzerland, has become one of the industrialized countries with the most restrictive abortion regulations. It is therefore not surprising that the fundamental conflict continues to exist as a matter of public controversy. The dispute intensified once again after 1980 with the establishment of the Conservative-Liberal government from which the opponents of reform expected an amendment. But the Christian parties were now reluctant to introduce a review of the reform because the Liberals (FDP), who had previously demanded the indication regulation, were now their coalition partner and there was therefore no prospect of a majority in favor of amendment.

DEMOGRAPHY OF ABORTION

The annual publication of the number of legal abortions, and above all of pregnancy terminations on the grounds of social hardship, repeatedly causes the polemic against the present abortion laws to flare up again. Data on the number of abortions by reasons and by marital status are presented in table 12.3.

Whereas the number of legal abortions was bound to increase with the beginning of legislation, if only because abortions were illegal before and took place abroad, nevertheless there is still a tendency for the number of abortions to increase on the grounds of social hardship. Another factor to consider is that physicians only register about half of the abortions performed at the Statistiches Bundesamt (Office for Statistical Information), although they are legally required to register all pregnancy terminations. Many physicians obviously feel pressured by the negative attitude of a great number of local authorities and medical associations, as well as by the permanent criticism not only of the social indication but also of the medical indication, which is considered to be 50 percent higher than it should be. Nonetheless, the attitude of a large number of physicians seems to have changed since the beginning of the 1970s. When in May 1986 the board of the Federal Association of Physicians submitted a resolution against the social indication, an overwhelming majority of delegates voted against it.

Depending on the political location, the high number of abortions on grounds of social hardship is used as proof that this law is abused by women, by physicians, and by nondenominational advisory institutions. The high numbers are further proof of the lack of effective assistance; they show that the present law only serves to deprive women of their right to assert themselves and that all the various legitimate motives for abortion cannot possibly be included in the indication regulation.

Compared with the year 1980 (87,702) the number of abortions in 1984 (86,298) fell by 1.6 percent. The number dropped further to 83,538 in 1985, a 3.2 percent decrease. In 1984 there were 147.9 abortions for every 1,000 live— and still—births as shown in table 12.4. In 1980, 72.2 percent of abortions compared with 84.0 percent in 1985 were obtained on grounds of social hardship. From 1981 the general medical indication was determined to a lesser extent but in the same proportion as the social indication rose. A little less than two-thirds of abortions were granted to women between eighteen and thirty years of age. The extreme lack of adequate sexual education in the Federal Republic must be partly responsible for the large number of women—36.2 percent—under twenty-five years of age who sought pregnancy termination. Meanwhile, the progress achieved in the field of sexual education in the 1970s has suffered a setback because of pressure from those who demand the most restrictive abortion regulations. Clearly, the majority of abortions take place in the first three to four months (see table 12.4), which is approximately the period for which the SPD-FDP coalition ultimately wanted to dispense completely with government intervention.

The largest group of women to have abortions in 1984 and who had never been pregnant before was the twenty to twenty-five age group, followed by the group under twenty years of age as shown in table 12.5. Altogether, the number of women with children who had an abortion in 1984 is greater than the number of women without children. In cases of women with children, they usually have two children already and they belong to the thirty to thirty-five age group; this group is closely followed by women with one child. Here the age group twenty-five to thirty predominates slightly.

SUMMARY

For over a century in Germany abortion was severely punishable by law. During this period there were few changes in the law, and these were only valid for a few years, as, for example, the stricter penalties for abortion under the fascist regime. A reform of the abortion law was not achieved until the period between 1970 and 1976, and then only amidst the greatest controversy. The opinions of both reformers and reform opponents produced unprecedented controversy in the FRG. The result of the reform was the indication regulation, on the grounds of which abortion within a certain period was legitimized. As a result of the new legislation, the number of illegal abortions and abortions obtained abroad was reduced, but women seeking pregnancy termination are still dependent on the physician's final decision and feel discriminated against by the administrative procedures which abortion entails. Compared with almost all other industrial societies, neither the law itself nor its implementation even after reform can be considered liberal in the Federal Republic. But neither this situation nor the fact that the number of abortions in West Germany is relatively low prevents the Conservative political power from attempting to reintroduce more restrictive regulations. A generally acceptable, and therefore stable, solution to the problem of abortion as has been found in some neighboring countries is still not in sight for the Federal Republic of Germany.

REFERENCES

Alternativ-Entwurf eines Strafgesetzbuches. Besonderer Teil (Straftaten gegen die Person). Tübingen: Erster Halbband, 1970.

Amendt, G. Abruptio inbegriffen: das Bremer Modell der Pro Familia. *Sexualmedizin*, 1978, 10, 803–810.

Arbeiterbewegung und Frauenemanzipation 1889–1933. Neudrucke zur sozialistischen Theorie und Gewerkschaftspraxis, Bd. 3, Frankfurt/M., 1973.

Bericht der Interministeriellen Arbeitsgruppe zum Programm "Schutz dese ungeborenen Lebens." Bundesministerium für Jugend, Familie und Gesundheit, Bonn, 1983.

Bericht der Kommission zur Auswertung der Erfahrungen mit dem reformierten §218 des Strafgesetzbuches. Unterrichtung durch die Bundesregierung, Deutscher Bundestag 8. Wahlperiode, Nr. 3630 vom 31.03.1980.

Bundesverfassungsgerichts-Urteil zum Normenkontrollverfahren wegen verfassungsrechtlicher Prüfung des Fünften Strafrechtsreformgesetzes (Fristenregelung) vom 25.02.1975, in: Bundesverfassungsgerichts-Entscheidungen, Bd. 39.

Evangelisch-katholische Stellungnahme "Das Gesetz des Staates und die sittliche Ordnung" vom 10.12.1970. In K. Panzer (Ed.) Schwangerschaftsabbruch §218 StGB. Dokumentation, Köln, 1972.

Gesetzentwurf der Bundesregierung vom 15.05.1972, Deutscher Bundestag 6. Wahlperiode, Drucksache Nr. 3434.

Gesetzentwurf der SPD/FDP-Fraktionen vom 21.03.1973, Deutscher Bundestag. Wahlperiode, Drucksache Nr. 375.

Heinsohn, G., Knieper, R., & Steiger, O. *Menschenproduktion. Allgemeine Bevölkerungslehre der Neuzeit*. Frankfurt/M., 1979.

Joachimsen, L. (Ed.). *§218—Dokumentation eines 100jährigen Elends*. Hamburg, 1971.

Ketting, E., & van Praag, P. *Schwangerschaftabbruch. Gesetz und Praxis im internationalen Vergleich*. Tübinger Reihe 5. Tübingen: Deutsche Gesellschaft für Verhaltenstherapie, 1985.

König, U. *Gewalt über Frauen. Berichte, Reportagen, Protokolle zur Diskussion über den Paragraphen 218*. Hamburg, 1980.

Kraiker, G. *Politischer Katholizismus in der BRD. Eine ideologiekritische Analyse*. Stuttgart, 1972.

———. *§218—Zwei Schritte vorwärts, einen Schritt zurück. Eine Analyse der Reform des §218 in der Bundesrepublik Deutschland*. Frankfurt/M., 1983.

Mehrheitsurteil—Bundesverfassungsgerichtsurteil [Decree of the Constitutional Court—majority decision], 1975, p. 6.

Müller, R., & von Paczensky, S. Familienplanungszentrum Hamburg. *Sexualpädagogik und Familienplanung*, 1982, 2, 15.

Noelle, E., & Neumann, P. (Eds.). *Jahrbuch der öffentlichen Meinung*. Allensbach, 1956.

Noelle-Neumann, E. (Ed.). *Jahrbuch für Demoskopie 1968–1973*. Allensbach, 1974.

von Paczensky, S. (Ed.). *Wir sind keine Mörderinnen! Streitschrift gegen eine Einschüchterungskampagne*. Reinbek, 1980.

Pfarr, H. *Das Erziehungsgeld ist nicht viel mehr als eine Gebärprämie*. Frankfurter Rundschau, Nr. 66, 19.03.1985.

Pressedienst des Bundesministers für Jugend, Familie und Gesundheit. Nr. 125a, 30.08.1985.

Pro Familia, Bremen (Ed.). *Wir wollen nicht mehr nach Holland fahren. Nach der Reform des §218 — Betroffene Frauen ziehen Bilanz*. Reinbek, 1978.

Protokolle des Bundestagssonderausschusses für die Strafrechtsreform, 6. Wahlperiode, 74.–76. Sitzung vom 10.–12.04.1972, Bonn: Deutscher Bundestag, 1972.

Stellungnahme der Deutschen Bischofskonferenz zur Strafrechtsreform vom 25.09.1970. In J. von Münch (ed.). Aktuelle Dokumente: Abtreibung. Reform des §218. Berlin/New York, 1972.

Stellungnahme des Kommissariats der deutschen Bischöfe zum Schutz des werdenden Lebens vom 23.06.1971. In J. von Münch (Ed.) Aktuelle Dokumente: Abtreibung. Reform des §218. Berlin/New York, 1972.

Stellungnahme des Weltärztebundes zur therapeutischen Schwangerschaftsunterbrechung vom 22.08.1970. In J. von Münch (Ed.). Aktuelle Dokumente: Abtreibung. Reform des §218. Berlin/New York, 1972.

Strafrechtsänderungsgesetz vom 15.05.1976. In Bundesgesetzblatt I vom 21.05.1976.

Verordnung zum Schutz von Ehe, Familie und Mutterschaft vom 09.03.1943. In Reichsgesetzblatt 1, p. 169.

Wort der Deutschen Bischofskonferenz zur Verantwortung für das menschliche Leben vom 23.09.1971. In K. Panzer (Ed.). Schwangerschaftsabbruch §218 StGB. Dokumentation. Köln, 1972.

Table 12.1
Women's and Advisers' Perception of Reasons for Abortion

Problem Category	Pro Familia and AW*	Protestant Organisations	Pro Familia and AW*	Protestant Organisations
Personal	35%	28,2%	47%	58,3%
Partner Relationship	10%	12,8%	17,7%	16,7%
Family Relationship	5%	12,8%	5,9%	5,6%
Professional	0%	2,6%	0,0%	0,0%
Financial	50%	41,0%	29,4%	19,4%
Miscellaneous	0%	2,6%	0,0%	0,0%

*Arbeiterwohlfahrt (Welfare association for the working class).
Source: *Bericht der Kommission*, 1980, p. 64.

Table 12.2
Pregnancy Terminations in the Federal Republic of Germany and Terminations Obtained by German Women Abroad Between 1977 and 1984

Year	German Federal Republic	Netherlands	England+ Wales
1977	54,309	55,000	1700
1978	73,548	44,000	1200
1979	82,788	32,000	700
1980	87,702	26,000	600
1981	87,535	21,000	500
1982	91,064	18,000	250(estimated)
1983	86,529	14,571	
1984	86,298	11,602	

Source: Statistisches Bundesamt (Office of Statistical Information).

Table 12.3
Number and Percentage of Abortions by Indications and Marital Status, FRG, 1978–84

Year	Total	General medical	%	Psychological	%	Eugenic	%	Criminal	%	Social hardship	%	Unknown
1978	73548	16872	22,9	3686	5,0	2731	3,7	104	0,1	49252	67,0	--
1979	82788	17261	20,8	2802	3,4	3162	3,8	101	0,1	58412	70,6	--
1980	87702	17655	20,1	2444	2,8	3053	3,5	101	0,1	63289	72,2	1160
1981	87535	15382	17,6	2524	2,9	2797	3,2	103	0,1	65466	74,8	1263
1982	91064	15214	16,4	2339	2,6	2306	2,5	74	0,1	70000	76,9	1131
1983	86529	12354	14,3	1861	2,2	1843	2,1	58	0,1	69436	80,2	977
1984	86298	10356	12,0	1242	1,4	1600	1,9	93	0,1	71904	83,3	1103

Indications (ground for granting abortion)

Indications by Marital Status, 1984

	Total	General medical	%	Psychological	%	Eugenic	%	Criminal	%	Social hardship	%	Unknown
Single	37104	2775	7,5	453	1,2	365	0,9	64	0,1	33015	89,0	428
Married	42559	6860	16,1	657	0,1	1132	1,1	25	0,1	33340	78,3	545
Widowed	469	86	18,3	7	0,1	6	0,1	-		364	77,6	6
Divorced	4759	477	1,0	94	2,0	66	1,4	4	0,1	4075	85,6	43
Unknown	1407	158	11,2	31	2,2	27	1,9	-		1110	78,9	81

Source: Statistisches Bundesamt (Office for Statistical Information).

Table 12.4
Number of Abortions by Age and Gestation Weeks, FRG, 1984

Age	Total	Indications (ground for granting abortion)					
		General medical	Psychiatric	Eugenic	Criminal	Social hardship	Unknown
under 15	97	7	1	1	3	83	2
15 - 18	3406	246	41	9	8	3065	37
18 - 25	27713	2124	316	342	38	24565	328
25 - 30	19261	1978	266	311	15	16460	231
30 - 35	16724	2271	277	335	13	13607	221
35 - 40	11347	1946	205	279	6	8766	145
40 - 45	5808	1325	108	220	6	4085	64
45 and over	1043	306	14	70	1	644	8
unknown	899	153	14	33	3	629	67
Gestation weeks							
under 6	4241	540	90	53	4	3520	34
6 - 8	27934	2952	285	408	33	23995	261
8 - 10	31498	3787	462	462	31	26397	359
10-13	14016	1820	210	315	11	1185	175
13-23	1106	226	66	196	1	600	17
23 and over	22	4	-	17	-	1	-
Unknown	7481	1027	129	149	13	5906	257

Source: Statistisches Bundesamt (Office for Statistical Information).

Table 12.5
Number of Abortions by Age of Women and Previous Pregnancies, 1984

	Total	Age Group								
		under 15	15 – 20	20 – 25	25 – 30	30 – 35	35 – 40	40 – 45	45 and over	unknown
No previous pregnancy	31957	96	8194	12855	6260	2698	1061	404	86	303
1 ...	17670	1	1018	5215	4915	3440	1986	803	118	174
2 ...	17477	-	165	2421	4367	4891	3400	1760	274	199
3 ...	9850	-	27	852	2197	2964	2189	1267	245	109
4 ...	4818	-	4	260	925	1463	1260	710	130	66
5 ...	2238	-	3	71	364	696	644	372	66	22
6 ...	1130	-	-	23	147	309	384	198	57	12
7 ...	548	-	-	6	44	152	192	124	27	3
8 and more	610	-	-	5	42	111	231	170	40	11
No live-birth	38667	97	8902	15337	8256	3735	1430	549	109	352
1 ...	17183	-	520	4107	4701	3973	2487	1016	153	181
2 ...	18826	-	81	1868	4399	5661	4132	2118	333	234
3 ...	7256	-	7	330	1416	2197	1900	1109	225	72
4 ...	2645	-	1	51	372	779	787	511	108	36
5 ...	1008	-	-	11	84	250	368	223	57	15
6 ...	419	-	-	3	25	93	145	110	38	5
7 ...	184	-	-	1	7	25	63	73	12	3
8 and more	110	-	-	-	1	11	35	54	8	1

13

GREECE

Anthony C. Comninos

Οὐδέ γυναιμί πεσσόν φθόριον δώσω
I will not give to a woman a pessary to cause abortion
—Hippocratic Oath

HISTORICAL DEVELOPMENT OF ABORTION POLICY

The problem of the unwanted pregnancy, whether legitimate or illegitimate, is by no means a contemporary one; it has existed throughout the ages, even though traditions, philosophies, and religions have varied. Almost all races and societies throughout history, civilized or otherwise, have practiced or described methods of controlling family size. Among the philosophic principles of Plato is to be found the suggestion that the population of the Republic of Athens should be restricted to no more than 5,040 citizens. Aristotle stated that "if it should happen among married people, that a woman who already had the planned number of children to become pregnant then before she feels foetal life the child should be driven out of her" (Georgoulis, 1962).

The long list of abortifacients mentioned in ancient Greek writings, as well as descriptions concerning the interruption of unwanted pregnancies, indicate that the Ancient Greeks were familiar with the act of abortion as well as its complications (Littré, 1839–61). Hippocrates, whose writings were rooted in the authority of observed facts, gives a clear description of septic abortion, which can be considered relevant even today. Hippocrates, whose teaching focused more on the diseased person than the disease, and tended more toward prevention than toward therapy, strongly objected to the idea of interrupting a pregnancy without any medical reason and condemned the practice of abortion. His philosophical, medical, humanistic, and ethical principles on abortion are embodied in the Hippocratic oath.

The attitude of the Greek societies in the following eras was of necessity influenced by their heritage and culture, particularly by the religious philosophies and moralities taught by the ancient Hebrew and Christian churches. In Greece the large majority of the population belongs to the Greek Orthodox Church which is the official church of the country. The Greek Orthodox Church believes that every human being, including the fetus, is entitled to life. The church considers abortion a crime and therefore prohibits and condemns the act of abortion as well as the avoidance of procreation.

The Rule of Elvira's Synod (early fourth century) forbids a woman who has induced abortion from receiving Holy Communion until the last moment of her life. According to the 21st Rule of Fasting John, a married woman who takes measures to prevent conception is barred from receiving Holy Communion for three years.

In 1937 Archbishop Chrysostomos and fifty-five metropolitans issued a circular letter on birth control in which they strongly protested and condemned every contraceptive device and the act of abortion, viewing them as threats to family life and as evil acts against God's will and rebellion against His laws (cited in Fagley, 1967; Moore-Cavar, 1974; Potts & Bhiwandiwala, 1979).

The only exception to the forced interruption of a pregnancy which the Greek Orthodox church accepts is risk of the pregnancy to the mother's life. The church also prohibits the use of drugs to induce abortion as well as any other measure to prevent conception. The church condones only abstinence and the "rhythm method."

A special church committee created to review the problem of abortion issued an encyclical stating that "the murderous trend of inducing abortion is threatening the nucleus of the family unit and endangering the survival of our union." It urged believers against "this destructive trend" and asked them to "realize that children in a family are a blessing not a curse" (Trichopoulos, 1975; WHO, 1983). Religious tenets have inevitably influenced legislation concerning induced abortion and have had a strong effect on the education, ethical teaching, and moral beliefs of the Greek physician.

The Greek Penal Code, articles 304 and 305 (legalized by law as No. 1492 on 17 August 1950), is very strict and spells out heavy penalties for persons involved in the practice of abortion, namely:

1. The person who performs abortions is punishable by imprisonment of up to ten years.

2. The person who performs an abortion is punishable by imprisonment of six months if the abortion is done with the consent of the pregnant woman and imprisonment up to ten years if done without her consent.

3. The woman who induces her own abortion or accepts the illegal interrution of her pregnancy is punishable by an imprisonment of up to three years.

The Greek Penal Code accepts only the following exceptions:

1. The pregnancy presents a threat to life or serious or permanent damage to the health of the pregnant woman.

2. The pregnancy is the result of rape or the woman is under the age of fifteen.

3. The pregnancy is the result of incest.

Until World War II, the Greeks were firmly opposed to induced abortion without a purely medical reason; therefore, it was rare in Greece and was practiced illegally under unsanitary conditions by unregistered midwives and some physicians known as abortionists. The morbidity and mortality rate of illegal abortion was considered high, although there are no official data available.

CURRENT STATUS OF ABORTION

After World War II, both public and physicians' attitudes changed. The practice of abortion in Greece was progressively taken over by the medical profession and became more frequent. The Greeks' attitudes were apparently changed by the long years of war and occupation by armies of various religions and moral beliefs, and by the long years of poverty and famine. The massive tourism following the war also influenced public attitudes to abortion. Year after year, the abortion law became more flexible in its application, despite the official heavy penalties, and year after year the number of induced abortions performed in the country increased, soon assuming epidemic proportions.

In 1978 the law on abortion was liberalized. The activities of the Family Planning Association of Greece and other organizations contributed positively to this change. The new law No. 821 of 13 October 1978 expanded the reasons for allowing therapeutic abortion and permitted the practice of abortion: (a) up to the twentieth week of pregnancy for eugenic reasons, namely, when a prenatal examintion and fetal screening using the most modern diagnostic methods available, reveals severe abnormalities in the fetus; and (b) up to the twelfth week of pregnancy in cases where the pregnant woman suffers severe mental health disturbances as certified by a state hospital psychiatrist. Abortion for social or economic reasons continued to be forbidden. As most of the abortions performed were illegal, there was no law covering parental consent in the case of minors.

However, the 1978 revision of the abortion law did not change the existing situation. The number of illegal abortions performed every year in the country continued to be rather high, a fact that led to the conclusion that the law needed to be changed once again so that it would correspond with the existing reality.

The provisions for granting abortions were further revised in July 1986 and put forth in the new abortion law No. 1609. Interruption of pregnancy is now permitted: (a) up to the twenty-fourth week in the case of fetal abnormalities; (b) if there exists an unavoidable danger to the woman's life or to her physical or mental health, and if this condition is certified by an appropriate specialist; (c) up to the nineteenth week of the pregnancy if the pregnancy resulted from rape, seduction of a minor girl, or incest (the minor must obtain the written consent of her parents or guardian); and (d) before the completion of the twelfth week of pregnancy on the request of the woman.

There is still a high rate of illegal abortions performed in Greece because the public is not fully aware of the new abortion law. In addition, the public is very poorly informed about the basic facts of reproduction as well as about the dangers of illegal abortion. There is also not enough education imparted in the benefits of the modern methods of contraception.

DEMOGRAPHY OF ABORTION

Today induced abortion is performed almost exclusively by practicing physicians in well-organized private clinics and hospitals under proper medical conditions. Accidents and complications from induced abortion are rare, and when they take place they are not recorded as such. Therefore, the exact number of induced abortions performed every year in Greece is not known because abortions are not registered and, consequently, no official statistical data on abortion are available. However, based on a number of reliable surveys on abortion published in medical journals, it is estimated that roughly 200,000 to 250,000 induced abortions are performed every year (Comninos, 1966, 1968, 1981; Papaevangelou, 1981; Trichopoulos et al., 1975a; Valaoras, 1969, 1974). This figure exceeds the number of live births, which is estimated to be approximately 150,000 per year: there is more than one induced abortion for every live birth (Comninos 1966, 1968, 1981; Danezis, 1981; Papaevangelou, 1981; Siampos & Valaoras, 1971; Trichopoulos et al., 1975).

Several statistical surveys on abortion reveal that 35 to 45 percent of the women in Greece reported they had at least one induced abortion in the past (Comninos, 1966, 1968, 1981; Papaevangelou, 1981; Roukas, 1979; Trichopoulos et al., 1975; and Valaoras, 1969a, 1969b). Abortion is performed more frequently in Athens and in other cities than in rural areas (Valaoras, 1969, 1974). Women living in urban areas have easier access to abortion than those living in rural areas, especially those living in small and remote villages and islands. In addition, the religious and moral taboos and traditions are still strong in villages and islands, and people living in these areas tend to have large families.

Reproductive rates are higher in rural than in urban areas (National Statistical Service of Greece, 1980a, 1980b, and 1981; Papadakis, 1981; Papaevangelou & Roumeliotou-Karayanni, 1979; Papaevangelou & Tsimpos, 1983; Siampos, 1969, 1973; Symeonidou-Alatopoulou, 1980; and Valaoras, 1974). It has also been found that induced abortion in Greece is more frequent among married women (49 percent) than single women (28 percent). The percentage of abortion increases progresively with parity and reaches the rate of 54.3 percent in women with two or more children (Comninos, 1966, 1968, 1981; Roukas, 1979; Valaoras, 1969a, 1969b).

Induced abortions have also increased among young girls and teenagers (table

13.1). One survey of university students gives a figure as high as 25 percent (Roukas, 1979). Education plays a considerable role in the abortion rate. The rate was found to be 36 percent for university graduates, 32 percent for women with college education, 55 percent for high school graduates, 53 percent for those with elementary school education, and 63 percent for illiterate women (Kavvos, Kapellakis & Comninos, 1983).

The abortion rate was also found to be related to income. The estimated rate of abortion was 35 percent for women with low income, 46 percent for women with average income, and 57 percent for those with high income (Kavvos, Kapellakis & Comninos, 1983).

ABORTION AND FERTILITY REGULATION

Greece has a declining population growth rate, with reproductivity continuously decreasing after the Second World War (Papadakis, 1981; Papaevangelou & Tsimpos, 1983; Siampos, 1969; Symeonidou-Alatopoulou, 1980; Valaoras, 1974). The population increase is estimated to fall to zero by the mid-twenty-first century unless the government institutes a pronatalist policy (Papadakis, 1981; Papaevangelou & Tsimpos, 1983; Siampos, 1969). Greece's Crude Birth Rate (CBR) dropped from 52 percent in the nineteenth century to 21 percent in the twentieth (Siampos, 1973) and even lower to 15 percent, in 1979 (Papaevangelou & Tsimpos, 1983; Valaoras, 1974).

The Total Fertility Rate (TFR) increased slightly in 1975 and reached a level of 2.37 live births per woman but subequently dropped again (National Statistical Service of Greece, 1980a, 1981). See table 13.2.

The decline in population has caused much official concern and the state has introduced a number of laws to support growth. For example, the government awards maternity benefits such as marriage payments, employment protection for pregnant women, working hours privileges, salary allowances, maternity leaves, tax deductions, children's financial allowances, and public nurseries. Several specific measures were also taken to support large families of three or more children.

At the same time no new measures to restrict abortion have been introduced, even though it is clear that induced abortion contributes substantially to Greece's declining population growth rate. The other contributing factor is the extremely large wave of emigration from Greece, mostly among young men and girls of marriageable age (Symeonidou-Alatopoulou, 1980; Trichopoulos et al., 1975; Valaoras, 1960; WHO, 1983). It is estimated that illegal abortions are responsible for approximately 40 percent of the recent decline in the birth rate (Trichopoulos et al. 1975; Valaoras, 1960).

The importance of informing and educating the public on family planning and on modern fertility regulation methods has been repeatedly emphasized by the Family Planning Associations of Greece. However, all three of Greece's Family Planning Associations were established by private initiative, and their functioning family planning centers are limited in number and are poorly organized. Therefore, their programs to disseminate information and to educate the public on family planning is restricted.

Until recently, modern aspects of fertility regulation methods were not included in medical school curricula; consequently, knowledge of modern contraception was limited even among practicing physicians.

Greece has no special legislation dealing in the importation and distribution of contraceptives. There is no law prohibiting the sale and use of mechanical (barrier methods) contraceptives. However, oral contraceptives are not manufactured domestically, and those imported until 1980 were advertised not as contraceptives but as menstrual regulators. In Greece oral contraceptives may be adminstered only by prescription, and only physicians may insert IUDs. These regulations are rarely enforced, however.

Until 1980, 0.8 percent of women aged fifteen to forty-four years used the pill and 0.7 percent the IUD (Danezis, 1980, 1981). All other contraceptives that have been introduced have limited use, with the exception of condoms which are promoted to prevent sexually transmitted diseases. The more popular contraceptive method in the country is coitus interruptus, the rate varying from 43 percent in urban to over 60 percent in rural areas, and the least favorite is voluntary sterilization—0.1 percent (Comninos, 1981; Danezis, 1980, 1981; Kavvos et al., 1983; Valaoras, 1969a, 1969b).

A more recent survey (Kavvos et al., 1983) on fertility regulation methods used by women living in the area of Athens, where more than one-third of the total population resides, showed that only about 10 percent of women use the pill and the IUD—8.2 percent using the pill and 2.4 percent the IUD. The survey also revealed that 43.5 percent used coitus interruptus and 20 percent used no contraception. Consequently, the induced abortion rate was found to be high (42 percent).

In 1980 the government introduced family planning legislation (Law No. 1036 on 15 March 1980) to combat the extremely high number of illegal abortions. The law mandates that the state disseminate information on the practical application of family planning. An Advisory Committee was established in the Ministry of Social Services to deal with questions of family planning policy. The goal can only be achieved when official educational programs and training seminars have been organized with the cooperation of the Family Planning Associations to educate physicians, midwives, and social workers in modern methods of fertility regulation and family planning.

The state's objective is to provide a good service for contraceptive advice and to encourage the public to make responsible use of the many safe contraceptive methods now available. Recently, the government announced that it is studying the problem of induced abortion with the intention of reforming existing legislation and liberalizing abortion.

MEDICAL SEQUELAE OF ABORTION

A statistical survey on the long-term consequences of abortion in 1,000 patients complaining of secondary infertility revealed a history of induced abortion in

530 (53 percent). In 475 of these 530 (78 percent), infertility was directly related to anatomical damage of the genital system following the induced abortion; 342 patients (64.5 percent) had no living children, while 188 (35.4 percent) had only one child. Of the childless women, 70 percent were rendered infertile following only one abortion (Comninos, 1973). See table 13.3.

All abortions mentioned were performed by practicing gynecologists under proper medical conditions. This suggests that even when performed under proper medical conditions, induced abortion can cause secondary infertility due to anatomical damage of the genital tract (Comninos, 1973).

SUMMARY

The practice of induced abortion is widespread in Greece, despite religious sanctions and legal restrictions.

The abortion law in Greece is strict in its formulation but flexible in practice. The reform of the law in 1978 permitting abortion for eugenic and severe mental health reasons did not influence the high illegal abortion rate. At present only abortionists, who charge high fees to perform the operation, benefit from this situation.

The exact number of induced abortions performed every year is not known because abortions are not registered. The estimated figure is 200,000 to 250,000, which corresponds to a rate of more than one abortion for every live birth.

Abortions in Greece are performed by gynecologists under proper medical conditions; therefore, operative and postoperative complications are rare. However, the long-term complications of induced abortion cannot be avoided. Tubal obstruction, endometrial adhesions, and cervical incompetence are common long-term complications leading to infertility. Induced abortion of the first pregnancy can render a woman permanently infertile (Comninos, 1973).

The question that remains is, Will legalization of abortions restrict the extremely high illegal abortion rate? It is doubtful that it will unless other supportive measures are taken together.

The public should be informed about the hazards of abortion and the benefits of proper family planning as well as the correct use of modern and safe contraceptive methods. Abortion should not be regarded as a method of fertility regulation but merely as a means of interrupting an unwanted or unplanned pregnancy. Sex education should be introduced in schools, and Family Planning Associations should be encouraged and supported by the state to create adequate centers to cover the needs of all geographical areas of the country.

Legalization of abortion will make registration of all operations possible and allow the medical profession and the state to collect valuable information and statistical data for scientific, demographic, and economic purposes. Furthermore, it will relieve women of guilty feelings and ensure their proper treatment at reasonable prices. However, legalization must overcome a difficult hurdle: the strong objections of the church and several other religious, legal, and medical groups, as well as the moral, philosophical, and humanistic beliefs of many influential members of society.

REFERENCES

Comninos, A. C. Criminal abortion and its complications. Proceedings of the Fifth Conference of the European and Near East Region of the IPPF, Copenhagen, July 1966. Preventive Medicine and Family Planning, Hertford: Stephen Austin and Sons, 1966, 112–114.

———. The problem of illegal abortion in Greece. Inaugural Address at Opening of the New Auditorium of the Queen Elizabeth Hospital, University of Birmingham, 7 October 1968.

———. Complications of induced abortion fertility and sterility. *Excerpta Medica*, 1973, 393–397.

———. *Abortions internationally and in Greece*. Seminar on Family Planning of the Ministry of Social Services, Athens, 9–20 March 1981 (in Greek).

Danezis, J. *Current views on contraception*. Symposium of Hellenic Fertility and Sterility Society. Athens, 15 May 1980 (in Greek).

———. Report of the Family Planning Advisory Committee. 1981. (Unpublished document in Greek.)

Fagley, R. M. Doctrines and attitudes of major religions in regard to fertility. Proceedings of the World Population Conference, Belgrade, August-September, 1965, 1967, 2 78–84.

Georgoulis, K. D. *Aristotelis Stageritis*. Thessaloniki: Foundation of Macedonian Studies, 1962.

Kavvos, J., Kapellakis, J., and Comninos, A. A statistical survey of fertility regulation methods used by women of the area of Athens. First Annual Meeting of the Society for the Avdvancement of Contraception. Cairo, 5–9 November 1983.

Littré, E. (Ed.). *Oeuvre Compléte d'Hippocrate*. Paris: Bailliere, 1839–61, Vol. 7, pp. 349–353.

Moore-Cavar, Emily C. *International inventory of information on induced abortion*. International Institute for the Study of Human Reproduction. New York: Columbia University, 1974.

National Statistical Service of Greece. The population of Greece during the second half of the 20th century. *Methodology Studies*, 1980a, Athens 14 (in Greek).

———. *Monthly Statistical Bulletin*, 1980b, 25, Bd. 1 (in Greek).

———. *Statistical almanac of Greece*. Athens, 1980c (in Greek).

Papadakis, M. E. Developments and prospects of the reproductivity of the Greek population. Ph.D. Thesis, Athens, 1979 (in Greek).

———. *Family planning and population phenomena*. Seminar of the Ministry of Social Services, Athens, 9–20 March 1981 (in Greek).

Papaevangelou, G. *Family planning and the demographic problem of Greece*. Seminar on Family Planning of the Ministry of Social Services, Athens, 9–20 March 1981 (in Greek).

Papaevangelou, G., and Roumeliotou-Karayanni, A. *Principles and methods of family planning*. Athens, 1979 (in Greek).

Papaevangelou, G., & Tsimpos, K. *Social and Public Health Consequences from the*

Demographic Evolutions of the Greek Population 1960–2001. Athens: Lambrakos and Pantazidou, 1983 (in Greek).

Potts, M., & Bhiwandiwala, P. *Abortion*. Cambridge: Cambridge University Press, 1979.

————. (Eds.). *Birth control: An international assessment*. Baltimore: University Park Press, 1979.

Roukas, K. Sexual relations and induced abortions in a studying population of Athens. Ph.D. Thesis, National Capodistrian University, Athens, 1979 (in Greek).

Siampos, G. S. *Demographic evolution in Greece 1950–1980*. Athens: Ministry of Co-ordination, National Printing Office, 1969 (in Greek).

————. *Demographic evolution of modern Greece 1821–1985*. Athens, 1973 (in Greek).

Siampos, G. E., & Valaoras, V. G. *Long term fertility trends in Greece*. International Population Conference, London, 1969, IUSSP, 1971, *1*, 598–609.

Symeonidou-Alatopoulou, H. *Fertility in Greece: Some explanatory factors in recent population change calling for policy action*. G. S. Siampos (Ed.). Athens: National Statistical Survey of Greece and ECPS, 1980, pp. 65–71 (in Greek).

Trichopoulos, D., Papaevangelou, G., Danezis, J., & Kalapothakis, V. *The population of Greece*. A Monograph for the World Population Year, 1974. Paris Committee for International Coordination of National Research in Demography (CICRED), 1975.

Valaoras, V. G. A reconstruction of the demographic history of modern Greece. *Milbank Memorial Fund Quarterly*, 1960 *38* (2), 115–139.

————. Greece: Postwar abortion experience. *Studies in Family Planning*, 1969a, *1*(46), 10–16.

————. *Epidemiology of abortion in Greece*. European Regional Conference of the IPPF, Budapest, September 1969b.

————. *Urban-rural population dynamic of Greece, 1950–1955*. NSSG and Athens: National Statistical Survey of Greece and CPER, 1974.

WHO. Family planning legislation. Report on a survey. EURO Reports and Studies 85. WHO Regional Office for Europe, Copenhagen, 1983.

Table 13.1
Abortion Rate in Unmarried Students by Age, Greece, 1978

Age In Years	Percentage With Sexual Relations	Abortions Per 100 Women	Abortions Per 100 Women With Sexual Relations
18	17	0	0
19	33	6	19
20	44	9	20
21	41	14	35
22+	51	17	33
Total	40	10	25

Source: Roukas, 1979.

Table 13.2
Total Fertility Rate (TFR) per 100 Women

1960	1965	1970	1975	1978
		T O T A L		
2.277	2.297	2.337	2.365	2.261
		U R B A N		Data not
1.718	2.045	2.136	2.104	available
		R U R A L		Data not
2.179	2.568	2.628	2.948	available

Source: NSSG, 1980a, table 23; NSSG, *Monthly Statistical Bulletin*, 1981, *26* (1), tables 4 and 6.

Table 13.3
Identified Cause of Secondary Infertility in 530 Cases of Induced Abortion

Identified cause	No of cases	Percent
Uterine adhesions	162	30.56
Endocervical adhesions	15	2.83
Uterine + endocervical adhesions	20	3.77
Tubal obstruction	138	26.03
Tubal obstruction + uterine adhesions + Anovulation	17	3.24
Tubal obstruction + uterine and Endocervical adhesions	55	10.37
Incompetent cervix	45	8.49
Anovulation	33	6.22
Luteal insufficiency	6	1.13
Congenital malformation	3	0.56
Male factor	5	0.96
Unspecified	31	5.84

Source: Comninos, 1973.

14

HUNGARY

András Klinger

HISTORICAL DEVELOPMENT OF ABORTION POLICY

Until the first half of the 1950s, abortion was illegal in Hungary as a means of birth control, having been proscribed by a law passed in 1878. Abortion was prohibited in order to protect the life of the fetus and the health of the mother, as well as to preserve the established moral order. An additional consideration was to attack the one-child system which prevailed in some regions of the country. The hospitals allowed abortion only for serious health reasons, and the annual number of these abortions did not even reach 2,000. The modern, effective methods of contraception, too, were not yet available, and there was no legal possibility of interrupting a pregnancy for birth control. As a result, by 1950 an estimated 100,000 to 150,000 illegal abortions were carried out yearly in Hungary. The law strictly prosecuted those who carried out the illegal operations; in 1953 about 1,500 persons were convicted for this activity.

The abortions were carried out under improper sanitary conditions and so were very dangerous for the pregnant woman's health and future reproductive ability. In 1953 the Ministry of Health, taking in view the protection of the females' health and the necessity of fighting against the illegal abortions, liberalized the legal conditions for abortion somewhat. At that time women were allowed to abort not only for health reasons, but in exceptional cases because of age or other important personal or family reasons. The regulations prescribed that the circumstances motivating the legality of the abortions be judged by committees established for that purpose. These committees worked in hospitals and clinics because pregnancies could be interrupted only in obstetrical and gynecological inpatient institutions. This provision remains in force today.

In June 1956 practically all conditions prohibiting abortion were removed. The official motivations for issuing this new decree were the greater protection of the females' health and the relaxation of the processes concerning the interruption of pregnancy. The 1956 amendment was necessary because, despite the 1953 decree which somewhat liberalized the authorization of abortions, the number of illegal abortions was still high. The abortion committees remained, but in 1956 they were no longer entitled to refuse applications. If the applicant insisted on the abortion, the committee was obliged to authorize it. Consequently, everyone who requested it could have the pregnancy interrupted until the twelfth week of gestation. In such a way induced abortions were authorized without conditions. The law did not change again until 1973.

LEGAL STATUS OF ABORTION

In 1973 the Hungarian government adopted comprehensive population policy measures within the framework of which the abortion law was revised with the purpose of reducing the harmful impact of induced abortions on the health of the mother and her future children. Another aim of this measure was to spread the notion that prevention rather than the interruption of the undesired pregnancy should be the means of birth control. To minimize the harmful effect of induced abortions, abortion could be performed only in certain cases and only in inpatient health institutions. The abortion committees were retained, and they were authorized to grant the abortion application only under the following circumstances:

—If it was medically motivated by health reasons of the parents or probable health reasons of the child to be born.
—If the woman was unmarried or had been separated for a long period.
—If the pregnancy resulted from a crime.
—If the pregnant woman and her husband, respectively, had no separate dwelling either privately owned or rented.
—If the woman had three or more children or had experienced three or more childbirths; or two living children and at least one further obstetrical event.
—If the pregnant female was thirty-five (the age was changed to forty in 1979) or older.

In addition, the law entitled the committee to consider the following cases on an individual basis:

—If the pregnant woman already has two living children but the viability of the child to be born from the existing pregnancy was imperiled.
—If the husband of the pregnant female was a regular soldier.
—If the pregnant woman or her husband was in prison.
—If it was motivated by other social reasons.

Induced abortions are authorized until the first twelve weeks but in the case of minors, until the eighteenth week. Two slight changes occurred in 1982 when (1) the age limit for authorizing abortions was decreased again from the earlier forty years to thirty-five; and (2) women were no longer required to ask the abortion committee for permission. For those who need special permission (e.g., the woman is thirty-five years old or older and she is not married) the chairman of the committee alone could authorize the operation.

The woman who has had an abortion is placed on the sick-list for at least two days, even if no complication develops. In most cases the woman has to pay for the operation (it is free only if authorized for health reasons or if the pregnancy resulted from a crime). When stating the amount, the reasons and circumstances are taken into consideration. The stated amount is in general 600 or 1,000 forints ($15 or $20).

ATTITUDES TOWARD ABORTION

The public did not oppose these measures, despite their restrictive character. An overwhelming majority, 60 percent, agreed with the decision restricting the authorization of induced abortions; and 20 percent believed it was necessary to revise the law during 1956–73 but considered the new rules too severe. The proportion of those who supported the unconditional authorization of induced abortions and the ratio of those who wanted abortions prohibited entirely were almost equal, 8 to 9 percent.

DEMOGRAPHY OF ABORTION

Levels, Trends, and Incidence

In 1950 fewer than 2,000 legal abortions were being carried out in Hungary yearly, and these were based solely on strict health reasons.

Following the issuance of the 1953 regulations, the number of induced abortions began to increase until in 1955 the figure reached more than 35,000. After the unconditional authorization of the operation was introduced in 1956, abortion operations became more widespread, totaling 83,000 in 1956 and 162,000 in 1960. In 1959 the number of induced abortions exceeded the number of live births in Hungary for the first time. After this date the number of abortions continued to grow, while the number of births decreased. In 1964 there were nearly 1,400 induced abortions per 1,000 live births, which also meant that nearly 60 percent of all pregnancies were being interrupted. In the following years the number of abortions continued to increase, reaching 207,000 operations in 1969. The statistics did not begin to drop until the use of oral and intrauterine contraceptive devices began to spread significantly in Hungary.

During 1956–73 abortions were granted on demand. Whereas 9 percent of applications for an abortion in 1957 cited health motives, at the beginning of the 1970s this proportion was down to only 2 to 3 percent. All other applicants named social reasons. (See table 14.1.)

In 1974 after the 1973 restrictions on abortions were adopted, the number of induced abortions fell by about 40 percent, and in 1975 fewer than 100,000 operations were carried out. In the following years the slow decline continued and at the beginning of the 1980s the annual figure had dropped to about 80,000.

The population policy measures adopted in 1973 greatly facilitated the prescription of oral contraceptives. Until 1973 only gynecologists could prescribe the pill, but after that date all physicians could do so. In 1975, 18 percent of the seventeen to forty-nine year old females and in 1982, 32 percent took the pill; the application of intrauterine devices also became more popular. In 1974 the state increased its contribution to the costs of childrearing with the purpose of stimulating the birth rate. As a result, the population did grow significantly, though only temporarily.

In 1981, 78,000 pregnancies were aborted in Hungary, which indicates that there were 35 induced abortions per 1,000 fifteen to forty-four-year-old females, 57 per 1,000 live births, and 36 induced abortions per 100 pregnancies. The above ratios have not changed materially in recent years.

After enactment of the 1974 regulation, 12 percent of women requested abortion for health reasons and over 25 percent because of their unmarried status. The proportion of those who applied for an abortion on the basis of the number of their children and of their age, respectively, was nearly the same—20 to 21 percent—while the share of those requesting an induced abortion for lack of a separate dwelling (where parents with their children can live alone) was much lower, that is, 13 percent. In 1979 the age limit for the authorization of the operation was increased from thirty-five to forty years. Thus, in these years number of applicants for age reasons decreased and the number of those who mentioned the number of their children as a motive grew considerably. In 1982, when the age limit for the authorization was again stated as thirty-five years, the earlier proportions returned, and the two most frequently cited reasons (22 to 23 percent) were unmarried status and number of living children, respectively. After this, age was mentioned most frequently, 18 percent; 15 percent requested an abortion for health reasons. Lack of a separate dwelling as a motivation represented 10 percent of the cases in 1982. See table 14.2.

Demographic Characteristics

The incidence of induced abortions differs by settlement type, educational level, and occupation. These differences developed under the impact of the contraception practice characteristic of the given subpopulation, differences in fertility norms, religion, and so on.

As is true of most other countries, abortions are more frequent in Hungary's urban than rural areas. In 1982 there were 44 induced abortions per 1,000 fifteen to forty-four year olds in the capital, 35 in the provincial towns, and only 31 in rural areas. The above order is valid for all age groups. The fertility sample surveys also show these proportions. A thousand married women under forty years of age had on the average 0.82 abortions in the course of their lives in the capital, 0.60 in the provincial towns, and 0.47 in rural areas.

With regard to socioeconomic groups, among the cooperative peasantry 41 of the 100 married women, 53 among nonmanual workers, and 63 among the working class had abortions in their lifetimes. In the case of nonmanual workers, nearly every second pregnancy ended in abortion. By 1980 each third pregnancy of the working-class women and each fifth pregnancy of the peasant women was interrupted.

A comparison of statistics by educational level shows that women of a higher educational level gave birth to their children mainly at twenty to twenty-four years of age, which means that a smaller proportion of them have abortions. However, among lower educated women childbirth begins at a younger age and ends in a later stage of the reproductive period of life; therefore, both for those under twenty and over twenty-five years of age abortions occur less frequently than among the more highly educated.

Age, Parity, and Marital Status

In Hungary abortion as a birth control method has been and remains characteristic of all the groups of females of childbearing age. The overwhelming majority of women of reproductive age are married, and the greatest number of induced abortions falls in their group. In the 1960s about 80 percent of all induced abortions were carried out among married women; 15 percent among single women; and 4 percent among widowed and divorced women. In 1973 there were 70 induced abortions per 1,000 married women of childbearing age and 45 per 1,000 unmarried women. The relatively frequent incidence of abortion among unmarried women indicates not only the tolerant attitude of the society toward extramarital sex, but also shows that the question of the contraception of young persons is not solved.

The restriction of authorization for induced abortions—introduced in 1973—affected mainly married women. Therefore, after 1974 the abortion rate decreased most among married women. In 1975 there were 35 induced abortions per 1,000 married females of childbearing age, which decreased to 30 in 1981. The rate of abortion among unmarried women also decreased from 45 in 1973 to 38 in 1975, to 33 induced abortions per 1,000 unmarried women of childbearing age in 1981.

Despite the drop in rates, the overwhelming majority—70 percent—of induced abortions is still performed among married women. But the share of single females has grown to 20 percent from 15 and that of ever married women to 9 percent of total abortions.

Interruptions of pregnancy were and are most frequent among twenty- to thirty-five-year-old women. However, while in the 1960s the incidence of induced abortions was three times as high in this age group as among the younger and older females, respectively, by the second half of the 1970s these differences decreased. In 1982 there were 41 induced abortions per 1,000 twenty to twenty-nine year olds and 26 per 1,000 fifteen to nineteen year olds. See table 14.3.

Abortion as a birth control method can be used both for the child spacing and child limitation. In the 1950s and 1960s, for example, 30 percent of the pregnancies of childless women, more than half the pregnancies of one-child mothers, and more than three-quarters of the pregnancies of women with two and more children were aborted. As noted earlier, one purpose of the 1973 population policy measures was to encourage women to use contraceptive devices for birth control rather than abortion which can be detrimental to the mother's health and future fertility. These policy measures increased the availability of modern contraceptives and somewhat restricted abortions which affected mainly those groups of married women who had not yet completed their families. In keeping with the government policy, the number of abortions decreased substantially, first among the childless and one-child women. In 1971 there were 28 induced abortions per 1,000 childless married women, and this rate further declined to 6 in 1980.

Among the one-child mothers, this ratio fell from 96 to 25, that is, in the above two groups the incidence of induced abortions declined by nearly 25 percent. Among the two-children mothers, the incidence of abortions fell by more than 50 percent, and among those with three and more children, 60 percent (table 14.4).

The ideal policy would be to reserve abortion as "the last means" among the birth control methods, allowing it only when contraception devices fail. If used as a separate, primary form of birth control, the repeated abortions can damage the health of the woman and impair her future pregnancies. Hence, study of the incidence of repeated abortions is important.

REPEAT ABORTION

As a result of the free abortion system introduced in Hungary in 1956, many women have undergone repeat abortions. By the mid–1960s more than half of all abortees had already had an abortion. By 1970 one-quarter of the aborting women had one, 15 percent had two, and 17 percent had three or more induced abortions; only about 40 percent were experiencing abortion for the first time.

Beginning in 1973—under the impact of the wide availability of modern contraceptives and the somewhat restricted abortion decree—the number of repeat abortees decreased, although the percentage of first-time abortees was still small at the start of the 1980s—50 percent. The greatest change was the decrease in the proportion of females who had three or more abortions previously.

By 1980, 75 percent of women who had undergone repeated abortions had no other obstetrical events such as childbirth between the two abortions. This was much the same situation in 1970. However, while in 1971 the interval between two successive abortions was less than two years in nearly half the cases, in 1981 this figure had declined to one-third.

The incidence of repeated abortions is different by demographic characteristics, too, because induced abortions are more frequent among older females of a lower educational level who have more children. By marital status it is the most frequent among women who were married at earlier ages, and naturally, its incidence is higher among the older women.

DURATION OF PREGNANCY, METHOD, AND COMPLICATIONS

An abortion is an operation, and the incidence of its early complications depends not only on the skill of the person performing the operation, but also on the duration of pregnancy and the method used.

In present-day Hungary abortion may be authorized within the first twelve weeks of pregnancy (except, as noted, for minors who may apply through the first eighteen weeks). Hence, 99 percent of abortions are performed in the first trimester and in two-thirds of the cases in the fifth through eighth weeks.

Until 1975 the only abortion method used in Hungary was dilatation and curettage (D&C). In recent years vacuum aspiration and intra-amnial filling up have been adopted to some extent. In 1982, the D&C method was used in 86 percent of abortions; vacuum aspiration in 11 percent, and intra-amnial filling up in 2 percent. Only 1 percent of the induced abortions was carried out with other methods.

With regard to the operative and the early complications of abortions, in Hungary special comparative studies have been performed to demonstrate the complications of the two most popular methods. The study proved that vacuum aspiration produced fewer complications than the D&C method. In operations using vacuum aspiration, only 7 of 1,000 operations ended in an operative complication, whereas the ratio was 13 per 1,000 in the case of intervention through curettage. With both methods bleeding and shock were the most frequent complication. Incidence of a perforated uterus was also less frequent with vacuum aspiration (0.8 per 1,000 compared to 2.5 per 1,000 with curettage) and only in those cases when evacuation of the uterus was not appropriate after use of the vacuum and subsequently a curettage was also performed.

The incidence of early complications was also less frequent with vacuum aspiration (1,059 per 1,000 abortions) than with curettage (1,284 per 1,000 operations). The ratio of bleeding (681) and inflammation of the lower pelvis (13.4) was only somewhat lower in the case of vacuum aspiration, but complications requiring repeated curettage—after termination of the abortion—were half as frequent in the case of vacuum aspiration.

During an abortion, a woman's reproductive organs may be injured, which may later lead to the abnormal implantation of the fertilized ovum, producing a midterm spontaneous abortion and a premature birth. Another complication may be secondary sterility. In the rare case, abortion can cause death; in recent years there have been 2 to 4 deaths per 100,000 abortions. Of great concern is the effect of repeated abortions on subsequent premature births and lower birth weight in newborns (under 2,500 g.). Among first-time abortees, fewer than 10 percent of subsequent births were premature, compared to 13 percent among those with one previous abortion and more than 20 percent among those who had undergone three or more previous abortions.

ABORTION AND FERTILITY REGULATION

In Hungary the decline in live births and the decrease in fertility have been observed since the 1880s. Hence, conscious birth control has been practiced there for a long period of time. Until the 1960s the so-called traditional methods of birth control were used, for example, coitus interruptus, the rhythm method, and vaginal irrigation. In addition, mechanical devices—mainly the condom, the vaginal pessary, and the cervix cap—and difference chemical contraceptives were applied.

As mentioned above, the interruption of unwanted pregnancies became legal only in the second half of the 1950s, and since that date conditions relating to the authorization of abortions have changed.

The fertility and birth control sample surveys show the birth control practices of women of childbearing age since the second half of the 1950s. Some favorable changes are apparent. Whereas in 1958 only one-fifth of all fifteen- to thirty-nine-year-old married women controlled the number of their pregnancies with a contraceptive method, in 1966 one-third and in 1977 more than half of them did so. Another important change is that already in 1977 only a slight share of the females (3 percent) never used any contraception, always resorting to abortion to terminate their pregnancies. In 1958, 17 percent of the women relied exclusively on abortion for fertility control. A large percentage of nonusers consists of the youngest females who used no contraception between marriage and the birth of their first child, but after it they will most probably use contraception. This is not valid for the 1958 data when the proportion of the female population who did not control the number of their childbirths was over 20 percent. This suggests that besides the young married women many other females did not try to affect the number of their children either by contraception or by abortion.

In 1971 nearly 75 percent of women who had undergone an induced abortion did not use any contraception, and by 1981 this proportion had fallen to 40 percent. Nearly half of the regular users became pregnant because they had temporarily stopped using contraception, while the other half got pregnant while using contraception, mainly because they used less efficacious methods (table 14.5).

Data from the fertility and birth control surveys also prove that during the last three decades women's attitudes toward contraception have changed considerably, in conformity with the nation's new population policy. The proportion of females using contraception increased from 59 percent to 73 percent during 1958–77. (The remainder consisted of pregnant women, those desiring a child, sterile women as well as nonusers.) Thus the proportion of those needing contraception but not using it decreased greatly. Another major change occurred in the late

1960s: use of modern contraceptive methods, notably oral contraceptives and intrauterine devices, became widespread, replacing the natural methods that had been used formerly. Thus, the regulations terminating the free abortion system and restricting the availability of induced abortions influenced the population to turn to other birth control methods. See table 14.6.

Despite such conditions, the number of abortions in Hungary remain high when viewed internationally. The effort to decrease abortions can be aided by expanding the birth control possibilities (e.g., using sterilization, which is not legal at present) and introducing new methods (e.g., reversible contraception of males). It will also be necessary to alter public attitudes toward abortion as a birth control method. The induced abortion should be considered a "last solution"and not a routine method of birth control.

Data Source

Hungary's system of authorization of abortions affords exact, detailed statistical data. In the 1956–70 period the statistical reports of the institutions carrying out abortions allowed the collection of relevant comprehensive data. Each application for abortion contains an individual data record which, besides the data on pregnancy, also registers demographic and other characteristics of women. One copy of these records is housed in the Hungarian Central Statistical Office.

The fertility sample surveys represent another source of abortion data; these surveys also contain the fertility history of the woman interviewed. However, in such retrospective surveys women do not acknowledge their abortions. Some women intentionally conceal this event, while others actually forget the number of abortions they have had. It is estimated that the women declare 50 to 60 percent of their induced abortions in the fertility surveys.

SUMMARY

Abortion was made legal in Hungary in 1956, thereby introducing the free abortion system. Before then, pregnancies could be terminated only for health reasons in health institutions. At the same time, illegal abortions were carried out in great number, often under poor health conditions. After legalization, the number of abortions grew rapidly, until the beginning of the 1960s when more abortions than live births were recorded. Many women considered induced abortion a primary birth control method, and they resorted to it not only to limit their families after the birth of the desired number of children, but also to time the birth of children. The complications and by-effects of abortion influence the health of the mother and the fetus to be born, and repeat abortions may also affect a woman's reproductive ability.

Because of these considerations, in 1973 the government began to restrict abortions somewhat. This effort coincided with the simplification of prescribing contraceptives. In the following years the incidence of induced abortions decreased by more than half, and the different modern forms of contraception proliferated. Since 1973 the 50-percent decrease in abortion has stabilized. In order for it to decline further, other methods of contraception and birth control will have to be expanded and attitudes toward abortion will have to be changed. Abortion should not be considered a routine method of birth control; rather, it should be used only as a last resort.

REFERENCES

Hungarian Central Statistical Office. *A vetélések adatai, 1971* [Data on abortions, 1971]. Statisztikai Kiadó Vállalat, 1973.

———. *A vetélések adatai, 1972–1973* [Data on abortions, 1972–1973]. Statisztikai Kiadó Vállalat, 1975.

———. *A vetélések adatai, 1974–1975* [Data on abortions, 1974–1975]. Statisztikai Kiadó Vállatat, 1977.

———. *Az 1977. és 1974. évi termékenységi, családtervezési és születés-szabályozási vizsgálatok eredményei* [Results of the 1977 and 1974 Fertility Family Planning and Birth Control Surveys]. Statisztikai Kiadó Vállalat, 1978.

———. *Terhességmegszakitások és spontán vetélések adatai, 1976–1977* [Data on induced and spontaneous abortions, 1976–1977]. Statisztikai Kiadó Vállalat, 1979.

———. *Terhességmegszakitások és spontán vetélések adatai, 1978–1979* [Data on induced and spontaneous abortions, 1978–1979]. Statisztikai Kiadó Vállalat, 1981.

———. *Egységes szülészeti adatszolgáltatási rendszer: terhességmegszakitások és spontán vetélések adatai, 1980–1981* [Unified obstetrical data supply system: Data on induced and spontaneous abortions, 1980–1981]. Statisztikai Kiadó Vállalat, 1983.

Hungarian Demographic Research Institute. *Népesedési kérdésekkel kapcsolatos közvéleménykutatás* [Public opinion survey concerning demographic questions]. Statisztikai Kiadó Vállalat, 1976.

Tietze, C., & Henshaw, S. K. *Induced abortion: A world review, 1986* (6th ed.). New York: Alan Guttmacher Institute, 1986.

Table 14.1
Births and Abortions, Rates and Ratios, 1950–84

Years	Number of		Ratio of		
	live births	induced abortions	live births per 1000 15–44 year old females	induced abortions per 1000 15–44 year old females	induced abortions per 1000 live births
1950	195 600	1 700	89.0	0.77	8.7
1951	190 600	1 700	86.8	0.77	8.8
1952	185 800	1 700	84.7	0.78	9.2
1953	206 900	2 700	94.6	1.2	12.9
1954	223 300	16 300	102.4	7.5	72.9
1955	210 400	35 400	96.8	16.3	168.2
1956	192 800	82 500	88.8	38.0	427.7
1957	167 200	123 400	78.6	58.0	737.9
1958	158 400	145 600	74.9	68.8	918.9
1959	151 200	152 400	71.5	72.1	1008.0
1960	146 500	162 200	69.1	76.5	1107.2
1961	140 400	170 000	65.5	79.4	1211.1
1962	130 100	163 700	59.8	75.2	1258.4
1963	132 300	173 800	59.7	78.4	1313.6
1964	163 100	184 400	58.9	82.2	1395.2
1965	133 000	180 300	59.1	80.1	1355.3
1966	138 500	186 800	61.4	82.8	1348.6
1967	148 900	187 500	66.0	83.1	1259.5
1968	154 400	201 100	68.2	88.8	1302.3
1969	154 300	206 800	68.0	91.1	1340.2
1970	151 800	192 300	66.2	83.8	1266.5
1971	150 600	187 400	65.4	81.3	1244.2
1972	153 300	179 000	66.4	77.5	1168.1
1973	156 200	169 700	67.7	73.5	1085.9
1974	186 300	102 000	80.9	44.3	547.7

Table 14.1 (Continued)

1975	194 200	96 200	84.7	41.9	495.3
1976	185 400	94 700	81.1	41.5	510.9
1977	177 600	89 000	78.1	39.2	501.7
1978	168 200	83 500	74.4	37.0	496.8
1979	160 400	80 800	71.3	35.9	503.6
1980	148 700	80 900	66.8	36.3	544.0
1981	142 900	78 400	64.4	35.3	548.8
1982	133 600	78 700	60.3	35.5	589.1
1983	–	78 600	63.8	35.5	–
1984	–	82 200	69.1	37.1	–

Source: Hungarian Central Statistical Office, 1981, p. 14; *Demográfiai évkönyv 1982* [Demographic yearbook 1982], Statisztikai Kiadó Vállalat, 1983, pp. 16, 36; Tietze & Henshaw, 1986; and partly unpublished data.

Table 14.2

Females Having Undergone an Induced Abortion by Reasons for Authorization

Years	health	Reasons for authorization						total
		the female does not live in marriage	lack of separate dwelling	3 living children or 2 living children + obstetrical event	the female is older than 40 years	other	unknown	
1957	8.6			91.4				100.0
1960	5.2			94.8				100.0
1970	3.0			97.0				100.0
1973	2.4			97.6				100.0
1974	11.6	26.9	12.8	20.4	20.9	6.1	1.3	100.0
1975	10.6	27.1	13.4	20.2	21.2	7.2	0.3	100.0
1980	15.6	25.1	11.6	29.8	6.2	10.4	1.3	100.0
1981	15.8	25.3	10.5	29.5	6.6	12.3	0.0	100.0
1982	15.1	23.7	9.6	22.9	18.0	10.7	0.0	100.0

Source: Hungarian Central Statistical Office, 1981, p. 14; *Demográfiai évkönyv 1978, 1981, 1982* [Demographic yearbook 1978, 1981, 1982], Statisztikai Kiadó Vállalat, 1979, 1982, 1983, pp. 162, 168.

Table 14.3
Interruptions of Pregnancy by Age Groups

Years	-19	20-24	25-29	30-34	35-39	40-X	Total
				Per cent			
1957	4.4	22.0	29.1	24.6	15.6	4.3	100.0
1960	5.1	22.2	28.5	24.1	15.5	4.6	100.0
1970	9.5	24.7	27.0	20.7	13.4	4.7	100.0
1973	10.0	24.6	23.2	20.0	14.0	8.2	100.0
1974	10.9	22.5	20.4	19.9	16.9	9.4	100.0
1975	10.6	23.5	21.0	19.6	16.9	8.4	100.0
1980	10.1	18.4	24.2	21.2	16.6	9.5	100.0
1981	10.3	18.0	24.5	22.1	16.5	8.6	100.0
1982	10.4	17.3	24.3	22.3	17.1	8.6	100.0

Interruptions of pregnancy per 1000 females of respective age

Years	-19	20-24	25-29	30-34	35-39	40-X	Total
1957	15	76	95	77	58	17	58
1960	22	102	127	102	63	29	76
1970	40	121	142	114	72	24	84
1973	38	98	106	95	69	38	74
1974	27	53	55	56	50	27	44
1975	26	50	52	52	47	23	42
1980	26	39	44	45	37	23	36
1981	26	39	43	43	36	20	35
1982	26	40	43	43	38	20	36

Source: Hungarian Central Statistical Office, *Demográfiai évkönyv 1980, 1981, 1982* [Demographic yearbook, 1980, 1981, 1982], Statisztikai Kiadó Vállalat, 1981, 1982, 1983, pp. 161, 181; and unpublished data.

Table 14.4
Ratio of Interruptions of Pregnancy of Married Females per Number of Children

Years	Number of live-born children					Total
	0	1	2	3	4-x	
Interruptions of pregnancy per 1000 married females with the respective number of children						
1971	28	96	108	107	131	94
1973	25	83	95	98	116	83
1980	6	25	42	63	70	35
1981	6	24	41	61	68	35
1982	6	25	40	61	70	35
Interruptions of pregnancy per 100 obstetrical events						
1971	31	54	83	79	69	55
1973	30	54	80	77	67	52
1974	23	25	65	66	56	35
1975	21	22	64	66	52	33
1980	19	23	70	72	59	35
1981	19	23	68	72	55	35
1982	20	25	70	73	58	37

Source: Hungarian Central Statistical Office, unpublished data.

Table 14.5
Women Who Underwent an Induced Abortion, by Their Previous Attitude Toward Contraception

Years	Regular users	Non-regular users	Non-users	Total
1971	18.9	9.7	71.4	100.0
1975	25.7	14.9	59.4	100.0
1980	39.8	13.1	47.1	100.0
1981	39.5	16.0	44.5	100.0
1982	41.6	17.6	40.8	100.0

Source: Hungarian Central Statistical Office, *A vetélések adatai 1971, 1975* [Data on spontaneous abortions, 1971, 1975], Statisztikai Kiadó Vállalat, 1973, 1977, pp. 81, 83, and partly unpublished data.

Table 14.6
Proportion of Married Females Using Contraception by Main Methods of Contraception

Main method of contraception	1958	1966	1977
Coitus interruptus	52.3	63.1	23.4
Other natural methods	15.0	9.1	5.2
Condom	21.2	17.5	5.9
Intra-uterine devices	–	0.1	13.1
Other mechanical methods	4.8	5.8	1.1
Oral contraceptive	–	0.2	49.3
Other methods	6.7	4.2	2.0
Total	100.0	100.0	100.0
Of 100 females			
users	59	67	73
non-users	41	33	27

Source: Hungarian Central Statistical Office, *Népesedés-népesseg* [Main demographic features of population], Statisztikai Kiadó Vállalat, 1982, p. 30.

15

INDIA

Prema Ramachandran

HISTORICAL DEVELOPMENT OF ABORTION POLICY

India is the world's largest secular democracy with an estimated population of 784 million. In spite of substantial inputs into maternal and child health and family planning over three decades, India still has a high birth rate (35 per 1,000) and maternal mortality rate (4 per 1,000) (*National Health Policy Statement*, 1982; *Pocket Book*, 1976). It has been reported that septic abortion is the cause of 20 to 30 percent of all maternal deaths in India (Baskar, Rao, 1980; Chandrasekhar, 1974).

Since the 1950s, there has been a growing concern over the problem of illegal induced abortion leading to high maternal morbidity and mortality. It was suggested that liberalization of abortion laws might lead to significant reduction in illegal abortion and a perceptible decrease in maternal morbidity and mortality rates. However, realizing that the liberalization of abortion laws has implications other than maternal health status impinging on socioeconomic, legal, moral, and religious aspects of life, the government of India felt that the issue had to be thoroughly investigated from all these angles before attempts were made to modify the existing legal provisions.

The government set up a study committee in 1964 to obtain information on (1) the prevalence of induced abortion in the country; (2) the health consequences of illegal induced abortion; (3) views of major religious groups in the country on induced abortion; (4) the opinion of the general population and professionals regarding liberalization of abortion laws; (5) the legal implications of such liberalization; (6) health personnel and infrastructure needs to cope with increasing demands for medical termination of pregnancy (MTP) following liberalized abortion laws; and (7) the health and fertility consequences of liberalizing MTP.

In India even birth and death records are not accurate. Under these circumstances, it was very difficult, if not impossible, to obtain reliable data on the incidence of spontaneous and induced abortions. The committee reviewed all available information and came to the conclusion that in India every year 6.5 million abortions take place (2.6 million spontaneous and 3.9 million induced) (*Report of the Committee*, 1967). Other investigators have arrived at essentially similar figures regarding the prevalence of induced abortion in India (International Planned Parenthood, 1974). The committee also concurred with the then available estimates that 20 to 30 percent of all maternal deaths were due to complications following illegal abortion. The committee expressed the hope that if MTP laws were liberalized, there might be substantial reduction in maternal morbidity and mortality.

The views of the Hindu, Muslim, Christian, and other religious groups on liberalization of induced abortion were ascertained. None of the religions favored induced abortion on demand. Except among Catholics, however, the consensus among the other religious leaders suggested that liberalization of MTP along the lines suggested by the committee might not be against the doctrine of these religions; subsequently, several publications confirmed this (Chandrasekhar, 1984; Mallick, 1974; Tahir, 1977).

A keen debate arose among professionals regarding the health hazards that would follow liberalized MTP laws. Some held the view that liberalized abortion laws might not result in any significant reduction in illegal abortions. Others felt that the physician's role was to save, not destroy, life, and opined that if MTP laws were liberalized, the physicians who did not want to do MTP should be exempted from performing it. However, the majority favored liberalized abortion laws and participated in the attempts to define and provide infrastructure and facilities for providing MTP services as a part of Maternal Child Health (MCH) activities in their institutions (Chandrasekhar, 1974; Mallick, 1974; *Report of the Committee*, 1967).

Opinion surveys among women suggested that the demand for abortion existend among all segments of the population. Women knew about persons and places where illegal abortions were being performed and utilized these services. Many felt that if safe abortion could be provided in hospitals, they would take advantage of it (Chandrasekhar, 1974; Mallick, 1974; *Report of the Committee*, 1967).

The committee reviewed all these findings and recommended liberalization of MTP laws. After several consultations between the Ministry of Health, Family Planning, and the Ministry of Law, the first Medical Termination of Pregnancy Act was introduced in 1969. It was emphasized that the major factor leading to liberalization of the abortion laws was the desire to decrease morbidity and mortality resulting from illegal induced abortion and rapid succession of unwanted pregnancies in women and that abortion should not be considered a method of regulating fertility. Abortion services were, therefore, to be provided under MCH care with the help of MCH personnel. Guidelines for recognition of hospitals where MTP services could be provided and physicians who could provide MTP services were laid down.

LEGAL STATUS OF ABORTION

The Medical Termination of Pregnancy bill was enacted in 1971 and went into operation on 1 April 1972. The act permits termination of pregnancies by a registered medical practitioner when the length of pregnancy does not exceed twelve weeks or by two medical practitioners acting together when the length of pregnancy exceeds twelve weeks but does not extend beyond twenty weeks. Termination of pregnancy beyond twenty weeks is not permitted.

Termination of pregnancy could be done if the medical practitioners believed that continuation of the pregnancy involved (1) risk to the life of the pregnant woman or risk of injury to her physical or mental health; or (2) a substantial risk that if born the child could suffer from physical or mental abnormalities as to be seriously handicapped.

Continuation of pregnancy is assumed to constitute a grave injury to the mental health of the pregnant woman, if the pregnancy has resulted from rape or from failure of any contraceptive method used either by the woman or by her husband for the purpose of limiting the number of children. Furthermore, in deciding whether continuation of pregnancy would involve risk to the physical or mental health of the pregnant woman, Indian law permits some consideration of the pregnant woman's actual or reasonably foreseeable condition. Thus, Indian law is quite liberal and is in consonance with the health and demographic needs of the nation.

DEMOGRAPHY OF ABORTION

Levels, Trends, and Incidence

Soon after the liberalization of MTP, the health services started a long-term program of training medical officers and equipping clinics for MTP. Initially, it was speculated that the demand for abortion might be so great as to outstrip the existing service facilities. However, the available data suggest that the demand for MTP has not been overwhelming.

In 1972, 24,000 MTPs were recorded; by 1977, the cumulative total had risen to 278,073 (*Facts and Figures*, 1978). By March 1979, 312,800 MTPs (the MTP rate being 2.3 per 1,000 women aged fifteen to forty-four and the abortion ratio 12 per 1,000 pregnancies) and by March 1981 388,400 MTPs had been performed (an MTP rate of 2.7 per 1,000 women aged fifteen to forty-four and an abortion ratio of 21 per 1,000 pregnancies) (*Family Welfare Programme*, 1981). The total number of abortions stood at 518,608 in March 1984 (*Family Welfare Programme*, 1985).

These figures suggest that, unlike other Asian countries such as Japan and Korea, India's liberalization of MTP laws was not followed by a marked increase in MTP over the next decade (Hong & Tietze, 1979; Tietze, 1983). This might be due to several reasons. In India, MTP facilities are readily available in large metropolitan cities, both in private hospitals and in government hospitals. MTP servies are available, though not as readily in most of the rural towns. But even in urban areas overcrowding of hospitals, lack of personal rapport, fear that the confidentiality of MTP might be compromised, and, in some cases, a long waiting time between request for MTP and actual performance of procedure do interfere with better utilization of available MTP facilities.

Facilities for MTP are yet to reach the rural areas where 80 percent of the Indian population reside. According to the statistics available from the Ministry of Health, until 1981, 3,000 physicians had been recognized for performing MTP and 6,200 physicians had been trained in MTP techniques. However, only 1,600 of these physicians are working in Public Health Clinics (PHCs). In spite of organized attempts to provide MTP facilities for PHCs, so far only 10 percent of all PHCs have been equipped for performing MTP (*Family Welfare Programme*, 1981). Because of exigencies in service and personnel, many PHCs possess the equipment needed for MTP but do not have a doctor trained in MTP and vice-versa. Lack of MTP services in rural areas might be one of the major factors responsible for the relatively low MTP rates in India.

Implementation of MTP law has been slow and geographically uneven. There are marked differences between different states in the number of institutions where MTP facilities are available. According to the official report published by the government of India in March 1978, a total of 2,615 institutions had been approved for performing MTPs. Of these, 16.7 percent were located in Maharashtra, 9.4 percent in Gujarat, and 8.6 percent in Karnataka. Uttar Pradesh, the largest and most populous Indian state, had no more than 8.7 percent institutions performing MTP (*Facts and Figures*, 1978) It is, therefore, obvious that wider population coverage is needed to ensure that women benefit from liberalized abortion laws.

Most of the private institutions, where MTPs are done, do not have secretarial assistance to maintain and periodically dispatch to the government the data on MTPs done in their institutions. It has been suggested that nearly two-thirds of all MTPs done by private practitioners go unreported to the Ministry of Health. It is, therefore, possible that underreporting might even be one of the factors responsible for the small number of MTPs reported to the Central Health Ministry.

In India the majority of MTP seekers are married parous women. Nearly 30 percent of all women undergo sterilization at the time of abortion, and another 50 percent accept reliable methods of contraception (*Family Welfare Programme*, 1985; *Report on Family Welfare*, 1978; *Report on the Collaborative Study*, 1981). The fact that the majority of abortion seekers to accept contraception might be yet another reason why MTP rates are at the current low level.

Among the reported cases of induced abortion, the majority were done for socioeconomic reasons or because of contraceptive failure (clauses 3, 4, and 5 of the MTP act) (*Facts and Figures*, 1978). Procedures for prenatal detection of fetal abonormalities require highly trained laboratory personnel and often expensive equipment. Very few women seek antenatal care early in pregnancy or have access to sophisticated tests for diagnosis of congenital malformation. As a consequence, the number of abortions performed in India on the basis of prenatal diagnosis of congenital malformation is at present extremely low. In Indian families male children are preferred, and most families want at least one male child. In antenatal clinics women with one or more girls often express their desire to find out whether the fetus is male or female, and continue the pregnancy only if it is male. Fetal sex determination after amniocentesis is a relatively simple technique. But in view of the health, moral, and demographic implications of selective abortion of female fetuses, the government of India has prohibited fetal sex diagnosis and selective MTP except in cases of sex-linked heritable disorders.

Demographic Characteristics

An insight into the profile of abortion seekers is an essential prerequisite for proper organization of abortion services. Data from numerous publications on the profile of MTP seekers and the India Council of Medical Research (ICMR) Collaborative study on sequelae of induced abortion indicate that the majority of Indian MTP seekers came from educationally and economically superior segments of the urban population (table 15.1). The majority were married women between twenty and thirty-five years of age with one or more children and who did not want another child (*Report on the Collaborative Study*, 1981). In this respect, the profile of the Indian abortion seeker is similar to that reported from East European countries and Singapore (Tietze, 1983).

Comparing the profile of MTP seekers with that of women admitted to hospitals with illegal abortion showed distinct differences between the two groups. The majority of the MTP abortion patients came from educationally and economically advantaged segments of the population from urban areas, while over three-fourths of septic (illegal) abortion cases were parous women who had no formal education and came from very poor segments of the population (*Report on the Collaborative Study*, 1981). Hence, it is obvious that even in urban areas MTP facilities have not yet reached the high-risk population who seek illegal abortions. Ways and means of carrying health education messages, including one to extend timely MTP services to these segments of the population, need be explored.

In India, the proportion of abortion seekers requiring MTP during the second trimester ranges from 10 to 40 percent in different centers. The majority of second-trimester MTP seekers were unmarried, widowed, or separated women or grand multipara coming from less educated and poorer segments of the population (*Report on the Collaborative Study*, 1981). It would appear that ignorance and inability to make a quick decision regarding termination of pregnancy might be the major causes of delay in all these cases. Lack of awareness of MTP facilities might also be one of the contributing factors.

Provision of an MTP clinic in the near vicinity might result in an increasing number of women seeking MTP in the first trimester. Health education to promote awareness of the advantages of MTP in early pregnancy is a crucial intervention.

Although the initial response among the illiterate poorer segments of population might be poor, with persistence over time this high-risk group might be persuaded to seek timely help. In spite of high morbidity rates, it is not possible either to refuse or to restrict second-trimester MTP in the hospitals because of the fear that these women might then seek an untrained abortionist and incur even greater risk in trying to get rid of an unwanted pregnancy.

REPEAT ABORTIONS

In many countries, following liberalization of MTP laws, there has been a marked increase in demand for repeat abortions (Tietze, 1983). The available meager data from India suggest that at the moment repeat abortion seekers form a very small proportion of abortion seekers, ranging from 5 to 15 percent in different regions (*Report on the Collaborative Study*, 1981). This might be mainly because the number of MTP seekers in India has remained at a relatively low level throughout last ten years. The fact that the majority of Indian abortion seekers were parous married women and nearly 75 percent of them had accepted some form of contraceptive at the time of MTP might also contribute to the relatively low repeat abortion rates.

Though small, the profile of women seeking repeated MTP is distinctive. Data from the ICMR study suggest that repeat abortion seekers are the older parous educated women from the middle-income group. Working women, be they manual laborers or members of the technical, administrative, or clerical cadre, resorted to repeat induced abortion more than housewives. Most of the repeat MTP seekers had three or more children, and the last pregnancy was terminated by MTP in at least two-thirds of the cases. Unlike the general population seeking MTP, nearly 50 percent of the repeat MTP seekers claimed they had used contraceptive measures earlier, and over one-fourth claimed the pregnancy was due to contraceptive failure (*Report on the Collaborative Study*, 1981). The number of repeat abortions might have been lower if these parous women had undergone tubal sterilization at the time of the earlier induced abortion. Since the Indian repeat abortion seeker is a married multiparous educated woman from more affluent segments of the population with previous experience in contraceptive usage, it might be relatively easy to convince these women about the dangers of repeat induced abortion and the importance of choosing adequate contraceptive measures at the time of MTP.

MEDICAL SEQUELAE OF INDUCED ABORTION

In India, over the last decade there has been an explosive increase in publications regarding the sequelae of induced abortion, indicating the concern not only of obstetricians and health personnel, but also sociologists, demographers, and psychiatrists and several other disciplines. It is difficult, however, to compile or compare these publications to find out the consequences of MTP because of the difference in methods of data collection. Realizing the need for a continued nationwide surveillance system for monitoring and evaluating the health hazards associated with MTP, so that appropriate remedial measures could be promptly initiated, the India Council of Medical Research initiated a series of studies. The report of the first of these surveys on MTP done in thirteen postgraduate teaching hospitals was published in 1981. The second survey, conducted in a larger number of institutions, has been completed and the data are being analyzed.

Data from all available sources and the ICMR study indicate that, in India, the overall incidence of complications of MTP, both immediate and delayed, was low. Hemorrhage (3.3 per 1,000), cervical injury (1.3 per 1,000), and uterine injury (3.1 per 1,000) were the most common immediate complications. The pelvic infection rate was high (26.6 per 1,000), but severe life-threatening sepsis occurred rarely (1 per 1,000) (*Report on the Collaborative Study*, 1981). The ICMR study reported a death to case rate of 68 per 100,000, with hemorrhage and sepsis as two major causes of death. Data from the study clearly demonstrated that morbidity and mortality associated with second-trimester abortion was severalfold higher than that of first-trimester abortion as shown in table 15.2.

The first ICMR survey was conducted in 1976–7. Available data from smaller studies conducted during subsequent years suggest that there might have been substantial reduction in morbidity and mortality associated with MTP. A substantial reduction in morbidity rates following MTP over time has been reported from many other countries as well. This might partly be attributable to more women seeking MTP in early pregnancy because of increasing awareness regarding the safety of early MTP. The increasing experience of physicians in MTP techniques might also play a role in the observed reduction in morbidity rates. Data from the second ICMR survey would provide some information regarding time trends in morbidity associated with MTP performed in teaching hospitals in India.

It has been suggested that termination of pregnancy prior to six weeks has many advantages and is likely to be associated with minimum morbidity. Data from the ICMR study (presented in table 15.3), however, show that the differences in complication rates between MTP done at six or eight weeks were not statistically significant. The report concludes that in the Indian context, the optimal period for MTP might be seven to eight weeks gestation (*Report on the Collaborative Study*, 1981).

Adequate cervical dilation is the crucial step for safe and successful termination of pregnancy in the first trimester. Although manual dilation is generally a safe and simple technique, it can be difficult and on rare occasions dangerous. Inadequate dilation of the cervix might be associated with excessive blood loss or incomplete evacuation of the uterus (*Cervical Dilation*, 1977; Ramachandran, 1980; *Report on the Collaborative Study*, 1981). However, rapid and excessive dilation might result in higher incidence of spontaneous abortions and premature deliveries in subsequent pregnancies (*Cervical Dilation*, 1977; Tietze, 1983). Slow dilation of the cervix using laminaria tents has been advocated by many prior to MTP. However, the fear that this procedure might be associated with the higher pelvic sepsis rate has blocked wider use of slow dilation of the cervix. Analysis of complication rates in the first-trimester abortion in relation to the method used for cervical dilation showed that in the ICMR study incidence of hemorrhage, uterine injury, and cervical trauma and pelvic sepsis rates were significantly lower in the laminaria tent group as shown in table 15.4.

One of the major problems preventing wider use of the laminaria tent was its cost. A low-cost disposable cervical dilator has been prepared, tested (Khanna, 1980), and marketed by Central Drug Research Institute in Lucknow, India, and is currently widely used in India.

The multiplicity of methods currently being investigated and the enormous number of publications in the field testify to the unsatisfactory status of the current methods of second-trimester termination. In India, over two-thirds of women requesting second-trimester MTP had two or more living children. Hysterotomy with concurrent sterilization was the most commonly used method of terminating pregnancy (43.1 percent) because the constraint that a scar on the uterus might adversely affect future obstetric performance was not present in these cases (*Report on the Collaborative Study*, 1981). Comparison of complication rates in relation to the method used for midtrimester termination showed that hysterotomy was associated with very few immediate complications. The mortality rate associated with hysterotomy (188 per 100,000) was much lower than the mortality rate associated with prostaglandins (456 per 100,000) or saline (502 per 100,000) instillation for midtrimester termination.

The low complication rates associated with hysterotomy in India were diametrically opposite to the findings reported in the Joint Program for Studies of Abortion (JPSA) where hysterotomy was associated with the highest morbidity rate among all methods used on the second-trimester MTP (Lewitt & Tietze, 1972; Tietze, 1983). The reason for the conflicting trends might range from differences in patient profiles to the gynecologist's experience in hysterotomy technique.

During the last few years, there have been reports indicating that dilatation and evacuation may be the safe method of inducing midtrimester abortion (Cates et al., 1977). Data from the ICMR study show that in India most obstetricians do not use dilatation and evacuation for termination of pregnancy beyond twelve weeks of gestation. Analysis of complication rates following dilatation and evacuation with those of hysterotomy showed that in the hands of Indian obstetricians, hysterotomy was the safer method of surgical termination.

Contraception and Abortion Sequelae

It is generally accepted that some form of contraception should be given to all women who seek MTP in order to ward off repeated MTPs. Since the majority of Indian MTP seekers had two or more children at the time of MTP, the need of concurrent contraception in this population is very high. It is essential, however, to determine whether concurrent contraceptive measures have any adverse effects on the sequelae of MTP. The ICMR study showed that at the time of the MTP 25 percent of women accepted sterilization, 27.8 percent the IUD, and 8.5 percent oral contraceptives (*Report on the Collaborative Study*, 1981). Calculation of complication rates in relation to concurrent contraception in this study showed that concurrent sterilization at the time of MTP was associated with an increase in some of the complications. However, the morbidity rates following concurrent sterilization were not higher than morbidity of MTP and sterilization done at two different times. The Indian data indicate that concurrent sterilization should preferably be done by abdominal route because vaginal sterilization was associated with a higher sepsis rate. Concurrent IUD insertion was associated with a significant increase in postabortal bleeding, but the Indian report suggested that since this is only a minor complication, concurrent IUD insertions might be carried out at the time of MTP. Concurrent contraception has two distinct advantages: (1) women are better motivated at the time of abortion to accept contraception, and (2) concurrent contraception at the time of MTP is helpful in overcoming domestic problems in parous women.

It is well documented that maternal morbidity and mortality have a definite socioeconomic gradient and that age and parity exert considerable influence on maternal morbidity and mortality rates. In the Indian study, the complication rate in MTP was calculated in relation to these factors. The prevalence of all complications, both immediate and delayed, followed socioeconomic and educational gradients; the lowest complication rates were noted in the higher income, college-educated women and the highest in low-income, illiterate women. Teenagers and women beyond thirty-five years of age, nullipara, and grand multipara had higher rates of complications. Complication rates were higher in women who had preexisting medical and/or obstetric complications and those who had undergone induced abortion earlier (*Report on the Collaborative Study*, 1981).

Sepsis following MTP is a problem that worries all obstetricians. Sulfa drugs, penicillin, tetracycline, and ampicillin were used either alone or in combination in many cases. Analysis of data from the study showed no differences in pelvic sepsis rate between those who received prophylactic antibiotic therapy and those who did not.

Long-Term Sequelae of MTP

Available global data on the long-term consequences of MTP such as secondary sterility, spontaneous abortion, premature labor, and psychological problems are conflicting (Tietze, 1983). There is very little information regarding the long-term sequelae of MTP in India. Under existing conditions in Indian cities, it is difficult to maintain long-term surveillance after MTP. The fact that nearly one-fourth of MTP seekers had undergone tubal ligation and another one-fourth had accepted the IUD prevents a full investigation of the fertility consequences of MTP. Even in studies where long-term consequences were investigated, it is difficult to arrive at any conclusion as to whether the observed effect was due to MTP or to concurrent contraception.

Because the majority of Indian abortion seekers have two or more children prior to MTP, the absence of information regarding long-term fertility consequences has not deterred Indian obstetricians from performing MTP. However, efforts are underway to assess the fertility consequences of MTP among the small but high-risk group of nulliparous MTP seekers.

Postabortion Contraception

The government of India has repeatedly emphasized that MTP should not be viewed as a method of family planning for the individual or as a method of reducing the national birth rate (Chandrasekhar, 1974). However, MTP provides an opportunity to ensure adequate contraceptive care services. Data from the ICMR study, presented in table 15.5, showed that prior to MTP over 75 percent of women had not used any form of contraception, but six weeks following MTP nearly two-thirds had accepted an effective form of contraception. With wider use of contraception, the MTP rate might be reduced. However, since both contraceptives and the people using them are subject to failure, abortion services will still be needed to cope with pregnancies due to contraceptive failure. A positive association between abortion and contraceptive use may be further strengthened if MTP services are provided as part and parcel of integrated maternal health and contraceptive care.

ILLEGAL ABORTION

One of the major reasons for liberalizing abortion laws in India was the concern over maternal mortality due to illegal induced abortion. There is very little information on the prevalence of illegal abortion in India after liberalization of MTP because it is difficult to obtain information on the incidence of illegal abortion. Several investigators have attempted to obtain data from community-based surveys, using a randomized response technique, surveys among abortion providers in rural communities, and hospital-based studies on septic abortion. The data from hospital-based surveys indicate that, over years, the incidence of septic abortion among hospital admissions has remained unaltered (Kolwani et al., 1979; Lakshmi Devi & Singh, 1981; Mathur & Rahatagi, 1981). The reason for the continued high septic abortion rates is still not clear. It is possible that legal abortion is not readily available to many women who continue to seek illegal abortion. An idea about the lack of effective utilization of MTP services may be obtained from the fact that every year only about 1 million MTPs are reported to the government, while the estimated illegal abortions are supposed to range from 4 to 6 million per year. Provision of adequate facilities and personnel to provide abortion care in rural areas is essential to lower the incidence of septic abortions in the community.

It is also possible that there might be a shift in type of persons performing illegal abortions, especially in urban areas. Unlike the traditional illegal abortionist who tends to use herbs and sticks, the quasilegal abortionist might be using uterine instruments to perform invasive procedures. This might lead to higher sepsis rates and contribute to the continued high prevalence of septic abortion.

Data from the ICMR study suggest that the sepsis rate is not low even in legal abortion (about 2.5 percent). Thus, legal MTP might also be contributing at least in part to the septic abortion admissions in the hospitals.

It is also possible that legal and illegal abortion might attract different kinds of women. All available data suggest that women currently making use of hospital facilities for MTP come from educated middle-income families in urban areas. Available information on the demographic profile of septic abortion cases admitted in hospital indicates that a large proportion of these cases were rural, poor, illiterate women. In addition, the small high-risk group of widows, single women, divorced, or separated women who had become pregnant might suffer secret abortion rather than legal abortion in the hospitals.

Provision of MTP facilities, both in urban and rural areas, and health education to promote awareness of the availability of safe legal abortion might be an essential prerequisite for reducing the prevalance of septic abortion in India.

SUMMARY

The government of India liberalized the laws governing medical termination of pregnancy in 1972, with a view to reducing illegal abortion and consequent maternal morbidity and mortality. Under this act, MTP could be done (1) if continuation of the pregnancy involved risk to the life of the pregnant woman or risk of injury to her physical or mental health; or (2) if a substantial risk existed that if the child were born, it would suffer from physical or mental abnormalities so as to be seriously handicapped. Most of the MTPs in India are done under the first provision.

The available data suggest that implementation of MTP laws in India has been slow and geographically uneven. According to figures available from the government of India, only about 1 million MTPs are performed annually, even a decade after liberalization of MTP laws. It is estimated that currently 6 million illegal abortions are performed annually in India. It would appear that liberalization of MTP has not yet resulted in significant reduction in illegal abortions.

In India, the majority of MTP seekers are educated, married, parous women between twenty and thirty years of age from urban middle-income group families. Second-trimester abortion seekers form 10 to 40 percent of MTP seekers. The majority of second-trimester MTP seekers are unmarried or widowed women or grand multipara from indigent, illiterate segments of the population. Repeat abortion seekers account for fewer than 10 percent of MTP seekers in India. Repeat abortion seekers were predominantly parous, educated working women from urban middle-income group families. In contrast, women admitted with complications of illegal septic abortions were illiterate parous women from poorer segments of urban or rural population. It is, therefore, obvious that existing

MTP facilities are either not available or not utilized by the population segments that seek illegal abortion.

The overall complications following induced abortions were quite low. However, midtrimester terminations were associated with higher morbidity and mortality rates. Data from the Indian study indicated that seven to eight weeks of gestation might be the optimal period for MTP. Use of laminaria tents for slow cervical dilation was associated with significantly lower complication rates. Contrary to the findings in other studies, hysterotomy with sterilization had the lowest complication rate when compared with all other methods of midtrimester MTP. Concurrent initiation of contraception at the time of MTP was not associated with any significant increase in complication rates. The Indian studies also demonstrated the existence of a readily identifiable high-risk group among abortion seekers who might need and benefit from intensive care by experts.

Data from the Indian studies suggest that it is imperative to expand MTP services in urban areas and to ensure provision of adequate MTP services in rural areas. Such an expansion is an essential prerequisite for achieving reductions in illegal abortion and in consequent morbidity and mortality.

Data from these studies indicate that the availability of abortion services might improve and reinforce consistent contraceptive use. The positive association between abortion and contraception might be further strengthened by providing abortion services as part of intregrated MCH and contraceptive care.

REFERENCES

Baskar, Rao K. Maternal mortality in India: A comparative study. *Journal of Obstetrics and Gynaecology, India*, 1980, *30*, 859.

Gates, W., Grimes, D. A., Schulz, K. F., and Tyler, C. W. Mid-trimester abortion by dilation and evacuation—A safe practical alternative. *New England Journal of Medicine*, 1977, *296*, 1141.

Cervical dilation—A review. Population Reports, 1977, Series F, No. 8.

Chandrasekhar, S. *Abortion in a crowded world—The problem of abortion with special reference to India*. Seattle: University of Washington Press, 1974.

————. The Hindu view on family planning and abortion. *Population Review*, 1984, *28*, 7–44.

Facts and figures on family welfare. New Delhi: Ministry of Health and Family Welfare, 1978.

Family welfare programme in India—Year Book 1979–80. New Delhi: Ministry of Health and Family Welfare, 1981.

Family welfare programme in India—Year Book 1983–84. New Delhi: Ministry of Health and Family Welfare, 1985.

Hong, S. B., & Tietze, C. *The increasing utilization of induced abortion in Korea*. Seoul: Korea University Press, 1979.

International planned parenthood federation surveys of world needs in family planning. London: IPPF, 1974.

Khanna, N. M. et al. Isaptent—A new cervical dilator. *Contraception*. 1980, *21*, 29–40.

Kolwani, B. G., and Padubidri, V. Septic abortions—5 year review. *Journal of Obstetrics and Gynaecology*, 1979. *34*, 593–597.

Konar, M., Lahiri, D., & Saha, K. Abortion mortality. *Journal of Obstetrics and Gynaecology*, India, *23*, 436–442.

Lakshmi, Devi Y. & Singh J. Increasing hazard of induced septic abortion in Manipur. *Journal of Obstetrics and Gynaeology*, 1981, *31*, 907–912.

Lewitt, S., & Tietze, C. Joint program for study of abortion—Early medical complications of legal abortion. *Studies in Family Planning*, 1972, *3*, 97–122.

Mallick, S., and Rao, K. G. Annotated bibliography on Indian studies on abortion problems. *Studies in Family Planning*, 1974, 380–426.

Mathur, V., & Rahatagi, P. Maternal mortality in septic abortion. *Journal of Obstetrics and Gynaecology*, 1981, *31*, 272–275.

National Health Policy Statement. New Delhi: Ministry of Health and Family Welfare, Government of India, 1982, 16.

Pocket Book of Health Statistics in India. New Delhi: Ministry of Health, 1976.

Prema, K. Blood loss during induced abortion. *Journal of Obstetrics and Gynaecology*, 1980, *30*, 613–616.

Report of the committee to study legalization of abortion. New Delhi: Ministry of Health and Family Planning, Government of India, 1967.

Report on the collaborative study on short term sequelae of induced abortion. New Delhi: Indian Council of Medical Research, 1981.

Report on family welfare achievements. New Delhi: Ministry of Health and Family Welfare, 1978.

Tahir, Mohamad. *Family planning—The Muslim view point*. Delhi: Vikas Publishing House, 1977.

Tietze, C. *Induced abortion: A world review, 1983* (5th ed.). New York: Population Council, 1983.

Tietze, C., & Henshaw, S. K. *Induced abortion: A world review, 1986* (6th ed.). New York: Alan Guttmacher Institute, 1986.

Uterine aspiration techniques. Population Reports, 1974, Series F, No. 8.

Table 15.1
Profile of MTP Seekers

Age (in years)		under 20	20–30	30+	
		5.6	59.9	39.5	
Marital Status	Single	Married	Widow	Divorced/ separated	
	5.4	93.0	0.8	0.8	
Education of wife	Illiterate	Primary	Precollege	College	
	19.1	25.7	40.6	14.6	
Education of husband	Illiterate	Primary	Precollege	College	not applicable
	7.1	15.1	40.7	30.4	6.7
No. of Previous pregnancies	0	1	2–4	5+	
	7.6	20.1	60.6	11.7	
No. of previous induced abortions	0	1	2+		
	93.5	5.8	0.7		
Period of gestation (in weeks)	under 6	6–12	13–16	17+	
	23.8	62.1	8.9	5.2	

Source: Indian Council of Medical Research, New Delhi, 1981.

Table 15.2
Complication Rates in First and Second Trimester MTP

Complications	First Trimester	Second Trimester
Immediate	(Rate/1000)	
Total number of cases	15133	2485
Hemorrhage	2.0	12.1^c
Cervical injury	0.7	4.8^c
Uterine injury	3.5	0.8^c
Minor complications	31.4	30.6^a
Delayed		
Total number of cases	14009	2247
Incomplete abortion	15.5	4.5^c
Pelvic infection	24.5	40.1^c
Minor complications	103.4	117.0^a
Death to case rate	26.4	321.9*

$^aP>0.05$, $^bP<0.05$, $^cP<0.01$
*Rate/1,000,000
Source: Indian Council of Medical Research, New Delhi, 1981.

Table 15.3
Complications Following Vacuum Suction at Six and Eight Weeks of Gestation

Complications	Period of Gestation	
	6 weeks	7-8 weeks
Immediate	(Rate/1000)	
Total number of cases	3233	5815
Hemorrhage	0.6	1.4*
Uterine injury	3.1	3.5*
Minor complications	47.0	31.9***
Delayed		
Total number of cases	2957	5328
Post-abortal bleeding	119.4	143.8***
Continuation of pregnancy	6.0	3.0**
Incomplete abortion	15.6	14.8*
Pelvic Infection	28.1	22.3*
Minor complications	113.6	131.9***

*$P>0.05$, **$P<0.05$, ***$P<0.01$
Source: Indian Council of Medical Research, New Delhi, 1981.

Table 15.4
Complication Rates in Relation to the Method of Cervical Dilation

Complications	Laminaria Tent	Manual Dilation
Immediate	(Rate/1000)	
Total number of cases	1747	1689
Hemorrhage	0.6	7.1[b]
Cervical injury	0.6	1.8[a]
Minor complications	4.0	55.7[c]
Delayed		
Total number of cases	1702	1490
Post-abortal bleeding	182.7	120.1[c]
Imcomplete abortion	10.6	24.8[c]
Pelvic infection	17.4	35.6[b]
Minor complications	26.4	181.9[c]

[a]$P>0.05$, [b]$P<0.05$, [c]$P<0.01$
Source: Indian Council of Medical Research, New Delhi, 1981.

Table 15.5
Contraceptive Acceptance (%) Prior to, at, and after MTP

	Prior to MTP	At the time of MTP*	At follow up*
Pill	3.7	8.5	9.0)
IUD	1.8	28.7	9.0)
Condom	15.9	-	24.6
Others	3.1	-	0.8
Sterilization	-	25.9	5.4
None	75.5	36.9	60.2
Total cases	17628	15241	5177**

*Women with previous injury/illness were not considered.
**Women who did not accept contraceptives at the time of MTP.
Source: Indian Council of Medical Research, New Delhi, 1981.

16

INDONESIA

H. Marsidi Judono, Sundraji Sumapraja, and F. A. Moeloek

HISTORICAL DEVELOPMENT OF ABORTION POLICY

Abortion has posed a major problem in Indonesia, not only for the medical and legal professions, but also for sociologists, psychologists, religious leaders, and the society at large. A large proportion of women in Indonesia consider pregnancy unwanted and seek to terminate it. This attitude represents an intricate background of social, economic, educational, and cultural factors. Those who want to induce abortion generally call on *dukuns* (traditional healers), midwives, or incompetent persons working under unhygienic conditions.

All abortions, regardless of the grounds, constitute criminal offenses in Indonesia for which all persons involved, none excepted, may be prosecuted. Nonetheless, the incidence of abortion remains constant, or may even be increasing in direct proportion to the increasing number of women who want smaller families, as is recommended by the government (Sampoerno & Sadli, 1974).

There are no official data on the incidence of abortion in Indonesia, but quite a few papers have been issued on the subject. During 1964–82, eighty-seven papers on abortion were registered in Indonesia (Utomo, Jatiputra, & Tjokronegro, 1983). Thirty-six of them covered the incidence of abortion, seventeen abortion laws, seventeen religious, ethical, and moral aspects of the problem, eleven the induction of menstruation, five family planning, and one another aspect.

This chapter seeks to present a profile on abortion in Indonesia, viewed principally from the aspects of legislation and the reform of abortion laws, epidemiology, and the links between contraception and abortion.

CURRENT STATUS OF ABORTION LAWS

Among the five nations with the world's largest population, Indonesia is the only one that has not yet legalized abortion, allowing no exceptions to its ban (Judono, 1975).

The law governing abortion is part of the Penal Code (Undang-Undang Hukum Pidana, UUHP) which was enacted on 1 January 1918 in the colonial period. It is patterned along the lines of the eighteenth-century French Penal Code (Hariadi, 1974; Soewondo, 1978). This Penal Code, and specifically the laws on abortion, have never been reformed, although many recommendations have been presented over the years. The law is based on the principles that prevailed in Dutch society in colonial times and is no longer relevant to present conditions (Soewondo, 1978).

The Penal Code dating from the colonial era (1918) consists of three books (Soesilo, 1973). The law governing abortion is found in the Penal Code Book II, Chapter XIV, articles 283 and 299, on moral crimes; and Chapter XIX, Articles 346, 347, 348, and 349 on crimes against human life. Moral offenses are dealt with in Book III, Chapter VII, Article 535. These articles do not elaborate on: (1) the meaning and definition of abortion, (2) the stages of pregnancy, (3) the nature of abortion, and (4) the grounds for abortion.

If the laws on abortion were being enforced strictly, including those governing abortion for medical indications to save the life of the woman concerned, many doctors would be prosecuted and brought to trial. In actual practice, the doctor who carries out therapeutic abortion will not be prosecuted as long as he or she is carrying out professional duties (Soedjati, 1974a). The position of a specialist being consulted by a general practitioner is precarious, however. If specialists recommend abortion, they can be prosecuted, and if they refuse to give their advice and the patient dies, they can be penalized for criminal negligence (Soedjati, 1974b).

A general practitioner is not permitted to perform surgery, except in emergency cases, when no competent surgeon is available. Thus, if a general practitioner performs therapeutic abortion through surgery, and the patient dies, he or she can be prosecuted for performing surgery, but not for performing an abortion. Abortion in itself is not a cause for prosecution.

The current laws on abortion cannot prevent women from committing *abortus provocatus*. Although no accurate and reliable statistics exist on clandestine abortions performed under unsanitary conditions by incompetent persons, based on the cases arriving in hospitals and being diagnosed as *abortus incompletus*, sometimes in critical condition, one may conclude that the incidence of abortion is quite high, resulting in unknown disease and death.

Judono (1974) has suggested that in order to reduce the incidence of clandestine abortions with their resulting complications and mortality, induced abortion should be legalized for medical indications. Beside providing legal protection for therapeutic abortion acts, the law would also prevent abuses (Budijanto, 1973). Such suggestions increased during the 1970s, especially following proposals presented by a Symposium on Abortion organized in Jakarta in 1964 by the Jakarta Chapter of the Indonesian Medical Association (IDI) and the Indonesian Society of Obstetricians and Gynecologists (Judono, 1974). Various organizations and institutions, including the IDI, the Society of Obstetricians and

Gynecologists, the Association of Women in the Republic of Indonesia, the PERSAHI (Association of Indonesian Lawyers), the Center for Criminal Research, and the Universitas Indonesia Faculty of law (Soewondo, 1978) organized symposia, seminars, conferences, and workshops.

These efforts culminated in the establishment of an interdepartmental committee comprised of representatives from the departments of Health, Justice, Religion, the Police Service, the Attorney General's Office, the Universitas Indonesia, the IDI, and the Society of Obstetricians and Gyneologists. This committee was appointed by the minister of health in January 1977, with the instruction to draft a law on abortion based on medical indications. After sixteen months, the committee presented a draft bill on Pregnancy Termination for Health Considerations, which was then presented in a seminar in Jakarta on 27–29 October 1978, organized by the Department of Health (Sumapraja et al., 1979).

Predictably, not all the parties involved agreed with these results. Some objected to the incomplete specification of medical indications, while others required the inclusion of economic indications. To this day the draft bill has not been presented to Parliament.

DEMOGRAPHY OF ABORTION

Incidence

No complete reports are available from hospitals, and the cases that come to the hospitals represent only a small fraction of the abortions that occur in the community.

Two denominators are used in computing abortion rates: number of pregnancies and number of births (World Health Organization, 1970). The number of pregnancies is obtained from the addition of abortion and pregnancy figures at the Obstetrics Department to the number of births in a given period. Some investigators compute the number of pregnancies by adding the total number of pregnancies of women having abortions up to the time the pregnancy is terminated (Effendi, 1980; Jatiputra et al., 1978; Lim, 1969; Saifuddin, Soekoprapto, & Wiknjosastro, 1980; Soetopo, n.d.,; Wiharto, n.d.). They found that the incidence of abortion at a number of hospitals from 1967 through 1980 ranged between 147 to 267 per 1,000 pregnancies, or 57 to 242 per 1,000 births (table 16.1).

According to the World Health Organization—WHO (1970), of every 100 pregnancies 15 to 20 will terminate by spontaneous abortion; we may therefore conclude that about half of these abortions have been induced abortions.

Only one report has endeavored to measure the number of women who have experienced abortions (Saifuddin & Bachtiar, 1979). A group of women selected by certain characteristics, having consultations at the Dr. Cipto Mangunkusumo Hospital, Obstetrics and Gynecology Department, in Jakarta, was randomly divided into two groups in order to determine whether they had experienced aborted pregnancies. One group (the control group) was interviewed directly, and the other (target) group was interviewed indirectly by the random response technique. The percentage in the control group which experienced aborted pregnancies was 18.7 percent. ($n = 353$); with the target group, the percentage was 32.7 ($n = 355$).

Based on a survey at eighteen hospitals (85.7 percent of all Jakarta hospitals) and twenty-two maternity clinics of hospitals (17.2 percent of all Jakarta maternity hospitals/clinics) in Jakarta, Jatiputra et al. (1978) found a rising trend in abortions, both with regard to the number of abortions and the proportion of abortions per every 100 births in the period 1972 through 1975. With the hospitals the rates were, respectively, 18.28, 19.74, 20.46, and 39.63 per 100 births, and for the maternity clinics 3.93, 5.68, 6.60, and 6.68 per 100 births in, respectively, 1972, 1973, 1974, and 1975 (table 16.2).

Karkata et al. (1979), surveying abortion cases at the Sanglah Hospital in Bali, reached similar conclusions. He also found an increase in infection cases.

Nature of Abortions

The diagnostic terms used in Indonesian surveys differed one from the other, and sometimes could not be reconciled, rendering comparisons difficult.

In 1980 surveys were conducted at the Dr. Cipto Mangunkusumo Hospital in Jakarta and the Hasan Sadikin Hospital in Bandung in order to compare the incidence of abortions, ectopic pregnancies, and *mola hydatidosa*. The results were, respectively, 25.7, 2.0, and 2.5 per 100 pregnancies at the Dr. Cipto Mangunkusumo and 24.6, 2.9, and 2.6 at the Hasan Sadikin Hospital (Saifuddin, Soekoprapto, & Wiknjosastro, 1980).

Several surveys showed the incidence of abortion by the stage at which the abortion was performed: complete (0.2 percent), incomplete (71.0–74.7 percent), incipient (15.9–11.3 percent), imminent (14.1–23.6 percent), and missed abortions (0.9 percent) (Lim, 1969; Saloheimo, Hutabarat, & Wilharas, 1973; Surya & Manuaba, 1980; Wiharto, n.d.). From the above reports it is apparent that the majority of abortion cases can be classified as incomplete abortions.

Several writers estimate that induced abortions occur in 7.9 to 35.0 percent of all abortion cases and spontaneous abortion in 64.8 to 90.2 percent of all cases (Effendi, 1980; Manuaba, 1979; Rattu, 1973; Sopacu, 1974; Surya & Manuaba, 1980).

CHARACTERISTICS OF ABORTION PATIENTS

The median age of women experiencing abortion in 1972–75 was about twenty-eight years, which reflected neither a rising nor declining tendency (Jatiputra et al., 1978). Viewed by the age distribution, the mode is the twenty to twenty-nine age group, ranging from 35.26 percent (Soetopo, n.d.) to 58.8 percent (Jatiputra et al., 1978) for all abortion cases. With regard to illegal abortions, the reported mode is the twenty-five to thirty-five age group, representing 40.16

percent of all illegal abortion cases (Rattu, 1978), or perhaps 50 percent of illegal abortion cases in the twenty-six to forty-five age group (Sopacua, Manuputty, & Wulur, 1974). Effendi (1980) found a bimodally shaped distribution, with the first mode covering the sixteen to twenty-five age group, and the second the thirty-five to forty age group. The proportion of abortion patients below the age of fifteen years is very small—only 0.1 percent of all abortion cases (Wiknjosastro, Harahap, & Wiknjosastro, 1973).

No attempt has been made to relate the age distribution of abortion cases to that of women giving birth. Affandi and Santo (1976) related the age distribution of women undergoing menstruation induction to that of the women confined at the Raden Saleh Clinic in Jakarta. They found that women giving birth are younger compared with those having menstruation inductions. Of the women giving birth, 81.7 percent are below thirty years old, while of those having menstruation inductions only 43.6 percent are younger than thirty years.

Surya and Manuaba (1980) report that a larger proportion of unmarried women have induced abortions rather than spontaneous abortions, while Rattu (1973) reports that 10.16 percent of all illegal abortion cases involve unmarried women. A larger proportion of abortion cases are from a lower socioeconomic level. Generally, the patients' husbands are farmers, farm workers, unskilled laborers, and fishermen. Only a very small proportion of abortion patients are illiterate. Generally, they have had one to nine years of education. Induced abortion patients are better educated than spontaneous abortion patients (Sopacua, Manuputty, & Wulur, 1974; Surya & Manuaba, 1980). The cause for this distinction is not clear, but it may well be related to higher awareness, and the availability of services and purchasing power.

The distribution of abortion cases by religion does not differ from the overall religious distribution of the population, with Muslim patients comprising 85 to 89 percent, Protestant 4 to 8 percent, and Catholic 2 to 8 percent of the total abortion cases.

Of the abortion cases at the Dr. Cipto Mangunkusumo Hospital in 1972–75, 52.3 percent had no to two living children, and about half (22.4 percent of all cases) had no living children. At the Pikkmi Maternity Clinic in the same period, 88.0 percent had no to two living children and about half (40.8 percent) had no living children. A high proportion were women with six or more living children (20.4 percent of all cases at the Dr. Cipto Mangunkusumo Hospital, 1972–75) (Jatiputra et al., 1978).

Wiknjosastro, Harahap, and Wiknjosastro (1974) state that 31.5 percent of the abortion cases had one to three parity, while Saifuddin, Soekoprapto, and Wiknjosastro (1980) had findings for the same parity number, with a proportion of 52.2 percent at the Dr. Cipto Mangunkusumo Hospital and 40.4 percent at the Hasan Sadikin Hospital. For all three above-mentioned hospitals, the zero parity was, respectively, 12.8 percent, 16.4 percent, and 21.0 percent, and the parity seven and over was, respectively, 8.4 percent, 18.6 percent, and 10.0 percent.

Other surveys reported the highest proportion with multiparous women (Lim, 1969; Manuaba, 1979; Surya & Manuaba, 1980).

Gestational Period

Most abortions occur at twelve weeks of pregnancy or less (Lim, 1969; Manuaba, 1979; Rattu, 1973; Saloheimo, Hutabarat, & Wilaras, 1973; Surya & Manuaba, 1980; Wiknjosastro et al., 1973). Apparently, there is no difference in the stage of pregnancy with all abortions and induced abortions.

Unwanted Pregnancies

Of the 881 abortion cases treated at the Dr. Soetomo Hospital in Surabaya, reportedly 60 percent can be categorized as unwanted pregnancies. Of those 60 percent, 23 percent had attempted to abort the pregnancies by taking medication or by massage. Also surveyed were 1,188 pregnant women being examined at the BKIA (Mother and Infant Welfare Clinics) in Surabaya, of whom 25.7 percent were unwanted pregnancies and 4.4 percent had attempted to terminate the pregnancy. It was also found that the percentage of unwanted pregnancies rose proportionally with the number of living children (Soedigdomarto, 1974).

Other surveys at the Dr. Soetomo Hospital in Surabaya, relating to 1,561 abortion cases treated between 1 June 1972 and 31 October 1973, examined attitudes toward the pregnancy (Soerjaningsih, Joedoseputro, & Soewondo, 1975). The percentage of unwanted pregnancies was 12.04 percent. Apparently, there is a distinct correlation between unwanted pregnancies and patient's age, parity status, number of living children, and youngest child's age. The motivation to abort increases with mother's age, number of living children, or occurrence of pregnancy when the previous child is younger than two years old.

Morbidity and Mortality

The mortality and morbidity rates for the abortions presented were quite limited. The figures referred only to cases coming to the hospitals, and therefore do not reflect the true situation in the communities. The cases coming to hospital obviously required care or medication. A further cause of this limitation is that the data do not cover information from all hospitals.

Abortion morbidity and mortality at the hospitals were inter alia due to action taken before the patients came to the hospital, or to action taken at the hospital, and all were affected by the patient's condition at arrival.

A number of reports have been published on patients' symptoms and signs at the first examination. The data reported for the 1,188 cases, for example, showed twenty-two cases or 1.9 percent with abortion sepsis (Lim, 1969). The surveys of 663 cases on arrival reported 66 cases (or 10 percent) with fever, hemorrhage, or shock, or uterus perforations, tetanus, or sepsis (Rattu, 1973). Of the cases coming to the hospital and suspected to be illegal abortions, the morbidity rate ranged between 6.6 and 74.2 percent (Effendi, 1980; Manuaba, 1970; Rattu, 1973; Sopacua, Manaputty, & Wulur, 1974; Surya & Manuaba, 1980).

Complications arising from vacuum suction were reportedly light. Wiknjos-astro et al. (1973) surveyed 214 cases that experienced vacuum suction and found 0.5 percent of the patients suffering adnexitis. According to Affandi et al. (1976b), 3.9 percent of the vacuum suction cases had complications, namely perforations of the uterine wall.

The reported causes of death included tetanus, septicaemia with circulation failures and renal failure, and diffuse peritonitis. Most patients arrived in critical condition. The mortality rates of abortion cases ranged between 0.17 percent and 3.36 percent (Karkata, Surya, & Duarsa, 1979; Lim, 1969; Rattu, 1973; Surya & Manuaba, 1980), the causes of death being encephalomalacia and coma; irreversible septic shock and meningitis; peritonitis; serious ilea with septic shock; and septic shock with serious icterus.

CONTRACEPTION AND ABORTION

Contraception and Occurrence of Abortions

Many of the abortion patients were using contraceptives at the time the abortion was being diagnosed. Saloheimo, Hutabarat, and Wilaras (1973) reported that of 100 cases surveyed, IUDs were found in four cases (in situ); 89 percent of the cases did not use any contraceptives. Other researchers reported several cases of spontaneous or induced abortions with IUD users, varying between 4.47 percent and 11.7 percent (Manuaba, 1979; Rattu, 1973; Surya & Manuaba, 1980). Sumampouw (1974) in Surabaya observed that 54 percent of the induced abortion cases could be regarded as contraception failures. There was no distinct difference in the proportion of contraceptive users between spontaneous and induced abortion cases. However, another investigator found that, with regard to the distribution of contraception modes, the difference was quite remarkable (Surya & Manuaba, 1980). (See table 16.3.)

Use of Contraceptives, Sterilization, and Abortion

To obtain data on the opinions of obstetricians and gynecologists on contraception, sterilization, abortion, and sex education, Sumapraja and Saifuddin (1974) sent out questionnaires to 137 respondents, of whom 80 (59 percent) responded. The results can be summarized as follows: 86.75 percent of the respondents always discussed contraception with their patients and 80.0 percent fitted IUDs. Forty-five percent of the respondents gave contraceptives to women. If IUDs actually constituted abortive devices, 37.5 percent of the respondents proposed a ban on IUDs as contraceptives, while 31.25 percent suggested that the physician's oath be amended.

Voluntary sterilization of married women who had three children, were over thirty-five years old, and had a harmonious marriage was supported by 63.75 percent of the respondents. Three respondents were opposed to sterilization on any ground. Induced abortion was approved by 82.50 percent of the respondents for ailing women, whose illness would be aggravated by pregnancy, while 50 percent of the respondents approved if the fetus was suspected of being mal-formed. In general, the respondents did not approve of abortion for teenagers with unwanted pregnancies (77.50 percent), or for unwanted pregnancies while using contraceptives (75 percent), and of abortions on request (81.25 percent).

Sex education was approved by 87.50 percent of the respondents.

Postabortion Use of Contraceptives

Menstruation induction is applied as backup for contraception (Sastrawinata, Agoestina, & Siagian, 1976). Surveys carried out at the Dr. Cipto Mangunku-sumo Hospital in Jakarta in 1975 found monthly increases in menstruation in-duction cases and a corresponding decline in confinements. The proportion of users of contraceptives among women having menstruation inductions was 79.3 percent and that of women giving birth 18.1 percent. All the menstruation induction cases had wanted to extend the interval between pregnancies but had failed, even though they were using contraceptives. Menstruation induction solved the problem for them (Affandi & Santo, 1976a). Voluntary sterilization following menstruation inductions for mothers who had their full quota of chil-dren was more acceptable than postpartum sterilization for those having their full quota of living children (Moeloek et al., 1979).

A greater number of septic abortion cases opted for postabortion contraception compared with the number of nonseptic abortions (Doodoh, 1975); according to Manuaba (1976), the septic abortion cases preferred voluntary sterilization after menstruation induction.

CONCLUSION

The population of Indonesia in 1981 numbered 148.8 million, making it the fifth largest nation in the world, after the People's Republic of China (985 million), India (784 million), the Soviet Union (268 million), and the United States (229.8 million) (Population Reference Bureau, 1981). Among these five nations Indonesia is the only one that bans abortion strictly, making no exceptions.

Like the other developing nations, Indonesia is facing a population problem, including high growth rate (2.4 percent per annum), uneven population distri-bution (60 percent of the population inhabiting the island of Java, which has only 7 percent of the total land surface area), low per capita annual income ($120), and high dependency rate. Accordingly, the government is planning to reduce the fertility by half by 1990.

The core of the population problem lies in the fertility rate. The best way to control the fertility rate is through a family planning program, but the results will not be visible immediately unless abortion is also included in a crash pro-gram, as is being done in Japan, India, Singapore, and other countries (Wi-knjosastro, Harahap, and Wiknjosastro, 1974).

Induced abortion still constitutes an illegal act under the existing laws in Indonesia. However, the incidence of abortion apparently remains constant or is ever increasing. Efforts to reform the laws have been made since the early 1970s, and are continuing to be made at present by certain circles, mainly among the medical and legal professions, by women's organizations, as well as by the government itself.

Official data on the incidence of abortions in Indonesia are not yet available; extensive data are received from hospitals but even these are incomplete. The hospital data reveal a trend toward abortions from year to year. It may be concluded that nearly half of the abortion cases refer to *abortus provocatus*, stemming from the society's increased acceptance of the small family norm in accordance with the government's recommendations.

Acceptance of effective contraceptives is increasing among those who do not want a larger number of children, and more so among those who have experienced abortion or menstruation induction.

REFERENCES

Affandi, B., & Santo, R. M. Induksi haid, effektivitas, profil sosiodemografi dan reproduksi. Naskah Lengkap Kongres Obstetri dan Ginekologi Indonesia ke III di Medan, 7–11 Juni 1976, Panitia Pelaksana Kongres. Medan, 1976.

Affandi, B., Wiknjosastro, G. H., & Santo, R. M. Pemakaian antibiotika pada "Suction Curettage." Naskah Lengkap Kongres Obstetri dan Ginekologi Indonesia ke III di Medan, 7–11 Juni 1976, Panitia Pelaksana Kongres. Medan, 1976b.

Budijanto, A. Masalah abortus provokatus dalam seminar kriminologi ke II di Semarang. *Majalah Kedokteran Indonesia*, 1973, 23–40.

Doodoh, A. Abortus incompletus 1975 (beberapa segi profil reproduksi). Skripsi, Bagian Obstetri dan Ginekologi Fakultas Kedokteran Universitas Indonesia. Jakarta, 1975.

Effendi, R. Tinjauan beberapa karakteristik dan aspek sosiomedis penderita abortus di rumah sakit Dr. Hasan Sadikin periode 1977–1979. Skripsi, Bagian Obstetri dan Ginekologi, Rumah Sakit Dr. Hasan Sadikin, Fakultas Kedokteran Universitas Padjadjaran. Bandung, 1980.

Hariadi, S. S. Pembahasan Atas Pasal-Pasal KUHP yang mengatur tentang masalah abortus (Pasal 299 dan Pasal 346 sampai dengan 349 KUHP). Skripsi, Jurusan Hukum Pidana Fakultas Hukum Universitas Airlangga Surabaya, 1974.

Jatiputra, S., Sampoerno, D., Hertonobroto, P., & Sabaruddin, S. Abortus di Rumah Sakit dan Bersalin DKI Jakarta 1972–1975. Fakultas Kesehatan Masyarakat Universitas Indonesia. Jakarta, 1978.

Jodono, H. M. Dokter, Abortus dan Patient (suatu pandangan). Kumpulan naskah-naskah ilmiah dalam simposium abortus di Surabaya 2 Agustus 1973. Departemen Kesehatan Republik Indonesia, Jakarta, 1974.

————. Peraturan-peraturan Hukum yang langsung berhubungan dengan kesuburan dan fertilitas. Laporan Seminar Nasional Hukum dan Kependudukan di Yogyakarta 26–29 Mei 1975. Badan Koordinasi Keluarga Berencana Nasional, 1975.

Karkata, K., Surya, I.G.P., & Duarsa, S. Abortus infektiosus di RSU Sanglah Denpasar. Seri Penerbitan Naskah Simposium/Diskusi Panel Kongres Obstetri dan Ginekologi Indonesia ke IV di Yogyakarta 10–15 Juni 1979, no. 21, Panitia Pelaksana KOGI IV. Yogyakarta, 1979.

Lim, B. H. *Abortus*, Skripsi, Bagian Kebidanan dan Penyakit Kandungan, RSUP. Medan, 1969.

Manuaba, I.B.G. Data-data klinik abortus di Bagian Obstetri dan Ginekologi Fakultas Kedokteran Universitas Udayana/Unit Pelayanan Ginekologi RSUP Sanglah Denpasar. Seminar Reproduksi Manusia, Keluarga Berencana, dan Dinamika Kependudukan. Fakultas Kedokteran Universitas Udayana, Denpasar, 1979.

Moeloek, F. A., Affandi, B. Santoso, S.I.S., & Sumapraja, S. Perbandingan penerimaan sterilisasi sukarela setelah induksi haid dan persalinan. *Majalah Obstetri dan Ginekologi Indonesia,* 1979, *4*, 226.

Population Reference Bureau. *World population data sheet*, Washington, D.C., 1981.

Rattu, R. B. Abortus provokatus kriminalis di RSU Manado. Naskah Lengkap Kongres Obstetri dan Ginekologi Indonesia ke II di Surabaya 29 Juli–3 Agustus, 1973, Panitia Pelaksana KOGI II. Surabaya, 1973.

Saifuddin, A. B., & Bachtiar, I. Penentuan insidens pengguguran kehamilan muda dengan "Randomized Response Technique." Seri Penerbitan Naskah Simposium/Diskusi Panel Kongres Obstetri dan Ginekologi Indonesia ke IV di Yogyakarta 10–15 Juni 1979, no. 23, Panitia Pelaksana KOGI IV. Yogyakarta, 1979.

Saifuddin, A. B., Soekoprapto, S. D., & Wiknjosastro, H. Beberapa perbandingan corak penderita abortus di Rumah Sakit Dr. Cipto Mangunkusumo, Jakarta dan Rumah Sakit Dr. Hasan Sadikin, Bandung. *Majalah Obstetri dan Ginekologi Indonesia,* 1980, *6* (4), 69.

Saloheimo, A., Hutabarat, H., & Wilaras, A. A preliminary report on social aspects in spontaneous abortions. Naskah Lengkap Kongres Obstetri dan Ginekologi Indonesia ke II di Surabaya, 29 Juli–3 Agustus, 1973, Panitia Pelaksana KOGI II. Surabaya, 1973.

Sampoerno, D., & Sadli, S. *Indonesia, proceeding of the Asian Regional Research Seminar on psychosocial aspects of abortus.* Kathmandu, 26–29 November 1974.

Sastrawinata, S., Agoestina, T., & Siagian, P.E.L. Induksi haid sebagai penunjang kontrasepsi di Rumah Sakit Dr. Hasan Sadikin Bandung. Naskah Lengkap Kongres Obstetri dan Ginekologi Indonesia ke III di Medan, 7–11 Juni 1976, Panitia Pelaksana KOGI III. Medan 1976.

Soedigdomarto, M. H. Pengguguran kehamilan atas indikasi sosio medik. *Majalah Obstetri dan Ginekologi Indonesia*, 1974, *1* (2): 88.

Soedjati, R. Abortus provocatus dipandang dari sudut Ilmu Kedokteran Forensik. *Majalah Kedokteran Diponegoro*, 1974a, *9* (1), 19.

———. Abortus provocatus kriminalis ditinjau oleh seorang dokter dan segi hukumnya. *Majalah Kedokteran Diponegoro* 1974b, *9* (2), 66.

Soerjaningsih, S., Joedoseptro, S., & Soewondo, H. Some aspects of unwanted pregnancy, a preliminary report on a survey at Dr. Soetomo hospital, Surabaya, Indonesia. *Majalah Kedokteran Surabaya* 1975, *12* (2), 42.

Soesilo, R. *Kitab Undang-Undang Hukum Pidana*. Penerbit Politeja, Bogor, 1973.

Soetopo, M.H.W. *The occurance of abortion in fifteen general hospitals in Indonesia (June-November 1972)*. Department of Epidemiology and Medical Statistics, National Institute of Public Health, Surabaya (n.d.).

Soewondo, N. *Abortion in Indonesia*. Report Prepared for the IPPF Ad Hoc Expert Panel Meeting on Abortion. Bellagio, Italy, February 1978.

Sopacua, A., Manuputty, J., & Wulur, F. Abortus provocatus di RSU Ujung Padang. *Majalah Obstetri dan Ginekologi Indonesia*, 1974, *1* (2), 93.

Sumampouw, H. Beberapa pengalaman abortus provocatus di Surabaya. *Majalah Obstetri dan Ginekologi Indonesia*, 1974, *1* (2), 110.

Sumapraja, S., & Saifuddin, A. B. Angket kontrasepsi, sterilisasi, abortus dan "Sex Education." *Majalah Obstetri dan Ginekologi Indonesia* 1974, *1* (2), 142.

Sumapraja, S., Saifuddin, A. B., Wibowo, B., Moeloek, F. A., & Affandi, B. Pengguguran kandungan berdasarkan pertimbangan kesehatan. *Majalah Obstetri dan Ginekologi Indonesia*, 1979, *5* (3), 46.

Surya, I.G.P., & Manuaba, I.B.G. Evaluasi Hospital Abortion Record di RSUP Sanglah Denpasar. Rapat Tahunan Kontributor Badan Kerja Sama Penelitian Fertilitas Indonesia. Surabaya, 1980.

Utomo, B., Jatiputra, S., & Tjokronegoro, A. Abortus di Indonesia: Suatu telaah pustaka. *Majalah Medika*, 1983, *5* (9).

Wiharto, W., Warsito, B., & Soerohardjo, M. *Tinjauan kasus abortus selama 10 tahun di Rumah Sakit Mangkuyudan Yogyakarta.* Bagian Obstetri dan Ginekologi Fakultas Kedokteran Universitas Gajah Mada. Yogyakarta (n.d.).

Wiknjosastro, H., Doodoh, A., Supardi, A. Wj., & Sudarman, E. Abortus di Bagian Obstetri dan Ginekologi Rumah Sakit Dr. Cipto Mangunkusumo, Jakarta. Naskah Lengkap Kongres Obstetri dan Ginekologi Indonesia ke II di Surabaya, 29 Junli3 Agustus 1973. Panitia Pelaksana KOGI II. Surabaya, 1973.

Wiknjosastro, H., Harahap, H., & Wiknjosastro, G. H. Induksi haid. *Majalan Obstetri dan Ginekologi Indonesia*, 1974, *1* (2), 114.

World Health Organzation. *Spontaneous and induced abortion.* Technical Report Series, No. 461. Geneva, 1970.

Table 16.1
Incidence of Abortions at Several Indonesian Hospitals

Location	Year	Abortions per 1000 pregnancies
RSU (General Hospital), Medan	1967-1968	147
15 Regency Hospitals	1972	267
Mangkuyudan Hospital, Yogyakarta	1968-1977	250
Hasan Sadikin Hospital, Bandung	1979	246
Dr. Cipto Mangunkusumo Hospital, Jakarta	1979	257
		per 1000 births
Hospital in Jakarta	1972-1975	242
25 Maternity Clinics, Jakarta	1972-1975	57
Sanglah Hospital, Bali	1979-1980	188

Source: Adapted from Effendi, 1980; Jatiputra et al., 1978; Lim, 1969; Saifuddin et al., 1980; Soetopo, n.d.; Surya & Manuaba, 1980; Wiharto, Warsito, & Soerohardjo, n.d.

Table 16.2
Rising Abortion Frequency at Hospitals and Maternity Clinics in Jakarta, 1972–75

Location	Y e a r	Abortions per 100 births
Hospitals	1972	18.28
	1973	19.74
	1974	20.46
	1975	39.63
Maternity Clinics	1972	3.93
	1973	5.68
	1974	6.60
	1975	6.68

Source: Jatiputra et al., 1978.

Table 16.3
Incidence of Abortions with User of Contraceptives, by Modes and Nature of Abortion

Mode of contraception	Nature of abortion			
	Spontaneous		Induced	
	Number	%	Number	%
IUD	65	74.7	13	46.4
OC	13	14.9	7	25.0
Injection	2	2.3	1	3.6
Sterilization	2	2.3	-	-
Condom	5	5.7	6	21.4
Coitus interruptus	-	-	1	3.6

17

ISRAEL

Eitan F. Sabatello and Nurit Yaffe

HISTORICAL DEVELOPMENT OF ABORTION POLICY

Before the establishment of the State of Israel in 1948, regulations concerning abortions in Palestine under the British Mandate were extremely rigid, as they stemmed from the English Offences Against the Person Act of 1861: A person inducing an abortion was liable, if convicted, to imprisonment for fourteen years, while an aborting woman was liable to seven years of jail. However, Palestinian courts seem to have dealt only very infrequently with abortion cases. In 1948 the British act was incorporated in the Israeli system. However, in 1952 the District Court of Haifa declared that induced abortion for bona fide medical grounds was permissible if done openly (Bachi, 1970). In consequence, the attorney general instructed the police not to prosecute cases of induced abortion (unless they were exceptional, if the woman's health or life were endangered), because such prosecution did not constitute an act of public interest. Later, any punishment for the aborting woman was abolished, while sentences for persons inducing an abortion were reduced to five years.

In practice, it is believed that abortion was used extensively in the 1950s and 1960s as a primary method of limiting births (Friedlander, 1974; Yaffe, 1976), though the discrepancy between written law and actual practice was considered undesirable by the policymakers (Bachi, 1970).

The prevailing stand of the various Israeli governments has consistently been one of moderate pronatalism, even if only rarely has it been codified into actual policy. In 1964 the prime minister set up a special Committee on Natality Problems, and its recommendations were published two years later. The report acknowledged that only sporadic cases of death were caused by abortive practice (on the average, about one case per year), because in general, abortions, though illegal, were performed by physicians in hospitals or private ambulatories under satisfactory hygienic and professional conditions. Still the report pointed out that

"induced abortion is an important and even a leading cause of different gynecological and obstetrical situations and complications" (Report, 1966). Various
governmental circles, as well as selected sectors of political and public opinion,
by then, felt that clear regulations of abortion practice should be introduced.

Two major currents have characterized the public stand toward abortion in
Israel. First, there was the perception that the Jewish religion prohibits fertility
control. In a 1974 study of married women by Friedlander and Goldscheider
(Yaffe, 1976), more than 80 percent of the respondents thought their religion
prohibited contraception, and it may be assumed that the perception of the attitude
of religion toward abortions was even more extreme. In fact, the religious parties
and some pronatalist associations (Ephrat, Zahavi) have consistently opposed
any legal or pragmatic concession to abortion. In their view, abortion should be
outlawed, except perhaps, for the rare well-defined case of health conditions.

The other current, which demanded the liberalization of abortion laws, was
led by a political party fighting to widen civil rights in Israel and by several
voluntary organizations, such as the Israel Family Planning Association which
concentrates on family planning services and means.

At the same time, abortion was actually available at the clinics of the General
Sick Fund (an extension of the labor movement), whose health insurance scheme
covered more than 70 percent of the Israeli population, and at the clinics of
private gynecologists. In 1977 the pro-abortionist parties and organizations got
a new bill through Parliament which basically formalized the actual practice of
abortion as performed at the General Sick Fund clinics, for a wide range of
medical, personal, and socioeconomic reasons. The bill, enacted under the Ministry of Health's regulations by February 1978, stated that committees composed
of two physicians and a social worker were to be established in any authorized
hospital or clinic and could grant a woman an abortion under one of the following
conditions:

1. The woman is under the legal marriage age, seventeen, or over forty

2. The pregnancy results from an illicit (rape, incest) or nonmarital relationship, regardless of the woman's marital status

3. The fetus is suspected to have physical or mental malformation

4. Continuing the pregnancy may endanger the woman's life or cause her physical or
   mental harm

5. Family or social conditions (economic conditions of the woman or her family's,
   presence of numerous or very young children, and so on) dictate an abortion.

Still, considerable autonomy was left to each committee, whose decisions
would reflect the general policy or outlook toward abortion of the hospital or
clinic in which the committee was set up. For example, a committee in a "re-
ligiously" oriented hospital might refuse an abortion that would be granted by
another. (For a similar pattern, see Blayo, 1979.)

Under the pressures of a small, but then politically powerful, religious (Orthodox) party, the bill was modified in 1980: the most conspicuous modification was the abolition of Article 5, which allowed abortion for "social" reasons.

Besides religious beliefs, the major concern of antiabortion circles seems to have been the overall impact of abortions on (Jewish) birth rates in the country, which have decreased almost continuously since the 1950s. Sustained fertility rates are perceived by different influential political and social settings as a major national goal (Friedlander, 1974).

Since the abolition of Article 5 of the 1977 bill, the antiabortionists have turned the public debate toward an extent of illegally performed abortions, and those abortions "socially" motivated and now disallowed by the law but allegedly performed and reported by physicians under one of the admitted articles. In their opinion, only truly health-related abortions should be permitted; in other cases, the parents should raise their unwanted child, with help if necessary, or (as in the case of unmarried women unable to do so) give it up for abortion (Davids, 1981).

Though never supported by scientific evidence, figures of over 40,000 abortions per year (including the 15,000 to 16,000 legal) during the early 1980s have frequently been circulated by religious leaders and political appointees at the Ministry of Health. Thus, they imply more than one abortion per two live births and 25,000 or more illegal abortions per year.

PAST PATTERNS OF ABORTION (1950s–70s)

Abortion among Maternity Cases

In 1959–60 and 1964, two surveys on family planning were carried out in Israel, both covering only selected areas of the country and pertaining to maternity cases only. From those sources, Bachi (1970), Bachi and Matras (1962), and Matras and Auerbach (1964) reported extensive results on abortion in Israel by several population subgroups. Induced abortion practices were found to be positively related (among the Jews) to age, parity, and perhaps education, and inversely related to "religious" observance and recency of arrival in the country. Jewish childbearing women of European origin practiced abortion more than those less "modern" ones who came from Middle East, Asian, and African countries. Arab women experienced, by far, fewer abortions than their Jewish counterparts.

The authors of those studies themselves mention the selectivity of their samples (delivering women only), which by definition should have included smaller shares of contracepting and aborting women than in the total female population of the country. For this and other reasons, those data could not provide a base for estimating the overall frequency of abortion within the population.

Abortion among Married Women

In a 1974 study of 3,000 Jewish women up to the age of fifty-four, married for the first time, and living in urban localities (where 90 percent of the Jewish population lived), the interviewees were asked if they ever had an induced abortion and when the first abortion was carried out. No distinction was made between legal and illegal abortions. It was found that 28 percent of all respondents had at least one abortion.

Peled's study (1978) found that a similar percentage of women experienced abortion in the past and that 60 percent of those abortions were performed by a private physician and not through medical committees. Application to the medical committees, however, was more popular among young couples. In addition, a majority of couples who had never experienced an abortion expressed an intention to apply to a medical committee, should the need arise.

Extrapolating her findings, Peled (1978) concluded that in the future more women intending to have an abortion would be likely to apply to a legal committee than in the past. In another study (Peled & Friedman, 1973) that investigated family planning and abortion patterns along a scale of "modernity-nonmodernity," it was found not only that the more modern the couples, the higher the positive attitude toward abortion (within each group, religious couples were less favorable to abortion), but also that the more modern the couples, the lower the proportion who actually experienced it, because of their more modern methods of contraception control.

Among women married prior to 1944 (i.e., married thirty years or more at the time of the survey), 34 percent had at least one abortion, with a conspicuous difference between women born in Europe or America—43 percent—and those born in Asian or African countries—21 percent only. The gap decreased in younger generations and was virtually nonexistant among women married in 1965–74 and around 17 percent in both origin groups (Yaffe, 1976).

Table 17.1 presents data on the extent of abortion practice by women's education and religiosity. With the exception of the recently married women, it seems that, generally, less educated women experienced abortion less frequently than better educated women.

More clearcut is the effect of religiosity. In every cohort of marriage, by far more nonreligious women had an abortion than religious women. For instance, 44 percent of the nonreligious women who married in the 1945–54 period (i.e., married twenty to twenty-nine years in 1974) had at least one abortion compared to only 14 percent of the religious women.

The 1974 survey included a large number of questions concerning contraceptive usage and thus enabled an assessment of the important linkage between the two major components of family size regulation: contraception and abortion.

Data on the percentage of women who used abortion as their only means of fertility control (out of all women defined as family planners—i.e., women who used abortion only, those who used contraception only, or those who practiced both) indicate that the percentage was slight—4.2 percent only of all planners and (with one exception) lower than 10 percent when women were differentiated by duration of marriage and origin (Yaffe, 1976).

From these and other data (Peled & Friedman, 1973), it follows that in the early 1970s abortion and contraception in Israel were not competitive means for regulating family size, but both were being used. The explanation of the seeming contradiction probably lies in the fact that less effective contraceptive means were used and that abortions were carried out when contraception had failed. The proportion of early and more modern contraception was found to be higher among young couples, which might mean a decreasing request for abortion.

DEMOGRAPHY OF ABORTION

Despite legalization since 1978, registration data available on abortion in recent years are very poor. They refer to number of abortions only (no information is available on the characteristics of the women or the number of applications refused) and are based on aggregate monthly reports from the hospitals and clinics, pooled by the Ministry of Health. The available annual information is tabulated by month of occurrence, clinic name (useful for yielding a geographical distribution), ownership of the clinics, and the law's articles justifying the abortions. Most of these data have recently been included in the annual *Statistical Abstract of Israel* (CBS, 1984).

No data based on personal files (such as age, marital status, or origin of the women) are available at present. However, for the sake of this study, we will assume that all the recorded abortions in Israel pertain to Jewish women only (83 percent of the total).

Estimates of illegal abortions in Israel in the early 1980s (1980–83) were obtained as the difference between estimates of total abortions and the annual average number of recorded legal abortions. Total abortions (i.e., legal and illegal together) were calculated through standardization: 1978–81 age-marital-status specific abortion rates on countries[1] selected to encompass the Israeli pattern in fertility control practice, were applied to suitable distributions of the female population of Israel (Sabatello, 1985).[2] For this purpose, the information collected by Tietze (1983) for several countries and data from some specific national studies (Blayo 1979; Muñoz-Perez, 1981) were availale.

Estimates of possible illegal (nonrecorded) abortions in those model countries were taken into account and proportionately added to the previous calculations.

INCIDENCE AND DEMOGRAPHIC CHARACTERISTICS OF LEGAL ABORTION

The first full year in which abortion data were collected under the 1977 law was 1979, when slightly fewer than 16,000 induced abortions were registered, or 23 abortions per 1,000 Jewish women of childbearing age. Between 1980 and 1983, the annual number of total legal abortions ranged between slightly less than 15,000 and almost 16,000—with the exception of 1982 (16,800 cases)—and averaged 15,400; in 1984 and 1985 they rose to about 19,000 or 26 abortions per 1,000 Jewish women of childbearing age. The available information does not suggest whether this recent rise reflects a further shift from illegal to legal abortion or a net increase of induced pregnancy terminations.

Table 17.2 shows the main basic data and indexes of abortions in Israel during the first six years since the enactment of the new law.

In terms of the general abortion rate (per 1,000 women aged fifteen to forty-four), Israel is in an intermediate position as compared with East European and West or North European countries, and near, for example, to Denmark and the U.S. white population. In terms of abortion ratio (per 100 live births or 100 known pregnancies), Israel ranks lower than most European countries, because of its relatively high natality and fertility patterns.[3]

The age and marital status composition of the legally aborting women in Israel may be estimated only indirectly through an analysis of the legal abortion data by the article justifying their performance: the underlying assumption is that the reporting of the abortions implying an age or marital status criterion for their authorization is correct. A possible allocation of legal abortions by large age group and by marital status is shown in table 17.3. (For details of allocation procedure, see Sabetello, 1985, from which it appears that about two-thirds of legal abortions have been performed on married women; the reasons usually invoked were medical circumstances.) The same table shows that abortion rates might be the highest at ages eighteen-nineteen and decrease thereafter. However, the age group twenty to thirty-nine is too wide to enable any clearcut conclusion, and more detailed evidence is needed.

ILLEGAL ABORTIONS: ALTERNATIVE ESTIMATES

Table 17.4 presents alternative numbers of abortions in Israel for 1980–83, as obtained by multiplying age-specific and marital status abortion rates from each of the model countries, by the appropriate female Jewish population of Israel in 1982 (details in Sabatello, 1985). Apparently, the frequency of abortion in Israel in the early 1980s did not exceed 27,000 cases if Hungary (which represents an extreme case of widespread approval and practice of abortion—see Leridon, 1981—is used as a model. It was more likely 20,000 to 22,000 according to three of the six countries chosen as model, that is, about half the volume of abortions currently claimed by antiabortion circles.

A very low illegitimacy rate and moderate frequency of premaritally conceived births in Israel (Sabatello, 1979; Sabatello, 1986) should raise expectations of a relatively widespread abortion practice among Israel's unmarried young women. This is not the case, however: teenage abortion rates in Israel are about the same as, or even lower than, those prevailing in most European countries, because premarital intercourse in Israel is less prevalent than in comparable countries (Autonowski et al., 1980), though use of effective contraception is perhaps more limited.

In total, in the 1980s the relative incidence of abortion in Israel seems to be quite close to that prevailing in Western Europe and North America, but unlike these regions, the share of illegal abortions is substantially higher—25 to 30 percent of the total, according to our estimates. The recency of the law and the more recent disallowment of abortions for social and family reasons might partly explain this high incidence of unauthorized induced abortions. Israeli policy in the coming years is likely to be directed toward curbing the incidence of disallowed abortions in the country.

The balance obtained by the difference between the (corrected) estimates (see table 17.4, column 2) of total abortion and the actual legal abortions in Israel represents the alternative estimate of illegal abortions in Israel. They range from 11,600 (Hungary) to zero (England), with the intermediate, quite close, and likely figures of about 4,500 to 7,000 cases according to the pattern of Czechoslovakia, France, and the United States. Denmark's pattern would yield a very small illegal practice. If an intermediate estimate of about 6,000 illegal abortions is retained, the corresponding annual estimate of total abortions in Israel for 1980–83 is 21,400, or 30 per 1,000 women in their childbearing ages (table 17.4).

ABORTION AND (JEWISH) FERTILITY

Has the legalization of abortion had any impact on recent fertility trends? The fertility of the Israeli Jewish population (83 percent of the total in 1984) has undergone an almost steady decrease since the early 1950s, as better educated and motivated women replaced in the childbearing population less educated women, usually originating from developing countries. Friedlander (1973) ascribes a major role to abortion in the earlier control of fertility among large section of the Israeli population, but by the late 1970s, contraception had probably become the leading method of limiting the number of children in the family. Table 17.5 shows several period indexes of fertility for the years just before the actual application of the 1977 abortion bill and for the seven years since its enactment. Together, they demonstrate that fertility declined faster before than since 1979, and the decreasing trend may have been reversed by 1982, just when abortion under the new law had become well established and accessible to most of the women "at risk."

CONCLUSIONS

This chapter has briefly reviewed information on abortion in Israel for the past thirty years; for the most recent years, the early 1980s, only quite undetailed data and overall estimates of legal and illegal abortion could be dealt with.

The evidence suggests that resort to abortion within the marriage should have lessened, and will likely decrease further, as younger, more "modern," more educated women replace those married in the 1950s and 1960s and as highly effective contraception became widespread. The data suggest that abortion in Israel has been practiced primarily as a corrective when inefficient contraception has failed.

Recent evidence on the family size norms and achievements of married women suggests that abortion might be lower in Israel than in other comparable countries. Table 17.6 shows that Israeli Jewish women use modern, effective contraception to about the same extent as women in most Western societies, but on the average, they idealize, plan, and actually achieve up to 50 percent more children (Sabatello, 1985). That is, an unwanted pregnancy in Israel is more likely than elsewhere to be eventually accepted by the couple and continued up to birth.

NOTES

Both authors work with the Israel Central Bureau of Statistics. Responsibility for the contents of this chapter belongs solely to the authors.

1. The "model" countries from which the abortion rates were borrowed were chosen from among those countries that are as developed or more developed than Israel and share with it a general cultural (European) background. The following specific criteria aided this search:

   1. Statistics on legal abortions are reliable, and/or estimates of illegal or other unreported abortions exist.
   2. Illegal abortions are relatively infrequent in those countries.
   3. The law regulating abortion is similar or more liberal than in Israel.
   4. Levels of contraception, its distribution by means used, family size intentions, and achievements are known; they encompass those prevailing in Israel.

2. For other approaches, see, among others, Goodhart (1969) and James (1971).
3. The sum of live births and of legal abortions (Tietze, 1983).

REFERENCES

Antonowksy, H. F., Kav-Venacky, S., Lancet M., Modan B., & Shoham I. *Adolescent sexuality*. Lexington, Mass.: 1980.

Bachi, R. Abortion in Israel. In R. E. Hall (Ed.), *Abortion in a changing world*. Vol. 1. New York: Columbia University Press, 1970, 274–283.

Bachi, R., & Matras, J. Contraception and induced abortion among Jewish maternity cases in Israel. *Milbank Memorial Fund Quarterly*, 1962, *40* (2), 207–229.

Bachi, R., Matras, J., Toaf, R., & Aylon, E. *Fertility and birth control among women in Tel Aviv-Jaffa* (in Hebrew). Tel Aviv: Hebrew University, Statistical Department, and Municipal Hospital, Department of Maternity, 1960.

Berman-Yeshurun, T. Trends in women's requests for induced abortions. *Briuth Hatsibur*, May 1975, *2* (in Hebrew).

Blayo, C. Les interruptions volontaires de grossesses en France en 1976. *Population*, 1979, *34* (2), 307–343.

CBS (Central Bureau of Statistics). *Statistical abstract of Israel*. No. 35 (1984), Jerusalem.

Davids, L. *Induced abortions today: Facts, problems and alternatives* (in Hebrew). Report presented to the Demographic Center, 1981.

Friedlander, D. Family planning in Israel: Irrationality and ignorance. *Journal of Marriage and the Family*, 1973, *35* (1), 117–124.

———. Population Policy in Israel. In B. Berelson (Ed.), *Population policy in developed countries*. New York: McGraw Hill, 1974, 42–97.

Goodhart, C. B. Estimations of illegal abortions. *Journal of Biosocial Sciences*, 1969, *1* (No. 3), 235–245.

James, W. The Incidence of illegal abortion. *Population Studies*, 1971, *25* (2), 327–339.

Leridon, H. Fertility and contraception in 12 developed countries. *Family Planning Perspectives*, 1981, *13* (2), 93–102.

Matras, J., & Auerbach, H. On rationalization of family formation in Israel. *Milbank Memorial Fund Quarterly*, 1964, *11* (4), 453–480.

Muñoz-Perez, P. Douze ans d'avortement légal en Angleterre-Galles. *Population*, 1981, *36* (6), 1105–1139.

Peled, T. *Behavior and preferences in family planning: Patterns of the young well-to-do social strata in Israel*. Jerusalem: Israel Institute of Applied Social Research, 1970 (in Hebrew).

———. A status report on induced abortion in Israel. *Psychosocial aspects of abortion in Asia*. Proceedings of the Asian Regional Research Seminar on Psychosocial Aspects of Abortion, Kathmandu, Nepal, November 1974, 33–46.

———. Psychosical aspects of abortion in Israel. In H. D. David, et al. (Eds.), *Abortion in psychosocial perspective*. New York: Springer Publishing Co., 1978, 57–76.

Peled, T., & Friedman, H. *Population policy in Israel: Perceptions and preferences among policy makers, service providers and the public*. Final Report, Washington, D.C./Jerusalem, 1973.

Peled, T., & Schimmerling-Bar, H. *Family planning in Israel: Behavior and attitudes of professionals*. Jerusalem: Israel Institute of Applied Social Reserach, 1970 (in Hebrew).

Report of the committee on natality problems. Submitted to Head of Government, Jerusalem, 1966 (in Hebrew).

Sabatello, E. F. Patterns of illegitimacy in Israel. *Jewish Journal of Sociology*, 1979, *21* (1), 53–65.

———. *Estimated abortion and fertility in Israel: An application of the Bongaarts model*. Paper presented at the Annual Meeting of the Population Association of America, Boston, March 1985, 36.

———. Premarital pregnancies in Israel: an exploratory assessment through record linkage. In U.O. Schmelz & G. Nathan (Eds.), *Studies in the Population of Israel*, in honor of R. Bachi, Scripta Jerosalemitana, Vol. 30, 70–88. Jerusalem: Magnes Press, 1986 (in Hebrew).

Schiff, G. S. The politics of fertility policy in Israel. In P. Ritterband (Ed.), *Modern Jewish fertility*. Leiden: E. J. Brill, 1981, 255–278.

Tietze, C. *Induced abortion: a world review*. New York: Population Council, 1973.

United Nations. *Fertility and family planning in Europe around 1970: A comparative study of twelve national surveys*. Population Studies No. 58. New York: 1976.

Yaffe, N. *Family Planning in Israel*. Jerusalem: Hebrew University, 1976, 55 (in Hebrew).

Yisai, Y. Abortion in Israel: social demand and political responses. *Policy Studies Journal*, 1978, 7 (2), 270–290.

Table 17.1
Percentage of Women Who Had at Least One Abortion, by Period of Marriage, Education, and Religiosity

Period of marriage	Years of Schooling		Religiosity	
	0-8	9+	Religious	Non-Religious
Total	30.5	26.5	12.3	32.9
-1944	32.4	35.2	12.5	46.2
1945-1954	33.2	38.3	14.4	43.9
1955-1964	31.6	32.7	12.3	38.0
1965-1974	18.3	13.8	7.7	16.1

Source: Yaffe, 1976.

Table 17.2
Selected Indicators of Legal Abortions in Israel, 1979–84

	1979	1980	1981	1982	1983	1984
Ground[a]						
Total numbers[b]	15,900	14,700	14,500	16,800	15,600	18,900
1	1,700	1,800	1,800	1,800	1,500	2,000
2	4,500	5,000	5,000	6,600	6,700	7,900
3	2,200	2,100	2,000	2,600	2,400	2,900
4	1,300	5,200	5,500	5,800	5,100	6,200
5[c]	6,300	650	–	–	–	–
Percentages	100.0	100.0	100.0	100.0	100.0	100.0
1	10.5	12.1	12.3	10.5	9.6	10.3
2	28.0	34.0	34.5	39.4	42.7	41.4
3	13.6	14.4	15.2	15.6	15.2	15.5
4	8.2	35.1	38.1	34.4	32.5	32.7
5[c]	39.8	4.4	–	–	–	–
Rates						
Per 1,000 women						
15–44	23.2	21.1	21.6	23.5	21.5	25.7
Per 100 live births	22.8	20.6	20.5	23.1	20.8	25.5
Per 100 known pregnancies	18.6	17.1	17.0	18.7	17.2	20.3

[a](1) Woman's age under 17 or over 40; (2) Pregnancy from illicit or nonmarital relationship; (3) Suspected malformation of the infant; (4) Danger to woman's health; (5) Social and family reasons.
[b]Rounded-off numbers.
[c]Disallowed by February 1980.
Source: Central Bureau of Statistics, 1985.

Table 17.3
Allocation of Legal Abortions Performed in Israel, 1980–83 (Average), by Ground of Abortion, Age Group, and Marital Status

	Legal Abortions[a,b]		Married women	Non-married women
Total[a,b]	15,400		10,400	5,000
			Percentages	
		100	68	32
Ground (1977 Law's article)				
1. Under 17 or 40+	1,700	100	68	32
2. Illicit or non-marital pregnancy	5,800	100	26	74
3. Infant malformation	2,300	100	98	2
4. Danger to woman's health	5,400	100	99	1
			Rates[c]	
Age group				
All ages	15,400	22	23	20
Under 20 years	2,350	19[d]	(14)	20
Thereof: 18-19 years	1,500	31	(15)	33
20-39 years	11,750	23	24	21
40 years and over	1,300	18	18	(15)

[a]Rounded-off 1980–83 averages.
[b]Includes abortions performed on ground 5 before abolition of the article in early 1980.
[c]Per 1,000 women in each group and marital status.
[d]Per 1,000 women 15–19 years old. The rate would be about 16 per 1,000 women aged 13–19.
Source: Sabatello, 1985.

Table 17.4

Annual Estimates of Total and Illegal Abortions in Israel, 1980–83, by "Model Countries," and Derived Abortion Indexes

Model country	Estimate by standardi- zation	Corrected for under registration	Estimated illegal abortions No.[a] %		Abortion rate per 1000 W15-44	Abortion ratios per 1000 Live Births	Known preg- nancies
Czechoslovakia	21,400	22,500	7,100	31	32	31	24
Denmark	15,300	16,100	700	4	23	22	18
England-Wales	9,100	11,000	X	X	15	15	13
France[b]	17,900	19,700	4,300	22	28	27	21
Hungary	25,500	26,800	11,600	43	38	37	27
U.S.A.	20,100	21,100	5,700	27	30	29	22
Intermediate (likely) Estimate		21,400	6,000	28	30	29	23

[a]Corrected estimates—15,400 legal abortions.
[b]After correction of age-specific abortion rates (Blayo, 1979).

276

Table 17.5
Fertility and Legal Abortions in Israel, 1970–85

Year	Total fertility rate[a] Total	Born in Israel	Age specific rate for women 35–39 years old	Legal abortions
1970	3.41	3.12	77.3	–
1972	3.25	2.96	71.4	–
1974	3.20	3.05	68.4	–
1976	3.20	3.11	68.1	–
1977	2.99	2.89	63.0	–
1978	2.82	2.78	58.3	–
After the enactment of the 1977 abortion bill				
1979	2.77	2.76	57.8	15,900
1980	2.76	2.76	58.9	14,700
1981	2.71	2.76	58.2	14,500
1982	2.79	2.90	60.7	16,800
1983	2.90	2.93	63.3	15,600
1984	2.84	2.85	63.0	18,900
1985	(2.86)[b]	–	–	19,700

[a]Jewish population; rates for 1983 and later were calculated on population adjusted after the 1983 Census.
[b]Author's estimate, unpublished.
These trends are hardly consistent with the alleged depressing influence of the 1977 abortion laws on current Jewish fertility in Israel.
Source: Central Bureau of Statistics, 1985.

Table 17.6
Percentage of Women Using Modern Contraceptives and Family Size Norm Desired and Achieved by Countries

Countries (1970's)	% using Pill, IUD[a]	Average number of children		
		ideal[b]	wanted[b]	born[c]
Israel	54	3.89	3.34	2.80
Denmark	46	2.50	2.61	1.77
England & Wales	51	2.41	2.59	1.72
France	50	2.44	2.17	1.72
Hungary	62	2.24	1.96	2.19
U.S.A.	59	2.67	2.80	1.80

[a]Per 100 contracepting women who constitute 60 to 70 percent of total women of childbearing age of the indicated countries.
[b]Couples married less than 4 (Israel: 5) years.
[c]Total fertility rate.
Source: Sabatello, 1985.

18

ITALY

Irene Figà-Talamanca

HISTORICAL DEVELOPMENT OF ABORTION POLICY

In prewar Italy, abortion was classified among crimes against the family. The law was part of the more general policy aimed at maintaining stability in the family by prescribing biological and partimonial unity and proscribing divorce and abortion. During the fascist regime, the emphasis was moved from the individual and the family to the ''race.'' The family and the individual (especially the females) were viewed as a mere vehicle to the creation of a large and strong population. Thus abortion, contraception, and even propaganda in favor of contraception became crimes against the race.

These laws survived the postwar republican constitution in 1948 and remained in power until the early 1970s. Abortion penalties included from two to twelve years of imprisonment for the person performing the abortion and one to five years for the woman undergoing it. In case of death from abortion, the penalty for the abortionist was from ten to twenty years. All penalties could be reduced by half, if the above crimes were committed in order to save someone's honor. These laws, however, were rarely enforced. In 1973, for example, there were fifty-nine convictions for illegally induced abortions. Conviction for abortion deaths was very rare. For many years it was thought that abortion was indeed a rare problem confined to very special groups of women such as unmarried teenagers, adulterous wives, prostitutes, or women from the privileged social classes.

The statistics, however, suggest that nothing could be further from the truth. Between 1961 and 1971, the average annual rate of increase of the population was 0.65 percent. In 1975 the crude birth rate was 14.8 per 1,000. Couples were obviously controlling their fertility, and abortion made a large contribution to their effort. In fact, all the studies conducted during those years showed that between 70 and 90 percent of couples tried to control their fertility by a combination of traditional contraceptive methods (especially withdrawal) and abortion (Figà-Talamanca, 1972). The rhythm method, the only birth control method tolerated by the Catholic church, was rarely known or used. Modern contraceptive methods were, of course, illegal and mostly unknown. They could only be prescribed and purchased under the pretense of therapeutic use. Spermicidal jellies and prophylactics, for example, were sold to "prevent infection" and oral contraceptives to "treat menstrual irregularities." Only the very privileged and well-informed couples had access to these methods.

Doctors, too, were hesitant to prescribe contraceptives, and not just because of legal restrictions. Many knew nothing about the subject, and others disapproved on moral grounds. Contraception was not included in the medical school curriculum, and this is still the case in some universities. A study among medical students in 1972 showed that their knowledge on the subject was superficial. There was no difference in knowledge of first-year and graduating medical students. A proportion of them (8 percent) felt contraception and abortion laws should not be changed (Modolo, Maruccini, & Marlunghi, 1973). Specialists in gynecology and obstetrics provided similar responses in a 1973 study. They felt that their specialist colleagues (and therefore indirectly themselves) did not have enough training in contraception. A large proportion of them (30 percent) also felt that there was no need to change the existing laws on contraception and abortion (Figà-Talamanca & Rugiati, 1974). The study showed that negative attitudes toward abortion and contraception were particularly prevalent among physicians with university appointments, that is, the professional and scientific leaders in the field.

In the 1970s, several researchers tried to estimate the dimension of the illegal abortion problem. Estimates varied widely, often reflecting the ideological position of the author. Somehow estimates focused on the figure of 100,000 abortions a year (Colombo, 1976), while proabortion exponents produced estimates ten to thirty times higher. Moderate estimates, which were proved reasonable by the statistics after abortion became legal, were about 340,000 illegal abortions per year (Figà-Talamanca, 1976).

The conflict between the church and laypersons on the issue of contraception and abortion became open at the beginning of the 1970s. In response to the papal encyclical *Humanae Vitae* which condemned the pill, a known woman activist published a popular book entitled *Inhumanae Vitae*, describing the inhuman conditions under which working-class women with large families had to abort repeatedly (Zardini de Marchi, 1970). Defying the law and the church, the Italian Association for Demographic Education distributed contraceptives and scientific information to the public. Its president was arrested, and the case was brought to the constitutional court in 1971. As a result, the article of law prohibiting the publicity of contraceptive methods was stricken off as unconstitutional.

Public pressure kept building up. Clandestine family planning clinics were now operating in all major cities without being disturbed by the authorities. The church, too, instituted clinics providing information on the methods accepted by ecclesiastic authorities, that is, periodic abstinence. In 1975 after a long and painful battle, the Parliament approved a law to legalize the de facto situation by officially instituting family planning services.

In the meantime, the topic of abortion began to stir public debate. It became the main cause of the movement for woman's liberation and of the radical party. Analogous events in France, amply covered by the Italian mass media, gave the movement further momentum. In 1973 hundreds of prominent women and doctors in France confessed to the crime of abortion. Court cases in Italy also made the headlines. Tragic cases such as those of a poor Sicilian mother of eight who had to spend four years in prison for having tried to avoid a ninth birth by abortion caused national debate (Borruso, 1982). Groups of women started to confess abortion and to organize public protests, sit-ins, and even hunger strikes. Risking instant arrest, activist women and doctors started operating free-standing abortion clinics. It is one of the few moments in the history of Italian feminism when all fronts were united.

In 1975 several exponents of the movement (presently all parliamentarians) were arrested off the stage of an auditorium while rallying for a new abortion law. The Parliament discussed several proposals of a new abortion law, but the opposition was still strong.

In the meantime, with the support of the press, the movement to liberalize abortion completed the difficult and unusual procedure required to bring an issue to a popular vote (referendum): It involves collecting, within the span of three months, half a million notary-public-authenticated signatures of citizens requesting modification of a law. Consequently, the Constitution requires citizens to vote for or against abrogation of the law in question within a given period of time. The referendum can only be avoided if, during the interim period, Parliament modifies the law in the requested direction.

Opinion polls now showed that most Italians, independent of their political beliefs, were in favor of reforming the abortion law (*Panoroma*, 1974). The commonly assumed association between disapproval of contraception and abortion and adherence to the Catholic church was not substantiated by research. In a sample of 568 women undergoing illegal abortions, 47 percent were practicing Catholics (Figà-Talamanca, 1972). No major political party favored the referendum, which would have been a costly and lacerating exercise at that moment. In the summer of 1978, and after numerous attempts and the fall of one government on the abortion issue, Parliament succeeded in passing a new law and thus avoiding the referendum.

THE PRESENT ABORTION LAW

The new law, entitled "Rules regarding the social prevention of maternity and the voluntary interruption of pregnancy,"is, at least on the formal level, a compromise. In its opening section, it guarantees women "the right to conscious and responsible procreation, recognizes the value of motherhood, and assures the protection of human life from its beginnings.'' It also urges health authorities to ''promote and develop social and health services to prevent abortion from being used as a form of birth control.'' In the ensuing articles, however, any woman over eighteen years of age is allowed to decide autonomously and independently that she is unable to continue her pregnancy for a broad range of health, social, and economic reasons. The woman is required to discuss the matter with a doctor, who must confirm the pregnancy; one week's waiting time is required between the first contact with the doctor and the abortion authorization. During this week the woman is expected to ''reflect'' on her decision. ➡

Minors below the age of eighteen may be granted an abortion if the request is approved by a parent, a guardian, or a judge acting in loco parentis.

Abortions can be performed only in public or privately authorized facilities. The standards of such facilities are subject to state and regional health regulations. Abortion is free of charge as part of the national health service.

Abortions cannot be performed outside the state-regulated procedure. This seemingly liberal and protective policy might also be viewed as an attempt to keep abortion under the control of the state, thus depriving the woman of the possibility of obtaining an abortion anonymously in a private service.

The most controversial part of the law is the ''conscience'' clause. Health workers (doctors, nurses, and health auxiliaries) who object to abortion on moral or religious grounds, after registering with the director or the institution in which they work, may be exempted from the tasks involved in the actual operation. This clause, which also applies to the future generations of health professionals, is considered a concrete obstacle to the application of the law. Within a month from the approval of the law, over 70 percent of doctors registered as conscientious objectors. A number of regions had, and still have, difficulty recruiting personnel to perform abortions.

This situation, together with the restrictions the law imposes on the minor's right to abortion, created the conditions for renewed protests and requests for modifying the law. At the same time, pressure from the Catholic community to abolish the law was mounting. In the spring of 1980, the Italian people were called to vote on two contrasting referenda, each attempting to abrogate different portions of the law. One aimed at making the law more liberal (extending abortion unconditionally to minors and abrogating the conscience clause), and the other aimed at restricting it (permitting abortion only under certain life-threatening conditions). Neither of these proposals was approved. The popular vote confirmed the abortion law in its original form. Indeed, the great majority of the people were satisfied with the solution which Parliament had devised for the abortion problem. Since that time no attempts have been made to modify the abortion law.

DEMOGRAPHY OF ABORTION

Statistics on legal abortion are collected and published annually by the Ministry of Health. Table 18.1 shows the number, rates, and ratios of legal induced abortions from mid–1978 (the year the law went into effect) to 1984 (the most recent year for which data are available). In the first three years, as services for legal abortions were being instituted, the number of abortions increased. In the 1980–81 period, however, the number as well as the rate and ratio of abortion remained stable. After a period of relative stability in 1980–81 the number as well as abortion rates and ratios rose in the period 1982–83. Thereafter the number, abortion rates, and ratios started to drop slightly in 1984.

The abortion law applies equally to all twenty regions of the country, but regional governments have autonomy in implementing national health policies. As a consequence, many regions are still reluctant to institute adequate and accessible abortion services. This situation is reflected in the statistics. In 1981, for example, abortion rates in the northern and central regions of the country were generally higher than those in the south and almost double those of the islands (table 18.2). On the other hand, the region of Puglia, (where Bari, an important large city, is located), although in the south, had an abortion rate five times higher than that of neighboring regions. These differences undoubtedly reflect differences in the availability of legal abortion services. This hypothesis is fully supported by a correlational analysis of abortion rates and availability of services. The two variables were closely correlated ($r = +0.810$) (Nobili, 1981). If this hypothesis is true, it would be safe to say that the official abortion statistics are an underestimate of the actual number of abortions taking place.

Nonetheless, when compared with those of other European countries, Italian abortion rates are not low. As shown in table 18.3, the abortion rates and ratios in Italy in 1979, the first full year in which the abortion law was in effect, was higher than those of France, Finland, England and Wales, and the Federal Republic of Germany, all countries with longer experience with a liberal abortion law. Italy continued to post higher abortion rates and ratios in 1984 compared to these countries as is evident in table 18.3.

The social and demographic characteristics of women undergoing legal abortions are shown on table 18.4. As far as age is concerned, the great majority of the women undergoing abortion are in the eighteen to thirty-five age group. The proportion of women under age eighteen (minors) is small, and it has in fact decreased from 4.1 in 1978 to 3.3 in 1983. Compared to other European countries, this proportion is low. Unfortunately, again age breakdown into different age groups does not allow a direct comparison with data from other countries. For the regions that did provide comparable data, however, it was shown that the proportion of teenagers (below age twenty) undergoing abortion was 8.2 percent for Italy, 27.7 percent for England and Wales, 24.4 percent for Norway, and 17.1 percent for Denmark (Tietze & Henshaw, 1986, p. 65). Likewise low is the abortion rate for this age group (5.3 per 1,000) (Landucci-Tosi et al., 1983). As we will discuss later, the legal requirement of consent by a parent or a judge is believed to constitute a barrier to legal abortion services for teenage girls.

Most women undergoing abortions are married (73.4 percent in 1983). This is particularly true of the less developed areas of the country where abortion

Figure 18.1
Fertility Rate in Italy, 1962–81

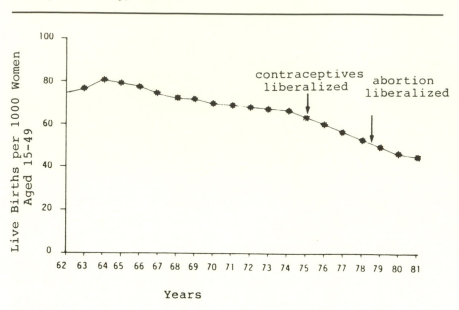

Years

services are scarce. In this respect, too, the situation in Italy is different from that of other European countries. In 1983 the proportion of single women undergoing abortion was 58.3 percent in England and Wales, 59.1 percent in Finland, and 44.4 percent in France (1982 data) (Tietze & Henshaw, 1986). In addition, most Italian women (76.2 percent) undergoing abortion have had at least one previous live birth. This figure too differentiates Italy from other countries where abortions are more frequently observed in nulliparous women. (Three-fourths of women obtaining abortions in 1983 had no previous abortion experience. It is difficult to evaluate this figure since the data from previous years are incomplete and since legal abortions became available only very recently. However, the question of repeat abortions requires further research in Italy. It is of great interest to those concerned with education and public policy.)

ABORTION AND FERTILITY REGULATION

In spite of the absence of contraception and abortion services, the fertility rate in Italy has been steadily decreasing in the postwar period (figure 18.1). The introduction of contraception services in 1975 and abortion services in 1978 has probably rendered fertility regulation more efficient and safe. A large number of women, however, are still deprived of such services.

According to the World Fertility Survey in 1979, withdrawal was still the most commonly used method in all age groups (WFS, 1979). More recent data from a national sample of female industrial workers confirms this finding (Figà-Talamanca, 1983). The WFS data also show that the types of contraceptives used by women who still plan to have another child and those who have completed their fertility are similar and again mostly ineffective. Seventy percent of couples who want no more children, for example, normally practice "natural methods" (mostly coitus interruptus). Only 16 percent of these women use the pill, and another 3.7 percent use the IUD. While the diaphragm and chemical methods are practically unknown, a relatively large proportion of couples use prophylactics (19 percent) while another 14 percent practice periodic or occasional abstinence. Hormonal contraceptives are used mostly by women with intermediate and higher education aged twenty-five to thirty-five; teenagers and older women and women with low educational levels use primarily withdrawal and prophylactics (Landucci-Tosi et al., 1981).

Family planning services (*consultori familiari*) are now available in most urban centers. They provide preventive services on all material and child health problems, including contraception. These services, however, have not yet earned the full confidence of the working-class housewives who are still too reserved to seek help for fertility control in a public service. Many of these women would probably accept more efficient contraceptives if they were sufficiently informed. In a number of regions, especially in the South, family planning services are not available even in urban settings. Financial constraints and lack of trained personnel have delayed the implementation of the 1975 law instituting such services. Abortion services here are also lagging behind. These areas are, in fact, experiencing a fertility rate, which, although not very high in absolute terms, is higher than that of the northern and central regions. The abortion rates, too, are lower here than in the rest of the country (table 18.2). This does not necessarily mean that women in the less developed regions choose to have more children and fewer abortions. It probably means that in the absence of effective contraception they end up with more pregnancies. It also probably means that in the absence of legal abortion services, they end up with illegal abortions as they did in the past.

UNRESOLVED PROBLEMS

The preceding discussion points out several of the problems that have not been adequately solved by the new abortion law. We will now discuss three of these problems in some detail: the problem of minors' accessibility to abortion; the problems created by the "conscience" clause; and the organizational problems in implementing the law.

The Problem of Minors

As shown in table 18.4, a progressively smaller proportion of minors tends to seek legal abortion. This proportion is lowest in the rural southern regions (1 percent in Molise) and higher in the more developed northern regions (7 percent

in Emilia Romagna). It is probable that the requirement of consent on the part
of a parent or guardian or judge is a major obstacle to minors seeking abortions.
In the past most minors who did request abortion had parental consent. In 1983
about 59 percent of minors who underwent an abortion did so on parental consent.
In the last year for which data are available (1981), there seems to be a marked
increase in the proportion of minors obtaining an abortion with the permission
of a judge. It may be that young women prefer to resolve their problem without
parental intervention. This would also indicate that services should make a greater
effort to provide pre- and postabortion counseling to these women. Data from
various regions also indicate another problem in connection with minors. Their
abortions are usually performed at a later gestational age than those of adult
women. Young women probably delay seeking an abortion because of inexperience, ambivalence, and hesitation to discuss the matter with their parents. The
requirement of consent from parents or from the judge also probably contributes
to delays in seeking abortion early in pregnancy.

The "Conscience" Clause

A great many health professionals working in services that could provide
abortions have chosen not to do so on the basis of the "conscience" clause. In
1981, 59 percent of physicians, 49 percent of anesthetists, and 32.8 percent of
nurses and other paramedical personnel were conscientious objectors. Although
incomplete, data seem to indicate that, in regions where public pressure to provide
abortion services is high, the number of doctors willing to provide abortion is
slowly rising. In many other regions, however, the situation is still very difficult.
In some regions as many as 90 percent of the doctors refuse to perform abortions.
Sometimes the conscience clause has even been interpreted to apply to tasks
extraneous to the intervention; some auxiliary personnel such as cooks or other
housekeeping workers refuse to provide their services to women in the abortion
ward. The lack of a sufficient number of medical staff in abortion services often
creates long waiting lists. The law prescribes that abortions have to be performed
in the first trimester and as emergency procedures. In many services, however,
overworked providers, under the pressure of increasing demand, have no choice
but to schedule abortions close to the first-trimester limit. A waiting period of
two to four weeks before the abortions can be performed is not unusual. As
shown in table 18.4, about half of the abortions are, in fact, performed after the
ninth week of gestation. Most women find this waiting period particularly stressful, and some shop around the services in the hope of obtaining an earlier
appointment.

Without doubt some doctors use the "conscience" clause for reasons other
than their moral and religious beliefs. Being a conscientious objector often means
doing less work, especially less unpleasant work. It also means not exposing
oneself to the criticism of the older and often more conservative supervisors. It
protects against stigma from fanatic antiabortion members of the community.
Besides, it involves no loss of income or prestige. The doctor performing abortion

has no advantage over his or her colleagues. On the contrary, such doctors expose themselves to all the above risks. Their only motivation is their personal dedication to help women in need. By removing the abortion practice entirely (often a lucrative one) from the private to the public sector, the new law eliminated the physicians' financial incentives. Previously, a number of physicians working in public services (hospitals, clinics, etc.) privately performed clandestine abortions for a fee. As long as the "conscience" clause gives them a way out at no loss, they have no reason to offer the services free of charge in the public sector.

It is also interesting to know that a health professional can claim and disclaim exception from abortion-related tasks on the basis of the "conscience" clause as many times as one wishes. Changes in "conscience" indeed do take place, and sometimes in coincidence with other career changes such as promotions, change of jobs, or change of supervisors.

Problems in the Organization of Services

In the last few years Italy has made impressive progress in the areas of family planning legislation. Both the law instituting family planning services and the law providing abortion practically on demand are among the most complete and most progressive in the world today. Nevertheless, legislation is not enough. The major problem now is to implement these laws. The difficulties are many: Financial problems have been becoming progressively more serious in recent years. Organizational problems are also pressing. There is urgent need to extend the services to all women and to render abortion a safe outpatient procedure. There is also need for training the personnnel and for educating the public to the correct use of available services.

Funds for abortion services are inadequate and are often used ineffectively. Preoperative and operative procedures make abortion a costly operation in Italy. According to the World Health Organization guidelines, preoperative laboratory examinations may be limited to hemoglobin determination and blood grouping (WHO, 1979). Preabortion laboratory examinations routinely requested in Italy include a long list of blood and urine tests, electrocardiograms, chest x-rays, and in some cases even pulmonary function tests.

Long waiting lists cause delays. Many women are operated on at the end of the first trimester and are subjected to D&C under general anesthesia. Most women are kept in the hospital for several days, thus considerably increasing the economic cost of abortion.

In addition to being costly, delays also increase the risk of postabortion complications. The data on this subject are incomplete because of poor followup. The available evidence indicates a rate of complications that does not exceed that of other Western countries. Many postabortion complications, however, would be avoided if more abortions were performed prior to the ninth week and under local anesthesia.

When the abortion law became effective, most hospitals were not equipped to perform induced abortions. Equipment, especially equipment for vacuum aspirations, was scarce and is still missing in some areas. There have been no organized training programs. Many physicians had to obtain their training informally from colleagues. Nor have providers been trained in abortion counseling. Most women requesting an abortion, of course, need minimal or no counseling. They must simply be informed in detail of the steps involved in the operation and of what is expected to happen. Expert counseling may be necessary in some cases, such as cases of young girls, of women having abortions for medical reasons or for fetal anomalies, or of women with particular social problems. Contraceptive counseling is also important. At present, abortion services in Italy are located in hospitals. They have no communication with the family planning clinics. Abortion patients are often lost to followup in both services. It is therefore necessary either to establish close collaboration between the two services or to provide effective contraceptive counseling at the abortion service.

Public education is another important priority. A very large number of Italian couples still rely on natural methods of fertility control. Unwanted pregnancies are terminated with abortion. Most such abortions are now legal and safe, but many of them would also be prevented by a change to better contraceptive practice. This change is slowly occurring in most urban and developed parts of the country; however, many rural areas of the South are still deprived of both services and information. The challenge for the future is to implement adequately the well-intended legislation, so that soon all abortions may become legal, and many of them may eventually be prevented by contraception.

SUMMARY

Liberal abortion legislation was introduced in Italy in 1978 following a long and bitter battle between pro- and antiabortion factions. The law was challenged and confirmed by popular vote in 1980. Legal abortion is now available free of charge to all women over the age of eighteen for a broad spectrum of health, social, and economic conditions. The abortion decision is left entirely up to the woman. Minors may have an abortion with the consent of a parent or a guardian, or with the permission of a judge. Abortion services are public and are operated according to precice standards. Abortions are not allowed in the private sector.

The number of abortions performed annually in Italy is about 220,000. It is hypothesized that in many areas of the South where abortion services are not available, abortions are still performed illegally. Women undergoing abortions are mostly adults, married, with previous births. Compared to other European countries, few teenagers resort to abortion in Italy. This may be due to the legal barrier which requires teenagers to present parental consent.

Most Italian couples use natural contraceptive methods (especially withdrawal). Oral contraceptives and the IUD are still used by relatively few and better educated women. Unwanted pregnancies are terminated by abortion. Abortion rates and ratios are low and declining.

Some of the problems still facing the legislature are the accessibility of legal abortion to minors and the lack of collaboration of the medical community in implementing the law. The majority of physicians refuse to perform abortions in the name of the "conscience" clause which exempts from the abortion service those who object to it for moral or religious reasons. Other aspects of implementation problems discussed include organization of services and training of personnel.

REFERENCES

Borruso, V. [Abortion in Italy.] Ila Palma Palermo, 1982.

Colombo, B. [On the diffusion of illegal abortions in Italy.] *Medicina e Morale*, 1975 (1/2).

Figà-Talamanca, I. [Attitudes and opinions about contraception and abortion.] *Educazione Sanitaria* 1972, *3*, 411–421.

―――. Induced aborting in Italy. *Pacific Health Education Reports* 1974, *4*, 1–139.

―――. Estimating the incidence of induced abortions in Italy. *Genus*, 1976, *22*(1–2), 91–107.

―――. [National survey of the reproductive health of industrial workers.] Rome: Istituto di Medicina Sociale, 1983 (unpublished data).

Figà-Talamanca, I., & Rugiati, S. [Survey on the attitudes towards contraception and abortion of a sample of Italian gynecologists.] *Difesa Sociale* 1974, *4*, 1–28.

Landucci-Tosi, S., Grandolfo, M. E., & Spinelli, A. [Voluntary interruption of pregnancy in Italy 1978–1980.] ISTISAN 1982/6.

Landucci-Tosi, S., Spinelli, A., Baldini, A., & Caroffi Perini, A. [Contraception in Italy: A sample study of family planning centres of seven different regions.] *Contraccezione Fertilità Sessualità*, 1981, *5*, 425–446.

Landucci-Tosi, S., Spinelli, A., Cortellessa, C. M., and Grandolfo, M. E., & Timperi, F. [Voluntary interruption of pregnancy in Italy 1981.] ISTISAN, 1983/6.

Modolo, M. A., Marcuccini, A. M., & Morlunghi, P. [Survey on the opinion of medical students at the University of Perugia on problems of contraception and abortion.] *Educazione Sanitaria*, 1973, 160–179.

Nobili, A. [First data after the voluntary abortion law in Italy.] Proceedings of the Seminar [*Incidence, trends and characteristics of induced abortion: International experience and the Italian situation.*] Rome, 2 May 1980, Institute of Demography of the University of Rome.

Tietze, C., & Henshaw, S. K. *Induced abortion: A world review, 1986* (6th ed.). New York: Alan Guttmacher Institute, 1986.

What Italians Think. *Panorama*, 1 August 1974, pp. 57–58.

World Fertility Survey. *Italy*, 1979. Rome: National Research Council, 1981.

World Health Organization. *Induced abortion guidelines for the provision of care and services.* WHO Offset publications No. 49, 1979.

Zardini de Marchi, M. L. *Inhumanae Vitae.* Sugar Ed. Milan, 1970.

Table 18.1

Legal Abortions, Abortion Rate and Ratio, and Fertility Rate, Italy, 1978–84

Year	Legal Abortions	Abortion[1] Rate	Abortion Ratio	Fertility Rate
1978[2]	137,400	10.1	17.2	58.7
1979	187,631	15.9	27.7	49.4
1980	222,499	18.7	34.5	46.6
1981	224,067	18.7	36.3	45.0
1982	234,800	19.6	38.2	-
1983	234,000	19.5	39.3	-
1984	227,400	19.0	38.8	-

[1]Abortion rates are calculated per 1,000 women aged 15–44.
[2]1978 figures were estimated on the basis of the experience of the second semester of that year.
Source: Data for this table were calculated on the basis of the following: Landucci-Tosi et al., 1982/6 and 1983/6; Tietze & Henshaw, 1986.

Table 18.2

Legal Abortions by Geographic Area, Italy, 1981

Area	Legal Abortions	Abortion Rate	Abortion Ratio	Fertility Rate
North	108,934	17.4	486	35.9
Central	51,133	19.4	486	39.9
South	48,052	14.5	245	59.2
Islands	15,948	9.9	175	56.6
Total	224,067	16.2	363	45.0

Source: Data for this table were calculated on the basis of the following: Landucci-Tosi et al., 1982/6 and 1983/6.

Table 18.3
Abortion Rates and Ratios for Some European Countries, 1979 and 1984

Country	Abortion Rates per 1000 women Aged 15-44		Abortion Ratio	
	1979	1984	1979	1984
Bulgaria	69.6	61.9	97.5	92.5
Hungary	35.9	37.1	52.5	69.1
Denmark	21.6	18.4	39.8	40.0
Italy	15.9	19.0	28.9	38.8
Finland	15.8	12.1	26.5	20.2
France	14.1	14.9	20.2	23.3
England and Wales	12.1	12.8	18.6	21.0
German Federal Rep.	8.8	7.3	19.3	16.8

Source: Tietze & Henshaw, 1986.

Table 18.4
Percentage of Selected Characteristics of Women Having Abortions in Italy, 1978–83

Age	1978	1979	1980	1981	1983
17 or less	4.1	3.3	3.6	3.0	3.3
18-35	73.4	73.9	73.4	71.1[1]	69.9[2]
36+	22.8	22.9	23.0	25.3[1]	26.8[3]
Marital Status					
Single	29.4	24.1	28.0	23.7	26.6
Married	70.6	75.9	72.0	76.3	73.4
Previous Births					
None	NA			24.9	23.8
1	NA			20.5	21.4
2	NA			32.2	31.8
3+	NA			22.4	23.0
Weeks of Gestation[4]					
8 or less	47.9	40.3	36.1	52.8	44.6
9-12	50.5	58.0	63.8	47.0	54.6
13 or more	1.5	1.7	1.1	0.4	0.9
Abortion Procedure					
D and C NA				20	NA
Vacuum Aspiration NA				61	NA
D and C plus instrumental evac. NA				18	NA
Others NA				16	NA

NA = not available.
[1]Age groupings 18–34 and 35 and over.
[2]Age groupings 18–34.
[3]Age groupings 35 and over.
[4]Data from selected regions.
Source: Landucci-Tosi et al., 1982/6 and 1983/6; Tietze & Henshaw, 1986.

19

JAPAN

Minoru Muramatsu

HISTORICAL DEVELOPMENT OF ABORTION POLICY

Prior to World War II, the political authorities in Japan took a highly restrictive attitude toward abortion. The Criminal Code of 1907 forbade all induced abortions except when they were judged to be absolutely necessary from the medical standpoint to save the life of the mother. Penal regulations were inflicted on abortees as well as those who performed an induced abortion illegally.

A national law promulgated in 1948, which was named the Eugenic Protection Law, changed the picture completely. The law was not introduced by the government itself; a small number of Diet members who were medical doctors at the same time submitted a bill to the Diet, and it was passed without extensive debate. Even in its original form, the Eugenic Protection Law of 1948 had a rather liberal attitude to abortion. In those years, the vast majority of countries in the world limited legal indications for abortion to narrowly defined medical conditions. The liberal handling of induced abortion in Japan thus attracted the attention of interested individuals in the world.

Since then, the law has undergone several amendments. Most important among them were the amendment enacted in 1949 which added an economic consideration to the legal grounds for abortion and the amendment of 1952 which enabled the physician in charge to perform abortion entirely at his or her own discretion without consulting a local official committee. With these two major amendments incorporated, the performance of induced abortion became further liberalized.

Even today there are differences of opinion as to the real motive for the establishment of such a liberal abortion law in 1948. A group of observers maintain that the law was conceived as part of a national policy that aimed at the curtailment of population growth. It is believed that, owing to a large-scale population movement into Japan immediately after the war, as well as the so-called postwar baby boom, overpopulation was a serious problem in Japan and induced abortion was regarded as a quick solution to it under such circumstances. Opposed to this opinion are those who interpret the enactment of the law as a health and welfare measure in order to safeguard women against the physical injury incurred by the increasing resort to criminal abortions in those years. At that time the government emphasized that the policy was officially adopted from this viewpoint of health and welfare, but, in due fairness, it could be argued that a demographic consideration was also an important underlying factor (Berelson, 1974).

For the past fifteen years or so, serious debates have been held as to whether or not the law should be modified in accordance with the change in the country's socioeconomic conditions. A number of political leaders, with strong support from certain religious groups, have repeatedly urged more rigid strictures on abortion. They claim the law is too liberal, focusing their arguments on such points as: induced abortion can be harmful; too many abortions are done, and this leads to the deterioration of the respect for life; birth rates in Japan have fallen too low and fertility should be restored; and, in particular, the "economic consideration" as a reason for abortion might have been necessary in those early years when the law was introduced, but in view of the remarkable economic progress of the country since then, it is no longer valid to retain such a clause.

Against this organized political move toward the restrictions over abortion, a group of influential citizens and private organizations have also repeatedly expressed their views in favor of maintaining some freedom in the choice of induced abortion. They base their arguments on such points as the following: the liberalization of abortion has been widely accepted in many advanced countries; abortions are not particularly harmful as long as they are performed by qualified medical practitioners; the "national economic progress" does not necessarily mean individual well-being and induced abortion cannot be forgone altogether; the number of children for each couple is entirely a matter of personal decision; more effective contraceptive methods, such as oral pills, should be made freely available before legal provisions concerning abortion are modified; and, in particular, a woman's right to privacy must be duly respected.

Both parties have been equally vocal in their own assertions. Under the circumstances, the Diet, which has often become a central arena of heated debates, is not yet in a position to draw a final conclusion. Thus, the abortion clauses contained in the Eugenic Protection Law remain unchanged. Women's organizations have also been very active in their pro-liberalization campaign in Japan.

LEGAL STATUS OF ABORTION

The Eugenic Protection Law of 1948, as it stands in 1984, prescribes in Article 14 the following indications for legal performance of abortion as major components:

1. Eugenic indications applicable in the case of mental diseases, hereditary physical diseases, hereditary mental diseases, and so on.

2. The so-called maternal health protection indication which states that an abortion can be performed when the mother's health will be seriously impaired due to physical or economic reasons if the pregnancy continues.

3. Humanitarian indications applicable in the case of pregnancy due to violence.

As can be seen from these indications, an induced abortion cannot be performed merely on request; the law does specify certain conditions required for the legal performance of abortion. However, in practice, the above-mentioned maternal health protection indication, which is a combination of medical and socioeconomic reasons, is loosely interpreted by the general public. The fact that more than 99 percent of all reported induced abortions are done under this indication suggests, in all likelihood, that a large number of abortions are likely being performed to terminate an unwanted pregnancy.

Japan has one unique arrangement with regard to the legal performance of induced abortion: not all licensed physicians are allowed to do the operation but only those with sufficient professional knowledge, skill, and facilities in obstetrics and gynecology who have been authorized by local medical associations can perform an induced abortion. This is known as the system of "designated physicians" and is believed to be of help in eliminating unsafe abortions done by unqualified invidividuals.

ATTITUDES TOWARD ABORTION

According to a national family planning survey conducted by the Mainichi Newspapers in 1981, 16 percent of a total of about 3,000 women surveyed indicated unconditional approval of induced abortion. Sixty-six percent said they would approve abortion under certain conditions, for example, to protect the life or the health of the woman, to terminate a pregnancy resulting from violence, or to terminate a pregnancy when serious hereditary diseases are associated. On the other hand, those who denied abortion under any circumstances represented 11 percent (Summary of Sixteenth National Survey, 1981).

In general, Japanese women show permissive attitudes to abortion. The number of women who disapprove has declined somewhat. As far as the general public is concerned, religion does not seem to play a significant role as a restraint on abortion.

DEMOGRAPHY OF ABORTION

Table 19.1 presents the number of induced abortions reported to the health authorities in Japan from 1949 to 1983. A peak was reached in 1955 when some 1,170,000 abortions were reported against about 1,731,000 live births officially registered. Thereafter, the numbers have generally continued to decrease; 590,000 abortions in 1982 as compared to 1,515,000 live births. It has been argued that these reported numbers do not represent the real total incidence, but no perfect methodology is available to arrive at reliable and indisputable estimates of abortion.

Table 19.2 represents the induced abortion rates per 1,000 women aged fifteen to forty-four for the period 1955–83. The rates for the period under observation fell almost steadily; the 1983 figure was slightly less than half of what it was twenty years before.

When the abortion rates are broken down by age, the rates decrease significantly from 1955 to 1982 in all age groups except the youngest group, less than twenty years, although the abortion rate in this age group is much lower than that in other groups (table 19.3). The increasing trend in abortion among teenagers has drawn the attention of many quarters of society, and the need for sex education designed for this particular population is being discussed.

Also available from the official statistics of abortion published by the Ministry of Health and Welfare is information about the period of gestation. If 567,500 reported induced abortions in 1983 were broken down in this respect, 52.2 percent were done up to the end of the eighth week; 42.3 percent during the ninth through twelfth week; 3.1 percent during the thirteenth through sixteenth week; and 2.4 percent seventeenth week and beyond. The vast majority of abortions are performed within the first trimester of gestation in Japan, but first-trimester abortions are more common among older women aged twenty-five and above who reported 94 percent to over 96 percent of the total in 1982. Younger women under twenty-four constitute eight out of every ten women who sought first-trimester abortions in the same year.

Furthermore, increasingly more women with low parity are among those obtaining abortions. The proportion of women with zero parity increased from 21 percent in 1961–65 to 41 percent during 1976–80. (The above discussion shows that in Japan typically married women with children seek abortion, but this characteristic seems to be changing.) According to data from the Congenital Anomaly Research Center (known as Human Embryos Data), 61 percent of the women who sought an abortion in 1980 had experienced one or more previous abortions (Shiota & Nishimura, 1982). The 1986 National Survey on Family Planning revealed that 30.6 percent of all women surveyed had experienced one or more prior abortions.

ABORTION AND FERTILITY REGULATION

For the past few decades, researchers have from time to time tried to estimate the roles played by induced abortion vis-à-vis contraception in the overall decrease in fertility in Japan. There are some differences among the results shown by them, but one common characteristic is the conclusion that the part played by induced abortion was very significant during the early years while that played by contraception had gained substantial weight in more recent years.

A typical example of studies conducted along this line may be seen in table 19.4. From this presentation the relative ratios between abortion and contraception in the prevention of births can be summarized. The results contained in this table are based on a pilot family planning study conducted by the late Dr. Hisao Aoki of the Institute of Population Problems, Ministry of Health and Welfare, some ten years ago. Using data obtained in the pilot study, the author first calculated the number of pregnancies that would have occurred in the absence of any fertility control method. Then, from this figure, the number of actually recorded live births was subtracted. The balance consisted of two groups of pregnancies: those prevented by contraception (including sterilization) and those prevented by induced abortion. Using data pertaining to the effectiveness of contraception also obtained by the study, the author estimated the number of pregnancies prevented by contraception. The balance then was the number of pregnancies that were prevented by induced abortion. Finally, all these figures were converted into percentages.

SUMMARY

A national law promulgated in 1948 prescribes certain indications for the legal performance of induced abortion in Japan. It does not allow an abortion on request, but in practice, people tend to interpret the law liberally. In addition, Japanese women by and large take a permissive attitude to abortion.

There have been heated debates as to the needs of modifying the legal grounds for abortion contained in the current law. Among other things, the so-called economic reason has been a matter of most serious controversy. Debates are not yet settled; no substantial changes have so far been effected.

The reported number of abortions in Japan has declined significantly since 1955. Abortion rates among young women aged less than twenty are on the increase, although they are low in comparison with those of other age groups. The majority of abortions are done within the first trimester. Only those medical practitioners who are deemed well qualified in obstetrics and gynecology can perform an abortion legally.

During the early period after the last war, abortion apparently was a significant factor in reducing births. In recent years, however, contraceptive practice has gained in influence over abortion.

REFERENCES

Berelson, Bernard (Ed.). *Population policy in developed countries*. New York: McGraw-Hill Book Co., 1974.

Muramatsu, M. *Japan's experience in family planning—Past and present*. Tokyo: Family Planning Federation of Japan, 1967.

————. An analysis of factors in fertility control in Japan—An updated and revised version. *Bulletin of the Institute of Public Health*, 1973, *22* (4), 228–236.

————. Estimation of induced abortions, Japan, 1975. *Bulletin of the Institute of Public Health*, 1975, *27* (2), 93–97.

————, & Kuroda, T. Japan. In B. Berelson (Ed.), *Population policy in developed countries*. New York: McGraw-Hill Book Co., 1974.

————, et al. Bird's-eye view of population and family planning in Japan. Tokyo: Japanese Organization for International Cooperation in Family Planning, 1980. 48–49.

Report of Eugenic Protection Statistics: Showa 57. *Japan*. Tokyo: Ministry of Health and Welfare, 1983.

Shiota Kohei, & Nishimura, H. Epidemiology of induced abortion. Paper presented at the International Conference on Reproductive Health Care, Maui, Hawaii, June 1982.

Summary of Sixteenth National Survey on family planning (in Japanese). Tokyo: Population Problem Research Council, Mainichi Newspaper, 1981.

Tietze, C., & Henshaw, S. K. *Induced abortion: A world review, 1986* (6th ed). New York: Alan Guttmacher Institute, 1986.

Tyler, C. W. Epidemiology of abortion. *Journal of Reproductive Medicine*, 1981, *26*, 459–469.

Table 19.1
Reported Induced Abortions, Japan, 1949–83

Year	Number	Year	Number
1949	246,104	1966	808,378
1950	489,111	1967	747,490
1951	638,350	1968	757,389
1952	805,524	1969	744,451
1953	1,068,066	1970	732,033
1954	1,143,059	1971	739,674
1955	1,170,143	1972	732,653
1956	1,159,288	1973	700,532
1957	1,122,316	1974	679,837
1958	1,128,231	1975	671,597
1959	1,098,853	1976	664,106
1960	1,063,256	1977	641,242
1961	1,035,329	1978	618,044
1962	985,351	1979	613,676
1963	955,092	1980	598,084
1964	878,748	1981	596,569
1965	843,248	1982	590,299
		1983	567,500

Source: Statistics concerning eugenic protection, Statistics and Information Division, Ministry of Health and Welfare, Japan; Tietze & Henshaw, 1986.

Table 19.2
Induced Abortion Rates per 1,000 Women Aged Fifteen to Forty-four, Japan, 1955–83

Year	Rate	Year	Rate
1955	55.5	1969	28.4
1956	53.9	1970	27.9
1957	51.2	1971	28.3
1958	50.6	1972	27.8
1959	48.4	1973	26.4
1960	46.7	1974	25.6
1961	45.3	1975	25.2
1962	42.1	1976	25.0
1963	39.5	1977	24.2
1964	35.4	1978	23.4
1965	33.4	1979	23.2
1966	31.5	1980	22.6
1967	28.9	1981	22.7
1968	29.1	1982	22.4
		1983	21.5

Note: Rates computed by the author, using abortion data published by the Statistics and Information Division, Ministry of Health and Welfare, and population data published by the Bureau of Statistics, Prime Minister's Office, Japan.

Table 19.3
Induced Abortion Rates per 1,000 Women by Age, Japan, Selected Years

	Less than 20	20-24	25-29	30-34	35-39	40-44
1955	3.4	43.1	80.8	95.1	80.5	41.8
1960	3.2	40.2	73.9	74.0	62.7	29.4
1965	2.5	31.1	56.0	56.0	38.8	21.2
1970	3.2	26.4	42.2	44.7	32.9	14.7
1975	3.1	24.7	34.3	38.4	29.2	13.8
1976	3.4	25.2	33.8	38.5	28.3	13.4
1977	3.5	24.2	32.3	36.4	28.2	13.5
1978	3.9	23.8	31.2	34.9	26.8	12.7
1979	4.3	23.8	30.5	34.5	26.8	12.4
1980	4.7	23.3	29.3	33.2	26.8	12.0
1981	5.5	23.5	28.9	32.8	27.1	11.9
1982	6.0	23.2	27.9	33.3	26.8	12.2

Source: Statistics concerning eugenic protection, Statistics and Information Division, Ministry of Health and Welfare, Japan.

Table 19.4
Relative Proportions of Births Actually Recorded, and Births Averted by Induced Abortion and by Contraception, Japan, Selected Years

	Of a Total of 100 Pregnancies Theoretically Expected		
	Proportion of Births Actually Recorded	Proportion of Births Averted by Induced Abortion	Proportion of Births Averted by Contraception
1955	44.9	37.4	17.7
1960	38.8	31.4	29.8
1965	38.2	19.8	42.0
1970	38.8	16.9	44.3

Source: Muramatsu et al., 1980.

20

SOUTH KOREA

Sung-bong Hong

HISTORICAL DEVELOPMENT OF ABORTION POLICY

The policy toward induced abortion during the Japanese occupation was strictly prohibitive. During this period Confucianism, which encouraged large families, prevailed among the people. This value system was maintained unchanged through the liberation in 1945 up to the outbreak of the Korean conflict in 1950. Indictments against induced abortion were reported sporadically during this period.

Before the implementation of the First Five-Year Economic Development Plan in 1962, population control was viewed as a prerequisite to achieve economic development. Hence, family planning programs were adopted as a government project. Aspiration for small family size has emerged along with the nationwide campaigns for family planning. Although the Penal Code against abortion was still in existence, actual judicial supervision was markedly attenuated.

The active participation of physicians in the small family program resulted in a steadily increasing demand for induced abortion. In 1966, four years after the government launched its family planning programs, the government, pressured by religious groups and politicians, proposed a new maternal and child health law which included the legalization of induced abortion. The second attempt at legalization was again defeated in 1970. However, on 30 January 1973 the Extraordinary State Council (the martial law authority) (Potts, 1977) passed the law against which the Korean Bishop's Association immediately protested. On the other hand, the Korean Associations of Protestant Churches, convened in 1974, declared their official acceptance of induced abortion.

The government considered a revision of the Maternal and Child Health Law to liberalize abortion, but it did not materialize because of political pressure from the Roman Catholic church. It was reported that the government planned to extend the scope of legalized abortion to include adolescents and indigents.

As suggested earlier, the actual practice of induced abortion had been liberal long before the law was enacted. Obstetricians and the majority of the medical profession as well as the judicial sector were generally favorable to legalized abortion, but the pediatric specialists opposed the legislation because it had nothing to do with child health. An editorial in the *Han-Kook Daily*, one of the leading newspapers in Korea, asserted that legalization was inevitable.

With regard to the religious sectors, the Catholic church has protested the abortion policy throughout the past two decades whereas the Protestant churches supported the legalization cautiously.

Even though the problem of abortion concerns women mainly, the majority of women's organizations have remained unresponsive to the issue, probably being satisfied with the present situation.

LEGAL STATUS OF ABORTION

According to the Korean Penal Code, articles 269 and 270, induced abortion is illegal. But the estimated number of induced abortions per year probably exceeds 1 million, which is ample evidence that the prohibitive law is meaningless in practice.

The Maternal and Child Health Law enacted 30 January 1973 set out the conditions under which abortions could be performed. Article 8 (United Nations Fund for Population Activities, 1979) permitted a physician to perform an abortion, with the consent of the woman and her spouse, in case of hereditary defect and certain infectious diseases; when the pregnancy results from rape or incest; and when, from the medical point of view, the continuation of pregnancy will severely damage the health of the mother. It did not permit abortion on socio-economic grounds.

The government has unsuccessfully attempted to liberalize induced abortion on several occasions. Reportedly, the government is preparing to extend the law to include induced abortion for adolescents, the unwed, and indigents.

ATTITUDES TOWARD ABORTION

Few illegal abortions were performed before the 1950s when the prohibitive Penal Code was strictly observed. Once the government family planning programs were fully functioning in 1962, the new small family goal was firmly established among the public. Along with the spread of contraceptive devices, induced abortion was increased gradually from urban to rural areas with lessened judicial enforcement against abortion, coupled with active participation by the medical profession.

The ratio (Hong, 1971) of induced abortion to live birth in Seoul shows that induced abortion increased during the 1960s in Seoul: 21.1 to 100 live births in 1961; 49.0 in 1963; 60.4 in 1967; and 74.8 in 1969. These figures reflect the whole picture of induced abortion in which providers, clients, and legal constraints are all interrelated. Under the circumstances described above, the Maternal and Child Health Law prescribed legalized abortion in January 1973. Around that time, leading figures in the medical profession opined that the nonfunctioning abortion law should be revised to cope with the reality.

As previously mentioned, within the religious sector, the Protestant church favored legalization of induced abortion, whereas the Catholic church protested legalization. An editorial in Korea's leading daily newspaper asserted that the abortion law should be revised to keep pace with changing reality.

In the earliest preparation phase of the new abortion law in 1966, the government had intended to include socioeconomic reasons for induced abortion but, succumbing to strong pressure from the religious sector and some politicians, it did not do so. However, beginning in 1974 the government programs subsidized menstrual regulation procedures for indigents; these programs are nothing but induced abortion in the very early stage of pregnancy. The number of menstrual regulation recipients subsidized between 1974 and 1981 was reported to be about 327,000, and the number of births averted was estimated to be as much as 236,000 (Ministry of Public Health and Social Affairs, 1982).

DEMOGRAPHY OF ABORTION

Prevalence of Induced Abortion

The number of induced abortions during the Japanese occupation and through the 1950s was presumably negligible under the strictly observed abortion law. However, with the initiation of national family planning programs in 1962 and the relaxation of judicial enforcement, the practice of abortion expanded from urban to rural areas.

As shown in table 20.1, the prevalence rate of induced abortion among currently married wives in Seoul based on surveys (Hong, 1976; Byun, 1979; Lim, 1982) was 25 percent in 1964, doubled in twelve years in 1976 to 50 percent, and rose to 58 percent in 1978. The rate in other cities was 15 percent in 1964, 34 percent in 1971, and 57 percent in 1978, the same level as in the Seoul area. (Denominators for the period 1964–68 are currently married wives aged twenty to forty-four, and for 1971–82 those aged fifteen to forty-four.)

In rural areas the prevalence was only 4 percent in 1964, 10 percent in 1968, 19 percent in 1971, and 38 percent in 1978. Thus, it grew ten times in fifteen years and was approaching a level comparable to that in urban areas. Thus, the marked difference by regions, urban versus rural, that was found at the outset had diminished.

With regard to the national rates, the figure was 7 percent in 1964, 14 percent in 1967, 26 percent in 1971, and 49 percent in 1978. In 1982 the proportion of Korean wives who experienced induced abortion was one-half of all wives (49.6 percent).

Induced Abortion Ratios

The induced abortion ratio (Hong, 1976; Byun, 1979) to pregnancies for ever married women aged twenty to forty-four before 1965 was 7 to 100 pregnancies, 1 to 5 for three consecutive years between 1966 and 1968, and about 1 to 4 for the next three years between 1969 and 1971. (See table 20.2.) Likewise, the abortion ratios to live births was 8.4 to 100 live births before 1965, and rose to 1 to 4 in 1966, 1 to 3 in 1969, 2 to 3 in 1973, and more than 4 to 5 in 1978. (Ratios of abortion for the period between 1973 and 1978 are based on the denominators represented by currently married women aged fifteen to forty-four.) Although data for the 1980s are not available, the ratio of abortion to births could very well be nearly 1 to 1 for 1982.

The remarkable increase in the abortion ratio of women in their twenties is illustrated in table 20.3. The abortion ratios to live births for women aged twenty to twenty-four are read on the first row horizontally. The ratio is 22 per 1,000 live births for wives aged forty-five to forty-nine (as of 1982 born in the mid–1930s), whereas the ratio rose to 296 for those aged twenty to twety-four (born in the mid–1950s). This was as much as a thirteenfold increase in twenty years.

Age-specific Induced Abortion Rates

The main reason which Korean wives reported for induced abortions was limitation of family size (in 73.4 percent) (Moon, Ham & Shin, 1982). The highest induced abortion rate is then expected among the age group which has completed family size.

As shown in table 20.4, throughout the period surveyed (Byun, 1979; Koh, Ham, & Byun, 1980; Hong, 1979), from 1963 to 1979 (except in 1978) the highest rate for currently married women was still recorded aged thirty to thirty-four. The rates for age twenty to twenty-four was 12 to 16 per 1,000 wives in the 1960s, and reached 88 in 1979. The rate for age twenty-five to twety-nine was from 29 to 155 per 1,000 wives, for age thirty to thirty-four from 58 to 188, for age thirty-five to thirty-nine from 40 to 127, and for age forty to forty-four from 31 to 69, respectively. In brief, between 1963 and 1979 the age-specific abortion rate for wives in their twenties increased as much as five- to sixfold, tripled for those in their thirties, and doubled for those in their forties.

The remarkable increase in the abortion rate for those in their twenties is attributable partially to the younger generation's wish for small family size. For example, 44 percent of induced abortions among wives in their twenties were for limitation of family size. Another reason for the increase was the termination of premarital conception. Among the married cohort in 1974–76, premarital conception (Lee, Park, & Choi, 1978) occurred in 26.0 percent.

The data cited so far are derived from the surveys collected from wives. However, the picture of induced abortion after the late 1970s would be incomplete without the inclusion of adolescents or unwed young adults. In this context, a survey of providers of abortion services (Hong, 1979) was carried out in 1979 in Seoul. Of 1,000 abortions, nulliparous women comprised 46.6 percent of the total; women aged twenty to twenty-four represented about 40 percent; and those twenty-five to twenty-nine about 25 percent of the total abortions. Thus, women in their twenties comprised two-thirds (65.2 percent) of all abortions in Seoul.

The proportion of aborters before marriage is estimated to range from 28.7 percent to 38.5 percent. Another provider's survey (Lim & Choi, 1979) in a middle-sized city, Chunju, reported in 1979 that single women accounted for 27.8 percent of total induced abortions.

Abortion Rates for All Women

As described above, abortion rates have increased particularly among wives in their twenties and level off somewhat among wives in their late thirties. As a whole, annual abortion rates have been rising throughout the last two decades. The rates (Tietze, 1979; Byun, 1979; Hong, 1979) for all women aged fifteen to forty-four are shown in table 20.5. The annual induced abortion total was estimated at 104,000 in 1961, 223,000 in 1965, and 331,000 in 1970.

The figures for 1973, 1977, and 1978 are based on the denominators representing currently married women; therefore, they are inappropriate for the direct comparison with the rates computed on all women in the same age as depicted for the 1960s. However, the trend obviously rose throughout the 1970s. As shown in table 20.5, the rate during the last decade surpassed 100 per 1,000 women aged fifteen to forty-four. A survey of providers of induced abortion in Seoul reported an astonishingly high figure—235 per 1,000 women aged fifteen to forty-four, more than twice the national figures produced by surveys of women at about the same time of observation.

Compared with the earlier estimates, this figure from the provider survey probably reflects the ever increasing trend in abortion in Seoul. It also reflects the exclusion of unmarried women from the sample population and underreporting by ever married respondents in the earlier surveys.

Demographic Characteristics

Table 20.6 indicates that more than half of the currently married women after age thirty have utilized abortion. The prevalence of abortion shows a direct association with age of wives in this survey, but the earlier surveys showed a peak mostly at age thirty-five to thirty-nine for all residence groups and the drop after age forty.

Having an abortion is directly related to the number of living children in a family, as table 20.6 indicates. Abortion prevalence reaches 58.4 percent for women with three children; whereas 15.7 percent of wives with no child have already had an abortion. Considering that 46.6 percent of all abortions in Seoul (Hong, 1979) were performed on women with no previous childbirth experience, some premarital abortion is certain.

The relationships between educational levels and utilization of abortion are blurred as indicated in table 20.6. In the 1982 survey, the prevalence is highest for the lower end of the educational distribution (51.4 percent) and lowest for the college level (44.5 percent). However, the abortion surveys done earlier, in the 1970s, had demonstrated a direct association between education and abortion prevalence, with greater utilization of abortion by better educated women. There had been some evidence of shrinking educational differentials in Seoul in the late 1970s survey. The reversed association between education and abortion prevalence in the 1982 survey would be indicative of the increasing effective contraception among the highest educational level.

As illustrated in table 20.6, wives of husbands who run their own shops are more likely to have utilized abortion than wives of farmers. In the earlier surveys (Hong, 1976) wives of husbands with white-collar jobs had been in the highest categories.

There is a direct association between economic status and abortion prevalence. Although the pattern of abortion prevalence by educational attainment and husband's occupation had become somewhat inconsistent in surveys in the late 1970s and early 1980s, the economic factor continues to retain a strong association with abortion prevalence.

Timing of Abortion

In the 1982 survey, induced abortion in the midtrimester occurred among 7.2 percent of women (Moon, 1982). The frequency was 12 percent in urban abortees but 21 percent in rural abortees in the 1971 survey (Hong, 1976). A decrease in midtrimester abortions is favorable from a medical point of view.

Contraceptive Practice Prior and Subsequent to Abortion

Pregnancy terminated by induced abortion may have resulted from contraceptive failure or from nonuse of contraception. The abortion may then be a point of change in contraception and a point of continuity for others. Although recent data on contraceptive practice rates before and after abortion are not available, patterns of contraception among abortees might be more or less similar to that found in the 1971 survey (Hong, 1976).

After their first abortion, 54 percent of women practiced contraception, but only 31 percent were practicing before it. The practice rate before the last abortion, 52 percent, increased to 66 percent afterward. Since abortion terminates unwanted pregnancy, contraceptive rates are obviously higher for aborted women than among all women.

Regardless of time reference to abortion, the current and ever user proportion for abortees in the 1971 survey was much higher than for all women: 42 percent and 76 percent for the abortees and 25 percent and 44 percent for all women, respectively. The current and ever contraceptive user proportion of all women in the 1982 survey (Moon, 1982) was 58 percent and 75 percent, respectively.

ABORTION AND FERTILITY REGULATION

The population of the Republic of Korea was doubled in thirty-three years and reached 40 million in 1983. Since 1962 when the national family planning programs were inaugurated, the annual growth rate decelerated from 2.9 percent in 1962 to 1.56 percent as of 1980. The reduction in the growth rate is considered to be mostly due to postponement of marriage, ever increasing induced abortions, and contraceptive use.

Nonetheless, Korea still ranks twenty-first in world population and third in its density (next to Bangladesh and Taiwan). The proportion of women of reproductive age remained at 46 to 47 percent until the early 1970s, and it rose to 53 percent in 1980. The rural population represented 72 percent of the total in the 1960s but declined to 43 percent by the early 1980s. At the same time, the urban population increased rapidy.

At the inception of the national programs in 1962, traditional methods such as foam tablets and condoms were distributed primarily through health centers, but they were soon discontinued owing to their low effectiveness (except for condoms). The programs were extended to include the IUD in 1964 and oral contraceptives in 1968. As illustrated in table 20.7, the governmental programs (Ministry of Public Health and Social Affairs, 1981) offer IUDs, surgical sterilizations, oral contraceptives, and condoms. The IUD and surgical sterilization for males and females are provided by designated private physicians, and condoms and oral contraceptives are distributed by health workers at the health centers located in each county. For indigents, menstrual regulation has been subsidized under the national programs since 1974.

ABORTION AND ADOLESCENTS

Abortion practice among teenagers was relatively low: 3.3 percent of all abortions in Seoul. The age-specific abortion rate for women aged fifteen to nineteen was 46 per 1,000 in Seoul as reported in the survey (Hong, 1979) of providers, but it was negligible—3 per 1,000 women—in a middle-sized city in 1979 as shown by a similar survey (Lim, 1979). As reported in the surveys of students (Min, 1978; Kim, 1975) and of adolescent female factory workers conducted in the late 1970s, the prevalence of sexual intercourse was 12.1 percent and 20.1 percent, respectively. With Korea's liberal position on sex, induced abortion among adolescents is expected to increase in the future.

REPEAT ABORTIONS

The percentage of repeat abortion (induced abortion experienced twice or more) by residential areas is shown in table 20.8. Among wives repeat abortion was experienced by 34.5 percent in the large cities, 32.1 percent in other cities, and 24.2 percent in rural areas (Lim, 1982). The frequency of repeaters was higher in Korea than in any other country for which such data (Tietze, 1983) are available. Many wives rely on induced abortion as a primary method of fertility regulation rather than as a backup measure when contraception failed. However, some reduction in the prevalence rates of repeaters is noted from the 37 percent figure in the 1978 survey (Byun, 1979) to one-third of wives in cities in 1982, contrasted with an increase by 3.2 percent in rural areas. The decrease in repeaters in cities would likely be due to increasing surgical sterilization and more appropriate contraceptive use.

ABORTION RESEARCH

The majority (91.9 percent) of induced abortions are performed at private (Lim, 1982) or free-standing clinics without any obligation of reporting. The utilization of medical records for the study is limited in scope and is only applicable for clinical study. Thus, the collection of data on abortion should rely on sampling survey.

In a setting in which abortion had risen rapidly and was quite openly admitted and discussed by the population, a sample survey was carried out in Seoul by the author in 1964 and a similar survey ensued in rural areas in 1968. Another survey was repeated in Seoul to evaluate the changing trend in abortion in 1970. A national survey on family planning and abortion was undertaken by the Korean Institute for Family Planning jointly with the author in 1971.

Two clinical studies of the sequelae of induced abortion on subsequent pregnancies sponsored by WHO (WHO Task Force on Sequelae of Abortion, 1979) was undertaken in collaboration with other European countries, but the results for Korea have not yet been published.

A study on sexual behavior and family planning among female factory workers and another study on sexual behavior among adolescents are in progress under the auspices of WHO.

ILLEGAL ABORTION

Since the enactment of the Maternal and Child Health Law in 1973, induced abortion has been legalized under limited conditions. Actual practice, however, contradicts the legal status. An estimated 1 million induced abortions are performed every year; induced abortion rates in 1978 reached 124 per 1,000 wives aged fifteen to forty-four.

Almost all induced abortions are undertaken by qualified physicians and pose no judicial problem. Several attempts by the government to liberalize induced abortion have failed because of protest from Catholic sectors. The menstrual regulation program has been subsidized by the government (Ministry of Public Health and Social Affairs, 1981) since 1974 for indigents and wives who become pregnant due to IUD failure.

SUMMARY

Korea's population growth has decelerated within a short period of time compared to other developing countries in Asia. A major contributing factor has been induced abortion which in a strict sense remains illegal except on medical and philanthropic grounds. But in practice, the prevalence of abortion in Korea surpasses the level in countries where abortion has been liberalized.

Induced abortion in Korea may be summarized as follows:

1. With the recognition of the consequence of unchecked population growth, the government adopted family planning as a national program in 1962. Induced abortion, which had been strictly prohibited until 1962, gradually became a routine medical practice. Such changes are supported by the medical profession and the majority of opinion leaders except the Catholic church.

2. Induced abortion was belatedly legalized on medical and philanthropic grounds with the provision of the Maternal and Child Health Law in 1973. Reportedly, the government is preparing to expand the scope to include socioeconomic indications.

3. In parallel with family planning campaigns since 1962, the medical profession as well as Protestant churches and others favored legalizing induced abortion. Since 1974 the government has subsidized the menstrual regulation procedure, which is nothing but an early induced abortion.

4. The proportion of Korean wives who experienced induced abortion was 49.6 percent in 1982.

5. The induced abortion ratio to pregnancies was 7 to 100 pregnancies before 1965 and rose to 1 to 4 in 1971. Likewise, the ratio to live births was 8.4 to 100 live births before 1965 and rose to 4 to 5 in 1978.

6. During sixteen years between 1963 and 1979, age-specific induced abortion rates for wives in their twenties increased as much as five- to sixfold, tripled for those in their thirties, and doubled for those in their forties. The remarkable increase in abortion rate for those in their twenties is partially due to the adoption of a small family ideal and to an increase in the termination of premarital conception.

7. The prevalence of induced abortion shows a direct association with wife's age, living standard, and number of children. However, the relationship between abortion and educational levels became inconsistent and blurred in the 1982 survey.

8. The number of induced abortions in the midtrimester decreased to 7.2 percent in 1982. In 1971 the proportion was 12 percent and 21 percent for urban and rural areas, respectively.

9. Contraception practice rates after and before the first abortion were 54 percent and 31 percent in the 1971 survey, whereas the rates after and before the last abortion were 66 percent and 52 percent, respectively.

10. National family planning programs were launched in 1962 with mostly traditional methods, which later extended to include IUD in 1964 and oral contraceptives in 1968. Surgical sterilization, intrauterine contraceptives, and menstrual regulation (the last-named being an induced abortion procedure in early pregnancy) are provided by designated physicians subsidized by the government.

11. The incidence of abortion among teenagers was relatively low in Seoul (3.3 percent of all abortions in Seoul) and was negligible in a middle-sized city in 1979. With the government's liberal stance toward sex, the number of induced abortions among adolescents is expected to increase in the future.

12. The repeat abortion figures were 34.5 percent of all abortees in large cities, 32.1 percent in other cities, and 24.2 percent in rural areas. Repeat abortions are more frequent in Korea than in any other country from which data on repeaters are available.

13. Since the reporting of abortion is not required, collection of data on abortion should rely on sampling surveys. In the last two decades relatively frequent surveys on abortion have been undertaken by the Korean Institute for Population and Health.

14. The circumstances surrounding induced abortion appear to be liberalized in actual practice, regardless of the existing conditional abortion law in Korea.

REFERENCES

Byun, J. H., & Koh, K. S. *1978 family planning and fertility survey*. Korean Institute for Family Planning, 1979, 508–526.

Hong, S. B. *Changing patterns of induced abortion in Seoul, Korea*. Seoul: Modern Medicine Publishing Co., 1971, 14–15.

————. Recent changes in patterns of induced abortion in Seoul. *Korean Journal of Obstetrics and Gyneology*, 1979, 22(9), 795–803.

Hong, S. B., & Watson, W. B. *The increasing utilization of induced abortion in Korea*. Korea University Press, 1976.

Induced abortion and legalization. *Han-Kook Daily News*, 29 April 1976, p. 2.

Kim, Y. J., & Koh, Y. A. Studies on sex and family planning among unmarried factory workers in urban areas. *The Modern Medicine*. Seoul: Modern Medicine Publishing Co., 1975.

Koh, K. P., Ham, H. S., & Byun, J. H. *1979 Korean contraceptive prevalence survey report*. Korean Institute for Family Planning, 1980, p. 523.

Lee, S. B., Park, B. T., & Choi, S. Analysis of fertility for premarital pregnant women. *Journal of Family Planning Studies*. Seoul: KIFP, 1978, *5*, 27–28.

Lim, J. K. Current status of induced abortion. *Journal of Population and Health Studies*. Seoul: Korean Institute for Population and Health, 1982, 2 (1), 166–179.

Lim, J. K., & Choi, B. O. *The socio-demographic study on induced abortion*. Seoul: Korean Institute for Family Planning, 1979, 33.

Min, B. K., Choi, S. C., & Lee, K. H. The attitudes and behaviors of Korean adolescents. *Adolescents in Korea Today*. Seoul: Chung-Ang University, 1978, 57.

Ministry of Public Health and Social Affairs. *Public health and social affairs: 1981*. Ministry of Public Health and Social Affairs, 1981, 382.

Moon, H. S., Ham, H. S., & Shin, H. S. *National family planning survey: 1982*. Seoul: Korean Institute for Population and Health, 1982, 37–42.

Potts, M., Diggory, P., & Peel, J. *Abortion*. Cambridge: Cambridge University Press, 1977, 410–453.

Tietze, C. *Induced abortion: 1979*. New York: Population Council, 1979, 30.

————. *Induced abortion: A world review, 1983*. New York: Population Council, 1983, 61–64.

United Nations Fund for Population Activities. *Survey of laws on fertility control*. UNFPA, 1979, 83–84.

WHO Task Force on Sequelae of Abortion. Gestation, birthweight and spontaneous abortion in pregnancy after induced abortion. *Lancet*, 1979, *1*, 142–145.

Table 20.1

Percentage of Currently Married Women, Aged Fifteen to Forty-four, Ever Having an Abortion, by Residence, 1964–82

Residence	'64[a]	'65[a]	'66[a]	'67[a]	'68[a]	'71[b]	'73[b]	'76[b]	'78[b]	'82[c]
Seoul	25	–	30	–	48	40	44	50	58	53
All cities	15	23	27	28	26	34	38	41	57	51
Rural	4	5	7	7	10	19	24	29	38	44
National	7	11	13	14	16	26	30	39	49	50

Denominators are currently married wives aged 20–44 for the period between 1964–68, and those aged 15–44 for the period 1971–82.

Source: [a]Hong & Watson, 1976, p. 37.
[b]Byun & Koh, 1979, pp. 510–512.
[c]Lim, 1982, p. 168.

Table 20.2

Induced Abortion Ratios to Pregnancies and Births in Ever-Married Women Aged Twenty to Forty-four, 1965–78

Ratios	before '65	'66	'67	'68	'69	'70	'71	'73*	'77*	78*
per 100 Pregnancies	7.1	19.1	22.1	21.3	24.9	26.2	24.5	–	–	–
Per 100 Births	8.4	25.5	31.1	29.1	36.9	39.6	36.3	40.6	70.9	85.5

*The figures from Byun and Koh's report and denominator are currently married women aged 15–44.

Source: Hong & Watson, 1976, p. 38; Byun & Koh, 1979, p. 522.

Table 20.3

Abortion Ratio per 1,000 Live Births of Age Cohort

Age at performance of abortion	Cohort of Women (age in 1982)				
	45–49	40–44	35–39	30–34	25–29
20 – 24	22	36	116	174	296
25 – 29	122	214	344	525	
30 – 34	374	724	1,455		
35 – 39	913	3,076			
40 – 44	2,614				

Source: Moon, Ham & Shin, 1982, p. 42.

Table 20.4

Trends in Age-Specific Abortion Rates for Currently Married Women, 1963–79

Age	1963[a]	68[a]	73[a]	75[a]	78[a]	79[b]	79[c]
20 –24	16	12	86	63	70	79	393
25 – 29	29	46	75	86	156	155	345
30 – 34	58	90	137	158	148	188	284
35 – 39	40	69	88	153	156	127	214
40 – 44	-	31	22	75	54	69	91
Total Marital Abortion Rates	0.72	1.24	2.05	2.34	2.92	3.5	-

Source: [a]Byun & Koh, 1979, p. 523.
   [b]Koh, Ham, Byun, 1980, p. 523.
   [c]Hong, 1979, p. 799.

Table 20.5

Induced Abortion Rates for All Women, Aged Fifteen to Forty-four, 1961–78

Year	Number of Abortion	Abortion Rate Per 1000 women 15-44
1961	104,000	19.5
1962	127,000	23.3
1963	152,000	27.2
1964	191,000	33.3
1965	223,000	37.9
1966	252,000	41.9
1967	264,000	42.9
1968	293,000	46.4
1969	315,000	48.8
1970	331,000	50.1
1973*	390,000	105.4
1977*	558,000	112.8
1978*	631,000	124.2
1977/78**	480,000	235

*Denominators for 1973, 1977, and 1978 are currently married women.
**An estimate based on providers survey limited to metropolitan area, Seoul.
Source: Byun & Koh, 1978; Hong, 1979; Tietze, 1979.

Table 20.6
Percentage of Currently Married Women Aged Twenty to Forty-four with Induced Abortion, by Demographic Characteristics

Characteristics	Percent
All	49.6
1. Wife's current age	
20 - 24	19.2
25 - 29	38.5
30 - 34	54.7
35 - 39	63.5
40 - 44	66.4
2. No of Living children	
0	15.7
1	23.2
2	50.4
3	58.4
4	53.5
5	56.0
6+	49.3
3. Education	
Primary	51.4
Middle	47.4
High	49.6
College	44.5
4. Husband's Occupation	
Managerial workers	49.2
clerical workers	50.3
sales & service	56.0
unskilled laborer	49.4
farmer & fisher	41.0
5. Annual income*	
1 million wons or less	46.3
1 - 2 million wons	45.8
2 - 5 million wons	50.1
5 million wons or more	55.8

*As of year-end 1987, $1 (US) was equivalent to about 800 won.
Source: Moon, Ham, & Shin, 1982.

Table 20.7
Governmental Family Planning Programs Achieved

Contraceptives	Period				
	1962–1966	1967–1971	1972–1976	1977–1980	Total (%)
I.U.D.	725.5	1,460.8	1,619.3	899.8	4.705.4 (42.5)
Male sterilization	82.3	84.9	156.1	144.6	470.0 (4.3)
Female Sterilization	–	–	65.6	749.2	812.7 (7.3)
Condoms (/months)	706.1	760.0	859.0	368.6	2,693.6 (24.3)
Oral pills (/months)	–	487.6	1,134.3	521.0	2,142.9 (19.4)
Menstrual Regulation	–	–	14.4	232.4	246.8 (2.2)
Total	1,513.9	2,793.3	3,848.7	2,915.6	11,071.4 (100.0)

Source: Ministry of Public Health and Social Affairs, 1981.

Table 20.8
Percentage of Married Women with Experience of Induced Abortion, by Residence, 1982

	No. of Induced Abortions Experienced				(N)	Average
	0	1	2	3		
large cities	47.0	18.5	15.1	19.4	100.0 (2158)	1.4
other cities	49.3	17.8	15.1	17.0	100.0 (1219)	1.2
Rural	56.6	19.2	11.2	13.0	100.0 (1965)	0.9

Source: Lim, 1982.

21

LATIN AMERICA

Benjamin Viel V.

Latin America is often considered a homogeneous region, but such is far from the reality. If there was indeed a certain ethnic similarity among the original inhabitants, then the Europeans' discovery and conquest of the region led to profound differences in racial composition. These differences were accentuated in the years that followed, a process facilitated no doubt by the high mountains and vast distances that hindered exchange and communications. The Wars of Independence and the subsequent atomization of the region into small countries had the effect of differentiating still further the customs of the people and their ways of life, so that today it is more proper to speak of a mosaic of nations rather than of one region of uniform characteristics.

Where once the great pre-Columbian empires held sway (as in Mexico and Peru), a high proportion of indigenous peoples continues to exist and to conserve ancestral customs within the Christianity to which they were converted. The tropical lowlands have a high proportion of black people, who were brought there during the era of the slave trade. Not only their folklore but also many of their present habits and customs show the influence of their African ancestry. The highlands as well as the temperate regions of the far south have a cold climate to which the black slave was poorly adapted. In contrast, the Europeans preferred the cool regions, as they continued to show during the great migratory wave of the second half of the nineteenth century and the first years of the twentieth century.

Ethnic diversity, varied climates, and differing traditions were translated into a variety of habits and customs that had their inevitable effects on sexual behavior and on the composition of the family. Table 21.1 shows crude birth rates and the percentage of illegitimate births in selected countries of Latin America in 1950, before the use of the contraceptive methods that have become available today. The table clearly indicates differences in reproductive behavior and in the concept of the family in the different societies of the region on the threshold of its demographic explosion.

High rates of illegitimacy in countries that considered themselves Catholic lead to the conclusion that the Christian concept of the family was not precisely observed at that time. The very high birth rates, except in three countries, are close to what one would expect in populations of young age structure that are doing nothing to control fertility. They thus lead to the suggestion that except in a few countries few had recourse to abortion before 1950.

HISTORICAL DEVELOPMENT OF ABORTION POLICY

Nothing is known about abortion in pre-Columbian America. Evidence exists that in the Aztec Empire (in Mexico and a part of Chile), human sacrifice was practiced. One supposes that in those communities infanticide was more frequent than abortion in view of the technical difficulties in surgical procedures. Yet folkloric medicines that seem to predate the discovery of America are still used by women who want to induce an abortion. They are of doubtful efficacy, and some have toxic qualities.

Letters from priests of the Spanish court in the first century after the conquest remark on the low fertility of indigenous women in contrast to the women united to the Spaniard—and even when indigenous. These are cited by a number of historians, including P. Ramos (1977). It would seem that in that epoch, wretched living conditions lessened women's desires for motherhood. Did they achieve their purposes by recourse to abortion? Was infanticide the method employed? Father Las Casas speaks of the use of a piece of wood covered with wax and introduced by the indigenous woman into the cervix. Of course, he says nothing about the frequency of this practice or of its geographical distribution.

In the colonial period as in the first century following independence, infant mortality was extremely high throughout all Latin America, as was mortality at young ages. According to Viel (1981), in the whole of the nineteenth century, the population only tripled—and that in spite of a strong European immigration, especially to the south of the region—while in the first eighty years of the twentieth century, it multiplied six times.

Throughout the nineteenth century, a period in which the principal energy source was human muscle and in a region that could well be considered under-populated, it is hardly likely that induced abortion was an important phenomenon. Early death regulated family size, while children had economic value from the moment they could participate in the work of the family—and subsequently as well, when they provided support to those few who managed to attain advanced age. If three or four children were to reach the fertile ages still alive, it was necessary to use woman's reproductive capacity to the maximum. Only among the upper classes was there any prejudice against unmarried mothers. There, too, abortion induced surgically was probably employed very little given the high danger of infection. What replaced it was the secret birth and the child delivered to a convent, which in that period served as the asylum for abandoned children.

LEGAL STATUS OF ABORTION

Under the undoubted influence of the Catholic religion as well as of the prevailing social conditions (high mortality, shortage of labor, underpopulated territories that were potentially productive), the penal codes as they were first elaborated by the newly independent countries of the region universally designated induced abortion as a crime, establising prison terms for both the person who performed it and the woman who received it. In the course of time, a number of countries modified their codes to the extent of legalizing abortion when it was performed to save the life of the mother. A few have gone further, legalizing it when the pregnancy is the product of rape or incest. In certain islands of the Caribbean that are still European colonies, abortion has been legalized and can thus be performed without fear of penalty. Among independent Caribbean countries only Cuba (1979) and Barbados (1983) have legalized abortion, making it available on request during the first three months of pregnancy and for medical reasons thereafter.

Yet even though the penal codes declare induced abortion to be a criminal procedure, the penalties specified are much less severe than those designated for someone who has killed a person already born. According to current laws, the destruction of a fetus *in utero* is a minor crime when compared with murder.

Somewhat arbitarily, 1930 is picked as the opening year of a period in which demographic and social changes, weakly evident as early as the beginning of World War I, began a strong acceleration. In a number of countries, the 1930s saw the initiation of a decline in general mortality which clearly began with a decline in infant mortality and in deaths at young ages. With the appearance in the 1940s first of sulfa drugs and then of antibiotics, both powerful weapons in the treatment of contagious diseases which have been the principal cause of death, the decline in mortality was accentuated—but with no corresponding modification in the birth rate. The inevitable result was a demographic explosion that raised population growth rates from an average of about 1 percent a year to close to 3 percent a year.

The food needs of this growing population demanded an increase in the productivity of cultivated lands which led to the mechanization of agriculture, and that, in turn, created unemployment in rural areas. The inevitable outcome was an increasing migration to urban areas. In some of the countries that were experiencing annual growth of 2.5 percent to 3 percent, there were cities that in the 1960s were growing at rates of 7 percent to 10 percent per year, giving rise to the spectacle of vast marginal communities.

Industrialization was stimulated by the need to provide employment to this expanding urban population, and a region that had been characterized primarily by agriculture and mining began to create an industrial base. With that, the urban proletariat began to exhibit increasing political strength.

The woman has generally been the more responsible element in a Latin American society that continues to be essentially *macho*. The woman saw an increase in the number of her children, their numbers no longer controlled by early death, with no corresponding increase in family resources. The rise in density within the home, relatively endurable in the spacious rural environment, became unbearable in the urban environment, and the woman had recourse to induced abortion to restore an equilibrium between the size of the family and its available resources. Indeed, a veritable "epidemic" of induced abortion took place in Latin America which, since it had become a social necessity, paid no attention to the reigning legal dispositions.

In Santiago, the capital of Chile, Viel (1980) investigated the relation, if any, between the decline in infant mortality between 1940 and 1964 and the increase in hospitalizations for complications resulting from abortion (table 21.2). In Chile, official statistics on population size, live births, and deaths of those younger than one year are fully reliable, as are hospital statistics, particularly with reference to the cause of hospitalization. Clearly, the best data are to be found in the capital of the country.

A certain portion of the hospitalizations was unquestionably from spontaneous and induced varieties. If the doctor should inscribe the abortion as induced, he or she would be required to report it to the police, and so the doctor merely inscribed a diagnosis of abortion without further specification. Since there is no reason why there should have been an upsurge in spontaneous abortions in the twenty-five years under review, they cannot very well be credited with the tremendous increase in hospitalized abortions that took place in that period. Complications from illegal, induced abortion, the frequency of which is believed to have been constantly on the rise, appear to be the most logical reason for an increase in the hospitalization rate of 46 percent. The cause of that was the decline in infant mortality. On noting that early death had gradually ceased to be the regulator of family size, the woman had recourse to induced abortion. The condom was then in use by the middle and upper classes, as was coitus interruptus, a practice rejected by the great majority of the people of a region where *machismo* prevailed. The newer methods that had come into use in the developed world were practically unknown in Chile.

Beginning in 1965 the government of Chile accepted the proposal of medical sectors that education in the use of reversible contraception should be facilitated in order to combat induced abortion. By 1964 induced abortion had become responsible for 50 percent of maternal deaths, and cases with complications were taking up one-third of all hospital beds in obstetrical and gynecological services. The initiation of contraceptive distribution in the government's maternal services was followed by a decline in the rate of hospitalized abortions, which by 1980 had reached a low of only 16.5 cases per 1,000 women of fertile age. This decline can be taken as evidence that the increase in the rate of hospitalized abortions between 1940 and 1964 was due principally to illegal induced abortions, which were less needed after the woman had access to effective methods of prevention.

What was observed in Chile should also have occurred in all those countries which in the 1930s began to experience a decline in mortality together with a rising trend toward urbanization. Unfortunately, hospital statistics are not available in all the countries that would make comparisons with Chile possible. It is known, however, that between 1960 and 1970 cases of septic abortion were occupying a high proportion of the beds in all the hospitals of the region, and one infers that the majority of these were induced abortions. During the same periods, half of the high maternal mortality was generally attributed to deaths from abortion.

In 1974 the Fourth American Congress on Social Security Medicine was held, and an analysis was presented of the mother-and-child care provided by the relevant institutions. On that occasion, Dr. R. Molina (1974) analyzed the hospitalizations for abortion among women covered by social security in their respective countries. To be sure, such women are not representative of the general community, and even less so in those countries where social security provides limited coverage. (See table 21.3.)

Even though these statistics apply to a highly selected population, the figures show that in only two countries was the percentage of abortions low enough to be within the parameters of spontaneous abortion. In addition, by the number of births taking place in hospitals—except for Chile, Colombia, and Mexico, and, to a lesser degree, Guatemala and Venezuela—one can conclude that in most of the region, the social security systems embraced only a very small number of women who were not of fertile age.

Hospital statistics can never be expected to show more than the tip of the iceberg. They are data dependent on the number of beds available and on the ability of the patients to gain access to them, since in countries where the procedure is illegal, only the cases suffering from complications end up in the hospital without reporting the number of procedures carried out without complications. It is also likely that the number of hospitalizations registered depends in large measure on what facilities exist.

Aroused by the increasing number of hospitalizations with a diagnosis of abortion, a group of Chilean doctors decided to undertake research that would elucidate the subject. Armijo and Monreal (1964) carried out a study on a random sample of women in the city of Santiago, and then in 1977 used the same technique to investigate the situation in other parts of the country. Both studies confirmed what was to be expected: that illegal induced abortion was at that time much more frequent than hospital statistics indicated. Differences appeared according to social class, educational level, and woman's age. There were also regional differences, with the practice occurring much more frequently in urban than in rural areas. Subsequently, Requena (1965) carried out a survey in a sector of Santiago showing that the woman who had had recourse to one induced abortion had a tendency to repeat the practice, even though she had suffered serious complications in the first instance. The study found no differences among Catholics, members of other religions, and unbelievers; even among Catholics, there was no discernible relationship between the practice of abortion and degree of religiosity. One deduces from this survey that the Chilean woman of that time viewed induced abortion as a social necessity regardless of what the law or religion had to say about it.

The seriousness of the problem in Chile was brought out strongly when Plaza and Briones (1963) showed what the treatment of hospitalized abortion had cost the National Health Service in 1962. Costs of hospitalization and expenses of treatment reached an estimated $1 million in that year, in which 30.4 percent of beds intended for obstetrical services were occupied by abortion cases, who had a death rate of 5 per 1,000 cases treated.

The studies carried out in Chile probably stimulated the Latin American Demographic Center to initiate a regionwide investigation to determine in greater depth the epidemiology in induced abortion. In the 1960s this institution conducted surveys in various countries of Latin America which greatly helped to ascertain how serious and how widespread the phenomenon of induced abortion was in that epoch. In an analysis of the surveys carried out by CELADE, Gaslonde (1973) showed that, wherever birth rates were lower, induced abortion was more frequently practiced and that it was more consistently practiced in urban than in rural settings.

The Population Studies Division of the Colombian Association of Medical School Faculties (ASCOFAME) (Lopez-Escobar et al., 1978) also made important contributions to the understanding of the epidemiology of induced abortion. A survey carried out by ASCOFAME in Bogota in 1973 investigated the termination of pregnancy in one year in accordance with the socioeconomic status of the pregnant woman, and the results are presented in table 21.4.

The greater number of induced abortions apparent in the middle and lower classes is explained by the simultaneous investigation carried out on the use of effective contraception in the various social classes, confirming that, at that time, contraceptive use was much more frequent in the upper class. The consequence of contraception is a lower number of pregnancies as the table shows—3,840 in the higher classes versus 53,280 in the lower class.

A figure of 5.8 induced abortions per 1,000 women of fertile age in Bogota in 1973 cannot be taken as representative of what was occurring at the same time in other cities of the region. The birth rate in Colombia was still high (40.6 per 1,000). In the same period in Buenos Aires, Argentina, with a birth rate 17 points lower than Colombia's, a retrospective study (Olivares & Surur, 1983) of women between thirty and fifty-five years of age revealed 1.2 induced abortions for every two children born alive. The two studies are not exactly comparable, yet they lead to the suspicion that induced abortion was employed a good deal more frequently in Buenos Aires than in Bogota, and that the same thing would have been found in other cities showing a lower birth rate than Bogota's in a period in which it was much more difficult to practice contraception than it is today.

The number of studies carried out in different countries in the 1960s and in the first years of the 1970s is so large that to cite them and to comment on each would exceed the intentions of this chapter. What is important to emphasize is that wherever the phenomenon was studied, its frequency was shown to be high, that there were regional variations as there were variations within regions; there were also differences according to socioeconomic status and to urban as against rural residence. It is important again to emphasize that the practice was affected neither by religious beliefs nor by legislative dispositions. The studies provide sufficient evidence showing that at the time they are carried out induced abortion was more frequent wherever crude birth rates were lower. The implication is that the woman of that epoch was using abortion to limit the size of her family.

It is also important to note that all the studies under review—although their methodological differences render them not strictly comparable—agree in finding that the great majority of the women who admitted having had recourse to abortion were married or living in stable unions, were older than twenty, and already had between three and four living children. This provides one more proof that induced abortion was then employed as a method for limiting family size in the face of demographic and social circumstances that had changed radically in the course of only a few years (as in declines in mortality and in accelerating urbanization).

An approach through surveys, whether retrospective or prospective, unquestionably provides more information than can be obtained from hospital statistics. At the same time, no one should suppose that surveys can indicate the true magnitude of induced abortion in a given country or region and at a determined moment with the same degree of precision provided by data obtained in countries in which abortion has been legalized and is carried out in authorized services by professional personnel.

With retrospective studies, forgetfulness can reduce the number of events. They can be reduced in prospective studies by a tendency to conceal them, a tendency that will be stronger the more induced abortion is perceived to be a sin or a crime. In Chile, the woman in lower economic strata will more readily admit to abortion than will the woman of the upper class, a stratum that generally refuses to reply to questions on this subject.

It would be a mistake to judge present events in Latin America exclusively in terms of the experience accumulated in studies carried out over the past ten or fifteen years. Changes have occurred in a number of countries that may well have diminished the frequency of induced abortion. In many countries today, family planning programs have been included in the health services provided by governments, and some of these programs include voluntary sterilization. Such services ought to reduce the need for abortion felt by the woman who formerly knew of no other way to limit the size of her family. In the current decade, Brazil, with a population almost one-third of Latin America's total population, is still without a family planning program that would provide education and contraceptive services. In a similar situation are to be found Argentina, Ecuador, Paraguay, and Peru, countries in which only private services are available and those of necessarily limited coverage. In these countries, one is led to believe that induced abortion is still widely practiced—and the more so the lower the crude birth rate happens to be.

If it is reasonable to recognize that family planning has reduced the incidence of induced abortion in countries where programs are in operation, one must also recognize that changes are taking place in the sexual behavior of the young that can bring about an increase in abortion. Hospital records throughout the region show that the age of women hospitalized for septic abortion is lower today than it was fifteen years ago. Moreover, a greater number of single women is to be noted, as of women living in ephemeral unions, and there are clear indications that an active sexual life is beginning at an earlier age than in the recent past. Such trends can lead to an increased incidence of induced abortion even in countries that have family planning programs. Adolescents are rarely in attendance at the clinics that offer these services.

To ascertain the extent of induced abortion at the present moment in the life of Latin America is as difficult as to find out the exact number of cases of measles occurring on a given day in the course of a measles epidemic. Hospitalization for complications is just one index, and it depends on hospital facilities and the quality of the diagnostic records. Surveys provide only partial information about what is going on at a given moment in a society undergoing change. Recent publications on the subject are largely expressions of guesswork, and it is not unusual to see fluctuations in the data from one author to another. Some researchers estimate that in Brazil the number of induced abortions cannot be less than 700,000 per year (Rodriguez, 1978). Even this total could be well below the reality. Retrospective studies carried out among limited samples of women in the State of Sao Paulo give results that, if extrapolated to the rest of the country, would substantially raise the total (Berquo, Oliveira, & Camargo, 1977).

A review of the data on hospitalization for abortion in countries for which the data exist suggests as an estimate that this diagnosis is being applied to 15 per 1,000 women of fertile age. If half of these are induced abortions, then its frequency—with complications—is some 7.5 per 1,000 women of fertile age. Previous studies have indicated that one case is hospitalized for every three induced abortions, representing around 22 per 1,000 women of fertile age per year. If this figure is applied to the estimated number of women of fertile age in the region (83 million in 1983), one is led to conclude that at the most conservative estimate, the annual number of induced abortions in Latin America cannot be less than 1.8 million. It would not be at all surprising if the actual figure were twice that considering all the difficulties that inhere in efforts to reach a reliable estimate.

One is only justified in concluding that induced abortion exists, that it is frequent, and that it is more frequent wherever low birth rates coincide with situations in which women are generally unprotected by effective contraception. In the countries in which it has thus far been carried out, the World Fertility Survey has shown that the proportion of women protected by effective contraception is still low in comparison with that in the developed countries. This is reflected in crude birth rates well above those characteristic of the industrial world and probably in a greater need for induced abortion as well.

ATTITUDES TOWARD ABORTION

To persuade legislators to interest themselves in abolishing futile legislation demands the pressure of public opinion, especially from groups of specialists such as obstetricians and gynecologists, midwives, and public health specialists, and in particular from women themselves. Little has been done in this regard. Only a few isolated surveys have been carried out, and these are difficult to compare because of differences in their methods. In Chile, a well-designed survey directed to medical specialists (Duhart & Ossandón, 1981) shows that a majority of the younger physicians are in favor of reforming the laws, while the weight of tradition means that the older doctors are still opposed to change. Some of the older doctors believe that the laws should be strengthened so as to bring them to bear on those who perform abortions. They have failed to consider that such a policy would doubtless increase the amount of self-induced abortion, which is the most dangerous type and the major source of morbidity and mortality.

Surveys taken on random samples of the general public have not been performed in sufficient quantity to provide valid conclusions. In the few that have been carried out, a majority is found in opposition to the legalization of abortion, and this can be explained to the extent that information channels have not demonstrated to the public the magnitude of the problem, the dangers of pregnancy at adverse ages, the limitations in the effectiveness of contraceptive methods, and especially the adverse conditions that confront the infant who is not wanted by its parents as is apparent in Latin America and ever more so where the birth rate is high. In a study carried out in a maternity hospital in Brazil, Etges (1975) reported that 50 percent of the women giving birth said they would have preferred that the child just born had not been born.

Without adequate information, the public will inevitably give replies that conform to religious convictions. Those who are Catholics respond negatively to proposals that the law be changed even when, confronted with an unwanted pregnancy, they themselves are disposed to have recourse to an illegal abortion. The influence of the church, which has considered all forms of abortion to be criminal only since 1869, weighs very heavily on public opinion but much less so on public conduct. Indeed, the influence of the church weighs even more heavily on governments, which are unlikely to be interested in making legislative changes that will place them in direct conflict with the church, especially when such changes are not yet supported by a clear majority in public opinion.

The mass media have not yet shown an interest in giving the public adequate information on the demographic problem, much less on the problem of abortion. The studies carried out to date go no further than the ambit of the scientific societies in which they are discussed. As long as the proper information has not been made available, it is unlikely that the subject of abortion will be discussed with the frankness it has received in the industrial countries. The great majority of the Latin American people do not know that there are countries in which abortion has been legalized, and they are even less aware of the reasons that induced governments to legalize abortion in such Catholic countries as France and Italy.

If a proposal were made today to legalize abortion in any country of continental Latin America, not only would it be fought by the Catholic church, but it would also be opposed with equal force by the military caste. Latin America denies that it is in the process of arming itself, and yet it is, and this is one of the reasons why so many countries find themselves in a financial crisis. The armed forces of Latin America still believe that for national defense the quantity of population is more important that its quality, and thus their attitudes continue to be openly pronatalist.

INCIDENCE OF INDUCED ABORTION

There is no city in Latin America where money cannot buy an abortion performed by competent professionals. Information about them is generally obtained from friends, who are happy to provide names and addresses. There are even cities in which the daily press contains advertisements offering the professional services of doctors or clinics in carrying out "an early diagnosis of pregnancy," words that everyone understands to mean that abortions are performed. Since early abortion (within the first ten weeks of pregnancy) is an ambulatory procedure, it is easily performed by those who are skilled at it and with its very low mortality rate, it remains a secret between the woman and the practitioner. The law that punishes induced abortion affects only those who have no money and those adolescent mothers who do not know where to go and who might have obtained money and information if they were not afraid to confess their pregnancy to their families.

The poorer the woman, the more difficult it is for her to obtain an abortion from a skilled professional. Unable to raise the money required, she has recourse to a backstreet operation at a lowoer price, or she herself will introduce an object into her uterus, a vegetable stalk or a knitting needle, to bring on a self-induced abortion. These are the women who furnish the maternal mortality associated with abortion and who are subject to the complications of abortion that require hospitalization.

Beyond the clear injustice produced by the legislation currently in force, one needs only glance at the numbers actually known, that is to say, of hospitalized abortions, to see clearly that what the present laws entail is impossible to enforce. In the first place, doctors are not inclined to report what they recognize as a complication of induced abortion. Second, if the crime were reported, no judicial system in any country in the region would have the capacity to handle the number of trials that would require judgment under the law. Third, nowhere in the region are jail facilities sufficient to deal with the hordes of the guilty who would be subject to imprisonment. Fourth, if the person found guilty of having induced an abortion would happen to be the mother of other young children, no facilities currently exist for taking care of these children during the term of imprisonment. For all these reasons, the law as written is not enforced, and the few trials that do take place follow from the death of the woman in an effort to flush out an incompetent practitioner. Clearly, such cases follow deaths that occur in hospitals where an autopsy is performed, or where the dying woman informs on the practitioner, an event of very rare occurrence.

Confronted with the impossibility of enforcing the law, the countries of the region, with rare and sporadic exceptions, prefer not to discuss the issue. The legislation has no effect on the moneyed classes, who are those with political influence, and all efforts to legalize abortion have thus far been quashed.

LATIN AMERICA IN THE YEAR 2000

The population of Latin America and the Caribbean in 1980 was estimated at about 380 million. For the year 2000, only twenty years later, the population is projected to reach 600 million if present growth rates persist, and some 550 million if growth should decline. The projections estimate that the trend toward urbanization will accelerate even more.

At the present time, the cities are faced with serious problems of public sanitation. They have severe housing deficits. Although the percentage of illiterates is tending to decline, their absolute numbers are increasing (Sanfuentes & Lavados, 1982). The Food and Drug Administration estimated that, even in 1980, 40 million children younger than six were suffering from malnutrition.

A population increase of between 170 million and 220 million in only twenty years in a region already showing serious evidence of decline in the quality of life can be counted on to produce fundamental changes. It can be foreseen that among such changes will be modifications in the present legislation concerning induced abortion. Already such changes are taking place in the islands of the Caribbean Sea. The very fact of their being islands intensifies their problems of population growth, and this explains the trend toward changes in their legislation. It is likely that something similar will soon be observed in the continental territories. Only fifteen years ago, very few countries of Latin America accepted the notion that governments were obligated to provide information and services on effective contraception, while today there are very few that do not accept that principle. It could well happen in the next twenty years that a movement to change unenforceable laws will find wide justification in the fact that the contraceptives provided by medical science are capable of reducing rates of induced illegal abortion but are not so good that such intervention is never required by those who become victims of unwanted pregnancy that preventive measures could not forestall.

SUMMARY

Except in Cuba and Barbados, abortion is illegal in Latin America, where penal codes establish prison terms for those who perform the operation and for those who receive it. The punishments prescribed for induced abortion, however, are always less than those established for the murder of someone already born.

Although there are variations within the region, it is apparent that the Latin American woman regards abortion as a social necessity. Its occurrence is impossible to ascertain with precision just because it is illegal and tends to be concealed. Indirect evidence indicates that the incidence is high—and even higher where effective contraceptives are difficult to get.

It is quite apparent that the laws that prohibit and punish abortion as a crime are unenforceable and that punitive attitudes have done nothing to diminish its frequent occurrence.

More adequate information on the magnitude of the problem and of its consequences, directed to both scientific groups and the public at large, would help to obtain changes in the present legislation, which, in the last analysis, affects only the poorest sectors of the population.

REFERENCES

Armijo, R., & Moreal, T. Epidemiologia del aborto provocado en Santiago. *Revista Médica de Chile*, 1964, *92* (3). Estudio Comparativo del Aborto Provocado en Diversas Ciudades Chilenas. *Actas de la Sociedad Chilena de Salubridad*, 1977.

Berquo, E., Oliveira, M., & Camargo, C. *A fecundidade en Sao Paulo. Caracteristicas demográficas, biólogicas e socio-economicas*. Sao Paulo, Brasil: Editorial Centro Brasileiro de Analise e Planejamiento, 1977.

Duhart, S., & Ossandón, J. *Actitudes de los medicos gineco-obstetras frente a la planificacion familiar: estudio comparativo 1968–1981*. ICARPAL, Mimeographed copy, 1982.

Etges, N. *Fecundidade humana no Rio Grande do Sud*. Rio Grande do Sud, Brasil: Universidade Valle dos Sinos, 1975.

Gaslonde, S. *Análisis preliminar de algunos datos sobre aborto provenientes de encuestas de América Latina*. Santiago, Chile: CELADE, 1973.

López-Escobar, G., Riaño-Gamboa, G., & Leniz-Nicholls, N. Interrogantes, comentarios y resultado parciales de algunas investigaciones colombianas. *Centro Regional de Población*, Vol. 8. Bogotá, Colombia, 1978.

Molina, R. Impacto de la planificación familiar en la atención Médica de la seguridad social. *Congreso Conmemorativo de los Servicios Medicos del Instituto Mexicano de Seguro Social*. México, D.F. Mimeographed copy, 1974.

Olivares, D., & Surur, A. Frecuencia del aborto provocado. *Contribuciones*, Vol. 6 (21). Buenos Aires, Argentina: Asociacion Argentina de Proteccion de la Familia, 1983.

Plaza, S., & Briones, H. Al Aborto como Problema Asistencial. *Revista Médica de Chile*, 1963, *91*, (4).

Ramos, P. *El peso de la tradicion en la explosión demográfica*. Ciudad de México. Pax México, 1977.

Requena, M. *Epidemiology of induced abortion in Santiago, Chile*. New York: Milbank Memorial Fund, April 1965.

Rodriguez, W. *Prevencao do aborto provocado nos programas de saude publica*. Rio de Janeiro, Brasil: Editorial Sociedade Civil Bem Estar Familiar no Brasil, 1978.

Sanfuentes, A., & Lavados, H. *Dimensions of poverty in Latin America and the Caribbean*. Santiago, Chile: Ed. UNICEF, 1982.

Viel, B. La población de Chile. Pasado, presente y futuro. *Revista Médica de Chile*, 1980, *108* (3).

———. *Crecimiento de la población de Europa y las Américas*. Bogotá, Colombia: Editorial Presencia, 1981.

Table 21.1
Crude Birth Rates and Percentage of Illegitimacy in Selected Countries of Latin America, 1950

Country	Birth Rate	% of Illegitimacy
Guatemala	50.9	73.2
Panama	33.3	73.0
Honduras	41.4	64.4
El Salvador	48.5	61.3
Dominican Republic	41.2	59.8
Venezuela	42.6	56.6
Nicaragua	41.2	56.3
Peru	47.1	43.3
Ecuador	46.7	32.7
Colombia	46.0	27.0
Mexico	45.6	24.1
Costa Rica	47.4	23.7
Chile	33.3	17.1
Argentina	26.4	--

Source: For natality, *United Nations Demographic Yearbooks*. Illegitimacy rates taken from G. Mortara, *Le Unioni conjugali libere nell America Latina* (Rome, 1961).

Table 21.2
Hospitalizations for Abortion in Santiago, Chile, between 1940 and 1964, and Rate of Infant Mortality per 1,000 Live Births

Year	Number of Women Age 15–44 (thousands)	Number of Hospitalized Abortion Cases	Abortion Rate per Thousand Women of Fertile Age	Mortality Rate of Children under One Year of Age per 1,000 Live Births
1940	215	7,515	34.9	174.4
1941	223	8,315	37.3	152.2
1942	231	8,732	37.8	151.5
1943	240	8,081	33.7	140.5
1944	249	8,951	35.9	113.2
1945	259	9,238	35.8	126.1
1946	268	10,231	38.2	114.2
1947	278	10,601	38.1	121.9
1948	288	12,557	43.6	116.3
1949	298	12,998	44.0	117.9
1950	308	13,549	42.3	103.8
1951	319	13,485	42.3	91.2
1952	330	13,650	41.4	88.6
1953	341	14,579	42.8	78.1
1954	353	15,068	42.7	89.3
1955	364	15,566	42.8	89.1
1956	376	16,929	45.0	72.4
1957	388	17,826	45.9	82.1
1958	401	19,860	49.5	91.0
1959	414	18,900	45.7	79.8
1960	426	20,349	47.5	84.8
1961	440	21,179	48.1	81.9
1962	451	21,414	47.5	79.2
1963	467	20,786	44.5	77.4
1964	480	24,427	50.9	81.8

Source: Office of the Census, hospital statistics, statistics of the Health Ministry.

Table 21.3
Number of Births and Number of Hospitalized Abortions among Beneficiaries of
Social Security Services in Selected Countries of Latin America

Country	Year	Births	Abortions	%
Bolivia	1972	2,165	437	20.2
Chile	1969	256,153	47,430	18.5
Colombia	1972	67,882	12,401	18.2
Costa Rica	1972	8,423	1,215	14.4
Ecuador	1972	4,548	737	16.2
El Salvador	1972	8,637	900	10.4
Guatemala	1972	12,998	1,861	14.3
Honduras	1971	2,686	595	22.2
Mexico	1972	377,986	51,210	13.5
Nicaragua	1972	6,154	785	12.8
Paraguay	1971	3,729	678	18.2
Venezuela	1972	35,209	5,959	18.9

Source: Molina, 1974.

Table 21.4
Pregnancies Occurring in the Preceding Year in Accordance with Their Manner
of Termination and Socioeconomic Class, Bogota, Colombia, 1973

Class	Number of Women	Number of Pregnancies	Abortion Spontaneous	Abortion Induced	Induced Abortion per 000 Women
High	36,992	3,840	448	64	1.7
Middle	120,982	11,809	1,446	723	6.0
Low	287,120	53,280	5,328	1,776	6.2
Total	445,094	68,929	7,222	2,563	5.8

Source: López-Escobar, Riaño-Gamboa, & Leniz-Nicholls, 1978.

22

THE NETHERLANDS

Jany Rademakers

HISTORICAL DEVELOPMENT OF ABORTION POLICY

In contrast with most Western countries, liberalization of abortion services in the Netherlands preceded an alteration of the law. This was possible because the existing abortion law of 1886 (which was elaborated in 1911) offered enough margin for interpretation in the reality of social change.

Abortion was inserted in the Penal Code as a capital offense in 1886, but because it was impossible to establish whether the aborted fetus had lived at the time of the operation, the legislation was extended in 1911, making abortion an ethical offense as well. The only exception made was for abortion due to medical necessity. No further definition was given as to the extent of the term "necessity": judgment was left to the physician.

In the 1960s under the influence of the more relaxed attitude toward sexuality, family life, and birth control, *abortus provocatus* (induced abortion) also became a subject for social discussion. Before then, individual physicians had set themselves up as advocates for a medically creditable aid service and liberalization of the abortion law, but the taboo and opposition were at the time so persistent that these efforts continued to retain an incidental character. From 1965 onward, the tide turned, and various publications and articles appeared in medical magazines. The discussions that ensued forced individual physicians to take a stand on the issue of the admissibility of abortion. In the discussion, a number of them took a less restrictive stand than had been expected of them.

The discussion on abortion was lifted to another level by a television debate in 1967. For the first time the taboo on abortion was broken in society as a whole. The debate caused a wave of abortion requests in a number of Dutch hospitals and university clinics. In the chaotic situation that resulted, characterized by absence of a common standpoint or policy on the one hand and great pressure caused by the number of abortion requests on the other, a number of "abortion teams" were established by way of an *ad hoc* solution. Through a multidisciplinary approach, these teams tried to make an objective assessment as to the indications of necessity for treatment. Operations were performed in hospitals on a limited scale. In 1970 eight of these teams were functioning throughout the Netherlands, their most important function being the partial filling of the gap between the growing demand for abortion and inadequate facilities that existed at that time and establishing a firm basis for a more adequate abortion service.

The methods of the abortion teams created so many problems (that is, lack of common criteria, too limited capacity to meet all demands, use of a time-consuming procedure) that this form of service disappeared by the early 1970s. In the meantime, especially under the influence of psychiatry, there was a change of attitude and policy regarding the system used to assess indications for treatment. It was a question of the disappearance of the so-called no, unless and the acceptance of the yes, unless policy. In other words, it would no longer be a question of searching for indications as to whether pregnancy termination should be performed, but that in principle termination should be granted at the woman's request unless there were clear contradindications. The legal conception of medical necessity was stretched to abortion at request. Literally speaking, this was contrary to the law, but at the same time by way of the argument that finally the woman alone could decide whether an abortion was a "necessity," it became legally possible. However, an alteration of the law had become urgent.

Around 1970, owing to dissatisfaction with the existing situation, a number of initiatives in the field of abortion care were being undertaken. Within the NVSH (Dutch Association for Sexual Reform), work was done to achieve a better system to transfer people seeking abortion to England. In addition, several practitioners themselves began to perform abortions in their consulting rooms. Common action was also taken by groups of physicians, first by exerting pressure on gynecologists and later by providing facilities where treatment could be given. These facilities can be regarded as "forerunners" of the future abortion poly-clinics. Even now abortion services in clinics are almost exclusively in the hands of general practitioners.

An initiative that would later become significant throughout the country was the founding in 1969 of STIMEZO (Foundation for Medically Responsible Abortion Care). The proclaimed aim of this institution was to create possibilities for abortion within the limits of the law and on a nonprofit basis. Just as important was their aim to break the taboo surrounding abortion within the medical world and within society as a whole. The plan to open an abortion polyclinic was to be a form of seeing these aims realized. A number of barriers had to be overcome: juridical, medical, and financial barriers. A publicity campaign was set up, its aim being to obtain strong social support that would be necessary in overcoming these barriers. In newspapers and magazines, people were asked for moral and financial support. Within one month between 3,000 and 4,000 people and institutions gave their moral support, a great number of which came from social groups, many of which were connected with Women's Lib. For the first time, these groups, which individually had had little influence on the abortion issues, had banded together. As a result, STIMEZO appeared to be quite a powerful organization, and the authorities took no measures to prevent the opening of the clinic. The medical community also began to adopt a more tolerant attitude toward the initiative.

The publicity surrounding STIMEZO reached its height in December 1970 when a progressive broadcasting organization arranged a radio and television campaign in behalf of STIMEZO. In the meantime a loan was supplied, so that the clinic could open in Rotterdam in the autumn of 1971. During this time polyclinics were also founded in other cities, and together they formed the STIMEZO association in 1973, to better achieve their common goals (Ketting, 1978). This association still exists today. In the course of time the participating members began to alternate.

At the present time fourteen of the nineteen Dutch abortion clinics are members of the association. They perform about 70 percent of the total number of abortions performed in the Netherlands. Furthermore, about 20 percent are treated in non-STIMEZO clinics (mostly women from abroad) and about 10 percent in general hospitals. (No illegal abortions have taken place in the Netherlands since the early 1970s (de Bruijn, 1979). STIMEZO has played an important role in the political struggle to liberalize the law, as well as in setting up a registration system that provides a factual basis for information and research. Within the association, the main objective was to develop criteria for and to uphold the quality of service. Consequently, a qualitatively high-leveled infrastructure of abortion services existed before the law was altered in 1981.

LEGAL STATUS OF ABORTION

In 1970 the first proposition to alter the abortion law was submitted, proposing complete legalization without substantial restrictions. It was never put to the vote. Six more propositions for liberalization followed, supplemented by more or fewer restricting regulations. It was not until 1981 that a proposition presented by liberals and Christian Democrats was accepted with the smallest possible majority, by which the already existing situation was legalized with some restrictions. The basic concept of the law is that abortion is to remain in the Penal Code but is not a punishable offense if and when legal regulations are met. The abortion law stipulates that an abortion is admissible only in case of an emergency that cannot be dealt with in another way. The woman, in consultation with the physician, decides whether the situation is an emergency. In practice, this amounts to abortion being available on request because every reason is accepted as a ground for abortion. The physician is expected to follow the procedure stipulated by law (i.e., to discuss the alternatives to abortion and to check whether the woman in question has made the choice of her own free will) in order to be assured that the decision taken is done so carefully.

Other requirements are as follows:

—Abortions may only be performed in licensed clinics or hospitals. The license is issued by the government if the said institutions meet a number of requirements (i.e., have a nonprofit basis).

—A waiting period of five days must be observed between the first visit to a physician regarding the abortion and the termination. This stipulation is also meant to guarantee a well-thought-out decision. The five-day period may be waived only if the woman's life is in immediate danger.

—Clinics and hospitals are obligated to register all cases, thereby preserving the woman's anonymity.

—There is no prohibition from performing abortions on women from abroad.

—No limit is stipulated as to the length of the pregnancy for performing the abortion. The criterion used is the viability of the fetus (in reality abortion is performed up to twenty-two weeks after conception). Clinics and hospitals that perform second-trimester abortions are required to meet a number of extra conditions.

It took more than three years before the requirements for performing abortions could be settled, so that it was not until 1 November 1984 that the law was actually enforced.

Workers in abortion services criticized mainly the requirement of a five-day waiting-time. This measure, which had originated from the necessity of a political compromise, was regarded as useless and pampering (Paling & Rademakers, 1986). The abortion services for women from abroad could be especially hampered by this rule. However, it is unlikely that a political debate on the subject of the abortion law will be renewed in the near future. After a struggle lasting eleven years, this law has become an acceptable compromise, through which the abortion services can practically continue their work on the same lines.

One advantage of the legalization of abortion is that the government finances the operation for Dutch women.

ATTITUDES TOWARD ABORTION

After the abortion law was liberalized, the subject practically disappeared as a topic of social interest. Only small devout religious groups and a rather active pro-life organization bring the subject up now and again in the media by tenaciously arguing against the right to choose an abortion.

The majority of the Dutch population has a reasonably tolerant and, above all, pragmatic attitude toward birth control in general, and, consequently, also toward abortion as an "emergency measure." Yet for most individuals abortion remains a controversial theme. The most important reasons are:

—The deep-rooted influence of religion in Dutch society

—The idea of failing in a society where sex education and contraceptives are easily obtainable

—Myths and fables that doggedly continue to cloud abortion

—Propaganda from pro-life organizations.

DEMOGRAPHY OF ABORTION

Data Source and Incidence

Since 1974 data have been systematically recorded for all women who have their pregnancies terminated in an abortion clinic. Most of the non-STIMEZO clinics also contribute to this registration. Since 1 January 1985 hospitals have also been legally obligated to register each case. Since data for 1985 have not been analyzed yet, we will present the figures for 1984. These are based on registered terminations, which in some cases are supplemented by the estimated number supplied by hospitals, based on research done among all Dutch gynecologists (Ketting & Leseman 1986). As shown in table 22.1, a total of ± 43,200 abortions were performed in the Netherlands in 1984 (of which 84 percent were registered and 5 percent were performed in other clinics and ± 11 percent in hospitals).

For the past few years there has been a systematic decrease in the number of abortions (table 22.2) partly caused by the reduced number of clients from West Germany and Belgium. We will proceed to give an account of the patients living in the Netherlands.

After an increase in the number of terminations in 1980–81, which was due mainly to a so-called pillpanic wave (Ketting, 1981), which was inspired by massive press attention on the health risks of the contraceptive pill, a steady decrease in the number of abortions began to take place. In 1984 the abortion rate per 1,000 women fifteen to forty-four was 5.6, which is the lowest known rate in the Western world. In addition, in 1982, 10.7 of every 100 known pregnancies were terminated by means of abortion; in 1984 this figure had declined to 9.6.

Age, Parity, and Marital Status

Data on abortions by age are presented in table 22.3. Nearly half of the Dutch abortion clients are found in the age group twenty to twenty-nine years. The high frequency of abortion in this age group is linked to two risk factors that have a reinforcing influence on one another: on one hand, the tendency toward a more active sex life by which the chances of (unwanted) conception increase; and on the other hand, the tendency to postpone the decision to start a family.

Married women account for more than one-third of the Dutch abortion population. In the last few years their share has decreased: in 1978, 43.6 percent;

in 1982, 38.9 percent; in 1984, 34.4 percent (table 22.4). This decrease is largely offset by an increase in the number of unmarried women living alone: in 1982, 19.6 percent; in 1984, 24.2 percent. The risk factors involved in this group have to do with the apparently less effective use of contraceptives stemming from the absence of a permanent partner, combined with the maintenance of varying and yet relatively highly sexually active relationships.

Pregnancy Experience and Length of Pregnancy

Nearly half of the abortion clients terminate their first pregnancy as shown in table 22.5. In other words, they have never had an abortion before and are not mothers. Furthermore, there is an increase in the number of women who have previously had an abortion (see table 22.6). This occurs mainly with clients from allochthonous population groups (Dutch inhabitants of foreign nationality) and is an indication of their less adequate contraceptive use. One of the remaining consistent—and welcome—tendencies concerns the gestational age at the time of the operation. An increasing number of pregnancies are terminated at an early stage: in 1978, 41.2 percent of the pregnancies were terminated at less than six weeks of gestation; in 1982, 49 percent; and in 1984, 55.1 percent. (See table 22.7).

This development can be attributed to the following factors:

—Better information on the possibilities for abortion, resulting in the decrease of un- necessary delay

—Increasing acceptance of abortion, making the decision to terminate the pregnancy quicker and easier

—Greater alacrity of general practitioners in referring women to the clinic

—Decline in the total number of clients, which gives the clinics more than enough capacity and ability to schedule women within a shorter time.

Use of Contraceptives

The registration of statistics takes note of which contraceptive means was applied in the six months previous to the operation. The information recorded in 1984 is presented in table 22.8.

These data can be used to make a comparison between the abortion population and the total figures on the use of contraceptives in the Netherlands, but they cannot be used to determine the (un)reliability of some methods (since no dis- tinction has been made between method-failures and patient-failures), or to de- termine the cause of the unwanted pregnancy (the question was: which contraceptive was mainly used in the previous six-month period). One of the most frequent causes of unwanted pregnancies is in fact that the woman stopped using a contraceptive or changed to another method.

In comparison with the total group of fertile women in the age group eighteen to thirty-seven, the use of extremely reliable contraceptive means (pill, IUD) is notably lower in the abortion population (total: 46 percent, abortion population: 27.5 percent), while the use of condoms is notably higher (total: 6 percent, abortion population: 20.9 percent). Condom users form an important risk group for abortion, partially because this method is less reliable, and there is a greater chance that users are unmotivated and use them inefficiently. The use of condoms occurs relatively more often in first sexual contacts and in the absence of a permanent partner.

Women who use rhythm or employ the withdrawal method run a greater risk of pregnancy. Together they form about one-fifth of the abortion clients, while the total number of fertile women in the Netherlands who apply these methods is less than 2 percent. The pill is the contraceptive chosen by most women after abortion (57.1 percent). A further 12.7 percent choose the IUD and 10.2 percent sterilization.

Use of contraceptives is connected primarily with the living situation, which is not surprising because it implies the regularity of sexual intercourse. Table 22.9 shows the association between contraceptive use and the sexual partner's living status with the woman.

Married and unmarried cohabiting couples are less likely to be nonusers of contraceptive methods. Traditional methods (rhythm and withdrawal) and condoms are most frequently used by married couples, which increases their risk of an unplanned pregnancy. Moreover, the unmarried (young) women living with their parents tend to use less reliable methods (rhythm/withdrawal and condoms) or no methods at all.

TEENAGE ABORTION

Although teenagers tend to form a group at risk for unwanted pregnancy and abortion, the situation in the Netherlands is far better than in the United States and other West European countries.

In 1984, 15.1 percent of all abortion clients were under twenty years of age (2,080). This percentage is showing a steady decrease over the years: in 1978 it was 18.4 percent, in 1982 16.4 percent. The abortion rate per 1,000 women under twenty years of age diminished from 6.9 in 1972 to 5.5 in 1982 and 4.7 in 1984. The same trend applies to the abortion ratio; in 1982, 40.2 of every 100 known pregnancies ended in abortion, and in 1984 38.8. The main reason for this decrease in teenage abortions is the effective use of contraceptives. In 1981, 43 percent used the pill during their first sexual intercourse, and another 27 percent used condoms.

One-fifth of the teenagers, however, reported they used no contraceptive method, which is an unacceptably high proportion, since almost every pregnancy in this age group is unwanted. Research is being done on how to further diminish this risk group.

SUMMARY

In the Netherlands a qualitatively sound abortion service preceded the liberalization of the law. This form of aid is concentrated in independent abortion clinics and is mainly in the hands of general practitioners. There are nineteen clinics in the Netherlands spread throughout the country. They are partly united in "STIMEZO Nederland," an "umbrella" organization that serves their common interests, and are engaged in documentation, sex education, and research in the field of abortion and contraception. In 1981 an amendment to the law legalized the existing abortion services, with a few restrictions, the most important of these being the obligatory five-day waiting period. Social discussion of abortion has practically disappeared since the amendment. Most of the Dutch have a tolerant and, above all, a pragmatic attitude toward contraceptives in general and toward abortion as an emergency solution.

In 1984 a total of ± 43,200 abortions were performed, of which 18,700 were on women living in the Netherlands. The abortion rate per 1,000 women (age fifteen to forty-four) is 5.6, and the abortion ratio per 100 known pregnancies is 9.6. Nearly half of the clients are found in the age group between twenty and twenty-nine. More than one-third of the women are married. In most cases it is their first pregnancy that is terminated. Yet the number of women who have had previous abortions is increasing, which is largely due to the ineffective use of contraceptives by allochthonous women. As to contraceptive use, women who use condoms, rhythm, or withdrawal are the most important risk categories. After the operation has taken place, women often choose the pill, IUD, or sterilization.

REFERENCES

de Bruijn, J. Geschiedenis van de abortus in Nederland. Ph.D. diss. Amsterdam: Van Gennep, 1979.
Giessen, G. J. van de. Onderzoek gezinsvorming 1982, voorlopige uitkomsten. Maandstatistiek van de Bevolking, 1983, 4/5, blz. 38–53.
Ketting, E. Over het kondoom. Stimezo-onderzoek 76–2, Den Haag, 1976.
———. Van misdrijf tot hulpverlening. Ph.D. diss. Samson, Alphen a/d Rijn, 1978.
———. De teloorgang van "De Pil." NISSO, Zeist, 1981.
Ketting, E., & Leseman, P. Abortus en anticonceptie 1983/1984. Stimezo-onderzoek, Den Haag, 1986.
Ketting, E., & van Praag, Ph. Abortus provocatus, wet en praktijk. NISSO, Zeist, 1983.
Paling, W., & Rademakers, J. De abortuswet kent een eigen praktijk. Welzijnsweekblad nr. 12, 21 March 1986, blz. 10–11.
Permanente Registratie Stimezo Nederland 1984.
Wet Afbreking Zwangerschap. Staatsblad, 1981, nr. 257.

Table 22.1
Registered and Estimated Total Number of Abortions in 1984, by Country of Residence (Absolute Figures)

Country of Residence	Registered[a]	Estimated Total[b]
Netherlands	13,821	18,700
W. Germany	9,949	11,300
Belgium/Luxembourg	4,372	4,900
Spain	7,299	7,300
Other countries	949	1,000
Total	36,390	43,200

[a]Data concerning abortions carried out in clinics that took part in the registration.
[b]Abortions carried out in clinics not taking part in the registration as well as abortions in hospitals.
Source: Ketting & Leseman, 1986.

Table 22.2
Number of Abortions Performed in Clinics and in Hospitals on Women Living in the Netherlands, 1977–84

Year	Abortion clinics	Hospitals	Total	Abortion rate per 1,000 women	
				Total population	Women 15–44
1977	12,100	(4,300)	16,400	1.2	5.5
1978	11,800	4,100	15,900	1.1	5.2
1979	13,200	(4,400)	17,600	1.3	5.6
1980	16,300	(5,000)	21,300	1.5	6.7
1981	16,100	(5,000)	21,100	1.5	6.5
1982	15,700	(5,000)	20,700	1.5	6.3
1983	14,800	4,700	19,500	1.4	5.9
1984	13,900	(4,800)	18,700	1.3	5.6

Source: Ketting & Leseman, 1986.

Table 22.3
Abortion by Age of the Women, 1984 (in percentage)

Age	% in 1984
≤ 14 years	0.2
15-19 years	14.9
20-24 years	26.4
25-29 years	22.3
30-34 years	18.1
35-39 years	13.4
40-44 years	4.2
≥ 45 years	0.5
total Netherlands	100.0
	N =13,821
Average age	27 years
Most frequent age	20 years

Source: Ketting & Leseman, 1986.

Table 22.4
Abortion by Marital Status and Living Situation, 1984 (in percentage)

Marital status/Living situation	% in 1984
Married	34.4
Married, in divorce	1.4
Never married, living with parents	21.7
Never married, living with partner	9.7
Never married, living alone	24.2
Divorced/widow, living alone	6.1
Divorced/widow, living with partner	1.5
Total Netherlands	100.0
N=	13,821

Source: Ketting & Leseman, 1986.

Table 22.5

Percentage of Abortion Patients by Number of Earlier Pregnancies, 1984

Number of earlier pregnancies	% in 1984
0	48.1
1	15.5
2	16.5
3	10.6
4	4.9
5 or more	4.4
Total Netherlands	100.0
N=	13,821

Source: Ketting & Leseman, 1986.

Table 22.6

Abortions by Number of Prior Abortions, 1984 (in percentage)

Number of prior abortions	% in 1984
none	80.9
one	15.4
two	2.7
three or more	1.0
Total Netherlands	100.0
N=	13,821

Source: Ketting & Leseman, 1986.

Table 22.7
Abortion by Weeks of Gestation, 1984 (in percentage)

Length of pregnancy	% in 1984
≤ 3 weeks	6.6
4-5	48.5
6-7	26.2
8-9	8.8
10-11	4.8
12-13	2.6
14-15	1.2
≥ 16	1.3
Total Netherlands	100.0
N=	13,821

Source: Ketting & Leseman, 1986.

Table 22.8
Percentage Distribution of Abortion Patients by Contraceptive Use During the Six-Month Period Prior to Unwanted Pregnancy, 1984

Contraceptive method	% in 1984
Pill, depoprovera	23.5
IUD	4.0
Condoms	20.9
Diaphragm/spermicides	2.6
Rhythm	19.6
Other contraceptive method	1.4
No method used	27.9
Total Netherlands	100.0
N=	13,821

Source: Permanent Registration, STIMEZO, 1984.

Table 22.9

Contraceptive Use Among Women Eighteen to Thirty-seven Years in 1984, by Sexual Partner's Living Status (in percentage)

	No method used	Pill, Depopro-vera	IUD	Condoms	Diaphragm/ spermicides	Withdrawal/ Rhythm	Other method
married	20,6	19,5	4,6	23,8	1,5	28,2	1,9
married, in divorce	43,3	24,2	5,7	8,9	1,9	14,6	1,3
never married, living with parents	37,5	18,1	0,9	21,8	0,5	21,0	0,3
never married, living with partner	21,8	29,4	6,5	23,2	5,2	13,2	0,8
never married, living alone	29,8	25,3	3,5	18,0	3,9	18,4	1,0
divorced/widow ,living alone	40,1	25,6	2,9	12,3	2,1	16,3	0,6
divorced/widow ,living with partner	32,4	25,6	3,4	15,9	1,7	19,3	1,7
Total Population	27,9	23,5	4,0	20,9	2,6	19,6	1,4

Source: Permanent Registration, STIMEZO, 1984.

23

NEW ZEALAND

Janet Sceats

HISTORICAL DEVELOPMENT OF ABORTION POLICY

Abortion legislation in New Zealand evolved from the laws of England and Wales and first appeared as part of the Offences Against the Person Act (1867), which was a direct copy of sections of an earlier English statute. Through successive revisions of this act in the Criminal Code Act (1893) and Crimes Acts (1908 and 1968), and until 1977, the laws relating to abortion remained substantially unchanged (Royal Commission on Inquiry, 1977). Based on both statute and case-law, abortion was not illegal if done in good faith for the preservation of the life of the mother or her physical or mental health (Williamson, 1970). The lack of definition of the concept "unlawful" was one of the factors that stimulated public debate prior to the change of the law in 1977.

Until the 1970s, however, induced abortion was considered primarily within the context of maternal mortality or of pronatalist concerns for population growth. Four governmental inquiries have focused on abortion. The first, in 1921, reporting on maternal mortality, noted "the abnormally high death rate due to septic conditions following on attempts to procure abortion." Policy recommendations were made to improve standards of maternal health but did not relate to abortion (Royal Commission of Inquiry, 1977).

In 1936 another committee, known as the McMillan Committee, investigated maternal deaths due to septic abortions. These were seen as a major public health problem (see section below, "Abortion and Fertility Regulation"). The McMillan Committee recommended as solutions the state provision of financial, domestic, and obstetric help, sex education for the young, encouragement of more tolerant social attitudes toward unmarried women and their children, and a prohibition on the advertising of contraceptives and their sale to young persons (McMillan, 1937).

In 1946 the Dominion Population Committee considered the question of abortion in the light of the recommendations made by the McMillan Committee, many of which had, by this time, been implemented. In endorsing the conclusions of the earlier report, this committee noted that, despite "strenuous endeavours to check the crime of abortion it continues to be a serious evil" (Dominion Population Committee, 1946).

Abortion did not surface again as a major issue until the late 1960s. It is difficult to assess the incidence of legal or illegal induced abortion at that time, but the renewed interest and the growth of pressure groups appear to have occurred primarily in response to events elsewhere rather than because of pressure to change the existing local system. Because New Zealand law relating to abortion was based on that of the United Kingdom, passage of the Abortion Act, 1967 (United Kingdom) attracted considerable attention, as did the liberalization of the abortion law in South Australia in 1969 (Royal Commission of Inquiry, 1977).

The first pressure group, called the Society for the Protection of the Unborn Child (SPUC), was organized in 1970 with the objective of preventing the introduction of any abortion law similar to that of the United Kingdom. It campaigned to bring public and political pressure against any move to liberalize the existing law (Stone, 1977).

In 1971 the New Zealand Abortion Law Reform Association (ARLANZ) was established, in part to counteract the effects of the anti-liberalization movement. Important aspects of its campaign were dissemination of information on the state of the law, attempts to obtain data on the incidence of induced abortion, and commissioning of pubilic opinion surveys. The arguments for reform were based on the lack of clarity in the existing law which produced variations in interpretation and application (Stone, 1977). ALRANZ also wished to extend the existing grounds for legal abortion to include risk of fetal abnormality and pregnancy resulting from a criminal act (Kirkwood & Facer, 1976).

Women's Abortion Action Committees were formed in a number of centers in 1972, and in 1973 the first National Women's Abortion Action Conference was held and the Women's National Abortion Action Campaign (WONAAC) came into being. The objective of this organization was the repeal rather than the reform of the existing law, and the campaign was based on "a woman's right to choose" (Stone, 1977).

Three of the major Protestant churches recommended reform of the abortion law: Baptists (1979), Presbyterians (1971), and Methodists (1974). The largest denomination, the Anglican church, had no official policy as each diocese is autonomous, but it commissioned a special report in 1973 to examine the legal, medical, social, and moral aspects of abortion. No specific recommendations were made, but the issue was recognized as controversial and was considered to be a matter of individual conscience. The Catholic and Mormon churches were strongly opposed to abortion (Facer, 1973; Kirkwood & Facer, 1976; Stone, 1977).

In 1974 a charitable trust opened the first private clinic to provide abortion services, and immediately a campaign began to force its closing. A bill, The Hospitals Amendment Act, was introduced into Parliament to limit the performance of abortions to public hospitals. While it was in passage, the police seized confidential records from the clinic, forcing its temporary closing and provoking a public outcry. These events intensified the abortion debate, and, as a result, the establishment of a Royal Commission to inquire into contraception, sterilization, and abortion was announced. In the meantime the Hospitals Amendment Act (1975) was passed and in its final form provided for abortions to be carried out only in hospitals that had been specially licensed by the Department of Health. It also set up the basis for the first systematic data collection system by requiring that a government agency be notified of each induced abortion.

The Royal Commission on Contraception, Sterilization and Abortion presented its report in 1977 after receiving a large number of submissions from individuals and organizations, including the churches, women's groups, and professional bodies. Although the findings, most notably the recommendation of a panel system to approve abortions, were widely criticized, the report formed the basis for important changes in the law. The commission also attempted to place the whole question of abortion within a broader context—the social, medical, and moral implications of fertility regulation—and to synthesize the varying viewpoints on what had become a deeply divisive issue.

In 1977, reflecting some of the recommendations of the Royal Commission, the Crimes Act (1961) was amended to provide a definition of the grounds under which it is lawful to perform an abortion. New legislation, the Contraception, Sterilization and Abortion Act (1977), was introduced to establish the procedures under which a woman could obtain an abortion and to set up a statutory body, the Abortion Supervisory Committee, to oversee the working of the laws relating to abortion.

This legislation had several immediate after-effects. It was criticized because it still failed to provide adequate clarification of the law and because the procedures were considered to be unworkable (Kember, 1978). Organizations appeared in a number of centers in late 1977 to assist women requiring abortions to travel to Australia (O'Neill, 1982). The Abortion Supervisory Committee complained of lack of cooperation from medical practitioners (Abortion Supervisory Committee, 1978).

Over the next eighteen months further amendments to the law were passed, which then gained greater acceptance from the medical profession. Public hospital abortion clinics, licensed to perform first-trimester abortions, were opened in two major cities in 1978 and in 1980, and in 1979 the original private clinic was granted a license and reopened. Migration data indicated that, as more facilities were established, the number of women going to Australia to obtain abortions was diminishing. By 1981 it was felt that this traffic had virtually ceased and that almost all abortions to New Zealand women were being performed in New Zealand licensed institutions (Abortion Supervisory Committee, 1982).

The rapid increase in abortion rates since 1978 has slowed, and public debate has subsided. Some attempts have been made to challenge the existing law through the courts (Bergin, 1983), and in October 1983 two Private Members Bills were introduced into Parliament. One of these bills was designed to restrict severely the legal grounds, and the other aimed to repeal the existing law and make abortion a matter between a woman and her doctor. Both bills were defeated.

Inequality of access to abortion services, either because of cost or geographic maldistribution, represents a problem of implementation. The first of these, cost, is of minor relevance in New Zealand where the overwhelming majority of abortions, 81 percent in 1982, are performed free of charge in public hospital facilities. Geographic maldistribution is more difficult to overcome in a country with a small and unevenly distributed population. Thus, the largest city has two clinics, and the capital city one; these three North Island facilities undertake approximately two-thirds of all abortions. The largest hospital in the South Island brings this total to 80 percent; the remaining 20 percent of abortions are carried out in public and private hospitals in both main islands.

LEGAL STATUS OF ABORTION

Grounds

The grounds for legal abortion as set out in the Crimes Act (1961) and in the Crimes Amendment Acts of 1977 and 1978 are as follows:

Serious danger . . . to the life or to the physical or mental health of the woman. . . .

Substantial risk that the child, if born, would be so physically or mentally abnormal as to be seriously handicapped. . . .

Pregnancy that is the result of incest or of sexual intercourse with a girl under care or protection

The woman or girl is subnormal

The following matters, while not in themselves grounds . . . may be taken into account in determining . . . whether the continuance of the pregnancy would result in serious danger to her life or to her physical or mental health:

a) the age of the woman . . . is near the beginning or the end of the usual child-bearing years

b) the fact . . . that there are reasonable grounds for believing that the pregnancy is the result of rape. (New Zealand Crimes Amendment Acts, 1977, 1978)

Procedure

Under the terms of the Contraception, Sterilization and Abortion Act (1977), a medical practitioner may apply to the Abortion Supervisory Committee to become a certifying consultant and thus is empowered to declare that a woman has legal grounds for having an abortion. A woman seeking an abortion must receive a letter of referral from her doctor to a certifying consultant. She must then obtain a certificate stating that she has legal grounds signed by two certifying consultants, one of whom must be an obstetrician/gynecologist. If one certifying consultant refuses, then the approval of a third may be sought. The agreement of the operating surgeon must be obtained, but this may be (and frequently is) one of the two certifying consultants.

The law provides that a woman should receive counseling from a trained counselor prior to her termination. In the abortion clinics, the whole procedure from approval, through counseling, to operation is carried out in the same institution, thus facilitating what appears to be a cumbersome process.

ATTITUDES TOWARD ABORTION

Between 1969 and 1977 more than thirty local, national, and special interest group surveys of attitudes toward abortion were conducted. No opinion survey results have been published since the law changed in 1977.

In 1972, 1974, and 1976 ALRANZ commissioned an independent research organization to undertake nationwide random sample opinion surveys. These surveys showed consistent majority support for the grounds specified in the existing law, and for these to be extended to include fetal abnormality and pregnancy resulting from a criminal act. The minority positions of either complete prohibition or of unrestricted availability of abortion were decreasingly popular. There was majority approval of abortion if a woman and her doctor decided continuation of the pregnancy was inadvisable, but support for this view declined somewhat over the period (Facer, 1977, pp. 7–8).

Other local and national surveys carried out in this period, but using different questions and methodology, confirmed these findings (Facer, 1977, pp. 8–12). More conservative attitudes were found among women, persons over fifty-five years of age, ethnic minorities, and Catholics (Kirkwood & Facer, 1976).

There have been three surveys of all medical practitioners (1969, 1975, and 1977), two surveys of obstetricians and gynecologists (1971, 1975), and one of psychiatrists (1975), with varying response rates. All surveys indicated strong support for existing grounds as well as the above-mentioned extensions (Royal Commission of Inquiry, 1977). The opinion that abortion should be a decision made by the woman and her doctor, although a minority view, gained increasing support from 39 percent (1975) to 50 percent (1977). The proportion agreeing that abortion was never justified remained very low (4 percent) but, as among the general public, there was little support for unrestricted availability (Kirkwood & Facer, 1976, pp. 34–36). The first survey, with the lowest response rate (51 percent) had found a high level of ignorance and confusion over the law among those medical practitioners interested enough to reply (Gregson & Irwin, 1971).

DEMOGRAPHY OF ABORTION

Data Sources

Unless otherwise specified, the data used here come from two sources: (1) notifications of abortions, available since 1976; and (2) a survey of 1,267 abortion patients undertaken by the writer in 1983.

Incidence

Because of lack of reliable data from the early 1970s, it is not possible to provide estimates of the incidence of legal abortions for this period, but interestingly the number of "therapeutic" abortions recorded in public hospitals (May 1974 to May 1976) was far less, 1,986, than in one private clinic, 4,655, during the same period when abortion debate had resumed and intensified. No figures are available for private hospitals for those years.

In 1978 and 1979, following the change in the law, the rates of induced abortion were very low (see table 23.1). This was the period of significant movement of women to Australia to obtain abortions. Thus, much of the growth between 1979 and 1980 is a product of the increasing provision and use of New Zealand's facilities, diminishing the importance of the Australian component of New Zealand abortions. From 1981 onwards, the data are thought to include virtually all abortions to New Zealand women.

By comparison with most other low fertility countries, levels of induced abortion in New Zealand are low (Tietze & Heushaw, 1986, pp. 30–42). Provisional data for 1984 do not show any great increase over the level in the previous two years.

Demographic Characteristics

The demographic characteristics of women obtaining abortions in 1983 are presented in table 23.2. The majority of these women were under age twenty-five, had never been married, or had had a live birth or a previous induced abortion. This pattern is consistent with patterns of previous years. In both 1981 and 1982, 94 percent of all induced abortions were performed in the first trimester by suction curettage. The 0.12 percent (1982) of more than twenty weeks' gestation were for very specific medical reasons.

Socioeconomic Characteristics

There are limited data based on a 1983 survey (see below) on employment status, occupation, and preabortion contraceptive use of a very large representative sample of women having abortions (see table 23.3). Because the appropriate 1981 detailed census tabulations are not yet available, it is difficult to compare these data with those for the population at risk. On the basis of provisional census tabulations, however, age-standardized percentages demonstrate that the survey population twenty to forty-four years was somewhat less well educated than the total female population of these ages. Tertiary educated women were overre-presented, however, among abortion patients fifteen to nineteen years of age.

Because unemployment levels have increased greatly since the 1981 census, it is not possible to make a meaningful comparison for employment status. It is of interest to note, however, that using an age-standardized percentage from the census, 5 percent of all women fifteen to forty-four would be expected to receive the Domestic Purposes Benefit paid to a single parent supporting dependent children, compared with 8 percent of abortion clients.

Preabortion contraceptive behavior was based on use in the month preceding conception. The abortion clients fall into three groups of approximately equal size: nonusers, users of hormonal or other modern methods, and users of mechanical or inefficient methods. More than half of the pill users were aware of irregular use. No data are available on postabortion contraception (Sceats, 1984).

ABORTION AND FERTILITY REGULATION

Population Dynamics

Much of the discussion in this section is drawn from two publications (Pool & Sceats, 1982; Sceats & Pool, in preparation). These show that two separate fertility transitions have occurred in New Zealand. For non-Maoris, the majority population primarily of European descent, the pattern has resembled that of the United States. In the late nineteenth century, there was a rapid decline from the high levels of the 1870s (TFR = 6.0), which was followed by a more gradual movement to very low levels in the Depression of the 1930s (TFR = 1.9). A prolonged "Baby Boom," during which a TFR of 4.0 was achieved, lasted from World War II until the 1970s, since which time there has been a rapid decrease to subreplacement (TFR = 1.9, 1982). For Maoris, who constitute 10 percent of the population, there were high levels of fertility (TFR = 6.0) until the 1960s, followed by an exceptionally rapid decrease (TFR = 2.6, 1981).

The late-nineteenth-century decline in non-Maori fertility resulted more from changing patterns of nuptiality than from marital fertility regulation. From the early 1900s, however, birth control (contraception plus abortion) within marriage was the more significant factor. During the 1920s and 1930s illegal induced abortion was a matter of considerable concern, being attributed as a prime cause of maternal mortality and reaching an estimated level of 20 per 100 live births (Royal Commission of Inquiry, 1977). This rate is quite low, however, by international standards, being similar to that of England and Wales and Finland in 1981 (Tietze, 1983, p. 26), while the possible impact on maternal health may have been exaggerated by factors such as problems of certification (Donovan, 1969). Nevertheless, this period appears to have been the only time when induced abortion played a significant role for non-Maori marital birth control (spacing and limitation).

In the "Baby Boom" decade, the impact of induced abortion on population dynamics must have been minimal. Similarly, until recently, Maori fertility levels have been so high that abortion would have been precluded as a significant means of fertility regulation.

The contribution of abortion to fertility regulation can be more directly assessed for recent years. The data presented earlier and below demonstrate that abortion is not a prime method of regulation. Given the reported very high levels of use of both hormonal contraceptives (oral and injectible) and sterilization (Trlin & Perry, 1981, pp. 24–47), this is hardly surprising.

In the New Zealand context, fertility regulation must be interrelated with ex-nuptial conception and ex-nuptial birth. The status "illegitimacy" does not exist in New Zealand family law (Cartwright, 1984). For the entire period for which satisfactory data exist, premarital conceptions followed by births in the first eight months of marriage have constituted an important component of first order births for young non-Maoris (Jacoby, 1961). This was particularly marked during the "Baby Boom" when the modal age for first marriage was very low. Recently, there have been changes in this pattern and in the related practice of birth control, resulting overall in a delay in the first birth. Ex-nuptial conception followed by precipitated marriage has decreased significantly, while ex-nuptial conception and birth have decreased slightly, except at very young ages (Pool & Crawford, 1980).

A comparison with Canadian data showed intervals between births in New Zealand to be much shorter (Sceats, 1981). The reason probably has more to do with prevailing norms than with poor contraceptive efficacy, given the high-level use of hormonal contraception. Abortion does not appear to be used to achieve a longer spacing, for women of low parity are underrepresented among abortion cases (Abortion Supervisory Committee, 1983).

Family Planning Programs and Policy

Since New Zealand has no national family planning program per se, these services are provided through private but subsidized medical consultation, with prescribed contraceptives being available free of charge. There is also an active, privately supported and government-subsidized Family Planning Association which provides clinics in many centers and plays an important role in preabortion pregnancy diagnosis (Sceats, 1984). The comprehensive welfare system, notably financial support for single parents and benefits for dependent children, makes childbearing and -raising a viable alternative to induced abortion. The McMillan Report strongly advocated that family allowances, first introduced in the 1920s, be extended for this purpose, a recommendation implemented in the 1940s (Chapman, 1981).

SPECIAL GROUPS

Adolescents

Levels of fertility among women under twenty are high by comparison with most other low fertility countries, but are declining (see table 23.4). Although rates for the younger ages (under sixteen) have decreased slightly, most of the decline has occurred among those seventeen years and over.

Abortion rates for women fifteen to nineteen years have increased steadily, apart from the aberration in the 1978 data (Cartwright, 1984). There has been little change, however, in the levels of abortion among those under fifteen years. Abortions to women under age twenty accounted for 28 percent of all abortions in 1982, while 10 percent of all live births were to women in this age group. An increasing proportion of known pregnancies to young women are ending in abortion, and for the under fifteen-year-olds abortions now outnumber live births in a ratio of 2:1 (see table 23.4). In 1982 for the first time there were more abortions than live births to women forty-five years and over, the only other age group to have such a ratio.

Induced abortion has played a role in the decline in fertility among older adolescents in New Zealand, but the major contribution would seem to be from increasing and more efficient use of contraception. Evidence to support this is found in the consistency and long-term nature of this decline. The Age-Specific Fertility Rate (ASFR) for fifteen to nineteen year olds fell steadily from 70 per 1000 in 1971 to 34 per 1000 in 1982, despite the changing availability of abortion during this period. The provision of contraceptive services and advice to persons under age sixteen is restricted under the Contraception, Sterilization and Abortion Act (1977), and it is in this age group with limited access to contraception that the least decline in fertility has taken place. The small decrease in fertility rates for those under sixteen in recent years are due to the increasing use of induced abortion to prevent births to this high-risk group. The known conception rates (based on total births plus abortions) for thirteen, fourteen, and fifteen years olds were the same in 1982 as they had been in 1979. By contrast, known conceptions among eighteen to nineteen year olds fell by 9 percent in this time.

Minority Groups

The only data currently available on the incidence of induced abortion among minority groups are drawn from the 1983 survey described above. Comparisons with the most recent census show that Maori and Pacific Island women were considerably overrepresented in the study population. Statistically significant relationships were found between ethnic group, age, and parity, with Maori and Pacific Island women being more likely to be older and of higher parity than the majority non-Maori population. There are, therefore, two markedly different patterns of induced abortion in New Zealand which correspond to the differences in family formation patterns. For the low fertility European-origin population, induced abortion appears to be used primarily for timing purposes by young (under age thirty) nulliparous women to delay the first birth. For the higher fertility minority populations, induced abortion is an adjunct to limitation for women who have achieved a desired family size (Sceats, 1984).

ABORTION RESEARCH

The various public inquiries, particularly the most recent, have summarized the available research on levels of abortion. Until notification data became available there was "an absence of any good data from which meaningful measures might have been calculated" (Pool & Sceats, 1982, p. 123). A number of researchers, however, had attempted, through surveys and other means, to estimate both levels and the numbers of women traveling to Australia (Kirkwood et al., 1979; Trlin, 1975). Prior to the change in the law, there were also a number of surveys of public and professional attitudes, as well as a few clinical studies (Pool & Sceats, 1982, pp. 123–124). Records from clinics have also been analyzed (Hunton & Salive, 1977; Sparrow, 1980). Apart from the national polls, these have all been local studies. Annual statistics are published by the Abortion Supervisory Committee (Abortion Supervisory Committee, 1978–1983).

The only national study of abortion patients is being undertaken by the writer, and involves both a detailed trend analysis of notification data and a survey of the experiences of women in obtaining an abortion. This survey was carried out from May to July 1983 on all women ($n = 1,267$, 93 percent response rate) having terminations in the four institutions, which together carry out 80 percent of all notified abortions. Questions covered pregnancy diagnosis, medical consultation, decision-making, counseling, and key demographic attributes (Sceats, 1984). Data from this study have been presented elsewhere in this chapter.

ILLEGAL ABORTION

The Royal Commission attempted to estimate the incidence of illegal abortion from a variety of sources and concluded that they could make no reliable estimate (Royal Commission on Inquiry, 1977). Maternal mortality, hospital morbidity data, or criminal prosecutions records do not suggest any significant illegal abortion figures currently in New Zealand. Travel to Australia, which, in the recent past, has been an alternative for women unable to obtain an abortion locally, has virtually ceased. This is perhaps the most important indication that, in spite of early criticism of the law and the acknowledged maldistribution of facilities, there is, at present, no apparent unmet demand for abortions that would lead women to seek these outside legitimate New Zealand channels.

SUMMARY

Induced abortion continues to be a controversial issue in New Zealand, although levels are comparatively low. It is not a major method of fertility regulation, and it appears to have played only a minor role in recent fertility declines. Abortion is legal if it poses serious danger to the life or physical or mental health of the woman and under a number of specific circumstances. The majority of abortions are performed free of charge within the public hospital system and occur in the first trimester. There has been no maternal mortality from this cause for many years, and there is little evidence of any illegal abortion. The majority of European-origin women who have abortions are predominantly young, single, and childless, while the minority groups, who are largely Polynesians, tend to be older and of higher parity.

REFERENCES

Abortion Supervisory Committee. *Annual reports. 1978–1982.* Wellington: Government Printer, 1978–1983.

Bergin, J. D. The abortion paradox. *New Zealand Medical Journal*, 1983, *96*, 768–771.

Cartwright, S. Law and population. In *Population of New Zealand* (ESCAP Country Monograph Series). Book in preparation. Bangkok: Popular Division, United Nations, 1984.

Chapman, R. M. From labour to national. In W. H. Oliver, with B. R. William (Eds.), *The Oxford history of New Zealand.* Wellington and Oxford: Oxford University Press and Clarendon Press, 1981.

Dominion Population Committee. Report. *Appendices to the Journal of the House of Representatives*, H45I. Wellington: Government Printer, 1946.

Donovan, J. W. Mortality in New Zealand. Ph.D. diss., University of Sydney, 1969.

Facer, W.A.P. *Attitudes to abortion in New Zealand.* Auckland: ALRANZ, 1973.

————. (Ed.). *Legal abortion in New Zealand: A review of opinions and policies, 1970–1977.* Auckland: New Zealand Rationalist Association Inc., 1977.

Gregson, R.A.M., & Irwin, J.R.M. Opinions on abortion from medical practitioners. *New Zealand Medical Journal*, 1971, *73*, 267–275.

Hunton, R. B., & Salive, H. T. Social characteristics of patients attending a private early pregnancy termination service in Auckland. *New Zealand Medical Journal*, 1977, *85*, 220–222.

Jacoby, E. G. Some demographic observations on first order births in the light of the cohort approach. *Economic Record*, 1961, *37*, (79), 308–319.

Kember, D. Abortion and the Crimes Amendment Act 1977. *New Zealand Law Journal*, April 1978, *6*, 109–117.

Kirkwood, B. J., Brown, R. A., Facer, W.A.P., Lawrence, G. M., & Hunton, R. B. Abortion experiences among New Zealand women. *New Zealand Medical Journal*, 1979, *90*, 294–297.

Kirkwood, B. J., & Facer, W.A.P. Public opinion and legal abortion in New Zealand. *New Zealand Medical Journal*, 1976, *83*, 43–47.

McMillan, D. G. Report of the Committee of Inquiry into the various aspects of the Problem of Abortion in New Zealand. *Appendices to the Journal of the House of Representatives*, H31A. Wellington: Government Printer, 1937.

New Zealand. *Crimes Act, 1961.* Wellington: Government Printer, 1961.

————. *Crimes Amendment Act, 1977.* Wellington: Government Printer, 1977.

————. *Crimes Amendment Act, 1978.* Wellington: Government Printer, 1978.

O'Neill, C. J. Contraception and abortion in New Zealand; A review article. *New Zealand Population Review*, July 1982, *8* (2), 51–60.

Pool, D. I., & Crawford, C. Adolescent ex-nuptial births and ex-nuptial conceptions in New Zealand. *New Zealand Population Review*, June 1980, *6* (2), 20–28.

Pool, D. I., & Sceats, J. E. *Fertility and family formation in New Zealand: An examination of data collection and analyses*. Wellington: Government Printer, 1982.

Royal Commission of Inquiry, *Contraception, sterilization and abortion in New Zealand: Report*. Wellington: Government Printer, 1977.

Sceats, J. E. Family formation in New Zealand: An analysis of the timing and spacing of pregnancies. *New Zealand Population Review*, October 1981, *7* (3), 29–47.

———. *Induced abortion in New Zealand, 1976–1983*. Wellington: Government Printer, 1985.

Sceats, J. E., and Pool, D. I. "Fertility Regulation." In *Population of New Zealand*, Vol. 1 (U.N. Economic & Social Commission for Asia and the Pacific Country Monograph Series, No. 12), New York, 1985, pp. 178–192.

Sparrow, M. The contraceptive practice of abortion patients. *New Zealand Medical Journal*, 1980, *91*, 104–106.

Stone, R. Group struggle in a value field: The comparative performance of New Zealand pressure groups. *Political Science*, 1977, *2a* (2), 139–153.

Tietze, C. *Induced abortion: A world review, 1983* (5th ed. New York: Population Council, 1983.

Tietze, C., & Henshaw, S. K. *Induced abortion: A world review, 1986* (6th ed.). New York: Alan Guttmacher Institute, 1986.

Trlin, A. D. Abortion in New Zealand: A review. *Australian Journal of Social Issues*, 1975, *10* (3), 179–195.

Trlin, A. D., & Perry, P. E. *Manawatu family growth studies* (Special Report No. 60). Wellington: Department of Health, 1981.

Williamson, N. W. Abortion: A legal view. *New Zealand Medical Journal*, 1970, *72*, 257–261.

Table 23.1

Number of Abortions, Abortion Rates, and Abortion Ratios, 1976–84

	1976	1977	1978	1979	1980	1981	1982	1983	1984
Number	4682	5433	2094	3635	5945	6759	6903	7198	7300
Rates/1000 Women 15-44	7.1	8.1	3.1	5.3	8.6	9.5	9.6	9.7	9.7
Ratio/100 Live Births	7.9	9.4	3.9	6.7	10.5	11.7	12.0	14.1	14.1

Source: N.Z. Department of Health, unpublished data, 1976–77; Abortion Supervisory Committee, 1976–83; Sceats, 1985.

Table 23.2

Percentage Distribution of Abortion Cases by Age, Marital Status, Parity, and Previous Abortions, 1983

Age	Under 15	15-19	20-24	25-29	30-34	35-39	40-44	45+
	1.1	26.0	31.2	19.6	12.7	6.7	2.7	0.3
Abortion Rate	–	13.2	15.8	10.9	7.5	4.3	2.4	–

Marital Status	Married	Widowed	Separated	Divorced	Never Married
	22.0	0.6	3.9	9.3	64.0

Parity	0	1	2	3	4	5	6 or more
	54.8	15.1	14.6	9.7	3.7	1.9	0.9

Previous Induced Abortions	0	1	2	3 or more
	87.8	10.6	1.2	0.4

Source: Abortion Supervisory Committee, 1983; Sceats, 1985.

Table 23.3
Percentage Distribution of Abortion Patients by Education, Employment Status, and Pre-Abortion Contraception

a)   Education

High School (Incomplete)	High School (Graduate)	University	Other Tertiary
37.3	35.0	11.1	16.4

b)   Employment Status

Home Duties	Unemployed	Student	Bene-ficiary	Full time employ.	Part time employ.
17.8	7.6	10.6	8.3	45.5	10.1

c)   Pre-Abortion Contraception

None	Pill	Inject.	Steril-ization	IUD	Condom	Dia-phragm	Other
38.0	22.2	0.3	0.8	5.7	17.5	4.0	11.5

Source: Sceats, 1985.

Table 23.4
Adolescent Fertility and Abortion

	ASFR/1000	ASAR/1000	% Known pregnancies ending in abortion	Ratio of Abortions/100 known pregnancies
		Under 15 Years		
1980	0.7	1.5	64.7	183.3
1982	0.7	1.4	66.9	202.3
		15-19 Years		
1976	51.2	9.5	16.0	19.3
1978	44.4	3.5	7.5	8.1
1980	38.0	11.5	23.3	30.4
1982	34.0	12.5	27.1	37.2

Source: Calculated by the author from special tabulations provided by N.Z. Department of Statistics.

24

NIGERIA

Stephen Nnatu

HISTORICAL DEVELOPMENT OF ABORTION POLICY

Although in most countries abortion law has been liberalized, a restrictive abortion law still exists in Nigeria and in other countries in the Sub-Saharan region. In contemporary Nigeria the alarming increase in unwanted and unplanned pregnancy is of obvious concern to parents, policymakers, and government. However, the government is obviously reluctant to initiate a liberal abortion law because of profound resentment from elders, religious leaders, and communities who have a strong pronatalist tradition. Despite these views and restrictive laws, illegal abortion is performed daily by both skilled and unskilled personnel who employ aseptic techniques and unorthodox methods with consequent high mortality and morbidity. While it is difficult to obtain national data on illegal abortion, hospital records on emergency admissions indicate that complications of abortion account for over 50 percent of their cases (Adewole, 1983; Aggarwal & Mati, 1982).

Since numerically hospital records represent the tip of the iceberg, the figures of complicated induced abortion suggest an unmet need to women of reproductive age in terms of contraceptive service and education. Nigeria, like most other African countries with restrictive laws, is currently at a stage of demographic transition when unwanted pregnancy and illegal abortion rates are high and access to contraceptive information and services is limited.

LEGAL STATUS OF ABORTION

Among the countries of the world, the legal status of induced abortion ranges from complete prohibition to elective abortion at the request of the pregnant woman. A major consideration advanced by advocates of less restrictive legislation in matters of abortion, and especially of abortion on request, has been the benefit to public health. In those countries with restrictive abortion laws, poor and high parity women and unmarried adolescents form the majority of women who seek illegal abortion, often with compromised reproductive capacity or death. Hence it is not surprising that the Nigerian Termination of Pregnancy Bill generated a lot of public interest and debate when it was presented in 1981 before the National Assembly.

The bill, while suffering from exceedingly unskillful drafting, did attempt to introduce into the law relating to abortion some useful reforms along the lines described above. However, the title of the bill is a misnomer, perhaps caused by a desire to avoid the unsavory connotations of the word ''abortion.'' A better title would have been the Abortion Law Reform Bill. This might have awakened the public to the fact that Nigeria had a law of abortion on the books and all that was needed was reform of that law. Section 1 (1) of the bill provides the following:

It shall be lawful and legal when a pregnancy is terminated by a registered medical practitioner if two registered practitioners are of the opinion formed in good faith
    (a) that the continuance of the pregnancy would involve risk to the life of a pregnant woman or of injury to the physical or mental health of the pregnant woman or any existing children of her family greater than if the pregnancy were terminated; or
    (b) that there is substantial risk that if the child were born it would suffer such physical or mental abnormalities as to be seriously handicapped.

Many individuals felt that the traditional law was entirely too strict and welcomed the liberalization effort, whereas others felt that such liberalization would lead to even more sexual permissiveness and promiscuity in an already morally lax society. Others objected strongly on religious grounds. Unfortunately, the Termination of Pregnancy Bill was aborted at its first reading without any parliamentary debate on the subject.

As presently formulated, Nigerian law regards any interference with pregnancy, however early it may take place, as criminal unless it is for therapeutic reasons as prescribed by the Criminal and Penal Codes (Nigeria Criminal Code, n.d.). The law is based on the argument that the fetus is a human life and must be protected by the criminal law from the moment the ovum is fertilized.

The relevant provisions of the Criminal Code applicable to the Southern States of Nigeria are stated in sections 228 and 229 therein. It provides that

Any person who with intent to procure the miscarriage of a woman whether she is or not with child, unlawfully administers to her or causes her to take any poison or other noxious thing, or uses force of any kind, or uses any other means whatever is guilty of a felony
. . . Any woman who with the intent to procure her own miscarriage, whether she is or not with child unlawfully administers to herself any poison or other noxious thing or uses force of any kind or uses other means to be administered or used to her is guilty of felony.

The only circumstance under the present law in which an abortion would not be unlawful is when it is performed for the preservation of the mother's life. See S.297 of the code, which states:

A person is NOT criminally responsible for performing in good faith and with reasonable care and skill a surgical operation . . . upon an unborn child for the preservation of the mother's life, if the performance of the operation is reasonable having regard to the patient's state at the time and all the circumstances of the case.

Similarly, the Penal Code whch applies to the Northern States of Nigeria provides in its Section 232 that "Whoever voluntarily causes a woman with child to miscarry shall, if such miscarriage be not caused in good faith for the purpose of saving the life of the woman, be punished."

CASE FOR ABORTION

The abortion debate is generally divided into two extreme views: those who regard abortion as virtually always evil and who thus advocate a restrictive abortion policy; and those who think abortion entirely innocent and thus advocate a permissive policy. The second view has been advanced chiefly by women's movements, although one need not be a feminist to espouse it. Their argument is that proscribing abortion does not promote celibacy, nor does liberalizing abortion promote promiscuity. The choice then for society, they state, is not between "abortion" or "no abortion," but between abortion in safe aseptic surroundings performed by qualified practitioners under the control and supervision of the law and abortion in filthy backrooms performed by unscrupulous operators who are discovered and brought to justice only when the operation irrevocably and tragically goes wrong. Private acts with ascertainable public consequences become a matter of legitimate concern to the public and a legitimate subject for legislation. Thus, as long as induced abortions have any consequences for society, for family life, and for the practice of medicine, society has the right to take a legal interest in them.

ATTITUDES TOWARD ABORTION, SEXUAL RELATIONS, AND CONTRACEPTION

In view of the current restrictive abortion law and the rather sensitive nature of sexual behavior and contraception, survey research conducted on attitudes toward sexual relations, contraception, and abortion is likely to reflect a considerable degree of underreporting. Nevertheless, available data from community and hospital studies show some pertinent trends. Earlier reports from Togo, Nigeria, Sierra Leone, and Ghana indicate that fewer than 5 percent of the women admitted having had induced abortions, although a considerably higher percentage of the respondents in most studies acknowledged knowing about traditional and modern methods of induced abortion (Caldwell, 1974; Caldwell & Igun, 1970; Harrell-Bond, 1975; Kume Kpor, 1970). For example, in 1969, 8,400 rural and urban men and women in Nigeria were surveyed. Only 7 percent of the men reported that their partners had undergone induced abortions, and only 1.3 percent of the women admitted having induced abortions. By contrast, 24 percent of the women and 38 percent of the men said they knew about modern and traditional abortion methods (Caldwell & Igun, 1970).

The subject of unwanted pregnancy and illegal abortion is topical in Nigeria. Limited existing data, most frequently obtained from hospital records, suggest that sexual activity among unmarried adolescents, particularly in urban areas, is increasing. Of significance too is the high percentage of adolescents in documented cases of illegal abortion (Akingba & Gbajumo, 1969; Ovin et al., 1984; Akinla & Adadevoh, 1969). A review of hospital records from University of Benin Teaching Hospital between 1 January 1974 and 31 December 1979 revealed that approximately 71.1 percent of induced abortion was among primary and secondary school students; only 9.8 percent were married. In an earlier study by Akingba and Gbajumo (1969), 60.8 percent of the patients were adolescent girls and 53.7 percent of them had had septic abortion. More than nine-tenths (91.2 percent) of the study population was unmarried. Oronsaye and Odiase (1983) who reported on attitudes toward abortion and contraception among secondary school girls in Benin City, Nigeria, revealed that 21.1 percent of respondents had their first sexual experience before the age of fifteen years, while 30.2 percent of 530 respondents admitted to having had illegally induced abortion. Among the abortion group 81.2 percent were single teenage girls aged fifteen to nineteen. In general, the study group had negative attitudes toward formal contraception. Only 6 percent ever used the "pill," while 44 percent had never used any contraceptive method.

A study entitled "Sexual Behavior, Contraceptive Practice and Reproductive Health Among the Young Unmarried Population in Ibadan, Nigeria," aged fourteen to twenty-five, was conducted between November 1981 to March 1982 (Ladipo et al., 1984). The sample was largely purposive, self-selected, and voluntary, and consisted of four distinct subgroups defined largely by age and education. A total of 959 respondents were males, while 841 were females. Eighty-one percent of all male respondents and 69 percent of female respondents approved of sexual relations before marriage, particularly among couples who are engaged to be married. Interestingly, only 66 percent of males contrasted with 78 percent of females also approved the use of contraception. Sexual activity among the respondents varied from 38 percent of female secondary students to 90 percent among working-class males. The mean age for initial sexual experience was sixteen years. Among all eighteen year olds, 51 percent of the women and 78 percent of the men had engaged in sexual intercourse.

Of the sexually active adolescents, the better educated reported more frequent use of contraception. Overall, 48 percent of sexually active males and 66 percent of sexually active females had ever used contraception. Nonusers overwhelmingly cited lack of knowledge about contraception as the main reason for not using any method, followed by concern over the safety of modern contraception. Consequently, it is not surprising that a high proportion of female respondents had experienced a pregnancy. Of all sexually active females, 45 percent reported having had at least one pregnancy, rising to 62 percent among working-class females.

Of 203 first pregnancies, 183 were interrupted by means of induced abortion. This figure, however, reflects some degree of self-selection, since in-school samples exclude women who became pregnant and elected to carry the pregnancy to term.

Despite the illegality of abortion in Nigeria, between one-fourth and one-half of the students surveyed said they would advise friends with unwanted pregnancy to opt for induced abortion. Over two-thirds of the working females would give such counsel, while only 25 percent of their male counterparts would do so. In an unpublished Monrovia Adolescent Study, 33 percent of the nonstudent community sample and 53 percent of the school sample have had abortion among those who have been pregnant (Ladipo et al., 1984). In a study by Oronsaye and Odiase (1983), the response that abortion was "wrong under any circumstances" (abortion is murder) was noted in only 15 percent of the control subjects and 50 percent of the abortion subjects, while 58 percent and 55 percent of respondents, respectively, favored induced abortion on medical grounds.

DEMOGRAPHY OF ABORTION

The typical patient seeking induced abortion is young, unmarried, and in school. Because many institutions dismiss pregnant school girls, the pregnant adolescent is likely to be forced to abandon her education unless some other solution is fund (Akingba, 1972; Akinla, 1970; Bleek, 1977). In most studies on induced abortion in Africa, the desire to complete school training or remain gainfully employed and the morbid fear of dismissal are the principal motivations for seeking to terminate unplanned pregnancy. Sixty-eight percent of the cases of induced abortion surveyed by Akingba and Gbajumo (1969) cited fear of dismissal as the reason why adolescents in Lagos sought clandestine abortion. Two-thirds of the adolescents surveyed by Oronsaye and Odiase (1983) cited similar reasons. Results from other West African studies are similar (Ampofo, 1970; Ayangade, 1984).

Other less frequently cited reasons for induced abortion are economic constraints, the taboo against illegitimate pregnancy, and pregnancy resulting from extramarital union.

Of interest as well is the tension between attitudes toward premarital sexuality and the premium set by Nigerian society on childbearing and parenthood. It is thought that many prospective bridegrooms demand proof of fertility from their fiancees or girlfriends as a prerequisite to marriage. Adolescents may thus feel obliged to establish their fertility through premarital sexuality. This explains in part why unwanted pregnancies among adolescents are on the increase and why illegal abortion is common despite Nigeria's restrictive abortion laws.

MEDICAL COMPLICATIONS OF ILLEGAL ABORTIONS

Illegal abortion is on the increase, particularly among adolescents, presenting a myriad of complications. Mortality and morbidity from clandestine illegal abortion are still high in developing countries due to unskilled abortionists and unhygienic facilities utilized for inducing abortion. The number of deaths from complications of abortion vary from 2.2 to 25.19 per 1,000 hospital admissions from hospital reports from various parts of Africa (Akingba, 1977; Ampofo, 1973; Lwanga, 1977; Oronsaye, 1984). As much as 50 percent of all maternal deaths are accounted for by complications of illegal abortions on adolescents in Nigeria (Akingba, 1972; Ojo, 1978). In a 1970 Study in Lagos, 11 percent of all teenaged women hospitalized with complications from induced abortion died (Akingba & Gbajumo, 1969). Morbidity of illegal abortion is more difficult to measure, although more common. Perhaps the most frequent complication of illegal abortion is incomplete evacuation, with a variety of complications.

Septic abortion constitutes a special problem in Nigeria's gynecological practice. Indeed, it is the most common life-threatening complication and the most common cause of death among women undergoing induced abortion, whether legal or illegal (Ojo, 1978; Adewole, 1983). The clinical picture is quite often that of a young unmarried school girl presenting with fever, abdominal pain, and foul-smelling, blood-stained vaginal discharge. She is usually moribund, apprehensive, and toxic. Some of these patients present in terminal stages of septicemic shock with varying degrees of heptorenal failure, jaundice, and occasionally severe bleeding due to disseminated intravascular congulopathy. A few cases may be frankly psychotic and restless, have flight of ideas, and exhibit frank grandiose delusion. The majority of these patients die because of inadequate facilities for investigation and management. The appropriate drug therapy is usually limited and too expensive for the average client. The few that survive septic abortion subsequently suffer chronic pelvic inflammatory disease with periodic acute exacerbation, congestive dysmenorrhea, and dyspereunia. This often leads to indiscriminate use of antibiotics and analgesic drugs at great cost, with varying degrees of symptomatic relief. In any culture, in particular in African society, the long-term effect of septic abortion resulting in compromised reproductive potential has serious social, economic, and psychological implications in view of the very high premium on childbearing and parenthood.

Trauma to the genital tract when illegal abortion is procured by instrumentation is often accompanied by visable and concealed hemorrhage leading to hypo-volumic shock and pallor. Perforation of the uterus with damaged viscus requires urgent exploratory laparotomy, while a turned cervix needs to be skillfully repaired. Overenthusiastic cervical dilatation often results in subsequent cervical incompetence with future reproductive failure due to recurrent midtrimester abortion. Subsequent poor reproductive performance often leads to regret, remorse, marital disharmony, depression, and ultimately divorce or separation.

The literature review indicates that women who have had repeated induced abortions may run increased risks of subsequent adverse reproductive outcome. Cates (1981) previously reviewed the possibility of higher risk of miscarriage, prematurity, and low birth weight and concluded that there was no demonstrable consistency about whether repeat abortion per se produces increased risk of adverse reproductive outcome in subsequent desired pregnancies. Rather, reviewed data imply that technical subleties of the abortion procedure may be the most important culprit affecting the outcome of published investigations, while uncontrolled differences in patient characteristics may explain in part the conflicting results among the studies.

The above complications vary from country to country depending to a large extent on the abortionist, facilities for inducing abortion, and gestational age. In general, where abortion is legalized, the safest effective technology is used and necessary safety precautions are observed, whereas in most countries with restrictive laws the client's only option is the clandestine practitioner who charges exorbitant fees with little consideration for the safety of the client. In a recent publication from University of Benin Teaching Hospital, Benin City, Nigeria, 90 percent of abortionists involved in cases of admitted induced abortions were quacks or charlatans (Oronsaye, 1984).

Noteworthy is the considerable drain on limited hospital resources by patients admitted for complications of induced abortion. The majority of the cases who survive the first forty-eight hours of admission occupy hospital beds for two to eight weeks depending on the nature of their complications (Oronsaye, 1984; Aggarwal & Mati, 1982). The cost of therapy in terms of drug therapy, blood transfusion, and operative management is staggering. In many developing countries, very few hospitals are adequately equipped to cope with complicated cases of illegal abortions, especially those that are associated with severe sepsis and hemorrhage—hence the high mortality associated with illegal abortions.

ABORTION AND FERTILITY REGULATION

The observed global change in sexual behavior, particularly among youths, is to a large extent responsible for the increased prevalence of unwanted pregnancy. In most African countries with restrictive abortion laws, the breakdown of traditional norms that regulate sexual behavior has led to staggering levels of unwanted pregnancy that is usually terminated illegally despite the risk of health. These countries also have a strong pronatalist position and hence low contraceptive usage for preventive purposes or termination of fertility.

Most developing countries are currently at a stage of demographic transition when induced abortion rather then effective modern contraception is widely used to limit family size. Experience from the University College Hospital, Ibadan, indicates that women who have had an abortion are more highly motivated than other women to use an effective method of contraception (Ladipo & Ojo, 1978). Other studies have also shown that abortion experience for most women is responsible for enhanced knowledge and practice of contraception (Akhter & Rider, 1984; Bhatia & Ruzicka, 1980; Maryolis et al., 1974; Potts, Diggory, & Peel, 1977). The relationship between abortion and contraception is complementary rather than competitive.

In a recently concluded study in Ibadan, Nigeria, the dynamics of the pituitary hormone (luteinizing hormone, follicular stimulating hormone, prolactin) and progesterone in normal adult Nigerian females during their first postabortal cycle indicated that 82 percent attained LH peak within the first twenty-two days after menstrual regulation. It is therefore important to stress the need for contraceptive counseling during this vulnerable period (Ostimehin, Otolorin, & Ladipo, 1984).

CONCLUSION

Induced abortion, the oldest method of human birth control, remains the major cause of maternal mortality and morbidity in Nigeria. Despite the restrictive abortion laws, the incidence is escalating because of lack of effective contraceptive knowledge and services, preference for smaller families, desire for higher education, increase in the number of women of childbearing age, and current economic crisis. Women seeking abortion are demonstrating an intense desire to avoid unwanted births. Therefore, the priority of governments with restrictive abortion laws is to politically recognize the adverse complications associated with illegal abortion and hence formulate rational policies that would accelerate reproductive health education and encourage the use of modern contraceptives. A more liberal policy on abortion would also considerably reduce the currently high mortality and morbidity associated with illegal abortion.

For any woman, illegal abortion is physically and psychologically traumatic with immediate risk to life and health and compromised further fertility. Undoubtedly, most women are ignorant of the varied risks, while enlightened others would rather accept the risk in a desperate attempt to avoid illegitimate birth. For the individual, the risks and costs are high. For the community, illegal abortion incurs both human and financial costs by imposing a heavy burden on limited health care resources. In communities where women play a major role in income-generating ventures, prolonged hospitalization for complicated abortion can result in loss of significant income.

REFERENCES

Acasadi G. T. Traditional birth control methods in Yorubaland. In J. F. Marshall and S. Polgar (Eds.) *Culture, natality and family planning*. Caroline Population Centre, 1976 (Monograph 21), 126–155.

Adewole, I. F. *Managment problems in Abortion*. Gynecological Commentary for FMCOG, 1983.

Aggarwal, V. P. Review of abortions at Kenyatta National Hospital. *Nairobi East African Medical Journal* 1982, *57*, 138.

Aggarwal, V. P., & Mati, J.K.G. Epidemiology of induced abortion in Nairobi. *Journal of Obstetrics & Gynecology, East Central Africa*, 1982, *1*, 54–57.

Akhter, H. N., & Rider, R. V. Menstrual regulation and contraception in Bangladesh: competing or complementary. *International Journal of Gynecology and Obstetrics* 1984, *22*, 137–143.

Akingba, J. B. The problem of unwanted pregnancies in Nigeria Today. Lagos: Nigeria University of Lagos Press, 1972, 133.

————. Abortion, maternity and other health problems in Nigeria. *Nigerian Medical Journal*, 1977 (4), 465–471.

Akingba, J. B. & Gbajumo, S. A. Procured abortion—Counting the cost. *Journal of the Nigerian Medical Association*, 1969, *6* (16).

Akinla, O. Abortion in Africa. In R. E. Hall (Ed.) *Abortion in a changing world.* Vol. 1. Proceedings of the 6th World Congress on Fertility and Sterility, Tel Aviv, 20–27 May 1968, Jerusalem, Israel. Israel Academy of Sciences and Humanities, 1970, 113–120.

Akinla, O., & Adadevoh, B. K. Abortion a medico-social problem. *Journal of the Nigerian Medical Association*, 1969, *6* (16).

Ampofo, D. A. The dynamics of induced abortion and the social implications for Ghana. *Ghana Medical Journal*, 1970, *9*, 295–300.

————. Epidemiology of abortion in selected African countries. Paper presented at the IPPF Conference on the Medical and Social Aspects of Abortion in Africa, Accra, Ghana, 12–18 December 1973, 22.

Ayangade S. O. Contraceptive knowledge and practice among induced abortion partients: Nigerian experience. Paper presented at the International Symposium on Reproductive Health Care, Maui, 10–15 October 1982. *Abstract in Contraception. Delivery System*, 1984, *3*, 419.

Bhatia, S., & Ruzicka, L.T. Menstrual regulation clients in a village based family planning programme. *Journal of Biosocial Science*, 1980, *12* (31).

Bleek, W. Family planning or birth control: The Ghananian contradiction. *Cultures et Development*, 1977, *9* (i), 64–81.

Caldwell, J. C. *The study of fertility and fertility change in tropical Africa.* Voorburg, Netherlands International Statistical Institute, May 1974. World Fertility Survey Occasional papers No. 7, 35.

Caldwell, J. C., & Igun, A. The spread of ante-natal knowledge and practice in Nigeria. *Population Studies*, 1970, *24* (1), 21–34.

Cates, W., Jr. Repeat induced abortions: Do they affect future childbearing. Presented at 37th Annual Meeting of the American Fertility Society, Atlanta, Georgia, 16 March 1981.

Harrell-Bond, B. Some influential attitudes about family limitation and the use of contraceptives among the professional group in Sierra-Leone. In J. C. Caldwell (Ed.), *Population growth and socioeconomic change in West Africa.* New York: Columbia University Press, 1975, 473–492.

Kume Kpor, T. K. Rural women and attitudes to family planning, contraceptive practice and abortion in Southern Tago. *Socio-demographic Study of the Republic of Tago*, 1970, Report 1, 30.

Ladipo, O. A., & Ojo, O.A. Menstrual regulation in Ibadan, Nigeria. *International Journal of Gynecology and Obstetrics*, 1978, *15*, 428–432.

Ladipo, O. A., et al. Reproductive health attitudes and practices—Nigeria. *Pathpapers*, 1984 (11), 10–15.

Lwanga, C. Abortion in Mulago Hospital, Kampala. *East African Medical Journal*, 1977, *53* (3), 142–148.

Maryolis, A., Rindfuss, R., Coughlar, P., & Rochat, R. Contraception and abortion. *Family Planning, Perspective*, 1974, *6* (56).

Mati, J.K.H. Abortion in Africa. In F. T. Sai (Ed.) *Family welfare and development in Africa*. London: IPPF, 1977, 74–79.

Nigerian Criminal Code, Chapter 28, Section 171, of the Laws of the Western region of Nigeria. (Government publication), n.d.

Ojo, O. A. Septic abortion in Ibadan: A ten year review of cases. *West Africa Medical Journal*, 26, 1978, 51–53.

Oronsaye, A. U. Maternal mortality due to abortions at UBTH, Benin City. *Tropical Journal of Obstetrics and Gynecology*, 1984, *5* (1), 23–26.

Oronsaye, A. U. & Odiase, G. I. Attitudes towards abortion and contraception among Nigerian Secondary School girls. *International Journal of Gynecology and Obstetrics* 1983, *21*, 423–426.

Ostimehin, B., Otolorin, E. O., & Ladipo, O. A. *Sequential hormone measurements after first trimester abortion in normal Nigerian women 1984*. In press.

Ovin, A. E., Oronsaye, A. U., Fall, M.K.B., & Asuquo, E.E.J. Adolescent induced abortion in Benin City, Nigeria. *International Journal of Gynecology and Obstetrics*, 1984, *19*, 10–15.

Potts, M., Diggory, P., & Peel, J. *Abortion*. Cambridge: Cambridge University Press, 1977, 490–527.

25

NORWAY

Hans Skjelle

HISTORICAL DEVELOPMENT OF ABORTION POLICY

In 1899 Norway's Department of Justice announced that induced abortion was legal only in the following instances: (1) When pregnancy posed a medical complication for the pregnant woman which could be avoided by terminating the pregnancy; and (2) a cephalopelvic disproportion was present (Grünfeld, 1973). This condition could be congenital or be caused by malnutrition or rickets.

In the civil law of 1902 the death sentence (which had been in the books for abortion since 1683) was changed to a prison sentence. Paragraph 245 recommended a three-year sentence for a woman who had had an illegal abortion, and it was strictly enforced.

In 1929 the abortion question was discussed at the Norwegian Surgeons Association's annual meeting, and in 1930 a committee from the Norwegian Medical Association suggested three indications for legally induced abortions: medical, humanitarian, and social (Grünfeld, 1973). The association's annual general meeting in 1930 asked the authorities to pass a law legalizing abortion in keeping with the legal trends of that time.

A suggestion for a new and more liberal law on abortion in the summer of 1934 by four consultants and four lawyers started a heated debate that continued throughout the year and following spring. In the 1920s and 1930s, doctors and lawyers were the action force behind the movement to liberalize the abortion laws, especially Dr. Tove Mohr, consultant surgeon Kristen Andersen, and gynecologist Louise Isachsen. One of the main concerns at the time was illegal abortion, with its high maternal mortality rate combined with the problems of poverty, social need, large families, and the lack of effective contraception. Work on the abortion laws stopped altogether during the war and occupation years in Norway, 1940–45.

In 1956, the Penal Law Council suggested a revision of the abortion laws.

Norway's first abortion law came into force on 1 February 1964. It had three main indications for a termination of pregnancy (legal abortion): medical, genetical, and humanitarian (Stortingsmelding, nr. 17). Social indications alone were not considered sufficient grounds for a termination. The woman's total life situation had to be evaluated. The decision was to be made according to Paragraph 6 by a board of two doctors, one of whom was to be the Hospital Department's consultant. The women's general practitioner had the right of appeal.

The practice of this law differed greatly from committee to committee, often unfairly so, but after a while the differences were resolved and the acceptance rate for applications rose throughout the country.

In June 1975 the Norwegian Parliament (Stortinget) passed the second abortion law, which went into effect on 1 January 1976 (Stortingsmelding, nr. 17). The new law granted an additional indication for terminating pregnancy—one built solely on social grounds, and formalized what had, in fact, been practiced for several years. The pregnant woman herself now had direct access to the deciding board; if she was refused, she had an automatic right of appeal, providing she didn't withdraw her application.

Bishop Per Lønning of the Norwegian Lutheran Church, resigned his post in protest of the law. Nonetheless, applications for abortion increased steadily in the three years the second law was in force. In 1978, 98.4 percent of all applications were accepted (*Statistical Yearbook*, 1979).

On 30 May 1978 Parliament passed a law on legal abortion with a majority vote of one! This was the third law on abortion in Norway. The Sunday after it was resolved, the bishops of the Norwegian Lutheran church, issued pastoral letters against induced abortions which were read aloud from pulpits all over the country.

Norway's first law on abortion, passed in 1964, was very restrictive, whereas the second law, made effective 1 January 1976, was much more liberal. In both instances the patient had to go before a board before being granted an abortion. With the third law, whch came into force on 1 January 1979, a woman could demand an abortion up to twelve weeks gestation. Applicants over twelve weeks gestation must still go before a board.

Two women played an especially important role in drafting a more liberal abortion law. The first, Katti Anker Møller, wrote many articles and gave several speeches on the subject, until 1930 when her daughter, a doctor, Tove Mohr, took over her work. Møller continued the campaign from within the ranks of the medical association and other committees and forums.

In 1970s the campaign for legal abortion attracted the support of women's liberation groups, the Socialist party, and many conservatives and individuals from the health service. In June 1974 the Educational Committee for Self Regulated Abortion was formed and was composed mainly of doctors and health workers. In 1973 legal abortion had been renamed self-regulated abortion in Norway. The above-mentioned groups for legal abortion became very visible, promoting their views through the press, radio, and television.

The opposition, composed of the People's Action Group Against Free Abortion, the Norwegian Pro Vita, the church, the Norwegian Christian Doctors Society, and many individuals, not only opposed liberalization of the abortion laws, but also wanted to restrict the existing one. The People's Action Group Against Free Abortion delivered a petition with 610,000 signatures before the law on legal abortion was passed. The action group for legal abortion did likewise with 10,000 signatures.

LEGAL STATUS OF ABORTION

The law on legal abortion that was passed in January 1979 gives a woman the right to terminate her pregnancy in the first twelve weeks gestation. After twelve weeks, the decison is made by a board of doctors.

Paragraph 14 of the law added a conscience clause under which hospital staff can be excused from participating in the actual termination but cannot refuse to help pre- and postoperatively.

In April 1983 the law had been in force four years when it was brought up for evaluation in Parliament. The majority opposed any new discussion of the laws (Stortingsmelding, nr. 17).

ATTITUDES TOWARD ABORTION

Since 1979 terminations have often been used to avoid having children at an inconvenient time. Some of the more common justifications for having an abortion are as follows:

1. The fetus is part of the mother's body up to twelve weeks gestation.
2. The quality of life offered to the child after birth is important and should be taken into consideration more than just its existence.
3. A woman should be responsible for all decisions concerning her own body.

An opinion poll in 1974 showed that for the first time more than 50 percent of the population favored legal abortion.

Christians and Abortion

In 1982 after a meeting of the bishops of Norway, a statement was issued, requesting reconsideration of the existing law on legal abortion. Even today the action group against legal abortion is actively trying to influence and change people's opinions.

As late as 1983 a Norwegian Lutheran State Church priest was removed from his position, first at the assizes and later by the High Courts, after refusing to execute his "state" duties as a priest in protest against the abortion laws.

The Medical Profession and Abortion

In 1979 the executive committee of the Norwegian Christian Doctors Association stated that the new abortion law was so contradictory to the basic principles of medicine that they would not be able to abide by it. To date thirty-two Norwegian health workers have registered their refusals to participate.

The problem of finding personnel to assist in induced abortions has so far been small and is diminishing.

DEMOGRAPHY OF ABORTION

There are 65 million terminations of pregnancy every year in the world. More than 14,000 legal abortions a year have been performed in Norway in the last three years. Table 25.1 shows that the introduction of legal abortion in January 1979 produced no increase in the abortion rate in Norway, and the legal abortion rate of women between the ages of fifteen and forty-four years decreased by 20.5 percent from 1974 to 1984. Thereafter the number of abortions and the rate of abortion, however, began to increase. There were 14,577 legal abortions in 1985, representing an abortion rate of around 14.8, and 15,400 abortions in 1986, or 15.4 abortions per 1,000 women, fifteen to forty-four years of age (*Statistical Yearbook*).

Abortion and Place of Residence

In the last few years every fifth pregnancy in Norway has ended in an induced abortion. In the capital, Oslo, the numbers are as high as every third pregnancy. The rate is also high in northern Norway; it is lowest in the west and southern Norway. The high rates in Oslo are probably due to many students and other young people resident there, as well as difficult living conditions.

Fertile Women/Women of Childbearing Age

In the fifteen years from 1968 to 1983, the number of fertile women (fifteen to forty-four years of age) rose every year, from 722,000 to 875,000. (See table 25.1.) If we then calculate that 400,000 to 500,000 women are exposed to the risk of an unwanted pregnancy and use contraceptive methods with a failure rate for 3 to 4 pregnancies for every 100 women, the number of unwanted pregnancies does equal the number of legal abortions per year in Norway.

The Number of Births/Conceptions

In the late 1960s 1,000 women in the age group fifteen to forty-four years gave birth to an average of 92.3 children per year (table 25.2). In 1978 the numbers had decreased to 64.5 births per 1,000 women, a reduction of 30 percent in approximately ten years. There was a corresponding decrease in the annual known pregnancies (live births plus legal abortions). In 1972 there were approximately 76,500 births and legal abortions, compared with approximately

67,000 in 1977, a reduction in the known pregnancies from 103 to 85 per 1,000 in the age group fifteen to forty-four years. This reduction is reasonable when we take into consideration that four or five women used a recommended contraceptive method.

The number of known pregnancies reached its height in 1972, after which the numbers declined radically. It may be concluded that the decreasing birth rates were caused by the increased use of contraceptives and to some extent the easy access to legal abortions.

Abortion/Age

The legal abortion rates per 1,000 women in Norway has been highest in the age group fifteen to nineteen years (table 25.3). In the last couple of years the abortion rates for the age groups fifteen to nineteen years and twenty to twenty-four years have been comparatively even.

In 1966, 30 percent of women applying for a legal abortion were under the age of twenty-five. In 1971 it was 40 percent, and in 1979 and the subsequent five years 50 percent. Approximately 3,500 pregnancies of women under twenty years of age are terminated every year. Half of the pregnancies of women under twenty years end in abortion and half in births. Applicants for legal abortions are therefore getting younger.

Parity/Abortion

Nearly half (46.5 percent) of those who applied for an abortion in Norway in 1982 were childless. Women who had given birth to two or more children accounted for nearly 38 percent of those who obtained an abortion.

Many Norwegian women today have completed their childbearing function at an early reproductive age. Birth statistics for the last fifty years show that the percentage of women with one to two children has not changed significantly.

Socioeconomic Status

Grünfeld (1975) and Walloe et al. (1978) showed that women of low social status had a marked higher incidence of abortion. However, in 1981 Kristiansen, while doing an analysis of the 1977 Fertility Study, discovered a connection between well-educated women and a higher abortion rate. Among women of higher education, who had had one to two pregnancies he found an increase in the percentage of abortions. A similar development had taken place in the United States and New York City (Tietze & Henshaw, 1986).

Abortion and Marital Status

The number of induced abortions among unmarried women increased from under 1,500 in 1968 to per 7,000 in 1978, a fivefold increase over the period (table 25.4). In 1983 the abortion rate for unmarried women (including divorcees and widows) was 13 percent higher than that for married women. The abortion rate for married women increased at a moderate rate from 1965 to 1975 and then began to decline. It is now only slightly higher than it was in 1960.

PRE- AND POSTCONTRACEPTIVE USE

Grünfeld (1973) found that women who had obtained induced abortions, married and unmarried, had used the least effective contraceptive methods. The 1977 Fertility Study (see table 25.5) revealed that 84 percent of women exposed to the risk of pregnancy in the four weeks preceding the interviews had used contraceptives (Noack & Østby, 1981): 34 percent had an IUD inserted, 20 percent used the pill, 22 percent used condoms, 10 percent coitus interruptus, and 6 percent the safe period (rhythm method). The reason why so many women apply for abortions must be that 13 percent have not used contraceptives at all and that a large percent used the least effective contraceptive methods.

Only in Taiwan and South Korea is there a higher percentage of women using IUDs than in Norway. It was mostly women in their twenties and early forties who had not used contraceptives.

Among those using contraceptives in all age groups under thirty-five years, over 50 percent used the pill or IUD. The proportion of pill users decreased from 30 to 10 percent from the youngest to the oldest age groups, while IUD use increased with the number of pregnancies.

Press and television coverage of serious complications in connection with use of the pill, along with legal action against some pharmaceutical companies after the deaths of some young women, may account for its low acceptance rate.

The condom is the most commonly used method of contraception among teenagers and women in their early forties. It is commonly used in Norway as it is in England and Finland, and the percentage of users increases through all age groups with standards of education.

Changes in the Contraceptive Pattern

Figure 25.1 shows the use of contraceptives by twenty to twenty-four years old in the years 1961 to 1977. In the mid–1960s there was a marked increase in the use of the IUD and the pill. The number of women not using contraceptives decreased dramatically in this period. The same changes are noticeable in the twenty-five to twenty-nine year group.

The increase in contraceptive use probably came about through the educational programs in the schools, youth clubs, and health centers, along with information from radio, TV, the press, and books on contraception.

In the 1970s there was a definite movement away from use of the pill to use of the IUD, and for many this was apparently a lasting decision. However, as a result of articles on the IUD and salpingitis, many nulliparas have gone back to using the pill.

Figure 25.1
Contraceptive Methods in Percent Use for Women Twenty to Twenty-four Years of Age, 1961–77

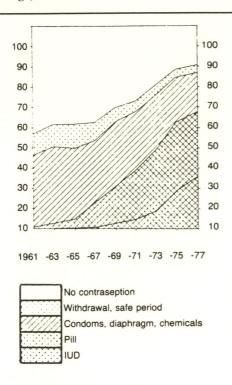

No contraseption
Withdrawal, safe period
Condoms, diaphragm, chemicals
Pill
IUD

Sterilization

Sterilization is, of course, the most effective contraceptive method. In Norway the number of sterilizations has increased tenfold between 1960 and 1980. There has been a similar increase throughout the rest of the world.

As of 1 February 1978, a person of "sound mind" over twenty-five years of age, resident in Norway, can apply directly for a sterilization.

The number of vasectomies performed increased dramatically in the early 1970s, but have stabilized around 2,000 per year. Nearly 10,000 men and women are sterilized in Norway every year. Sterilization is becoming the most common form of contraception for married couples over the age of thirty (as it is in England). A stable relationship is very characteristic of these couples: 75 percent of them have been married more than ten years.

ABORTION AND FERTILITY REGULATION

The increase in contraceptive use has been accompanied by a marked reduction in the fertility rate: from 3 births per woman in 1965 to 1.75 in 1977 and to

1.66 births per woman in 1983. A rate for 2.10 is needed to ensure reproductivity; the rate in Norway was below this figure in 1975. The reproduction rate has decreased by 43 percent since 1965 in Norway (Noack & Østby, 1981).

Of the women who are at the end of their reproductive life, 30 percent have two children and 7 percent have more than three children, a dramatic reduction in the number of women with three children or more.

PREVENTION OF UNWANTED PREGNANCIES

The 1979 law on legal abortion contains a clause requesting that the society should ensure that its children have a secure childhood. A woman's right to contraceptive advice after an abortion is also included in the law. Parliament has given additional grants to be used in family planning campaigns.

In 1950 "Mødrehygienekontoret" was established in Oslo as the first advice bureau for abortion applicants in the country. Since 1969 several offices have been established to give advice and help relating to contraception, venereal disease, and abortion. In 1980 Norway had 1296 health centers, 60 percent of which had family planning services. Health and social service personnel must convey the principles cited in the World Health Organization's definition of sexual health: "Sexual health is comprised of the bodily, emotional, intellectual and social aspects of sexuality that should enrichen and strengthen the personality, communication and love."

Approximately 135 of the 453 local councils in Norway run youth clubs. Considering the high abortion rate of women under twenty years, they play an important role in promoting sex education and family planning.

REPEAT ABORTIONS

In 1978, 80 percent of those who obtained an abortion were doing so for the first time. But the proportion of women with initial abortions has continued to drop since then, approaching 77 percent in 1983. As shown in table 25.6, 16 to 18 percent had had one abortion before and only 3 to 4 percent had two or more. Women who have undergone an abortion probably use the more effective methods of contraception later.

ABORTION RESEARCH

In 1957 in a post-operative examination of 135 women who had had an induced abortion, Kolstad found that 83 percent were satisfied with their decision, 10 percent had some doubts, 3 percent knew it had been necessary but were sad, and 4 percent regretted the termination.

Grünfeld (1973) interviewed 230 women six months after they had had an induced abortion. Approximately 60 percent of them felt no guilt connected with the termination and 32 percent experienced slight regrets immediately afterwards.

Grünfeld found serious regrets/guilt reactions in 11 percent and serious psycho-logical disturbances in 1 percent after the termination. He believes that the premorbid personality determines unfavorable psychological reactions after a termination.

In a study of intrauterine contraception in connection with induced abortion, Sundsbak and Skjelle et al. (1979) found a higher continuity rate after six months in women who had the IUD inserted at the time of the abortion than in those who got the IUD three weeks later.

PRE- AND EARLY POSTOPERATIVE COMPLICATIONS

During the abortion and subsequent four weeks, the incidence of somatic complications is 10 percent. Various surveys conducted during the period be-tween 1970 and 1981 report complications in 14 to 19 percent of abortion cases, notably perforation of the uterus in 0.4–0.5 percent, and lacerations of the cervix in 0.2 to 0.3 percent. Serious complications average 3 to 4 percent in Norwegian material.

In Norway in the 1964–83 period, 216,045 abortions have been performed (see table 25.1), 144,340 of them during 1973–83. Three women have died as a direct cause of the abortion (one in 1971 and one in 1976). This is a mortality rate of 1.4 per 100,000 induced abortions.

Approximately 550 to 600 second-trimester abortions are performed every year in Norway. Fylling and Jerve (1983) prefer intra-amniotic instillation of prostaglandin whenever possible. They use vaginal pessaries early in the second trimester (thirteen to fifteen weeks). They found less marked side-effects of extra-amniotic instillation of Sulprostone (PGE_2) than of other PG compounds they tried.

ILLEGAL ABORTIONS

Legal abortions have been registered in Norway since 1964. In the 1920s and 1930s illegal (criminal) abortions were an immense medical problem. They were said to number around 10,000 annually in the 1930s, and approximately 95 women died every year as a result.

A survey by Reigstad and Arnesen proved that illegally induced abortions accounted for 35 percent of all abortion patients admitted to Ullevål Hospital in 1960. Not one such patient was admitted to hospital in 1972–73. In about 1970, 30 to 40 percent of those who had been refused an abortion did not give birth at the expected time. Many have probably obtained abortions illegally. This was marked in the unmarried group.

In 1968 when England introduced the most liberal abortion law in Europe, Norwegian women who wanted an abortion traveled there, and some also went to the Netherlands.

It is unlikely that illegal abortions are performed in Norway today. However, women who have been refused a second-trimester abortion might then try abroad.

SUMMARY

In 1683 Danish/Norwegian law enforced a death sentence for induced abortion. A Norwegian penal did not change this law to a prison sentence until 1902.

In 1913 Katti Anker Møller demanded the woman's right to decide about abortion.

In the 1920s and 1930s mostly health personnel were engaged in the abortion debate. Doctor Tove Mohr, consultant surgeon Kristen Andersen, and gynecologist Louise Isachsen were the "driving force" behind the movement to liberalize the abortion laws. All work on the laws stopped during the occupation years in Norway (1940–45).

Norway's first law on abortion came into being on 1 February 1964, and it was very strict. An induced abortion could be granted only after the applicant had gone before a board at the hospital consisting of two doctors.

Norway's second law on abortion was only in force three years, from 1 January 1976. It was a more liberal law, but it did not allow for free/legal abortion. The hospital board still had the final decision.

Free abortion up to twelve weeks gestation went into effect with the third law on abortion on 1 January 1979.

In 1974 an opinion poll showed that for the first time more than 50 percent of the population were in favor of legal abortion.

Terminations are often used to avoid having children at an inconvenient time. The introduction of legal abortion has not led to an increase in the number of abortions in Norway. In the last few years every fifth pregnancy in Norway has ended in an induced abortion. Applicants for legal abortion are getting younger. Since 1979 half of the pregnancies of women under twenty years have ended in abortion.

The staff's right to refuse to assist at an abortion has not been a problem.

A liberal abortion law has apparently removed the problem of illegal (criminal) abortion and thereby reduced the morbidity and mortality rates of abortion. Even in Norway, legal abortion is not the main reason for the decline in birth rates. The reduction is also due to the increase in the use of contraception.

REFERENCES

Aanesen, E. Ikke send meg til en kone doktor. Forlaget Oktober A/S, Oslo, 1981.

Fylling, P., & Jerve, F. Experience with PG for therapeutic abortion in Norway. *Acta Obset. Gynecol. Scand.*, 1983, Suppl. 113, 113–116.

Grünfeld, B. Legal abort i Norge. *Universitetsforlaget. Oslo*, 1973.

Kristiansen, J. E. Abort og sosial bakgrunn: Sammenhengen som forsvant? *Tidsskrift for samfunnsforskning*, 1981, Bind 22, 383–405.

Molne, K., et al. Somatiske komplikasjoner etter ab. prov. *Journal of the Norwegian Medical Association*, 1976, *94* (8), 483–488.

Noack, T., & Østby, L. Fruktbarhet blant norske kvinner. (The Norwegian Fertility Study, 1981) Oslo: Central Bureau of Statistics, 1981.

Reigstad, A., & Arnesen, E. Febril og illegalt provosert abort. *Journal of the Norwegian Medical Association*, 1974, *92* (16), 1064–1068.

Statistical Yearbook. Central Bureau of Statistics, Oslo, 1979–84.

Stortingsmelding, nr. 17. Oslo: Sosialdepartementet, Oslo, 1982–83.

Sundsbak, H. P., Skjelle H., et al. Intrauterin prevensjon ved abortus provocatus. *Journal of the Norwegian Medical Association*, 1979, *97* (34–35–36), 1787–1789.

Tietze, C., & Henshaw, S. K., *Induced abortion: A world review, 1986*, (6th ed.). New York: Alan Guttmacher Institute, 1986.

Walløe, L., et al. Seksualitet, familieplanlegging og prevensjon i Norge. Oslo: Universitetsforlaget, 1978.

Table 25.1
Number of Women Fifteen to Forty-four Years, Number of Legal Abortions,
Abortion Rates, and Abortion Ratios in Norway, 1964–86

Year	Number of women 15–44 years	Number of abortions	Abortion rate per 1000 Total population	Women 15–44 Years	Abortion ratio per 1000 Known Pregnancies
1964		2662			
1965		3455			
1966		4537			
1967		5108			
1968	721992	5259	1.4	7.3	72
1969	727436	6458	1.7	8.9	89
1970	732308	7941	2.0	10.9	109
1971	739364	10402	2.7	14.1	137
1972	748329	12203	3.1	16.4	162
1973	756909	13680	3.5	18.2	185
1974	766209	15169	3.8	20.0	208
1975	775204	15132	3.8	19.7	217
1976	785044	14754	3.7	18.9	220
1977	795628	15528	3.8	19.6	233
1978	808376	14783	3.6	18.4	221
1979	821249	14456	3.5	17.7	222
1980	834829	13531	3.3	16.1	209
1981	849402	13845	3.4	16.2	213
1982	856278	13496	3.3	15.8	208
1983	875080	13646	3.3	15.6	215
1984		14070	3.4	15.9	219
1985		14577			
1986		15400			

Source: Statistical Yearbook.

Table 25.2
Norwegian Fertility Rates

Year	Live births per 1000 women 15–44 years	Total fertility Rates
1961–1965	89.3	2.94
1966–1970	92.3	2.73
1972	86.4	2.39
1974	78.3	2.13
1976	68.5	1.86
1978	64.5	1.77
1983		1.66

Source: *Statistical Yearbook*.

Table 25.3
Legal Abortion Rates by Age of Women at Termination and Total Abortion Rates in Norway, 1976–84

Years	19 or less	20–24	25–29	30–34	35–39	40 or more	Total abortion rate
1976	22.8	24.2	19.0	17.5	15.5	10.0	545
1977	25.5	24.9	19.1	17.6	15.9	10.2	566
1978	25.4	23.3	18.1	16.0	13.8	9.5	530
1979	24.4	23.4	18.1	15.3	12.3	8.5	510
1980	22.6	22.1	16.2	13.7	11.0	6.8	459
1981	23.1	21.8	16.9	14.3	10.7	6.2	462
1982	20.9	22.1	15.5	13.9	11.4	6.6	445
1983	20.7	23.1	16.1	13.8	10.6	6.4	454
1984	21.0	24.4	17.0	13.7	10.7	6.1	465

Source: *Statistical Yearbook*; Tietze & Henshaw, 1986.

Table 25.4
Marital Status at the Time of Abortion in Numbers and Percentage in Norway, 1971–83

Year	Currently married	Previously married	Never married
1971	61.9		
1973	58		
1975	53.1		
1977	45.6	8.0	46.4
1978	(6427) 43.8	(1173) 8.0	(7061) 48.2
1979	(5957) 42.6	(990) 7.1	(6757) 50.3
1980	(5216) 40.5	(948) 7.3	(6341) 52.2
1981	(5238) 39.4	(903) 6.6	(6613) 54.0
1982	44.0	7.4	48.6
1983	43.5	7.2	49.3

Source: *Statistical Yearbook*; Tietze & Henshaw, 1986.

Table 25.5
Percentage Use of Contraception by Method

Contraceptive Type	Percent
Total Used	84
Pill	20
IUD	34
Condoms	22
Diaphragm	1
Withdrawal	10
Safe period/Rhythm method	6
Chemicals/Spermicides	1
None Used During Last 4 Weeks	13
Of Nonusers Who Wished or Would Not Mind Becoming Pregnant	6

Source: Noack & Østby, 1981.

Table 25.6
Percentage Distribution of Legal Abortions by Number of Prior Induced Abortions in Norway, 1978–83

Year	0	1	2 and 3	4 or more
1978	81.5	15.6	2.7	0.2
1979	78.9	17.6	3.3	0.2
1980	78.2	18.2	3.4	0.2
1981	77.9	18.0	3.9	0.2
1982	77.0	18.8	4.3	
1983	76.9	18.8	4.3	

Source: *Statistical Yearbook*; Tietze & Henshaw, 1986.

26

POLAND

Marek Okólski

HISTORICAL DEVELOPMENT OF ABORTION POLICY

Until 1932 any interruption of pregnancy was prohibited by law in Poland. On 11 July 1932 the president of the Republic of Poland decreed the Penal Code (articles 231–234) in which the legislation on induced abortion was modified. The code permitted induced abortion under two conditions: (1) the operation had to be performed by a physician and (2) the relevant pregnancy resulted from a crime (rape, incest) or endangered the life or health of the pregnant woman,[1] But the physician performing the abortion had to receive a relevant certificate from two other physicians, a condition that was not feasible in most villages and in most towns and prohibitive for poorer women. The solution written into the 1932 Penal Code was an outcome of the work of the Codifying Commission established in 1919 and in a way a settlement of a comprehensive and controversial discussion that gained momentum after the first code's project was published in 1929 (Wolinska, 1962).

A conservative view strongly opposed to any relaxation of the existing law concerning induced abortion seemed natural in predominantly Catholic and rural Polish society. The conservative view prevailed, even though no organized antiabortion campaign took place. Between 1923 and 1931, however, in some professional circles (e.g., the Criminologist Society, the Lawyers Congress, and the Warsaw Gynecologist Society) far-reaching postulates that aimed at widening access to abortion (for social, eugenic, and legal indications) were voiced. Initiated by the end of 1929, a spectacular press campaign led by an influential journalist and writer, Tadeusz Boy-Zelenski, awoke public interest and drew strong support for the idea of relaxing the "abortion law," particularly among physicians, the liberal-minded intelligentsia, and women's organizations. The central thesis of the liberals was that because of the misery of poverty and the situation of too many children or unmarried motherhood, induced abortion had already reached a mass scale despite its criminal status. On the other hand, precisely because of the criminal status of abortion, many operations were performed by unqualified persons or under unacceptable sanitary conditions and often ended in health complications or the child's or mother's death. Such arguments resulted in changes in the Penal Code relative to its initial project.

In the 1946–50 period a discussion on the abortion issue was revived (e.g., within Poznan Medical Society, Bygoszcz Medical Society, Polish Lawyers Society, Polish Gynecologist Society, and some clerical circles as well as in the media). At that time, the arguments of those who advocated a total ban of abortion were more audible than before. They included demographic concerns (heavy population loss during the war) added to the moral questions that had been raised earlier. Some specialists pointed to the excessive size abortion had reached during the war years when the legal practice was even more relaxed, and persisting after the war. The most specific resolution in that respect was perhaps one adopted by the Congress of Polish gynecologists in 1948 which proposed a clearer specification of the health indications allowed to obtain an abortion, tightening medical control over the operations, sharpening the sanctions in case of breaching the law, and, at the same time, increasing maternal and child care along with economic assistance (in particular to the benefit of unmarried mothers).

In 1950 the dispute, like all public debates of that period, was suppressed by the government. The law and practice remained unchanged, that is, abortion was illegal (except for special and rare situations), but it was performed on a large and apparently growing scale.

In November 1955, immediately after the abortion law was relaxed in the Soviet Union, Polish Radio and some central newspapers started a new wave of discussion (Parzynska, 1955a; 1955b; ZET, 1956), Trzebuchowski, 1956). At that time it meant an almost unidirectional support for legalization of induced abortion on very broad grounds in the name of salvaging a pregnant woman's health or life and with the declared aim of curbing the illegal practice. It appeared that opponents of liberalization were not free to speak in public; the only two Catholic (small-circulation) journals published few articles and a symbolic number of letters to the editor. After a very short time, in April 1956 the government proposed the Abortion Act, which on 27 April of the same year was adopted by the Parliament (Seym).[2] In its spirit the act provided for an almost unlimited abortion by introducing a vague notion of operation permitted on social grounds. The Roman Catholic church, however, instantly denounced it as an encouragement to commit infanticide. Nevertheless, to a part of the society a seemingly unlimited liberalization of abortion looked quite natural as a sanctioning of long-lasting everyday practice and a reaction to anachronously high fertility recorded in the first half of the 1950s (Okólski, 1983a).

Neither the 1956 act nor the ordinance of the minister of health which followed was sufficient to effect a radical shift from illegal to legal practice. According to some researchers, the relevant legal documents were imprecise and too general, and in reality they left the decision about induced abortion in the hands of physicians, not the women concerned. The medical practice tended toward ever growing restrictiveness; many reports from various regions indicated that the scale of illegal abortion had increased, as had the number of related complications.

The opponents of abortion (a number of physicians, Catholic intellectuals, clergy) immediately proposed canceling the 1956 act arguing that, being morally harmful in itself, it did not eliminate postoperation health complications and thus proved to be a misconceived means in the accomplishment of the officially declared task. On the other hand, some physicians, jurists, and journalists suggested fuller implementation of the 1956 act by demanding appropriate executive regulations that would reduce the formalities involved in any application for an abortion. The discussion that climaxed in 1958 and 1959 was strictly limited to professional circles, and it hardly spread to the mass media.

The new ordinance announced by the minister of health on 19 December 1959 gave the pregnant woman a practically exclusive right to decide on the mode of pregnancy termination. The new regulations concerning abortion were substantially supported by the family planning program initiated by the government and implemented through the activity of numerous state-run institutions and associations like the Society for Conscious Motherhood, the Women's League, the Society for Popular Knowledge, the Society for Fostering Secular Culture, youth organizations, and so on, which not only provided the public with information and medical and legal advice on abortion but also popularized contraception which so far had been virtually neglected (Ziolkowski, 1974).

During 1960–80, no changes in abortion policy were made. In the 1960s apart from the family planning program discussed above, a large part of the mass media launched a campaign in which big families and parents with many children were derided and labeled as anachronisms. An antinatalist climate became overwhelming within many groups of the society. On the other hand, the dissemination of information on contraception has taken place slowly, and the supply of contraceptives has been constantly insufficient, which created a gap in family planning that could only be filled by more and more abortions.

Beginning in 1967, there was growing pressure on the government to restrict access to abortion.[3] Some intellectual circles were deeply disturbed by the apparently careless attitudes toward abortion, particularly among young women, and by reports that the number of abortions had begun to exceed the number of live births. Some physicians observed an increasing incidence of infertility, pregnancy complications, and other health pathologies that were clearly connected with recurring interruptions of pregnancy, while some sociologists pointed to disruption of family and other unwelcome social phenomena as a possible outcome of excessive abortion. A number of demographers suggested that a dramatic drop in fertility in 1960s could in large part be explained by the too liberal abortion law (Okólski, 1983a, 1983b; Ziolkowski, 1974).

Between 1967 and 1973 a number of articles that approached the problem of abortion policy within the wider context of population and social policy appeared in the press (Czesninowa, 1964; Waszynski, 1972). In a bimonthly journal *Problemy Rodziny*, published by the Society for Conscious Motherhood, some authors strongly suggested that the 1956 act might have been abused in the sense that induced abortion had become a major means of fertility regulation (Bednarski, 1961; Grabowiecka, 1962; Rozewicki et al., 1971). In a weekly medical journal *Sluzba Zdrowia* and specialized journals like *Problemy Lekarskie, Ginekologia Polska*, and *Zdrowie Publiczne*, various authors on the basis of hospital inquiries presented the first evidence that the health side-effects of abortions had greatly increased in the 1960s. Catholic journals like *Wiez, Kierunki*, or *Tygodnik Powszechny*, in an even stronger tone than before, repeated the uncompromising antiabortion stand of the church and Catholic intelligentsia. Few journals continued to present the antinatalist viewpoint and to defend the abortion act, a notable exception being the government weekly *Polityka*.

By the end of 1960s, however, a new form of church activity in the area was initiated. Premarital and marital counseling centers were established in all decanates, and most parishes carried out obligatory courses prior to marriage. Begun by Cardinal Karol Wojtyla in Krakow, a network of diocesan motherhood houses was set up in which unmarried and helpless pregnant women could live and work before and after childbearing.

Under heavy pressure in 1973, Parliament sent the 1956 act to its standing Commission on Health and Physical Culture for revision,but on the basis of a special investigation the commission decided to make no amendments to the existing law. Instead, the commission maintained that the 1956 act had extended the rights and personal freedom of women; shifted practically all induced abortions to adequately equipped clinics, thus making operation safer; contributed to the elimination of criminal abortion, suicides by pregnant women, and infanticide; and led to a decrease in the number of deaths following abortion. Furthermore, without even studying the intensity of abortion in private clinics, it determined that the number of abortions obtained on social grounds had gradually begun to decline. As the leading newspaper observed, the commission, faced with a possible increase in the number of illegal abortions resulting from a restrictive abortion law, decided to choose the "lesser evil," an argument brought up when the original act was ratified by the Parliament (Maziarski, 1973).

Although they did not disturb the integrity of the 1956 act, the conclusions of the parliamentary commission have marked a new stage in population policy, which from that time on has been based on social and economic measures favoring large families. In order to facilitate a new pronatalist policy, in 1974 and 1976 two specialized governmental agencies, the State Population Commission and the Family Council, were founded (Dzienio & Latuch, 1983).

After 1973 opposition to the Abortion Act intensified further. A militant but rather obscurantist article published in 1976 in a popular newspaper triggered off the debate on depopulation. The ideas of that article were discussed and at least in part adopted within many professional circles and other groups.

The church has radically broadened its antiabortion activities. Through parish teaching concerning the value of human life and the importance of having off-spring and siblings, it has undertaken to shape the attitudes of all followers, including small children. Premarital courses composed of twenty lectures on the theology of family and marriage as well as on conception planning became a huge nationwide endeavor involving several thousand qualified instructors.

Since 1980 church activity has been extended to more open and general statements not only in the flourishing Catholic press, but also in governmental journals, and to more specific antiabortion programs. Catholic groups organized seminars on the "natural" methods of birth spacing, published their own lit-erature, and distributed the literature of other antiabortion groups. They also tried to influence patients waiting for contraceptive or abortion counseling in the clinics. Already in the late 1970s the Movement for the Protection of the Unborn Life, inspired by one of the committees established by the primate, was set up. Its regional branches, including Gaudium Vitae (Gdansk), Pro Familia (Warsaw), Troska o Zycie (Katowice), or Oazy (Krakow), work with youth and offer diversified forms of assistance to pregnant women ranging from telephone con-fidences to financial support. It has challenged the activities of the Society for Conscious Motherhood sponsored by the government (Campbell White, 1981).

In 1980 and 1981 Poland's minister of health issued new instructions con-cerning interruptions of pregnancy in hospitals whose aim was to curb the number of abortions. In addition, the minister announced proposals to significantly restrict the abortion law. These proposals have not been yet made operational, however.

LEGAL STATUS OF ABORTION

The legal basis of induced abortion is at present the Abortion Act adopted by the Parliament (Seym) on 27 April 1956.[4] The law had been implemented under the terms of a series of ordinances issued by the minister of health. According to the first of them (11 May 1956), any woman eighteen years of age or older was eligible for abortion during the first trimester of pregnancy. In other situations (younger age or longer duration of pregnancy), unless recommended by a phy-sician a court verdict was necessary. Apart from cases of criminal assault resulting in pregnancy and the threat to the pregnant woman's health or life (both of which had already been considered by law between 1932 and 1956), induced abortion was made permissible on broadly conceived social grounds. The final decision, however, concerning each application for interruption of pregnancy was trans-ferred to the special local commission composed of physicians and social work-ers, and an applicant had no right to appeal the commission's verdict in case of refusal. Normally, the commission expected the applicant to provide certificate(s) confirming her unfavorable social conditions (Okólski, 1983a; Dzienio & Latuch, 1983).

Induced abortions were to be performed by specialized physicians (obstetri-cians, gynecologists, and surgeons) in the state maternity hospitals and, in the event there were no maternity hospitals or they were of insufficient capacity, in private outpatient clinics. Only when performed in state hospitals was abortion free of charge (within the national health insurance system). Regardless of the place, the patient was entitled to a paid sick leave (usually five to seven days). Physicians were required to keep a record of all operations and to deliver a quarterly report on the number of induced abortions to the health department of the local national council. The managers of the private clinics also submitted such reports to the fiscal authorities. The hospital records of abortions contained some information about the patient's social and demographic status, whereas the records kept in private clinics were devoid of such data.

According to the ordinance of 19 December 1959 which repealed the ordinance of 11 May 1956, the only proof needed to obtain an abortion on social grounds was the applicant's declaration, which was often accepted in oral form. A physician performing an operation no longer had to consult the commission, and the operation became his or her sole responsibility. Any refusal made on medical grounds was subject to an appeal to the health commission. At the same time, ambulatory facilities run by medical cooperatives joined state and private practice.

As noted before, in 1973 the Parliament sent the 1956 act to its standing Commission on Health and Physical Culture for revision. The commission voted against any amendments to the existing law, however.

The third ordinance which altered the regulations concerning induced abortion was issued on 2 December 1980 only. It introduced minor changes to the ordinance of 19 December 1959. The most important change was the one limiting the right to perform operations to obstetricians and gynecologists who passed national proficiency tests (the so-called specialization of the first or second degree). Nevertheless, that ordinance was followed by a letter from the minister of health to all health departments of the regional national councils and state hospitals encouraging physicians to resist pressure from pregnant women to undergo abortion, especially in case of a first pregnancy. On 21 September 1981 the four ministers—those of health, defense, interior, and transportation—jointly issued an instruction to all state hospitals insisting that physicians severely restrict access to induced abortion. In this instruction the physicians were required to inform pregnant woman about all possible side-effects of an abortion as soon as possible, that is, during a preliminary medical examination, and the emphasis was placed on the thorough investigation of each application.

The proposals reportedly announced by the minister of health in February 1981 included a ban on outpatient clinic abortion and stated that the physician had the right to refuse to perform an abortion on moral grounds. Such proposals have not been enforced.

ATTITUDES TOWARD ABORTION

The official attitudes of particular professional, religious, or social groups to abortion have been constant over time. No group unconditionally approves of abortion. While practicing Catholics are absolutely opposed to it, other groups, for example, part of the medical profession, consider abortion a lesser evil, at the same time pointing to its health, mental, and social side-effects. A small but strong proabortion lobby exists among physicians who, by running private clinics, make large amounts of money on abortions (Mazur, 1981; Okólski, 1983b).

Disapproval of abortion is widespread. According to the 1972 national survey, almost two-thirds of married women of reproductive age disapprove of abortion. However, the differences between various social groups are sometimes striking. Nearly two-thirds of the women interviewed in small towns, more than half of the women in medium-sized and large towns (20,000 to 500,000 people), and a little more than one-third of women in cities opposed abortion. Yet the highest percentage of disapproval, 77 percent in 1972, was recorded in villages. This figure is not consistent with the results of the survey conducted in 1978, which covered the rural population only. This survey indicated only 35 percent disapproval. It is highly improbable that such a great change in attitude could take place in six years. On the other hand, in 1978, 69 percent of the women interviewed stated that in case of "emergency," that is, an unwanted pregnancy, they would rather save a conceived child; 23 percent were hesitant and only 8 percent favored abortion. These figures demonstrate that, at least among the rural population, attitudes toward abortion are ambiguous.

DEMOGRAPHY OF ABORTION

Trends in the magnitude and incidence of abortion are almost impossible to discern. The specialists (demographers, physicians, etc.) generally feel that the official figures published by the Central Statistical Office are greatly underestimated. For instance, the press and the medical profession widely maintained that before 1956 400,000 to 500,000 clandestine abortions were performed every year. During the first year after legalization of induced abortion (1957), however, only 122,000 operations were registered, as shown in table 26.1.

The phenomenon of a large-scale number of unreported abortions can be almost entirely attributed to the lack of proper control over the private outpatient clinics. Physicians who run such clinics reported only 13.7 thousand induced abortions in 1982, which means some six to seven operations per one clinic during the whole year while, according to some estimates, for many clinics this number is performed weekly or fortnightly (Demographic Situation of Poland, 1983; Okólski, 1983a).

Even the officially published data extracted from hospitals are of poor quality and do not permit an analysis of abortion according to such fundamental characteristics as age, marital status, occupation, and parity. The only conclusion that seems legitimate on the basis of the official statistics is that there has been a continuous and significant shift in induced abortions from hospitals to ambulatory facilities (see table 26.1).

A number of estimates concerning the magnitude of induced abortions have been made since 1956, most of them based on the ratio of abortions to all terminations of pregnancy observed in randomly selected hospitals. This ratio was most often within the range of 0.7 to 1.0, leading to the "true" number of induced abortions of about 400,000 to 600,000 as compared with the official figure of 140,000 to 160,000 (Czesninowa, 1964; Lech, 1974).

The most reliable estimate so far seems to be that based on the 1977 national survey (Smolinski, 1981). It was found that 23.8 percent of all married women below the age forty-five were pregnant. As the number of married women of this age in 1977 was nearly 5 million, about 1.2 million legitimate (within marriages) pregnancies might have been expected during the twelve-month period (Okólski, 1983a). Meanwhile, only 630,000 legitimate births were registered, which suggests that the number of abortions within a population of married women was 570,000. Assuming that 20 percent of all abortions were performed on unmarried women, one may arrive at an estimate of 700,000 of all interruptions of pregnancy and 620,000 of all induced abortions. Therefore, the 1977 ratios would be: 90 interruptions of pregnancy and 75 induced abortions per 1,000 women aged fifteen to forty-four.

There seems to be sufficient evidence to claim that the above assumed shares of abortions made on unmarried women in all abortions is underestimated. For instance, a survey conducted in 1974, which covered about 2,000 graduate university students (mostly unmarried) in three principal cities—Warsaw, Lodz, and Wroclaw, indicated that, depending on city, 48 to 52 percent of women already underwent at least one induced abortion. Moreover, more than 99 percent of reported operations were performed in a private clinic. (Population Policy, 1983).

WARSAW OBSTETRIC HOSPITAL SURVEY

More information on abortion can only be obtained from hospital inquiries. This source is seriously biased, however, for it underrepresents younger and unmarried women and women of higher social status or educational attainment (Tucholska-Zaluska, 1982). Nonetheless, a study conducted in 1968 in one of Warsaw's obstetric hospitals might be helpful here. This study investigated 2,248 women (all patients who were admitted to that hospital), 1,307 of whom were childbearing and 941 were undergoing an abortion.

The data reveal that hospital patients undergoing an abortion are typically around the age of thirty and are distinctly older than those childbearing. The median age of patients is 31.5 years at abortion and 25.4 at birth. The average number of live births per childbearing woman is only slightly lower (1.4) than the corresponding figure for a woman undergoing an abortion (1.9) (both sets of figures being consistent with the 1970 national data), whereas the average number of pregnancies is significantly higher for the latter group of women (4.2), compared with 1.9 for the childbearing women. Such a discrepancy is clearly due to the inability to effectively control conception by aborting women. On the basis of the same survey, it might be added that, although 88 percent women who had an abortion practiced contraception before the last pregnancy, as much as 40 percent admitted a failure, irregularity, or other imperfection in practicing a given method. Moreover, 67 percent of individual cases of methods applied were those falling into the categories of calendar rhythm or withdrawal. The other important feature of the analysed phenomenon is a remarkably high frequency of abortions among women who have achieved the goal of a certain small number of children; in the younger marriage cohort, most women terminate pregnancy through abortion after giving birth to the first child. Most childbearing women, regardless of age, have never had an abortion, and the abortion ratio per 100 women is rather low in this category. Only in the group thirty-five years or more is it close to 100. In the category of women undergoing an abortion the ratios are distinctly higher, that is, between 161 and 259 (compared with 17 to 92 abortions per 100 childbearing women), and the frequency of those who had three or more operations sharply increases with age to reach 44 percent in the group thirty-five years or more (Sternadel, 1982).

A study completed in 1982 which covered all induced abortions performed at the Institute of Obstetrics and Gynecology in Warsaw between 1 January 1978 and 31 March 1980 (1,104 cases) revealed that 17 percent of the patients had never given birth and 50 percent had had a previous abortion, of which 44 percent occurred within two years.

ABORTION AND FERTILITY REGULATION

Although Poland's fertility is currently among the highest in Europe, it has decreased considerably during the last thirty years. The role of induced abortion in this decline seems almost impossible to judge because of the paucity of reliable data on changes in the number and intensity of induced abortions. There are wide differences of opinion on that subject. Some authors claim that the liberalization of the abortion law has been the major factor in the postwar fertility decline, while others claim that the relaxation of the law did not significantly contribute to the rise in the number of abortions, its only serious effect being in shifting most of the operations from nonprofessional facilities to medical clinics (Okólski, 1983a, 1983b).

On the other hand, family planning policy and specific programs in this area had an important effect on fertility trends. These programs started in the second half of 1950s only. Before that date the idea of family planning was nearly totally obscured, the incidence of contraceptive practice was very low, particularly in marital intercourse, and no contraceptives were available on the market. Meanwhile, immediately after Parliament adopted the 1956 abortion act, medical institutions, mainly obstetric clinics and health advice centers for women, launched a program whose aim was to instruct women on how to prevent unwanted pregnancy. In 1957 the Society for Conscious Motherhood (renamed the Society for Family Planning in 1970 and the Society for Family Development in 1980) was founded. The society, supported by the government and affiliated with the International Planned Parenthood Federation, set up branches and counseling centers in all regions, started to spread knowledge about contraception and human sexuality, and to produce and disseminate contraceptives (spermicides and other). By the end of 1950s the government had formulated plans for training family planning instructors and expanding the information network, and the state industry launched large-scale production of condoms, distributed brochures to teenagers, and initiated special classes for high school students. Contraceptives (condoms and spermicides) were sold in newspaper stands everywhere in the country, and a number of vending machines were installed. Generally, the idea of fertility regulation attracted constant attention in the press.

After the spectacular attempts to promote fertility regulation by means of contraception, which culminated in 1968 when domestic production of the pill was started, a backward trend began in the production of contraceptives and the provision of family planning services.

At the beginning of 1980s, the idea of family planning no longer attracted media attention. Since the late 1960s the Society for Conscious Motherhood has hardly expanded its activities and it has apparently lost direct appeal to the public. The provision of services by health centers also lags behind need because of the decreasing capacity of the health system. Printed matter for adolescents devoted to sexuality and fertility regulation, and other pamphlets about family planning, are now difficult to obtain. Furthermore, the contraceptives that were introduced in the 1950s are now old-fashioned, and their quality standards have deteriorated. Except for condoms, contraceptives (irregular in supply and smaller in quantity) are now available only in crowded pharmacies that have no self-service section.

In 1976 the Supreme Court of Control (the highest independent body that monitors and supervises state activities) concluded after an extensive investigation that there existed permanent shortages of contraceptives on the market and that both physicians and the general public were not well informed about modern and newly developed methods. There were no official imports of contraceptives, however, except for small quantities of the pill (less than 100,000 boxes in 1976). Imported IUDs, which are sold in hard currency shops, seem much too expensive for most couples. No wonder, then, that in 1978 domestic production of the pill may have served the needs of only 2.3 percent of women aged fifteen to forty-nine who were practicing fertility regulation.

In spite of the obstacles, the results of all fertility and family planning surveys carried out in the 1970s indicate that Poles have widely adopted the idea of family planning and have pursued fertility regulation. According to the 1977 national survey of a sample of 9,799 currently married women below the age of forty-five, more than 80 percent of fecund couples where the wife was not pregnant were practicing contraception. Couples who had been married less than five years had the lowest frequency of contraceptive use (76 percent), while for couples married five years or more no significant differences were encountered in respect of marriage duration (frequencies just above 80 percent). It is re-markable that among childless fecund couples where the wife was not pregnant, 51 percent were controlling conception.

In that survey, nine different contraceptive methods were distinguished, and each of them was investigated separately. Of women sampled, 7,370 reported 10,920 methods of current or recent contraceptive practice. The most widely used methods among women practicing contraception at the time of the survey were calendar rhythm (35.0 percent), withdrawal (34.4 percent), condom (15.1 percent), pill (6.9 percent), and temperature rhythm (3.2 percent). The remaining methods (i.e., spermicide and jelly, IUD, cervical cap, and diaphragm) had frequencies below 3 percent.

The heavy reliance on rhythm is striking. Dependence on rhythm is quite rare in Europe, being restricted mostly to countries (or regions) with a predominantly Catholic population. Nevertheless, the percentage of Polish couples who prac-ticed contraception in 1977 by means of rhythm (38.2 percent) was unprecedented even among Catholic countries. The other feature that deserves mention is the extremely low frequency of pill use, which seems entirely consistent with the data on domestic pill production and sales (table 26.2).

As shown in table 26.2, the contraceptive method used differs markedly when examined on the basis of wife's education. As education increases, there is a reversal in the use of withdrawal and rhythm. No significant differences, how-ever, can be noticed for contraceptives sold on the market (condom, pill, other), although the percentage of couples using marketed contraceptives is by far larger in towns than in villages. For instance, in 1977, 37 percent of highly educated urban couples (a wife with postsecondary education) relied on those methods, compared to only 25 percent of rural couples with the same educational status, even though the incidence of contraception was somewhat higher in villages (87 percent versus 84 percent in towns). The probable explanation is that, despite chronic shortages that undoubtedly affect all educational groups, the availability of contraceptives, like most manufactured goods, has been greater in towns than in villages.

The contraception pattern in Poland is particularly unfortunate for couples who do not want to have more children. Indeed, according to the 1977 national survey, the incidence of contraception is very high among these couples (87 percent of those exposed to the risk of pregnancy), but the majority of the methods used are the traditional, inefficient ones. This is above all a result of the gov-ernment's failure to provide modern contraceptives and family planning services. Traditional methods in turn frequently lead to unwanted pregnancies and ulti-mately to abortions. For it might be argued that when no more children are desired, women, once they get pregnant, tend to seek induced abortion.

HEALTH CONSEQUENCES OF ABORTION

In-depth research on the health consequences of abortion did not begin until the 1970s. It would be difficult, and perhaps premature, to summarize the results of already completed or ongoing studies. It might be mentioned, however, that some of them lead to similar conclusions.

The results of two studies published in 1973 and 1976 suggest that the frequency of bleeding during pregnancy among women who underwent an earlier abortion is five to seven times higher than among those who did not have an operation, the frequency of spontaneous abortions and extrauterine pregnancies is three times higher, and the frequency of premature deliveries is two times higher. In addition, as the other study (1982) indicates, direct postabortion complications often lead to injuries, and indirect complications sometimes end in sterility. The studies whose results were revealed in 1973 and 1974 imply that perinatal and early neonatal mortality is four times higher when the mother had an abortion before the actual pregnancy, health complications during the newborn's first month of life occur twice as frequently, and asphyxia appears 1.5 times more frequently. Pregnancy pathologies resulting from past induced abortions involve a high frequency of a low birth weight and retarded mental development of newborns (Dziewulska, 1973; Fijalkowski, 1983; Zrubek et al; 1976).

SUMMARY

Abortion has been a controversial issue in Poland for a long time. Since 1960 access to abortion has been almost unlimited and the incidence of abortion is probably very high. Paradoxically, Poland is a predominanatly Catholic country whose citizens largely disapprove of abortion, and the authorities responsible for abortion policy seem to be aware of the negative health, mental, and social consequences of repeat abortions. A high incidence of abortion is due mostly to lack of effective contraception, rather than to public ignorance or negligence. The government has been unable to provide modern contraceptives and family planning services in sufficient quantity.

NOTES

1. See *Dziennik Ustaw*, no. 60, 1932, position 571.
2. A tiny group of independent Catholic MPs voted against the act.
3. As a breakthrough, one can regard a conference devoted to population policy held in 1967 in Tarda and organized by the Polish Academy of Sciences during which the antinatalist policy based on the wide use of abortion was sharply criticized.
4. See *Dziennik Ustaw*, no. 12, 1956, position 61.

REFERENCES

English Language

Abortion laws: A survey of current world legislation. Geneva: World Health Organization, 1971.

Campbell White, A. Church pressure in Poland. *People*, 1981, *2*.

David, H. P., & McIntyre, R. J. *Reproductive behavior: Central and Eastern European experience*. New York: Springer, 1981.

Mazur, D. P. Contraception and abortion in Poland. *Family Planning Perspectives*, 1981, *4*.

Okólski, M. Demographic transition in Poland: The present phase. *Oeconomica Polona*, 1983a, *2*.

————. Abortion and contraception in Poland. *Studies in Family Planning*, 1983b, *11*.

Ziolkowski, J. Poland. In B. Berelson (Ed.), *Population policy in developed countries*. New York: Population Council, 1974.

Polish Language

Bednarski, B. Brief balance sheet and perspectives of the activity of the Society for Conscious Motherhood. *Problemy Rodziny*, 1961, *1*.

Czesninowa, M. There are a quarter of a million. *Sluzba Zdrowia*, 1964, *1*.

Demographic situation of Poland: The 1983 report. Warsaw: State Population Commission, 1983.

Dzienio, K., & Latuch, M. *Population policy of European socialist countries*. Warsaw: State Economic Publishers, 1983.

Dziewulska, W. The undergone abortions and the course of next pregnancy: The health of newborn. *Ginekologia Polska*, 1973, *44*.

Fijalkowski, W. Ecology of fertility. Paper presented at the seminar "Population policy— for the betterment of a human being and the Polish society." Warsaw, 6 June 1983.

Grabowiecka, L. Analysis of the implementation of the abortion act. *Problemy Rodziny*, 1962. *4*.

————. Causes and consequences of the slow development of contraception in Poland. *Problemy Rodziny*, 1967, *3*.

Jarosz, A. False shame and true troubles. *Sluzba Zdrowia*, 1983, *5*.

Jedruszek, B. Abortion—an attempt to balance sheet. *Zycie i Mysl*, 1977, *2*.

Klonowicz, S. Liberalization of the abortion law and the dynamics of natality in Poland. *Studia Demograficzne*, 1974, *36*.

Kloszewicz, P. On abortion. *Wiez*, 1969, *1*.

Kozakiewicz, M. Why I am against . . . *Zycie Warszawy*, 9–10 May 1981.

KTT. Contraception. *Zycie i Nowoczesnosc*, 9 September 1971.

Lakomy, T. On the problem of abortion. *Ginekologia Polska*, 1964, *3*.

Lech, M. An estimate of a percentage of pregnant women in the urban population. *Zdrowie Publiczne*, 1974, *11*.

Lobodzinska, B. *Family in Poland*. Warsaw: Interpress, 1974.

Malanowski, J. The attitude among the society toward natural increase. Warsaw: Center for Investigation of Public Opinion, 1966.

Maziarski, J. Legally or illegally? *Polityka*, 1973, *14*.

Mikrut, W. The effect of induced abortion on sexuality of women. *Problemy Lekarskie*, 1983, *1–2*.

Parzynska, M. Not only medical indications. *Zycie Warszawy*, 6–7 November 1955a.

————. What are we fighting for. *Zycie Warszawy*, 3 December 1955b.

Population policy—for the betterment of a human being and the Polish society. Seminar organized by the Polish Academy of Sciences on June 6, 1983 in Warsaw (unpublished report on the discussion).

Rozewicki, S., et al. Some problems related to contraception and abortion. *Problemy Rodziny*, 1971, 2.

Salij, J. On twenty five years of the abortion act. Warsaw: Warsaw Metropolitan Curia, 1980.

Skretowicz, B. Natality in villages: Procreative attitudes and attitudes towards fertility control. Paper presented at the seminar "Population theory and the determinants of human reproduction in socialism," Jachranka, 26–28 May 1980.

Smolinski, Z. Fertility regulation. *Zdrowie Publiczne*, 1974, 3.

————. Fertility regulation. *Polityka spoleczna*, 1981, 7.

Sternadel, Z. Studies on effectiveness of basic methods of fertility regulation. In *Medical conditions for protection of conception, maternity and family*. Poznan: Economic Academy, 1982.

Szamotulska, K. On the estimates of annual number of induced abortions in Poland. *Studia Demograficzne*, forthcoming.

Tarnawski, M. On the proper protection of conceived human life. *Tygodnik Powzechny*, 1983, 31.

Trzebuchowski, P. Before an important decision. *Tygodnik Powszechny*, 1956, 5.

Tucholska-Zaluska, H. Interruption of marital pregnancies on social grounds in the light of empirical investigation (selected hospital population). Warsaw: unpublished manuscript, 1982.

Waszynski, K. Analysis of the implementation of the 1956 Abortion Act in Warsaw in the 1957–68 period. *Ginekologia Polska*, 1972, 3.

Wielowieyski, A. Let them live. *Polityka*, 1971, 41.

Wolinska, H. Abortion in the light of criminal law. Warsaw: Polish Scientific Publishers, 1962.

ZET. Victims of illegal operations. *Zycie Warszawy*, 5 January 1956.

Zrubek, H., et al. Induced abortions and the course of next pregnancy and delivery. *Ginekologia Polska*, 1976, 47.

Table 26.1
Number and Percentage of Induced Abortions and Miscarriages, and the Relevant Abortion Ratio in Poland, 1957–82

| Year | Total number A | Induced abortions in hospitals | | Induced abortions in ambulatory facilities or private clinics D | Miscarriages E | Percentages | | | | Total abortion (A) ratio per 1000 women aged 15–44 | Induced abortion (B+C+D) ratio per 1000 women aged 15–44 |
		social reasons B	medical reasons C			B/A	C/A	D/A	E/A		
1957	122.000	NA	NA	NA	N/A[a]	NA	NA	NA	NA[b]	19.7	NA
1960	223.800	146.400[a]	4.000[a]	73.400[a]	-[b]	65.4[a]	1.8[a]	32.8[a]	28.4	36.0	NA
1965	235.400	131.500	3.200	33.800	66.800	55.8	1.4	14.4	30.7	33.9	24.2
1970	214.000	107.400	1.700	39.200	65.700	50.2	0.8	18.3	34.5	28.7	19.9
1975	212.100	79.500	1.700	57.700	73.300	37.5	0.8	27.2	34.8	26.8	17.5
1978	223.300	74.800	1.800	69.000	77.700	33.5	0.8	30.9	33.7	28.0	18.2
1980	199.812	64.795	1.807	65.977	67.233	32.4	0.9	33.0	35.7	24.9	16.6
1982	216.030	67.723	1.559	69.695	77.053	31.3	0.7	32.3		26.9	17.3

[a]Includes a number of miscarriages

[b]There were no separate categories for miscarriages in 1960.

Source: *Rocznik statystyczny ochrony zdrowia* [Statistical yearbook of health protection] (Warsaw: Central Statistical Office of Poland, consecutive volumes); and *Sytuacja demograficzna Polski: Raport 1983* [Demographic situation of Poland: The 1983 report] (Warsaw: State Population Commission, 1983).

Table 26.2
Contraceptive Methods of Couples in Poland by Education of Wife, 1977 (in percentage)

Contraceptive method	Educational level of wife				
	Elementary not completed	Completed elementary	Vocational	Secondary	Postsecondary
Withdrawal	52.8	43.3	34.4	26.3	17.8
Calendar rhythm	26.0	30.6	35.1	39.2	40.8
Temperature rhythm	1.0	2.4	3.2	3.8	5.7
Condom	13.7	14.6	14.9	15.7	15.9
Pill	3.1	4.7	7.4	8.6	11.0
Other	3.4	4.4	5.0	6.4	8.8
Number of methods	292	3,979	2,167	3,916	566
Number of women	214	2,754	1,448	2,604	350

Source: *Dzielnosc kobiet w Polsce* [Natality in Poland] (Warsaw: Central Statistical Office of Poland, 1980).

27

SINGAPORE

S. S. Ratnam and R. N. V. Prasad

Singapore is a small country. Yet this city-state with a population of 2.5 million has attracted a good deal of attention from family planners worldwide, for it has had immense success in controlling its population growth. Various factors have contributed to this success story: bold and imaginative government policies and legislation, a literate population, a high gross national product, increasing recognition of the status of working females, and easy accessibility of services and media to all parts of the country.

The legalization of abortion has been an important factor in the rapid fall in the population growth rate. Singapore has very liberal abortion laws which grant abortion on demand. The development of these abortion policies and their impact on demographic trends will be discussed in this chapter.

HISTORICAL DEVELOPMENT OF ABORTION POLICY

Before 1949, Singapore had no organized program for the dissemination of family planning knowledge. Between 1949 and 1965 family planning was provided by a voluntary organization (the Family Planning Association) comprising a group of housewives, doctors, social workers, and others interested in family planning. The Singapore Family Planning and Population Board (SFPPB), a government Statutory Board, was inaugurated in January 1966.

In 1967 the Medical Committee of the SFPPB advocated the legalization of abortion, especially for contraceptive failures. The government also felt that the population decline over the preceding years (1949–66) had not been rapid enough, even though the targeted numbers of contraceptive acceptors had been reached. In late 1967 the government therefore decided to legalize abortion.

The government decision provoked much public debate. There were letters published in the newspapers (*Straits Times*, 1967) from interested individuals, the Singapore Medical Association (*Sunday Mail*, 1967), the Graduates' Fellowship (*Straits Times*, 1967), and the Conference of the Methodist Church. The views expressed were mixed, and those favoring abortion advocated proceeding in a cautious manner. After much lively discussion in Parliament, the House passed the Abortion Bill by majority vote on 29 December 1969. Induced abortion therefore became legal in Singapore on 20 March 1970 under the provision of the Abortion Act of 1969. Under this act, all requests for abortions had to be reviewed and approved by an eleven-member Termination of Pregnancy Authorization Board. The abortion had to be performed by registered medical practitioners, and approval had to be sought in all cases except where the woman's life was in immediate danger due to her pregnant status. The board was empowered to authorize abortion on medical (up to twenty-four weeks), eugenic (up to twenty-four weeks), social (up to sixteen weeks), and financial grounds. In fact, between 20 March 1970 and 31 December 1970, 2,596 women out of 2,726 applications (i.e., 95 percent) were approved on social grounds. (Saw, 1980)

No serious problems were encountered in the first years after legalizing abortion, and there appeared to be widespread public acceptance of the legislation. However, there was unnecessary delay in performing the abortion while awaiting board approval. In many cases the delay caused the abortion to be performed as a midtrimester termination. For these reasons, the government decided to abolish the board and liberalize the abortion law.

LEGAL STATUS OF ABORTION

When the Abortion Act, 1974, went into effect, the Termination of Pregnancy Authorization Board was disbanded. Abortion can now be performed at the request of the pregnant woman up to twenty-four weeks. There is no stipulated minimum age for giving consent, and any woman, however young, may lawfully seek abortion. The spouse's consent is unnecessary, and secrecy is ensured. The fee for abortion has been fixed at S$5 (US $2) if performed at a government institution. The new laws cut red tape and eliminated unnecessary delay for abortion seekers. Moreover, the septic abortion rate fell after legalization from 75.1 in 1967 to 34.2 septic abortions per 1,000 abortions in 1976, and criminal abortions became almost nonexistent in the later years.

DEMOGRAPHY OF ABORTION

Incidence

Doctors are compelled by law to notify the government of all abortions on a prescribed notification form. Even so, some degree of underreporting is inevitable, especially in the private sector. The majority of abortions are reported, however, and these statistics have helped the government plan its strategy as regards population and family planning services.

In the initial years of legalization of abortion there was a rising trend. Table 27.1 shows that this trend has settled at a legalized abortion rate of around 28 per 1,000 in the last five years. The number of abortions took a sharp upturn in 1985 when 23,510 abortions or 35 percent of all pregnancies were terminated.

Age, Parity, and Marital Status

Table 27.2 presents statistics for the years 1970–83 showing the percentage of legal abortion by age of women and parity at the time of treatment. Women seem to be seeking abortion at a younger age. Women between thirty and thirty-nine years comprised 54.0 percent of the abortees in 1970, but this figure fell to 31 percent in 1983. However, the percentage of younger women (twenty to twenty-nine years) undergoing abortion rose from 27.7 percent to 56.4 percent during the same period. Statistics from the University Department of Obstetrics and Gynecology show that this percentage for women aged twenty to twenty-nine years remained fairly stable between 50 and 60 percent (table 27.3) from 1976 to 1983.

More significantly, the number of women seeking abortion for their very first pregnancy is rising. Only 0.5 percent of the abortees in 1970 were nulliparous, and 51 percent had at least five previous children. By 1974 the proportion of nulliparous women seeking abortion had increased to 7 percent and, with the liberalization of abortion in 1975, continued to rise phenomenally to 26 percent in 1977. The current sexual mores, emancipation of women with increasing numbers becoming gainfully employed, coupled with the economic needs of setting up an independent nuclear family unit encourages the seeking of abortion should pregnancy occur at an inconvenient time. A breakdown of single and married women seeking abortion in the University Department of Obstetrics and Gynecology's Fertility Control Clinic is shown in table 27.4. Although married women exceed the number of single women, the percentage of single women seeking abortion has steadily risen from 8.6 percent in 1976 to 12.8 percent in 1979 to 15.6 percent in 1982.

Gestation

The majority of abortions performed in both government hospitals and private institutions are first-trimester abortions. Table 27.5 shows the breakdown of the figures. After the liberalization of abortion in 1975, 15 percent of the abortions performed in government institutions were second-trimester terminations. With easy availability, wider social acceptance of abortion, and health education, there has been a steady decline in second-trimester terminations of pregnancy, and such abortions accounted for only 7 percent in 1981.

Private Abortions versus Abortions in Public Hospitals

Private institutions are playing an increasingly important role in providing an abortion service in Singapore. The average Singaporean seems affluent enough to be able to afford the charges, which vary anywhere from S$150 to S$450

(US $70 to US $200) for a first-trimester abortion and S$350 to S$1,000 (US$160 to US$450) for a second-trimester abortion.

Even though abortions are cheaply available (S$5, or US$2), in government hospitals there is a rising trend for abortees to seek private abortions for various reasons. Abortions are more private and personalized. They are also immediately available unlike the case in government hospitals where a separate appointment for abortion is given. In addition, confidentiality is ensured, and general anesthesia is more readily available on request. Moreover, private sector costs have also fallen considerably since abortion became legal. Whatever the reason, there is a definite rising trend in the number of private abortions from 7 in 1970 to 9016 in 1981, and for the first time in 1982 abortions performed in approved private institutions (50.6 percent) exceeded those carried out in government hospitals.

ABORTION AND FERTILITY REGULATION

The demographic goal of the first five years of the national program (1966–70) was to reduce the crude birth rate (CBR) from 29.5 births per 1,000 population in 1965 to around 20 per 1,000 by 1970. By 1970 the CBR had indeed been reduced to 22.1. There was an increase, however, in the total fertility rate from 3.045 children per woman in 1971 to 3.052 in 1972.

The increase caused the government to introduce strong measures in 1972. Extensive family planning education aimed at priority groups, a widely publicized policy of advocating a two-child family, and the introduction of new as well as an intensification of current disincentives and incentives to encourage family limitation were introduced. These incentive/disincentives were aimed at discouraging high order births and included measures in the areas of maternity leave, accouchement fees, income tax, housing, education, and work permits. These strict measures succeeded in reducing family size.

The demographic goal of the program's second five-year plan (1971–75) was to reduce the CBR to 18.0 by 1975. From 1972 to 1975 Singapore experienced another sharp decline in birth rates (figure 27.1). The legalization of abortions had a definite effect here. During the period 1970 to 1977 some 66,365 legal abortions were performed. The proportion of abortions to live births also increased progressively from 7.66 percent in 1972 to 42.86 percent in 1977 and reached a level of 44.8 percent in 1982.

Other factors that contributed to the fall in births are the ready availability of sterilization (60,689 women and men being sterilized between 1970–77), improvement in social conditions, emancipation of and increase in the number of working women, social disincentives to large families, and increased public awareness of the benefits of a small family. From 1972 to 1975 the total fertility rate fell from 3.052 to 2.104, the net reproduction rate from 1.410 to a below-replacement level of 0.978, and the crude birth rate from 23.1 to 17.8. The goal of the second five-year plan was therefore reached.

Figure 27.1
Live Births and Crude Birth Rate, Singapore, 1960–82

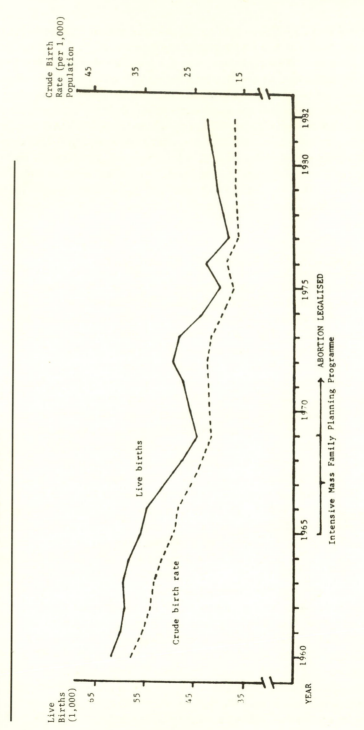

The long-term objective of the national program is to achieve zero population growth by maintaining replacement-level fertility (a net reproduction rate of 1.0, or a two-child family average), which was achieved in 1975. It is projected that zero population growth will be achieved around the year 2030 when the projected population would have stabilized at 3.4 million. The liberal abortion policies have acted synergistically with the family planning program to produce Singapore's birth control success story. With such liberal abortion laws, roughly 44.8 percent of births are presently being averted annually, and this has made a very significant contribution to achieving Singapore's targeted demographic goals rapidly.

ABORTION AND ADOLESCENTS

Abortion in adolescents, especially among the very young, is fraught with problems. Although some researchers (Cates, 1980) have shown that at similar stages of gestation, the risk of immediate complications or of death from legal abortions is no greater for teenagers than for older women, adolescent girls do run increased risks inasmuch as they tend to present for abortion later in pregnancy. Therefore, as a group, adolescent abortion does carry higher morbidity when compared with abortion in women of other ages. The long-term complications and emotional sequelae of abortion in this age group are also ill understood. Adolescent abortions therefore are a matter for concern. Table 27.6 shows the number of abortions in Singapore performed on young women. There has been a rise in the abortion rate over the years, and legalization of abortion has enabled them to use the services freely. The majority of these teenagers seeking abortion are unmarried, and in 1976 single teenage abortions accounted for 77 percent of total teenage abortions (Saw, 1980).

Teenage abortions, although significantly high in Singapore, have not yet reached figures observed in other countries with liberal abortion policies. For example, the teenage abortion rates in 1975 were higher in European countries ranging from 11 to 30 abortions per 1,000 compared with 7.5 for Singapore. The rate in Singapore has stabilized at around 11 per 1,000.

REPEAT ABORTIONS

Most clinicians view repeat abortions with some concern as some believe that morbidity and mortality increase with each subsequent abortion. As yet, there is no hard evidence for this position. Others (Beresford, 1979) feel that repeat abortions should be an acceptable alternative to women, as first-trimester abortions have become very safe.

Figures for repeat abortions are not presently available for Singapore. However, the University Department of Obstetrics and Gynecology statistics (table 27.7) show that roughly 37 percent of women who present to the department for abortion have had at lease one previous induced abortion, with 10 percent of them having undergone at least two earlier terminations. These women are all counseled and motivated to accept contraception. Interestingly, all women who have come for repeat abortions have knowledge about contraception.

NULLIPAROUS ABORTIONS

Forceful dilatation of the nulliparous cervix prior to abortion may damage the internal cervical os, possibly leading to later cervical incompetence. To reduce this potential problem, nulliparous women seeking first-trimester abortion are routinely pretreated with prostaglandin analogues (Karim & Prasad, 1979a) to soften and dilate the cervix prior to vacuum aspiration. Nulliparous women form roughly one-fifth of all those seeking abortion at the University Obstetrics and Gynecology Unit. The majority of these women are unmarried teenagers, but nulliparous abortions have been performed on women over thirty-five years of age.

ABORTION RESEARCH

Since the legalization of abortion in Singapore, health services and clinical research have been conducted by family planners and clinicians. Some of this research is detailed here.

Knowledge, Attitudes, and Practice Survey (KAP Survey)

The government conducted a KAP survey in 1973. This First National Survey on Family Planning was conducted by means of a two-stage stratified sample design on 2,167 married women who were interviewed between 7 and 29 September 1973. The response rate was 96 percent, and 2,078 women were successfully interviewed. At the time of this KAP survey, the Abortion Act had been in operation for three and a half years. More than half of them (55.3 percent) knew that abortion was legal and 44 percent knew where to obtain legal abortion. There was a positive correlation between educational level and awareness of the abortion law.

About 52 percent of the women surveyed disapproved of abortion outright, and only 23.1 percent approved of it. Most women in the survey said they preferred contraception to abortion. More recent KAP studies on abortion are not available, but the acceptance of abortion and knowledge of the liberal laws are now felt to be more widespread among the population.

Outpatient versus Inpatient Abortion

When abortion became liberalized, the demand was so overwhelming that it became difficult to provide inpatient abortion services with the existing hospital facilities. Approximately 20 to 25 percent of all gynecological beds were required to cater for patients requesting abortion in the first three years.

In conjunction with the World Health Organization, abortion as an outpatient procedure was tested in a randomized controlled trial and proved to be a safe procedure in healthy multiparous women in 1974 (Cheng, Ng., & Ratnam, 1976; Adolsek et al., 1977). As a result, 60 percent of abortions in the University Department, Kandang Kerbau Hospital, are now performed on an outpatient basis under paracervical block anesthesia.

Clinical Research in Abortion

Since 1971 the University Department of Obstetrics and Gynecology has conducted research in the use of prostaglandins and their analogues for induced abortion (see Karim, 1976, for review). They have been used very effectively for medical menstrual regulation by the vaginal and intrauterine routes (Karim & Prasad, 1979b). For first-trimester abortions, vacuum aspiration is still the method of choice, but prostaglandin analogues are used to pretreat nulliparous women to make cervical dilatation easy (Karim & Prasad, 1979a). Prostaglandin analogues are the method of choice for second-trimester abortion. Research on the efficacy, safety, and reduction of the induction–abortion interval with synthetic prostaglandins given by various routes and in combination with laminaria tent insertion is continuing in the University Department (Karim et al., 1983).

With the availability of easy and legal abortions, the dreaded complications of criminal abortions are virtually nonexistent in present-day Singapore (Lim et al., 1979). However, continual research on abortion morbidity is being conducted in the department (Cheng et al., 1977; McCarthy, 1981). Apart from physical complications, the incidence of psychological complications of abortions also has been studied. In contrast to the literature, the Singapore studies have shown that the psychological sequelae of abortion are uncommon (Tan, 1978, 1979; Tsoi et al., 1976).

ABORTION COUNSELING

Induced abortion is essentially a procedure with potential complications. Hence, it is important for anyone who provides such a service to give adequate counseling so that abortion seekers are able to practice adequate contraception after abortion. Today planning and social workers routinely provide this health education to women presenting for abortion in government hospitals in Singapore.

The Fertility Control Clinic of the University Department of Obstetrics and Gynecology realized the need for abortion counseling from its inception and has employed a team of social workers to motivate and counsel women seeking abortion. Over the years, these workers have managed to change the attitudes of abortion seekers. Women who have never practiced contraception before have accepted the methods offered, and women previously practicing less effective methods of contraception (e.g., the rhythm method, condoms) have been induced to accept more effective methods (e.g., oral pills, IUD, and sterilization). Table 27.8 shows this change in contraceptive practice in women seeking abortion attending the University Department's Clinic. It is clear that the time spent counseling these women is not wasted.

TRENDS IN MORTALITY FROM INDUCED ABORTION

Deaths from abortion have been the major cause of maternal mortality in Singapore over the years (Lim et al., 1979; Cheng et al., 1971). (See table 27.9.) Lim (1979) has worked out the mortality figures for first- and second-trimester abortions to be between 2 and 3 per 50,000 abortions. The major cause of deaths from abortion is sepsis. There has been a falling trend in abortion deaths since 1964—from 0.12 per 1,000 deliveries in 1964 to 0.08 in 1970. It is difficult to interpret the significance of this change because of the small numbers involved. Rising socioeconomic standards and improvement in hospital care standards could account for the fall in the early years, but in the later years legalization of abortion and the virtual elimination of criminal abortion has led to the drop in abortion deaths (Lim et al., 1979).

SUMMARY AND CONCLUSIONS

Abortion was successfully legalized in Singapore in 1970. Although there was some expected initial resistance to the law, it was generally well accepted leading to its complete liberalization in 1975. This abortion on demand policy has been instrumental in helping the government achieve quickly the demographic goals it set for itself in its population control effort. Singapore's success is unique and may not be applicable to other developing countries where rural conditions and low literacy levels may hamper wide implementation of population policies.

Induced abortion has now become part and parcel of Singapore's family planning armamentarium, and it has become very safe to have one nowadays with the modern techniques available. Liberal abortion laws have also abolished criminal abortion with its attendant hazards and has made cheap abortion readily available to all Singapore women.

ACKNOWLEDGMENTS

The authors wish to thank Miss Arunthathi Mylavaganam and Miss Heng Siaw Huang for their help in data collection and analysis. We are also indebted to Miss N. Prema for her expert secretarial assistance.

REFERENCES

Andolsek, L., Cheng M. C. E., and Hren M., et al. The safety of local anaesthesia and outpatient treatment: A controlled study of induced abortion by vacuum apiration. *Studies in Family Planning*, 1977, 8 (5), 118–124.
Beresford, T. Abortion counselling. In G. I. Zatuchni, J. J. Sciarra, & J. J. Spiedel

(Eds.) *Pregnancy termination—Procedures safety and new developments.* New York: Harper & Row, 1979, 89.

Cates, W. Adolescent abortion in the United States. *Journal of Adolescent Health Care,* September 1980.

Cheng, M. C. E., Choo, H. T. Vengadasalam, & Sidhu, Singh. Changing trends in mortality and morbidity from abortion in Singapore (1964–1970). *Singapore Medical Journal,* October 1971, *12* (1).

Cheng, M. C. E., Ng, A., & Ratnam, S. S. The safety of outpatient abortions: A controlled study. *Annals of the Academy of Medicine,* 1976, *5* (3): 245–248.

Cheng, M. C. E., Andolsek L., Ng, A., Shan, Ratnam, et al. Complications following induced abortion by vacuum aspiration: Patient characteristics and procedures. *Studies in Family Planning,* 1977, *8* (5), 125–129.

Karim, S. M. M. Obstetrical and gynaecological use of prostaglandins. In S. M. M. Karim (Ed.) *Proceedings of the Asian Federation of Obstetrics and Gynecology 1st International Congress,* Vol. 1. Singapore: Eurasia Press, 1976.

Karim, S. M. M., & Prasad, R. N. V. Preoperative cervical dilation with prostaglandins. In S. M. M. Karim (Ed.) *Practical applications of prostaglandins and their synthesis inhibitors.* MTP Lancaster Press, 1979a, 283–289.

————. Menstrual regulation with prostaglandins. In *Proceedings of Towards 2.1% Thai Family Planning Seminar.* Bangkok, 1979b, 8–15.

Karim, S. M. M., Prasad, R. N. V., Ratnam, S. S., et al. Enhancement of the efficacy of 15(S) 15 methyl $PGF_2\alpha$ in termination of second trimester pregnancy by laminaria. *Singapore Journal of Obstetrics and Gynaecology,* 1983, 14 (3), 211–214.

Lim, L. S., Cheng, M. C. E., Rauff, M., & Ratnam, S. S. Abortion deaths in Singapore (1968–1976). *Singapore Medical Journal,* 1979, *20* (3), 391–394.

McCarthy T. Abortion complications and their management. *Singapore Family Physician,* 1981, 7 (3), 77–79.

Public policy and population change in Singapore. Peter Chew and James Fawcett (Eds.). New York: Population Council, 1979.

Ratnam, S. S. & Prasad, R. N. V. Abortion in the adolescent. In *Proceedings of International Planned Parenthood Federation Consultation on Adolescent Fertility Regulation Services,* Milan, Italy, 25–29 July 1983.

Saw, S. H. Induced abortion. In S. H. Saw (Ed.), *Population Control for zero growth.* London: Oxford University Press, 1980, 72–95.

The Straits Times, 2, 9, 13, and 14 September 1967.

Sunday Mail, 13 August 1967; *Eastern Sun,* 13 August 1967.

Tan, S. B. The psychosocial sequelae of abortion in Singapore. Ph.D. diss., University of Singapore, 1978.

————. The psychosocial sequelae of abortion. *Singapore Journal of Obstetrica and Gynaecology,* 1979, *10* (2), 7–16.

Tietze, C., & Henshaw, S. K. *Induced abortion: A world review, 1986* (6th ed.). New York: Alan Guttmacher Institute, 1986.

Tsoi, W. F., Cheng M. C. E., Vengadasalam, & Seng, K. M. Psychological effects of abortion. *Singapore Medical Journal,* 1976 7 (2): 68–73.

Table 27.1
Legalized Abortions in Singapore, 1970–83[a]

Year	No. of Menstrual Regulations	Number of Abortions	Total No. of Legalized Abortions	Legalized Abortion Rate
1970	–	1913	1913	4.2
1971	–	3407	3407	7.2
1972	–	3806	3806	7.7
1973	–	5252	5252	10.3
1974	–	7175	7175	13.6
1975	1768	11105	12873	23.3
1976	2566	12930	15496	27.5
1977	2681	13762	16443	28.3
1978	2952	14294	17246	28.4
1979	2144	14855	16999	27.1
1980	3728	14491	18219	28.4
1981	3615	15275	18890	28.8
1982	3562	15548	19110	28.6
1983	–	–	19100	28.1

[a]Legalized abortion rate = (Total number of legalized abortions per year × 1,000) ÷ (Mid-year population of women aged 15–44)

Source: Adapted from Singapore Family Planning Population Board (SFPPB), 17th Annual Report, 1982; Tietze & Henshaw, 1986.

Table 27.2
Percentage Distribution of Legal Abortions in Singapore by Age Group and Number of Living Children, Selected Years, 1970–83

Characteristics	1970	1972	1974	1976	1978	1980	1982	1983
Age Group								
15-19	1.8	2.7	6.1	7.5	8.3	8.8	7.8	8.0
20-24	10.5	13.8	19.9	26.1	28.4	28.4	27.7	27.4
25-29	17.2	19.9	24.6	27.3	28.0	27.8	29.2	29.0
30-34	29.5	29.4	22.4	17.3	17.9	20.4	21.0	20.6
35-39	24.2	22.1	17.6	13.6	11.0	9.2	9.6	10.5
40 & above	16.8	12.1	9.4	8.2	6.4	5.4	4.7	4.4
Mean Age	32.8	31.6	29.8	28.5	-	-	-	-
Number of living Children								
0	0.5	1.1	7.5	24.6	29.8	33.8	37.0	38.4
1	2.7	4.7	13.3	15.8	18.6	18.5	18.7	18.4
2	7.4	15.6	23.5	24.3	26.1	26.8	27.1	27.0
3	16.5	19.8	18.7	14.8	12.0	12.1	11.2	10.9
4	19.5	18.6	12.7	8.2	6.1	4.8	3.6	3.2
5 or more	53.4	40.2	24.3	12.3	7.4	4.0	2.3	2.1
Mean	5.2	4.6	3.4	2.4	-	-	-	-

Source: Saw, 1980; Tietze & Henshaw, 1986.

Table 27.3

Percentage Distribution of Abortions by Age Group, University Department of Obstetrics and Gynecology, Singapore, 1976–83

Age Group	1976	1977	1978	1979	1980	1981	1982	1983
< 19	5.4	6.3	7.9	8.2	9.4	8.9	7.7	8.0
20–29	62.8	59	62	58.4	54.3	53.9	57.3	54.0
> 30	31.8	34.7	30.1	33.4	36.3	37.2	34.8	38.0

Table 27.4

Number and Percentage of Abortions by Marital Status, University Department of Obstetrics and Gynecology, Singapore, 1976–83

Marital Status	1976 No	1976 %	1977 No	1977 %	1979 No	1979 %	1980 No	1980 %	1981 No	1981 %	1982 No	1982 %	1983 No	1983 %
Single	40	8.6	80	10	231	12.8	731	17	784	17.6	447	15.6	324	15.0
Married	422	91.4	724	90	1575	87.2	3568	83	3673	82.4	2422	84.4	1834	85.0
Total	462	100	804	100	1806	100	4299	100	4457	100	2869	100	2158	100

Table 27.5

Percentage Distribution of Legalized Abortion in Singapore Government Hospitals, by Period of Gestation, 1970–81

Gestation Period (weeks)	1970	1971	1972	1973	1974	Year 1975	1976	1977	1978	1979	1980	1981
Total No	1886	3343	3694	5089	6681	10659	11665	12744	13120	12008	11280	9874
12 and less (%)	91	92	92	94	93	84	86	85	79	81	92	93
13 and above (%)	9	8	8	6	7	15	12	13	16	17	8	7
Unknown	+	+	+	+	+	1	2	2	5	2	+	+

+ Less than 1 percent.

Source: Ministry of Health Statistics, Singapore.

Table 27.6
Number of Adolescent Abortions in Singapore, 1970–82

Year	Age Under 15	15–19	Teenage Abortion Rate*
1970	2	33	0.8
1971	2	96	0.8
1972	7	96	0.8
1973	4	180	1.4
1974	5	432	3.2
1975	22	1032	7.5
1976	6	1134	8.1
1977	17	1303	9.4
1978	9	1408	9.9
1979	18	1357	9.7
1980	26	1578	11.5
1981	8	1509	11.2
1982	13	1479	11.3

*Teenage abortion rate = (Total teenage abortions $\times$ 1,000) $\div$ (Number of women aged 15–19)
Source: Ratnam & Prasad, 1983.

Table 27.7
Repeat Aborters at the Fertility Control Clinic, University Department of Obstetrics and Gynecology, 1976–82

YEAR	Number of previous induced abortions						Total No	Percentage with 2 or more previous abortions
	0	1	2	3	4	Unknown		
1976	314	109	28	3	5	3	462	7.8
1977	460	267	61	13	2	1	804	9.5
1978	1164	504	108	18	7	5	1805	7.4
1979	3111	946	189	33	14	6	4299	5.5
1980	3034	1101	253	49	16	4	4457	7.1
1981	2146	913	297	50	16	3	3425	10.6
1982	1723	758	219	61	17	1	2869	10.4

Table 27.8
Contraceptive Practice (in Numbers of Women) Before and After Abortion, University Department of Obstetrics and Gynecology, Singapore, 1976–83

Contraceptive used		None	Oral Pills	IUCD	Condoms	Sterilization	Others*
1976	Before ab.	96	71	6	155	2	132
	After ab.	15	168	144	46	10	79
1977	Before ab.	145	112	13	271	2	253
	After ab.	9	154	361	43	23	214
1978	Before ab.	430	173	40	498	7	658
	After ab.	46	272	790	144	63	491
1979	Before ab.	922	309	54	1044	3	1967
	After ab.	205	616	814	573	188	1903
1980	Before ab.	846	370	77	1070	8	2086
	After ab.	176	845	980	370	188	1898
1981	Before ab.	712	285	70	917	7	1434
	After ab.	101	919	769	256	137	1243
1982	Before ab.	653	220	61	696	5	1243
	After ab.	74	433	780	174	96	1312
1983	Before ab.	546	131	48	538	2	893
	After ab.	53	431	502	141	41	990

*Includes rhythm method, combination of methods, injectibles, other methods, and unknown.

Table 27.9
Causes of Maternal Deaths in Singapore, 1968–79

Causes of Death	1968–70		1971–73		1974–76		77–79
	No	%	No	%	No	%	%
Abortion	15	29.4	13	37.1	9	34.6	17.6
Hemorrhage	15	29.4	12	34.3	5	19.2	47.1
Toxemia	8	15.8	3	8.6	4	15.4	0.0
Ectopic Pregnancy	4	7.8	2	5.7	5	19.2	11.8
Others	9	17.6	5	14.3	3	11.6	23.4
Total	51	100	35	100	26	100	100
Maternal Mortality Rate	0.37 per 1000		0.24 per 1000		0.20 per 1000		0.04 per 1000

28

REPUBLIC OF SOUTH AFRICA

F. F. W. van Oosten and Monica Ferreira

HISTORICAL DEVELOPMENT OF ABORTION POLICY

Prior to 1975, the South African law of abortion was governed by the Roman-Dutch common law (De Wet & Swanepoel, 1960, p. 217 ff.; Hunt, 1970, p. 303 ff.; Hawthorne, 1982, p. 203 ff.). Criminal abortion was defined as the intentional and unlawful killing and/or causing the expulsion of the live fetus of a pregnant woman. Whether a mere killing of the fetus or a mere causing the expulsion of the fetus sufficed is a bone of contention (Van Oosten, 1986, p. 51 ff., and the authorities cited and discussed therein). Despite this uncertainty, the legal interest protected by the crime of abortion was (and still is) generally held to be the life of the fetus. The only legally recognized ground of justification was necessity and then only when the life of the mother was endangered by the continuation of the pregnancy. In practice, however, abortions were often performed by medical practitioners, without prosecution by law enforcement agencies, on other grounds, most of them similar to those incorporated in the act (Hunt, 1970, pp. 309–310; Middleton, 1972, p. 398). In turn, this state of affairs resulted in strong judicial pleas for a reform of the law of abortion (*S.* v. *King*, 1971; *S.* v. *Van Druten*, 1972, p. 59 ff.).

In 1975 the Abortion and Sterilization Act No. 2 of 1975, which replaced the common law in most respects, came into operation after extensive investigations and lengthy debates in Parliament (Armstrong, 1973, p. 247 ff.; Hawthorne, 1982, p. 238 ff.; *S.* v. *Kruger*, 1976). The act was designed to give legal affirmation to a practice of therapeutic abortion that had for many years become settled in the medical profession. Various aspects of the act have been subjected to severe criticism, and, although some amendments have been introduced by the legislators, a number of unsatisfactory issues remain (Smit, 1976, p. 156 ff.; Stassen, 1976, p. 260 ff.; Bertrand, 1977, p. 263 ff.; 1978, p. 263 ff.; Van Oosten, 1977, p. 376 ff.; D'Oliveira, 1982, p. 321 ff.; Milton, 1982, p. 315

ff.; Hawthorne, 1982, p. 248 ff.; Snyman, 1983, p. 387 ff.; Strauss, 1984, p. 226 ff). According to the act, criminal abortion consists in the unlawful abortion of a live fetus of a woman with the intent to kill such fetus (see sections 1, 2, and 10). A "live fetus" for the purposes of the act means a fetus as from the moment of conception until birth (see *S*. v. *Collop*, 1981). As noted above, whether a mere causing the expulsion (with the intent to kill) of the fetus suffices is a moot point (see Van Oosten, 1986, 48 ff. and the authorities cited therein). An unlawful abortion is one that is procured otherwise than in accordance with the provisions of the act (Section 2).

LEGAL STATUS OF ABORTION

The act stipulates that, to qualify as lawful, an abortion must (cf. also sections 6(2) and (6), 7 and 8), among other things, be procured by a medical practitioner (Section 3(1)) in a state hospital (Section 5), and then only where the pregnancy: (1) endangers the life of the woman; (2) constitutes a serious threat to the physical or mental health of the woman; (3) creates a serious risk that the child to be born will suffer from so great a physical or mental defect that he or she will be irreparably seriously handicapped; (4) is alleged to be the result of unlawful carnal intercourse, that is, rape or incest (Section 1); or (5) is the result of illegitimate carnal intercourse with a woman who, due to a permanent mental handicap or defect, is unable to comprehend the consequential implications of or bear the parental responsibility for the fruit of coitus (Section 3(1)(a)-(e)).

In all of these circumstances, the act requires that two other medical practitioners (one of whom must have practiced for at least four years) certify in writing that the abortion is necessary for the reason specified (Section 3(1) and (2)). The following provisions are specified: (1) Where the abortion is procured to protect the mental health of the woman, one of the medical practitioners must be a state psychiatrist, and it must be certified that the continued pregnancy creates the danger of permanent damage to the woman's health. (2) Where the risk of a physical or mental defect to the child to be born exists, it must be certified that such a risk exists on scientific grounds. (3) Where rape or incest is alleged, one of the medical practitioners must be the district surgeon who examined the woman if a complaint in regard thereto has been lodged with the police; the woman must be interrogated in regard to the alleged rape or incest (Section 3(1)(a)-(e) and 3(3)(a)-(c)); and the medical practitioner who is in charge of the state hospital, who may be one of the certifying medical practitioners and whose written approval to procure the abortion is required (Section 6(1) and 6(3)), must be furnished with a certificate, issued by a magistrate in whose district the offense is alleged to have occurred, to the effect that the magistrate is satisfied (a) that a complaint relating to the alleged unlawful carnal intercourse has been lodged with the police or, if no complaint has been lodged, that there is a good and acceptable reason for it; (b) after an examination of any relevant documents submitted to the magistrate by the police and after such interrogation

of the woman concerned or of any other person that the magistrate may consider
necessary, that, on a balance of probability, the alleged unlawful carnal intercourse did in fact occur; and (c) in the case of alleged incest, that the woman
is within the prohibited degree related to the person with whom she is alleged
to have committed incest (Section 6(4)(a)). In addition, the magistrate must
certify that the woman alleges in an affidavit submitted or a statement under
oath to the magistrate that the pregnancy is the result of rape or incest, as the
case may be (Section 6(4)(b)).

A medical practitioner who has issued a certificate is prohibited from participating or assisting in the abortion in question. In addition, such certificate is
invalid if issued by members of the same partnership or persons in the employ
of the same employer, unless such persons are employed by the state (Section
3(2)(a) and (b)).

No medical practitioner (other than the one who is in charge of the state
hospital and whose written approval is required), nurse, or other person falling
within the terms of the act is obliged to participate or assist in an abortion
(Section 9).

Despite the replacement of common law abortion by the act, there remains a
residual area in which the common law rules are still operative, that is, attempted
abortion (e.g. where the fetus, unknown to the abortionist, is already dead at
the time of the act in question: see *R*. v. *Davis*, 1956); complicity in abortion
(e.g., by the pregnant woman, where she consents to the abortion, her consent
affording neither herself nor the abortionist a defense: *R*. v. *Freestone*, 1913,
p. 769; *R*. v. *Thielke*, 1918, p. 378; *R*. v. *Owen*, 1942, p. 392; *R*. v. *P*.,
1948, p. 109; *R*. v. *Voges*, 1958, p. 417); and abortion defenses outside the
provisions of the act. As concerns the last-named, the defense of necessity will
continue to avail the abortionist if an emergency renders the abortion in question
imperative in circumstances where compliance with the requirements of the act
is physically impossible (Van Oosten, 1976, pp. 394–395; Bertrand, 1977,
p. 285; Milton, 1982, p. 321).

INCIDENCE OF LEGAL ABORTION

The number of legal abortions performed each year is officially recorded in
the annual reports of the Department of Health and classified separately for the
four ethnic groups in South Africa. The total number of abortions on women of
any age and for all ethnic groups performed was 625 in 1976; 539 in 1977; 541
in 1978; 423 in 1979; 347 in 1980; 381 in 1981; and 464 in 1982 (Department
of Health, Annual Reports, 1976–82). The total number of abortions performed
on women aged fifteen to forty-four years in 1983, 1984, and 1985 was 451,
542, and 689, respectively (Department of Health, Annual Reports, 1983–85).

Of the abortions performed during each of three consecutive years, 1983–85,
an average of 40 percent were performed on unmarried women, 52 percent on
married women, and 8 percent on divorced or widowed women. Four-fifths of

the abortions performed during each of the same three years were performed on white women and the remainder on Asian, black, and coloured women—3 percent, 4 percent and 13 percent respectively (Department of Health Annual Reports, 1983–85).

The average percentage of abortions performed each year during the period 1983–85 on the grounds of (1) the continued pregnancy endangering the life of the woman or constituting a serious threat to her physical health was 13 percent; (2) the continued pregnancy constituting a serious threat to the mental health of the woman, 49 percent; (3) a serious risk existing that the child to be born would suffer from a physical or mental defect, 32 percent; (4) the fetus allegedly having been conceived in consequence of alleged rape or incest, 5 percent; and (5) the fetus allegedly having been conceived in consequence of unlawful carnal intercourse with a female idiot or imbecile, less than 1 percent.

Of the abortions performed on the grounds of the continued pregnancy constituting a serious threat to the mental health of the woman, 90 percent were performed on white women. Four-fifths of abortions on the grounds of a serious risk that the child could be born with a physical or mental defect were performed on white women.

The high percentage of legal abortions performed annually on white women suggests that non-white women are restricted in their access to lawful abortions, either through ignorance of the possibility of a legal abortion or lack of knowledge about where to obtain a legal abortion.

INCIDENCE OF ILLEGAL ABORTION

An estimate of 200,000 illegal abortions a year in South Africa has been cited, although the basis for the estimate is unclear. Statistics from surveys of admissions to gynecological wards at major hospitals indicate that many of these admissions are for illegal abortions that result in medical complications (Dyer, 1979; Mbere & Rubin, 1979).

Analyses of the notifications of operations for the removal of the residues of a pregnancy in the annual reports of the Department of Health, 90 percent of which operations are generally considered to be the result of backstreet abortions, reveal that over a period of three consecutive years, 1983–85, 95,000 such operations were performed. The average percentages of the total number of these operations performed annually during this period on women of the four ethnic groups were whites, 21 percent; coloureds, 13 percent; Asians, 6 percent; and blacks, 60 percent. The figures suggest that substantially more black women than women of other ethnic groups resort to backstreet abortions. This is probably a result of the unequal opportunity for nonwhite women to obtain a legal abortion and complex procedures that discriminate against these women. The official figures reflect only illegal abortions that result in complications requiring medical treatment.

Despite the restrictive abortion law, thousands of women in South Africa apparently resort to backstreet abortions despite their illegality (Kunst & Meiring, 1984). The average number of prosecutions for illegal abortion in a year is only thirty-four (Strauss, 1984, p. 236). A number of women travel to Britain to procure an abortion (Bertrand, 1977; Bourne, 1980; *OPCS Monitor*, 1982).

The medical profession cites the consequences of illegal abortions as one of the major reasons for the need to review South Africa's abortion legislation (Mbere & Rubin, 1979). Other consequences of illegal abortions that have been noted include an estimated mortality rate of 5 to 10 per 1,000 illegal abortions (Larsen, 1978); permanent infertility and disability (Mbere & Rubin, 1979); a drain on medical resources (Botes, 1973); and the expenditure of public funds (Dyer, 1979).

ABORTION RESEARCH

Negligible research has been undertaken in South Africa on legal and illegal abortion practice. The bulk of the studies that have been conducted have (1) debated the Christian principles and ethical problems surrounding abortion (Du Toit, 1978; Swanepoel, 1983); (2) investigated the problem of abortion from a social work perspective (Rode, 1974; Mark, 1981; Price, 1984; and (3) argued the legal philosophy of abortion or perceived shortcomings of the act (Smit, 1976; Bertrand, 1977; Strauss, 1980; Kunst & Meiring, 1984).

Because abortion is illegal and not socially legitimated in South Africa, the results of surveys of the attitudes of various ethnic groups toward abortion (Lötter & Glanz, 1980), as well as changes, shifts, and trends in attitudes and public opinion (Venter, 1981, 1982) probably do not reflect actual attitudes toward abortion. Apart from a study among gynecologists by Dommisse (1980), there are no comprehensive survey findings reflecting the attitude of the medical community toward abortion.

Only rudimentary demographic data on legal abortions are available and are found in the annual reports of the Department of Health. No comprehensive epidemiological studies have been undertaken of either legal or illegal abortions, and there is a lack of reliable information on morbidity and mortality rates associated with abortion and on wider measurements of the characteristics of abortion populations.

OPPOSITION TO AND SUPPORT OF THE ABORTION LAW

Both opposition to and support of the Abortion Act and its implementation by individuals and groups are apparent. Proabortion lobbyists are mainly represented by the Abortion Reform Action Group (ARAG). ARAG campaigns "for a humane law for the right of every woman of every race in South Africa to terminate undesired pregnancy . . . without delay, without stigma, with proper health care and with proper privacy" (ARAG leaflet, n.d.). Women's organizations that have declared their support of the abortion reform movement in

South Africa include the National Council of Women, the Afrikaanse Christelike Vrouevereniging, Soroptomists International, the Women's Legal Status Committee, the International Federation of University Women, the South African Society of Medical Women, Business and Professional Women, the Black Sash, the Garment Workers and Industrial Union, and the Women's Bureau (Kunst & Meiring, 1984).

Antiabortion campaigners support pro-life and right-to-life movements and organizations. These organizations are strongly Christian-based and backed by religious groups. The organizations generally claim to stand for a ban on abortion on any grounds, including rape.

Since 1980 pro-abortion groups and parliamentary lobbyists have pleaded for a commission of inquiry into the workings and effects of the act, under the chairmanship of a judge and including experts from various fields, of both sexes and of all ethnic groups. Incumbent ministers of health have repeatedly turned down the requests. Although a draft bill was published in 1981 that would have allowed abortion following failed sterilization, this clause in the amendment bill was withdrawn before debate. Incumbent ministers of health and antiabortion parliamentary lobbyists have remained adamant that the act will not be submitted to a judicial inquiry and that Christian ethics preclude the government from allowing abortion on request.

Generally, opposition to any liberalization of the abortion law in South Africa comes from right-wing, conservative groups on moral and religious grounds. Churches base their opposition on the conviction that the moment of fertilization is synonymous with the creation of a new life and that liberalization of the abortion law will lead to wide-scale immorality. Strauss (1980) points out that, although it is not the function of the law generally to enforce religious dogma, the present legislature in South Africa does not readily legislate in opposition to the consensus of church opinion.

ABORTION AND FERTILITY REGULATION

In the face of growing recognition of demographic pressures in the country (Report of the Science Committee on Demographic Trends, 1983), future progress in family planning and the reduction of fertility may depend on the provision of abortion as an additional means for facilitating choice behavior in fertility regulation (Ferreira, 1985; Mostert & Van Tonder, 1986). On the basis of the findings of research on unplanned pregnancies, Mostert and Van Tonder suggest that there is a latent need among women of all ethnic groups in South Africa to use abortion on demand if it is available and needed. The response of the government is that it chooses to promote contraception to effect fertility reduction through its population development program, of which the family planning program is one of a number of components of a comprehensive development strategy directed at improving the quality of life of all people in South Africa, and not permit abortion. Until recently, the objectives of the family planning program were far more explicit, and efforts to promote development and upliftment were comparatively understated. The reason for the shift in emphasis has been government suspicions that the black population may be antagonistic to the family planning program and resistant to motivation to practice contraception, as they perceive the aims of the program are politically inspired and directed at reducing the number of blacks in the country relative to the number of whites.

SUMMARY

The present South African government is not contemplating changes in its restrictive abortion law. The act is perceived by some to restrict the categories of women that qualify for an abortion and to be complicated and time-consuming in its implementation. It is argued that the act does not fulfill the multifaceted requirements of South African society. Low-income and nonwhite women are perceptibly hardest hit by restricted access to lawful abortions. Backstreet abortion practice is evident in the number of women, particularly black women, who are admitted to state hospitals for the treatment of complications arising from such abortions.

Because abortion is illegal in South Africa, there is no opportunity for the social and personal legitimation of abortion. For the larger part, there has been no visible shift from a moral-religious view of abortion as immoral and criminal to the interests of the individual and society as a whole. The moral-religious view remains the basis of the controversy or debate on abortion and is reinforced by the body politic, suggesting a political expediency in maintaining the status quo of abortion. Public discussion of the problematics of abortion has been minimal, and the discussion that exists is seldom related to a factual basis.

Despite the government's recognition of the urgent need to decrease the population growth rate, it finds itself unable to permit abortion as an additional means of fertility regulation. South Africa is, however, currently undergoing political and social reform in many areas. The present abortion legislation reflects the values and norms of the whites. With increased sharing of power and decision-making by the nonwhite populations under a new dispensation—populations that may reveal a desire for a liberalized abortion law—the status of abortion may change.

REFERENCES

Armstrong, N. W. The new Abortion Bill—Medicine and society. *Responsa Meridiana*, 1973, 247.

Bertrand, A. R. L. The Abortion and Sterilization Act 2 of 1975: A third opinion. *South African Journal of Criminal Law and Criminology*, 1977, 263; 1978, 263.

Botes, M. Septic abortion and septic shock. *South African Medical Journal*, March 1973, 432.

Bourne, D. E. Abortion statistics. *South African Medical Journal*, 1980, *24*, 852.

De Wet, J. C., & Swanepoel, H. L. *Die Suid-Afrikaanse strafreg*. Durban: Butterworths, 1960.

D'Oliveira, J. Vrugafdrywing as nog 'n regverdigingsgrond. *De Jure*, 1982, 321.

Dommisse, J. South African gynaecologists' attitudes to the present abortion law. *South African Medical Journal*, July 1980, *57*, 1044–1045.

Du Toit, D. M. *Die Christen en Aborsie*. Pretoria: NG Kerkboekhandel, 1978.

Dyer, M. The Abortions' Act—a plea for a commission of inquiry. *Social Work* 1979, *15*(4), 185–190.

Ferreira, M. *Abortion and family planning: A literature study*. Pretoria: Human Sciences Research Council, 1985 (Report S–126).

Hawthorne, L. The crime of abortion: A historical and comparative study. Ph.D. diss. Pretoria: University of Pretoria, 1982.

Hunt, P. M. A. *South African criminal law and procedure*. Vol. 2. Cape Town: Juta, 1970.

Kunst, J., & Meiring, R. Abortion law—A need for reform. *De Rebus Procuratoriis*, 1984, 265.

Larsen, J. V. Induced abortion. *South African Medical Journal*, May 1978, 853.

Lötter, J. M., & Glanz, L. *Sekere houdings jeens aborsie*. Pretoria: Human Sciences Research Council, 1980 (Report SN–11).

Mark, G. A follow-up of therapeutic abortions—a social work perspective. M.A. thesis, Pretoria, University of South Africa, 1981.

Mbere, J. M., & Rubin, A. *South African Journal of Hospital Medicine*, 1979, *5*, 193.

Middleton, A. J. Abortion. *De Rebus Procuratoriis*, 1972, 397.

Milton, J. R. L. *South African criminal law and procedure*. Vol. 2. Cape Town: Juta, 1982.

Mostert, W. P., & Van Tonder, J. L. *Die voorgestelde Suid-Afrikaanse bevolkingsprogram van die Presidentsraad: Insette ter bereiking van fertiliteitsdoelwitte*. Pretoria: Human Sciences Research Council, 1986 (Report S–142).

OPCS Monitor. Office of population census and surveys. September 1982 (Reference AB79/2).

Price, H. *Psychological adjustments of pregnant adolescents who seek legal abortions*. M.A. thesis, Johannesburg, University of Witwatersrand, 1984.

R. v. Davies, 1956(3) S.A. 52(A).

R. v. Freestone, 1913 T.P.D. 758.

R. v. Owen, 1942 A.D. 389.

R. v. P., 1948(4) S.A. 103(C).

R. v. Thielke, 1918 A.D. 373.

R. v. Voges, 1958(1) S.A. 412(C).

Rode, H. L. *Enkele aspekte van aborsie: 'n Literatuurstudie*. Pretoria: Department of Welfare and Pensions, No. 1, 1974.

S. v. Collop, 1981(1) S.A. 150(A).

S. v. King, 1971(1) P.H.H. 103(T).

S. v. Kruger, 1976(3) S.A. 290(A).

S. v. Van Druten, unreported, *Journal of Contemporary Roman-Dutch Law*, 1972, 59.

Smit, P. C. Aspekte van die Wet op Vrugafdrywing en Sterilisasie, 1975. *Journal for Juridical Science*, 1976, 156–164.

Snyman, C. R. *Criminal law*. Durban: Butterworths, 1983. South Africa, Department of Health. *Annual reports*, 1976–85.

South Africa. *Report of the Science Committee of the Presidents' Council on Demographic Trends in South Africa*. Cape Town: Government Printer, 1983 (P.C. 1/1983).

Stassen, J. C. Die Wet op Vrugafdrywing en Sterilisasie 2 van 1975. *Journal of South African Law*, 1976, 260.

Strauss, S. A. *Doctor, patient and the law*. Pretoria: Van Schaik, 1980, 1984.

Swanepoel, A. M. E. Aborsie as etiese probleem. M.A. thesis, Pretoria, University of Pretoria, 1983.

Van Oosten, F. F. W. Abortion—Adieu common law?. *South African Law Journal*, 1976, 393.

————. Regmatige vrugafdrywing. *De Jure*, 1977, 376.

————. Vrugafdrywing: 'n misdaad sonder omskrywing en met 'n twyfelagtige inhoud?. *De Jure*, 1986, 48.

Venter, J. D. Houdings van en houdingsveranderings by Blanke Suid-Afrikaners ten opsigte van aborsie. *Humanitas*, 1981, *7* (2), 131–141.

————. Die houdings en houdingsveranderings van Kleurlinge ten opsigte van aborsie. *Die Suid-Afrikaanse Tydskrif vir Sosiologie*, 1982, *13* (1), 62–78.

29

SRI LANKA

N. Kodagoda and Pramilla Senanayake

HISTORICAL DEVELOPMENT OF ABORTION POLICY

Cultural as well as religious attitudes toward abortion in Sri Lanka have been restrictive. Even so, in recent times, the subject has come to be more openly and objectively discussed.

In 1977 a publication on population law for medical students expressed the following concern:

It would appear that it is really women from middle to low socio-economic groups who have to get their pregnancies terminated surreptitiously by quacks. . . . It is also people from these groups who have the least awareness of contraceptive techniques. Though the exact incidence of criminal abortion is yet unknown, it has been reported that illegal abortions are done in this country under primitive and unhygienic conditions, resulting in high mortality and chronic ill-health. (Jayasuriya & Kodagoda, 1977, p. 15)

The publication also referred to the flexibility of the spirit of the law, where legal abortion was allowable on a psychiatrist's certificate, stating that "the probability is high of the woman committing suicide, if the pregnancy were to continue" (Jayasuriya & Kodagoda, 1977, p. 17).

In general, the effectiveness of the law began to be doubted, and the moralistic stand on abortion was subjected to rational analysis. It was in this environment, and encouraged by it, that several organized bodies turned their attention to the law on abortion.

LEGAL STATUS OF ABORTION

The law relating to abortion in Sri Lanka was enacted in 1883, based on the Indian Penal Code, and remains substantially the same today (Penal Code, 1956). It is a highly restrictive law, legally allowing abortion only in order to *save the life* of the mother. The law proceeds to lay down a greater punishment if the woman be "quick with child."

The term "miscarriage," used synonymously with "abortion," is left undefined in the Penal Code, but it has generally been taken to mean a premature expulsion, or even a threat at expulsion, of the contents of the uterus. "Quick with child" is left undefined too; it has been used in contrast to the phrase "woman with child." It is thus taken to signify a more advanced stage of pregnancy where there is perception of the intrauterine movements of the fetus. A woman who causes herself to miscarry is also within the meaning of this section of the law. The Supreme Court of the island has taken the view that a person could be convicted of abetment of the offense, even if there is no evidence that the woman had in fact been pregnant (*King* v. *Fernando*, 1925). Absence of consent is an enhancing factor for criminality—that is, regardless of whether or not the woman is "quick with child."

Where the death of a woman is caused by an act performed with intent to cause miscarriage, the person so doing can be charged with culpable homicide. This liability exists even if the person did not know that the act performed is likely to cause death. The consent of the woman in this instance is immaterial, although the Indian law did draw a distinction.

The law does not define the persons lawfully entitled to perform a legal abortion to save the life of the mother; neither does it specify the nature of the premises in which it may be done.

As with other criminal offenses, with abortion too, intent is paramount. Caselaw in Sri Lanka has held that it is not essential to prove that the accused caused a miscarriage; what is material is the intent to cause one (*Queen* v. *Waidyasekera*, 1955). The burden of proof of the objective of the action to be in good faith, to save the life of the mother, rests with the accused. Under the provisions of the law, it would appear that an abortion or other surgical procedure amounts to an offense termed "hurt." However, free consent from the party is a valid defense for this charge.

Generally, then, it is desirable to obtain the written consent of the person undergoing a legal abortion, and, when possible, it is preferable to obtain the consent of the partner as well. Even so, acts done in "good faith" for the benefit of a person, without consent, due to the impossibility to signify consent or incapability to give consent, are not treated as offenses.

Reappraisal of the Law

The Medico-Legal Society of Sri Lanka was early in the field of reappraising the law on abortion, and appointed a committee to examine the present-day implications. The committee carried out an objective study and reported on it. The following year the parent body recommended that the existing law be extended to include the following: (1) prevention of grave injury to the physical and mental health of the pregnant woman; (2) pregnancies resulting from rape and incest; and (3) abortion where there is substantial risk that the child, if born, would suffer from such physical or mental abnormalities as to be seriously handicapped in life.

A National Seminar on Law and Population (Family Planning Association of Sri Lanka, 1974) concluded that the existing law on abortion as contained in the Penal Code was very restrictive. The meeting further declared that no new statute on abortion, like the abortion acts of England, Singapore, and India, was indicated for Sri Lanka, but that present law should be amended to bring certain other situations (additional to saving the life of the mother) within the bounds of "legal" abortion. In this respect, the recommendations of the Medico-Legal Society were endorsed. The seminar was also of the opinion that the Penal Code ought to be amended to provide specifically that any termination of pregnancy should be done only by a registered medical practitioner.

In December 1975, at a seminar on Population Problems of Sri Lanka in the Seventies, liberalization of abortion laws was said to deserve careful consideration (Sri Lanka Foundation, 1975). On this occasion, over and above the considerations in the previous seminar, liberalizing the law to cover situations such as contraceptive failure and economic difficulty was stated as desirable. The seminar on Population Law and the Medical Profession (University of Sri Lanka) aligned itself with the recommendations outlined above, in stating that the law should permit a woman to procure abortion for social, economic, eugenic, and humanitarian reasons, and in instances of contraceptive failure.

Both then and later, several surveys were done with the object of ascertaining the views of professionals on the subject of liberalizing abortion. A survey carried out among a group of thirty-seven doctors, nineteen lawyers, and three law enforcement officers revealed that 93.2 percent were of the opinion that the existing law required amendment. The specific reasons that they recommended for allowing abortion were as follows: poverty—94.5 percent; risk of deformed children—90.9 percent; pregnancies due to rape or incest—81.8 percent; large family—72.7 percent; social and humanitarian reasons—36.4 percent; contraceptive failure—38.2 percent; improvement of family health—30.9 percent; for birth control—14.5 percent; and for checking population increase—7.3 percent (Jayasuriya, 1976).

Kodagoda (1984) conducted a survey among a group of Western medical practitioners, with a view to ascertaining their views on the law of abortion. The sample comprised 346 doctors, in private as well as state practice. Both sexes, all religions prevalent in the country, and all grades of qualifications and services were represented. Of the respondents, 64.5 percent advocated a change in the law with a view to liberalizing abortion. Among those who advocated change, the reasons for which liberalization was recommended were as follows: ill-health of mother—99.6 percent; pregnancy from rape—96.4 percent; pregnancy from incest—78.9 percent; contraceptive failure—76.2 percent; and financial reasons—53.8 percent. It is noteworthy that 43.9 percent recommended a change in the law to accommodate legal abortion on demand by both parents and 23.3 percent on demand by the mother alone.

The indigenous medical practitioners responded to suggested changes in the law with much less conviction. The indication for liberalizing legal abortion which they most favored was an excessive number of children. Economic difficulties and wishes of the parents followed, in order of preference, but considerably behind; pregnancy from rape came next; and the wish of either parent was considered last in the list of preferred indications. The reticence of these practitioners is understandable, for they are tradition-bound, practicing in rural areas; most are elderly; and many of them have had no institutional training. On the other hand, considering these factors, the proportion of indigenous practitioners favoring liberalization for one reason or another seems highly significant in the assessment of trends toward change.

The Ministry of Plan Implementation (1983) has conducted an in-depth interview of a small number of consultant gynecologists on the matter of liberalizing abortion. Among the fears they expressed in the event of a relaxation of the law were a decline in the use of contraceptive methods, development of a casual public attitude toward abortion, inability of state institutions to cope with demand (and subsequent lengthening of the already long waiting lists for gynecological operations), and an increase in the number of unqualified persons practicing abortions. Regardless of these reservations, the consultants considered abortion a major public health issue, and called for urgent and meaningful intervention.

The Ministry also interviewed a group of women community leaders. This attitude assessment, however, was carried out after they had heard the question of abortion discussed by a panel. They all came to hold the view that the law should be modified to enable procurement of abortion for maternal health reasons. Rape, incest, and probability of fetal malformation were also rated high. A consideration that came lower down the list, but one not encountered in other interviews, was when a woman becomes pregnant by a man whom she does not subsequently want to marry.

In the course of time, pressures from professionals and others involved in family planning activities came to influence politicians. In 1978 several government parliamentarians introduced a Private Members' Bill in Parliament to reform the abortion law. Opposition to the move arose, not only from members of the public, but also from other parliamentarians, and the move had to be abandoned.

Current Status of Abortion Laws

As seen from the above considerations, although the matter of abortion law has been the subject of much discussion, liberalization seems remote. Barriers to liberalization are tangible, stemming from moral, religious, and social attitudes. The political explosiveness and implications of these factors play an important part in withholding any substantial change to abortion law in Sri Lanka.

It would be futile to attempt an analysis of the abortion policy in Sri Lanka, for none has been proclaimed—that is, apart from the definitive and stringent stand of the law already detailed.

Tradition-bound peasants totally abide by their religious convictions and consider willful abortion tantamount to the taking of life. The fertilized ovum is considered to have life in that sense. Whether a fetus in whom consciousness has not been implanted can be considered a life form, the destruction of which comprises killing, continues to be a matter for debate. The philosophical question as to when consciousness begins in a fetus has also not been indisputably answered—anywhere. Yet, the general impression that destruction of a fertilized ovum, at whatever stage, is killing, remains unshaken in Sri Lanka.

ATTITUDES TOWARD ABORTION

A small-scale survey by questionnaire was conducted with the objective of assessing young peoples' attitudes toward abortion (Kodagoda & Senanayake, 1982). The vast majority of 150 unmarried men desired to get married early and preferred small families. Inquiry as to what they would do if their girlfriend got pregnant revealed that only 0.7 percent of 150 respondents would resort to abortion; 35.3 percent were uncertain of what they would do.

In answer to the question "What did their parents think of abortion?," 46 percent did not know what their parents thought; 28.6 percent thought they would disapprove of abortion under any circumstances; and only 18.7 percent felt they might approve, but only under certain circumstances.

Of this group of respondents, 41.3 percent were unaware of what their male friends thought of abortion, while 54.7 percent were unaware of the attitudes of their female friends; 18.7 percent felt their male friends would disapprove of abortion under any circumstances; and 14.7 percent thought their female friends would disapprove.

The authors also carried out a parallel survey of attitudes among a group of 200 young women. Questioned as to what they would do if they became pregnant, 64 percent did not respond, possibly indicating a reticence about the subject. Of those who did respond, 48.6 percent said they would have the child; only 1.4 percent thought they would decide to have an abortion; and 42.1 percent felt that their parents would disapprove of abortion under any circumstance. In the female group, too, ignorance of other people's attitudes was marked; 31.8 percent, 68.9 percent, and 34.5 percent of the sample were unaware of the attitudes of their parents and their male and female friends, respectively (Kodagoda & Senanayake, 1982).

Although the samples referred to above are small and have elements of built-in preselection, it is justifiable to deduce a sizable social bias against abortion, even among young people. It is also possible to recognize an element of secrecy from these results, since discussions on the subject, even among friends, appear to be limited.

The media do not appear to have a definite policy about the question of abortion. The matter does attract bold headlines from time to time, particularly when abortion is associated with crime, or when the police detect a sensational case of criminal abortion. The subject of abortion also receives publicity in the media when an important personality makes a strong statement either for or against it. The common factor that pervades all such instances is that the topic is treated in a sensationalist manner rather than objectively.

A content analysis of printed mass media during a three-year period, conducted by the Ministry of Plan Implementation, has revealed the following information. Out of 244 relevant newspaper reports, 40 were about the subject of abortion, 29 of which had reported that the woman died following an induced abortion. Of these abortions, 44 percent had been induced by quacks and 20 percent by non-Western medical personnel, functioning under the assumed title of "doctor" (Ministry of Plan Implementation, 1983). Apart from such revelations, two other matters given wide publicity dealt with a lecture by an eminent pediatrician and a seminar, both of which had made a case for liberalization.

Following the publicity given to arguments for liberalization and a mild attempt in 1978 by a deputy minister to initiate discussions on the subject, much was said and written in the media by a variety of persons. Among the articles published, 9 percent were unbiased, 37 percent advocated liberalization, and 32 percent were opposed.

The Sri Lanka law requires that any citizen can bring the commission of a crime, or one about to be committed, to the notice of the relevant authorities. In fact, not to do so would amount to abetment. Even so, it would not be common practice for a villager to take such action in the event of an abortion. The same attitude appears to have pervaded medical ethics as well.

Ethical propriety demands that information pertaining to one's patient gathered in the course of medical practice not be divulged to a third party, barring a few exceptional instances. The law, however, does not consider criminal abortion to be an exception. On the contrary, case-law requires that, with regard to a criminal offense, a medical practitioner has the duties of a responsible citizen first and the ethics of a doctor second. Nonetheless, the general practice is to maintain silence regarding perpetration of an illegal abortion on one's patient. A doctor is more likely to take the initiative to inform the authorities when the act has been performed clearly against the woman's consent or by a known backstreet abortionist, or when, as a result of interference, the patient's life is threatened. Doctors may find it necessary to take that course of action in order to be safeguarded from the possibility of a future charge of abetment or, indeed, of complicity.

DEMOGRAPHY OF ABORTION

Only recently has the subject of abortion entered polite conversation. With the aura of secrecy, religious stricture, and social stigma, a reliable and comprehensive assessment of abortion incidence has not yet been undertaken in Sri Lanka. Relevant in this connection is the fact that only a certain proportion of cases are managed in institutions where statistical records are maintained. Some may indeed be managed with no trained medical assistance at all. Because of the stern legal view on the matter, it is natural to expect an assessment of the incidence of criminal abortion to be even more difficult.

Various impressionist, that is, sociological, assessments of abortion have been made. One such analysis arrived at a figure of 500 illegal abortions per day in the City of Colombo (female population 260,584) (*Ceylon Daily Mirror*, 1981). This figure has since been hotly challenged. A recent unofficial public statement from the Ministry of Health places the figure at a comparable level.

One of the earliest reliable records of the incidence of abortion outlined the situation that existed in a major women's hospital in Colombo in 1973. In comparing the number of deliveries and abortions in the Castle Street Hospital for women (a major city hospital in Colombo), the abortion to delivery ratio was found to vary between 1:5 to 1:7.8 during the period 1968 to 1972. It was also noted that the percentage of criminal abortions as a total of all abortions varied between 6.7 and 8.0 at this hospital during the same time period (Rajanayagam, 1973). These figures are understandably limited by the well-known factors that confound abortion statistics.

Abortion figures collected from a group of twenty general practitioners in a small town 100 kilometers from Colombo (area 190 sq. km.; estimated population of about 161,533) revealed the following information. Questioned as to the number of women who presented with unwanted pregnancies, eight responded with monthly averages of 150, 50, 13, 20, 22, 23, 10, and 4, respectively. The highest figure of 150 was given by a practitioner situated in the town center, while the lowest numbers were from those in more outlying locations. It is well known that, when faced with "difficult" situations, rural people tend to seek medical advice from doctors in towns.

If it is assumed that the practitioners who did not respond faced situations that were comparable to those who did, and therefore had come across similar numbers of unwanted pregnancies, then the total in the area of survey would be 730 per month. This amounts to 54 unwanted pregnancies per 1,000 population per year. This figure could be erroneously high by wrong diagnoses, and by the same woman going to more than one practitioner for the same episode. On the other hand, it could reflect an underestimation because the women who went to quack practitioners, or government institutions, would not be reflected here. Interrogation of the three pharmaceutical shops in the area with regard to requests for abortifacient drugs yielded an estimated figure of 57 for the month.

The results of these rather superficial surveys indicate that unwanted pregnancies do occur more commonly than is believed, and that a sizable proportion of women with such pregnancies try to get rid of them.

Kodagoda and Senanayake (1982) conducted another island-wide survey by questionnaire, among 401 indigenous practitioners, of whom 10,000 are registered with the state and at least another 10,000 are unregistered. A little over one-half (52.9 percent) said they had been consulted for an unwanted pregnancy during the three-month period before the survey; 40.9 percent said they had not; and the rest did not respond. The 212 practitioners who gave a positive response stated that during the period, 1,932 women came to them with an unwanted pregnancy and that 82.5 percent of them clearly indicated they wanted an abortion.

The above survey also yielded a profile of women seeking abortion. Of 1,083 women whose marital status was known, 75.1 percent were married. The ages of abortion seekers were available in 742 cases, and a breakdown indicated the particular vulnerability of younger age groups.

A total of 63.2 percent were between fifteen and twenty-nine years of age. No age seemed exempt however, for there were occasional instances of those aged fifteen years and under and forty-five years and above. The highest prevalence of abortion seekers was among those with no children. (Out of 637 cases, 29.8 percent presented with one to four weeks of amenorrhea.) The majority, 47.1 percent, presented between the fifth and eighth weeks, while 14.8 percent were nine to twelve weeks pregnant. There were isolated instances of thirty-three and thirty-six weeks of amenorrhea.

The Ministry of Plan Implementation has made further observations on fifty women who received menstrual regulation in the city of Colombo. An analysis of their monthly income has revealed a preponderance in the 300 to 700 (12 to 28 US$) rupee range. (An unskilled laborer's income would be about $1.50 per day, while a white-collar worker's about $35 to $50 US per month.) This study also reports that 16 percent sought abortion following contraceptive failure, 20 percent because of economic reasons, 12 percent because they had already attained their desired family size, and 20 percent felt that the previous child was too young to have a sibling. Altogether, sixteen had had a previous abortion. Those conducting the study felt that, although unadmitted, social stigma (for instance, in the case of a widow and in several cases where previous children were already grown up) was the reason for turning to menstrual regulation.

ABORTION AND FERTILITY REGULATION

As far back as the 1940s, the government had become sensitive to the need for population regulation measures. This trend is reflected in the Immigration Bill and in the Bill for Registration of non-Ceylonese, both of which were introduced in the country's legislature in 1941.

Even though definite steps have been taken with regard to the problems of immigration, it should be noted that it was not with the objective of population regulation. Regardless of the restrictions imposed, the population continued to grow rapidly.

The first policy statement regarding population regulation was issued in 1949, when the minister of health of the first government of independent Sri Lanka, addressing the Second World Health Assembly, said; "There is a growing need for the consideration of the problem of birth control on an international plan. . . . I do suggest . . . that a beginning be made in the preparation of the necessary statistics and data'' (WHO, 1949). This plea did not find much international favor at the time.

A comprehensive analysis of the implications of rapid population growth was contained in the ten-year plan of 1959, which made the following statement: ''It is clear that unless there is some prospect of a slowing down in the rate of population growth, and of relative stability in at least the long run, it is difficult to envisage substantial benefits from planning and development.'' This ten-year plan further suggested that the question of population policy be made the subject of a nationwide discussion, through the medium of a competent committee of inquiry.

When it took office in 1977, the present government included four policy imperatives: (1) recognition of the necessity to control the growth of population; (2) provision of more services in family planning; (3) provision of financial incentives; and (4) promotion of voluntary acceptance of family planning.

An important facet of the country's family planning policy is its acceptance at a level above political party differences. Contraceptives are freely available and at low cost. A beginning has been made in family life education in schools.

The budget speech of 1979 committed the government to the concept of a small family with the following words of the finance minister: ''It is my intention to introduce further tax disincentives to larger families. Population growth must be curbed if we are to achieve our objectives of eliminating unemployment, shortages of food and housing, and the depletion of our natural resources. Tax policy will be geared to this end.''

The unison and readiness with which politicians of varying ideologies cried for action spurred a senior government minister to remark that ''Twenty years ago no government, whatever political view they had, would have dared to make public statements about it.'' The minister for family health, chairing the Third Asian and Pacific Population Conference held in Colombo in 1982, outlined the future strategy as follows: ''What we expect to do is to persuade each respective government to take necessary steps to reduce population, and ensure population stability.'' On that same occasion, the minister also made the following pleas to all Asian nations: ''If we can get together on matters of population, we can get together on other issues'' (Atapattu, 1982).

Although such political commitment and unanimity does exist in the country, a counterinfluence is discernible. One source of such negative opinion is the inevitable ultramoralistic group, mainly religious, which tends to associate family planning with permissiveness. Another group of objectors believes that the adoption of family planning practices by sections of the population would ultimately alter the ethnic balance.

Objections to population control measures, and the attitude of successive governments to such objections, are clearly depicted in the following words of a former prime minister:

Family planning and population control have their proponents and opponents in Sri Lanka as well as in other parts of the world. I am aware that there are religious prejudices against family planning. I am also aware that there are groups in Sri Lanka who, apart from any religious bias, oppose family planning on the grounds that if implemented on a big scale, it will mean the extermination of one race or another. I do not think a properly planned programme of family planning will mean the extermination of any race. Control, solely, does not mean eradication or extermination.

Implicit in the government's actions is the theory that wider availability of family planning services will reduce the number of unwanted pregnancies and therefore illegal abortions. No government has so far committed itself to bringing about legal change in the availability of abortion. As mentioned earlier, this could be because of the religious, cultural, and moral views on abortion prevalent in the country.

CRIMINAL ABORTION—INCIDENCE AND MORTALITY

As the law stands in Sri Lanka, any abortion willfully induced with an intent other than that of saving the life of the mother amounts to criminal abortion. What has been stated regarding the accuracy of assessment of the incidence of abortion in general is even more true of criminal abortion; for in addition, there are the fears of criminal liability. In practice, indictment in cases of criminal abortion takes place only rarely; convictions are rarer still. This is illustrated by available figures from the Prisons Department, quoted by the Plan Implementation Ministry, according to which, between 1977 and 1981, there have been only seventeen convictions for abortion.

Atapattu (1983) presented more realistic figures at the Scientific Sessions of the College of Obstetricians and Gynaecologists in 1983. During the latter half of 1974, the number of women admitted to his hospital who had had abortions was 508. Of these, 8.0 percent were criminally induced abortions. During 1982 and the first half of 1983, the same hospital treated 222 cases of septic abortion, in 34.7 percent of which there was a history of "interference." The total number of inpatient days of treatment was 2,309, and surgery had to be performed in 85.1 percent.

Kodagoda analyzed the causes of death in a medico-legal unit during a specified period of time. The study investigated a total of 1,250 deaths, of which 494 were unnatural and 2.8 percent of these deaths from unnatural causes were due to abortions. In comparison, 38.9 percent of deaths were due to accidents. In this study all fourteen abortion deaths occurred in women between the ages of eighteen and thirty years, with the majority under twenty-five. At autopsy, 64.2 percent revealed genital lacerations, commonly in the region of the cervix, indicating mechanical interference by untrained hands. One of the cases had the instrument used still in situ. In one, a paste containing arsenic had been used to pack the vagina, presumably with the intention of causing irritation of the uterus, making it contract and expel its contents. In another, quinine had been used as an abortifacient.

The most common cause of death was hemorrhage. Next was infection, with five of the fourteen women dying of tetanus. The one in whom arsenic was used had absorbed enough of the drug to cause death before effective contractions of the uterus had begun.

The traditional methods used in Sri Lanka to induce nontherapeutic abortion are not different from those used in other parts of the developing world. Several local substances are believed to have abortifacient properties, the most common one being the unripe pineapple. The majority of other substances claimed to be abortifacient are, if at all, used by indigenous practitioners; however, very strong laxatives are sometimes used.

An "instrument" commonly used locally to disturb the intrauterine situation is the stalk of the common castor plant. It could be considered effective, if only judging from its popularity. The castor stem probably has a dual mode of action, first as a mechanical device and then as an irritant, by virtue of the latex it secretes. It is also easy to use (and difficult to detect) because of its smooth surface, suppleness, and small diameter which allows introduction into the uterus without the need for dilation.

SUMMARY

In Sri Lanka, the government has accepted fertility regulation as a priority measure for the promotion of health and develpment. This acceptance has superseded party political interests. The law on abortion, almost a century old, allows abortion only to save the life of the mother.

Public attitudes to abortion are highly culture bound, and, at least superficially, there appears to be resentment toward it. The mass media have not apparently adopted a firm policy on the subject.

The incidence of abortion is probably higher than is commonly thought. A rural survey places the figure for unwanted pregnancies where interference is sought at a minimum of 54 per 1,000 population per year.

Those seeking abortion are mostly young women, the majority having fewer than two children. The most common time at which they present for possible abortion is between five and eight weeks of amenorrhea. Most of these women seek abortion following contraceptive failure, because of economic reasons, because desired family size has been reached, or because the elder child is still too young. Convictions for criminal abortion have not been common; deaths, though small in number, are significant, the young being most at risk.

Over the past decade, attitudes toward the law on abortion, both among professionals and laypersons, have changed. Health and economic factors, contraceptive failure, rape, and incest are some of the reasons for which liberalization of abortion is suggested. The subject being of great religious, sociocultural, and political significance, it is likely that moves toward liberalization will take a long time to materialize.

REFERENCES

Atapattu, J. A. F. *Proceedings of the Sri Lanka College of Obstetricians and Gynaecologists.* 1983.

Atapattu, R. *Speech at the Third Asian and Pacific Population Conference.* Colombo, September 1982.

Ceylon Daily Mirror, 20 March 1981.

Family Planning Association at Sri Lanka. *Proceedings of the Seminar on Law and Population in Sri Lanka.* 1974.

————. *Proceedings of Seminar on Population Law and the Medical Profession, Colombo, 27 Nov. 1976.* Colombo, 1976.

Jayasuriya, D. C. *Attitudes to abortion law reform in Sri Lanka: Views of the medical and legal professions.* Report of the Seminar on Population Law and the Medical Profession in Sri Lanka, Colombo, 27 November 1976, 56–59.

Jayasuriya, D. C., & Kodagoda, N. *Population law for medical students.* Colombo: Family Plannsing Association of Sri Lanka, 1977.

Kodagoda, N. WHO/IPPF Multicentre survey on choice and use of contraceptives. 1983. (Unpublished.)

————. *Attitudes of doctors to abortion and family planning.* Colombo, Sri Lanka. Ministry of Information—Family Planning Communication Strategy Project, 1984.

Kodagoda, N., & Senanayoke, P. *Some aspects of abortion in Sri Lanka.* London: IPPF, 1982.

Ministry of Plan Implementation. *Perspectives on abortion in Sri Lanka.* Colombo: Ministry of Plan Implementation, 1983.

Penal Code (Cap.19), Secs. 303–307. Vol. 1, Revised (1956) edition of the Legislative Enactment of Sri Lanka.

Rajanayagam, S. The problem of illegal abortions in Sri Lanka. *Ceylon Medical Journal,* 1973, *18,* 123–129.

R. v. Fernando (1925), 27 *New Law Reports,* 181.

R. v. Waidyaskera (1955), 57 *New Law Reports,* 202.

Sri Lanka Foundation and United Nations Fund for Population Activities. Seminar on the Population Problems of Sri Lanka in the Seventies, 1975.

University of Sri Lanka, Department of Forensic Medicine, Sri Lanka Law and Population Project and FPA of Sri Lanka. Report of the Seminar on Population Law and the Medical Profession in Sri Lanka, Colombo, 27 November, 1976.

WHO Off Record, No. 21, 4th Plenary Session. *WHO 2nd world health assembly.* 13 June–2 July 1949, 84.

30

SWEDEN

Kajsa Sundström-Feigenberg

HISTORICAL DEVELOPMENT OF ABORTION POLICY

In Sweden, as in other European countries, in the past social control of fertility was rigorous. The only justification for sexuality—at least in women—was reproduction. Only marriage could render a child legitimate, and unmarried mothers were condemned by the church as well as by society. At the same time, inducing abortion was strictly forbidden. Once a woman became pregnant, she was expected to give birth. Consequently, the methods available for birth control were illegal abortion and infanticide, or giving away or neglecting the newborn. Contraceptive measures were regarded as sinful and contrary to nature.

Inducing abortion was still a crime at the beginning of this century, and both the sale of contraceptives and dispensing information about them were banned by law in 1910. It was not until 1938 that contraceptives could be discussed in public, and in the same year the first Abortion Act in Sweden stated that abortion could be permitted under certain conditions.

These two changes were part of an enlightened program of family policy in the wake of low birth rates in the 1930s. Alva and Gunnar Myrdal (1934) had written a book on Sweden's "population crisis" and proposed a number of social reforms to support the family, including maternity benefits, public maternal and child health care, and child allowances.

It was envisaged that social reforms would pave the way to a higher birth rate. For this purpose, efforts concentrated on improving the health of mothers and children. This drive included the promotion of family planning by making contraceptives as well as abortion (subject to certain condition) legal.

LEGAL STATUS OF ABORTION

The 1938 Abortion Act

The first Abortion Act, passed in 1938, remained in force with some some minor amendments until 1975. It stated that abortion was forbidden in principle but could be permitted for specific indications, namely, eugenic, humanitarian, or medical reasons.

The act stipulated that abortion prior to the twentieth week of pregnancy required approval by the National Board of Health and Welfare or joint approval by two physicians, and that after the twentieth week it always had to be approved by the central authority, that is, the board. The twenty-fourth week constituted an absolute limit, which could be exceeded only in cases where the woman's life or health was at risk.

Abortion was not allowed solely for social reasons. The indications restricted it to cases of hereditary disease, rape, or incest, or cases where the woman had a medical disease (e.g., severe heart failure or turberculosis) or was in a poor physical state after many childbirths. In those days an illegal abortion was still the only solution for most women with unwanted pregnancies, particularly those who were poor, young, and unmarried.

In 1946 the act was amended to admit a sociomedical indication. This was interpreted as physical or mental risk in the pregnant woman, or the prediction of such risk if she had to bear the child. It was also stipulated that a woman who wanted an abortion should have a consultation with a social worker. These abortion counselors were to investigate the woman's situation and scrutinize her reasons, help her to formulate her application, and append the social worker's own assessment. It was also expected that the social worker should offer social and economic assistance so that a woman could reconsider her decision or—as was often the case—provide her with support if her application was refused by the physician or the central board.

In 1963 "injury to the fetus" was added as a justification for abortion. This amendment was made after a test case had caused intense public debate in the United States and in Sweden. An American woman wanted an abortion because an interuterine infection meant that the fetus was liable to be malformed; having been refused in the States, she applied for and obtained the abortion in Sweden— and the Swedish legislation was changed.

Although the principle and the phrasing of the Abortion Act remained the same, the interpretation of the law and the handling of these cases in the health care system changed considerably over the years. In the 1950s, having an abortion was a long and often humiliating procedure. Having been assessed and examined by an obstetrician, a psychiatrist, and a social worker, the woman had to apply to the National Board of Health and Welfare whose approval might or—usually— might not be granted. Social circumstances, however adverse, never sufficed alone; there had to be medical reasons, too. Just by threatening to commit suicide or by obtaining a psychiatric diagnosis such as depression or mental instability, the woman could be sure of approval from the National Board.

The abortion consultations were free of charge in the public health system, and having obtained approval, a woman could be operated on without cost in a public hospital. But she might have to wait for a place and could have difficulty finding a doctor who was willing to do the operation. At some hospitals the chief obstetrician was an outspoken opponent of abortion and refused to admit such cases. Women with money and the right connections could pay for a private consultation with a psychiatrist and have the operation in one of the three or four private clinics in the country. For all those who were less well off, however, the only way out was a hazardous abortion by a quack or layperson.

In the early 1960s attitudes toward induced abortion were still very restrictive among physicians and the medical and health authorities. Many women went abroad, for example, to Poland, to get an abortion. These more or less organized abortion trips to Poland caused a fierce public debate, accompanied by growing opposition to the official policy from radical women's organizations and some liberal and left-wing politicians and progressive doctors. As a result, in 1965 the government appointed a subcommittee to review the legislation.

In the late 1960s and early 1970s a less strict interpretation of the law resulted in a rising number of induced abortions. This reflected a radical change in attitudes among people in general, the women concerned, and the medical establishment. There was a growing recognition of the legitimacy of interrupting a pregnancy that was not desired. ''I don't want a child right now'' or ''I don't want a child with that man'' were seen as acceptable reasons for requesting abortion. In the medical profession, where opposition to abortion had been fierce in the past, a growing number of doctors were implementing the law more liberally. Abortions certified by two doctors, without referral to the National Board, became increasingly common. The case would be handled by a psychiatrist and the obstetrician who subsequently undertook the operation. Social considerations were accepted as the sole ground in practice, accompanied by a psychiatric diagnosis to comply with the law. Most women, particularly teenagers, could count on getting an abortion if they turned to doctors in the public health service. But the procedure was liable to be protracted and demanding. The approach also differed in different parts of the country.

An important consequence of this altered policy was that it did away with illegal abortion. From the beginning of the 1970s onwards practically no illegal abortions have been performed in Sweden.

Preparation of New Legislation

The terms of reference for the governmental committee appointed in 1965 involved studying the application of the 1938 Abortion Act and considering alternatives for future legislation as well as measures by the public sector to prevent abortions. As is often the case in Swedish political life, the committee did a thorough job but took a long time to arrive at its conclusions. It was not until 1971 that the committee presented its report, ''The Right to Abortion.'' This report proposed that a woman should have an unconditional right, without any time limit, to decide that she should have an abortion. It also contained many suggestions about family planning services in the public health system.

The report was referred in the usual way to competent organizations and agencies. Many of these bodies found the proposals too radical. In the lively public debate that followed, however, wide acceptance was gradually gained for the principle that a decision about abortion was a matter for the woman.

The debate also stimulated demands that family planning services should be a public responsibility. Previously, family planning had not attracted a great deal of attention in the public health service. The introduction of oral contraceptives and IUDs in the mid–1960s involved an increased need for qualified medical services. There was a great demand for pills in particular, but access was restricted. Some doctors refused to prescribe contraceptives if the woman was young or single. Fees were high in private practice and public health alike, and contraceptives were expensive.

Opinions about abortion in the medical profession were of major importance in preparing the new legislation. The question was discussed in detail by the various organizations, particularly the Swedish Society of Gynecologists and Obstetricians. A fierce struggle was waged between opponents of abortion and advocates of ''abortion on demand.''

The disparate attitudes in the medical profession meant, as mentioned earlier, that the current Abortion Act was implemented differently in different parts of the country. The desirability of a uniform practice throughout Sweden was frequently advocated as one reason for amending the law.

The New Abortion Act

It was not until May 1974, after further preparation, adaptation, and revision of the proposals, that the Swedish Parliament approved the new legislation on abortion. The bill was passed by a fairly large majority, but there were differences of opinion in every political party and a minority voted against the bill. Parliament also approved proposals to step up efforts on behalf of services and information about family planning.

The main principle of the new Abortion Act, which came into force as of 1975, is that abortion is no longer a crime but free on demand. Briefly, the act specifies:

—If a woman asks for an abortion and the operation does not involve a risk to her life or health, the abortion may be carried out up to the end of the eighteenth week of pregnancy.

—Before the twelfth week, the woman need only consult a doctor. After that date, she is also required to discuss the matter with a social worker.

—For an abortion after the end of the eighteenth week of pregnancy, it is necessary to obtain the approval of the National Board of Health and Welfare, and there must be special grounds for this approval. Neither may such approval be granted if the fetus is judged to be viable.

The act also states that only a qualified physician is entitled to perform an abortion and that the operation must take place at a hospital or at medical institutions approved by the National Board of Health and Welfare.

The new act applies in principle only to women who are Swedish citizens or resident in the country. In special circumstances, however, the National Board can give permission for an abortion to a nonresident foreign national.

Efforts to Prevent Abortion

To encourage a buildup of family planning services, the new legislation on abortion was accompanied by the Act Concerning Compensation for Certain Birth Control Activities as well as a number of legislative amendments. The provision of grants from the public health insurance system meant that contraceptive services—in the public health care system as well as from private organizations and clinics—became free of charge for the person seeking advice. Contraceptives such as diaphragms and IUDs were dispensed without a charge; the price of oral contraceptives was limited in the same way as other drugs prescribed by a physician.

With government subsidies, a system of family planning services integrated with Maternity Health Care was built up all over Sweden. Special youth clinics have also been established at about thirty locations for all sorts of counseling, including contraceptive services. Boys and girls can also obtain advice about contraceptives from school physicians and school nurses.

Training of Midwives

To increase the effectiveness of the family planning services, a training program for midwives was initiated early in the 1970s. A shortage of doctors for health care was one reason for this program. Another was that many physicians considered family planning services to be less important or urgent than medical and health care in general.

Postgraduate training for midwives who were already practicing antenatal care in the Maternal Health System was arranged by the National Board of Health and Welfare. The same subjects were also integrated with the curriculum at schools of midwifery. All midwives who graduated after 1975 have studied family planning as part of their basic training.

After some additional in-service training, the midwife is entitled to run a family planning unit independently, providing services and information about all kinds of contraceptives, such as the insertion of IUDs, and instruction about barrier methods. In the event of complications, the midwife can consult the physician in charge at the Maternal Health Center.

Oral contraceptives cannot be obtained in Sweden without a prescription. To start with, trained midwives were not entitled to make out such prescriptions. If a woman asked for the pill, the midwife, after the consultation, prepared the prescription but it had to be signed by a doctor.

In 1978, following discussions with the physicians' professional organizations and with support from the obstetricians/gynecologists who were familiar with and appreciated the way midwives worked, the law was amended to give midwives with appropriate training the legal right to prescribe medical drugs for contraceptive use. This includes oral contraceptives as well as injectibles.

Of the 3,000 or so qualified midwives in Sweden, almost one-third work with antenatal care and contraceptive services in the Maternal Health Care system. More than 1,000 are now qualified to prescribe oral contraceptives in addition to other kinds of family planning services.

In their capacity as service providers, midwives are appreciated both by the doctors with whom they work and by those who require contraceptives. The midwives often attain better results—as regards both acceptance and continuation rates—than physicians working in this field. The midwives are easy to reach by appointment or for a telephone consultation. The fact that most of them are women also contributes to their popularity.

Midwives have performed very successfully in the family planning program. Since the beginning of the 1980s, they have been undertaking 70 percent of consultations on contraceptives in Sweden.

Public Information on Family Planning

When the Swedish Parliament approved the 1975 Abortion Act, it also allocated grants to the National Board of Health and Welfare for a five-year information program on family planning. The program was carried through by the board's Health Education Committee.

One component of the program concerned the production of basic information material on contraceptives, for health personnel as well as the public. Pamphlets, booklets, and periodicals were produced and adapted for those defined as target groups, for example, women after childbirth and abortion, adolescents, parents of teenagers, immigrants, and so on, but they were also aimed at the mass media, male politicians, teachers, youth leaders, and so on.

Methods for communication and information, aimed at motivating and influencing attitudes toward sexuality, gender roles, human relationships, and family planning, have been developed and tested in different settings. Local projects were initiated in some counties to supplement the more general forms of information to the public.

In one such broad family planning project, on the Island of Gotland in the Baltic, the buildup of contraceptive services was combined with intensive training and education of all categories of social, school, and health personnel. The intention here was to reach the public through the professionals—an education process that spreads the message like rings on water. An analysis of the results has been published as *Living Together* (1978).

Impact of the New Abortion Act

Many years of discussion and public debate preceded the new 1975 Abortion Act. In the meantime, people's attitudes toward abortion and family planning had changed considerably. The act can be said to have formalized a practice that had been implemented for some time in many parts of the country. It was therefore unlikely that, for instance, the abortion rate would change much, though many debaters had warned that free abortion would lead to an increase.

There were two main respects, however, in which the new act did change the situation. One concerns the completely new legal principle that there is nothing criminal about abortion. Every woman has the right to decide whether or not to have a child. Society and its representatives are not entitled either to initiate or refuse an abortion.

The other aspect concerns the vigorous efforts for preventive measures that accompanied the act. Society has assumed responsibility for family planning programs. Abortion on demand is accompanied by contraceptive services that are accessible and free of charge.

The provisions of the act and the preventive measures express the policy of society: the individual has the right to decide freely on the number and spacing of children. This means in turn that every child has the right to be wanted, and it is understood that this goal is to be attained in the first place with preventive measures, using abortion as a last resort.

As we will see, the abortion rate has not changed much since the new act became effective. What has changed is the procedure for examinations and care in connection with an abortion, resulting in less mental strain not only for the woman who undergoes an abortion, but also for the health service personnel who handle these cases.

DEMOGRAPHY OF ABORTION

Abortion Rates in Scandinavia

More liberal legislation on abortion has also been introduced in other Scandinavian countries in recent decades, though certain national differences do exist concerning the requirements for a legal abortion. Contraceptives are readily accessible in Scandinavia, and most people know about methods for birth control, for example, result of sex education in school.

The birth rate is falling in all these countries except Iceland. The methods in use for regulating fertility are the traditional and—to a growing extent—modern technical contraceptives, supplemented with induced abortion. Illegal abortion and journeys abroad to get an abortion are rare.

The development of abortion in the Nordic countries (see figure 30.1) is a clear illustration of the following finding in *Induced Abortion* (WHO, 1978): "Available data lend no support to the concern sometimes voiced that a large proportion of couples have abandoned contraceptive efforts after legal abortion has become more accessible." The report describes what happens when restrictive legislation is made more liberal: " . . . both induced abortion and contraceptive use increase, but while induced abortion may make a relatively large initial contribution to the decline in the birth rate, it is overtaken by contraception within a few decades" (p. 35).

Figure 30.1
Abortion Rates per 1,000 Women Fifteen to Forty-four Years of Age, Nordic Countries, 1968–81

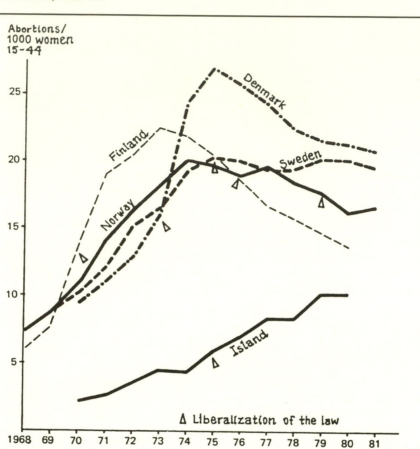

Source: *Family Planning and Abortion*. Report from the 1980 Abortion Committee, SOU, 1983.

The Nordic countries have evidently reached the stage where contraceptive use has become increasingly common and the abortion rate, after the initial increase, has remained constant or started to fall.

Nativity in Sweden has demonstrated a falling trend since the beginning of this century, punctuated by temporary increases. In the early 1930s the birth rate was lower than ever before. The annual number of births averaged 87,000, which represented a total fertility rate of 1.7 children per woman. Fertility picked up again in the mid–1930s and the rise continued in the 1940s.

The Situation under the First Abortion Act

In 1939, the first year in which the law permitted abortion, about 450 legal abortions were performed. Illegal abortions continued, of course, on a much larger scale. Their exact number is not known, but indirect estimates—based on the number of infected "spontaneous" abortions treated in hospital, samples from limited populations, court records, and so on—suggest that in the 1930s between 15,000 and 20,000 abortions were undertaken annually. During the 1940s the legal grounds for abortion were exercised more and more, and the number of legal abortions rose to more than 5,000 annually, giving a crude abortion rate of 0.7 per 1,000 population.

By the end of the 1940s, it is calculated that illegal abortions had decreased to 10,000 annually. After that, they increased again as the Abortion Act was implemented more strictly and the number of legal abortions fell. In 1951 more than 6,000 legal abortions were performed, giving a crude abortion rate of 0.9, and a decade later the number had been more than halved to a crude rate of 0.4 (table 30.1). This was accompanied by a diminishing birth rate in the 1950s, from 15.2 to 13.9 births per 1,000 population. Still, the decrease was somewhat smaller than might have been expected, in that it was the small birth cohorts from the 1930s that reached fertile age at this time.

Big Changes in the Sixties . . .

The medical establishment's restrictive implementation of the abortion law led, as mentioned, to strong opposition in the early 1960s. When the handling of abortion applications had been changed in the mid–1960s, the number of approved abortions increased markedly.

In 1966 the abortion rate climbed back to the level in the early 1950s, 0.9 per 1,000 total population. More than 7,000 legal abortions were performed in that year, while five years later the number had reached almost 20,000, giving a crude abortion rate of 2.4.

It was not until the mid–1960s that illegal abortions started to decrease appreciably. In 1965 they are estimated to have totaled about 5,000 (Pettersson, 1968). The number fell continuously after that, and by the early 1970s it can be said that the statistics on legal abortions reflect the real number of interrupted pregnancies in Sweden.

The birth rate rose in the first half of the 1960s from around 14 to 16 per 1,000 total population. It then fell very sharply, however, in 1968 and 1969. This development is reproduced in figure 30.2, which gives a picture of total fertility and abortion rates. It will be seen that in these two years in the late 1960s the abortion rate rose but not to the same extent as the number of births fell. The result was a drop in the number of registered pregnancies per woman.

In this context it can be mentioned that when the modern methods of birth control—oral contraceptives and IUDs—became available in the mid–1960s,

Figure 30.2
Average Number of Children and Abortions per Woman, Sweden, 1962–82

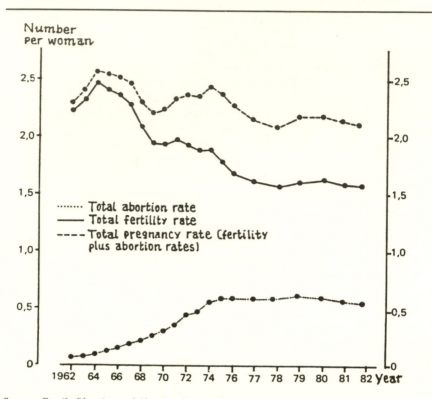

Source: *Family Planning and Abortion*. Report from the 1980 Abortion Committee, SOU, 1983.

they were adopted very quickly. By 1969 the pill was being used by almost 400,000 women, almost one in four of all women aged fifteen to forty-four years.

... and More So in the 1970s

The age-specific pregnancy rate (the sum of abortions and births) rose in the early 1970s, reflecting a strong increase in legal abortions, which was partly a consequence of the shift from illegal abortions. The total fertility rate declined slowly, to 1.9 in 1974, followed by a more appreciable fall in nativity. The combination of a rising abortion rate and a falling birth rate in this period meant that the abortion ratio per 100 live births doubled from 16.8 in 1971 to 32.9 in 1976 (table 30.1).

From 1975 to 1978 there was a steep fall in the birth rate. The number of births dropped below 100,000 in 1976, when the total fertility rate was 1.7 per woman. In 1978 the fertility rate was 1.6 or even less than the low from the

1930s. In 1979 and 1980 the number of births picked up slightly but then began falling once more. In 1982 there were 92,000 births, giving a total fertility rate of 1.62.

The sharp increase in abortions in the first half of the 1970s has been followed since 1975 by a fairly constant rate of around 32,000 abortions a year, giving a crude abortion rate of 4.0 per 1,000 total population. A slight increase in the period 1979–81 is largely explained by a greater number of women of fertile age in those years.

The general abortion rate per 1,000 women of reproductive age (fifteen to forty-four years) was 20.2 in 1975, followed by a maximum of 20.7 in 1979 and a minimum of 18.9 in 1982, which dropped further to 17.7 in 1984 (table 30.2). The corresponding general fertility rate fell from 64.4 births per 1,000 women (fifteen to forty-four years) in 1975 to 53.7 in 1982.

The abortion ratio per 100 live births has ranged between 30 and 35 since the mid–1970s, that is, 1 abortion per 3 births. At the beginning of the 1970s, there was 1 legal abortion per 6 live births. Thus, the average number of abortions per woman today is 0.6. Together with an average of 1.6 births, this gives us a total pregnancy rate of 2.2 per woman.

Age-Related Abortion Rates

Since 1975 when the new legislation made abortion on demand available, the general abortion rate has stabilized, but there are some differences between age groups. The abortion rate fell from 29.7 in 1975 to 17.6 in 1984 among young women aged nineteen or less and increased from 23 to 24.1 during the same period among those at the end of their fertile period. The trend is clearest for those under twenty, whose age-specific abortion rate has decreased continuously. In the age group twenty to twenty-four years, where abortion peaks in absolute as well as relative terms, the rate has been fairly stable (around 27), apart from a slight increase in 1980 when it was 28.5 abortions per 1,000 women. In this five-year group, the rate is highest for twenty year olds and decreases with age. Nativity is high in this age group, but more and more twenty-year-old women are choosing to have their first child later than was customary some decades ago. In recent years there has been a shift in nativity from the early twenties to twenty-seven to thirty-two years of age, which reflects a general tendency to postpone childbearing.

On the average, the abortion rate has been stable in the twenty- to thirty-four year band, whereas it has increased slightly among women over thirty-five. Since the latter group has a very low total pregnancy rate, the effect on the general abortion rate is slight.

Among women over twenty-five, the abortion rate increased temporarily in 1979 and 1980, but in 1981 and 1982 it decreased again toward the level from 1978.

To illustrate the pattern of abortions at different stages in a woman's life and

Figure 30.3
**Abortions in Percentage of the Total Number of Pregnancies (Live Births and
Legal Abortions Half a Year Earlier), One-Year Groups Fifteen to Forty-four
Years of Age, Sweden, 1970, 1975, and 1981**

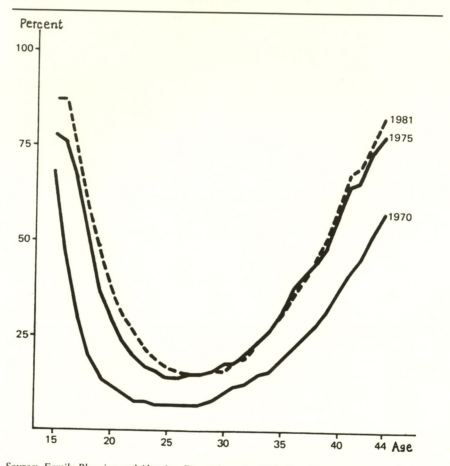

Source: *Family Planning and Abortion*. Report from the 1980 Abortion Committee, SOU, 1983.

how it has changed in the past decade, figure 30.3 shows the number of abortions
as a percentage of all known pregnancies in 1970, 1975, and 1981.

As one might expect, the proportion of pregnancies that are interrupted is
greatest among the youngest and the oldest women. It is smallest between the
ages of twenty-four and twenty-six years, which is when most pregnancies occur
as well as when most women wish to have their children.

From 1970 to 1975 the abortion percentage rose in practically all age groups,
whereas the changes from 1975 to 1981 were slight. In the latter period, however,
the proportion of abortions continued to rise among women under twenty-five
and over thirty-eight, respectively. Nowadays a majority of women in these age

groups try to avoid pregnancy and tend to choose an abortion if they do become pregnant. Of all pregnant eighteen year olds, 20 percent had an abortion in 1970, 50 percent in 1975, and 60 percent in 1981. In the case of thirty-eight year olds, one in three chose to interrupt the pregnancy in 1970, while one in two did so in 1975 and 1981.

REPEAT ABORTIONS

The statistics show that the proportion of women who have more than one abortion has been rising. Of the women who had an abortion in 1984, 33.5 percent had undergone an abortion before. Two-thirds of the latter group had had one previous abortion, and the others (10 percent of all women having an abortion in that year) had already had two or more abortions.

Women whose earlier abortion were illegal do not appear in the statistics on recurrent abortions. With the prevailing tendency and the complete registration of all abortions, the proportion of women with more than one abortion during their fertile life will increase. Like the relatively high abortion rate, this has to do with attitudes to birth control and family size. Most women today are not prepared to accept more than two children and if contraceptives fail, they prefer an abortion to completing an unplanned pregnancy.

The probability of a woman finding herself in an abortion situation increases if she has had an abortion before (Tietze & Jain, 1978; Tietze & Henshaw, 1986). Whereas first abortions occur and are computed in relation to the total population of women of fertile age, the repeat abortions belong in a population that consists of proven fertile, sexually active women who use contraceptives and bear children to an extent that exceeds the average for women of fertile age and who have already considered and accepted abortion as a solution to an undesired pregnancy.

GEOGRAPHICAL AND ETHNIC DIFFERENCES

Family structures and fertility patterns differ in different parts of Sweden, and abortion and birth rates also display regional variations. The abortion rate is highest in the three metropolitan areas, just as there are other urban, industrial districts where it is higher than in the surrounding rural areas.

The lowest abortion rates, often combined with a relatively high birth rate, are to be found in some agricultural districts in the south of Sweden and in a sparsely populated county in the far north. These areas are similar in cultural and socioeconomic respects and have a free church tradition.

Some immigrant groups have an above-average abortion rate. Recent immigrants from countries in the eastern Mediterranean have an abortion rate that is approximately twice that of other women in Sweden. This reflects different attitudes toward sexuality and family planning. As contraceptives are difficult to obtain in those countries, birth control is commonly practiced with abortion (usually illegal).

Immigrant groups, including those from countries outside Europe, who have spent some time in Sweden do not differ, however, from the rest of the population as regards birth rates, abortion rates, and the use of contraceptives. The same is true of immigrants from the other Nordic countries, of whom Finns are the largest group.

EARLY AND LATE ABORTION

Abortion before the Eighteenth Week of Pregnancy

The procedure for an abortion has been simplified in recent years, and abortions are being done at an increasingly early stage of pregnancy. This development has been promoted by a general awareness that abortion is a right and that the risk involved is smaller if the abortion is done early.

The mean duration of pregnancy at termination dropped from 14.1 weeks in 1968 to 9.9 weeks in 1980. In 1968 about 40 percent of all abortions were performed before the end of the twelfth week of gestation. By 1984 the figure had risen to more than 95 percent, using vacuum aspiration, which involves a minimum of strain and risk for the woman. More than 80 percent of all abortions were done on an outpatient basis.

The abortion procedure is an integral part of general gynecological care. The patient's fee for the first consultation is the same as for other outpatient gynecological care, and hospital costs are fully covered by public health insurance.

A woman who is considering an abortion can turn to a gynecologist or a general practitioner in the primary health care system or apply directly to a gynecology clinic at a hospital. If she so wishes, an appointment can always be arranged with a social worker so that she can talk the matter over.

The operation is performed at a hospital. If the pregnancy is in an early stage, vacuum aspiration is done and the woman usually goes home the same day. For an abortion in the second trimester, the woman stays in the hospital and labor is induced with saline solution or prostaglandin; after the expulsion, followed if necessary by instrumental evacuation, she stays on for a day or so.

Contraceptive services are always offered, and if the woman wants to have an IUD, this will be inserted after the evacuation.

Abortion after the Eighteenth Week of Pregnancy

The Abortion Act gives women the right to abortion on demand until the end of the eighteenth week of pregnancy. An abortion later in pregnancy requires approval from the National Board of Health and Welfare.

Today late abortions make up a very small share of the total. In 1971 abortions after the end of the eighteenth week still made up almost 6 percent (1,000 abortions); in 1982 the share had fallen to 0.8 percent or 250 abortions.

From 1975 onwards about 400 women a year applied for a late abortion under "especially compelling reasons," for example, fetal damage, diagnosed by amniocentesis, severe social problems, or low age. Approximately 80 percent of the applications were usually approved, and between 250 and 350 late abortions were done each year. Since 1980 the number of applications based on the youth and immaturity of the woman has decreased, whereas those citing established fetal damage have increased. Of the 250 late abortions that were done in 1982, approval was granted for 70 owing to injury to the fetus.

ABORTION AND FERTILITY REGULATION

Fertility Patterns and Use of Contraceptives

With the family planning and family patterns that prevail in Sweden, the number of abortions is bound to be relatively high. Statistically, the average woman has 1.6 children and 0.6 abortions in her lifetime. As some women have several abortions, it is approximately true to say that one woman in two in Sweden will have at least one abortion. In other words, abortions are not associated with women of a particular type. Every woman is liable to consider an abortion.

In 1982 the situation concerning birth control was as follows:

Births: 93,000

Abortions: 32,600

Contraceptives used by 1.1 million women and/or their partners, of whom approximately

400,000 or 36 percent used oral contraceptives.

300,000 or 28 percent used IUDs.

250,000 or 23 percent used condoms.

60,000 or 5 percent used spermicides.

45,000 or 4 percent used diaphragms.

45,000 or 4 percent were sterilized.

It will be seen that the birth rate is low and the use of contraceptives high. Society condones sexuality in youth and extramarital relations. It is usual for women, including those with young children, to go out to work.

Most women have sexual relationships from their teens onward and give birth to one or two children at the most. It follows that couples in general have to prevent an undesired pregnancy over a period of twenty-five to thirty years. Even with modern contraceptives and their widespread use, there is bound to be a risk of conception occurring at some time during such a long period. In addition, the efficiency of any contraceptive method is an individual matter and depends in large measure on the motivation of the user and the couple's fertility.

Highly fertile women may fail time and again, even though they are extremely careful and use a contraceptive that is very reliable in theory.

As we have seen, more than 1 million couples in Sweden use contraceptives—mainly those that are highly effective. In practice, it is inevitable that some of them will fail in their efforts to avoid pregnancy. A failure rate of 5 percent, which is a low figure, is equivalent to 50,000 undesired or at least unplanned pregnancies. In other words, the abortion rate in a particular population is dependent not only on access to contraceptives and proper foresight, but also on the extent to which unplanned pregnancies are tolerated. This depends in turn on the society and the age in which we are living.

ABORTION AND ADOLESCENTS

The process of industrialization and urbanization in recent decades has been accompanied by changes in the sexual behavior of young people, leading to an increasing number of abortions and young, single mothers. Teenage pregnancies are causing concern in many countries. In Sweden one of the strongest motives for the preventive measures that accompanied the new Abortion Act was the rapidly increasing abortion rate among teenagers in the early 1970s.

Not long ago, attitudes in Sweden were entirely different toward youth sexuality and toward young people living together. In the 1950s a teenage girl who became pregnant was expelled from school and had little chance of getting a legal abortion. Many young girls resorted to illegal abortion or in their desperation committed suicide, so as not to bring shame on their parents.

in the 1960s parents tended to react in a more supportive manner. They tried to help their pregnant daughter and arranged a marriage as soon as possible with the boyfriend—without asking the girl what she wanted. Grandmother looked after the baby so that the girl could finish her schooling.

Since the mid–1970s the situation of a pregnant girl has changed again. It is no longer a social disgrace to be a young, unmarried mother. A pregnant teenager can readily obtain an abortion, but if she does decide to keep the baby, she will have to look after it herself without assistance from her family. She can decide—without the earlier pressure from society—whether she prefers to live alone or with the child's father.

As mentioned earlier, the trend for teenage pregnancies changed during the 1970s. A rapid increase in abortions and a decrease in births in the early 1970s were followed by a fall for both. Since 1975 both the abortion rate and the birth rate for women under twenty have decreased year by year. This falling trend for teenage pregnancies, which is also apparent to some extent in other Scandinavian countries but not, for instance in the United States, indicates an altered attitude toward sexuality and a change in contraceptive behavior among teenagers.

The complexity of the situation is evident from the fact that the late 1970s were characterized by more sexual activity among adolescents, reduced frequency of venereal diseases, better use of contraception, higher incidence of unmarried mothers, and rising unemployment among young women.

The multifactorial course of changes in fertility patterns and contraceptive behavior among teenagers requires further study. It seems that young people today manage to prevent unwanted pregnancies more effectively than a decade ago. Since Sweden has had twenty-five years of compulsory sex education in school, there must be more to this than knowledge about sexual relations and contraceptives.

One important factor may be the long-term health education program that the government initiated in 1975 to reduce the number of abortions and influence attitudes about sexuality and living together. Teenagers have been one of the main target groups in this program.

EVALUATION OF THE 1975 ABORTION ACT

In the early years there was no substantial opposition to the new abortion legislation, and it seemed that abortion on demand had been more or less accepted by the medical establishment and people in general. At the end of the 1970s, however, resistance to abortion grew, as in other Western countries, and organizations were formed to combat free abortion actively and have the law changed.

These groups tended to borrow arguments from U.S. counterparts such as pro-life movements and Right-to-Life. In general, however, resistance to abortion was relatively weak in Sweden. Still there was an occasion in 1979 when some leading politicians expressed anxiety about the development of abortions and a desire for a return to earlier legislation. This evoked vigorous protests, not least from women in their own parties.

In 1980 the government appointed a parliamentary committee to evaluate the 1975 Abortion Act. The terms of reference involved reviewing the consequences of the act and the preventive measures that had been linked to it. In particular, the committee was to consider what the act had meant for women, their partners, and health care personnel, besides describing the frequency of abortions, the organization and quality of the care system for abortion, and the efforts that have been and are being made to avoid abortion. But neither the time limits under the act nor the principle that abortion is a woman's right were to be questioned.

The Abortion Committee presented its final report in June 1983 in a book called *Family Planning and Abortion*. Starting from a wealth of background material on family planning and abortion, the committee's report concludes that the Abortion Act has resulted in a number of improvements, not least for women facing an abortion situation as well as for health care personnel.

The committee found that the overall abortion rate had not increased and noted with approval that teenage pregnancies had fallen sharply throughout the 1970s and that, with the new act, the number of teenage abortions had decreased continuously since 1975.

The committee established that, contrary to what some politicians and observers had feared, abortion is not used deliberately as an alternative to contraceptives. The pregnancy rate has been falling for a number of years without a corresponding increase in abortion. The report also observes that the procedure for an abortion is now simpler, and the strain is considerably less for the women who consider and have an abortion.

The committee believes that the trend toward earlier abortion confers great medical and psychological advantages on the woman. Early outpatient abortions are also less of a mental strain for health care personnel and incur less public expenditure.

The committee found that the quality of advisory services differs between different parts of the country and tends to concentrate on providing support *before* the abortion. The committee considered that increased support must be provided for the woman and that, to achieve its purpose, it must have a voluntary foundation in the woman's wishes and needs. Consideration should also be paid to the need to support the partner as well as health care personnel. With regard to preventive measures, the report notes that contraceptive services have been greatly extended.

With continued drive for contraceptive services and purposeful, outreaching education work, the committee considers that under favorable conditions it will be possible to make further progress in preventing undesired pregnancies and reducing the present abortion rate.

The evaluation of the Abortion Act and the committee's ample documentation of the favorable development since 1975 have been of great importance in refuting opponents of abortion with factual arguments.

REFERENCES

Familjeplanering och abort: Erfarenheter av ny lagstiftning. Stockholm: The 1980 Abortion Committee, 1983. SOU, 1983, 31.

Living together: A family planning project on Gotland. Sweden, 1973–76. Stockholm: National Board of Health and Welfare, 1978.

Myrdahl, A., & Myrdahl, G. *Kris i befolkningsfrågan.* Stockholm: Albert Bonniers förlag, 1934.

Pettersson, F. *Epidemiology of early pregnancy wastage.* Stockholm: Norstedt, 1968.

Rätten till abort. Stockholm: The 1965 Abortion Committee, 1971. SOU, 1971, 58.

Sundström-Feigenberg, K. *Fri abort och frivilligt föräldrarskap.* Läkartidningen 1980, 77, 522–525.

Tietze, C., & Henshaw, S. K. *Induced abortion: A world review, 1986* (6th ed.) New York: Alan Guttmacher Institute, 1986.

Tietze, C., & Jain, K. The mathematics of repeat abortion: Explaining the increase. *Studies in Family Planning,* 1978 9 (12), 294–299.

WHO. *Induced Abortion.* WHO Technical Report, Series No. 623. Geneva, 1978.

Official statistics of Sweden
Abortions, 1978. (SM HS 1980:8). Socialstyrelsen, Stockholm.
Abortions, 1980. (SM HS 1982:5). Socialstyrelsen, Stockholm.
Abortions, 1982. (SM HS 1983:9). Socialstyrelsen, Stockholm.
Annual reports on population: Befolkningsförändringar, 1982 (1–3) SCB. Stockholm,
    1983; Folkmängd, 31 December 1982. (1–3) SCB.

Table 30.1
Number of Live Births, Birth Rates, Number of Abortions, Abortion Rates, and Abortion Ratios, Selected Years, 1951–84

| | Live Births | | Abortions | | |
Year	Number	Rate/1000 Total Popul	Number	Rate/1000 Total Popul	Ratio/100 Live Births
1951	110,200	15.5	6,300	0.9	5.7
1956	108,000	14.7	3,900	0.5	3.6
1961	104,500	13.9	2,900	0.4	2.8
1966	123,400	15.9	7,300	0.9	5.9
1971	114,500	14.3	19,300	2.4	16.8
1976	98,300	11.9	32,400	3.9	32.9
1981	94,000	11.2	33,300	4.0	35.4
1982	–	–	32,600	3.9	35.3
1983	–	–	31,000	3.7	33.4
1984	–	–	30,800	3.7	32.8

Source: Official Statistics, National Central Bureau of Statistics, S–11581 Stockholm, Sweden; Tietze & Henshaw, 1986.

Table 30.2
Number of Live Births, Birth Rates, Number of Abortions, Abortion Rates, and Abortion Ratios, 1975–84

Year	Live Births Number	Live Births Rate/1000 Women 15–44	Abortions Number	Abortions Rate/1000 Women 15–44	Ratio/100 Live Births
1975	103,600	64.4	32,500	20.2	31.4
1976	98,300	60.7	32,400	20.0	32.9
1977	96,000	58.8	31,500	19.3	32.8
1978	93,200	56.4	31,900	19.3	34.2
1979	96,200	57.3	34,700	20.7	36.1
1980	97,000	57.4	34,900	20.6	35.9
1981	94,000	55.1	33,300	19.5	35.4
1982	92,700	53.7	32,600	18.9	35.2
1983	–	–	31,000	17.9	33.4
1984	–	–	30,800	17.7	32.8

Source: Official Statistics, National Central Bureau of Statistics, S–11581 Stockholm, Sweden.

31

UNITED KINGDOM

Colin Francome

The law in operation in England, Wales, and Scotland is the Abortion Act of 1967. Although this law does not give women the right to choose an abortion, the grounds for abortion are wide and practice is relatively liberal. There are currently several areas of controversy, one of which is whether the time limit should be reduced. Currently, this stands at twenty-eight weeks in England and Wales, being governed by the Infant Life Preservation Act of 1929. There is no upper time limit in Scotland. A second area of debate is whether the act should be extended to give women the right to choose an abortion up to a specific time in pregnancy. This is the aim of various women's groups and some doctor's organizations. A third area of concern is about facilities for the provision of abortion. Many people believe that extra funds should be provided to allow more abortions through the National Health Service. They argue that poor women are put to great financial hardship having to seek abortions in the private sector or within one of the charitable abortion services. In Northern Ireland the 1967 Abortion Act does not apply, and so the country is still controlled by the Offences Against the Person's Act of 1861. Abortion is available for such conditions as rape or incest. Eire was governed by the same law until 1983 when abortion was prohibited by the Constitution after a referendum.

HISTORICAL DEVELOPMENT OF ABORTION POLICY

Until 1803 abortion was legal at least until quickening, the time when movement is felt; indeed, some argued that it was legal throughout pregnancy (Means, 1971). The act of 1803 was part of a very restrictive measure known as the Irish Chalking Act which introduced the death sentence for a whole range of offenses. This act was amended on two occasions before the 1861 Offences Against the Person's Act. In one amendment, Section 58, any pregnant woman who intended to "unlawfully" administer to herself any poison or noxious thing or any person who tried to unlawfully abort a woman whether or not she was pregnant by giving her any poison or other noxious thing would be liable to be kept in penal servitude for life. Section 59 provided that whosoever lawfully supplied or procured any poison or other noxious thing for an abortion would be guilty of a misdemeanor and have a liability to three years' imprisonment.

The wording of the act seems to imply that the main concern was against the abortifacient herbs and pills that were sold in the nineteenth century. A common drug for the use of abortion was saving oil of juniper. There is some controversy about the extent of abortion in the first part of the nineteenth century. In 1837 Professor D. Thomson said that the medicines taken to procure abortion sometimes worked but that he felt the incidence was rare. However, seven years later a doctor wrote to the *British Medical Journal*'s predecessor, saying that he had attended three unmarried females who had used herbs to abort and that the number of cases was increasing (Francome, 1984a, p. 32). By the middle of the century, it seems that abortifacient pills were well established, and an editorial in the *Lancet* (30 July 1853) reported that handbills about pills were dropped down in the kitchen areas addressed to the domestic help. The 1861 act does not seem to have reduced the sale of pills at all. In fact, at the turn of the century the *Lancet* began a great campaign against newspapers that advertised pills, and in its 25 February 1899 it reported it had discovered over a hundred newspapers containing such advertisements.

Although abortions were occurring, there was no real debate about them. The two groups that might have been expected to fight for abortion rights were the socialists and the neo-Malthusians. However, the socialists were opposed to fertility control on the grounds that what was needed was radical change in the social structure, and the neo-Malthusians pressed for contraception which they felt would eliminate the need for abortion. After the First World War, the neo-Malthusians increasingly supported abortion, and the first recorded call for legalization was published in the *Malthusian* in March 1915. The author of the article was Stella Browne who was a feminist socialist as well as a neo-Malthusian. She was involved with various attempts by women's groups to extend the law. In 1934 she was active in persuading the annual meeting of Cooperative women, attended by 1,360 delegates, to call on the government to amend the abortion laws and to give amnesty to women in prison for these offenses (*New Generation*, 1934, p. 78). In 1936 the Abortion Law Reform Association (ALRA) was set up to work for an extension of the law. It had its first success two years later through a challenge to the law. At least from the First World War, legal abortions were carried out for women who could afford to visit Harley Street doctors. However, ALRA wanted the law to be extended more formally to allow abortion for rape. Aleck Bourne, a consultant at St. Mary's Hospital in London, agreed to help. In 1938 a teenager under the age of fifteen was raped by two soldiers in Whitehall and became pregnant. Bourne aborted her and the police were informed. He was charged with performing an illegal abortion but was acquitted and the decision passed into English case-law. It is this Bourne Amendment to the 1861 act that is now in operation in Northern Ireland.

After the Second World War, there was renewed pressure to liberalize the British law. A number of bills were introduced without much chance of success until David Steel introduced his in 1966. ALRA was the major pressure group working for the change, and it set out to decide whether or not to work for a woman's right to choose an abortion or whether simply to extend the grounds. After a meeting at the House of Lords in 1964, it decided to pursue an extension of the grounds. There were a number of reasons why Steel's bill succeeded while others failed. First, the climate of opinion was more sympathetic, and politically the Labour government was friendly to reform. The husband of the chairwoman of ALRA was in fact in the cabinet. The timing of the election meant that the parliamentary session was unusually long, and so there was time for the measure to succeed. The main opposition to the bill came from the antiabortion pressure group, the Society for the Protection of Unborn Children (SPUC), and from the medical profession. A short time before the second reading of the bill, the Royal College of Gynecologists produced a report suggesting that a major change in the law was not necessary because its members would not hesitate to perform an abortion if continuation of the pregnancy would be detrimental to the physical or mental welfare of the woman.

A number of debates arose about the facts surrounding abortion. One was over the number of illegal operations. David Glass (1940) estimated that there were around 100,000 illegal abortions a year, and this figure was the one most widely quoted. However, the antiabortionists argued this was an overestimate. They also argued that it was more dangerous to have an abortion than to continue the pregnancy, and it was this argument that seems to have affected the final wording of the British law. As women were not being given the right to choose an abortion, the question arose as to what was the acceptable risk to a woman's health for her to be allowed a legal abortion under the terms of the act. Lord Parker, the lord chief justice, who was generally opposed to the bill, argued that to use phrases like "grave risk" or "serious risk" would cause problems of definition in the courts. He proposed that abortion should be legal if the risk to life or to health was greater by continuing the pregnancy than by ending it. Now if abortion were more dangerous than childbirth as the antiabortionists were claiming, it would mean abortion would only be carried out in very restricted circumstances. However, if, as many would argue, abortion is more safe than childbirth, then a woman would always have grounds for an abortion under the terms of the act.

The act received the Royal Assent in October 1967 and became effective on 27 April 1968. Three years after its introduction, Peter Huntingford, a well-known gynecologist, announced that he was performing "abortion on demand" and that this was legal under the terms of the act (Francome, 1984a, p. 169). Others have followed suit but with less publicity. However, the terms of the act also allowed people to opt out of performing abortions if they had a conscientious objection, and in some areas it is difficult to gain access to the operation.

Antiabortionists have made numerous attempts to restrict the act. The main one was in 1979 when John Corrie, MP for Bute and North Ayrshire, introduced a bill. It failed to become law, however, and the antiabortionists' best chance at restriction had gone.

Debate in Ireland

In Eire a significant change occurred in 1974 when the Supreme Court ruled that a law forbidding the importation of contraceptives was unconstitutional. A group of campaigners went by train to the north and came back waving their purchases with the police just standing by. After a long debate, a bill became operative in November 1980 which allowed the sale of contraceptives for the first time. However, there were still a number of restrictions, and even nonmedical kinds of birth control were to be available only on doctor's prescription and purchased at a chemist's. In February 1980 the Woman's Right to Choose Campaign was set up, and a few months later British SPUC sent two representatives and so Irish SPUC was launched. In April 1981 the Pro Life Amendment Campaign (PLAC) was established and initially proposed to guarantee "the absolute right to life of every unborn child." However, it had to be modified as it did not allow for procedures like an ectopic pregnancy which the Catholic church allowed. In the end the amendment was worded: "The state acknowledges the right to life of the unborn and with due regard to the equal right to life of the mother guarantees in its laws to respect, and, as far as practicable by its laws to vindicate and defend that right."

A reason for introducing the amendment at a time when abortion was already illegal was provided by antiabortion activist John O'Reilly who said, "The Pro Life amendment to the Constitution was the answer to the abortion problem in Ireland. It must be won while the vast majority of the Irish people were still opposed to abortion and while abortion was not too politically divisive" (*Irish Catholic*, 1 April 1982).

In the end, the amendment did raise a great deal of debate and controversy. The major Protestant and Jewish groups objected to Catholic doctrine being written so explicitly into law. Abortion, contraception, and sexuality were discussed openly for the first time and in a way that would have been unthinkable a few years earlier. Voting was held on 7 September 1983, with just over half the electorate voting. The majority in favor of the amendment was 2 to 1, and so it seems that Irish women seeking abortion will have to continue traveling to Britain.

In Northern Ireland the Ulster Pregnancy Advisory Service was started by an English woman in 1971. In the spring of 1980 the Northern Ireland Abortion Campaign (NIAC) was set up and began campaigning to extend the 1967 Abortion Act. However, their progress is likely to be inhibited as eleven out of twelve Northern Irish MPs oppose the extension of abortion rights; since direct rule,

the British government has felt it should not change the law without evidence
of broad support from people in the province.

ATTITUDES TOWARD ABORTION

In 1985 Marplan was commissioned to carry out an opinion poll on abortion.
The interviewing was conducted during 23–28 May on a quota sample of 1,493
people. The exact question was: "Do you think that the choice as to whether
or not to continue a pregnancy should or should not be left to the woman in
consultation with her doctor?" The responses are presented in table 31.1.

The results show that nearly four people out of five supported the right of the
woman to choose after consultation with a doctor, while only just over one in
ten opposed the right. Women were 5 percent more likely to support the right
to choose than were men. This question has now been asked on five separate
occasions, and on only one of these has the men's support for the right to choose
been higher than the women's and then it was only by 2 percent in 1982.

The replies to the question by age showed a curious division, with the greatest
support for abortion rights in the middle-age ranges and less support among the
young and the old. In fact, the percentage of those in the middle-age range
agreeing with the question is the highest on record, while that of the over sixty-
fives is the lowest from the five polls. The reason is not clear, but a clue is
given by the number of older people who replied "don't know." The over sixty-
fives were four times as likely to reply this way than were those in the twenty-
five to forty-four age group.

The Gallup Poll commissioned in 1983 in conjunction with ALRA provided
details of the attitude breakdown according to social class. In Britain four categories of class are normally given. They are upper middle (AB), lower middle
(C1), upper working (C2), and lower working (DE). On each previous occasion
the DE group of semiskilled and unskilled workers have taken a less liberal line
on abortion. This poll proved to be no exception. Seventy percent said women
should be able to make the choice, compared to 74 percent of the total sample.
Nearly one in five (19 percent) said women should not be able to make the
choice, and 12 percent said they did not know.

One of the interesting questions is how far religion affects attitudes toward
abortion. Religion was not asked in this latest poll, but it was in the 1979 and
1982 Gallup studies. The answer to the question about whether the decision on
an abortion should be left to the woman in consultation with her doctor is
presented in table 31.2.

The results showed that more than two-thirds of each of the denominations
support abortion rights. However, in some cases the figures come from a small
base, and people may identify with a group even when not practicing. Catholics
were the group most opposed to abortion rights, and more than one in four were
against the right to choose.

One of the problems with opinion polls on abortion is that the wording of the questions and the number of categories available can make great difference to the replies. In 1980 Gallup in Britain, Ireland, and the United States asked a very similar question which is useful for comparative purposes. In the United States and Ireland the question was, "Do you think abortion should be legal under any circumstances, only under certain circumstances, or illegal in all circumstances?" In Britain the phrase "legal under any circumstances" was replaced by "available on demand" but otherwise was identical. The replies are analyzed in table 31.3.

The results show that the percentage of people who agreed with abortion in all circumstances or on demand is much lower than for the question in the previous survey. This is in part due to the wording. The most ardent supporters of abortion could think of circumstances in which they would not agree to a legal abortion—for example, if it were against the woman's wishes or if the medical care would be inadequate. Moreover, the use of three categories makes the middle one "legal in certain circumstances" appear moderate. What is of interest in the results, however, is the great variation between the countries. In 1980 the percentage of people who said abortion should be illegal in all circumstances was 12 percent in Britain, 18 percent in the United States, 63 percent among Northern Ireland Catholics, and 80 percent in Eire. Such a wide variation to the same wording is very surprising. Less than one in eight British people thought abortion should be totally illegal compared to four out of five in Eire.

In a 1983 poll commissioned for SPUC, it was found that the percentage of British people disagreeing with abortion in all circumstances had fallen to 8 percent or one in twelve of the population. The percentage of people who agreed that abortion should be "available on demand" had risen to 26 percent. This suggests a liberalization of attitudes in the past few years, although this was not found in the first series of surveys discussed above. So it is probably safe to say there was little change in public opinion over the four years 1979–83.

The change for which there is evidence is the attitude of the medical profession. Before the act became operative, there was opposition as discussed above. Within a few years of the introduction of the act, however, the polls were showing that doctors and gynecologists had changed their attitudes and begun to support the 1967 Abortion Act. There is now an active group working for an extension of the law called Doctors for a Woman's Choice on Abortion.

DEMOGRAPHY OF ABORTION

The first year of full operation of the Abortion Act was 1968, and table 31.4 shows the number of abortions on indigenous women in England and Wales in successive years.

The data show a steady rise in the number of abortions until 1973, presumably owing largely to the transfer of the operation from the illegal to the legal sector. The number of deaths from illegal abortion fell over this period from forty-seven in 1966 to eight in 1973. In 1975 the government introduced free birth control through the National Health Service available to people regardless of their marital status. This was probably the primary force in the reduction of the abortion rate from 1975 to 1977. However, there was quite a large rise in the number of abortions from 103,000 in 1977 to 141,101 in 1985. The reasons for this are not totally clear. However, the scare about the pill was probably a large factor, and many women switched their method of birth control to less efficient forms. A further factor is the age structure. The increase in the number of women in their late teens was a crucial factor as their demand for abortion is much higher than the overall average for the age group fifteen to forty-four. Other less important influences on the overall rate were an increase in the incidence of rubella leading to abortion for fetal deformity and possibly the use of English addresses by Irish women seeking abortions in England.

The data show that married women outnumbered single women in 1969 but that since that time it has been otherwise. This suggests that in the early days after the act was passed abortion was used by those who may have completed their family size. However, in later years there was greater use by single women who probably did not want a baby at that stage of their lives but would expect to have a family at a later stage when they were better able to cope with it.

Abortions in Britain can either be free through the National Health Service (NHS), or women can have their operation in one of sixty approved places in the country. The cost of a first-trimester abortion in the private sector or one of the charitable abortion clinics is around £120. Whether or not a woman is given a free abortion depends to a large extent on which of the fifteen Regional Health Authorities she lives within. The percentage of abortions in the NHS according to region in 1982 is shown in table 31.5.

The figures show that almost nine out of ten women in the Northern region had their abortions through the NHS. However, in the West Midlands the figure is just over one in five. There was a large increase in NHS provision in Mersyside, and whereas just over one in four (27 percent) of women had free abortions in 1980, in 1982 it was more than half (52 percent). This was due to the opening of a new day care unit. The decrease in the percentage of NHS abortions in Wessex in 1982 was due largely to the fact that the Regional Health Authority made an arrangement with one of the large charitable abortion clinics that they should carry out the abortions on an agency basis. The abortions would still be free to the women concerned.

ABORTION AND ADOLESCENTS

The age-specific birth rates for teenagers in postwar years show a number of trends, but two main ones are evident. Between 1951 and 1961 there was a rise from 21 per 1,000 women under the age of twenty to 37 per 1,000 (Francome, 1984b). This rise continued to 48 per 1,000 in 1966 and 51 per 1,000 in 1971. However, then the trend changed and there was a marked fall in the birth rate to 28 per 1,000 in 1982. A detailed analysis of the changes during the decade

1970–79 is presented in Francome, 1983. This covered much of the period when the Abortion Act was first in operation. Over the seven years 1971–77 inclusive, the birth rate for women under the age of twenty fell from 51.5 to 30.0 per 1,000. Therefore, the fall in births was 21.5 per 1,000. The abortion rate did increase over the period, but only from 12.1 per 1,000 to 15.1 per 1,000. Therefore, only one-seventh of the decline in births can be attributed to an increase in the number of abortions. Unless there was a reduction in teenage sexual activity over the period, which seems unlikely given the evidence of the sex surveys, then it is clear that the change is largely due to the more effective use of birth control. With the scare over the pill in 1977 there was a slight rise in births, but the trend then began to move downwards again. A crucial influence on the outcome of a teenage pregnancy is the girl's age, and this becomes clear from table 31.6.

The figures show that for teenagers aged fifteen and under nearly three-quarters of the pregnancies end in abortion. However, as the age of the group increases there is a steady decline in the percentage until by the age of nineteen it is only one in four. A proportion of the older teenagers will be in stable relationships and may well have decided that they want to start a family. The latest data for those aged fifteen years in England and Wales are for 1982 and show an abortion rate of 7.43 per 1,000 and a birth rate of 2.42 (*Hansard* 8th November 1983).

ABORTION IN IRELAND

The number of Irish women registered as coming to Britain for their abortions is shown in table 31.7. The data show that the number of women traveling from Northern Ireland for their abortions has remained relatively constant at between 1,200 and 1,600 a year. However, the number of women from Eire has shown a continuing rise, although in recent years the rate of increase has tailed off. Figures released by the Ulster Pregnancy Advisory Association and published in Breaking Chains (April 1984) gave some details of the breakdown of 1,005 abortion cases for 1983. In all, 68 percent said they were married and 16 percent single. The Protestant groups accounted for 65 percent of the total and Catholics 30 percent. Nearly one in three of the women were referred by their general practitioner, and 69 percent were not using any method of contraception at the time they became pregnant.

ABORTION IN SCOTLAND

Table 31.8 gives the figures for Scottish women having abortions in their own country. The data show only a slight increase in the number of abortions between 1971 and 1978. The rise from 7.4 thousand in 1978 to 9.0 thousand in 1981 suggests that there may well have been an effect from moving to less efficient forms of contraception. At 8.3, however, the abortion rate per 1,000 women at risk is relatively low. In part, this is because Scotland has relatively few private abortions, and so women not able to get an NHS operation may well decide to travel to England. In 1981, 998 Scottish residents had their abortions in England, and 898 did so in 1982. If trends for the first nine months are considered in 1983, the number may well have been below 820. However, by adding the two figures together, we find that Scotland had an overall abortion rate of 9.2 per 1,000 in 1981, which is only three-quarters of the rate for England and Wales. For countries with liberal laws, Scotland has the lowest abortion rate in the world except for Holland.

The abortion rate per thousand women does vary greatly between regions. Tayside has a rate of 12.3 per 1,000 and Grampian one of 10.8. In contrast, the rate for the Western Isles was 4.9 and Lanarkshire 5.3. So there are wide differences. One striking fact about Scottish abortions is that they entail a mean stay in hospital of 3.7 days, which is in striking contrast to countries such as the United States and Holland where day care is the norm.

REPEAT ABORTIONS

Between 1982 and 1984 I carried out a random sample of abortion patients in Britain and the United States using the same questionnaire. The results will be written up more fully later, but it is instructive to consider the background to those receiving repeat abortions in Britain. The respondents were asked, "Have you had previous abortions? If so please specify how many." The replies are present in table 31.9.

The results show that just under one in five of the total sample were presenting for their second or subsequent abortion. Women who have had more than one abortion may well be those who have found particular problems with birth control methods. They may also mention the difficulty of obtaining a sterilization. One of the questions about repeat abortion is whether the group contained a disproportionate share of those who were careless or whether those presenting for more than one abotion had simply been unlucky in terms of contraceptive failure. For comparative purposes, birth control usage was noted according to the number of abortions. The results are shown in table 31.10.

The results show that two in five of the women in for their first abortion had always used birth control and that the percentage rose slightly for those in for their second abortion. In fact, only just over one in five of the women in for their second abortion were not using birth control at all. This suggests that the group contained a disproportionate percentage of women who had "bad luck," in terms of birth control failure. When the group of women are considered who are presenting for their third or more abortion, it can be seen that only one in five was always using abortion. This was a small group, and so it is important not to draw too many conclusions. However, the survey suggests there may be a group of women and their partners who continue to ignore the necessity of regular birth control to prevent unwanted pregnancies. There may be grounds for further research into this area.

ABORTION RESEARCH

Several useful reports have been published in recent years. John Ashton (1978) carried out a valuable study of women presenting for abortion from the Wessex Regional Health Authority; and Clarke, Farrell, and Beaumont (1983) analyzed the views and experiences of women having NHS and private treatment in the Camden area of London. Alberman and Dennis (1984) edited a report for the Royal College of Gynecologists (RCOG) on late abortions which was critical of some of the delays in the British service. For example, one in five women having their abortion at twenty to twenty-three weeks had seen the first doctor at twelve weeks. This delay was in large part due to the insistence of the current British law on the consent of two doctors, and there are delays while the woman is obtaining this approval. On the thorny issue of teenage pregnancy, there have been several research projects, and Judy Bury published a review of the available evidence in 1984.

Several research projects are currently being conducted. The RCOG is co-operating with the Royal College of General Practitioners in evaluating the long-term consequences of abortion; this study should produce some important findings as to potential risks with the operation. I have been carrying out a survey on abortion patients in Britain and the United States using an identical questionnaire in both countries. It is hoped that this will enable us to identify differences in sexual behavior and birth control use that leads to the American abortion rate being more than twice the British one.

CONCLUSION

This chapter shows some of the differences between the British and Irish experience of abortion. A strong case can be made for the simplification of the method of obtaining an abortion in Britain. This could come either by a change in the law or by a different interpretation of the 1861 Offences Against the Person's Act. In Ireland the issue has been decided for the time being, so the ferry services will continue to do business with women forced to travel for their abortions. How long this situation will continue is a matter of conjecture. A Gallup Poll in 1980 showed that 80 percent of people in Eire opposed abortions in all circumstances compare·to 12 percent in England and Wales and 18 percent in the United States (Francome 1982). The referendum campaign may have changed attitudes to some degree, but it is clear that the country still has strong antiabortion feelings.

The data also suggest that the abortion controversy is likely to be important for a number of years. The debates over the right to choose will continue, as will the arguments of those who believe abortion to be murder. One change that is likely to come within the next few years is for a movement toward day care abortions with local anesthetic to bring British practice more in line with that in some other countries. In terms of emotion it is likely that the most acrimonious debates will occur in Ireland.

REFERENCES

Alberman, E. & Dennis, K. J. *Late abortions in England and Wales*. RCOG, 1984.

Ashton, J. R. *The attitudes of Wessex women obtaining abortions outside their own region*. Southampton University, 1978.

Bury, J. *Teenage pregnancy in Britain*. Birth Control Trust, 1984.

Clarke, L., Farrell, C., & Beaumont, B. *Camden abortion study*. 1983.

Francome, C. *Gallup on abortion*. Abortion Law Reform and Doctors for a Woman's Choice on Abortion, 1982.

————. *Abortion freedom*. Allen and Unwin, 1984a.

————. Teenage pregnancy. *Novum*. May 1984b.

Glass, D. V. *Population policies and movements in Europe*. Frank Cass, 1940.

Means, C. The Phoenix of abortion freedom. *New York Law Forum*, 1971, *17*, 335–410.

Table 31.1
Do You Think That the Choice as to Whether or Not to Continue a Pregnancy Should or Should Not Be Left to the Woman in Consultation with Her Doctor?

Response	Sex		Age				Total
	Male	Female	15-24	25-44	45-64	64+	
			(in percentage)				
Should	76	81	73	83	83	69	79
Should not	12	11	12	12	11	11	11
Don't know	12	8	15	5	6	20	10

Table 31.2
Whether the Decision on an Abortion Should Be Left to the Woman in Consultation with Her Doctor (in percentage)

	1979		1982		
	Should	Should not	Should	Should not	Number
Church of England	75	15	85	11	602
Church of Scotland	92	5	77	16	82
Free Church	73	11	70	21	59
Catholic	72	19	69	27	123
Other	70	8	71	19	72
None	85	8	81	12	104

Table 31.3
Abortion Attitudes in the United States, Great Britain, and Northern Ireland (in percentage)

	U.S.A.	Britain	Eire	Northern Ireland Catholic
Legal in all circumstances (i.e. on demand)	25	23	2	0
Legal in some circumstances	53	61	13	35
Illegal in all circumstances	18	12	80	63
Don't know/no opinion	4	4	5	2

Table 31.4
Abortions by Number and Marital Status, England and Wales (Residents)
(in thousands)

year	all	single	married	widowed, divorced separated	Rate per 1000 women 15-44
1969	49.8	22.3	23.0	4.6	5.3
1970	76.0	34.5	34.3	7.2	8.1
1971	94.6	44.3	41.5	8.7	10.1
1972	108.6	51.1	46.9	10.6	11.5
1973	110.6	52.9	46.8	10.9	11.5
1974	109.4	53.3	45.2	10.9	11.5
1975	106.2	52.3	43.1	10.6	11.0
1976	101.0	50.5	39.9	10.6	10.4
1977	102.8	51.8	39.6	11.2	10.4
1978	111.9	56.4	42.2	13.3	11.3
1979	119.0	63.0	43.0	14.0	12.0
1980	128.9	68.7	44.3	15.9	12.8
1981	128.6	71.0	43.0	14.6	12.5
1982	128.3	71.8	40.5	14.3	12.3
1983	127.4	74.3	38.9	14.2	11.9
1984	136.4	82.3	39.2	14.8	12.6
1985	-	-	-	-	13.1

Source: Office of Population Censuses and Surveys (OPCS), ref. AB 85/3, August 1985. Unknown status distributed in proportion.

Table 31.5
National Health Service Abortions in Different Regions (in percentage)

Region	1982	1981	1980
Northern	88	89	88
Yorkshire	37	40	38
Trent	55	55	54
East Anglia	77	76	75
NW Thames	41	40	40
NE Thames	51	50	50
SE Thames	50	49	48
SW Thames	40	39	36
Wessex	46	52	50
Oxford	50	50	51
South-Western	78	77	75
West Midlands	21	21	22
Mersey	52	30	27
North Western	41	42	42
Wales	60	59	57

Source: OPCS monitors AB 84/1 and AB 85/5.

Table 31.6
Abortion Rate per 100 Pregnancies, by Age in 1980

Age	Percent Pregnancies ending in aborton
15 and under	73.9
16	59.5
17	42.5
18	31.4
19	25.0
All cases under 20	36.7

Source: Francome, 1984b.

Table 31.7
Irish Women Seeking Abortions in Britain

	1970	1974	1976	1978	1980	1981	1982	1983
Northern Ireland	199	1102	1142	1311	1565	1447	1509	1460
Eire	261	1406	1821	2548	3320	3603	3650	3677

Source: OPCS monitor series.

Table 31.8
Scottish Abortions by Marital Status

	1971	1978	1979	1980	1981
			(in thousands)		
Married	3.3	2.9	3.0	2.8	3.0
Single	2.4	3.7	3.8	4.2	4.9
Widowed/Divorced/Sep	0.6	0.8	1.0	0.9	1.1
All	6.3	7.4	7.8	7.9	9.0
Rate per 1,000 15-44	6.3	7.0	7.3	7.3	8.3

Source: *Scottish Abstract of Statistics*, no. 12, 1983, HMSO, Edinburgh, p. 21.

Table 31.9
Previous Abortions for the Total Sample

	Number	Percentage	corrected percentage
None	492	75.8	81.9
one	98	15.1	15.4
two	14	2.2	2.2
Three	1	0.2	0.2
Four	2	0.3	0.3
Not known/none	42	6.5	-
Total	649	100.0	100.0

Table 31.10
Birth Control and Repeat Abortions

	First Abortion		Second Abortion		Third or more Abortion	
	Number	%	Number	%	Number	%
thinking of using birth control	43	9.6	6	6.4	2	14.3
using a method sometimes	99	22.0	31	33.0	7	50.0
always using a method	177	39.3	40	42.6	3	21.4
not using a method	127	28.2	15	16.0	2	14.3
not known	3	0.7	2	2.1	-	-
Total	450	100.0	94	100.0	14	100.0

32

UNITED STATES OF AMERICA

Christopher Tietze, Jacqueline Darroch Forrest, and Stanley K. Henshaw

HISTORICAL DEVELOPMENT OF ABORTION POLICY

Abortions before ''quickening'' were permitted in the United States by traditional common law until 1845, when the first of many states passed laws prohibiting all or most abortions. The campaign to restrict abortion was led by physicians who had two concerns: women's health and their own interest in establishing medicine as a profession and banning from practice those who were not formally trained ''regular'' physicians, primarily midwives who frequently performed abortions. By the turn of the century, almost all states had passed laws restricting abortion, a situation that lasted into the second part of the 1900s. In the early 1960s, for example, one state, Pennsylvania, prohibited all abortions. The majority of states (forty-four) only allowed abortions if the pregnant woman's life would be endangered if the pregnancy were carried to term, and the remaining states permitted abortions only if the woman's life or physical health was in jeopardy or (one state) in cases of rape. Fourteen states explicitly made obtaining an abortion, as well as performing an abortion, a crime.

In spite of such restrictions on abortion, many women were obtaining them, but the exact number cannot be determined. In 1930 abortion accounted for 18 percent of all maternal deaths in the United States. Respondents to Kinsey's nationwide survey in the 1940s reported that 22 percent of married women had had one or more abortions between the time they were married and age forty-five, and about nine to ten who reported premarital pregnancies said that they had been terminated by abortion. Estimates of illegal abortions in the 1960s range from 200,000 to 1.2 million per year. In 1965 illegal abortions accounted for 20 percent of all deaths related to pregnancy and childbirth (Alan Guttmacher Institute, 1982).

During the 1960s and early 1970s many organizations called for repeal or reform of state laws outlawing abortion. These groups included numerous health and social welfare organizations, and medical, legal, religious, and women's groups. In part, these groups were protesting the toll illegal abortions were taking on women's health and lives.

In 1967 Colorado was the first state to reform its antiabortion law, permitting abortion in cases in which the woman's life was endangered, her physical or mental health imperiled by the pregnancy, the fetus would be born with severe physical or mental defect or the pregnancy had occurred from rape or incest. By 1972 twelve other states had adopted such laws, and four states had passed laws allowing abortion if the woman and her physician felt it was necessary. In all but five other states, bills to reform or repeal abortion laws had been introduced. Women from throughout the country, when they could afford it, traveled for abortions to those states where it was legal, especially to California, the District of Columbia, and New York. In 1972 about one-third of the 600,000 legal abortions were to women who had traveled from their home states.

In 1973 the Supreme Court invalidated all state antiabortion laws by holding that the constitutional right to privacy included a woman's decision to terminate a pregnancy in consultation with her physician. Although organized opposition to the decision appeared in succeeding years, the court has reaffirmed its decision in many subsequent decisions which further defined the limits of governmental authority to restrict abortion. Attempts to amend the U.S. Constitution to overturn the Supreme Court decisions have been unsuccessful, in part because of divisions within the antiabortion movement. However, the Supreme Court remains sharply divided on the issue, and if the Reagan administration succeeds in its policy of appointing antiabortion justices the court may reverse its position. A reversal would probably mean a return to the pre–1973 situation in which the legal status of abortion was determined by the states.

LEGAL STATUS OF ABORTION

The Supreme Court's 1973 decisions declared that during the first trimester of pregnancy, the decision to terminate a pregnancy is primarily a medical one and must rest with the physician. States may regulate the conditions under which abortions are performed as long as these procedures are treated like all other medical procedures. They may, for example, require abortions to be done by licensed physicians and in licensed facilities. States may regulate abortion to protect the woman's health once abortion is more dangerous to the woman than childbirth, generally after the beginning of the second trimester. As a result, many states required that abortions past the first trimester be performed in hospitals, but these laws were declared unconstitutional in 1983 after it was shown that outpatient abortions were as safe as those performed in hospitals. After the fetus is capable of sustained independent existence, states may restrict all abortions except those necessary to preserve the woman's life. Almost half of the states have prohibited all abortions except those needed to protect the life or

health of the woman, but even in the others, abortions are rarely performed near
viability.

ATTITUDE TOWARD ABORTION

Since 1972, the year before nationwide legalization of abortion, about two-
thirds of U.S. adults have approved of legalizing abortion (Jaffe et al., 1981).
The proportion approving of legal abortions varies, however, according to the
circumstances involved. In 1984, 90 percent approved if the woman's health
were seriously endangered by the pregnancy; 80 percent if the pregnancy resulted
from rape or if the baby would be born with a serious defect; 43 to 46 percent
approved if the family were poor and could not afford more children, if the
woman were unmarried, or if a married woman did not want more children; and
39 percent approved for any reason (Alan Guttmacher Institute, 1984).

While about two-thirds of adults in the United States consistently feel abortion
should be available legally, there are differences between those of different
backgrounds. While the difference by religion is fairly small (69 percent of
Protestant women over age eighteen support legal abortion compared to 61
percent of Roman Catholics and 67 percent of all U.S. women), women of higher
education and family income are more likely to approve. Some surveys have
found blacks less approving of abortion than whites, but others have found the
opposite. Urban and suburban residents are more likely to support legal abortion
than those living in small towns or rural areas. The United States is a very
religious country, with 42 percent of women attending services at least once a
week. Those who do so are less likely than infrequent attenders to approve
making abortion legal (Henshaw & Martire, 1982:54).

INCIDENCE OF LEGAL ABORTION

The total number of legal abortions in the United States increased from an
estimated 50,000 in 1969 to around 200,000 in 1970, with most of the increment
in the second half of that year when New York State, mainly New York City,
and several other areas made legal abortion available to nonresidents. The number
increased each year through the 1970s passing the 1 million mark in 1975 and
approaching 1.6 million in 1980–85. In 1982 abortions were obtained in the
United States by about 5,400 residents of Canada, about 2,000 residents of
Mexico, and about 1,600 women from other areas, mainly the Caribbean Islands
(Henshaw et al., 1987b). Because the number of women of reproductive age
also increased during the period, the abortion rate per 1,000 women aged fifteen
to forty-four years rose somewhat less rapidly than the number of abortions, for
example, by only three-fourths from 1973 to 1979, compared with a doubling
of the numbers, and by only 1.7 percent from 1979 to 1980, compared with a
3.8-percent increase in the number of abortions (table 32.1). The rate peaked at
29.3 in 1980 and 1981, and then fell slightly, to 28.0 in 1985.

A different way of looking at these statistics is to relate the number of abortions to the number of known pregnancies, that is, legal abortions plus live births six months later. In 1985 three out of ten known pregnancies were terminated by legal abortion, compared with less than one in five in 1973. Since probably not more than 2.1 million of the 3.3 million births conceived in 1978 were intended at the time of conception, it would appear that about one-half of the unwanted or mistimed pregnancies were aborted in that year. In 1982 about 56 percent ended in abortion (Tietze & Henshaw: 1986).

It cannot be emphasized too strongly that the rapidly increasing number of legal abortions in the United States during the early and mid–1970s did *not* reflect an equally rapid increase of the total number of induced abortions. Many legal abortions have replaced unwanted births, but large numbers—estimated as somewhere between a half million and a million—have replaced illegal abortions. Other factors involved have been increasing proportions of women of reproductive age who are unmarried, increasing sexual activity among teenagers and repeated "pill scares" resulting—in some age groups of women—in changing patterns of contraception.

AVAILABILITY OF ABORTION SERVICES

Prior to the implementation of restrictions on federal funding for abortion, passed by Congress in 1976 and fully implemented, after judicial review, in 1978, indigent women and others with low incomes could obtain legal abortions under the Medicaid program, funded jointly by the federal government and the several states. In 1978 federal funding was, for all practical purposes, limited to abortions on strict medical indications, present in about 1 percent of all cases. However, roughly 85 percent of all Medicaid-eligible women lived in states continuing to pay for these services, while 15 percent lived in states where all public funding had become unavailable. The number of abortions funded by Medicaid also declined in those states where state funds were still available, probably because of widespread confusion among pregnant women and among providers of abortion services concerning the availability of Medicaid funding. Based on the experience of three states, it has been estimated that among the 295,000 Medicaid-eligible women nationwide in 1978, 194,000 obtained Medicaid-funded abortions, some 84,000 could not obtain Medicaid-funded abortions but were able to obtain legal abortions in the private sector, about 14,000 gave birth, and fewer than 3,000 obtained abortions from illegal (nonmedical) practitioners, mostly in states where public funding had been curtailed (Cates, 1981). Comparable estimates for more recent years have not been published.

As shown in table 32.2, about 52 percent of all legal abortions in the United States in 1973 took place in hospitals, 46 percent in nonhospital clinics, and 2 percent in doctors' offices. By 1985 only 13 percent of all abortions were reported from hospitals, 83 percent from clinics, and 4 percent from doctors' offices. In addition, almost four-fifths of all abortions in hospitals were performed as outpatient procedures. In absolute terms, the number of abortions in hospitals remained about 400,000 during 1973–77 and then dropped to about 200,000 by 1985. In 1985 only 21 percent of all non-Catholic general short-term hospitals and 17 percent of public hospitals provided *any* abortion services. If hospitals reporting fewer than one abortion every two weeks are excluded, these percentages are reduced by about one-third. In 1980 in seventeen states more than 50 percent of all women aged fifteen to forty-four lived in counties without abortion facilities, while in only nine states more than 90 percent lived in counties where such services were available.

An important characteristic of abortion facilities in the United States is their high degree of concentration. In 1985 a mere 38 hospitals and 461 clinics, representing 19 percent of all providers of abortion services, with 1,000 or more abortions per year and an average of about 20 abortions per week per provider, accounted for 77 percent of all legal abortions. This concentration probably increases the experience and competence of the professionals involved and the quality of the services. On the other hand, followup care is fragmented, with possible unfavorable effects on the patient.

Around two-fifths of all legal abortions obtained in the United States in 1972 were performed outside the state of the woman's permanent residence. By 1982 the share of out-of-state abortions had declined to about 6 percent (Henshaw et al., 1987). However, many women obtaining abortions had to travel, often considerable distances, to other communities within their state of residence. This handicap applied particularly to women living in smaller cities and towns or in rural areas. In each year from 1973 through 1985, at least 95 percent of all abortions were performed in metropolitan areas (Henshaw et al., 1987).

DEMOGRAPHY OF ABORTION

The demographic profile of women having abortions in the United States has not changed dramatically since 1973 (Henshaw, 1987). A majority are young (62–66 percent under twenty-five years), unmarried (71–81 percent), childless (55–58 percent), and white (67–74 percent). However, some trends can be discerned. The proportions of teenagers and of women in their late thirties and early forties declined, while the share of women in their twenties rose from about 50 percent to 56 percent in 1983, reflecting changes in the age distribution of the female population. Unmarried women, including single, separated, divorced, and widowed women, increased from 71 percent of the total in 1973 to 81 percent in 1983, and women with no prior live births, from 55 percent to 57 percent. Both trends probably reflect changes in the sexual activity of unmarried women as well as rising age at marriage and first birth. Conversely, abortions to women with three or more prior births dropped from 15 percent to 8 percent, probably a result of the growing acceptance of surgical sterilization by women and men. The share of nonwhite women rose from 26 percent in 1973 to a peak of 33 percent in 1976, and then dropped to around 30 percent in 1980–82, which may reflect variations in access to publicly funded abortion services (Henshaw & O'Reilly, 1983).

It is instructive to compare the age patterns of abortion rates per 1,000 women and of the percentage of known pregnancies terminated by abortion (table 32.3). In 1983, for instance, the abortion rate increased with age from 4.5 for women under fifteen years of age (computed per 1,000 women aged thirteen to fourteen years) to the very high level of 60 per 1,000 at eighteen to nineteen years of age, followed by a steady decline to 3.1 for women over forty years of age (computed per 1,000 women aged forty to forty-four years). The proportion of known pregnancies terminated by abortion, on the other hand, was 42 percent among women under fifteen years of age, drorpped to 23 percent at twenty-five to twenty-nine years when most women would be building their families, followed by a rise to 51 percent among the relatively few pregnancies to women in their forties.

Abortion rates per 1,000 women aged fifteen to forty-four years and the proportions of known pregnancies terminated by abortions were 4.7 and 6.8 times higher, respectively, in 1983 for unmarried women than for married women (table 32.4). Abortions and births used in the computation are defined in terms of the woman's status at the time of the event. It must be remembered, however, that the pregnancy of an unmarried woman can end in a nonmarital birth, a nonmarital abortion, or marriage, usually followed by a birth. If it were possible to classify abortions and births by marital status at conception, the percentage of known pregnancies terminated by abortion would be increased for the married and substantially reduced for the unmarried.

In regard to parity, as shown in table 32.5, the highest proportion of known pregnancies terminated by abortion has been consistently reported during recent years among women with no prior birth (37 percent in 1983). Many of these were pregnancies to unmarried women. Among women with one prior birth, the share of abortions dropped to 22 percent, rose again to a higher level at parities 2, 3, and 4, followed by a marked decline back to 21 percent among women with five or more prior births because women who avoid abortion for religious or other reasons are overrepresented among women of high parity. Owing to the high correlation of parity and age, this pattern is entirely obliterated in the parity-specific abortion rates per 1,000 women fifteen to forty-four, which declined from a high among the nulliparous women to a low among those with five or more prior births.

While white women represent a substantial majority of women obtaining legal abortions in the United States during 1973–83, both the abortion rate per 1,000 women aged fifteen to forty-four years and the percentage of known pregnancies terminated by abortion are consistently higher among blacks and other minorities (table 32.6). This differential reflects primarily a higher proportion of unintended pregnancies among blacks, rather than a greater acceptance of abortion as a means of resolving such pregnancies (Henshaw & O'Reilly, 1983).

REPEAT ABORTIONS

The issue of repeat abortion is a matter of concern, since most people feel that abortion is unacceptable as a primary method of fertility regulation and should be used only as a backup measure when contraception has failed. Others fear that even minor adverse effects on the health of the woman or on the outcome of later pregnancies would be accumulated by multiple abortion experiences.

Table 32.7 presents data on repeat abortions in the United States. The information on prior induced abortions was obtained from women seeking a subsequent termination and is, therefore, subject to response error and, in some cases, deliberate denial or understatement. It is believed that few women report abortions obtained in illegal settings. The importance of this source of underreporting declines as the number of years since legalization increases.

The number and percentage of repeat abortions increased rapidly in the United States from 1974 to 1983. Their share among all abortions was even higher in such places as New York City where legal abortion on request became available earlier and where the abortion rate (among residents) has been much higher than in the country as a whole. The upward trend does not reflect a progressive change from contraception to abortion as the primary method of fertility regulation but, to a large degree, the fact that growing numbers of women who have had a first legal abortion are now at risk of having a repeat abortion. As shown in figure 32.1, the number of women at risk in 1980 was 3.5 times higher than in 1974, an increase almost equal to the increase of repeat abortions (3.7 times).

PERIOD OF GESTATION AND METHOD OF TERMINATION

One of the most important factors in the evaluation of adverse effects associated with abortion is the period of gestation at which the pregnancy is terminated. The traditional division has been between abortions in the first trimester and those in the second trimester, generally defined as those abortions performed at twelve weeks or less from the onset of the last menstrual period (LMP) and those at thirteen weeks or later. However, accumulating experience has made it clear that this dichotomy is not sufficient because the frequency of adverse effects increases with the progress of gestation within each trimester.

In the United States, the period 1973–83 has seen a trend toward earlier performance of legal abortions, especially from 1973 to 1977 (table 32.8). In 1983 more than one-half of all terminations were performed eight weeks from LMP or earlier, more than nine-tenths at twelve weeks or earlier, and more than 99 percent at twenty weeks or earlier. Midtrimester abortions represent a smaller proportion of all legal abortions in the United States than in other countries where termination is permitted up to the point of viability of the fetus (Tietze, 1983).

The trend toward earlier abortion reflects not only a recognition by women and physicians that it is less stressful and safer (and also less expensive) than

Figure 32.1
Repeat Abortions and Women at Risk of Repeat Abortion: United States, 1974–80

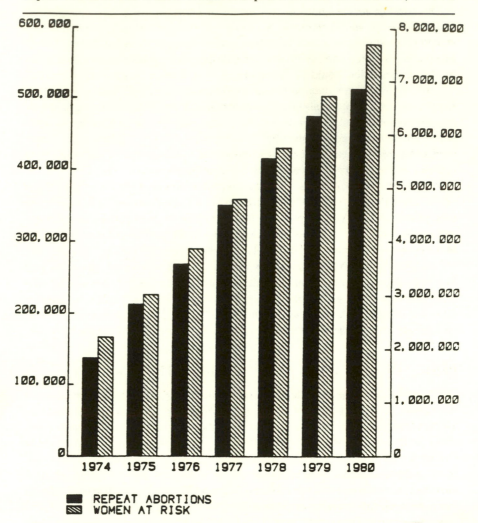

REPEAT ABORTIONS
WOMEN AT RISK

termination later in pregnancy, but also easier access to abortion services. This is illustrated by the statistics for New York State. In 1973 about 16 percent of all abortions obtained by residents were performed at thirteen weeks or later, dropping to 11 percent in 1980. The corresponding fraction for nonresidents rose from 25 to 34 percent. Apparently, women in other states were increasingly able to obtain first-trimester abortions, generally available in clinics, but not second-trimester procedures which in many places were restricted, by law or medical tradition, to hospitals.

Late abortions occur most frequently among the youngest women (table 32.9).

In 1980 only one-third of women under fifteen years of age obtained abortions at eight weeks or earlier, while 3 percent obtained them at twenty-one or more weeks of gestation. The corresponding fractions for women in their early thirties were 64 percent and 0.5 percent. Conversely, almost one-half of all abortions at twenty-one or more weeks gestation and 44 percent of all second-trimester procedures involved teenagers, compared with less than one-fourth of all abortions at eight weeks or earlier.

The strong inverse association of period of gestation and woman's age reflects the inexperience of the young in recognizing the symptoms of pregnancy, their unwillingness to accept the reality of their situation, their ignorance as to where to seek advice and help, and their hestiation to confide in adults. Economic considerations and/or laws or regulations prohibiting surgery on minors without parental consent also contribute to delays.

The slight decline in the proportions of abortions performed at eight weeks or earlier among older women reflects primarily the associations of high order pregnancies with economic and cultural deprivation. Abortions on medical grounds are also more common among older women, and some women in their forties may misinterpret the amenorrhea of pregnancy as the onset of menopause.

Parental diagnosis is rarely possible prior to sixteen weeks of gestation, and in some cases a definitive determination may not be available before twenty-two to twenty-four weeks of gestation, at the borderline of fetal viability. The importance of such procedures lies in the fact that findings are negative in more than 95 percent of cases. Although it is never possible to guarantee a perfect baby, the prospective parents can at least be reassurred that their child will not suffer from the disorder that had been suspected or feared. Prenatal diagnosis backed up by selective abortion thus makes procreation possible for couples who might otherwise avoid childbearing, perhaps by aborting all pregnancies.

At present, the number of abortions performed on the basis of prenatal diagnosis is quite small. Because the procedures have been in use only since 1968, most prospective parents and even some physicians are not aware of them, and comparatively few centers exist where they can be carried out. In the United States, about 125 prenatal diagnosis programs were active in 1978, but only ten to fifteen laboratories were adequately staffed and equipped for the diagnosis of Tay-Sachs disease or neural tube defects. The number of diagnostic amniocenteses performed in that year was on the order of 15,000, compared with 150,000 to 200,000 pregnancies at risk under currently accepted criteria. By 1982 the number of programs had risen to at least 155 and the number of amniocenteses to at least 30,000. The number of abortions then performed on the basis of prenatal diagnosis may have been on the order of 1,500, or one-tenth of 1 percent of all legal abortions in the United States. However, each of these abortions has averted a major catastrophe for a family.

Table 32.10 shows the methods used for the termination of pregnancy in the United States. The overwhelming majority of legal abortions during 1973–83 and virtually all first-trimester abortions were accomplished by instrumental evacuation, including suction curettage (also called vacuum aspiration or VA), surgical curettage (D & C), and "dilatation and evacuation" (D & E), designating procedures at thirteen or more weeks gestation. Suction curettage is by far the most widely used technique. Medical induction includes instillation of hypertonic saline, prostaglandin (PG), urea, or combinations of these into the amniotic cavity as well as a small number of PG abortions by other routes, such as vaginal suppositories. The decline of this category of abortions from 9.7 percent in 1973 to 3.1 percent in 1983 reflects in part the trend toward earlier termination, but also a shift from medical induction to instrumental evacuation, especially during the early part of the second trimester, that is, at thirteen to fifteen weeks gestation. A substantial proportion (more than two-thirds in 1972–78) of these procedures are performed in nonhospital clinics (Cates et al., 1982). Major surgical procedures (hysterotomy and hysterectomy) have never been used extensively in the United States as methods of abortion during the period under consideration; by 1978 their share had dropped to one-tenth of 1 percent of all legal abortions.

SUMMARY

Abortion was legalized nationwide in the United States by decision of the U.S. Supreme Court in 1973. Services became available quickly thereafter, and the number of legal abortions increased sharply while illegal, nonphysician abortions dropped to very few in number.

Abortion services are currently available from almost 3,000 sites, but service remains highly concentrated in the larger metropolitan areas and most abortions are provided by a small proportion of large providers.

Over four-fifths of the abortions in the United States occur in free-standing, nonhospital clinics, and few involve an overnight hospital stay. Fifty percent occur at eight or fewer weeks from the last mentrual period, and 91 percent occur at twelve weeks gestation or less, even though abortion is legal through the second trimester.

The abortion rate in the United States is about 28 per 1,000, higher among adolescents, unmarried women, and blacks. The proportion of known pregnancies terminated by abortion, three in ten overall, is highest among the youngest and oldest women, black, unmarried women, and those with no prior births. Abortion is used most commonly by women seeking to postpone or space childbearing rather than by those who want no more children.

As a result of abortion having been available legally for a number of years, and relatively high rates of abortion in those years, the proportion of all abortions to women who have had a previous abortion has increased steadily. This does not, however, indicate use of abortion instead of contraceptives as the primary method of fertility control.

After the Supreme Court decision legalizing abortion nationwide, opposition to abortion service availability solidified. While unsuccessful in making abortion illegal, it has caused restrictions of federal and most state funding for abortion to cases endangering the health and life of the pregnant woman.

In spite of vocal opposition, public opinion over the years since 1973 has been remarkably stable, with two-thirds of adults supporting the current legal status of abortion and as many as nine in ten supporting its legal availability in some cases.

REFERENCES

Alan Guttmacher Institute. Abortion in the U.S.: Two centuries of experience. *Issues in Brief*, January 1982, *2*(4), 1–4.

———. Supreme Court reaffirms right to abortion, strikes down local restrictions. Washington Memo, 22 June 1983a, 1–4.

———. 10 years after Roe v. Wade: Responses to concerns raised about abortion. *Issues in Brief*, February 1983b, *3*(1), 1–6.

———. Most Americans remain opposed to abortion ban and continue to support woman's right to decide. *Family Planning Perspectives*, September/October 1984, *16*(5), 233–34.

Cates, W., Jr. The Hyde Amendment in action. *Journal of the American Medical Association*, 4 September 1981, *246*(10), 1109–1112.

———, et al. Dilatation and evacuation procedures and second-trimester abortions: The role of physician skill and hospital setting. *Journal of the American Medical Association*, 6 August 1982, *248*(5), 559–563.

Henshaw, S. K. Characteristics of U.S. women having abortions, 1982–1983. *Family Planning Perspectives*, January/February 1987, *19* (1), 5–9.

Henshaw, S. K., & Martire, G. Abortion and the public opinion polls. *Family Planning Perspectives*, March/April 1982, *14*(2), 53–62.

Henshaw, S. K. & O'Reilly, K. Characteristics of abortion patients in the United States, 1979 and 1980. *Family Planning Perspectives*, January/February 1983, *15*(1), 5–16.

Henshaw, S. K., et al. Abortion services in the United States, 1984 and 1985. *Family Planning Perspectives*, March/April 1987, *19*(2), 63–70.

Jaffe, F. S., et al. *Abortion politics: private morality and public policy.* New York: McGraw-Hill, 1981.

Tietze, C. *Induced abortion: A world review, 1983* (5th ed.). New York: Population Council, 1983.

Tietze C., & Henshaw, S. K. *Induced abortion: A world review, 1986* (6th ed.). New York: Alan Guttmacher Institute, 1986.

Table 32.1
Legal Abortions Reported to Alan Guttmacher Institute, United States, 1973–85

	1973	1974	1975	1976	1977	1978	1979	1980	1981	1982	1983	1984	1985
Number (1,000s)	745	899	1,034	1,179	1,317	1,410	1,498	1,554	1,577	1,574	1,575	1,577	1,589
Percent increase from prior year	na[1]	20.7	15.1	14.0	11.7	7.1	2.6	3.8	1.3	-0.2	0.1	0.1	0.8
Rate per 1,000 women aged 15–44 years	16.3	19.3	21.7	24.2	26.4	27.7	28.8	29.3	29.3	28.8	28.5	28.1	28.0
Percent of known pregnancies[2]	19.3	22.0	24.9	26.5	28.6	29.2	29.6	30.0	30.1	30.0	30.4	29.7	29.8

[1]Not applicable.
[2]Legal abortions plus live births six months later.

Table 32.2
Legal Abortions by Type of Services, United States, 1973–82, 1984–85

Type of Service	1973	1974	1975	1976	1977	1978	1979	1980	1981	1982	1984	1985
Number (1,000s)[1]												
Hospitals	386	418	413	417	391	351	348	341	306	281	222	208
Clinics	343	455	585	721	872	999	1,087	1,145	1,199	1,219	1,292	1,315
MD's offices[2]	15	25	35	41	54	60	63	68	72	74	63	65
Percent of total												
Hospitals	51.8	46.5	40.0	35.3	29.7	24.9	23.2	21.9	19.4	17.9	14.1	13.1
Clinics	46.1	50.7	56.6	61.2	66.2	70.8	72.6	73.7	76.0	77.4	81.9	82.8
MD's offices[2]	2.1	2.8	3.4	3.5	4.1	4.3	4.2	4.4	4.6	4.7	4.0	4.1

[1]Because of rounding, numbers in this and subsequent tables may not add up to totals in table 32.1.
[2]Physicians' offices reporting 400 or more abortions a year are classified as clinics.

Table 32.3
Legal Abortions by Age of Woman, United States, 1973–83

Age (years)	1973	1974	1975	1976	1977	1978	1979	1980	1981	1982	1983
Number (1,000s)[1]											
14 or less[2]				16	16	15	16	15	15	15	16
15–17	244	292	340	153	166	169	179	183	176	168	166
18–19				210	231	250	266	261	257	250	245
20–24	241	287	332	392	450	489	526	549	555	552	548
25–29	130	163	189	220	247	266	284	304	316	326	328
30–34	73	90	100	110	124	134	142	153	167	168	172
35–39	41	49	53	57	62	65	65	67	70	73	78
40 or more[2]	17	19	21	21	22	21	20	21	21	21	21
Percent of total[1]											
14 or less[2]				1.3	1.2	1.1	1.1	1.0	1.0	0.9	1.0
15–17	32.8	32.5	32.9	13.0	12.6	12.0	11.9	11.8	11.2	10.7	10.6
18–19				17.8	17.5	17.7	17.8	16.8	16.3	15.9	15.5
20–24	32.3	31.9	32.1	33.3	34.2	34.7	35.1	35.4	35.2	35.0	34.8
25–29	17.4	18.1	18.2	18.7	18.7	18.9	19.0	19.6	20.0	20.7	20.8
30–34	9.7	10.0	9.7	9.3	9.4	9.5	9.5	9.8	10.6	10.7	10.9
35–39	5.5	5.4	5.1	4.8	4.7	4.6	4.3	4.3	4.4	4.7	5.0
40 or more[2]	2.3	2.1	2.0	1.8	1.7	1.5	1.3	1.3	1.3	1.4	1.4

	1973	1974	1975	1976	1977	1978	1979	1980	1981	1982	1983
Rate per 1,000 women[1]											
14 or less[2]				3.9	3.9	3.8	4.3	4.3	4.3	4.2	4.5
15–17	23.9	28.2	32.5	24.2	26.2	26.9	28.8	30.2	30.1	30.1	30.8
18–19				49.3	54.1	58.4	61.9	61.0	61.8	60.0	60.4
20–24	26.2	30.4	34.3	39.6	44.3	47.2	49.9	51.4	51.1	51.2	51.1
25–29	16.4	19.6	21.8	24.1	26.9	28.4	29.6	30.8	31.4	31.5	31.1
30–34	10.9	13.0	14.0	15.0	15.7	16.4	16.5	17.1	17.7	17.7	17.8
35–39	7.1	8.4	8.9	9.3	9.8	9.8	9.4	9.3	9.5	9.3	9.6
40 or more[2]	2.9	3.3	3.6	3.7	3.9	3.6	3.4	3.5	3.4	3.3	3.1
Percent of known pregnancies[3]											
14 or less[2]					41.1	40.9	43.0	42.7	43.7	42.9	42.3
15–17	25.6	29.0	33.4	35.8	38.7	39.7	41.3	42.4	42.2	42.0	43.2
18–19					37.9	39.3	40.1	40.1	40.3	40.5	41.4
20–24	17.6	20.0	22.8	25.0	27.6	28.7	29.4	30.1	30.4	30.6	31.4
25–29	13.2	15.4	17.2	18.6	20.2	20.8	21.1	21.8	22.0	22.3	22.5
30–34	18.7	21.7	23.5	23.1	23.7	23.5	23.0	23.3	23.9	23.2	23.0
35–39	28.3	32.8	35.4	36.6	38.5	38.6	37.3	37.2	35.7	34.2	34.2
40 or more[2]	39.7	44.4	48.6	50.2	52.5	51.6	50.4	51.7	51.3	51.4	51.4

[1]By reported age at abortions.
[2]Rates computed per 1,000 women aged 13–14 and 40–44 years, respectively. Rates for women aged 19 years or less in 1973–75 are computed per 1,000 women aged 15–19 years.
[3]By estimated age at conception.

Table 32.4
Legal Abortions by Marital Status, United States, 1973–83

Marital status[1]	1973	1974	1975	1976	1977	1978	1979	1980	1981	1982	1983
Number (1,000s)											
Married	216	248	272	290	300	331	322	320	299	300	295
Unmarried[2]	528	650	762	889	1,017	1,079	1,175	1,234	1,279	1,274	1,280
Percent of total											
Married	29.0	27.6	26.3	24.6	22.8	23.5	21.5	20.6	18.9	19.1	18.7
Unmarried[2]	71.0	72.4	73.7	75.4	77.2	76.5	78.5	79.4	81.1	80.9	81.3
Rate per 1,000 women aged 15–44 years											
Married	8.0	9.2	10.0	10.6	10.9	12.0	11.6	11.3	10.5	10.5	10.3
Unmarried[2]	28.4	33.4	37.5	41.7	45.8	46.1	48.7	49.7	50.1	48.6	48.4
UM/M ratio[3]	3.5	3.6	3.8	3.9	4.2	3.8	4.2	4.4	4.8	4.6	4.7
Percent of known pregnancies											
Married	7.0	8.3	9.6	9.4	9.8	10.4	9.9	9.8	9.2	9.5	9.3
Unmarried	57.0	59.9	62.3	64.2	66.0	65.4	66.0	64.9	64.5	63.4	63.2
UM/M ratio[3]	8.1	7.2	6.5	6.8	6.7	6.3	6.7	6.6	7.0	6.7	6.8

[1] At abortion or birth.
[2] Never married, separated, divorced, and widowed women.
[3] Unmarried/married ratio.

Table 32.5
Legal Abortions by Prior Live Births, United States, 1973–83

Prior live births	1973	1974	1975	1976	1977	1978	1979	1980	1981	1982	1983
Number (1,000s)											
None	411	483	542	629	742	798	868	900	912	903	890
One	115	155	194	229	249	271	287	305	312	321	329
Two	104	130	156	176	186	198	207	216	220	223	228
Three	61	70	78	81	80	83	82	83	84	82	83
Four	29	32	34	34	33	33	30	29	29	28	
5 or more	26	28	30	30	25	26	23	22	20	18	
Percent of total											
None	55.2	53.7	52.4	53.4	56.4	56.7	58.0	57.9	57.8	57.3	56.5
One	15.4	17.3	18.8	19.4	18.9	19.2	19.2	19.6	19.8	20.4	20.9
Two	13.9	14.5	15.1	14.9	14.2	14.0	13.8	13.9	13.9	14.1	14.4
Three	8.1	7.8	7.5	6.9	6.1	5.9	5.5	5.4	5.4	5.2	5.3
Four	3.9	3.6	3.3	2.9	2.5	2.4	2.0	1.8	1.9	1.8	1.8
5 or more	3.5	3.1	2.9	2.5	1.9	1.8	1.5	1.4	1.2	1.1	1.1
Rate per 1,000 women aged 15–44 years											
None	21.8	24.7	26.3	29.4	33.6	35.2	37.3	37.7	u[1]	u	u
One	16.3	21.3	25.9	29.4	31.3	33.0	33.7	34.7			
Two	13.0	15.8	18.5	20.2	20.5	21.0	21.1	21.2			
Three	11.1	12.9	14.5	15.2	14.8	15.2	14.8	14.8			
Four	9.4	10.8	11.8	12.0	12.0	12.3	11.4	11.1			
5 or more	8.0	9.0	10.5	11.0	10.1	10.8	10.5	10.8			
Percent of known pregnancies											
None	24.0	26.4	29.1	31.3	34.8	35.5	36.2	36.6	36.8	36.6	36.9
One	10.6	13.3	16.3	17.8	19.0	19.8	20.1	20.8	20.8	21.1	21.7
Two	19.1	22.5	25.7	26.7	27.4	27.8	27.8	28.4	28.4	28.4	29.1
Three	23.5	27.4	29.7	30.1	29.7	29.9	28.9	28.8	29.0	28.1	28.7
Four	23.6	27.2	29.6	29.7	29.8	30.1	28.1	27.4	27.1	26.1	26.8
5 or more	18.4	21.4	24.9	25.7	24.6	25.2	23.2	22.4	22.0	20.9	20.7

[1]Data not available.

Table 32.6
Legal Abortions by Woman's Race, United States, 1973–83

Woman's race	1973	1974	1975	1976	1977	1978	1979	1980	1981	1982	1933
Number (1,000s)											
White	549	629	701	785	889	969	1,062	1,094	1,108	1,095	1,084
Other	196	269	333	394	428	440	435	460	470	479	491
Percent of total											
White	73.7	70.0	67.8	66.6	67.5	68.8	70.9	70.4	70.2	69.6	68.8
Other	26.3	30.0	32.2	33.4	32.5	31.2	29.1	29.6	29.8	30.4	31.2
Rate per 1,000 women aged 15–44 years											
White	14.0	15.7	17.2	18.8	20.9	22.3	24.0	24.3	24.3	23.8	23.3
Other	31.2	41.4	49.3	56.3	59.0	58.7	56.2	56.8	55.9	55.5	55.8
O/W ratio[1]	2.2	2.6	2.9	3.0	2.8	2.6	2.3	2.3	2.3	2.3	2.4
Percent of known pregnancies											
White	17.4	19.6	21.5	23.0	25.0	26.1	27.1	27.4	27.4	27.1	27.4
Other	25.9	31.6	35.9	38.9	40.4	39.6	38.2	39.2	39.2	39.2	40.1
O/W ratio[1]	1.5	1.6	1.7	1.7	1.6	1.5	1.4	1.4	1.4	1.4	1.5

[1]Other/white ratio.

Table 32.7
Legal Abortions by Prior Induced Abortions, United States, 1974–83

Prior induced abortions	1974	1975	1976	1977	1978	1979	1980	1981	1982	1983
Number (1,000s)										
None	762	822	911	973	996	1,025	1,043	1,023	994	964
One	113	170	213	272	317	352	372	310	398	406
Two	17	30	40	54	70	86	97	113	122	138
3 or more	7	11	14	19	26	34	41	52	59	66
Percent of total										
None	84.8	79.5	77.3	73.9	70.7	68.4	67.1	64.9	63.2	61.2
One	12.5	16.5	18.1	20.6	22.5	23.5	24.0	24.7	25.3	25.8
Two	1.9	2.9	3.4	4.1	5.0	5.8	6.3	7.1	7.8	8.8
3 or more	0.8	1.1	1.2	1.4	1.8	2.3	2.6	3.3	3.7	4.2

Table 32.8
Legal Abortions by Weeks of Gestation, United States, 1973–83

Weeks of Gestation	1973	1974	1975	1976	1977	1978	1979	1980	1981	1982	1983
Number (1,000s)											
8 or less	284	399	481	560	658	708	749	800	810	806	792
9–10	222	257	290	334	361	388	413	416	424	420	424
11–12	131	135	151	171	180	188	204	202	204	205	210
13–15	44	44	46	49	52	63	70	73	76	76	83
16–20	53	54	56	55	54	51	49	50	50	54	53
21 or more	10	10	10	10	12	12	13	13	14	14	12
Percent of total											
8 or less	38.2	44.5	46.5	47.4	50.0	50.2	50.0	51.5	51.4	51.2	50.3
9–10	29.7	28.5	28.1	28.3	27.4	27.6	27.6	26.8	26.9	26.7	26.9
11–12	17.5	15.0	14.6	14.5	13.6	13.3	13.6	13.0	12.9	13.0	13.3
13–15	6.0	4.9	4.4	4.2	4.0	4.5	4.7	4.7	4.8	4.8	5.3
16–20	7.2	6.0	5.4	4.7	4.1	3.6	3.3	3.2	3.1	3.4	3.4
21 or more	1.4	1.1	1.0	0.9	0.9	0.8	0.8	0.8	0.9	0.9	0.8

Table 32.9
Legal Abortions by Age of Woman and Weeks of Gestation, United States, 1980

Woman's age (years)	Weeks of Gestation					
	8 or less	9-10	11-12	13-15	16-20	21 or more
Number (1,000s)[1]						
14 or less	5.2	4.1	2.6	1.5	1.4	0.5
15-17	67.6	54.3	33.6	13.8	10.9	3.1
18-19	113.4	78.1	41.7	15.0	10.6	2.7
20-24	282.4	151.0	71.1	25.1	15.8	4.0
25-29	180.0	74.2	31.3	10.7	6.1	1.4
30-34	97.3	34.8	13.2	4.4	2.7	0.7
35-39	41.2	15.3	6.2	2.0	1.5	0.3
40 or more	12.9	4.8	2.0	0.6	0.5	0.1
Percent by weeks of gestation, within woman's age						
14 or less	33.9	26.5	17.2	10.0	9.3	3.1
15-17	36.9	29.6	18.3	7.5	6.0	1.7
18-19	43.4	29.9	15.9	5.7	4.1	1.0
20-24	51.4	27.5	12.9	4.6	2.9	0.7
25-29	59.3	24.4	10.3	3.5	2.0	0.5
30-34	63.6	22.7	8.6	2.9	1.7	0.5
35-39	61.8	23.0	9.4	3.1	2.2	0.5
40 or more	61.9	23.0	9.4	3.0	2.2	0.5
Percent by woman's age, within weeks of gestation						
14 or less	0.7	1.0	1.3	2.1	2.9	3.7
15-17	8.4	13.0	16.7	18.9	22.0	24.1
18-19	14.2	18.8	20.7	20.4	21.4	20.9
20-24	35.3	36.2	35.2	34.3	31.9	31.1
25-29	22.5	17.8	15.5	14.6	12.4	11.3
30-34	12.2	8.3	6.5	6.0	5.4	5.6
35-39	5.1	3.7	3.1	2.8	3.0	2.5
40 or more	1.6	1.2	1.0	0.9	1.0	0.8

[1]Distribution estimated by iterative adjustment of data for thirteen states in 1979 to marginal totals for 1980.

493

Table 32.10
Legal Abortions by Method of Termination, United States, 1973–83

	1973	1974	1975	1976	1977	1978	1979	1980	1981	1982	1983
Number (1,000s)											
Instrumental evacuation[1]	668	805	949	1,101	1,236	1,334	1,422	1,487	1,518	1,519	1,525
Medical induction[2]	73	89	82	75	78	74	75	66	58	54	49
Uterine surgery[3]	4.1	5.0	3.6	2.7	2.3	1.6	1.1	1.2	1.1	1.1	0.9
Percent of total											
Instrumental evacuation	89.7	89.5	91.7	93.4	93.9	94.6	94.9	95.6	96.2	96.5	96.8
Medical induction	9.7	9.9	8.0	6.4	5.9	5.3	5.0	4.3	3.7	3.4	3.1
Uterine surgery	0.6	0.6	0.3	0.2	0.2	0.1	0.1	0.1	0.1	0.1	0.1

[1]Includes vacuum curettage, surgical curettage, and dilation and evacuation (D&E) at 13 weeks gestation or later.
[2]Hypertonic saline, prostaglandin, urea, and combinations. Also includes a small number of terminations by "other methods."
[3]Hysterotomy and hysterectomy.

33

YUGOSLAVIA

Lidija Andolšek

HISTORICAL DEVELOPMENT OF ABORTION POLICY

Yugoslavia is a multinational community with many regional, ethnic, and cultural diversities in its population of 22,424,711 (the latest, 1981 census), living in an area of 255.804 square kilometers. Different historical developments in individual regions as well as the influence of different civilizations and cultures on Yugoslav nations and nationalities have created considerable regional differences in terms of local socioeconomic development and demographic trends, which are also reflected in abortion trends.

The state policy after 1918 prosecuted abortion severely. From 1929 on, abortion was allowed for strictly limited medical reasons only. After the Second World War, the nation's rapid socioeconomic development dramatically changed the social structure of the population. The consequences of this rapid development were also reflected in an increase of illegal abortions with high mortality and morbidity.

On women's initiative, in 1950 a public debate on the legalization of abortion was started. At that time, some progressive gynecologists represented a strong pressure group and support to women in their struggle for a change in existing regulations. In 1952 abortion on demand was not accepted, but abortion was allowed under certain restricted conditions. Since then, abortion legislation has been amended several times with the aim of increasing the availability of abortion in response to the increased demand.

The mass media have played a significant role in disseminating information on the advantages of contraception as well as on abortion, especially women's and youth journals which have popularized modern methods of family planning among broad segments of the population.

LEGAL STATUS OF ABORTION

The 1974 Yugoslav Constitution defines free decision-making on childbirth (which also includes the right of abortion) as a human right (Ustava Socialističke, 1974). The implementation of this right is within the competence of republics and provinces. Their legal regulations reflect the local conditions and govern either all medical aspects of fertility regulation—contraception, abortion, sterilization, and treatment of infertility (Slovenia, Croatia)—or only the conditions for medical termination of pregnancy (Serbia, Vojvodina, Macedonia, Bosnia and Herzegovina, Kosovo, and Montenegro).

If the duration of pregnancy does not exceed ten weeks, abortion must be done on women's request in all republics. The termination of pregnancy beyond ten weeks, however, is regulated in each republic differently. According to the Slovene and Croatian legislation, abortion beyond ten weeks may be performed only if approved by a special committee (*Zakon o zdravstvenih*, 1977; *Zakon o zdravstvenim*, 1978). The decision of this committee is based on the relative risk which continuation or termination of her pregnancy poses to the woman's life, health, and potential future motherhood. Regulations of other republics and provinces authorize the committee to make a decision on the basis of a wide range of indications (*Legal Abortion*, 1978).

ATTITUDES TOWARD ABORTION

As in every other country, attitudes toward abortion in Yugoslavia have gone through a considerable evolution, influenced mostly by women's attitudes and gynecologists' opinions. Women's organizations regard the right of abortion mostly from the point of view of equality, the woman's position in society, and human rights (Tomšič, 1975). During the past thirty years, gynecologists' attitudes toward abortion have become more and more positive, mostly because of the progress of medical technology in this field, which has made abortion in the first trimester a relatively safe procedure.

In the evolution of attitudes toward abortion, there have, of course, also been some hindrances and conservative opinions, conditioned by the attitudes of the Catholic and other churches and the fear of the influence of abortion on the population (*Drugi kongres*, 1968; Mirković et al., 1972; Žarković, 1971). In the 1980s most medical professionals accept abortion on demand as a right of the woman, although they still consider it an inadequate method of fertility regulation.

DEMOGRAPHY OF LEGAL ABORTION

Between 1950 and 1954 the natural population increase in Yugoslavia was 17 per 1,000 inhabitants; in 1981, however, it was only 8 per 1,000. These average statistics conceal considerable regional differences, mainly due to differences in the birth rates.

As mentioned earlier, Yugoslavia is characterized by great differences among individual regions, so that practically all the demographic processes and dilemmas of the modern world's demographic policy may be found in it. In regions with very low fertility, fertility control is very efficacious, practiced mostly by induced abortions applied for both limitation and spacing of the family.

Although abortion was legalized in Yugoslavia as early as 1952, exact data on abortion trends for the entire country do not exist. In 1966 a total of 133,000 abortions were registered, and in 1968 (the latest year of central statistics on abortion trends for the entire country) 254,800 abortions, that is, 46 per 1,000 women of fertile age.

Partial data available for some individual regions reveal that since the late 1960s the number of legal abortions has increased significantly everywhere. The dynamics of this process was different in each region, however. Generally, legal abortion increased substantially after 1975, mostly as a consequence of the new Constitution (adopted in 1974) and more liberal abortion laws (adopted mostly in 1977). According to data provided by the Federal Public Health Institute of Yugoslavia, in 1971 there were 261,905 abortions, or 69.9 abortions per 100 live births, while in 1978 the total number of abortions was 335,102, or 87.9 per 100 live births (*Statistics on Abortion*, 1984).

Table 33.1 shows the total number of abortions in 1971 and in 1981 separately for each republic and province, as well as the number of abortions per 100 live births. Without exception, the total number of abortions and the abortion/live birth ratio have increased. The highest number of abortions is registered in Serbia (narrow) where in 1971 there were 156.3 abortions per 100 live births and in 1978, 187.8, representing an increase of 20.2 percent.

In the republic of Serbia, the crude birth rate dropped by almost half in recent years (from 27.4 in 1952 to 14.6 in 1980). There has been a constant increase in the number of legal abortions, and in the last ten years the childbirth/abortion ratio increased from 1/1.5 to 1/1.8. In the province of Vojvodina the childbirth/legal abortion ratio was 1/1.4 by 1978. An increase of abortions is also reported from the republic of Croatia. In 1965 the ratio of legal abortions was 46.7 per 100 live births, while in 1981 this ratio was 77.1 per 100 live births. On the other hand, in Montenegro the number of legal abortions in 1982 was relatively low (0.5 abortions per 1 birth).

The lowest rate of abortions is recorded in the Autonomous region of Kosovo, but the abortion/live birth ratio increased 45 percent in the period 1971–80 (from 10.8 to 15.7 per 100 live births).

The most exact data on abortion trends are available for the republic of Slovenia, the second smallest Yugoslav republic. Its territory of 20.256 square kilometers holds 1,891.864 inhabitants, among whom are approximately half a million women of fertile age. For a better understanding of the Slovene situation, here are some demographic data provided by the Republic Public Health Institute for 1981 (Republic Health Institute, 1983):

Crude birth rate	16/1,000
Crude death rate	10/1,000
Crude rate of natural increase	6/1,000
Infant mortality rate	13/1,000
Maternal mortality rate	0.8/10,000

As can be seen from table 33.2, the number of legal abortions increased until 1965, when it reached its peak. After 1965, there was a decrease owing to an increased use of contraception, especially oral contraceptives. The next period (1968–74) was characterized by a relatively stable total number of abortions (with only minor fluctuations). Thus, in 1975 a total of 12,350 abortions were registered, with only a slight increase of legal abortions. Since 1975, however, because of the abortion liberalization and restrictions in prescribing oral contraceptives to smokers and women over thirty-five, the number of legal abortions has nearly doubled. In 1980 a total of 22,489 abortions were registered, which is 63 percent more than in 1965, when the first peak occurred. The increase should be ascribed mainly to the increase of legal abortions, as the number of "others" has decreased considerably since 1975 and represented only 14 percent of the total number of abortions in 1980. The 1981 unofficial statistics display the same trends. Particularly important is a further decrease of "other" abortions to 13 percent in 1982.

Similar trends can be observed in Croatia. There was a constant increase from 9.52 legal abortions per 100 live births in 1960 to 60.5 in 1970. From 1971 on, a slight decrease was observed which lasted until 1975. After the last liberalization of the abortion law, the number of legal abortions rose constantly, reaching 77.1 per 100 live births in 1981. This trend is reflected in the dynamics of other abortions in Croatia, where the percentage of "other" abortions dropped from 61.9 (1960) to 7.0 (1980).

Table 33.3 shows the incidence of abortions per total population, live births, and registered pregnancies for Slovenia. Although the number of legal abortions is still increasing, during 1965–80 in Slovenia only 1.7 to 3.4 percent of all legal abortions were performed in the second trimester. These abortions are performed mostly in the early second trimester (thirteen to fourteen weeks gestation), almost exclusively for medical reasons.

During the period discussed (1955–80), the distribution of legal abortions changed by age and parity. Before 1970 the largest number of abortions (70 percent) was performed in women aged twenty to thirty-five years. The majority of women requesting abortion were married (80 percent), and the predominant parity was two children.

After 1975, however, an increase of legal abortions in the group of women aged twenty to twenty-four years and in the group of adolescents was noticed.

The proportion of nulliparas under age nineteen increased from 5.5 percent in 1965 to 9.6 percent in 1970 to 10.7 percent in 1980.

ABORTION AND FERTILITY REGULATION

In Yugoslavia the family planning movement developed from the early movement for abortion liberalization and affirmation of contraception.

Although contraception was introduced in the entire country as part of public health at the primary health care level as early as the second half of the 1950s, it was not uniformly accepted in the various regions. The awareness gradually spread that family planning implied much more than just giving advice on contraception or performing an abortion; it began to be seen as a part of an interrelated social system. A parallel development was the concept of family planning as a human right. Several Yugoslav representatives were very active in creating this concept on the international level as well.

These long-lasting endeavors were given official recognition by the Resolution on Family Planning, adopted by the Federal Assembly in April 1969. It established the contents and objectives of family planning, declaring it a fundamental human right and duty.

The family planning program is implemented through the medical health service (family planning is an essential part of primary health care), the educational system (although it is still dealt with mostly outside the regular school system), the mass media (disseminating information on responsible parenthood), and the social welfare system (operating on all levels of Yugoslav society).

Despite impressive achievements in family planning in some regions, much remains to be done in order to expand services and change public attitudes toward family planning. This action is coordinated by the Federal Council for Family Planning, established in Yugoslavia as early as 1963, and the corresponding committees in each republic.

ABORTION IN ADOLESCENCE

Yugoslavia has approximately 1.9 million adolescents (those aged fifteen to nineteen). In 1975 a small difference between male and female adolescents still existed, but this difference tends to disappear. The percentage of adolescents varieis between 8 and 11 percent, while the population under age twenty represents 28 to 53 percent of the total population. There are great differences among individual republics and provinces.

The general increase of abortion in individual regions has been accompanied by an increase in adolescent abortions. But the proportion of adolescent abortions in the total number of abortions varies from region to region. The latest available data on the number of adolescent abortions for the entire country are from 1974, and they are estimated to be 5.2 percent of all abortions.

Again, the most data on adolescent abortion trends are available for the republic of Slovenia. Peterlin reports an increase in both adolescent childbirth and adolescent abortion (Peterlin, 1978, 1983). In 1965, 18.4 percent of abortions in pregnant adolescents were registered, whereas in 1980 as many as 39.3 percent of pregnant adolescents terminated an unwanted pregnancy.

The number of adolescent abortions is also seen to be on the increase when compared to the total number of abortions. In 1965 adolescent abortions represented 3.41 percent of all abortions, while in 1980 they increased to 9.19 percent. Between 1965 and 1974 the number of adolescent abortions increased at an unequal rate; a faster increase was noticed after 1975 and particularly after 1980s.

Slovenia has experienced a growing incidence of abortions, especially in the age group fifteen to seventeen, but most of these terminations are performed in the first trimester of pregnancy. Other Yugoslav republics still report a great number of adolescents requesting termination of advanced pregnancy.

In the province of Vojvodina an increase of second-trimester abortions from 10 to 30 percent was observed after 1972 (Ferenčević-Nikašinović, 1975). A similar trend was observed at the Department of Obstetrics and Gynecology of Belgrade University (in the republic of Serbia), where second-trimester abortions in adolescents represented 20.15 percent of all abortions performed (Husar, 1983).

REPEAT ABORTIONS

Partial data available from the former Family Planning Institute of Ljubljana show that in the period 1968–74 approximately 30 percent of women requesting an abortion had undergone one or more earlier terminations of pregnancy; approximately 10 percent of them were having their third or higher order abortion (Macek, 1983). Since 1975 the likelihood of a previous abortion has been even greater. In compliance with existing legal regulations, women are no longer asked about their previous abortions. Therefore, we can only estimate that the number of repeat abortions is still on the increase. According to some estimates, they have recently approached 50 percent, but the exact incidence of repeat abortion is still open for discussion (University of Ljubljana, 1975).

ABORTION RESEARCH

Organized research on abortion has been conducted mostly in Slovenia, although some individual investigations have analyzed selected aspects of abortions in other parts of the country.

In Slovenia, the Republic Public Health Institute carries out research on sociodemographic aspects on abortion, while the former Family Planning Institute, now part of the University Department of Obstetrics and Gynecology in Ljubljana, mostly studies medical aspects of induced abortions. In cooperation with national agencies (the Boris Kidrič Fund, the Research Foundation of Slovenia) and/or international agencies (World Health Organization, International Fertility Research Program), between 1968 and 1983 this institution conducted a series of twenty-five studies, encompassing about 25,000 women. The main topics of these studies were optimization of the abortion technique and procedure, identification of factors that influence early and late sequelae of abortion, and, consequently, optimization of abortion service.

Among these studies are five that deserve special mention; their findings have been published elsewhere (Andolšek, 1974; Andolšek et al., 1976, 1977; Cheng et al., 1977; Pompe-Tanšek, Andolšak, & Tekavčič, 1982).

ILLEGAL ABORTION

Data on legal and other abortions are presented in table 33.1. The column "Other Abortions" includes all spontaneous and illegal abortions. Although the data on illegal abortions for the entire country are not available, they are estimated to have increased after the last change in the abortion legislation in comparison with the previous years.

While in 1961 a total of 286 (5.1 percent) illegal abortions were registered in Slovenia, this number decreased to 34 (1.0 percent) in 1971 and in 1981 to 3 (0.1 percent) of illegal abortions. At the same time, the proportion of other abortions has declined in Croatia from 61.9 percent in 1960 to around 7 percent in the period 1977–81.

In comparison with the data on illegal abortions registered in Slovenia before the first liberalization of abortion regulation (91.9 percent of illegal abortions in 1955), such a significant decrease of illegal abortions is considered the first most important result of liberalizing abortion in Yugoslavia.

The second most important result is the reduction of abortion mortality. After 1961, postabortal mortality declined significantly in Slovenia and in other parts of the country. In 1964 there were 5.2 deaths per 10,000 abortions in Slovenia, while in 1979 postabortal mortality was only 0.5 per 10,000 abortions. Postabortal mortality for 100,000 women of fertile age was 1.9 in 1964 but only 0.2 in 1979. A similar trend is reported for Croatia where there were 18 deaths per 10,000 abortions in 1960 and only 0.4 deaths per 10,000 abortions in 1977. Postabortal mortality for 100,000 women of fertile age decreased from 30 in 1960 to 0.2 in 1977.

SUMMARY

In Yugoslavia, abortion is still the most frequent method of regulating fertility. National data on abortion are fragmentary; statistics are fully available only for Slovenia. The number of abortions is still on the increase, which may be ascribed to various factors, the first being the very liberalized abortion legislation. The right of abortion in the first ten weeks is a constitutionally recognized human right in Yugoslavia. After the tenth week, it is regulated by legislation, which varies from republic to republic. All abortions, regardless of gestational age, are performed in public health institutions. Women participate in abortion costs, although more or less merely symbolically. The participation varies in different regions.

Although the demographic characteristics of women seeking abortion did not change significantly between 1955 and 1975 (mostly they were married, twenty to thirty-five years old, with two children on the average), since 1975 there has been an increase of abortions in adolescents and women aged twenty to twenty-four.

Several studies have confirmed that an abortion performed at a public health institution prior to the tenth week of gestation is a relatively safe procedure. While in some regions the number of second-trimester abortions is negligible, in others there are still too many terminations of advanced gestation, especially in adolescents. There has also been an increase in the number of repeat abortions, which are estimated to account for at least 50 percent of all cases.

The gradual liberalization of regulations with regard to legal abortions, as well as the increase of their number, has almost completely eliminated mortality after illegal abortions and has significantly decreased portabortal morbidity. From the point of view of preserving the health of women of fertile age, this achievement may be considered an important one.

ACKNOWLEDGMENTS

The author wishes to thank Professor Stanka Krajnc-Simoneti, M.D., chief of MCH service of the Republic Public Health Institute, for providing all statistical data on the abortion dynamic in Slovenia and for giving so many suggestions for preparing the manuscript.

The author also thanks the following for help in gathering data from other republics and provinces: Professor Dubravka Štampar, M.D. (for Croatia), Milena Dragović, M.D. (for Montenegro), Professor Marta Husar, M.D. (for Serbia), and Milica Marjanović, M.D. (for Vojvodina).

REFERENCES

Andolšek, L. (Ed.). *The Ljubljana abortion study 1971–1973: Comparison of the medical effects of induced abortion by two methods, curettage and vacuum aspiration.* Final report. Ljubljana: National Institute of Health Bethesda, 1974.

Andolšek, L. et al. A comparison of flexible and nonflexible plastic canulae for performing first trimester abortion. *International Journal of Gynecology and Obstetrics*, 1976, *14*, 199–204.

———. *The safety of local anesthesia and outpatient treatment: A controlled study of induced abortion by vacuum aspiration.* Studies in Family Planning, 1977, *8*, 118–124.

Cheng, M., et al. Complications following induced abortion by vacuum aspiration: Patient characteristics and procedures. *Studies in Family Planning*, 1977, *8*, 125–129.

Drugi kongres slovenskih zdravnikov, Ljubljana 18–20 April 1968. Povzetki referatov. Ljubljana: Slovensko zdravniško društvo, 1968.

Ferenčević-Nikašinović, S. Demografsko-medicinske i socijalno-ekonomske osnove planiranja porodice u SAP Vojvodini. Doktorska disertacija, Novi Sad, 1975.

Husar, M. Personal communication. Belgrade, 1983.

Legal Abortion in Europe—Yugoslavia. Correspondent: Karel Zupančič, Ljubljana. *IPPF Europe Regional Information Bulletin*, Supplement, January 1978, 7(1), 7–8.

Maček, M. Personal communication. Ljubljana, 1983.

Mirković, A., et al. Sadašnje stanje pobačaja u Srbiji. In VII kongres ginekologa opstetričara Jugoslavije, Beograd, 9–11 October 1972. Zbornik radova I., Galenika, Beograd, 1972, 183–191.

Peterlin, A. *Nosečnost in porod v adolescenci—Vpliv mladoletnosti matere na novorojenčka.* Magistarski rad. Zagreb, maj 1978.

———. Umetna prekinitev nosečnosti pri adolescentkah in vpliv na pojavnost spontanega splava, trajanje nosečnosti in porodno težo novorojencev. Doktorska disertacija, Zagreb, 1983.

Pompe-Tanšek, M., Andolšek, L., & Tekavčič, B. *Utjecaj artificijalnog abortusa na tok i ishod slijedeće trudnoće.* Jugoslav. ginek. opstet. 22, 1982, 118–120.

Republic Public Health Institute of Slovenia. Selected statistical reports. Ljubljana, 1983.

Statistics on abortion trends. Beograd: Federal Public Health Institute, 1984.

Tomšič, Vida. *Status of women and family planning in Yugoslavia.* In Selected articles and speeches on the status of women and family planning in Yugoslavia. Published by the Federal Conference of the Socialist Alliance of the Working People of Yugoslavia—Federal Council for Family Planning. Ljubljana, 1975, 9–29.

University of Ljubljana, Medical Centre, Family Planning Institute. Statistical report. Ljubljana, 1975.

Ustava Socialističke Republike Jugoslavije. Uradni list SFRJ, Beogradsko izdavačko-grafiški zavod, Beograd, 1974.

Zakon o zdravstvenih ukrepih pri uresničevanju pravice do svobodnega odločanja o rojstvu otrok. Uradni list SRS, št. 11, 19.5.1977, 570–573.

Zakon o zdravstvenim mjerama za ostvarivanje prava na slobodno odlučivanje o radjanju djece. Narodne novine, broj 1252–1978, Zagreb, 21.travnja 1978.

Žarković, G. *Zdravstvo u SFR Jugoslaviji krcz prizmu zdravstvenih interesa gradjana.* In Zbornik III. kongresa lekara Jugoslavije, Bled 5–8 October 1971. Savez lekarskih društava Jugoslavije, Slovensko zdravniško društvo. Ljubljana, 1971, 15–52.

Table 33.1
Number of Women in Fertile Age, Number of Live Births, and Abortion Ratios, by Republic and Province, 1971 and 1981.

Republic or province	Number of women in fertile age		Number of live birth		Number of all abortions		Number of abortions/100 live birth		Increase of No. of abortions/100 live birth ratio (%)
	1971	1981	1971	1981	1971	1981	1971	1981	
Bosnia and Herzegovina	986.183	1.106.551	82.694	70.928[3]	28.676	46.874[3]	34.7	66.1[3]	90.5[3]
Montenegro	134.967	151.056	10.866	10.365[2]	4.590	5.689[2]	42.2	54.9[2]	30.1[2]
Croatia	1.174.488	1.152.704	64.891	67.455	41.104	55.887	63.3	82.9	31.0
Macedonia	421.227	491.236	37.904	39.784[3]	17.284	26.726[3]	45.6	67.2[3]	47.4[3]
Slovenia	451.193	476.888	27.432	29.220	12.593	23.274	45.9	79.7	73.6
Serbia (narrow)	1.484.793	1.459.961	77.900	80.916[1]	121.733	151.961[1]	156.3	187.8[1]	20.2[4]
Kosovo	270.050	351.396	47.060	53.147[3]	5.076	8.327[3]	10.8	15.7[3]	45.4[3]
Vojvodina	535.531	517.100	26.170	28.681[3]	30.846	43.369[3]	117.9	151.2[3]	28.7[3]

[1]Data for year 1978. [2]Data for year 1979. [3]Data for year 1980.
Source: Federal Public Health Institute, data extracted from yearly statistical reports, 1971–81.

Table 33.2
Incidence of Legal and Other Abortions in Slovenia, 1955–80

Year	Total No. of abortions	Legal abortions No.	%	Other abortions No.	%
1955	5.451	441	8.1	5.010	91.9
1960	13.762	8.229	59.8	5.533	40.2
1965	15.987	9.904	61,9	6.083	38.1
1970	12.046	8.505	70.6	3.541	29.4
1975	12.350	9.063	73.5	3.273	26.5
1980	22.489	19.339	86.0	3.150	14.0

Source: Republic Public Health Institute of Slovenia, data extracted from yearly statistical reports, 1955–80.

Table 33.3
Legal Abortion Rates and Ratios in Slovenia, 1955–80

Year	Abortion Rates			Early Fetal Mortality Ratio	
	Per 1,000 population	Per 1,000 women aged 15 – 49	Per 1,000 women 15–44	Per 1,000 live births	Per 1,000 registered pregnancies
1955	0.5	2.0		24.9	21.3
1960	5.2	20.2		259.7	197.9
1965	6.0	23.9		323.8	212.7
1970	5.0	18.8	21.6	310.0	215.4
1975	5.0	19.9	22.7	321.5	223.6
1980	10.2	40.6	46.8	646.6	376.3

Source: Republic Public Health Institute of Slovenia, data extracted from yearly statistical reports, 1955–80.

INDEX

CONTRIBUTORS

Halida Akhter
Program Associate, Ford Foundation, Ramna, Dhaka, Bangladesh.

Jean-Jacques Amy
Professor and Head, Department of Gynecology, Andrology and Obstetrics, Academisch Ziekenhuis, Vrije Universiteit Brussel, Belgium.

Lidija Andolšek
Professor, University Medical Center Ljubljana, Department of Obstetrics and Gynecology, 61000 Ljubljana, Šlajmerjeva, 3, Yugoslavia.

Anthony C. Comninos
Professor of Obstetrics and Gynecology, University of Athens, Greece.

Monica Ferreira
Senior Researcher, Human Sciences Research Council, Pretoria, Republic of South Africa.

Irene Figà-Talamanca
Researcher and Lecturer, Facoltà di Scienze M.F.N., Instituto di Fisiologia Generale, Università degli Studi di Rome, Italy.

Jacqueline Darroch Forrest
Director of Research, Alan Guttmacher Institute, New York, United States of America.

Colin Francome
Senior Lecturer, Department of Sociology, Middlesex Polytechnic, The Burroughs, London, United Kingdom.

Lars Heisterberg
  Professor, Department of Gynecology, Bispebjerg Hospital, University of Copenhagen, Denmark.

Stanley K. Henshaw
  Deputy Director of Research, Alan Guttmacher Institute, New York, United States of America.

Paula E. Hollerbach
  Associate, Center for Policy Studies, Population Council, New York, United States of America.

Sung-bong Hong
  Professor and Chairman, Department of Obstetrics and Gynecology, Korea University Hospital, Seoul, South Korea.

H. Marsidi Judono
  Professor Emeritus, Department of Obstetrics and Gynecology, School of Medicine, University of Gajah Mada, Jogyakarta, Indonesia.

András Klinger
  Chief, Population Statistics Department, Hungarian Central Statistical Office, 1525 Budapest, Hungary.

N. Kodagoda
  Professor of Forensic Medicine, University of Colombo, Sri Lanka.

Gerhard Kraiker
  Institut für Soziologie, Universität Oldenburg, Ammerländer Heerstrasse 67–99, Oldenburg, Federal Republic of Germany.

K. H. Mehlan
  Professor Emeritus, Schliemannstrasse 41, Rostock, German Democratic Republic.

F. A. Moeloek
  Senior Lecturer, Department of Obstetrics and Gynecology, School of Medicine, University of Indonesia, Jakarta, Indonesia.

Minoru Muramatsu
  Director, Department of Public Health Demography, Institute of Public Health, Tokyo, Japan.

Pirkko Niemelä
  Professor, Department of Psychology, University of Turku, Finland.

Stephen Nnatu
  Senior Lecturer, Department of Obstetrics and Gynecology, College of Medicine, University of Lagos, Nigeria.

Marek Okólski
: Professor, Faculty of Economics, University of Warsaw, Poland.

R. N. V. Prasad
: Senior Lecturer and Consultant, Obstetrics and Gynecology, National University of Singapore.

Jany Rademakers
: Research Coordinator, Stimezo Nederland, The Hague, The Netherlands.

Prema Ramachandran
: Deputy Director General (ECD), Indian Council of Medical Research, Ansari Nagar, New Delhi, India.

S. S. Ratnam
: Senior Professor and Head, National University of Singapore, Department of Obstetrics/Gynecology, Singapore.

Eitan F. Sabatello
: Director, Division of Population, Demography, Health and Immigrants Absorption, Israel Central Bureau of Statistics, Jerusalem, Israel.

Paul Sachdev
: Professor, School of Social Work, Memorial University of Newfoundland, St. John's, Newfoundland, Canada.

Janet Sceats
: Medical Demographer, Epidemiology Unit, Waikato Hospital, Hamilton, New Zealand.

Pramilla Senanayake
: Medical Director, International Planned Parenthood Federation, London, United Kingdom.

Stefania Siedlecky
: Senior Adviser, Family Planning & Women's Health, Commonwealth Department of Health, Woden, Canberra, Australia.

Hans Skjelle
: Spesiallege, Department of Gynecology, Gjøvik Hospital, Gjøvik, Norway.

Jiři Šráček
: Krojská nemocnice s poliklinikou v Ostravě, Ostrava-Zábřeh, Czechoslovakia.

Sundraji Sumapraja
: Senior Lecturer, Department of Obstetrics and Gynecology, School of Medicine, University of Indonesia, Jakarta, Indonesia.

Kajsa Sundström-Feigenberg
VC Kronan, Sundbyberg, Sweden.

Marleen Temmerman
Visiting Obstetrician and Gynecologist, Department of Gynecology, Andrology and Obstetrics, Academisch Ziekenhuis, Vrije Universiteit Brussel, Belgium.

Michel Thiery
Professor and Chairman, Department of Obstetrics, Academisch Ziekenhuis, Ruksuniversiteit-Gent, Belgium.

Christopher Tietze
Senior Consultant, Population Council, New York, United States of America (now deceased).

Chi-hsien Tuan
Professor, East-West Population Institute, East-West Center, Honolulu, Hawaii, United States of America.

F. F. W. van Oosten
Professor, Department of Criminal Law, University of Pretoria, Republic of South Africa.

Benjamin Viel V.
Providencia 2457, Santiago de Chile, Chile.

Nurit Yaffe
Chief Assistant to the Director, Division of Census of Population and Housing, Israel Central Bureau of Statistics, Jerusalem, Israel.